Loraine Boettner

Dr. Boettner was born on a farm in northwest Missouri. He is a graduate of Princeton Theological Seminary (Th.B., 1928; Th.M., 1929), where he studied Systematic Theology under the late Dr. C. W. Hodge. Previously he had graduated from Tarkio College, Missouri, and had taken a short course in Agriculture at the University of Missouri. In 1933 he received the honorary degree of Doctor of Divinity, and in 1957 the degree of Doctor of Literature. He taught Bible for eight years in Pikeville College, Kentucky. A resident of Washington, D. C., eleven years, and of Los Angeles three years, his present home is in Rock Port, Missouri.

His other books include: *The Reformed Doctrine of Predestination, Studies In Theology, Immortality,* and *The Millennium.*

ROMAN CATHOLICISM

ROMAN CATHOLICISM

By Loraine Boettner

Author of

Immortality
The Reformed Doctrine of Predestination
Studies in Theology
The Millennium

THE PRESBYTERIAN AND
REFORMED PUBLISHING COMPANY

PHILADELPHIA   PENNSYLVANIA

1962

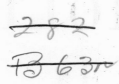

Second Printing

COPYRIGHT 1962 ©
By Presbyterian and Reformed Publishing Co.

Library of Congress Catalog Card Number 61-11748

Printed in the United States of America

CONTENTS

ROMAN CATHOLICISM

I. INTRODUCTION

1. Historical Background. 2. Roman Catholicism a Poor Defense Against Communism. 3. Romanism an Age-long Development. 4. Protestantism and First Century Christianity. 5. Contrast Between Protestant and Roman Catholic Countries.

1. HISTORICAL BACKGROUND

In our twentieth century America few among us seem to realize what a priceless heritage we possess in the freedom of religion, freedom of speech, freedom of the press, and freedom of assembly that is an integral part of our everyday life. Nor are many aware of the bitter and prolonged struggles our forefathers went through at the time of the Reformation and later to secure these freedoms. Instead it is quite the common thing to take these for granted and to assume that they are the natural rights of all men. But truly those of us who call ourselves Protestants are the inheritors of a great tradition. And in a country such as the United States our Roman Catholic friends also share these freedoms, little realizing what it means to live under a clerical dictatorship such as their church imposes wherever it has the power.

Roman Catholics often attempt to represent Protestantism as something comparatively new, as having originated with Martin Luther and John Calvin in the sixteenth century. We do indeed owe a great debt to those leaders and to the Reformation movement that swept over Europe at that time. But the basic principles and the common system of doctrine taught by those Reformers and by the evangelical churches ever since go back to the New Testament and to the first century Christian church. Protestantism as it emerged in the 16th century was not the beginning of something new, but a return to Bible Christianity and to the simplicity of the Apostolic church from which the Roman Church had long since departed.

The positive and formal principle of this system is that the Bible is the Word of God and therefore the authoritative rule of faith and practice. Its negative principle is that any element of doctrine or practice in

1

the church which cannot be traced back to the New Testament is no essential part of Christianity.

The basic features of Protestant belief therefore are:

1. The supremacy of the Bible in all matters of faith and practice.
2. Justification by faith, not by works, although works have their necessary and logical place as the fruits and proof of true faith.
3. The right of the individual to go directly to God in prayer apart from the mediation of any priest or other human intermediary.
4. Individual freedom of conscience and worship, within the authority of the Bible.

For more than a thousand years before the Reformation the popes had controlled Europe and had said that there was only one way to worship God. That period is appropriately known as the "Dark Ages." In the church and, to a considerable extent, in the state, too, the priests held the power. They suppressed the laity until practically all their rights were taken away. They constantly pried into private affairs, interfering even between husband and wife and between parents and children by means of the confessional. All marriage was in their hands. They interfered in the administration of public affairs, in the proceedings of the courts, and in the disposition of estates. The revenues of the state built new churches and paid the salaries of the priests in much the same manner as in present day Spain. Anyone who dared resist ran the risk of losing his job, his property, and even his life. Life under such tyranny was intolerable. From that condition the Reformation brought deliverance.

One of the first and most important results of the Reformation was that the Bible was given to the people in their own languages. Previously the Bible had been kept from them, on the pretext that only the church speaking through the priest could interpret it correctly. Luther translated the Bible into his native German, and edition followed edition in rapid succession. Similar translations were made in England, France, Holland, and other countries.

Protestants of our day who have not been called upon to suffer or to make any sacrifices to secure this rich heritage are inclined to hold these blessings lightly. But the advances that Romanism is making today in this nation and in other parts of the world should cause even the most careless to stop and think. It seems that as Protestants we have forgotten how to *protest* against those same religious and political abuses that were common before the Reformation. We need to acquaint ourselves with and to teach the principles of our faith if we are not to be overwhelmed by a religious despotism that, if it gains the upper hand, will be as cruel and oppressive as ever it was in Germany, Italy, France, or Spain.

✕ Our American freedoms are being threatened today by two totalitarian systems, Communism and Roman Catholicism. And of the two in our country Romanism is growing faster than is Communism and is the more dangerous since it covers its real nature with a cloak of religion. This nation has been well alerted to the dangers of Communism, and it is generally opposed by the radio, the press, and the churches. But Romanism has the support of these to a considerable extent; and even the Protestant churches in many places take a conciliatory and cooperative attitude toward it. Most people have only a very hazy notion as to what is involved in the Roman system. And yet the one consuming purpose of the Vatican is to convert the entire world, not to Christianity, but to Roman Catholicism. Its influence is being applied vigorously at every level of our local, state, and federal government. It is particularly significant that in this country the hierarchy has taken as its slogan, not, "Make America Christian," but, "Make America Catholic." And in that slogan are the strong overtones of a full scale attack upon our Protestant heritage and those precious rights of freedom of religion, freedom of conscience, and freedom of speech.

We cannot adequately understand this problem unless we realize that the kind of Roman Catholicism that we see in the United States is, for the most part, not real Roman Catholicism at all, that is, not Roman Catholicism as it exists where it is the dominant force in the life of a nation, but a modified and compromised form that has adjusted itself to life with a Protestant majority. Here it is comparatively reticent about asserting its claims to be the only true church, the only church that has a right to conduct public religious services, its right to suppress all other forms of religion, its superiority to all national and state governments, its control over all marriage, its right to direct all education, and the obligation of the state to support its churches and schools with tax money. That this is no visionary list of charges, but a cold and realistic appraisal, is shown by the fact that in Spain, which is governed under the terms of a concordat with the Vatican, and which is often praised by Roman Catholic spokesmen as the ideal Catholic state, the Roman Church is now exercising most of these so-called "rights" or privileges.

In order to see clearly what Roman Catholicism really is we must see it as it was during the Middle Ages, or as it has continued to be in certain countries such as Spain, Portugal, Italy, France, Southern Ireland, and Latin America, where it has had political as well as ecclesiastical control. In those countries where it has been dominant for centuries with little or no opposition from Protestantism, we see the true fruits of the system in the lives of the people, with all of their poverty, ignorance, superstition, and low moral standards. In each of those countries a dominant pattern is discernible. Spain is a particularly good example, for it is the most Roman Catholic country in Europe, yet it has the lowest standard of living of any nation in Europe. The Latin American nations have been predominantly Roman Catholic for four centuries, and today the illiteracy rate ranges from 30 to 70 percent. The veteran radio political analyist, Howard K. Smith, recently reported that, "The average per capita income in the United States is eight times that of any country in South America" (March 3, 1960). The average per capita income in South America is $280, one-ninth that in the United States.

But even in those countries we do not see the ultimate fruits of the system. For over a period of years they have been influenced to some extent by Protestantism and they have been receiving assistance from the Protestant nations, particularly from the United States and England, so that their present condition, economic, social, political, and religious, is not nearly as bad as it would have been had they been left to themselves. Substantial aid has been given since the close of the First World War. Senator Harry F. Byrd, of Virginia, is authority for the statement that American foreign aid since the Second World War through 1960 extended to the various nations has amounted to 65 billions of dollars, plus 30 billions more in military aid (Radio address, February 19, 1961). The Roman Catholic nations of Europe and Latin America have profited greatly through this assistance.

American Catholicism, so different on the surface from that found in Spain, Italy, and Latin America, is, nevertheless, all a part of the same church, all run from Rome and by the same man who is the absolute ruler over all of the branches and who has the authority to change policy in any of those branches as he deems it safe or expedient. If he chose to give his subjects in Spain or Colombia relatively more freedom and better schools, such as are enjoyed by those in the United States, he could readily do so by directing his priests and financial resources to that end. Undoubtedly Romanism in the United States would be much the same as that found in other countries were it not for the influence of evangelical Christianity as set forth by the Protestant churches.

2. ROMAN CATHOLICISM A POOR DEFENSE AGAINST COMMUNISM

We have no hesitation in saying that most of the Roman Catholic nations, had they been left to themselves, long ago would have fallen victims of Communism. In all probability both Italy and France would have turned Communist at the close of the Second World War had it not been for American aid and all of the political influence that our government could lawfully exert toward those nations, and even then the result was in doubt for some considerable time. The Vatican had supported Mussolini's Fascist and military policies, including the conquest of Ethiopia (which conquest had been condemned by the League of Nations and by practically all of the civilized world), his open and extensive support of Franco in Spain with troops and arms, and his invasion of Albania and Greece. After Italy entered the war on the side of Nazi Germany the Roman Church supported the Italian war effort, which meant, of course, that our work of carrying the war to a successful conclusion was made just that much harder. During the war pope Pius XII gave his blessing to large numbers of Italian and German troops who appeared before him in uniform. With the defeat of Germany and Italy those policies caused strong popular resentment. It is probable that in the turmoil that followed the ignominious fall of Mussolini the Roman Catholic Church would have been overthrown in much the same way that the Orthodox Catholic Church in Russia was overthrown when the Czarist regime fell at the end of the First World War had not American military forces then in Italy preserved order. In Russia a dead, formalistic church had lost the respect of the people and had become identified with the despotic rule of the Czar since he was the head of both the state and the church. When the people rose up in anger and threw out the political government they threw out the church with it and turned to the other extreme, atheism. That has often been the case where the people have known only one church. When that became corrupt they had no alternative but to turn against religion altogether.

In the critical Italian election held after the war, in April, 1948, the Communists made a strong effort to gain control of the government, but a coalition of other parties managed to gain the majority. Today the biggest Communist party outside of Russia and Red China is found in Roman Catholic Italy, seat of the papacy, precisely where, if Roman Catholicism is the effective defense against Communism that it claims to be, we should find the least Communism. Approximately one-third of the voters in Italy today are Communist, as are approximately one-fourth of those in France.

Roman Catholicism opposes Communism, of course, as one totalitarian system opposes another. And for propaganda purposes she even attempts to present herself as the chief opponent of, and the chief bulwark against, Communism. But the fact is that during the past fifteen years Communism has made its greatest gains in Roman Catholic nations, both in Europe and in Latin America, while the Protestant nations, the United States, Britain, Canada, Holland, Norway, Sweden, and Denmark, have been its most effective opponents. It is in reality only a short step from a totalitarian church to a totalitarian state, since the people have been trained to accept authority as it is imposed upon them rather than to think for themselves and to manage their own affairs.

In his very informative book, *American Freedom and Catholic Power,* Paul Blanshard, American sociologist and journalist who has written extensively on church-state relations, says:

> "In several great crises in Europe the Vatican has, through passive and active collaboration with fascism, thrown the balance of power against democracy. . . . It has aligned itself with the most reactionary forces in Europe and Latin America. Surely it is not by accident that the two most fascist nations in the world today—Spain and Portugal—are Catholic nations whose dictators have been blessed by the pope and are conspicuously loyal to him! The Vatican's affinity with fascism is neither accidental nor incidental. Catholicism conditions its people to accept censorship, thought control, and ultimately dictatorship" (Rev. ed., 1958, p. 291; Beacon Press, Boston).

And Count Coudenhove-Kalergi, a former Roman Catholic, says:

> "Catholicism is the fascist form of Christianity of which Calvinism represents its democratic wing. The Catholic hierarchy rests fully and securely on the leadership principle with the infallible pope in supreme command for a lifetime. . . . Like the Fascist party, its priesthood becomes a medium for an undemocratic minority rule by a hierarchy. . . . Catholic nations follow fascist doctrines more willingly than Protestant nations, which are the main strongholds of democracy. Democracy lays its stress on personal conscience; fascism on authority and obedience" (*Crusade for Pan-Europe,* p. 173).

If the United States should become Roman Catholic the result undoubtedly would be the rapid conquest of this country and the rest of the world by Russian Communism. In view of the weak defense that the Roman Catholic countries are able to put up intellectually, morally, or militarily, we are safe in saying that one of the surest ways to turn this nation Communist would be to turn it first to Roman Catholicism. We have acted as a strong restraint in keeping Roman Catholic nations from going Communist. But who would restrain this nation? There would be no other to serve that purpose, and our descent would be sure and swift.

The fact is that much of the popular support that the puppet governments behind the Iron Curtain have received has been given because they have forbidden the Roman Catholic Church to take any part in political affairs or to control the schools. In several countries, both in Europe and in Latin America, the only choice the people have is either Romanism or Communism. Protestantism, as an alternative choice, is practically non-existent. Those people have been taught hatred for Protestantism from childhood, and few of them would try it. Many vote Communist, not because they believe in the program, but because it is the only effective instrument they have to oppose Roman Catholicism.

On the other hand, to see what the effect of Protestantism is upon a people we turn to the United States, where with complete separation of church and state the Reformation has made its greatest advance, and to Britain and the other nations where Protestantism has long been the dominant religion. These we find are unquestionably the most enlightened and advanced nations of the world; and in the main it is from these nations, where the people are accustomed to think and act for themselves and to govern themselves in both church and state, that the opposition to Communism has come.

3. ROMANISM AN AGE-LONG DEVELOPMENT

One of the first things that we want to point out in this study is that the Roman Catholic Church has not always been what it is today. Rather, it has reached its present state as the result of a long, slow process of development as through the centuries one new doctrine, or ritual, or custom after another has been added. Even a superficial reading of the following list will make clear that most of the distinctive features of the system were unknown to Apostolic Christianity, and that one can hardly recognize in present day Romanism the original Christian doctrines. Not all dates can be given with exactness since some doctrines and rituals were debated or practiced over a period of time before their formal acceptance.

SOME ROMAN CATHOLIC HERESIES AND INVENTIONS
and the dates of their adoption over a period of 1650 years

1. *Prayers for the dead,* began about A. D. 300
2. Making the *sign of the cross* 300
3. *Wax candles,* about 320
4. *Veneration of angels and dead saints,* and use of *images* 375
5. *The Mass,* as a daily celebration 394
6. *Beginning of the exaltation of Mary,* the term "Mother of God" first applied to her by the Council of Ephesus 431
7. Priests began to dress differently from laymen 500
8. *Extreme Unction* 526

42. *Infallibility of the pope* in matters of faith and morals, proclaimed by
the Vatican Council 1870
43. *Public Schools condemned* by pope Pius XI 1930
44. *Assumption of the Virgin Mary* (bodily ascension into heaven shortly
after her death), proclaimed by pope Pius XII 1950

Add to these many others: monks—nuns—monasteries—convents—forty days Lent—holy week—Palm Sunday—Ash Wednesday—All Saints day—Candlemas day—fish day—meat days—incense—holy oil—holy palms—Christopher medals—charms—novenas—and still others.

There you have it—the melancholy evidence of Rome's steadily increasing departure from the simplicity of the Gospel, a departure so radical and far-reaching at the present time that it has produced a drastically anti-evangelical church. It is clear beyond possibility of doubt that the Roman Catholic religion as now practiced is the outgrowth of centuries of error. Human inventions have been substituted for Bible truth and practice. Intolerance and arrogance have replaced the love and kindness and tolerance that were the distinguishing qualities of the first century Christians, so that now in Roman Catholic countries Protestants and others who are sincere believers in Christ but who do not acknowledge the authority of the pope are subject to all kinds of restrictions and in some cases even forbidden to practice their religion. The distinctive attitude of the present day Roman Church was fixed largely by the Council of Trent (1545-1563), with its more than 100 anathemas or curses pronounced against all who then or in the future would dare to differ with its decisions.

Think what all of this means! Each of the above doctrines or practices can be pin-pointed to the exact or approximate date at which it became a part of the system. And no single one of them became a part of the system until centuries after the time of Christ! Most of these doctrines and practices are binding on all Roman Catholics, for they have been proclaimed by a supposedly infallible pope or church council. To deny any doctrine or practice so proclaimed involves one in mortal sin.

What will be next? Indications are that it will be another proclamation concerning Mary. Two new doctrines are under discussion: Mary as Mediatrix, and Mary as Co-redemptrix. Important Roman Catholic authorities have already indicated that these will be the next doctrines officially proclaimed. Mary is being presented in current Roman teaching as a Mediator along with Christ. She is said to be the "Mediatrix of all graces," and the people are being told that the way to approach Christ is through His mother. "To Christ through Mary," is the slogan. Her images outnumber those of Christ, and more prayer is offered to her than to Christ.

It is also being said that Mary's sufferings, particularly those at the cross, were redemptive in the same sense that Christ's sufferings were redemptive. It would seem that these two doctrines, if adopted, would in effect place Mary as a fourth member of the Godhead, along with the Father, Son, and Holy Spirit. And presumably these doctrines, if adopted, will be officially announced by the pope, for he was proclaimed infallible in this regard in 1870 and therefore no longer needs the authority of an ecumenical council.

And still the Roman Church boasts that she never changes or teaches new doctrines! *Semper idem*—"Always the same"—is her motto! The fact that not one of the doctrines in the above list has any support in the Bible disproves conclusively the claim of the priests that their religion is the same as that taught by Christ and that the popes have been the faithful custodians of that truth.

The fact is that many of the above listed rites and ceremonies were taken directly from paganism or from Old Testament Judaism. Some scholars say that as much as 75 percent of the Roman ritual is of pagan origin. John Henry Newman, later cardinal, in his book, *The Development of the Christian Religion,* admits that "Temples, incense, oil lamps, votive offerings, holy water, holy days and seasons of devotion, processions, blessings of fields, sacerdotal vestments, the tonsure (of priests, monks and nuns), images, etc., are all of pagan origin" (p. 359).

While the Roman Church has been so free to hurl the name "heretic" at all who differ with her, the above list shows that the real heretics are the Roman Catholics themselves, and that the true orthodox are the evangelical Christians. Says the Scripture:

"But in vain do they worship me, Teaching as their doctrines the precepts of men. . . . Making void the word of God by your tradition, which ye have delivered: and many such like things ye do" (Mark 7:7,13).
"To the law and to the testimony! if they speak not according to this word, surely there is no morning for them" (Is. 8:20).

Surely the apostle Paul knew the human tendency to add to the Word of God when he gave this warning to the early church:

"I know that after my departing grievous wolves shall enter in among you, not sparing the flock; and from among your own selves shall men arise, speaking perverse things, to draw away the disciples after them" (Acts 20:29,30). And even more strongly: "But though we, or an angel from heaven, should preach unto you any gospel other than that which we preached unto you, let him be anathema" (Gal. 1:8).

4. PROTESTANTISM AND FIRST CENTURY CHRISTIANITY

Ever since New Testament times there have been people who accepted the basic principles now set forth in Protestantism. That is, they took the Bible as their authoritative standard of belief and practice. They were not called Protestants. Neither were they called Roman Catholics. They were simply called Christians. During the first three centuries they continued to base their faith solely on the Bible. They often faced persecution, sometimes from the Jews, sometimes from the pagans of the Roman empire. But early in the fourth century the emperor Constantine, who was the ruler in the west, began to favor Christianity, and then in the year 324, after he had become ruler of all of the empire, made Christianity the preferred religion. The result was that thousands of people who still were pagans pressed into the church in order to gain the special advantages and favors that went with such membership. They came in in far greater numbers than could be instructed or assimilated. Having been used to the more elaborate pagan rituals, they were not satisfied with the simple Christian worship but began to introduce their heathen beliefs and practices. Gradually, through the neglect of the Bible and the ignorance of the people, more and more heathen ideas were introduced until the church became more heathen than Christian. Many of the heathen temples were taken over by the church and re-dedicated as Christian churches.

Thus in time there was found in the church a sacrificing and gorgeously appareled priesthood, an elaborate ritual, images, holy water, incense, monks and nuns, the doctrine of purgatory, and in general a belief that salvation was to be achieved by works rather than by grace. The church in Rome, and in general the churches throughout the empire, ceased to be the apostolic Christian church, and became for the most part a religious monstrosity.

There remained, however, some groups, small in numbers, usually in isolated places, and later primarily in the mountains of northern Italy, who maintained the Christian faith in reasonable purity. There were also individuals throughout the church in all ages, usually more or less independent of the church at large, who continued to hold quite correct ideas concerning the Christian faith. But the half paganized condition continued through the Middle Ages and on into the sixteenth century when the religious revival in the West, known as the Reformation, shook the church to its foundations. At that time some scholars began to study Bible manuscripts that had been brought to light by the forced flight of eastern monks from their monasteries as the Mohammedan invasions extended into Europe, and these scholars saw how far the church had departed from its original Scriptures.

First there came the Renaissance, which was primarily a revival of learning, followed shortly by the Reformation. Some of the scholars in the church were called "Reformers." They called the people back to the Bible, and there they saw how wrong and contrary to Scripture was the use of images, holy water, priests saying mass, and church services in Latin which the people could not understand. The Reformers strongly attacked the ignorance and superstition that had become such a large part of the church program, and gave the people a service in their own language with preaching based on the Word of God. Protestant-ism, therefore, was not a new religion, but a return to the faith of the early church. It was Christianity cleaned up, with all the rubbish that had collected during the Middle Ages thrown out.

The Reformation, under Luther, Zwingli, Calvin, and Knox, was literally a "back-to-the-Bible" movement, a return to apostolic Chris-tianity. Evangelical Christianity has established itself as the historic faith of the first century, which came down through the ante-Nicene Fathers and Augustine, which was largely obscured during the Middle Ages, but which burst forth again in all its glory in the Reformation, and which has continued to grow and increase down to our own time.

The very name "Protestant," first applied to those Reformers who pro-tested against the decrees issued by the Council of Spires, implies in its broader sense that the churches led by the Reformers "protested" against the false doctrines and practices that were contrary to the teachings of the New Testament. They demanded a return to the purity and sim-plicity of New Testament Christianity. Protestantism did not begin with Luther and Calvin. It began with the Gospel, with the life and death and resurrection of Christ. It teaches what the New Testament teaches, nothing more and nothing less. It was not founded on the writings of Luther, or Calvin, or any of the later writers, although those writings proved helpful in the work of the church. Evangelical Protestantism cannot change greatly, for it is founded on an unchanging Book, com-pleted in the first century and declared in the creeds of all evangelical churches to be the Word of God. The names of Protestant churches are not very old, and the denominations differ in regard to some doctrines; but the churches are in quite close agreement concerning the essentials of the faith, each attempting to hold in its purity the teachings of Christ and the apostles. The disagreement and conflict which Rome at-tempts to picture as existing between Protestant denominations is for the most part exaggeration, and is due largely to Rome's failure to under-stand what Protestantism really is.

How, then, do we know whether or not any particular system sets forth true Christianity? By comparing it with a recognized standard, especially with the Bible which is the ultimate authority. Judged by that standard evangelical Protestantism is the same system of truth that was set forth in the New Testament and practiced by the first century Christians. All accretions, such as purgatory, the authority of tradition, the priesthood, the papacy, the worship of the Virgin Mary and the saints, the veneration of relics, auricular confession ("auricular" —pertaining to the ear; auricular confession, therefore, means confession in the ear of a priest), penance, etc., are totally without Scriptural basis and should be branded as false.

5. CONTRAST BETWEEN PROTESTANT AND ROMAN CATHOLIC COUNTRIES

It is a fact beyond challenge that the Protestant countries of Europe and the Americas have been comparatively strong, progressive, enlightened, and free, while the Roman Catholic countries have remained relatively stationary or have stagnated and have had to be aided economically and politically by the Protestant nations. The Middle Ages were dark because Romanism was dominant and unchallenged. The light that we enjoy, which was first manifested in Europe and then in America, we owe to the Protestant Reformation. How appropriate the inscription on the Reformation monument in Geneva—*Post tenebras lux*, "After the darkness, light"!

The lesson of history is that Romanism means the loss of religious liberty and the arrest of national progress. If after living in the United States one who was not aware of the contrast between Protestant and Roman Catholic cultures were to visit some Roman Catholic countries in Europe or Latin America, not merely to see places that have been fixed up to attract tourists but to live for some time among the common people, it would make him sick at heart to see the ignorance, poverty, superstition, illiteracy, suppression of religious freedom, and legalized prostitution which particularly in Latin America is found in practically every town of any size, a fairly consistent pattern in all of those areas— characteristics of heathenism, characteristics of Romanism.

In Latin America, where the Roman Church has been dominant for four centuries with practically no competition from Protestantism, it has had ample opportunity to bring forth the true fruits of the system. And there, as a church, it has failed miserably. About 90 percent of the people have been baptized in the Roman Catholic Church, but probably not more than 10, or at most 15, percent are practicing Roman Catholics. The present writer is in receipt of a letter from a missionary in Bolivia who writes: "The Roman Catholic Church in Bolivia is not a Christian church at all but an unholy device for keeping the people in ignorance and poverty." He added that Romanism the world over is one unified system, all under the control of the pope in Rome, and that it probably would be as bad in the United States if it were not for the restraining influence of the evangelical churches. Strong words those, but he was writing of a situation concerning which we know but little in this country.

Governments in Roman Catholic countries have been extremely unsteady. Repeatedly the people shoot up their governments or overthrow them. Practically all of those countries have been ruled by dictators at various times, and sometimes for long periods of time. Since the Second World War France has had repeated governmental crises, until a more stable situation was reached making General de Gaulle president and giving him dictatorial powers. Italy has had 15 governmental crises in 14 years, usually, as in France, characterized by resignation of the government, followed by a period of uncertainty and paralysis until a new election was held or a new alignment of parties was worked out. Spain, which is often pointed to as the model Catholic state, is governed under a concordat with the Vatican, has only one political party, the clerical-fascist party of General Franco, and has been under the dictatorship of Franco since 1938. Portugal, too, is a clerical-fascist state, under dictator Antonio Salazar. In that country the fall of the monarchy in 1910 was followed by a period of economic and political chaos, with 40 governmental changes in 18 years, until Salazar became minister of finance in 1928 and prime minister with dictatorial powers in 1932, which position he has held ever since. In the Latin American nations the overthrow of national governments, followed by periods of dictatorship, has occurred repeatedly during the past 15 years—those in Argentina, Brazil, Colombia, Venezuela, Peru, El Salvador, and Cuba having been the most recent.

It cannot be passed off as mere chance that governments in Protestant countries, such as the United States, Britain, Canada, Holland, and the Scandinavian countries, have been so stable over long periods of time while those in the Roman Catholic countries have been so unstable. The result follows in part at least because of the contrasting doctrines of the relation that should exist between church and state. Protestantism holds that the church and the state are each of divine origin, that each is supreme in its own sphere and independent of the other. Romanism holds that power comes to the state through the church, that the church and state should be united with the church holding the superior position, that the pope as God's representative on earth is above all temporal rulers, above all kings, presidents, and governors, that it is the duty of the state to maintain a political atmosphere favorable to the Roman Catholic Church, supporting it with public money while placing restrictions on all other churches, and that the state should do the bidding of the church in punishing heretics. Such doctrines undermine governments by weakening the confidence of the people in them, while the Protestant doctrines strengthen and support them.

Throughout history the Roman Church has sought to gain power from the state, but has never willingly relinquished power to the state. It has always resented paying taxes to the state, even on purely commercial properties that are owned and operated by it, and it has resented any laws requiring its priests to pay income taxes. The continual meddling of the Roman Church in politics, even to the extent of sponsoring Roman Catholic political parties where it is strong enough to do so (usually known as the "Christian Democratic" party, or a similar name, as in Italy, France, Germany, Holland, Belgium, etc.), has caused much resentment. That, no doubt, is also its plan for the United States if and when it becomes strong enough. Usually a political party is not instituted unless it can control at least one-fourth of the total vote. How can any unprejudiced person face these facts and still not see the contrast between the two systems?

We behold a strange phenomenon in the world today. While people in the predominantly Roman Catholic countries are struggling to throw off the yoke of the Roman Church, Protestant countries are welcoming it with open arms and allowing it to dictate policies of state, education, medicine, social life, entertainment, press, and radio. And in no Protestant country is this tendency more clearly seen than in the United States. For 32 years, 1928-1960, one of our great political parties had an unbroken line of national party chairmen who were members of that church, and in 1960 it succeeded in electing a Roman Catholic president of the United States. Although the Constitution makes it illegal to favor one church above another, repeatedly in recent years bills have been passed by Congress and signed by nominally Protestant presidents granting very substantial favors to the Roman Catholic Church. More than $24,000,000 in public money has been given to the Roman Catholic Church in the Philippines since the close of the Second World War, allegedly for war damages, while hardly one-tenth that amount has been given to Protestant, Jewish, and other church groups in that country. In June, 1956, Congress passed, and President Eisenhower signed, a bill giving the Vatican nearly one million dollars ($964,199) for the refurnishing of the pope's summer home at Castel Gandolfo, just outside the city of Rome, Italy—allegedly as war damages inflicted by American air raids, although the State Department has held that this country has no legal obligation for such damages. In election years, when no one wants to vote against the Roman Catholic Church, Congress is particularly vulnerable to such pressures. But nothing was appropriated to restore Protestant churches in Italy or in the other war ravaged countries! Those had no lobby in Washington to represent their cause.

About 80 percent of the money provided by the government under the Hill-Burton bill for the building and operation of sectarian hospitals in the United States ($112,000,000 during the first ten years of its operation) went to Roman Catholic institutions as that church eagerly took such money while most Protestant churches, desirous of maintaining the principle of separation of church and state, were reluctant to accept it. In various places, particularly in the bigger cities governed by Roman Catholic officials, public properties, such as schools, hospitals, building sites, etc., have been turned over to the Roman Catholic Church at give-away prices. Similar things happen in England, where, for instance, parochial schools receive 95 percent of their total costs from the public treasury— but even so, the hierarchy is not satisfied and is demanding complete financial equality with the public schools, which, of course, is fair warning of what the Roman Church would like to achieve in this country.

The hold that Roman Catholicism is able to maintain over large numbers of people, not only in Europe and Latin America but also in the United States, is due in part to its appeal to unregenerate human nature. The Roman concept of sin is quite different from that of Protestantism. Rome does not demand reform in her people. As long as they acknowledge the church and meet the external requirements they are allowed to do about as they please. In our country witness the many corrupt politicians and gangsters in our cities in recent years who have been members of that church and who have remained in good standing while continuing their evil course over long periods of time. A case in point is that of Tom Pendergast, in Kansas City, who with a large number of his accomplices finally was sent to the penitentiary. When he died the Roman Catholic priest who conducted his funeral praised him as a friend and commended his loyalty to his church, because, it was said, he had not missed mass in 30 years. It can be assumed that Roman Catholicism will remain popular as long as the majority of men remain unregenerate.

But the real cause of Roman Catholic growth and success is not to be found so much in its aggressive policy in infiltrating governments, schools, press, radio, etc., nor in its lax moral code. It is to be found rather in *the indifference of Protestants and their lack of devotion to their own evangelical message.* Modernistic and liberal theology has so enervated many of the churches that they have little zeal left to propagate their

faith. Let Protestantism return to its evangelical message and to the
type of missionary zeal that governed the early Christians, and let
Protestants challenge Rome to full and open debate regarding the distinctive doctrines that separate the two systems, and it will be seen that the
one thing Rome does not want is public discussion. Rome prefers to
assert her alleged "rights" and to have them accepted without too much
question. But Protestantism has the truth, and can win this battle any
time that it is willing to force the issue.

In this regard J. Marcellus Kik, former associate editor of *Christianity
Today*, has written:

> "That there is still a remnant of paganism and papalism in the world
> is chiefly the fault of the church. The Word of God is just as powerful
> in our generation as it was during the early history of the church. The
> power of the Gospel is just as strong in this century as in the days of
> the Reformation. These enemies could be completely vanquished if the
> Christians of this day and age were as vigorous, as bold, as earnest, as
> prayerful, and as faithful as Christians were in the first several centuries
> and in the time of the Reformation" (*Revelation Twenty*, p. 74).

Protestants do not desire controversy merely for the sake of controversy, and often shrink from engaging in it. But in this time of rising
tensions certain issues must be faced. Rome continues to press her
propaganda drive. Where she is in the majority she takes special
privileges for herself and places restrictions on, or prohibits, other
churches. Where she is in the minority she asks for special favors,
favors which by no stretch of the imagination are ever given to Protestants
in Roman Catholic countries, and seeks quietly to infiltrate the government, schools, press, radio, hospitals, etc. When Protestants are in the
majority they tend to ignore those things. But when some major issue
arises, such as the nomination of an American ambassador to the Vatican,
or the nomination of a Roman Catholic for President of the United
States, Protestant opposition does become vocal. A few years ago when
President Truman sent the name of General Mark Clark to the Senate
for confirmation as American ambassador to the Vatican, there was
vigorous protest and a full scale debate was fast arising when General
Clark requested that his name be withdrawn. All that the hierarchy
could do was to run for cover and cry "bigot" and "persecutor" at anyone
who opposed such a tie-up with the Vatican. They definitely did not
want a public debate. But the result of such events is to bring out into
the open the issues which normally are more or less kept under cover,
and to afford opportunity for discussion of the issues on their merits.

The kind of society that Roman Catholicism has produced in other

countries where it has been dominant should serve as a fair warning
as to what we can expect if it becomes dominant here. What clearer
warning do we need? Let us take a good look at conditions in those
countries and then ask ourselves if a Roman Catholic America is the
kind of heritage we desire for ourselves and the kind we want to pass on
to later generations. Through the indifference of Protestants and the ag-
gressiveness of Romanists we are in danger of losing the very things
that have made this nation great.

Scripture quotations throughout this book for the most part are from
the American Standard Version of 1901 rather than the King James Version since the former is generally conceded to be more accurate. Quotations from the Roman Catholic Confraternity Version are designated as
such.

II. THE CHURCH

1. DEFINITION

The Bible teaches that Christ founded His church, the Christian church, and that He is both the foundation on which it rests, and the head of the church which is His body: "For other foundation can no man lay than that which is laid, which is Jesus Christ" (I Cor. 3:11); ". . . being built upon the foundation of the apostles and prophets, Jesus Christ himself being the chief corner stone" (Eph. 2:20); "And he put all things in subjection under his feet, and gave him to be head over all things to the church, which is his body" (Eph. 1:22,23); ". . . Christ also is the head of the church" (Eph. 5:23).

The church is composed of all who are true Christians, those who have been "born again," or "born anew" (John 3:3), from all nations and denominations. Local "churches of Christ" (Rom. 16:16) are congregations of Christians who gather together for worship and for missionary activity. And, while they are many, they are all members of the one church of Christ: "For even as we have many members in one body . . . so we, being many, are one body in Christ" (Rom. 12:4,5). This is the true church.

A truly broad and charitable definition of the church is given for example, in the Westminster Confession of Faith, which says:

> "The visible church, which is also catholic or universal under the gospel (not confined to one nation, as before under the law), consists of all those throughout the world, that profess the true religion, together with their children; and is the kingdom of the Lord Jesus Christ, the house and family of God, out of which there is no ordinary possibility of salvation" (XXV: 2).

And the Larger Catechism, in answer to the question, "What is the visible church?" (Q. 62), says:

"The visible church is a society made up of all such as in all ages and places of the world do profess the true religion, and of their children."

The marks of a true church are:
1. The true preaching of the Word of God.
2. The right administration of the sacraments. And,
3. The faithful exercise of discipline.

John Calvin insisted repeatedly on "the ministry of the Word and sacraments" as the distinguishing marks of a true church. To these are generally added the exercise of proper discipline, although minor errors and irregularities of conduct do not in themselves give sufficient cause to withhold acknowledgment of a true church. Dr. Louis Berkhof says concerning the faithful exercise of discipline: "This is quite essential for maintaining the purity of doctrine and for guarding the holiness of the sacraments. Churches that are lax in discipline are bound to discover sooner or later within their circle an eclipse of the light of the truth and an abuse of that which is holy" (*Systematic Theology*, p. 578).

In the Bible the word "church" never means a denomination. The Bible has nothing to say about denominations. Whether a local church chooses to remain strictly independent, or to enter into a working agreement with one or more other local churches, and if so on what terms, is not discussed in Scripture, but is left entirely to the choice of the church itself. And we find that in actual practice churches range all the way from those that remain entirely unrelated to any other, to the other extreme of those that subject themselves to some hierarchy of denominational overlords who own the property and send the minister.

Surely the local church should own the building and grounds that it has developed and paid for. Such ownership serves as a shield against undue denominational pressure being brought to bear upon it. And, as it has the right to decide whether or not it will join a denomination, so it should have the right to withdraw from the denomination if it so chooses.

Usually the word "church," as used in the New Testament, means a local congregation of Christians, such as "the church of God at Corinth," "the church in Jerusalem," "the churches of Galatia," "the church in thy house." At other times it may refer to the church at large, as when we are told that "Christ loved the church, and gave himself up for it" (Eph. 5:25). Or again it may refer to the whole body of Christ in all ages, as when we read of "the general assembly and church of the firstborn who are enrolled in heaven" (Heb. 12:23).

When our Lord prayed for unity, "that they may all be one" (John 17:21), it was primarily a spiritual unity, a oneness of heart and faith, of love and obedience, of true believers, and only secondarily a unity of ecclesiastical organization, that He had in mind, as is made clear by the fact that He illustrated that unity by the relationship which exists between Himself and the Father—"even as thou, Father, art in me, and I in thee." Unity of faith must be achieved before there can be unity of organization. The ideal, of course, would be for the church to be one in both faith and organization. But it clearly is not yet ready for that. Much work remains to be done in teaching God's Word before that can be accomplished. As Christians become more closely united in doctrine they work together more harmoniously and want to be united more closely in organization. But unity of doctrine must always remain primary, for that relates to the very purpose for which the church was founded. The alleged tragedy of disunity of organization is more than offset by the real tragedy of disunity of doctrine that results when conservative and modernistic churches are combined in one organization.

It is just here that the Romanists, who claim to be the only true church, err in attempting to bring all churches, even to force all churches, into one external and mechanical organization. The oneness for which Christ prayed was not external and visible, but spiritual and invisible. There can be and actually is real spiritual unity among Christians apart from organizational unity. The church is not a mechanism, but a living organism, whose head is Christ; and any unity that is mechanical and forced is bound to hinder the very thing that it is designed to promote. When we hear the pope and occasionally other church leaders talk about uniting all churches into one super organization, the words they employ and their method of approach make it clear that what they have in mind is not a spiritual unity of believers but an ecclesiastical and mechanical unity of believers and unbelievers, designed primarily for what they think would be greater efficiency of operation.

And after all perhaps the diversity of churches, with a healthy spirit of rivalry within proper limits, is one of God's ways of keeping the stream of Christianity from becoming stagnant. History is quite clear in showing that where there has been enforced uniformity the church has stagnated, whether in Italy, Spain, France, or Latin America. The confinement of religious life to a dead level of uniformity does not solve our problems.

2. "CATHOLIC"

Something should be said concerning the meaning of the term "catholic," which the Roman Church tries to appropriate exclusively to itself. Dr. J. G. Vos, editor of *Blue Banner Faith and Life*, gives this definition:

"THE CATHOLIC CHURCH: The universal church of God, as distinguished from a particular branch, congregation or denomination of that church." "The Church of Rome," he continues, "has wrongly appropriated to itself the term 'Catholic'; it is self-contradictory to call a body 'Roman' (which is particular) and at the same time 'Catholic' (which means universal)."

A *Catholic Dictionary* gives this definition:

"*Catholic.* The word is derived from the Greek, and simply means universal."

Dr. John H. Gerstner, Professor of Church History in Pittsburgh Theological Seminary, in *The Gospel According to Rome,* says:

"Strictly speaking 'Roman Catholic' is a contradiction of terms. Catholic means universal; Roman means particular. It is the Protestant and not the Romanist who believes in the catholic church. Protestants believe the church is universal or catholic; Rome cannot discover it beyond her own communion. Our formula is: '*Ubi Spiritus ibi ecclesia*'—'Where the Spirit is there is the church.' Her motto is: '*Ubi ecclesia ibi Spiritus*'— 'Where the (Roman) church is there is the Spirit.'

"It is because of the proper historic use of the word 'catholic' that Protestants do not hesitate to recite it in the Apostles' Creed. We cling to the word because we cherish the concept. Rome has no monopoly on it; indeed, as we have suggested, it is a question whether she has any right to it" (p. 14).

All those who believe in Christ as Saviour, regardless of what denomination they belong to, are in fact members of the Christian catholic church. Evangelical Protestants are the truest "catholics," for they base their faith on the New Testament as did the early Christians. The Roman Church has added many doctrines and practices that are not found in the New Testament, and anyone who accepts those becomes, to that extent, a Roman catholic, and by the same token ceases to be a Christian catholic. Since the word "catholic" means "universal," the true Christian catholic church must include *all* true believers, all who belong to the mystical or spiritual body of Christ ("the church, which is his body"—Eph. 1:22,23). But there have been, and are, millions of Christians who have never had any connection with the Roman church. The Roman Church, is, after all, a local church, with headquarters in Rome, Italy and is limited to those who acknowledge the authority of the pope. Even in her most extravagant claims the Roman Church claims only about one in eight of the population of the world, and in the professedly Christian world she has cut herself off from and broken communion with perhaps more than half of Christendom, so that there are probably more professed Christians who reject her authority than acknowledge it. And geographically she fails utterly to prove her claim to universality. Even in the nominally Roman Catholic countries such as Italy, France, Spain, and Latin America, Rome today probably does not have effective control of more than fifteen percent of the people. In any event the Roman Church clearly is not universal, but is only one among numerous others and is outnumbered by the effective membership of the various Protestant and Eastern Orthodox churches.

Bishop J. C. Ryle, of Liverpool (England), has well said:

"There are many 'churches,' but in the New Testament only one true church is recognized. This true church is composed of all believers in the Lord Jesus. It is made up of God's elect—of all converted men and women—of all true Christians. It is a church of which all the members are born again of the Holy Spirit. They all possess repentance toward God, faith toward our Lord Jesus Christ, and holiness of life and conversation. They all draw their religion from one single book—the Bible.

"It is the church whose existence does not depend on forms, ceremonies, cathedrals, churches, vestments, organs, or any act or favor whatever from the hand of man. It has often lived on and continued when all these things have been taken from it. This is the universal church of the Apostles' Creed, and of the Nicene Creed. This is the only church which is truly *universal*. Its members 'are found in every part of the world where the Gospel is received and believed."

And Rev. Stephen L. Testa, a former Roman Catholic, and founder of The Scripture Truth Society, has said:

"The Lord Jesus Christ founded His church (Matt. 16:18), which was evangelical Christian. He was to be the Head, the Holy Spirit the Guide, and the Bible the only rule of faith and practice. It was made up of His followers who were born again and pledged to continue His work of redemption in the world. It was *catholic* in that it was *designed for all the people of the earth*. The church remained pure and faithful to the Gospel for about 300 years, which was the golden age of martyrs and saints, who were persecuted by pagan Rome. After the so-called conversion of emperor Constantine (310 A.D.) Christianity was declared the state religion, and multitudes of pagans were admitted to the church by baptism alone, without conversion. They brought with them their pagan rites, ceremonies and practices which they gradually introduced into the church with Christian names, all of which corrupted the primitive faith and the church became Romanized and paganized. What makes a church truly catholic is its adherence to the Gospel of Christ and the Apostles' Creed. The Roman Church has added popery and so many other pagan doctrines and practices that many people think it no longer either Christian or catholic.

"The Reformation of the 16th century was a protest against those pagan doctrines, a wholesale withdrawal from the official church and a return to the primitive catholic Christianity of the New Testament. The Roman Church today can become again a truly catholic church by renouncing popery and those dogmas and practices which are contrary to the Word of God and holding fast to its primitive foundation, on which basis the reunion of all Christian churches could be realized. The name 'catholic,' when applied to the Roman Church exclusively, is a misnomer, for it befits better those Protestant churches which hold fast to the Bible and the Apostles' Creed without any additions whatever. 'For I testify unto every man that heareth the words of the prophecy of this book, If any man shall add unto them, God shall add unto him the plagues which are written in this book: and if any man shall take away from the words of the book of this prophecy, God shall take away his part from the tree of life, and out of the holy city, which are written in this book' (Rev. 22:18-19).

"The true church of Christ is invisible, made up of truly converted people who are to be found in all the visible churches and whose names are written in heaven, and the visible churches exist to train saints for the kingdom of Christ" (Booklet, *Is Romanism in the Bible?* p. 3).

3. WHAT IS A "SECT"?

Another trait of the Roman Church is her attempt to brand all other church groups as "sects," and as schismatic. First, let us fix clearly in mind precisely what a "sect" is. Dictionary definitions tend to emphasize the divisive, schismatic, heretical elements in defining a sect. Hence we would define a sect as a group that shuts itself in as God's exclusive people, and shuts all others out. By its exclusiveness a sect cuts itself off and isolates itself from the main stream of Christian life. On that basis the Roman Church, with its bigoted and offensive claim to be "the only true church," its readiness to brand all others as heretics, its anathemas or curses so readily pronounced against all who dare to differ with its pronouncements, and its literally dozens of heresies and practices which are not found in the New Testament, automatically brands itself as the biggest and most prominent of all the sects.

This sectarianism is shown, for instance, in statements such as the *Syllabus of Errors,* issued by pope Pius IX, in 1864, and still in full force where the Roman Church can enforce its will. The hierarchy in the

United States plays down this Syllabus, and for many years has conducted a subtle campaign designed to hide many of its distinctive doctrines and so to gain favor with the American public. But here are its claims in plain language. Some of the most distinctive articles in their affirmative form are:

15. "No man is free to embrace and profess that religion which he believes to be true, guided by the light of reason."
17. "The eternal salvation of any out of the true church of Christ is not even to be hoped for."
18. "Protestantism is not another and diversified form of the one true Christian religion in which it is possible to please God equally as in the Catholic Church."
21. "The Church has power to define dogmatically the religion of the Catholic Church to be the only true religion."
24. "The Church has the power of employing force and (of exercising) direct and indirect temporal power."
37. "No national Church can be instituted in a state of division and separation from the authority of the Roman Pontiff."
42. "In legal conflict between Powers (Civil and Ecclesiastical) the Ecclesiastical Law prevails."
45. "The direction of Public Schools in which the youth of Christian states are brought up . . . neither can nor ought to be assumed by the Civil Authority alone."
48. "Catholics cannot approve of a system of education for youth apart from the Catholic faith, and disjoined from the authority of the Church."
54. "Kings and Princes [including, of course, Presidents, Prime Ministers, etc.] are not only not exempt from the jurisdiction of the Church, but are subordinate to the Church in litigated questions of jurisdiction."
55. "The Church ought to be in union with the State, and the State with the Church."
57. "Philosophical principles, moral science, and civil laws may and must be made to bend to Divine and Ecclesiastical authority."
63. "Subjects may not refuse obedience to legitimate princes, much less rise in insurrection against them."
67. "The marriage tie is indissoluble by the law of nature; divorce, properly so called, cannot in any case be pronounced by the civil authority."
73. "Marriage among Christians cannot be constituted by any civil contract; the marriage-contract among Christians must always be a sacrament; and the contract is null if the sacrament does not exist."
77. "It is necessary even in the present day that the Catholic religion shall be held as the only religion of the State, to the exclusion of all other forms of worship."
78. "Whence it has been unwisely provided by law, in some countries called

Catholic, that persons coming to reside therein shall enjoy the free exercise of their religion."
80. "The Roman Pontiff cannot and ought not to reconcile himself to, or agree with, Progress, Liberalism, and Modern Civilization."

These statements are from the pope who just six years later established the doctrine of papal infallibility! The Roman Church here condemns freedom of religion, freedom of speech and of the press, the separation of church and state, asserts the authority of the church over the state and of the pope over civil rulers, the right of the church to direct all education, the right of the church to suppress other faiths, condemns the public school system, and many other things which are integral parts of our American way of life. Let no one say that this *Syllabus of Errors* belongs to a former age and that it is not to be taken seriously. Even today it forms a part of the ordination vows of every Roman Catholic priest in the world. Every priest takes an oath on the Bible that he believes and will defend the eighty articles of this Syllabus. No part of it has ever been repudiated. Hence it contains official Roman Catholic doctrine. With the church committed to this Syllabus *how can anyone at one and the same time be a member of the Roman Catholic Church and a loyal American citizen?*

In this Syllabus the Roman Church displays a bitter, sectarian spirit in its relations with other churches. In every local community Roman Catholic priests refuse to join ministerial associations or to cooperate with ministers from other churches in any form of religious observances, and they not infrequently refuse to cooperate even in non-religious community projects.

On the other hand most Protestant churches are remarkably free from sectarianism. Most of them take a broad, tolerant attitude in acknowledging as true Christians any of their fellow men who base their hope for salvation on faith in Christ and live a good Christian life—in which case, as we have just seen, they are "catholic," ecumenical in the best sense of the term.

It may be charitably assumed that there are good Christians in all denominations, including the Roman Catholic. For any one branch of the church to claim that those within its fold alone constitute the body of true Christians is both crude and impudent, and is inconsistent with the principles of love and charity so clearly commanded in the Scriptures.

The intolerance and sectarianism of Romanism is also shown in her attempt to use the word "church" for herself alone, as a synonym for the Roman Catholic Church, thereby unchurching all others, and by referring to Protestants as "non-Catholics." Protestants are too lax in allowing the Roman Church to deprecate them with terminology which implies that they have no place in the church universal. The correct meaning of the term "church" and "catholic" should be pointed out, and doctrinal and historical evidence cited to show that the Roman Church herself is the church of schism and innovation, that by adding a host of unscriptural doctrines she has departed from the simplicity of the Gospel and from apostolic practice. It can be shown that more than half of Rome's present creed was unknown to the early church. Consequently, she has neither the moral nor the logical right to appropriate to herself the terms "church" and "catholic."

We suspect that it is just because the Roman Church knows that so much of her doctrine and so many of her practices are unscriptural or anti-Scriptural that as a matter of self-defense she attempts to appropriate these terms to herself. A more appropriate name for this church, one that we have used frequently, is, the Roman Church, or the Church of Rome. These terms are accurate, and moreover they are terms which appear frequently in her own literature, written by representative Roman Catholics. Hence Protestants do that church no injustice in speaking of it under these terms.

Furthermore, in its official title—the Holy Roman Catholic and Apostolic Church—the Roman Church seeks to appropriate the word "apostolic." But again she has no right to call herself apostolic, since she bears so little resemblance to that church, more than half of her present doctrines and practices being unknown to the apostolic church. She applies to herself the term "holy," but the fact is that through the ages and in her official capacity the Roman Church has been guilty of the most atrocious crimes, practiced in the name of religion, including murder, robbery, persecution of all kinds, bribery, fraud, deception, and practically every other crime known to man. Such crimes have been practiced not merely by church members, but by popes, cardinals, bishops, and priests who, as a study of church history will show, undeniably were evil men. Those crimes still are practiced where the Roman Church is attempting to suppress Protestantism—in Colombia, for instance, since 1948, when the liberal government was overthrown and a new government came into power with the support of the Roman Catholic Church and a concordat with the Vatican, 116 Protestant Christians have been killed because of their faith, 66 Protestant churches or chapels have been destroyed by fire or bombing, over 200 Protestant schools have been closed, and Protestant work of any kind forbidden in approximately two-thirds of the country which has been

designated "mission territory" (See Report of the Evangelical Confederation of Colombia, Bulletin No. 50, June 26, 1959).

The assumption of Roman Catholic writers that theirs is the true
church, and that it is the same orthodox, martyr, missionary church of
apostolic times is manifestly false. The claim that the popes are in the
direct line of succession from St. Peter—even if such a claim could be
proved, which it cannot—would mean but little without imitation of
the lives of the apostles and conformity to their doctrines. Jeremiah
rebuked the foolish confidence of the Jews in his day who cried, "The
temple of Jehovah, the temple of Jehovah . . . are these" (7:4), and called
on them rather to prove their devotion to God with righteous and holy
living. Caiaphas was in the line of Aaron and was the successor of many
pious priests, but that did not make him and the Jews who crucified
Jesus the true church. John Calvin called the Church of Rome in his
day a foul harlot rather than the spouse of Christ, because of the low
moral standard practiced and tolerated by her priests. Her pretensions
to be the true church of Christ were shown by her actions to be false.
How could she be the kingdom of Christ when her way of life was at
such variance with His Word?

4.   CHURCH GOVERNMENT

As Protestants we believe in and practice democracy in Church
government as well as in state government. We have local organizations in which ministers and laymen with equal voting rights handle
local church problems, and for the denominations at large, general
assemblies or conventions or conferences, composed of ministers and
elders, usually in equal numbers, who are the elected representatives
of the churches. Both the New Testament and the history of the church
during the first four or five centuries make it abundantly clear that
Christianity is essentially democratic in tendency. That tendency becomes manifest wherever the spiritual life of the church is free to assert
itself.

The New Testament church was an organized band of baptized believers practicing New Testament ordinances and actively engaged in
carrying out the Great Commission. Of that organization Christ alone
was the Head. Believers were related to Him and to each other as
members of the body. Each local church appears to have been a self-
governing body. As the church in Jerusalem grew and needed more
organization, that was provided, not by hierarchical appointment, but
in a democratic way without consulting any other church. We read:
"The twelve called the multitude of the disciples unto them, and

said, . . . Look ye out therefore, brethren, from among you seven men of good report" (Acts 6:2-3). There was no dictation by Peter, nor by any other apostle, nor by the apostles as a group. Rather it was "the multitude of the disciples," that is, the membership of the church, who made the decision. Likewise, the church at Antioch sent out missionaries from its own membership (in this instance, Paul and Barnabas), without seeking permission or advice from any other body (Acts 13:1-4).

But while the New Testament churches were autonomous, there were certain ties which bound them together, such as that of maintaining doctrinal purity, for which purpose the Jerusalem conference was assembled (Acts 15:1-29), that of ministering to the material needs of the saints in sister churches in time of crisis (Acts 11:27-30; II Cor. 9:1-5); and a fellowship of worship (Acts 2:46-47; 20:6-7; Heb. 10:25). A study of the church as it is set forth in the New Testament shows that it was absolutely dependent upon the Word of God for its existence. It was, therefore, completely subordinate to that authority in matters of doctrine.

The fact of the matter is that we are told but very little about the organization of the early church or about the relations that existed between the various bodies, no doubt because the new congregations started in an elementary way and the problems that developed within the congregations or between congregations depended upon local circumstances. Elders were appointed in all the churches, and these had the general oversight of their respective churches as regarded teaching, preaching, and the administration of congregational affairs, including their relations with other congregations. We are inclined to believe that the early church was neither Episcopal, nor Presbyterian, nor Congregational, but a combination of all three, and that local churches then as now may have differed considerably in their manner of government. In any event it is quite clear that the Roman Catholic Church, with its hierarchical form of government, was *not* the New Testament church, for the institution of the papacy, with a sacrificing priesthood, did not develop until some five centuries later.

The spurious logic of the hierarchy through which it lays claim to supreme authority over all Christians finds no support in Scripture. In fact the idea of a totalitarian church in which the laymen has no vote and no voice in the formulation of doctrines, laws, and policies, a church in which he is *told* what to believe and what to do but in which he is never invited to discuss or help work out those beliefs and practices, seems to be the extreme opposite of that set forth in the New Testament.

It is a basic tenet of Protestantism that the Word of God as given in the Scriptures is to be put into the language of the people and that it is sufficiently clear so that the individual Christian has a responsibility to read and to think for himself. He has the right of private judgment in spiritual affairs. He cannot surrender his conscience to the church or to a priest, but must think, speak, worship, and act in such a manner that he can give an account to God for what he is and does. This does not mean that he is to ignore the teaching of the church or the rich heritage of theological knowledge that has been accumulated over the centuries. Rather within proper limits he will seek the fellowship of the church with its accumulated wisdom and will further his spiritual life in that atmosphere of mutual love and helpfulness which comes through association with other Christians.

In the typical Roman Catholic countries the essence of the church is composed of the bishops and priests, to the exclusion of the laity which, while expected to provide the financial support, is kept in the dark and in abject subservience to a power-hungry hierarchy. The lay people are purely passive in the life of their church: they have no say in the choice of their priests and almost no say in the administration of the material possessions of the church. Very little emphasis, if indeed any at all, is placed on Bible study. Instead, moral standards are inflexibly set by the church. The individual must submit his conscience and his intelligence to this external authority, which tells him what is right and what is wrong. From childhood he is trained to accept the domination of the priest over the whole realm of his moral, social, and political life. He is told what to do and how to do it, even as regards personal and family affairs. Needless to say, not all Roman Catholics obey these dictates, particularly if they have some contact with Protestant ideals of freedom of religion and conduct. But the attitude of subservience is the ideal which the hierarchy seeks to maintain in its people. Few Roman Catholics, even in a Protestant country such as the United States, realize what a great debt they owe to Protestantism. Instead they support their church in fighting Protestantism.

5. THE CHURCH IN POLITICS

The Protestant ideal is that church leaders and church assemblies are altogether distinct from the civil magistracy, and that they have no jurisdiction whatever in civil and political affairs. It is, however, the duty of the church to teach her people, through her ministry and laity, their duties in the state as Christians. Her ministry as regards the state focuses at that point, and stops right there. She does not seek to become a political power rivaling the state, nor to become a state within a state. She must not allow herself to be used as a pressure group for the securing of certain rights and temporal benefits for men, nor to pressure the state for reform measures, even though such reforms may be needed and desirable from the Christian veiwpoint. Christians as individuals are indeed to work for whatever reforms may be needed. But the church is not to do so in her corporate capacity. Such action on the part of the church almost invariably will detract from her primary mission of the proclamation of the Gospel and ministering to the spiritual needs of men, and will tend to give people a wrong conception as to what her true mission really is. And finally, she must not pressure the state for public funds to support her local churches, schools, and other institutions.

The Westminster Confession of Faith sets forth the role of the church in these words:

> "Synods and councils are to handle or conclude nothing, but that which is ecclesiastical: and are not to intermeddle with civil affairs which concern the commonwealth, unless by way of humble petition in cases extraordinary; or by way of advice for satisfaction of conscience, if they be thereunto required by the civil magistrate" (XXXI: 4).

Protestantism asks nothing of the state except such liberty and independence as it already enjoys in most Protestant countries, and which, chiefly through Protestant influence, the Roman Catholic Church also enjoy in those same countries.

In almost total contrast with this, the Roman Catholic Church seeks to exert a controlling influence in both the church and the state. This has been well expressed by Avro Manhattan, a critic of Romanism, in *The Vatican in World Politics:*

> "The better to exert its double activity (religious and political), the Catholic Church has two facets: first, the religious institution, the Catholic Church itself; secondly, the political power, the Vatican. Although they deal separately, whenever convenient, with problems affecting religion and politics, the two are in reality one. At the head of both stands the pope, who is the supreme religious leader of the Catholic Church as a purely spiritual power, as well as the supreme head of the Vatican in its quality of a world-wide diplomatic-political center and an independent sovereign state" (p. 19; Gaer Associates, New York; 1949).

The Roman Catholic Church is both a church and a political system. As such it attempts to exert its influence in every sphere of human activity, expediency alone determining whether it moves as a religious institution or as a political institution. These activities may be exercised separately or in unison, depending on the purpose to be accomplished and the type of people with whom they have to deal. On the lower level, through its local congregations, it presents itself as a religious organization, and its appeals for money and support and public trust are made on that basis. But in its higher branches, as its influence is exerted through the hierarchy, it becomes increasingly a political organization, until in the Vatican it is concerned almost exclusively with political affairs and seeks to exert a controlling influence over the affairs of nations. It has a Papal Secretary of State who visits other governments and functions in much the same way that our American Secretary of State functions in Washington. It sends ambassadors and ministers to other nations, and receives ambassadors and ministers from other nations. All of this political activity is, of course, utterly without Scriptural support, and is in fact contrary to what the New Testament teaches concerning the nature and purpose of the church.

C. Stanley Lowell, associate director of Protestants and Others United for Separation of Church and State, has recently said:

> "The fact is that the Vatican is a state-church hybrid which alternately poses as a church and as a state depending on which will prove the more profitable at the moment. The Vatican claims all prerogatives as a state, but denies all responsibility as a state because it is a church" (*Christianity Today*, Feb. 1, 1960).

To describe this activity there has been coined a word, "clericalism," meaning the organized political power of the higher clergy exerted in the affairs of a nation. This preoccupation of the hierarchy with temporal affairs has led some to declare, with good reason, that the Roman Church is not a church at all, but *primarily a government,* a political-commercial system which cloaks itself with religion to give it an air of respectability. The fact is that the Roman Catholic Church professes to be a state, without accepting the responsibilities of a state government; and at the same time it professes to be a church, without accepting the limitations which the New Testament sets for the church.

This double function has led to the conception of the Roman Church as an institution needing rulers after the manner of the state. Hence the concentration of power in the hands of the priests, bishops, and particularly in the hands of the pope as the coordinator of this vast world system, and the blind obedience expected from the laity in all countries to a foreign potentate of a clerical-fascist state.

A specific example of what papal control can mean is seen in the issuance of a directive, in April, 1958, by the pope to all Roman Catholics in Italy, just prior to the election in that country, forbidding them to vote for any party or candidates not favored by the Roman Catholic Church and declaring that anyone who did so vote would be subject to excommunication. The important thing about that directive is the principle involved. If the pope can issue a political order telling the Roman Catholics in Italy how to vote, he can do the same thing to those in the United States or in any other country. They all owe him the same kind and degree of obedience. The pope himself, of course, is the judge as to what parties or candidates are "Communistic" or otherwise not acceptable to the Roman Church. In Latin America Roman Catholic propaganda has long sought to identify Protestants and Communists as one and the same. That again serves as a clear warning as to what can happen here if Romanism comes into a position of dominance.

6. A CHURCH UNDER FOREIGN CONTROL

It has been 186 years since the United States gained her independence. While all other American churches that were in existence at that time have long since been granted their independence or have declared their independence from the parent churches in the country of their origin, the Roman Catholic Church remains as firmly as ever under the control of the pope in Rome. Furthermore, there are no democratic processes of any kind in the Roman Church by which the people can indicate their preferences or desires to the Vatican, nor even so much as express to the bishop of their diocese a choice regarding their own local priests. Everything is autocratically controlled by the hierarchy. However, it is true that while the local congregation has no official part in the matter of choosing a priest, as a matter of practical church management the wishes and advice of members of the congregation often are sought and taken into consideration.

At the head of this organization, with almost unlimited power, is the pope. The next ranking officials, the cardinals, often called the "princes of the church," are appointed by the pope. There is no veto power, either in the district or country over which the cardinal is to preside, or anywhere else in the church, by which his appointment can be rejected or even questioned. If the cardinal was a bishop or archbishop before his appointment he continues to hold that office and to exercise that authority after his appointment.

The number of cardinals has varied somewhat, the full number having remained at 70 for the past several centuries, until pope John XXIII, in 1960, increased the number to 85. The pope alone decides how many cardinals there shall be. Throughout most of history a majority, often a large majority, have been Italians. At the present time the Italians number 33 (several of those are from the city of Rome), still far more than any other country, the next highest being 8 from France, then 6 from the United States, 5 from Spain, 4 from Germany, 3 from Brazil, 2 each from Britain, Canada, Portugal, and Argentina, and 1 each from 18 other countries—surely not a very representative arrangement either numerically or geographically. While only 6 of these are Americans, an increase in 1959 from 4, the American branch of the Roman Church is by all odds the strongest and most influential and, from all indications, furnishes considerably more than half of the world revenues of the Vatican.

At the death of a pope the cardinals meet in Rome in the so-called College of Cardinals, and elect a new pope. This is their most important function. Usually one is chosen from their own number. After the election of a new pope the cardinals individually pledge their complete allegiance to him, even to the extent of prostrating themselves on the floor before him and kissing his foot as a symbol of submission. What a servile act that is! They then disband and return to their respective countries. They have no authority to re-assemble, or to remove a pope from office no matter what he may do. In the meantime they remain subject to him, and can be removed from office by him at any time, without any explanation whatever if he so desires.

Bishops are usually nominated by the cardinals but receive their appointments directly from the pope and remain immediately subject to him. Each bishop is required to appear before the pope in Rome for ordination and to make his vows of allegiance personally to him. They too pledge complete allegiance in an impressive and colorful ceremony, also prostrating themselves before him and kissing his foot. They are the pope's chief liaison officers through which he maintains contact with the church throughout the world. Each reports regularly to the pope concerning the affairs of the church in his diocese, that is, the district over which he has charge, and each must present himself in person to the pope at least once every five to ten years.

Next step down the ladder are the priests. They are immediately subject to the bishop of the diocese. The bishop supervises their course of training, inquires into the fitness of candidates, chooses those who shall be ordained, ordains them, assigns them to churches, transfers them, and removes them from office as he sees fit, without explanation if he wishes. Each priest pledges complete allegiance to his bishop, and submits reports to him. No priest who has had difficulties with his bishop will be accepted for work in any other diocese until he has made satisfaction to his own bishop. He must at all costs remain on good terms with his bishop, otherwise he is helpless.

The people in turn are expected to obey the priest, and to support him and the church through their services and money. They are trained and disciplined to that end from childhood. No one is to question the authority of the priest, even in domestic or family affairs. Democratic processes are discouraged. Lay organizations have only very limited scope, usually are not encouraged, and are excluded from authority in the church at large. Such lay organizations as do exist have clerical sponsors.

While in Protestant churches the people usually have the final say in regard to the choice of ministers and the powers granted to them, in the Roman Church the laity has no part at all in the ordination and calling of the clergy. The Council of Trent, in a decree directed in part against Protestantism, placed that power safely in the hands of the clergy, with the pronouncement: "In the ordination of bishops, priests, and of the other orders neither the consent nor vocation nor authority of the people . . . is required" (Sess. XXIII, Ch. 4), and even pronounced a curse upon anyone claiming such rights for the laity (Canon 7).

The Roman Catholic Church is, therefore, a totalitarian, autocratic organization from top to bottom. And the pope, claiming jurisdiction over from 300 million to 450 million Roman Catholics, the owner of fabulous wealth, and holding life tenure in his office, is by all odds the most absolute ruler in the world. And through the years the people, even in freedom loving America, have shown amazing docility in accepting the rule of the hierarchy.

In every Roman Catholic diocese, unless there are special corporation laws in the state favorable to the hierarchy, the title to all church property—grounds, churches, schools, monasteries, convents, cemeteries, and commercial businesses and properties owned by the church— is held by the bishop as an individual, often as a "corporation sole," which is a legal device by which he is permitted to hold church property. He can mortgage, lease, or sell such properties at will without consulting the people or the local church or diocese, nor does he render any financial report to the people concerning such sales or transactions. He reports only to the pope in Rome. Local church finances are in the hands of the priest, or of the bishop to whom he reports. Control of church finances and property by lay trustees such as is the custom in practically all Protestant churches is forbidden, having been abolished by papal decree in the last century. The bishop in turn, under Canon Law, that is, Roman Catholic Church law, holds the property in trust for and subject to the control of the pope.

The purpose of the Roman Church in having all such property recorded in the name of the bishop rather than treating it as a corporation is to avoid the necessity of making public financial reports. Canon law does not permit the incorporating of such properties unless the laws of the state are so drawn that they grant special favors to the hierarchy—which in this Protestant country they usually do not.

Where the money comes from, and where it goes, is all a deep, dark secret—enabling the hierarchy to accept money from various sources and for various causes which if known might subject it to public criticism; also enabling it to channel money into various projects at home and abroad to suit the purpose of the hierarchy without the criticism that would be sure to arise if it were generally known how the money was used. The implicit trust demanded by the Roman Church extends not only to theological and ecclesiastical matters, but to financial matters as well.

In contrast with the secrecy practiced in the Roman Church most Protestant churches voluntarily make public reports at least once each year of all funds received and expended, both locally and in the denomination at large. These reports are included in the annual minutes, and sometimes are published in newspapers and magazines. If anyone doubts that the finances of the Roman Church are a closely guarded secret, let him try to find out how much money is received, where it comes from, how it is expended in the local church, how much is given to the bishop, and how much is sent to Rome. He will find that the priest reports only to the bishop, and that the bishop reports only to the pope. Ironical as it may seem, this nation, mostly Protestant, is the main support of the Roman Catholic Church in her world work. But it does at least point up the fact that Roman Catholicism does better spiritually and economically where it has to stand on its own feet, where it is not supported by the state but is in competition with other churches.

In regard to the ownership of church property, a present day case that has attracted considerable attention is that of the De La Salle Institute, of Napa, California. There a group of Roman Catholic monks producing wine and brandy operate the largest brandy distillery in the United States, under the trade name Christian Brothers. Until recently they had not paid income taxes for thirty years. They have an outlet through the Seagrams company, one of the largest whiskey distributors in the industry. The Bureau of Internal Revenue has ruled that this company is subject to income tax, the amount involved being more than $1,840,000. The Christian Brothers have claimed exemption from corporate taxes on the profits of this commercial liquor business on the ground that the distillery is church property, "an integral part of the Roman Catholic

Church," held in trust for the benefit of the pope in Rome. When this case was given some publicity Christian Brothers paid part of the tax, $490,000, for the years 1952, 1953 and 1956, then filed a claim to recover the money. But after a prolonged court trial the claim was rejected. Net corporate profits in the three years involved were $3,250,000. See *Church and State*, July-August, 1961.

Various other church businesses over the country come under this same classification, two prominent ones being a radio and television broadcasting station in New Orleans, which accepts commercial advertising, operated by Jesuit priests at Loyola University, and another in St. Louis, also operated by Jesuit priests. Exemption from taxation, of course, gives such companies a substantial advantage over other companies that pay taxes. Such exemption is discriminatory and unfair and is an offense against all people and corporations that do pay taxes.

7. THE UNITY AND DIVERSITY OF PROTESTANTISM

It has long been Roman Catholic policy to represent Protestantism as composed of many denominations which are hopelessly divided and constantly quarreling among themselves. In view of the Romanist emphasis on unity and solidarity, the Roman Catholic laity has indeed found it hard to understand how there can be various Protestant denominations, and this has presented a real stumbling-block to many who are inclined to leave the Church of Rome. They have been taught to believe that each Protestant denomination claims to be exclusively the true church (as does their own) and that one cannot be saved unless he belongs to that church. The puzzle looks insolvable. They simply would not know where to turn.

It is true, of course, that the right of private judgment or private interpretation, which is claimed by all Protestant churches, has resulted in the rise of a great many denominations. But the remarkable thing is that in Protestantism there is a strong undercurrent of spiritual unity. Mechanical and organizational unity is a secondary thing with them. The great proportion of Protestant denominations do not claim to be the only true church, but readily and gladly acknowledge that salvation is to be found in any church where the Gospel is faithfully preached.

The various Protestant denominations agree quite fully on practically all of the essentials of the faith. They believe that the Bible and the Bible alone is the Word of God, and they accept it as the authoritative guide in church affairs. They believe in the deity of Christ, in His sacrificial death on the cross as a substitute for those who place their faith in Him, and that He alone is the Head of the Church. They are in general agreement concerning the meaning of the sacraments, baptism, and the Lord's Supper. They believe in the personal and visible return of Christ, the resurrection of the body, a future judgment, heaven and hell. Their ideas concerning moral character, spiritual life, and the relationship that should exist between church and state are quite similar. Whether called Baptists, Methodists, Lutherans, Presbyterians, or what not, they all belong to one body, the church of Christ, just as the 50 states of the United States have various names and local governments but all belong to one nation. Their basic attitude toward one another is not that of opposition and competition but rather of cooperation and friendship. Ministers of one denomination are often invited to speak or to conduct the entire service in churches of other denominations, and the laity is free to attend churches of which they are not members. Union services, particularly in evangelistic meetings, are common, often with all of the Protestant churches in a city cooperating, as witness the famous Billy Sunday evangelistic campaigns of a few years ago and the Billy Graham meetings in more recent years. On various radio programs the listeners are scarcely aware of the denomination to which the speaker belongs. Protestants thus acknowledge fellow Protestants in other denominations as true Christains. And they are united in rejecting what they believe to be the errors of the Roman Church, such as the priesthood, mass, confession, purgatory, worship of the Virgin Mary, etc.

On the other hand, the teachings that divide Protestants, while sometimes important in themselves, are minor compared with their differences with Romanism. They may differ in regard to the form of baptism or the Lord's Supper; some are Calvinists while others are Arminians; their form of church government may be Episcopal, Presbyterian, or Congregational. But when the Bible is taken as the authoritative guide, the liberty that each has to think through his own religion and arrive at conclusions for himself does not make for such sharp divisions as some might expect.

No one has expressed more beautifully the unity of the Protestant churches than that venerable Presbyterian theologian, Dr. Charles Hodge. Said he:

> "These separate churches remain one: (1) because they continue to be subject to the same Lord, to be animated by the same Spirit, and to possess the same faith; (2) because they recognize each other as churches, just as every Christian recognizes every other Christian as a fellow believer, and consequently recognize each other's members, ordinances, and acts of discipline; (3) they continue one body because they are subject to one common tribunal. The tribunal at first was the apostles,

now the Bible and the mind of the church as a whole, expressed some-times in one way and sometimes in another" (Article, reprinted in *Eternity* magazine, June, 1958).

The unity of spirit among Protestants minimizes very substantially the denominational differences. Consequently, when Roman Catholics leave their church and become Protestants they usually are surprised at the unity of faith and worship which they discover. The fact is that there is often more unity in Protestantism than in Romanism. The rivalry that for centuries has existed between the Dominicans and the Franciscans, between both of those orders and the Jesuits, and between various orders of monks and nuns, especially in countries in which there were no Protestant churches, has often been sharp and bitter. Such rivalries, how-ever, usually are suppressed by the pope so that they do not come to public attention.

Listen to the testimony of a former priest, now superintendent of Me-morial Hospital, Phoenix, Arizona, concerning the unity that he finds in Protestantism and the contrast between Romanism and Protestantism as regards the participation of the laity in church services. Emmett Mc-Loughlin, in his best seller book, *People's Padre*, which was published in 1954 and which now has passed the 250,000 mark, says:

"To me the differences among Protestants, though doctrinal, are superficial and non-essential. Their unity is greater than their diver-gency. . . .

"To me, the outstanding characteristic of all Protestant forms of wor-ship is their enthusiasm. Whether in a revival tent, in an ivy-covered church, or in an impressive cathedral, the members of the congregation show a spontaneity in praying, singing, and listening that does not exist in Roman Catholic churches. The reason is obvious: Most Protestants go to church because they want to; Catholics generally are there be-cause they are afraid not to be. Missing mass deliberately on only one Sunday is for Catholics a mortal sin and damns their souls to hell. The mass is a stereotyped Latin ritual that somehow is supposed to placate God. Protestant services of any denomination, even the silent Quaker service, calls for an active and voluntary participation of all those present. . . .

"The Protestant clergy—and I know many of them intimately—seem far more sincere and personally dedicated than the average Roman Catholic priest. This is probably because they are in the ministry through adult choice, not drawn into it when too young to know better. Protestants remain in the ministry because they wish to, not because they are bound irrevocably by laws of their churches or because of threats of divine and human reprisals if they leave the ministry" (pp. 272, 273)

And Walter M. Montano, a former editor of *Christian Heritage,* and also a former Roman Catholic, says:

"One of the outstanding marks of Protestantism is its *unity in diversity.* This is a characteristic inherent in its very nature, but unfortunately, is poorly understood by many of its beneficiaries.

"This diversity creates and stimulates freedom of action within the limits of what is right before God and man. The dissenting groups or congregations, when released from their Roman shackles, learn for the first time the blessings of freedom of expression. Diversity blocks the road to any religious monopoly, and prevents any man from standing in the place of God to rule the community with that totalitarian despotism that in the lexicon of the Roman Church is called 'papal infallibility.'

"In this concept of Protestantism there is no room for anyone with the investiture of a pope, and for this very reason, organic unity is a foreign element to Protestantism. The lack of organic unity is the strength, not the weakness, of Protestantism, and assures to us our freedom before God. . . . Unity and liberty are in opposition; as the one diminishes, the other increases. The Reformation broke down unity; it gave liberty. . . . America, in which of all countries the Reformation at the present moment has farthest advanced, should offer to thoughtful men much encouragement. Its cities are filled with churches built by voluntary gifts; its clergy are voluntarily sustained, and are, in all directions, engaged in enterprises of piety, education, mercy. What a difference between their private lives and that of ecclesiastics before the Reformation!

"Unfortunately, Protestants themselves at times succumb to a superficial criticism of our lack of organic unity without realizing that it is the safeguard of our liberty in Christ. We deplore the fact that in some isolated quarters there exist ideas and ambitions to establish a 'super-church' with a Protestant hierarchy and its well constituted ecclesiastical army. This will never happen as long as Christian Protestants remain loyal to the principles upon which Protestantism was founded. There is an essential and vast difference between organic unity, the boast of the Roman Church, and the spiritual unity, which identifies Protestant Christianity. Organic unity produces a machine which is an end in itself. Spiritual unity, on the other hand, the unity of the one true church of Jesus Christ, binds the hearts of all under one Head, the Lord Jesus Christ, while at the same time preserving the identity of each member" (*Christian Heritage,* October, 1958).

Unfortunately among Protestants there are some who are so absorbed with the idea of church union that they even hope for an eventual union with the Roman Catholic Church. Concerning these Dr. Montano says:

"These are foolish men who choose to walk in darkness. They cannot see the right path because they have chosen to be blind to the evils of the Roman Church, both past and present. Both of these concepts the desire for a Protestant 'super-church' and the desire for union with the Vatican, are the very antithesis of Protestantism and will destroy the very thing that gave life to the Reformation. . . . Only a militant Protestantism can save America and the world."

It is not surprising that there are many branches of the Christian church. The process of division started even in apostolic times, for we are told that Paul and Barnabas, though loyal friends and faithful co-workers in the church, disagreed because Barnabas insisted on taking Mark with them. In Acts 15:39 we read: "And there arose a sharp contention, so that they parted asunder one from the other."

In his first Epistle to the Corinthians Paul complained about divisions in the church because some said, "I am of Paul . . . I am of Apollos . . . I am of Peter . . . Is Christ divided" (1:12-13). That process has been going on through the centuries. The church has never been one solid organization. From the first centuries there have been schisms, and what are called heresies. Furthermore, those often arose not outside of but within the Christian church and were defended by members within the church. The church still has a long way to go before spiritual unity becomes a reality. In the present state of the church it is inevitable that there should be divisions. In answer to the Roman Catholic claim to be the one true church, we reply, Nonsense! The Roman Church is only one branch of a much larger body. The Eastern Orthodox Church is older and has a more direct connection with apostolic Christianity than does the Roman. Each Protestant denomination is as much a unit within itself as is the Roman Catholic or Eastern Orthodox Church. And most Protestant churches have a record of much truer devotion and loyalty to the Scriptures, and of having produced a higher morality and spirituality among their people than does either the Roman Catholic or Eastern Orthodox Church.

There is but one way to prevent divisions in the present day church, and that is by making unity a higher virtue than truth. The Roman Church achieves unity by eliminating religious liberty. A member of that church who will not subordinate his judgment to that of the pope is excommunicated. But that kind of unity has no attraction for men of strong religious convictions. When that alternative was presented to Martin Luther he promptly showed his contempt for a church that would make such a demand by burning the papal bull and denouncing the pope who had issued it as Antichrist.

It is to be acknowledged that many of the divisions that have occurred in the Christian church have been unnecessary and that some
have been detrimental. Some have arisen because of evil motives on
the part of certain groups, or because of the personal ambitions of
strong willed leaders. But many others have arisen because of natural
circumstances, such as those of race, language, nationality, geography,
or honest difference of opinion. If we have true spiritual unity, the lack
of outward unity will not seriously hamper Christian life and practice.
The spiritual unity that characterizes evangelical Protestants is more
important than the organizational diversity that places them in different
denominations. Religious liberty by its very nature is sure to bring
some degree of disunity, precisely as political liberty does; for we
do not all think alike or act alike. But to suppress that liberty is to
destroy the very basis for evangelical theology.

It is also true that this freedom on the part of Protestants has often
placed them at a disadvantage as they are confronted by an aggressive
Roman Catholic Church under unified leadership. But that is precisely
the same problem that we face in the political realm. It often happens
that in local, state, or federal government a well organized minority
pressure group pushes through its program and imposes its will on an
unorganized majority. We have seen that particularly in the big city
political machines where time and again and sometimes for long periods
of time corrupt and unscrupulous minority groups have been in control. But nowhere is such action more reprehensible than in the church
as minority pressure groups intimidate elected assemblies, the press,
radio, television, the movies, and other media that can be used to
their advantage. The remedy for such abuse, however, is not to
abolish liberty, but, in the state, to inform and arouse the electorate
so that it will choose clean, honest officials; and in the church, to so
evangelize the membership and develop a wholesome Christian conscience that such abuses will be impossible.

The primary point of cleavage between the Roman Catholic and
the other churches seems to be the fact that the Roman Church is
hierarchical and authoritarian in its form of government, while the
others are essentially democratic and place the control of church affairs
in the hands of the people. It was the Vatican Council of 1870, with its
pronouncement of papal infallibility, that sounded the death-knoll of
any democratic processes in the Roman Church and placed it irrevocably
on the road to totalitarianism.

III. THE PRIESTHOOD

1. The Office of the Priest. 2. No New Testa-
ment Authority for a Human Priesthood. 3.
Claims of the Roman Priesthood. 4. The Chris-
tian Ministry not a Sacrificing Ministry. 5.
Training for the Priesthood. 6. Groups Within
the Priesthood and Within the Laity. 7. Leaving
the Priesthood. 8. Renouncing Priestly Vows.

1. THE OFFICE OF THE PRIEST

The office or work of the priest is perhaps the most difficult to present
and the least understood of any part of the Christian system. In
the Old Testament the work of Christ was prefigured under the three
offices of prophet, priest, and king. Each of these was given special
prominence in the nation of Israel. Each was designed to set forth
a particular phase of the work of the coming Redeemer, and each
was filled, not by men who voluntarily took the work upon themselves,
but only by those who were divinely called to the work.

The prophet was appointed to be God's spokesman to the people,
revealing to them His will and purpose for their salvation. The priest
was appointed to represent the people before God, to offer sacrifices
for them and to intercede with God on their behalf. And the king
was appointed to rule over the people, to defend them and to restrain
and conquer all His and their enemies. In the present study we are
concerned only with the priesthood.

The essential idea of a priest is that of a mediator between God and
man. In his fallen estate man is a sinner, guilty before God, and
alienated from Him. He has no right of approach to God, nor does
he have the ability, or even the desire, to approach Him. Instead,
he wants to flee from God, and to have nothing to do with Him. He
is, therefore, helpless until someone undertakes to act as his representative before God.

In ancient Israel the priests performed three primary duties: they
ministered at the sanctuary before God, offering sacrifices to Him in
behalf of the people; they taught the people the law of God; and they
inquired for the people concerning the divine will. Under the old

43

covenant the men who held the offices of prophet, priest, or king were only shadows or types of the great Prophet, the great Priest, and the great King who was to come. With the coming of Christ each of these offices found its fulfillment in Him. And with the accomplishment of His work of redemption each of these offices, as it functioned on the human level, reached its fulfillment and was abolished. As regards the priesthood Christ alone is now our Priest, our one and only High Priest. He fulfills that office in that He once offered up Himself a sacrifice to satisfy divine justice, thereby making unnecessary and putting an end to all other sacrifices. He paid the debt for the sin of His people, and so opened the way for renewed fellowship between them and God. And as the risen and exalted Saviour of His people He intercedes effectually for them with God the Father.

All of this is clearly set forth by the writer of the Epistle to the Hebrews who in the ninth chapter says that "Christ having come a high priest of the good things to come, through the greater and more perfect tabernacle, not made with hands, that is to say, not of this creation, nor yet through the blood of goats and calves, but through his own blood, entered in once for all into the holy place, having obtained eternal redemption" (vss. 11, 12); that we are redeemed through "the blood of Christ, who through the eternal Spirit offered himself without blemish unto God" (vs. 14); that "Christ entered not into a holy place made with hands, like in pattern to the true; but into heaven itself, now to appear before the face of God for us" (vs. 24); that "now once at the end of the ages hath he been manifested to put away sin by the sacrifice of himself" (vs. 26); and in 8:1,2, that "We have such a high priest, who sat down on the right hand of the throne of the Majesty in the heavens, a minister of the sanctuary, and of the true tabernacle, which the Lord pitched, not man."

Thus under the figure of Israel's sacrificing priesthood, particularly through the figure of the high priest who entered into the holy of holies on the day of atonement with blood that had been offered, we are shown that Christ, who is our High Priest, has entered into the heavenly sanctuary with the merits of His atoning sacrifice, that its atoning and cleansing power may be constantly applied to all who put their trust in Him.

In accordance with this New Testament change in the priesthood, through which the old order of ritual and sacrifice which prefigured the atoning work of Christ has been fulfilled and Christ alone has become our true High Priest, the human priesthood as a distinct and separate order of men has fulfilled its function and has been abolished. Furthermore, all born-again believers, having now been given the right of access to God through Christ their Saviour, and being able to go directly to God in prayer and so to intercede for themselves and others, themselves become priests of God. For these are the functions of a priest. This we term *the universal priesthood of believers*. And this is the distinctive feature of Protestantism as regards the doctrine of the priesthood.

"Ye also," says Peter, "as living stones, are built up a spiritual house, to be a holy priesthood, to offer up spiritual sacrifices, acceptable to God through Jesus Christ. . . . Ye are an elect race, a royal priesthood, a holy nation, a people for God's own possession" (I Peter 2:5,9). In making that statement Peter was not addressing a priestly cast, *but all true believers*, as is shown by the fact that his epistle was addressed to Jewish Christians who were scattered throughout the various nations, "sojourners of the Dispersion" (1:1), even to those who are as "newborn babes" in the faith (2:2). And in Revelation 1:5-6, John, writing to the seven churches in Asia Minor, says: "Unto him that loveth us, and loosed us from our sins by his blood: and he made us to be a kingdom, to be priests unto his God and Father."

The sacrifices offered by the Christian in the exercise of this priesthood are, of course, not for sin, as professedly are those of the Roman Catholic mass. Christ offered the true and only sacrifice for sin, *once for all*. His sacrifice was perfect. When He had completed His work of redemption upon the cross and was ready to give up His spirit He said, "It is finished" (John 19:30). With His sacrifice God was fully satisfied. It therefore does not need to be repeated, nor supplemented, nor modified in any way.

The sacrifices offered by the Christian are termed "spiritual," and they relate to worship and service. First, there is the sacrifice of praise: "Through him then let us offer up a sacrifice of praise to God continually, that is, the fruit of lips which make confession in his name" (Heb. 13:15). This offering of thanks and praise to God in worship, which expresses the gratitude of the heart, is an acceptable offering. Second, there is the sacrifice offered through our gifts, as our substance is given for the support of God's work. He has declared that it is His pleasure to receive such gifts when they are given willingly and with pure motives: "But to do good and to communicate forget not [i.e., sharing with others, helping those who are in need]; for with such sacrifices God is well pleased" (Heb. 13:16). And third, there is the offering of ourselves, our bodies, our lives, in Christian service: "I beseech you therefore, brethren, by the mercies of God, to present your bodies a living sacrifice, holy, acceptable to God, which is your spiritual service" (Rom. 12:1). Furthermore, we are sons of God through faith in Christ (I John 3:1-2). As no longer servants but sons in His family we have direct access to Him as our Father and no longer need the mediation of any order of human priests. To depend upon priestly mediation is by that much to return to Judaism and to introduce an element of apostasy into Christianity.

Thus the New Testament sets forth a new and different kind of priesthood: first, Christ, the true High Priest, who is in heaven; and second, the universal priesthood of believers, through which they offer the "spiritual" sacrifices of praise, of gifts, and of themselves in Christian service. It thereby repudiates the pretentious claims of the Roman priesthood, which would perpetuate the Jewish priesthood and limit it to a few chosen men who are set apart from the laity, who profess to offer literal sacrifices in the mass, and who supposedly are nearer to God than are other men.

Every believer now has the inexpressibly high privilege of going directly to God in prayer, without the mediation of any earthly priest, and of interceding for himself and for others. We are told: "Ask, and it shall be given unto you; seek, and ye shall find; knock, and it shall be opened unto you" (Matt. 7:7); "If ye shall ask anything of the Father, he will give it you in my name" (John 16:23); "Whosoever shall call on the name of the Lord shall be saved" (Acts 2:21).

The believer, of course, approaches God not in his own merits but only through the merits of Christ who has made a perfect sacrifice for him. It is precisely at this point that the Roman Catholic fails to see God's true way of salvation; for he thinks that man still must approach God as in Old Testament times through a priest, or now perhaps through Mary or some saint whose merits can work for him. But Paul says, "By grace have ye been saved through faith; and that not of yourselves, it is the *gift of God*" (Eph. 2:8). Christians have, by virtue of their union with Christ, free access to God at all times. This right is one of the finest things in the Christian faith, and it is a present possession. Yet Rome would rob us of this privilege and would interpose her priests and dead saints between the soul and God. Rome's teaching and practice is heresy, for in many places the Bible invites us to come to God through Christ, without any reference to priests or other intercessors.

The Bible teaches that, "There is one God, and one mediator between God and men, the man Jesus Christ" (I Tim. 2:5). The Church of Rome teaches that there are many mediators, the priests, Mary, a host of saints, and the angels, and that it is right and proper to pray to them. But to any honest priest in the Church of Rome it must become more and more apparent that Christ is the only true Priest, the only true Mediator, and that in serving as a priest, in pretending to offer the sacrifice of the mass and to forgive sins, he is merely acting the part of an imposter.

2. NO NEW TESTAMENT AUTHORITY FOR A HUMAN PRIESTHOOD

The really decisive answer to all theories concerning a human priesthood is found in the New Testament itself. There we are taught that the priesthood, along with the other elements of the old dispensation, including the sacrificial system, the ritual, the Levitical law, the temple, etc., has served its purpose and has passed away. With the coming of Christ and the accomplishment of redemption through His work, the entire Old Testament legalistic and ritualistic system which had prefigured it became obsolete and passed away as a unit. It is very inconsistent for the Roman Church to retain the priesthood while discarding the other elements of that system.

An enlightening article that appeared in the *Chicago Lutheran Theological Seminary Record,* July, 1952, somewhat abbreviated has this to say about the priesthood:

"The writers of the New Testament had two separate words for *elder* and *priest*. They do not mean the same thing at all, and the New Testament never confuses them. It never says *presbuteros,* elder, when it means *priest*. The New Testament word for priest is *hiereus*. In Greek, from Homer down, this word had a singular meaning. It meant a man appointed, or consecrated, or otherwise endowed with power to perform certain technical functions of ritual worship, especially to offer acceptable sacrifices, and to make effectual prayers. Likewise in the Septuagint *hiereus* is the regular if not invariable translation of the Old Testament *kohen* and *kahen,* the only Hebrew word for priest. It occurs more than 400 times in the Old Testament in this sense. In the New Testament *hiereus* always means priest, never means elder. There is not anywhere in the New Testament the shadow of an allusion to a Christian priest in the ordinary sense of the word, that is, a man qualified as over against others not qualified for the special function of offering sacrifices, making priestly intercessions, or performing any other act which only a priest can perform. The Epistle to the Hebrews attributed both priesthood and high-priesthood to Christ and to Him alone. The argument of the Epistle not only indicates that a Christian priesthood was unknown to the writer, but that such a priesthood is unallowable. It is to Jesus only that Christians look as to a priest. He has performed perfectly and permanently the function of a priest for all believers. His priesthood, being perfect and eternal, renders a continuous human priesthood both needless and anachronistic."

Paul enumerates the different kinds of ministers and agents in the Christian church, and the office of priest is not among them: "And he gave some to be apostles; and some, prophets; and some, evangelists; and some, pastors and teachers" (Eph. 4:11). And again, "And God hath set some in the church, first apostles, secondly prophets, thirdly teachers. . . ." (I Cor. 12:28). There is never any mention of priests. The only mediatorial priesthood recognized in the New Testament is that of Christ, the great High Priest, and to Him alone is the title "priest" *(hiereus)* given: "Thou art a priest for ever, after the order of Melchizedek" (Heb. 7:17); "But he, because he abideth for ever, hath his priesthood unchangeable. Wherefore also he is able to save to the uttermost them that draw near unto God through him, seeing he ever liveth to make intercession for them. For such a high priest became us, holy, guiltless, undefiled, separated from sinners, and made higher than the heavens; who needeth not daily, like those high priests, to offer up sacrifices, first for his own sins, and then for the sins of the people: for this he did *once for all,* when he offered up himself" (Heb. 7:24-27). "For by *one offering* he hath perfected *for ever* them that are sanctified" (Heb. 10:14).

Since the priesthood occupied such an important place in the Old Testament dispensation and in the thinking of the Jewish people, it is inconceivable that had it been continued in the New Testament dispensation God would have made no mention of it at all—how priests were to be chosen, and ordained, and how they were to carry out their functions in this radically different dispensation. The fact of the matter is that the Old Testament priesthood was the human, Aaronistic priesthood, and that by its very nature it was, like the sacrificial system and the elaborate temple worship of which it was a part, a temporary affair, a mere shadow and prefigurement of the reality that was to come. And so, with the coming of Christ and the establishment of His priesthood, it fell away, as the stars fade before the rising sun, and as the petals fall away before the developing fruit. The priesthood as an order of clergy has been abolished.

In the Epistle to the Hebrews several chapters are devoted to showing that the Old Testament priesthood has been abolished and that there is no place in Christianity for a sacrificing priesthood, because Christ, "through his own blood, entered in *once for all* into the holy place, having obtained eternal redemption," and that He has offered *"one sacrifice for sins for ever"* (9:12; 10:12). The many human priests with their innumerable animal sacrifices were effective in their work of reconciling the people to God only because they represented the true High Priest and the one true sacrifice that was to come. But after the reality appeared there would be no more need for the shadows and types that had preceded it. Hence we read concerning the sacrifice of Christ: "But now *once* at the end of the ages hath he been manifested to put away sin by the sacrifice of himself" (Heb. 9:26); and again: "We have been sanctified through the offering of the body of Chirst *once for all*" (Heb. 10-10).

The sacrifice of Christ was therefore a "once-for-all" sacrifice which only He could make, and which cannot be repeated. By its very nature it was final and complete. It was a work of Deity, and so cannot be repeated by man any more than can the work of creation. By that one sacrifice the utmost demands of God's justice were fully and forever satisfied. Final atonement has been accomplished! No further order of priests is needed to offer additional sacrifices or to perpetuate that one. His was the one sacrifice to end all sacrifices. Let all men now look to that one sacrifice on Calvary! Any continuing priesthood and any "unbloody repetition of the mass," which professes to offer the same sacrifice that Christ offered on Calvary, is in reality merely a sham and a recrudescence of Judaism within the Christian Church.

The abolition of the priestly caste which through the old dispensation stood between God and man was dramatically illustrated at the very moment that Christ died on the cross. When He cried, "It is finished," a strange sound filled the temple as the veil that separated the sanctuary from the holy of holies was torn from top to bottom. The ministering priests found themselves gazing at the torn veil with wondering eyes, for God's own hand had removed the curtain and had opened the way into the holy of holies, symbolizing by that act that no longer did man have to approach Him through the mediation of a priest, but that the way of access to Him is now open to all.

But the veil which had been torn by the hand of God was patched up again by priestly hands, and for forty years, until the fall of Jerusalem, sacrifices continued to be offered in a restored temple service, and in Judaism the veil continued to stand between God and men. In our day the Roman priesthood has again patched up the veil. Through the use of spurious sacraments, the sacrifice of the mass, the confessional, indulgences, and other such priestly instruments it insists on keeping in place the curtain that God Himself has removed. It continues to place fallible human priests, the Virgin Mary and dead saints as mediators between the sinner and God, although the Bible declares most clearly that "There is one God, and *one* mediator between God and men, himself man, Christ Jesus" (I Tim. 2:5).

Hence the continuing priesthood in the Church of Rome is absolutely unscriptural and unchristian. It owes its existence solely to a man-made development that can be traced in detail in the history of the church, for it was not until the third or fourth century that priests began to appear in the church. That system has been a source of untold evil. But papal dominance has been built up on that practice and is dependent on its continuance. Without an hierarchical priesthood the papal system would immediately disintegrate.

The apostle Peter, far from making himself a priest or a pope, was content to call himself one of the many elders, a *presbuteros*. And he specifically warned the elders against that most glaring error of the Roman Catholic priests, lording it over the charge allotted to them. He urged rather that they serve as examples to the flock: "The elders therefore among you I exhort, who am a fellow-elder, and a witness of the sufferings of Christ, who am also a partaker of the glory that shall be revealed: Tend the flock of God which is among you, exercising the oversight, not of constraint, but willingly, according to the will of God; nor yet for filthy lucre, but of a ready mind; neither as lording it over the charge allotted to you, but making yourselves ensamples to the flock" (I Peter 5:1-3).

As regards priestly innovations that have been made by the Roman Church, Dr. R. Laird Harris, Professor of Old Testament in Covenant Theological Seminary, in St. Louis, writes:

> "First century Christianity had no priests. The New Testament nowhere uses the word to describe a leader in Christian service. The Jewish priesthood was changed, we are told in Hebrews 7:12. Christ is now our 'priest forever after the order of Melchizedek' (Heb. 5:10). It is true that the Douay but not the Confraternity version does use the word 'priest' (in a Christian connection), but the Greek never uses the word 'hiereus' (priest), nor does the Latin so use 'sacerdos' (priest). It is good that this clear mistranslation of the Douay has been corrected in the newer Roman Catholic Confraternity edition. Christian priests are a Roman Catholic invention" (Booklet, *Fundamental Protestant Doctrines*, II, p. 3).

But the doctrine of the universal priesthood of believers is not merely a negative teaching abolishing an order of clergy. For along with that freedom which makes the believer responsible only to God for his faith and life, there is an added responsibility. We are members of a Christian community, "an elect race, a royal priesthood, a holy nation, a people for God's own possession" (I Peter 2:9). As Christians, then, we are not "laymen," not mere spectators of the Christian enterprise who may or may not engage in it as we choose, but "priests," and therefore responsible to God for the faith and lives of others. We are under obligation to make known this message of salvation. The word "layman" is not found in the New Testament, nor is there any "layman's movement" in the Bible. A priest is inevitably involved in the lives of others, and is responsible to God for others. He has the high privilege and duty of making God known to others. This priesthood, therefore, applies to *all* believers, and consists of two things: (1) Immediate access to God in prayer for one's self; and (2) The right and duty of intercession for others. Only as we grasp these ideas can we appreciate the full, rich meaning of the doctrine of the universal priesthood of believers.

Furthermore, we are a *royal* priesthood. That means that we have been called, chosen, by the King of Kings to be His priests before our fellow men. We are not first of all clergy and laymen. We are first of all a royal priesthood, under obligation *individually* to make known the message of salvation. And the strength of Protestantism lies precisely here, in the willingness of its people to accept this strange office and all that it means, and to serve in the household of God as the royal priests that we really are.

3. CLAIMS OF THE ROMAN PRIESTHOOD

The Council of Trent, whose decrees must be accepted by all Roman Catholics under pain of mortal sin or excommunication, says:

"The priest is the man of God, the minister of God. . . . He that despiseth the priest despiseth God; he that hears him hears God. The priest remits sins as God, and that which he calls his body at the altar is adored as God by himself and by the congregation. . . . It is clear that their function is such that none greater can be conceived. Wherefore they are justly called not only angels, but also God, holding as they do among us the power and authority of the immortal God."

In a similar vein a Roman Catholic book, carrying the imprimatur of the Archbishop of Ottawa, Canada, says:

"Without the priest the death and passion of our Lord would be of no avail to us. See the power of the priest! By one word from his lips he changes a piece of bread into a God! A greater fact than the creation of a world.

"If I were to meet a priest and an angel, I would salute the priest before saluting the angel. The priest holds the place of God."

To millions of Christians who are outside the Roman Church such words border on blasphemy, if indeed they are not blasphemy. Surely such declarations are a usurpation of the power that belongs only to God.

It is surprising how little Scripture authority even the Roman Church cites as a basis for her doctrine of the priesthood. Her main and almost only support is found in two verses, Matthew 16:18-19—which she has misinterpreted, and then, by adding one human tradition to another, has built up an elaborate system which not only has no real support in Scripture but which acutally is contrary to Scripture. And by teaching her people this one interpretation and denying them the right to read or hear any other, she has misled millions so that they have come to believe that this is true Christianity. These verses read:

> "And I say unto thee, thou art Peter, and upon this rock I will build my church, and the gates of hell shall not prevail against it. And I will give thee the keys of the kingdom of heaven; and whatever thou shalt bind on earth shall be bound in heaven, and whatever thou shalt loose on earth shall be loosed in heaven" (Confraternity Version).

There are various interpretations of these verses. Suffice it to say here that this passage contains symbolical language and that the interpretation of the "rock," the "keys," the "gates of hell," and the "binding" and "loosing" adopted by Rome is by no means the only one, nor even the most plausible one. We shall treat these verses more fully in connection with the discussion of Peter as the alleged head of the church on earth.

There is probably no other doctrine revealed in Scripture that the Roman Church has so obviously turned upside down as that of the priesthood. The function of no New Testament minister or official resembled that of a priest of the Roman Church. The titles of "archbishop," "cardinal" ("prince of the church," as they like to be called), and "pope" are not even in the Bible. The term "bishop" (overseer, or shepherd of the flock) designated an entirely different office than does that term in the present day Roman Church. In fact the terms "bishop" *(episcopos)* and "elder" *(presbyteros)* were used interchangeably. Elders could be of two kinds—what we term the teaching elder, or pastor, and the ruling elder, who represented the congregation in the general affairs of the church.

Paul ordained elders in the newly established churches and gave his assistants, Timothy and Titus, instructions for choosing and ordaining elders in every city (I Tim. 3:2-7; Titus 1:5). During the Middle Ages the teaching elder became a priest at the altar, and the function of the ruling elder was usurped by bishops, cardinals, and the pope, until practically no authority was left in the hands of the congregation, which of course is the condition that continues in the Roman Catholic churches of today. Rome has robbed the laity of nearly all of its privileges.

Christ intended that His church, which consists of all true believers, should enjoy all of the rights and privileges that were conferred by Him. But Rome withdraws those rights and privileges from the people, and invests them in an order of priesthood. Christ bade His followers practice humility, acknowledge one another as equals, and serve one another (Matt. 20:25-28; 23:8; I Peter 5:3; II Cor. 4:5). But Rome denies this equality and sets up the priest as a dictator belonging to a sacred order, altogether apart from and superior to the people of the parish. The loyal Roman Catholic must heed what the priest says, for priestly dignity is above all. The priest dictates to his people concerning their church, school, marriage, children, family affairs, political activities, what literature they should read, and so on, all of which he may inquire into intimately in the confessional. From before birth until after death that influence continues. As father confessor and "director of conscience," and as God's spokesman to the people, his word is not to be questioned.

The feeling of fear and dread of the priest, so characteristic of the people in Romanist lands, is comparable only to the fear and dread that pagan people have for the witch doctor. Says one from Southern Ireland who has had ample opportunity to observe from within the workings of that system:

"You who have never been under this influence, who have from childhood been allowed freedom of speech, liberty of conscience, and who see no distinction between your clergy and laity, you cannot, you never will understand the influence that Roman Catholic priests have over the laity of their own nationality" (Margaret Shepherd, *My Life in the Convent*, p. 46).

Romanism puts the priest between the Christian believer and the knowledge of God as revealed in the Scriptures, and makes him the sole interpreter of truth. It puts the priest between the confession of sins and the forgiveness of sins. It carries this interposition through to the last hour, in which the priest, in the sacrament of extreme unction, stands between the soul and eternity, and even after death the release of the soul from purgatory and its entrance into heavenly joy is still dependent on the priest's prayers which must be paid for by relatives or friends. The Roman priests, in designating themselves, the Virgin Mary and the saints as mediators, and in making membership in their church the indispensable requirement for salvation, place a screen between God and the people. And where does Christ come in in this system? If you search you will find Him in the background, behind the priest, behind the Virgin, behind the church. The inevitable result is that the spiritual life of the Roman Catholic is weak and anemic, and that Roman Catholic countries, such as Spain, Italy, Southern Ireland, Quebec, and Latin America, are immersed in spiritual darkness.

No matter what the moral character of a priest, his prayers and his ministrations are declared to be valid and efficacious because he is in holy orders. The Council of Trent has declared that, "Even those priests who are living in mortal sin exercise the same function of forgiving sins as ministers of Christ"—such a declaration was necessary at that time, in the middle of the sixteenth century, if the Roman Church was to continue to function at all, because of the general and well known immorality of the priests. Just as the medicine given by the doctor is supposed to cure the patient regardless of the moral character of the doctor, so the priest's official acts are supposed to be valid and efficacious regardless of his personal character. He is accounted a "good priest" so long as he remains loyal to the church and the rituals and ceremonies performed by him are correct. Says one writer, "When you see the way the system of the priesthood works out in daily life, be glad you are a Protestant."

Few Protestants realize the nature and significance of the vast chasm which separates the Roman Catholic priesthood from the people. No such gulf exists between the Protestant clergyman and his congregation. A fiction of sacerdotal wisdom and holiness, particularly as displayed in the sacrifice of the mass, sets the priest apart from the awed and reverent Catholic laity. Yet the Roman Church seeks to have the world believe that a close unity exists between the clergy and the laity. And an almost total ignorance on the part of the Catholic people concerning the political machinations of the hierarchy leaves them usually not only willing but even proud to be identified with whatever program is put forth in the name of the Roman Church.

In our method of choosing a minister, which we believe is in harmony with the teaching of Scripture and the practice of the early church, we choose a man not because he is of a superior order, but because of our belief that he is capable of ministering the things of the Spirit to his fellow men and because we believe he will live an honest, humble, sincere, and upright life. Ordinarily the minister marries and dwells in a family because this is the natural state of man, and hence he is closer to his people than is the celibate priest. He is chosen by the people, not, however, to govern according to the will of the people, but according to the will of Christ as revealed in the Scriptures. He is among the flock as a spiritual leader, friend, and counsellor, not to be ministered unto, but to minister.

4. THE CHRISTIAN MINISTRY NOT A SACRIFICING MINISTRY

We have said that it is the work of a priest to represent man before God, to offer sacrifices, to intercede for men, and so to make God propitious, that is, favorably inclined toward them. In all pre-Christian religions, Judaism included, there were two common elements: (1) a human priesthood; and, (2) the teaching that the salvation provided was incomplete. In the very nature of the case their sacrifices were of limited value and therefore deficient. In the pagan religions this usually led to belief in a future round of existence after death wherein the still unsaved sinner would have to make further expiation for his sins. In Judaism it was shown in the never ending cycle of those sacrifices as day after day the same ritual was repeated.

Now, Roman Catholicism, although it professes to be Christian, possesses those same two elements. It claims a human priesthood; and, it teaches that salvation in this life is not complete, but that after death the soul must suffer a longer or shorter time in purgatory and that repeated masses must be said to pay the debt for sin. But Protestantism teaches that with the coming of Christ and the completion of His work on Calvary a new element was added, one which completely eliminates the other two, namely, the evangel, or the "good news" that because Christ was both God and man His sacrifice was of infinite value, and that it was, therefore, *complete, efficacious, and final.*

This is the clear teaching of the Epistle to the Hebrews, for there we read:

> "By which will we have been sanctified through the offering of the body of Jesus Christ *once for all.* And every priest indeed standeth day by day ministering and offering oftentimes the same sacrifice, the which can never take away sins: but he, when he had offered *one sacrifice* for sins *for ever,* sat down on the right hand of God; henceforth expecting till his enemies be made the footstool of his feet. For by *one offering* he hath *perfected for ever* them that are sanctified" (10:10-14).

And again:

> (Christ), "who *needeth not daily,* like those high priests, to offer up sacrifices, first for his own sins, and then for the sins of the people: for this he did *once for all,* when he offered up himself" (7:27).

Here we are taught, first of all, that the pre-Christian element of an incomplete salvation was superseded by the complete salvation obtained through the one efficacious sacrifice offered by Christ; and, secondly, that the human priesthood offering daily sacrifices for the sins of men was eliminated, having been done away through the *once for all* sacrifice for sins when Christ offered up Himself. This means further that sin cannot persist as something to be expiated for after death; that we are saved completely, not half-saved; and that therefore there can be no such place as purgatory.

In the Jewish priesthood, (1) there were many priests; (2) they were men of infirmity; and (3) it was necessary that they repeat their sacrifices many times, for their own sins and for those of the people. These same reasons apply with equal force against the Roman priesthood: (1) they too are many; (2) they too are men of infirmity; and (3) they too repeat their sacrifices many times for themselves and for the people. In the nature of the case there could be nothing permanent about the work of the Jewish priesthood, for it was merely a foreshadowing or a prefiguring of the work that was to be accomplished by Christ. But the "one sacrifice," offered "once for all," by Christ paid the penalty for the sin of His people and so fulfilled the ritual and made all further sacrifices unnecessary. There is, therefore, no place for a sacrificing priesthood in the Christian dispensation.

This same truth is taught when we are told that after Christ had completed His work he "sat down" on the right hand of God, thus symbolizing that His work was finished, that nothing more needed to be added. In Hebrews 1:3 we read: "who being the effulgence of his glory, and the very image of his substance, and upholding all things by the word of his power, when he had made purification for sins, sat down on the right hand of the Majesty on high"; and in Hebrews 10:12-13: "But he, when he had offered one sacrifice for sins for ever, sat down on the right hand of God, thenceforth expecting till his enemies be made the footstool of his feet."

The greatness and completeness and finality of Christ's sacrificial work is seen in His royal rest. The fact that He has sat down is of special interest since in the tabernacle and the temple there were no seats or benches on which the priests could ever sit down or rest. Their work was never done. Their sacrifices had to be repeated daily because there was no saving power in them. Therefore their task was endless. But the work of Christ was entirely different. His sacrifice of Himself was "once for all." By that one sacrifice He made perfect provision both for the sinner and for the sin. Therefore, as our High Priest, He sat down in the place of authority, and is now waiting until His enemies are brought into subjection and His kingdom is brought to fruition.

It is interesting to notice that when Christ sent out His apostles He commanded them to preach and teach, but that He said not one word about sacrifice. In the Great Commission He said: "Go ye therefore, and make disciples of all the nations, baptizing them . . . teaching them . . ." (Matt. 28:19-20). Yet the most prominent feature of the Roman priesthood is its sacerdotal or sacrificial character. The mass is the very heart of the service. In the first part of the ordination service for a priest he is addressed as follows: "Receive thou the power *to offer sacrifices* to God, and to celebrate masses, both for the living and for the dead. In the name of the Lord. Amen."

In the Book of Acts there are many references to the founding of churches, preaching the Word, the assembling of Christians, the governing of the churches, and the matter of controversies with those who advocate error. But there are no references whatever to a sacrificing priesthood. Paul likewise through his epistles gave many directions concerning the duties of the ministry. But nowhere is there even a hint that the ministers were to offer sacrifices, nowhere even an allusion to the mass! The Greek word for priest, *hiereus,* as we have noted, is never applied to New Testament ministers. Strange indeed, if this was the work of the early ministers, that in Scripture we find no references whatever to it!

But in contrast with this, in later ages, after the Roman Catholic Church had developed, we find the writings of the spokesmen for the church filled with references to the mass—how, when, how often, and under what circumstances it is to be administered. It became during the Middle Ages, as it is today, the most distinctive feature of the Roman worship, the primary thing that they profess to do. Surely it is clear that the sacrifice of the mass is a later development, a radical perversion, and that the Roman Catholic priesthood is following a system quite foreign to that of the early church.

Some Roman Catholics who have turned to Protestantism have said that before they left the Roman Church the charges which hurt them most were those which declared that the Bible does not reveal a teaching authority with the pope and the priesthood as its divinely authorized agents, and, that the blessed sacrament of the altar does not exist in the New Testament. But with further investigation they were forced to conclude that such was the case and that in truth the sole support of the priesthood was nothing other than the traditions of men.

Our conclusion concerning the priesthood must be that Christ alone is our true High Priest, the only Mediator between God and men, the reality toward which the entire Old Testament ritual and sacrifice and priesthood looked forward, and that when He completed His work that entire system fell away. Consequently, we reject all merely human and earthly priests, whether in the Roman Catholic Church or in heathen religions, and look upon their continued practice as simply an attempt to usurp divine authority.

5. TRAINING FOR THE PRIESTHOOD

There are approximately 54,000 Roman Catholic priests in the United States. And there are 227 bishops, archbishops, and cardinals who make up the American hierarchy, according to *The Official Catholic Directory* (May, 1960). The large proportion of the priests, about 33,000, are what are termed diocesan priests, whose work is in the local churches, while the remainder, some 21,000, are in the various religious orders, such as the Franciscan, Dominican, Benedictine, and Jesuit. Those in the various orders tend to specialize in some specific work, e.g., the Franciscans dedicating themselves to the relief of suffering and want, the Dominicans to theological and ministerial studies, the Benedictines to service in the schools and churches, and the Jesuits to the field of education, although the various fields overlap considerably. There are about 35,000 Jesuits in the world, some 8,000 of whom are in the United States. There are also about 168,000 nuns in the United States who work primarily in the schools and hospitals, although some are cloistered.

Many people find it difficult to understand why so many young people choose to dedicate themselves for life to the rigorous system of the Roman Catholic Church as priests and nuns. The answer is that most of them do not enter as a result of free personal choice, but are recruited while quite young, usually between the ages of sixteen and eighteen, with greater or lesser degrees of leading or persuasion by the priests who are instructed to keep their eyes open for promising boys and girls. The confessional, which affords the priests an opportunity to know intimately the personalities, ambitions, and problems of the young people, affords an excellent opportunity for such leading. The church seeks candidates for its personnel and tries to gain their commitment at that period in the lives of boys and girls when spiritual ideals are strongest but illusive and superficial. That is the age when the ambitions of youth soar highest and when they feel the urge for self-sacrifice in building a better world. The ones the church wants are, for the most part, selected by the priests, cultivated over a period of time, sometimes even for years, and so led into the various fields of service, although the priests are by no means successful in getting all they want. The result is that many a boy and girl who had never felt any natural inclination toward the priesthood or convent life has found himself or herself following that road and more or less committed to it before realizing the consequences.

Most of those who eventually enter the priesthood are recruited from the middle or lower class families, boys who for the most part would not have much chance for higher education or for advancement in life, and to whom ordination means promotion to a position of prestige which their family status would not likely attain for them. Training is for the most part provided without cost. In their new positions, with their handsome rectories, luxurious vestments and beautiful automobiles they can feel superior to their parishioners. Those become most beholden to the hierarchy for the advantages that they have received, and are the most easily controlled. Having been drilled and disciplined into the system, they feel powerless to change. This is especially true of those who come from orphanages, whether priests or nuns. They are the real victims of the system. That is an unhealthy situation and deeply unjust, but one that is difficult to control or remedy.

A former English priest, Joseph McCabe, in his book, *The Popes and Their Church*, says that the Jesuits and Benedictines, who control large schools, appeal more to the middle class, but that as a rule they fail to secure the more intelligent of their pupils, that the intellectual and moral level of priests is not nearly as high as, for instance, that of teachers and doctors, and that only a minority have any exceptional ability or deep religious feeling. Other writers have said substantially the same thing. Furthermore, the idea has been promoted among Roman Catholics that it is a special honor to have in one's family a priest or nun, and unusual privileges and favors, sometimes quite substantial, are directed by the church toward the families of those so chosen. Getting into the service of the Roman Church is not so difficult; getting out after one has committed himself or herself is the real problem.

In order to understand why Roman Catholic priests act as they do, and why the priesthood is able to hold them so firmly, it is necessary to know something about the training they receive. That has been set forth clearly by Mr. McLoughlin, and we present in considerable detail the account of his training in St. Anthony's Seminary, at Santa Barbara, California, which he informs us was during the years 1922-27. He says:

"When a boy enters a seminary, he begins twelve years of the most thorough and effective intellectual indoctrination the world has ever known. It begins gently, with a blending of the legitimate pleasures of boyhood, the stimulus of competition in studies, and the pageantry of the forms of an ancient religion unseen in an ordinary parish church. It ends twelve years later, with a mental rigidity and acceptance of medieval superstitions and religious concepts as archaic as those of the Buddhist monks upon the isolated, frozen mountains of Tibet. It may surprise non-Catholic Americans to learn that the story of Tibet in Lowell Thomas' *On Top of the World* has its counterpart in the hundreds of Roman Catholic seminaries flourishing in the cities and countrysides of America.

"The course of training for the priesthood is roughly divided into two periods. The first six years are spent in the junior seminary—four years of high school and two years of what would be considered college work. The senior seminary provides the last college years, devoted mainly to Catholic philosophy, plus four years of training in all the intricacies of Catholic theology. Between the junior and senior seminaries in religious orders (Franciscans, Dominicans, Vincentians), there comes a year devoted entirely to religious indoctrination. This is the novitiate. . . .

"All our textbooks, even in high school courses, were written by Catholic authors. No daily newspapers were permitted, and no non-Catholic magazines. All incoming mail was opened by the Prefect of discipline, a priest; if he deemed advisable, the letters were confiscated. All outgoing mail had to be placed in the Prefect's office in unsealed envelopes. Along with newspapers and movies, radios were forbidden for the use of junior seminarians. The priests in their supervised recreation hall were permitted a radio—but we were not admitted to that hall. Not only were we gradually withdrawn from the world but we grew to feel that the non-Catholic public disliked us and, if given opportunity, would persecute us. . . .

"During these junior years, the boy has no official ties binding him to the Church. He may leave the seminary at any time, without penalty. Many boys do so; and others are dismissed as being too worldly or intellectually unqualified for the intense indoctrination ahead. . . .

"With one magnificent gesture, the ceremony of entering the novitiate sweeps aside the centuries. The aspirant for the priesthood in the Franciscan Order finds himself, in spirit, walking the ancient streets of Assisi, eating in its hallowed monastic halls, and chanting the sixth-century hymns of Gregory the Great. . . . To symbolize more effectively the repudiation of the 'old' man and the start of a 'new' spiritual life, even our names were changed. I had been christened John Patrick. I was now named Emmett—or, in Latin, Emmatus—in memory of an obscure saint in early Irish and French history. . . .

"During this year our seclusion from American life and our indoctrination in the 'spirit' of the Catholic Church became so intensive that I came to feel that I alone was a true Christian, privileged to commune with God. I believed that the American way of life was pagan and sinful, a rebirth of the Roman Empire and destined to the same disgraceful doom in the ashes of history. I came to believe that the American government was to be tolerated though wrong—tolerated because it gives unlimited freedom to the Roman Catholic Church, wrong because it gives freedom to other churches. I believed the ideal form of government was the one in which I was living in the seclusion of my spirit—the era when the papacy made kings because the power to govern came from God to the king through his 'representative,' the pope. My boyhood concept of civics—of the right of man to the processes of law and government through the consent of the governed—faded away under the constant repetition of the teachings of Thomas Aquinas and the moral theologians. The Constitution of my country and the laws of its states dimmed into trivialities in comparison with the all-powerful Canon Law of the Roman Catholic Church. I became in all truth a citizen of the Church, living—by accident—in the United States.

"Such intensive indoctrination was unknown to the Western world outside the Roman Catholic Church until it was copied by Fascism, Nazism, and Communism. The training for the priesthood goes on, after the novitiate year, for six more years. We were no longer permitted to visit our homes, even for vacations, unless a death occurred in our families. . . .

"The process of indoctrination in all seminaries is intensified by the use of the Latin language. All textbooks of Catholic philosophy and theology are in Latin. The lectures by professors (at least in my day) were in Latin. Examinations were conducted in Latin. We reached the point where we were thinking in Latin, the language of the early centuries of Christianity. Subconsciously we were living not in the age of presidents and politicians, or labor unions and capitalists, but in the age of masters and slaves, of kings and serfs, of popes, representing God, and the faithful, who meekly acquiesced in their decisions as coming from the throne of God himself.

"The chains with which the religious orders of the Roman Catholic Church bind their priestly aspirants to a lifetime of service are the three vows of obedience, poverty, and chastity.

"The vow of obedience is the most important of the three. It identifies all ecclesiastical superiors with the Church, and it identifies the Roman Catholic Church with God. Every command by the superior of a religious community or by a church pastor, no matter how petulant, how ill-advised, or how unjust, must be considered as a command from God Himself and must be obeyed as such under penalty of sin. . . .

"The robe of every Franciscan monk is girded with a rope. One strand hangs from his side. It has three knots on it symbolizing the three vows—poverty, chastity, and (the bottom knot) obedience. The young Franciscan is trained that when the Provincial Superior greets him he must kneel on one knee and kiss the lowest knot on the Superior's cord, and then his hand. It is the token of complete, abject, unreasoning obedience. . . .

"The student priest must learn to crush the desire of the flesh by fasting, self-denial, and even physical pain. Many Americans have read of the ascetics and hermits of the early middle ages of Christianity who mortified the flesh by wearing hair shirts, fastening chains about their waists, and sleeping on boards or in bare coffins. But it might surprise these Americans to know that in the senior seminaries for Franciscan priests in the United States there hangs, inside the door of every cell or bedroom, a scourge or whip. It is made of several strands of heavy cord, each knotted at the end. Each Monday, Wednesday, and Friday evening at 5:45 o'clock we closed the doors of our cells; to the chant of the 'miserere' we disrobed and 'scourged our flesh to bring it into submission.' The Superior patrolled the corridors to listen to the sound of beating— the assurance of compliance. . . .

"The distinction between the licit and the illicit was so elusive in our minds that we could not discern it. We were warned constantly about the danger of any association with women. The saints had characterized them as tools of the devil, devils themselves in beautiful forms, instruments permitted by God to exist and test man's virtue of chastity" (*People's Padre*, pp. 7-18).

At the conclusion of the book Mr. McLoughlin says:

"To non-Catholic America, I have attempted to portray life within the priesthood as it actually is. I have emphasized the long, narrow, effective mental indoctrination of the seminary, taking young boys from their families, walling them off from society, from world events, from modern education through the formative years of adolescence, and then turning them out into the 'vineyard' after ordination as thoroughly dedicated as a Russian envoy to the United Nations. I have pictured the tyranny of fear that chains these men to their religious posts long after they have become disillusioned and yearn for the freedom and normal life of America. I have tried to show, through my own experience and through correspondence, the miasmic fog which the Church has intentionally spread to conceal the truth from the Roman Catholics who blindly follow it—stifling their freedom of thought, of worship, of action, and of life itself. I contend that this foreign thing is far more subtle, far less forthright, but just as inimical to the American concept of life as Communism itself. It is often the indirect cause of Communism by keeping whole nations in ignorance and poverty and by developing techniques of fear, indoctrination, and mental tyranny that the Kremlin exploits. The Inquisition led by the Catholic Church in the sixteenth century finds its parallel in the political persecution by the Communists in Czechoslovakia, Poland, and Russia" (p. 279).

We urge everyone who possibly can to read this very informative and interesting book by Mr. McLoughlin. It is written in a truly Christian spirit by one who knows intimately the Roman Catholic Church, written not in spite, or hatred, or vindictiveness, but to acquaint Roman Catholics themselves with the truth concerning the secret inner workings of their hierarchy, and to inform those outside the Roman Church concerning the nature of this growth that has spread so luxuriously in our free and hospitable land while at the same time choking freedom of thought and action in those lands which it controls.

We should add that the priestly course of preparation reaches its climax in a colorful and solemn ordination ceremony, in which the bishop pronounces the awesome words: "Thou art a priest forever, according to the order of Melchizedek." To himself and to the Roman Catholic world the young priest becomes an *alter Christus*, "another Christ," offering in the mass the same sacrifice that Christ offered on the cross. People bow before him and kiss his hands as a token of respect and submission. Ordinarily a priest is not ordained before the age of 24, although ordination can be performed earlier by special permission. According to Canon Law, a priest once ordained can never lose his ordination. Even if he leaves the Roman Catholic Church, renounces it, and becomes a Protestant minister, he still remains a priest, although unable to function as a priest until he returns and repents.

6. GROUPS WITHIN THE PRIESTHOOD AND WITHIN THE LAITY

After the new recruits have finished their long course of preparation and are ordained as priests, what is their reaction to the environment in which they find themselves? Dee Smith, a former Roman Catholic layman who writes with an intimate knowledge of conditions within the Roman Church, finds that when they emerge from the seminary they gradually evolve into three fairly distinct groups which may be classified as: (1) the naive; (2) the disillusioned; and (3) the aggressive. He says:

1. "The naive are worthy souls so honest themselves that they never question the honesty of others. Even repeated experiences of hypocrisy and corruption among their priestly brothers are insufficient to shake their faith or extinguish their inexhaustible charity. Such priests never advance to high rank among the clergy. They are found in poor city parishes, lonely country stations, or out in the mission field, sharing the meager life of their parishioners.

2. "What of the disillusioned? Emmett McLoughlin estimates that about 27 percent of the priests would like to leave not only the priesthood but also the church. . . . Not all who leave have the stamina to stay with it. The memory of indolent, well-padded living is too beguiling. Expecting

the same thing, plus adulation, in the Protestant camp and not finding it, these feeble characters inevitably return to Rome.

"In their eagerness not to jeopardize their cushy sinecure a second time they cravenly accept the hypocritical 'penances' handed out to them and become the most ardent of Rome's propagandists. Nevertheless it would be unfair to judge harshly all disillusioned priests who fail to break with Rome. When one considers the scurrilous attacks which will be made upon them in the Roman Catholic press, the boycott pressures which will starve them out of a means of livelihood, the malignant persecution which will seek them out and hound them wherever they go, one can readily understand that the decision to leave is a more heroic one than most of us are ever called upon to make. It cannot be denied that some of these priests are good men who, to atone for their lack of courage, do what they can to comfort, encourage, and assuage the lot of the duped and betrayed Catholic people.

3. "Nothing, however, can be said in extenuation of the aggressive cohort of the priesthood, the class which comprises the hierarchy and upper clergy as well as many of the lower. No man can rise very high in the ranks of the Roman Catholic priesthood unless he is of this class. In fact, the savagery of their intolerance against all who stand in the way of ruthless ambition extends far beyond their hatred of their tacit opponent, the non-Catholic world, and intimately permeates their own relationships. The viciousness of their tactics against one another in the competition for promotion is precisely the same quality as that of medieval cardinals who hired prisoners and assassins to dispose of their rivals in the Consistory.

"Their objective is not merely a life of privilege, luxury, and carnal self-indulgence. In fact, there are among them men of rigid ascetic character. But each and every man of them is driven by an insatiable lust for power. Each sees himself as a factor to be reckoned with in a globe-dominating force. Having lost the capacity for love, they seek the fear of their fellow-men—the more abject the headier. Is it any wonder that the hierarchy's own security demands an impassible gulf between the decent, well-meaning Catholic people and these men with the hearts and spiritual nature of wolves, these men with no God but Greed, no religion but Power? (*Christian Heritage*, May, 1959).

The chief victims of the Roman Catholic system are the people themselves, who are schooled to accept the teachings of their church implicitly and who are almost totally ignorant of the political machinations of their clergy. Again we are indebted to Dee Smith for an analysis which, with some degree of overlapping groups the Roman Catholic laity as follows:

1. First there is that comparatively small group of people whom we may designate as "converts" to Romanism, or "joiners," those who when

they see the Roman Church growing in influence "jump on the band wagon." Such as these would join most any movement, even the Communist if it appeared to offer them advancement. They have only a nominal Christianity, and usually have suffered frustration in some form. In Romanism they become the center of attention and gain a position of influence that would not otherwise be attainable to them.

2. A second group, much the largest group in the Roman Church, consists of those whom we may designate as spiritual suicides. They shrink from any serious thought concerning religious truths which they do not want to face, truths which if followed through might involve them in arduous spiritual effort. In the Roman Catholic Church they gain a promise of heaven through the payment of money and the recitation of sterile formulas. They are content simply to float along and to leave the spiritual and intellectual problems to others.

3. A third group consists of those who are genuinely naive. For them, as Dee Smith says, "the beautiful music, gorgeous trappings, fragrant incense, majestic temples, and eye-filling spectacles perform the office for which Rome designed them, namely, to lull the senses into a state of euphoria which the victim mistakes for heavenly transport. Like wide-eyed children at a circus, the victims of this form of mass hypnosis see nothing of the shoddy meanness behind the glitter."

4. There are those whom we may term the "practical Catholics," those who for personal reasons make a career of their church connections. They are the typical members who are always ready to do the bidding of the clergy, serving as a front against the non-Catholic world, bullying bookstores into refusing to handle anti-Catholic literature, organizing boycotts, coercing business men to support Catholic charities, posing the threat of the "Catholic vote," etc.

5. Another group is that of the "nominal Catholics," those who are members of the church simply because they were born such. They follow the rules of the church only so far as it suits their convenience. They are not critical of the church, but neither do they have any particular devotion for it. They generally attend mass, and they vote for Roman Catholic candidates. They are, however, unsteady and a source of concern to the clergy.

6. There is a comparatively small group of real liberals, men of integrity who try to reconcile the teachings of their church with their consciences as long as possible, but who in a showdown between church and conscience follow their conscience and walk out of the church.

7. Lastly, there is the group, consisting of perhaps one-third of the membership, who by any standard are good, honest, self-respecting people. They are, to be sure, somewhat naive, but they are good neighbors to their Protestant fellow-citizens and are the kind of people for whose sake Protestants sometimes resent any insinuations against the Roman Catholic Church. They are people who, if they knew the true purpose, motives and character of their church's leadership, would leave in

disgust at the betrayal of their faith. They are good not because they are Roman Catholics but in spite of that fact. They are the kind of people who, not going to the trouble to investigate the doctrinal tenets of the faith they profess, would be good in any faith in which they might have membership. Innocently and unknowingly they serve as a perfect smoke-screen for the hierarchy. By using the good character and sincere faith of these followers, and by surounding themselves with a stage-setting of exalted faith, the priests are able to create the illusion of true religion for their entire system. But that system in its basic reality remains like the magnificent Hollywood temples, so impressive and awesome to the untrained eye, but in reality nothing more than plywood and canvas (cf., *Christian Heritage*, May, 1959).

Protestants who have made any effort to talk with Roman Catholics about spiritual things know that they have received but very little Bible instruction from their priests. But that lack of Bible knowledge is but a natural consequence of the fact that the priests themselves have only a minimum of Bible study in their seminary training. L. H. Lehmann, a former priest who founded *The Converted Catholic Magazine* (now *Christian Heritage*), says that only in the last years of their training in seminary did they have any Bible study, and that even then it was in Latin. "The Scripture course itself," he says, "was merely an apologetic for papal interpretation of certain texts of Scripture to suit the past historical development and aims of the papal power. Nothing was taught or indicated to us about the spiritual, individual message of Christ in the Gospel itself. Hence, what was sought in teaching the Bible was a glib use of tag-ends of texts in defense of papal power. The *letter* of texts, apart from their content, supplied the pretext for Roman Catholic use of Scripture. The *spirit* of the word was overlooked" (*The Soul of a Priest*, p. 54).

A further word about the different orders of priests: As we have in-dicated earlier, there are two classes: (1) Secular or Diocesan priests, who are responsible only to the local bishop, and who usually are assigned to churches; and (2) Religious priests, who belong to an order, and who in most cases are responsible to an abbot who rules the monastery. Secular priests take the vows of chastity and obedience, but not of poverty, and so may own property. Members of religious orders take the three vows, poverty, chastity, and obedience, and are of two classes: monks, who withdraw from the world for religious motives, usually live in a monastery, and engage in meditation, study, writing, etc.; and the plain religious priests, who engage in various public activities for the order to which they belong. Those belonging to an order, taking the vows of poverty, chastity, and obedience, but not being ordained as priests, are called *Brothers*. These may teach in church schools, or engage in other kinds of church work. The Jesuits belong to an order but are not monastic, and usually are engaged in educational work in the colleges and seminaries.

As a rule the monks have a reputation for being lazy; the Jesuits for being industrious. The Jesuits are tightly organized under a military type of discipline, and their number is relatively fewer than those of the other orders. Their influence, however, has been out of proportion to their numbers. For centuries they have been the real power behind the papacy, often determining the election of popes, but apparently not trusted by their fellow priests and not being able to elect any of their own number. They have been the object of much criticism because of their advocacy of questionable moral principles, the word "Jesuitical" having entered the dictionary as a synonym for that which is crafty, deceptive, cunning. On various occasions the Jesuits have been banned from practically all of the European and South American countries, from Catholic as well as from Protestant countries. On one occasion the order was condemned and dissolved by a pope, but was restored by a later pope. Often there is bitter rivalry between them and the other orders, which they tend to look upon as inferior, or at least as less efficient.

A custom of the Roman priesthood offensive to Protestants is that of having people address them as "father," and particularly that of calling the pope the "Holy Father" (capitalized)—which we term simply blasphemy. In this connection Christ Himself commanded in the clearest language that the term "father" in a spiritual sense should not be used when addressing our fellow men. "Call no man your father on the earth," said He, "for one is your Father, even he who is in heaven" (Matt. 23:9). Yet the priests continually and openly violate that command.

7. LEAVING THE PRIESTHOOD

The priesthood is the *real crux* of the Roman system. Most of those men, even during their seminary course, as we have indicated, have but very little Bible study; and much of what they do have relates to disconnected portions of Scripture and is given primarily with the purpose of preparing them to answer the arguments that Protestants make against the Roman system. Such has been the testimony of various ones who have left the priesthood. There is in this regard a great contrast between the Protestant and Roman Catholic training for the ministry or the priesthood. Rome simply does not like Bible study either for her priests or for her people, for they find too many things there that are not in accord with their church.

We believe that if these men could be persuaded to make an unprejudiced study of the Bible many would be convinced of the error of their system and would turn from it. An encouraging feature in this regard is that a considerable number, after years of useless priestly ministry, have on their own accord made a serious study of the Bible and have found that it not only does not teach the distinctive doctrines of their church but that it contradicts those doctrines. When an honest priest studies Protestantism without prejudice, in the light of the Word of God and not of Roman tradition, he cannot but recognize that it is Christianity in its purity and in its originality. Much to his surprise and contrary to all that he has been taught he finds that Protestantism is very simple, very clear, and profoundly attractive. He finds that its doctrines are based solidly on the Bible, which is the true manual and code of Christianity. Says Lucien Vinet, a former Canadian priest:

> "In the Church of Rome faith is based on the authority of a man, the Pope, and the traditions of men, namely the opinions of former theologians such as the Fathers of the Church.
> "In Roman Catholicism, Christianity is the doctrines and practices of men; in Protestantism, Christianity is the doctrines of Christ as revealed to us, not by fallible men, but by the infallible Bible" (*I Was a Priest*, p. 126).

Many a priest, struggling against moral degradation and frustration of mind (and one who spends much time in the confessional has an abundance of both), has had an intense battle within himself as to whether or not he should remain in the Church of Rome. He possesses a Bible, but in accordance with the rules of his church he usually does not dare to read it apart from the assigned notes and commentaries, and so remains ignorant of its saving message. How difficult it is for him to realize that all that anyone has to do to receive forgiveness from sins and to experience the joy of salvation is to confess his sins to Christ and to put his trust in Him alone! When he does read the Bible he finds that most of the doctrines that he has held and taught either were perversions of the Scripture or that they were the inventions of men. Would that thousands of those men could be persuaded to turn from that false and subversive system to the clear teachings of Scripture! The key to the whole problem is the priest. And the task before us is to persuade him to read the Bible with an open mind.

It may seem surprising that it takes so long for a priest to discover the truth. But the fact is that a candidate for the priesthood enters the twelve year course of training from parochial school as just a boy —the preferable age is 16—that during his training he is quite effectively cut off from the surrounding world, and that he is an adult before he completes his training. He has not known any other kind of life. During that long and intensive course practically all of those who show signs of independent thinking, those whose dispositions indicate that they might not be obedient to their superior, and those in whose make-up there are any traits which might indicate lack of perseverance or failure for any reason, are weeded out. Not all who finish the course are chosen by the bishop for ordination. But those who are chosen are pretty much of a type that can be reasonably depended upon to continue loyal and submissive to the church. Those who become priests are not so much those who have volunteered for that service but rather those who have been chosen by the hierarchy and carefully screened and trained for that occupation. They are what we may term "hard core Romanists."

Becoming a Roman Catholic priest is a far different thing from becoming a Protestant minister. Everything possible has been done to impress upon the Roman priest the idea that if he breaks with the Roman Catholic Church he will not be trusted by anyone, either within or outside of the Roman Church, and that he cannot make his way in the commercial world for which he now is so entirely unfitted. His intensive training in Latin, doctrine, liturgics, and church history, is of comparatively little value in the outside world, and in fact has been in part designed to unfit him for anything except the priesthood. He has been disciplined for that particular work, and his soul is in a real sense held captive within the walls of Roman Catholic dogma and within the bonds of the priesthood. It is an exceedingly difficult thing for one who has been so trained, and who has committed himself to that system, to break those bonds and to come out into a new kind of life—even into the freedom of the Gospel, for he does not know what that means. This is particularly true if he does not reach that decision until middle age or later. Furthermore, the Roman Catholic people are forbidden to have anything to do with one who has left the priesthood. Getting into, or getting out of, the priesthood is no easy task.

Certainly there are many priests who do not believe what they are teaching, at least not all that they are teaching. Many are ill at ease, and a considerable number are struggling against a real sense of frustration. But they usually remain in the priesthood because they feel more or less helpless and do not have the courage to break away.

Emmett McLoughlin, in an address in Constitution Hall, in Washington, D. C., in 1954; said:

"It is not unusual for people to change their religious affiliation, but it is considered very unusual for Roman Catholic priests to leave the priesthood. Yet one-third of the class of which I was ordained have deserted the hierarchy. I know ten priests who have quit St. Mary's Church in Phoenix where I lived for fourteen years. The number of priests quitting the priesthood is kept as secret as possible. . . . According to the best estimate I have been able to find, at least 30 percent of all Roman Catholic priests leave Rome."

In his *People's Padre* he says:

"The hold of the Roman Catholic hierarchy over most of the clergy, as I have observed it, is not the bond of love, or of loyalty, or of religion. It is the almost unbreakable chain of fear—fear of hell, fear of family, fear of the public, fear of destitution and insecurity. I firmly believe that, in place of the 30 percent of the clergy who probably leave the priesthood today, fully 75 percent would do so if it were not for fear. . . .

"Most priests, torn between the intellectual realization that they have been misled by the hierarchy and the fear of family reaction, hesitate and live on through barren years in the priesthood. . . . Every priest is taught through the years that anyone who leaves the priesthood will be not only cursed by God but rejected by the public. The priest believes that people will sneer at him as one who has violated his solemn promises and therefore cannot be trusted with responsibility. In Catholic circles mention is never made of ex-priests who are successful—only of those who have strayed, who have starved, and who have groveled back to the hierarchy, sick, drunken, broken in spirit, begging to do penance for the sake of clothes on their backs and food in their bellies" (pp. 98-100). "Hundreds of priests quit the church every year. Hundreds more would if they had the means of earning a living" (p. 203).

And again:

"My experience has proved that an ex-priest can overcome his own fears and survive the most concentrated attacks of Roman Catholicism. That experience proves also that the American non-Catholic public still believes strongly in freedom of thought, freedom of religion, and freedom of the right to change one's means of livelihood—and that it will support a man who exercises that right. There is no need for any disillusioned priest or nun to seek the protective anonymity of Los Angeles, New York, or Detroit. He needs only the courage of his convictions, a willingness to work, a deep confidence in America, and a solid faith in God" (p. 261).

Lucien Vinet gives the following analysis as to why priests remain in the priesthood:

"There is no doubt that the great majority of the Roman priests in the ministry of their church have come to realize, just as many ex-priest have done, the hypocrisy, intrigue and falsehood of Romanism. There are various reasons why so many intellectual men still cling to a false religious system and even spend much time and energy in defending this un-Christian religious organization.

"Priests who remain in the priesthood can be classed in four categories:

1. "There are some priests who really are convinced that Christ founded the Roman Church and that 'Out of the Church of Rome there is no salvation.' They explain the contradiction between the doctrines of Christ and those of Rome as apparent only and believe that the traditions of the Roman Church have equal doctrinal value as the words of the Holy Spirit in the Bible. They excuse the many scandals of Romanism as a necessary human factor in the organization of the Church of God on earth. They believe in the infallible teaching authority of the pope and therefore placate their conscience in relying on the Pontiff of Rome for their spiritual and doctrinal convictions. We met very few priests during the nine years of our life in the priesthood, who could be sincerely classed in this category. Most priests know just as well as we do that Christ is the only Teacher of Christianity and that Romanism is anti-Christian in its doctrines and practices.

2. "There are priests who are fully convinced of the falsehood and hypocrisy of the Roman priesthood, but find it impossible to leave the priesthood. . . . Many of them hope that some day an opportunity will be given them to quit Romanism. They realize that their training in the Seminaries provides no preparation whatever for a proper position in life that will enable them to earn a decent living. Their knowledge of Latin, Greek, History of the Church, and Roman Theology is to them of very little use to obtain a decent position in our modern world. By the time they fully realize that their priesthood is a usurpation of the *only priesthood* of Christ and that of the priesthood of believers, they are usually too old to start a new training for a proper career in life. Their health might not be as good as it used to be and they fear that if they leave the comfortable existence they now enjoy, they might land in the poor house.

"The greatest incentive that keeps priests in the priesthood is fear. They fear the curse and persecution of Rome, the rebukes of some of their Roman Catholic friends and the loss of esteem and association of their families. Some of them, of course, fear hard work.

3. "There are now the priests who stay in the priesthood because they like the comfort and pleasure that the Roman ministry affords them. It is the very life of a priest that they like. They command the respect and obedience of many credulous Roman Catholics and they enjoy to the utmost dictating to them. . . . Their life is assured and they have no financial troubles. Even if they cannot accept all the doctrines of the

Church, they do not have to admit it publicly. They can travel extensively in distant lands where their identity is not known and where they can enjoy life as any other human being would do. . . .

4. "Finally there is a group of priests who remain in the priesthood, not on account of their Roman religious convictions and not because they find material comfort in the Roman ministry, but because they experience indescribable mental and sexual pleasure in the very exercise of their Roman ministry. These priests appear to the world as deeply religious and ascetic. They seldom indulge in material comforts and no one can accuse them of any actual sins of any visible form whatsoever, but they are spiritual perverts. The greatest satisfaction or pleasure of their lives is not 'Wine, women and song,' but the torturing of human souls in confession and in spiritual direction. They love to explore secrets of souls and hearts. They experience sordid pleasure in embarrassing female penitents by impertinent questions and prescriptions. Only the Roman system of confession can provide them with the means of indulging in these criminal and sordid pleasures" (*I Was a Priest*, pp. 75-80).

Mr. Vinet also recalls the suggestion of an old priest that if the priests in Canada were given ten thousand dollars each there would not be enough priests left to man the churches. We don't suppose anyone is going to offer that kind of an inducement for them to leave the priesthood, either in Canada or in the United States. But undoubtedly the fear of not being able to make a livelihood has kept many in their positions.

8. RENOUNCING PRIESTLY VOWS

We do not hesitate to say that a priest who becomes disillusioned and finds that the Church of Rome has deceived him with false pretensions should repudiate his vows, declare his independence, and make a new start. In such a case the church has misrepresented herself to him, the ideal that she held before him has proved deceptive and fruitless, and he therefore is not bound to continue in such a relationship. He has not failed the priesthood; the priesthood has failed him, and has been revealed as something other than that which it was represented as being at the time of his ordination. He was led to believe that the Roman Church was the only true church, God's chosen and exclusive instrument for the salvation of souls. She has failed to substantiate her claim to be the only true church, and has been found rather to be a mixture of truth and error, with error in many cases overshadowing the truth.

In so far as the Roman Church has extracted vows that are unscriptural and unreasonable, it is right that those vows should be repudiated. This principle applies not only to priests and nuns, but also to parents who in signing a marriage contract that was forced upon them have pledged away the religious freedom of their children even before they were born. No man has the right to swear away his own religious or civil liberty or that of others and so to place himself or those who are given into his care in a state of subjection to a fellow-mortal. Human slavery, whether physical or spiritual, is wrong and cannot be tolerated. Enforced spiritual servitude of one's self or of one's children to another person or institution can be as degrading and galling as physical servitude. "Ye were bought with a price; become not bondservants of men," says the Scripture (I Cor. 7:23). "Ye were redeemed . . . with precious blood . . . even the blood of Christ" (I Peter 1:18-19). "No man can serve two masters" (Matt. 6:24). Christ is our true Master; He has set us free, and no other person or organization has the right to usurp that freedom.

It is universally acknowledged that when one party to a contract breaks that contract and makes impossible its normal functioning, the other party is not under obligation to continue fulfilling its terms. Yet that is the condition in which many a priest and nun has found himself or herself. Even in human contracts only those obligations continue to be binding which the person to whom the promise was made wishes us to observe them; and certainly in this field of promises to God it is only reasonable to suppose that we are not bound to do what God does not want us to do, merely because we were led through false pretenses or false motives to promise that we would do it. In this instance the priest has made an unscriptural vow of complete obedience to another man, the bishop, and has pledged himself to a service that in reality does not exist. We have already seen that with the coming of Christ and the completion of His work on Calvary the human priesthood was abolished forever. Hence the Roman priesthood is in reality nothing but a sham and a delusion.

On these grounds all priestly vows are to be considered null and void. This was the position taken by the Reformers, Luther, Calvin, Zwingli, and others, as they renounced the authority of Rome, and the Gospel became the proclamation of liberty to the captives and the opening of the prison to those who were bound.

Those who leave Romanism for this reason are not traitors to the church of Christ, as the Roman Church attempts to make them believe. On the contrary they are enlightened and intelligent men, courageously following the path of duty. "The real traitor," says Lucien Vinet, "is the

Roman priest who knows the wickedness of Romanism and yet clings to it for material gain" (*I Was a Priest,* p. 10).

"It must come as a shock to non-Catholics," says McLoughlin, "to realize the possessiveness of even the lay Catholics toward their clergy. It is accepted practice among Protestant, Mormon, and Jewish groups to recognize a clergyman's right to change his vocation. Rabbis become merchants, Mormon bishops enter politics, and ministers in unknown numbers exchange the pulpit for farming, law, mining, teaching, trade, or just plain loafing. But not so a former Roman Catholic priest" (*People's Padre,* p. 176).

McLoughlin expresses as follows his justification for leaving the priesthood:

"Many letters from Roman Catholics had lamented that I had broken my solemn vows, my word to God. But I felt no guilt. I had entered sincerely into a contract, a bilateral contract, when I solemnly vowed poverty, chastity, and obedience. I was one party to the agreement. The Provincial Superior claimed to represent God. My indoctrination trained me to believe that he did. I know now that he did not. The contract was null and void" (p. 183).

And again:

"I was an unsuspecting pawn or tool in the greatest swindle of all history. . . . I have not defied God—I have rejected an organization that has usurped the prerogative of God and claims an exclusive right of speaking in His name. My only regret is that it took me so many years to come to my senses" (pp. 203, 204).

IV. TRADITION

1.   WHAT TRADITION IS

Protestantism and Roman Catholicism agree that the Bible is the inspired Word of God. But they differ widely in regard to the place that it is to have in the life of the church. Protestantism holds that the Bible alone is the authoritative and sufficient rule of faith and practice. But Romanism holds that the Bible must be supplemented by a great body of tradition consisting of 14 or 15 apocryphal books or portions of books equivalent to about two-thirds the volume of the New Testament, the voluminous writings of the Greek and Latin church fathers, and a huge collection of church council pronouncements and papal decrees as of equal value and authority—a veritable library in itself.

It is very evident that this difference of opinion concerning the authoritative basis of the church is bound to have radical and far-reaching effects. The agelong controversy between Protestantism and Roman Catholicism comes to a head regarding the question of authority. Right here, we believe, is *the basic difference between Protestantism and Roman Catholicism.* And, we may add, we believe that in its use of tradition is to be found the Achilles heel of Roman Catholicism. For it is in this that Romanism finds the authority for its distinctive doctrines.

Every religious movement that develops some unity and continues to live has its traditions. These traditions gather up the beliefs, thinking, practices and rules of the group, particularly as these are expressed in its doctrinal standards and forms of government. In this manner the movement gives stability to and regulates its own manner of life, and hands that stability and manner of life on to the next generation.

We do not reject all tradition, but rather make judicious use of it in so far as it accords with Scripture and is founded on truth. We should, for instance, treat with respect and study with care the confessions and council pronouncements of the various churches, particularly those of the ancient church and of Reformation days. We should also give careful attention to the confessions and council decisions of the present day churches, scrutinizing most carefully of course those of the denomination to which we belong. But we do not give any church the right to formulate new doctrine or to make decisions contrary to the teaching of Scripture. The history of the church at large shows all too clearly that church leaders and church councils can and do make mistakes, some of them serious. Consequently their decisions should have no authority except as they are based on Scripture.

Protestants differ from Roman Catholics in that they keep these standards strictly subordinate to Scripture, and in that they are ever ready to re-examine them for that purpose. In other words they insist that in the life of the church Scripture is primary and the denominational standards are subordinate or secondary. They thus use their traditions with one controlling caution: they continually ask if this or that aspect of their belief and practice is true to the Bible. They subject every statement of tradition to that test, and they are willing to change any element that fails to meet that test.

In contrast with this, Roman Catholics hold that there are two sources of authority: Scripture, and developing tradition, with the church being the judge of Scripture and therefore able to say authoritatively what the right interpretation of Scripture is. This, in effect, gives three authorities: The Bible, tradition, and the church. The primacy is in the hands of the church since it controls both tradition and the interpretation of Scripture. This, therefore, is the basis on which the Roman system rests. If this can be shown to be erroneous, it will be seen that the whole system rests on a false basis.

As Roman Catholicism works out in actual practice, the traditions of the church at any time are what the church says they are, Scripture means what the church says it means, and the people are permitted to read the Bible only in an approved version and within the limits of a predetermined interpretation. But when the Christian message is thus shackled by tradition and ecclesiastically dictated interpretation it ceases to be the free grace of God offered to repentant sinners, and becomes an instrument in the hands of the clergy for the control of the people. In professing to interpret the Bible in the light of tradition, the Roman Church in reality places tradition above the Bible, so that the Roman Catholic is governed, not by the Bible, nor by the Bible and tradition, but by the church itself which sets up the tradition and says what it means. Theoretically, the Roman Church accepts the Bible; but in practice she does not leave her members free to follow it. The errors that are found in her traditions obscure and nullify much of the truth that she professes to hold. To cite but one example of what this means in actual practice, while the Roman Catholic Church, in professing allegiance to the Bible, must agree with the Protestant churches that there is "one mediator also between God and man, himself man, Christ Jesus" (I Tim. 2:5), she introduces a host of other mediators—the Virgin Mary, the priests, and hundreds of saints and angels—which effectively sets aside the truth contained in the Scripture statement.

2.   HOW TRADITION NULLIFIES THE WORD OF GOD

We give credit to Rome for this: she professes to hold that the Bible is the Word of God. She repudiates and denounces modernism, which in reality is a more or less consistent denial of the supernatural throughout the Christian system and which unfortunately has come to have a strong influence in some Protestant churches. Modernists seek to reduce some of the historical accounts of the Bible, as for example those of the creation of man and of the fall, to mere myths or legends. Also, modernists usually say that the Bible *contains* the Word of God, but deny that it is in all its parts actually the Word of God.

But having said that, we must point out how Rome also nullifies or destroys the Word. She maintains that alongside of the written Word there is also an unwritten Word, an oral tradition, which was taught by Christ and the apostles but which is not in the Bible, which rather was handed down generation after generation by word of mouth. This unwritten Word of God, it is said, comes to expression in the pronouncements of the church councils and in papal decrees. It takes precedence over the written Word and interprets it. The pope, as God's personal representative on the earth, can legislate for things additional to the Bible as new situations arise.

The Council of Trent, the most authoritative of all Roman councils and the one of greatest historical importance, in the year 1546, declared that the Word of God is contained both in the Bible and in tradition, that the two are of equal authority, and that it is the duty of every Christian to accord them equal veneration and respect. Thus while modernism takes away from the Word of God, Romanism adds to it. Both are in error, and each would seem to be about equally bad. It would be hard to say which has done more to undermine true religion.

The untrustworthiness of oral tradition, however, is apparent for several reasons. In the first place the early Christians, who were closest to Christ and the apostles, and whose testimony therefore would have been most valuable, wrote but very little because of the persecutions to which they were exposed. And what is found in the writings of the second and third centuries has but little reference to the doctrines which at present are in dispute between Protestants and Roman Catholics. Tradition, therefore, for hundreds of years allegedly was transmitted by mere *report*. And it is this which Rome receives as of equal authority with the written Word. But so unreliable is report that it has become a proverb that " a story never loses in its carriage." In other words, a story seldom retains its original character without addition and exaggeration. Fortunately, we have a remarkable instance in the New Testament itself in which report or tradition circulated a falsehood, showing how easily oral tradition can become corrupted, how in a particular instance it did become corrupted even in the apostolic age. In John 21:21-23 we read: "Peter therefore seeing him (John) saith to Jesus, Lord, and what shall this man do? Jesus saith unto him, If I will that he tarry till I come, what is that to thee? follow thou me. This saying therefore went forth among the brethren, that that disciple should not die: yet Jesus said not unto him, that he should not die; but, If I will that he tarry till I come, what is that to thee?" Surely we cannot build a church on such an insecure foundation as oral tradition!

Furthermore, that the body of tradition is not of divine origin nor apostolic is proved by the fact that some traditions contradict others. The church fathers repeatedly contradict one another. When a Roman Catholic priest is ordained he solemnly vows to interpret the Scriptures only according to "the unanimous consent of the fathers." But such "unanimous consent" is purely a myth. The fact is they scarcely agree on *any* doctrine. They contradict each other, and even contradict themselves as they change their minds and affirm what they previously had denied. Augustine, the greatest of the fathers, in his later life wrote a special book in which he set forth his *Retractions*. Some of the fathers of the second century held that Christ would return shortly and that He would reign personally in Jerusalem for a thousand years. But two of the best known scholars of the early church, Origen (185-254), and Augustine (354-430), wrote against that view. The early fathers condemned the use of images in worship, while later ones approved such use. The early fathers almost unanimously advocated the reading and free use of the Scriptures, while the later ones restricted such reading and use. Gregory the Great, bishop of Rome and the greatest of the early bishops, denounced the assumption of the title of Universal Bishop as anti-Christian. But later popes even to the present day have been very insistent on using that and similar titles which assert universal authority. Where, then, is the universal tradition and unanimous consent of the fathers to papal doctrine?

The men who wrote the books of the Bible were inspired by the Holy Spirit and so were preserved from error. But the traditions of the church fathers, the church councils, and the popes are of a lower order and contain many errors and contradictions.

Bellarmine (1542-1621), a Jesuit and a noted Roman Catholic writer, divides tradition into three classes: divine, apostolic, and ecclesiastical. Divine traditions are those which it is alleged Christ Himself taught or ordained, which were not written but were handed down generation after generation by word of mouth. Apostolic traditions are those which were taught by the apostles but not written. And ecclesiastical traditions are those council pronouncements and papal decrees which have accumulated through the centuries. We insist, however, that it would have been utterly impossible for those traditions to have been handed down with accuracy generation after generation by word of mouth and in an atmosphere dark with superstition and immorality such as characterized the entire church, laity and priesthood alike, through long periods of its history. And we assert that there is no proof whatever that they were so transmitted. Clearly the bulk of those traditions originated with the monks during the Middle Ages.

When the leaders of the Reformation appealed to Scripture and thundered against the errors of the Roman Church, that church had to defend herself. And since she could not do so from the Bible alone, she resorted to these other writings. The result is that the most prominent doctrines and practices of the Roman Church, such as purgatory, the priesthood, the mass, transubstantiation, prayers for the dead, indulgences, penance, worship of the Virgin Mary, the use of images in worship, holy water, rosary beads, celibacy of priests and nuns, the papacy itself, and numerous others, are founded solely on tradition.

It is on such a basis as this that the Roman Church seeks to establish herself as "the only true church." But when the Roman Catholic layman searches his Bible for confirmation of the distinctive doctrines of his church, he finds either absolute silence or a distinct negative. The Bible, for instance, has nothing to say about the pope or the papacy as an institution; and it is emphatic and uncompromising in its commands against the use of images or idols in worship. It is natural that the Roman Church does not want to give up tradition. It cannot. If it were to give up tradition the whole system would fall to the ground, so much of its doctrine and practice has no other foundation.

Technically, the Roman Church does not claim that the pope receives new revelations or that he is inspired by the Holy Spirit as were the prophets and apostles when they wrote Scripture. In fact it denies that it formulates any new doctrines at all. Rather it insists that in *ex cathedra* pronouncements the Holy Spirit enables the pope to draw out and proclaim what belonged to the original revelation. But it does claim a divine presence of the Holy Spirit in the giving of *ex cathedra* pronouncements and in the formulation of traditions—which we would say is precisely the same in principle as claiming inspiration. At any rate, by this device it professes to maintain the unchangeability of the church while in reality it adds new doctrines.

It is obvious how inaccessible the Roman rule of faith is. No priest has the rule of his faith, which he vows to accept at ordination, unless he has all these numerous and ponderous volumes. No one could possibly master such a mass of materials, even if they contained no contradictions. And such a rule of faith is utterly beyond the reach of the laity.

3. THE APOCRYPHA

The 14 or 15 books that the Roman Catholic Church adds to the Bible and pronounces equally inspired and authoritative are known as the Apocrypha. These are printed as a part of the Bible and must be accepted by all Roman Catholics as genuine under penalty of mortal sin.

The word Apocrypha is from the Greek *apokrupha*, meaning hidden things, and is used by ecclesiastical writers for matters which are, (1) secret or mysterious; (2) or unknown in origin, forged, or spurious; or, (3) unrecognized, or uncanonical. It is primarily in the sense of spurious or uncanonical that we use the term. The books had this name before they were officially approved by the Council of Trent, and so it is not a name given them by Protestants. They are listed as follows:

1. The First Book of Esdras
2. The Second Book of Esdras
3. Tobit
4. Judith
5. The additions to the book of Esther
6. The Wisdom of Solomon
7. Ecclesiasticus, or the Wisdom of Jesus the Son of Sirach
8. Baruch
9. The Letter of Jeremiah
10. The Prayer of Azariah and the Song of the Three Young Men
11. Susanna
12. Bell and the Dragon
13. The Prayer of Manasseh
14. The First Book of Maccabees
15. The Second Book of Maccabees

Of these only the First and Second Books of Esdras (the latter of which contains an emphatic denial of the value of prayers for the dead, 7:105), and The Prayer of Azariah, were not officially accepted by the Council of Trent. The books accepted add a volume of literature about two-thirds the size of the New Testament, or if the entire 15 be included, about 84 percent of the size of the New Testament. By way of comparison a word count of the Old Testament in the King James Version shows a total of 592,439 words, the New Testament 181,253 words, and the Apocrypha 152,185 words. And since the Apocryphal books are pre-Christian, having been written between the close of the Old Testament and the coming of Christ, the effect of such an addition is to give greater prominence to the Old Testament and therefore to Jewish life and thought, and to decrease relatively the importance of the New Testament.

The Hebrew Old Testament was completed some four hundred years before the time of Christ. In the second century B. C., a Greek translation by Hebrew scholars was made in Alexandria, Egypt, and was called the Septuagint because the translators numbered 70. There developed an important difference, however, between the Greek translation and the Hebrew canon since the Septuagint contained a dozen or more Apocryphal books interspersed among the books of the Hebrew Bible. But not all copies contained the same books—suggesting that there was no general agreement among the translators as to which of these additional books were authoritative.

The Septuagint translation came into general use in Palestine, and that was the popular version at the time of Christ. But the Palestinian Jews never accepted the Apocryphal additions. And Protestants accept only the 39 books of the Old Testament that were in the Hebrew Bible at the time of Christ.

There is no record that Christ or any of the apostles ever quoted from the Apocryphal books or that they made any reference to them, although they undoubtedly knew of them. There are in the New Testament about 260 direct quotations from and about 370 allusions to passages in the Old Testament; yet among all of those there is not a single reference either by Christ or any of the apostles to the Apocryphal writings. They quote from every major book of the Old Testament and from all but four of the smaller ones. They thus set their stamp of approval upon the Jewish Old Testament. Christ quoted it as authoritative, and said, "The Scriptures cannot be broken" (John 10:35). But the reason that neither He nor the apostles ever once referred to the Apocryphal books is obvious. They did not regard those books as Scripture, and they did not intend that those legendary books should become a part of the Bible. Romanists sometimes charge Protestants with having "cut those books out of the Bible." But the record makes it clear that if anyone cut them out it was Christ Himself.

This is all the more significant when we remember that the language commonly spoken in Palestine in the days of Christ was not Hebrew, but Aramaic, that Greek was one of the spoken languages of Palestine at that time, that bilingual Christians who spoke both Aramaic and Greek probably were in the church from the first, and that Christ Himself probably could speak Greek as well as Aramaic. Furthermore, the New Testament books were written in Greek, and in those books we find that while some of the quotations were from the Old Testament reflecting the direct use of the Hebrew, the prevailing practice was to quote from the Greek of the Septuagint. Hence the writers undoubtedly were familiar with the Apocryphal books and undoubtedly would have made some quotations from them if they had been regarded as Scripture.

So, we find that at the time of Christ there were two versions of the Old Testament current in Palestine, the more liberal Alexandrian Septuagint, including the Apocryphal books, in Greek, and the more conservative Hebrew version which included only the canonical books of the Jews, and that the Roman Catholic Bible follows the Alexandrian while the Protestant Bible follows the Hebrew version.

The loose talk of some Roman Catholic writers about the "Greek Bible," the form of the Septuagint that originated in Alexandria, Egypt, being the Bible of the early church, is no credit to scholarship, for it ignores the most important point of all, namely, that so far as the evidence goes, Jesus and the New Testament writers did not consider the Apocryphal books canonical but instead accepted the Palestinian version of the Old Testament.

Furthermore, Josephus, the noted Jewish historian, about 90 A. D., gave a list of the books of the Jewish law and prophets, but he did not include the Apocryphal books. Other Jewish sources support Josephus. The Apocrypha was rejected by Origen, who is generally acknowledged to have been the most learned man in the church before Augustine, by Tertullian, an outstanding scholar in the early third century, by Athanasius, the champion of orthodoxy at the Council of Nicaea and by Jerome, the translator of the Latin Vulgate which became the authorized Roman Catholic Bible.

Jerome declared emphatically that the Apocrypha was no part of the Old Testament Scriptures. However, against his wishes and his better judgment, he allowed himself to be persuaded by two of his bishop friends who admired the books of Tobit and Judith to make a hurried translation of those. He is said to have translated the former at one sitting, and neither of them received the careful attention that had been given to the books which he considered canonical. But it is unfortunate that he did make the translations, for they were later bound up with his

Vulgate, and served to encourage the addition of other Apocryphal books. Augustine alone of the prominent scholars in the early church was willing to give the Apocrypha a place in the Bible, but it is not certain that he considered it authoritative in all cases. Yet in spite of all of these things, the 53 bishops of the Council of Trent, in the year 1546, pronounced the Apocryphal books canonical and deserving "equal veneration" with the books of the Bible.

Even within the Roman Church opinion regarding the canonicity of the Apocrypha has been divided. We have pointed out that Jerome categorically denied that it formed any part of the inspired Scriptures. Cardinal Cajetan, Luther's opponent at Augsburg in 1518, in his *Commentary on all the Authentic Historical Books of the Old Testament,* which he dedicated in 1532 to pope Clement VII, approved the Hebrew canon as over against the Alexandrian. And within the Council of Trent itself several of its members were opposed to the inclusion of these books in the Bible. Thus, even within the papacy, the Apocrypha was not considered canonical until the Council of Trent added it to the Old Testament and pronounced it so—nearly 2000 years after the Old Testament was completed and closed.

Dr. Harris writing on this subject says:

"Pope Gregory the Great declared that First Maccabees, an Apocryphal book, is not canonical. Cardinal Zomenes, in his Polyglot Bible just before the Council of Trent, excluded the Apocrypha and his work was approved by pope Leo X. Could these popes have been mistaken or not? If they were correct, the decision of the Council of Trent was wrong. If they were wrong where is a pope's infallibility as a teacher of doctrine?" (*Fundamental Protestant Doctrines,* I, p. 4).

The real reason for the addition of the Apocryphal books to the Bible by the Roman Church, as we have said, is to be found in connection with events at the time of the Reformation. The Reformers vigorously attacked doctrines which they regarded as unscriptural. The doctrine of purgatory in particular was in need of defense, and the Roman scholars thought they found support in II Maccabees 12:40-45, which tells of the work of Judas Maccabeus, who after a battle sent money to Jerusalem to offer a sacrifice for soldiers who had died while guilty of the sin of idolatry. But, as we shall show when we discuss the doctrine of purgatory, this passage really does not support the Roman Catholic position at all. For idolatry is a mortal sin, and according to Roman Catholic doctrine those dying in mortal sin go directly to hell. Only those who are guilty of venial sin go to purgatory and so only they can be helped by masses and prayers. This again illustrates the desperate nature of the search for support of the distinctive Roman Catholic doctrines.

4. THE NATURE OF THE APOCRYPHAL BOOKS

What, then, is the nature of these books that have caused so much dispute? In the first place they are useful in giving a history of Judaism as it existed between the close of the Old Testament and the opening of the New Testament, and in that regard they are on a par with the writings of Josephus and Philo and other authors of the time. They do not give a continuous history, but particularly in I and II Maccabees they narrate important phases of Jewish history. Most of the books, however, must be classed as religious novels, pious fiction, abounding in repetitions and trivial details which are of little interest to the average reader. They contain doctrines that are unscriptural, and stories that are fantastic and incredible. The colorful tale of Tobit, for instance, is clearly fictitious, written by a pious Jew about 190-170 B. C., and intended to provide religious and moral instruction in the form of an adventure story. Judith, another popular story, is also clearly fictitious. Ecclesiasticus has historical value in that it pictures many aspects of the Judaism of Palestine during the second century B. C.

But none of the writers claim inspiration for their works, and some explicitly disclaim it (Prologue to Ecclesiasticus; I Mac. 4:46; 9:27; II Mac. 2:23; 15:38). They add nothing essential either to the record of God's dealings with His people Israel as recorded in the Old Testament, or to the Christian Gospel as recorded in the New Testament.

Some examples of the numerous errors in these books are: Judith, chapter 1, vss. 1-7, calls Nebuchadnezzar king of the Assyrians and declares that he reigned in Nineveh. But we know that he was king of Babylon (Dan. 4:4-6, 30). In Tobit an angel is represented as telling a lie, claiming that he is Azarius, the son of Ananias. But an angel is a created spirit and cannot be the son of any human being. The book of Baruch purports to have been written by a man of that name who was secretary to Jeremiah (1:1). But he quotes from Daniel, and the book of Daniel was not written until long after the time of Jeremiah, for Jeremiah wrote at the beginning of the 70 year captivity and Daniel at its close.

In answer to the question as to why these books were never accepted by the Jews as canonical, Dr. Edward J. Young, Professor of Old Testament in Westminster Theological Seminary, Philadelphia, says:

"The answer must be that these books were never regarded as divinely inspired. . . . Both Judith and Tobit contain historical, chronological and geographical errors. The books justify falsehood and deception and make salvation to depend upon works of merit. Almsgiving, for example, is said to deliver from death (Tobit 12:9; 4:10; 14:10-11).

"Judith lives a life of falsehood and deception in which she is represented as assisted by God (9:10,13). Ecclesiasticus and the Wisdom of Solomon inculcate a morality based on expediency. Wisdom teaches the creation of the world out of pre-existent matter (11:7). Ecclesiasticus teaches that giving of alms makes atonement for sin (3:4), and in I Maccabees there are historical and geographical errors. This is not to deny many fine and commendable things in the Apocrypha, but the books nevertheless show themselves at points to be at variance with divinely revealed truth. They were consequently never adopted by the Jews as canonical" (*Revelation and the Bible,* p. 167).

Dr. Allan MacRae, Professor of Old Testament in Faith Theological Seminary, Philadelphia, says:

"The so-called Apocryphal books of the Old Testament are books written by godly Jews and containing only their fallible human ideas. They are in no sense the Word of God, nor can they ever become the Word of God. The Jews did not consider these books as part of the Word of God. Jesus Christ did not set His seal upon them as He did upon the actual books of the Old Testament. They are never quoted in the New Testament. There is no evidence that any of the apostles ever considered any of the books as, in any sense, a part of the Word of God.

"It is true that many people in the Middle Ages became confused and thought that some of these books were part of the Word of God. This is because they were included in copies of the Vulgate. However, the man who translated the Vulgate into Latin from the original Hebrew never intended that they should be so included. St. Jerome, the learned translator of the Vulgate, wrote an introduction in which he strongly and clearly expressed his belief that only the books that are today included in our Old Testament belonged in the Bible, and that the so-called Apocrypha are in no sense a portion of God's Word."

The Westminster Confession of Faith, which presents the views of the Presbyterian and Reformed churches, in a statement not designed to forbid reading of the books of the Apocrypha, but to differentiate between their proper and improper use, says:

"The books commonly called Apocryphal, not being of divine inspiration, are no part of the Canon of Scripture; and therefore are of no authority in the Church of God, nor to be otherwise approved, or made use of, than other human writings" (Ch. 1; sec. 3).

The Lutheran Church in Germany made no official pronouncement regarding the Apocrypha, but in the Bible prepared by Martin Luther, which for centuries remained the standard Bible of the Lutheran churches at home and abroad, it was included but was printed at the end of the Old Testament and in smaller print, which was generally understood to mean that it was considered as of secondary importance as compared to the Old and New Testament.

The Church of England and the Episcopal Church in the United States do not accept the Apocrypha as fully canonical, but they do include some readings from those books in their church manual—which indicates that they assign those readings a position higher than they give to the good writings of outstanding church leaders and near equal authority with the Old and New Testament. The sixth of the Thirty-nine articles calls the Apocryphal treatises books which "the Church doth read for example of life and instruction of manners; but yet doth it not apply them to establish any doctrine."

The position of the Eastern Orthodox Church is not clear. It has debated the issue through its long history, but has made no final decision. In practice it has tended to accept the Apocrypha as authoritative, but it has not subjected itself to the rigid ecclesiastical control of doctrine as has the Roman Church, and the result is that some church fathers and theologians quote it authoritatively while others reject it. The Septuagint version of the Old Testament is still in use in the Eastern Orthodox Church.

The British and Foreign Bible Society, in 1827, ruled against including the Apocrypha in its Bibles, and the American Bible Society has followed that example. Nearly all Protestant churches today oppose the use of the Apocrypha.

There were also a considerable number of New Testament Apocryphal books which at times circulated among the Jews or the Christians or both. These were written during the period from the second to the eighth century, and were designed primarily to supplement, or in some instances to correct, the canonical books. Dr. Bruce M. Metzger, Professor of New Testament in Princeton Theological Seminary, says concerning these books:

"Because the four Gospels say little of Jesus' infancy, childhood, and early manhood, and are silent altogether regarding His experiences during the three days in the tomb, several Apocryphal gospels were produced to satisfy the pious curiosity of Christians regarding these two periods of Jesus' life. . . . Still other gospels were written to support heretical doctrines, such as Docetism (the view that Jesus only seemed to be human) in the Gospel of the Egyptians, or to minimize the guilt of Pilate, such as the Gospel according to Peter and the Gospel of Nicodemus. . . .

"The most cogent proof that these books are intrinsically on a different plane from the books of the New Testament is afforded by reading them side by side with the books of the New Testament and allowing each to make its own impression. Then, in the words of M. R. James, 'it will very quickly be seen that there is no question of anyone's having excluded them from the New Testament: they have done that for themselves.' . . . The authors did not hesitate to elaborate marvelous tales, and, in the credulous temper of that age, almost anything was believed" (*Introduction to the Apocrypha*, pp. 249, 250, 262, 263).

Some of the New Testament Apocryphal or pseudonymous books were: The General Epistle of Barnabas, First Epistle of Clement to the Corinthians, Second Epistle of Clement to the Corinthians, Apostolic Constitutions, First Book of Hermas, Second Book of Hermas, Third Book of Hermas, various epistles of Ignatius, The Gospel of the Infancy of the Saviour, a mutilated and altered Gospel of John, and the Gospel of the Nativity of Mary.

These spurious writings, however, were never included in the Roman Catholic Bible. The Council of Trent evidently selected only books that would help them in their controversy with the Reformers, and none of these gave promise of doing that. Furthermore, these books are important, not as a reliable source of historical information about the age with which they purport to deal (that is, the first centuries of the Christian era), but because of what they reveal about the age in which they were produced, showing something of the legend, folklore, ignorance, and superstition so prevalent in that age in which many of the distinctive doctrines of the Roman Church have their roots. That such tales could have been believed shows the depth of the ignorance and superstition to which the people were accustomed.

5. THE VULGATE AND MODERN TRANSLATIONS

The official Bible of the Roman Catholic Church is the Latin translation of Jerome, called the *Vulgate* (meaning "common"). Jerome was commissioned by pope Damasus near the close of the fourth century to prepare a standard Latin version of the Bible, and his purpose was to put the Bible into the common language of the people in accurate, readable form. Had the Roman Catholic Church continued to promote the study of the Bible by the common people how different might have been the course of church and world history! But unfortunately that course was reversed by later popes, the Bible was withheld from the people, and to a large extent even from the priests. Only in recent years has Rome given the Bible to the people in some countries, and then mostly because of Protestant pressure.

The church historian, A. M. Renwick, of Edinburgh, Scotland, in his book, *The Story of the Church,* says: "Jerome (340-420), one of the most interesting and picturesque figures in church history, was born in northern Dalmatia (now Yugoslavia). He produced the Latin Vulgate Version of the Bible, which, even today, is the only version recognized as authentic by the Roman Church. . . . He spent thirty-four years at Bethlehem, where he lived mostly in a cave as a hermit and carried out his immense literary and scholarly labors" (p. 5).

The Roman Church seems to hold the Latin Vulgate translation of about 400 A. D., to be infallible. The Council of Trent decreed: "If any one receive not, as sacred and canonical, the said books entire with all their parts . . . as they are contained in the Old Latin Vulgate edition . . . let him be anathema!" The Vatican Council of 1870 (the council that set forth the doctrine of the infallibility of the pope) reaffirmed the declaration of the Council of Trent that "these books of the Old Testament and New Testament are to be received as sacred and canonical, in their integrity, with all their parts, as they are enumerated in the decree of the said council, and are contained in the ancient Latin edition of the Vulgate," adding that "they contain revelation, with no admixture of error" (Chapter II).

In the year 1590 Sixtus V issued an edition of the Vulgate which he declared to be final, and prohibited under an anathema the publication of any new editions thereafter unless they should be exactly like that one. However, he died soon after, and scholars found numerous errors in his edition. Two years later a new edition was published under pope Clement VIII, and that is the one in general use today. Clearly Sixtus V was in error—another example of the absurdity of that doctrine which holds that the pope is infallible in matters of faith and morals. This doctrine of the authority or infallibility of the Vulgate has caused Roman scholars much difficulty in recent years, because many errors have been pointed out and are now acknowledged by all scholars.

The Roman Catholic Douay version of the Bible (New Testament, 1582, and Old Testament, 1609) was made from the Latin Vulgate, as are the Roman Catholic translations into modern languages. The recent Confraternity version of the New Testament (1941) carries the notation: "Translated from the Latin Vulgate." The inaccuracies of Jerome's Vulgate are legion, as measured by present day scholarship, and the text has not been revised for centuries. So even the best of present day Roman Catholic versions, according to the notation on its own flyleaf, is *a translation of a translation*—an English translation of a Latin translation of the original Greek.

Roman Catholics pride themselves on a long history. Yet how much more accurate are the Protestant translations of the Bible! Protestant scholars go back to the original Greek and Hebrew Scriptures, which are much older than the Vulgate to which Roman Catholics are bound, and they use all the aids that modern scholarship and research can provide. Yet the priests tell their people that it is a mortal sin to read a Protestant Bible, and they destroy Protestant Bibles wherever possible, allegedly on the grounds that they contain error! In 1957 a large stock of Bibles in Madrid, Spain, belonging to the British and Foreign Bible Society was seized and burned. Yet as Protestants we would not dream of destroying Roman Catholic Bibles. Rather we acknowledge that despite their limitations they are quite good translations, and that they contain God's truth in clear enough revelation to enlighten any who will read them in a sincere search for truth, that apart from their interpretative notes they are surprisingly like our King James and American Standard versions. After all, the most distinctive features of the Roman Catholic religion come not from their Bibles but from their traditions.

6. THE QUESTION OF AUTHORITY

We have said that the most controversial issue between Protestants and Roman Catholics is the question of authority—*What is the final seat of authority in religion?*—and that Protestants hold that the Bible alone is the final rule of faith and practice, while Roman Catholics hold that it is the Bible and tradition as interpreted by the church. In actual practice the Roman Church, since the infallibility decree of 1870, holds that the final seat of authority is the pope speaking for the church.

But we need only read church history to discover that when another source of authority is placed alongside Scripture as of equal importance, Scripture eventually becomes relegated to the background. Whether that other source be reason, emotion, or tradition, the inevitable result is that it supplants Scripture and causes it gradually to fade away. If that other source be reason, we get rationalism. If it be emotion, we get mysticism. And if it be tradition, we get ecclesiastical dictation or clericalism. In each case the Bible, while still given lip service, is effectually superseded.

At the time of the Protestant Reformation Martin Luther took his stand solidly on the Bible and refused to be moved unless it could be shown that his teaching was contrary to the Bible. Summoned to appear before the Diet of Worms to give an account of his beliefs, the closing words of his masterful address were: "Here I take my stand; I can do no other; so help me, God." It could not be shown that his teaching was contrary to the Bible, and his position was unassailable.

The primary and almost immediate result of the Reformation was to bring the doctrines of Scripture clearly before men's minds as the Reformers based their teaching squarely on the Scriptures to the exclusion of all accumulated tradition. While the Church of Rome declared that "it belongs to the church to judge of the true sense of Scripture," the Reformers, both on the Continent and in England, declared that even lay people, with the guidance of the Holy Spirit, can interpret Scripture by diligent and prayerful searching and reading.

It is true, of course, that the person who has not been born again, that is the one who has not been the object of the regenerating power of the Holy Spirit and who therefore is not a Christian, is not able to understand spiritual truth. This too is clearly taught in Scripture: "Now the natural man receiveth not the things of the Spirit of God: for they are foolishness unto him; and he cannot know them, because they are spiritually judged" (I Cor. 2:14). But every born again Christian has the gift of the Holy Spirit, and is therefore able to understand the basic essentials of what God has written. It is also true that many people, even among born again believers, differ on minor points. But that is because they have not read the Scriptures carefully enough and compared the various parts. The remedy for that is more devoted, patient, diligent Bible study. In any event there is no reference whatever in the Bible that even hints that God has delegated the interpretation of Scripture to any one individual or group of individuals.

If it be asked how the Church of Rome, which contains important elements of truth, has become honeycombed with paganism, how even a professedly Christian church has managed to build up a semi-pagan organization, the answer is that the illegitimate authority that Rome has given to uninspired tradition has produced the effect. That development had an almost exact parallel in the nation of Israel. Israel had the inspired prophets, but she preferred the pleasing and flattering teachings of the false prophets, and so developed a set of traditions which in time came to supplant the true teachings of the prophets. In the teachings and writings of the false prophets the rulers of the Jews found the things they wanted, just as the popes and bishops have found in the man-made traditions of their church things which appeal to their selfish and prideful natures and which gave them what they wanted under the cover of religion. A study of religious errors will show that they have this common characteristic: They consist either of additions to Scripture, or of subtractions from Scripture, or perhaps a mixture of the two.

We do not deny, of course, the statement of the Romanists that much of what Jesus said and did is not recorded in the Gospels. John says plainly: "Many other signs therefore did Jesus in the presence of his disciples, which are not written in this book: but these things are written that ye may believe that Jesus is the Christ, the Son of God; and that believing ye may have life in his name" (20:30-31). But we do maintain that *that which is written is sufficient.* It is Protestant doctrine that the Bible contains all that is necessary to salvation, and no other writings or church pronouncements are to be regarded as having divine authority.

Numerous references set forth the sufficiency of Scripture. Nowhere do we find even a hint that these need to be supplemented by church councils or papal decrees of any kind. Some of these are as follows:

"To the law and to the testimony: if they speak not according to this word, it is because there is no morning for them" (or as the King James Version says, "it is because there is no light in them") (Is. 8:20).

"All scripture is given by inspiration of God, and is profitable for doctrine, for reproof, for correction, for instruction in righteousness" (II Tim. 3:16).

"Ye search the scriptures, because ye think that in them ye have eternal life; and these are they which bear witness of me" (John 5:39).

Our Lord proclaimed the infallibility of Scripture, for He said: "The scriptures cannot be broken" (John 10:35).

The brothers of the rich man had sufficient evidence because, said Jesus, "They have Moses and the prophets" (Luke 16:29).

Jesus' rebuke to the Sadducees was, "Ye do err, not knowing the scriptures" (Matt. 22:29).

When Jesus reasoned with His disciples after His resurrection in regard to the purpose and necessity of His death, we are told: "And beginning from Moses and from all the prophets, he interpreted to them in all the scriptures the things concerning himself" (Luke 24:27).

Peter wrote: "And we have the word of prophecy made more sure; whereunto ye do well that ye take heed, as unto a lamp shining in a dark place. . . . For no prophecy ever came by the will of man: but men spake from God, being moved by the Holy Spirit" (II Peter 1:19,21).

James quoted Scripture in the Council of Jerusalem to settle the question that was at issue (Acts 15:16-18).

Paul repeatedly appealed to Scripture, as when he asks: "For what saith the scripture?" (Rom. 4:3). And to Timothy he wrote: "From a babe thou hast known the sacred writings which are able to make thee wise unto salvation" (II Tim. 3:15).

The diligence of the Bereans in testing all things by Scripture is commended: "Now these were more noble than those in Thessalonica, in that they received the word with all readiness of mind, examining the scriptures daily, whether these things were so" (Acts 17:11). The Scriptures which the Bereans had were the Old Testament. They compared Paul's teachings about Jesus with what the Old Testament had predicted. They were not theologians or scholars, but ordinary religious people, and yet the writer of the book of Acts (Luke) implies that by comparing the teachings of the great apostle Paul with Scripture they were able to determine whether he was right or wrong.

And the book of Revelation pronounces a blessing on both the reader and those who hear: "Blessed is he that readeth, and they that hear the words of the prophecy, and keep the things that are written therein: for the time is at hand" (1:3).

Thus the sufficiency of Scripture is everywhere assumed. In all these cases our Lord and the New Testament writers referred to Scripture as clear, authoritative, and final. Never once did they say or imply that extra-Scriptural tradition was needed to supplement Scripture, or that any man or group of men was authorized to give authoritative interpretations of Scripture.

7. TRADITION CONDEMNED BY THE SCRIPTURES

In New Testament times the Jews had a great body of tradition, the accumulation of centuries, which they gave precedence over Scripture. But Jesus never mentioned tradition except to condemn it and to warn against it. He rebuked the Pharisees with these words: "Ye leave the commandment of God, and hold fast the tradition of men. . . . Ye reject the commandment of God, that ye may keep your tradition . . . making void the word of God by your tradition" (Mark 7:8,9,13). "And he answered and said unto them, Why do ye also transgress the commandment of God because of your tradition. . . . Ye have made void the word of God because of your tradition. . . . But in vain do they worship me, teaching as their doctrines the precepts of men" (Matt. 15:3,6,9).

Thus our Lord rebuked the Pharisees for doing precisely what the Church of Rome does today, for substituting a body of human teachings and making it equal to or even superior to the Word of God.

Early in the Old Testament Moses warned against this same danger: "Ye shall not add unto the word which I command you, neither shall ye diminish from it, that ye may keep the commandments of Jehovah your God which I command you" (Deut. 4:2). Paul gave a clear warning against the use of tradition: "Take heed lest there shall be any one that maketh spoil of you through his philosophy and with deceit, after the traditions of men, after the rudiments of the world, and not after Christ" (Col. 2:8). And John, in the final book of the New Testament set forth the severe penalty for adding to or taking away from the Word of God: "I testify unto every man that heareth the words of the prophecy of this book, If any man shall add unto them, God shall add unto him the plagues which are written in this book: and if any man shall take away from the words of the book of this prophecy, God shall take away his part from the tree of life, out of the holy city, which are written in this book" (Rev. 22:18,19).

In the Roman Church of today we have a perfect illustration of the attitude which characterized the Pharisees and scribes, who substituted a body of human teachings and made them equal to or even superior to the Word of God. In Jesus' day traditionalism had become so perverse and powerful that it finally crucified Him. Religion was so blinded by its own distortions of the Word of God that it took the cross to expose it and upset it and to reveal the truth once more. In a similar way the Church of Rome is following a set of traditions that she has accumulated through the centuries, which by her own pronouncements she has elevated to equal authority with, or even to superiority over the Word of God. Her purpose, of course, is to justify doctrines and practices which have no basis in Scripture, or which are in violation of Scripture commands.

In order for Rome to defend her use of tradition, which admittedly came into use long after the New Testament was completed, it was necessary for her to assert that the authority of the church is superior to that of the Scriptures. Protestantism holds that the Scriptures are the infallible rule of faith and practice, and that the church as an institution and all believers must be governed by that authority. The Church of Rome, on the other hand, holds that she is the supreme authority in matters of faith and practice. She even attempts to say that the Roman Catholic Church produced the Bible, and that the pope as the vicar of Christ on earth has the right to legislate for the church. But such claims are absurd, because the New Testament was completed in the first century of the Christian era while the Roman Catholic Church with its distinctive features and its separate existence did not come into being until about four centuries later. Furthermore, the sin and corruption that have characterized the Roman Church, particularly during the Middle Ages when so many of her doctrines and practices originated, is proof that she is in no sense superior to the Bible but quite the contrary. But because of that teaching the average Roman Catholic may not be particularly impressed when it is pointed out to him that the doctrines of purgatory, the mass, indulgences, penance, the use of images, etc., are not in the Bible or even that they are contrary to the Bible. He believes these things not because he has Scriptural authority for them, but because the church teaches them. This again shows how pernicious can be the use of tradition.

The reason that the Jews had departed from their Scriptures was that they accepted tradition and the decisions of their councils as their guide of faith. The Roman Church has made the same mistake. She, too, has compromised the truth of the Bible in order to follow tradition. When she began putting herself on a par with Scripture she found it impossible to stop there. The next step was to place herself *above* Scripture, and she has assumed that position ever since.

8. THE PROTESTANT ATTITUDE TOWARD THE BIBLE

The first complete English Bible was translated by John Wycliffe, "the morning star of the Reformation," about 1382. Before his time there was no Bible in English, although a few fragmentary portions had been translated. Wycliffe knew only the Latin Bible, so his version, like the Roman Catholic versions even to the present day, was a translation of a translation. The first English New Testament translated from the original Greek was that of William Tyndale, in 1525-26. That work was made possible through the publication of the Greek New Testament by Erasmus a few years earlier. But since the church authorities in England (Henry VIII was king and also the head of the church) did not want the people to have the Bible in their own language Tyndale was forbidden to carry on his work in England. He went instead to Germany, where the work of Luther had provided a hospitable environment for such a venture. His work was completed and published in the city of Worms, in 1526. However, it was condemned by the English government, and in order to gain entrance into England had to be smuggled in a few copies at a time.

But Tyndale eventually paid with his life for his devotion to the Bible. Having taken up residence in Antwerp, Belgium, opposition to his work began and continued until he was arrested and condemned. In 1530 he was put to death by strangling and his body was burned. His dying words were, "O God, open the king of England's eyes." That prayer was answered, and God opened the eyes of Henry VIII. In 1536 there appeared the *Miles Coverdale* version of the Bible, which also was published outside England, but which circulated with considerable freedom in England. And in 1539 the second edition was published in England and circulated freely. Coverdale was the friend and colleague of Tyndale, and the translation was largely Tyndale's.

The next important translation was the *Geneva Bible,* translated during the reign of Roman Catholic Queen Mary, by a group of English scholars in Geneva, Switzerland, hence its name. This became the Bible of Cromwell's army and the Scottish Covenanters, of John Bunyan and John Knox. It was the Bible of the Puritans, and was brought to this country by the Pilgrims. The next most important English Bible was the *King James* version, translated in 1611, which to the present day continues to be the most popular of all the versions.

Up until the time of the Reformation the Bible had been a book for priests only. It was written in Latin, and the Roman Church refused to allow it to be translated into the languages of the common people. But when the Reformers came on the scene all of that was changed. Luther translated the entire Bible into German for the people of his native land, and within 25 years of its appearance one hundred editions of the German Bible came off the press. It was also soon translated into most of the vernacular tongues of Europe, and wherever the light of the Reformation went it became the book of the common people. Decrees of popes and church councils gave way to the Word of Life. The Protestant churches of Europe and America have labored earnestly to put the Bible into the hands of the people in their own languages and have urged the people everywhere to read it for themselves. Protestant Bible societies now circulate more copies of the Bible each year than were circulated in the fifteen centuries that preceded the Reformation.

More than 8,000,000 copies of the complete Bible are now sold in the United States each year. During the last 150 years it has been translated into all of the major languages of the world. According to the report of the 1960 annual meeting of the American Bible Society the complete Bible, Old and New Testament, is now available in 219 languages and dialects, the complete New Testament is available in 271 more, and at least one book of the Bible, usually one of the Gospels, has been translated into 661 more, for a total of 1151 languages and dialects into which the Bible has been translated in whole or in part. Today the Bible is available in whole or in part in the native tongues of probably 95 per cent of the people of the world.

Dr. Hugh Thompson Kerr, late Presbyterian minister in Pittsburgh, has well said:

"Protestants have been the pioneers in Bible translation and have organized and supported the great world-encircling Bible societies. They believe that the Bible needs no other interpreter than the Holy Spirit. The Bible read under the guidance of the Holy Spirit is the Christian's authoritative guide. Protestants therefore claim that they truly represent and interpret Christianity as it is set forth in the Bible. They hold that anyone who will read the Bible prayerfully, with the aid of the best scholarship, will reach the conclusion that Protestantism honestly interprets the teachings and confirms the practice of early Christianity" (Booklet, *What Protestants Believe*, p. 8).

And another says:

"The fact is, the Bible was written for the common people. The language of the Old Testament was the language spoken in the homes and market-places of the Hebrews. The New Testament Greek was not the classical Greek of an earlier period but the Greek spoken by the common people. It was called the *koine*, which means the common language, what we would call today 'newspaper language.' This shows that God intended the common people to understand the Bible. Any man with ordinary intelligence and able to read English can read and learn that Jesus is the Saviour of sinners" (Edward J. Tanis, booklet, *What Rome Teaches*, p. 9).

The Protestant ideal is that everyone should read the Bible. Right here, we believe, is the reason that the Protestant nations, the United States, England, Scotland, Holland, and the Scandinavian nations have followed one line of development, while the Roman Catholic nations, Italy, Spain, France, and the Latin American nations have followed a distinctly different pattern. Protestants believe that those who study the Bible in sincerity and with prayer will have no difficulty in understanding its basic truths. The words of Jesus, previously quoted, imply that the common people should know the Bible and that they are able to understand it.

It is virtually axiomatic that where there is an open Bible, men will not long remain in bondage. But by the same token where the Bible is a closed book men soon find themselves in darkness and servitude. Everywhere it has been the precursor of civilization and liberty, driving out barbarity and despotism as bats and vermin flee from the sunshine. In every land where its free and unrestrained reading has been encouraged it has dispelled ignorance and superstition.

9. THE ROMAN CATHOLIC ATTITUDE TOWARD THE BIBLE

In contrast with the Protestant attitude toward the Bible, the Roman Church has traditionally opposed its free use by the people. Even today in the predominantly Roman Catholic countries it keeps the Bible from the people, or at least makes no effort to provide it for them. The result is that the people in those countries know practically nothing about the Bible except as some Protestant organizations have gone in and distributed copies. In countries where the Roman Church is in keen competition with Protestantism it has allowed the people to have the Bible if there is a demand for it, but it has always insisted strenuously that the version must be the Douay, or more recently the Confraternity, each of which contains a set of notes printed on the same page with the text and giving the Roman Catholic interpretation of disputed passages. Even to this day any other version, even the Bible as such without note or comment, is condemned. The alleged reason is that these versions contain "errors." But the real reason is that the Church of Rome does not want the Bible read apart from her interpretative notes.

The Bible was first officially forbidden to the people by the Church of Rome and placed on the *Index of Forbidden Books* by the Council of Valencia (a cathedral city in southeastern Spain) in the year 1229, with the following decree:

> "We prohibit also the permitting of the laity to have the books of the Old and New Testament, unless any one should wish, from a feeling of devotion, to have a psalter or breviary for divine service, or the hours of the blessed Mary. But we strictly forbid them to have the above-mentioned books in the vulgar tongue."

Here we see that the Bible was forbidden to the laity, except for the Psalms or breviary (book of devotions), and even then it could be only in Latin—which of course placed it beyond the reach of the common people. That decree was passed at the time the Waldensians were gaining strength, and it was enforced with bitter persecution.

The Council of Trent reaffirmed that decree and prohibited the use of the Scriptures by any member of the church unless he obtained permission from his superior. The decree read as follows:

> "In as much as it is manifest, from experience, that if the Holy Bible, translated into the vulgar tongue, be indiscriminately allowed to everyone, the temerity of men will cause more evil than good to arise from it; it is, on this point, referred to the judgment of the bishops, or inquisitors, who may, by the advice of the priest or confessor, permit the reading of the Bible translated into the vulgar tongue by Catholic authors, to those persons whose faith and piety, they apprehend, will be augmented, and not injured by it; and this permission they must have in writing."

To this decree, as to more than a hundred others passed by this council, was attached an anathema against anyone who should dare to violate it, and also penalties were fixed against the illegal possessor or seller of those books. Here we observe particularly the statement that the read-

ing of the Bible in the native tongue will do "more evil than good"!
Imagine that, as the deliberate teaching of a church professing to be
Christian! How insulting to God is such teaching, that His Word as read
by the people will do more evil than good! That attitude toward the
Word of God is the mark, not of a true church, but of a false church.

While it has been the policy of the Roman Church to withhold the
Bible from the people, Peter, the alleged founder of that church, refers
to Scripture as "the word of prophecy made more sure," and likens it to
"a lamp shining in a dark place" (II Peter 1:19). What a blessing it
would be to the world if the Roman Church would *really* follow the
teaching of Peter!

Early in the history of Israel God instructed Moses to make the words
of the law known and easily accessible to all the people: "And thou shalt
teach them diligently unto thy children, and thou shalt talk of them
when thou sittest in thy house, and when thou walkest in the way, and
when thou liest down, and when thou risest up. . . . And thou shalt
write them upon the door-posts of thy house, and upon thy gates" (Deut.
6:7-9). Another verse which expresses the preciousness of Scripture and
its importance to the individual is Psalm 119:11: "Thy word have I hid
in my heart, that I might not sin against thee."

Even where permission to read the Bible is granted by the Council
of Trent, to those who presumably are so thoroughly indoctrinated with
Roman Catholicism that nothing will shake their faith, that permission
must be in writing!

Ligouri, one of the highest authorities on Canon Law, whose books
probably are considered more authoritative and probably are quoted
more often than those of any other writer, says:

> "The Scriptures and books of Controversy may not be permitted in
> the vulgar tongue, as also they cannot be read without permission."

Four different popes during the eighteenth century made pronouncements against giving the Bible to the people in their own language,
typical of which was that of Clement XI (1713) in the Bull *Unigenitus*:
"We strictly forbid them (the laity) to have the books of the Old and
New Testament in the vulgar tongue." As for the Encyclical of Leo XIII
(1893) on "The Study of the Bible," sometimes quoted by Roman
Catholics as a statement urging the laity to study the Bible, it should
be observed that: (1) the Bible which was cited for study was the Latin
Vulgate, which of course was not available to the common people nor
understood by them; (2) the statement forbade them to interpret it
otherwise than as the church interpreted it; and (3) it did not rescind

or modify the prior law of the church which refused the free use of the Scriptures to the laity.

Such was the teaching and practice of the Roman Church for centuries. For one to possess or read the Bible in his native tongue without permission in writing from his superior and under the watchful eye of the bishop was a mortal sin, for which absolution could not be granted until the book was delivered to the priest. As the top-heavy structure of law and ritual developed, the Bible had to be denied to the people. Otherwise they would have seen that it was merely a man made structure. On the other hand the Bible had to be preserved as a reference book for the theologians and priests in order to sustain the power of the priesthood by plausible and elastic interpretations of certain texts. But so far as the people were concerned it might as well have been forgotten. Small wonder it is that ignorance, superstition, poverty, and low moral conditions have been so characteristic of Roman Catholic countries.

In Protestant countries, however, in recent years a considerable change has taken place in Roman Catholic practice, and, shamed into a different attitude because of Protestant criticism, the Roman Church now grants her people the privilege of reading the Bible, and even stocks it in the book stores—using, of course, only the approved versions. The Roman Church does not wish to appear to be the foe of the Bible, so indefensible is that position. An annual "Catholic Bible Week" has been instituted, and indulgences granted for reading the Bible at least fifteen minutes each day. But this appears to be an unnatural emphasis, by no means given with a clear conscience, permitted but not looked upon favorably by the authorities in Rome. Significantly, no similar program of Bible reading has been instituted in the predominantly Roman Catholic countries. Only in Protestant countries, and primarily in the United States, is this policy followed. And it certainly comes very late in the long, long history of the Roman Church. One can easily guess what the result would be if for some reason the Protestant influence were removed.

Unfortunately, it still is a mortal sin for a Roman Catholic anywhere to read the King James, American Standard, Revised Standard, or any other Protestant version. So, even the Bible as such remains on the Index of Forbidden Books! It is made fit for a Roman Catholic to read only when it is annotated by an authorized theologian! What St. Paul wrote, if it stands by itself, is on the Index. What was written by St. Peter himself, who according to Roman Catholic tradition was the first pope, is on the Index unless some Roman Catholic annotates his writing. Yet the Roman Church does not claim infallibility for the theologian who annotates it! So here we have the very height of absurdity—it takes the work of a theologian who is not infallible to correct and edit and make lawful and orthodox the text of those who wrote by divine inspiration!

The attitude of the Roman Church toward the Bible societies has been one of sustained opposition. Several acts of the popes have been directed exclusively against them. In 1824 pope Leo XII, in an encyclical letter said: "You are aware, venerable brethren, that a certain society called the Bible society strolls with effrontery throughout the world, which society, contrary to the well-known decree of the Council of Trent, labors with all its might and by every means to translate—or rather to pervert—the Scriptures into the vulgar tongue of every nation. . . . We, in conformity with our apostolic duty, exhort you to turn away your flock by all means from these poisonous pastures." In 1844 pope Gregory XVI again condemned these societies, and pope Pius IX, author of the decree of papal infallibility, who died in 1878, denounced "these cunning and infamous societies, which call themselves Bible societies, and give the Scriptures to inexperienced youth."

But in reality who can estimate the vast good that these noble organizations and their faithful colporteurs have brought to the nations of the world? Most prominent among these have been the British and Foreign Bible Society, the American Bible Society, the Bible Society of Scotland, and that of the Netherlands, which have translated the Scriptures into hundreds of languages and dialects, and which now circulate millions of copies of the Bible every year. Many times Bibles have been publicly burned by the priests. That the real attitude of the Vatican toward the Bible has not changed is shown by the fact that in 1957 the depot of the British and Foreign Bible Society in Madrid, Spain, was closed and its stock of Bibles confiscated and burned. After the Spanish civil war, which brought Franco and the Roman Catholic Church to power, Spanish children returning from hospitable Swiss families with Bibles in their pockets were forced at the Spanish frontier to hand those precious books over to the local priest. Time and again in Colombia during the past ten years Bibles have been taken from Protestants by fanatical Romanist groups and burned, almost always at the instigation of the local priests, usually in communities where new Protestant churches were being formed. The fact remains that only in those countries where Protestantism is dominant does the Bible circulate freely. Think of the popes, who profess to be God's representatives on earth, forbidding their people and all others to read God's own Book of Life! Surely the Church of Rome by such action proves itself apostate and false.

So, for a thousand years, from the early sixth century to the sixteenth century, while the Roman Church held sway, the Bible remained a closed book. The Roman Church, instead of being a kingdom of light, became a kingdom of darkness, promoting ignorance and superstition and holding the people in bondage. In most Roman Catholic countries today the Bible remains a closed book. Only since the time of the Protestant Reformation has it circulated freely in any country.

Among evangelical Christians in the United States there are thousands of classes studying the Bible. But among Roman Catholics such groups are very rare. Even a brief discussion with Roman Catholics will reveal that they know very little about the doctrines or the history of their church, and that they know almost nothing at all about the Bible.

Rome's traditional policy of seeking to limit the circulation of the Bible and in anathematizing or destroying all copies that are not annotated with her distinctive doctrines shows that she is really afraid of it. She is opposed to it because it is opposed to her. The plain fact is that she cannot hold her people when they become spiritually enlightened and discover that her distinctive doctrines are merely man made inventions.

A curious fact in regard to the Index of Forbidden Books is that the Roman Church permits the reading of some books by ecclesiastical writers outside her fold when those books contain nothing contrary to her doctrines. Even some heathen books are allowed to adults, because of their "elegance and propriety." But not the Bible—unless it carries her interpretation! The traditional attitude of the Roman Catholic Church toward the promotion and study of the Bible has been, we believe, the greatest spiritual and cultural tragedy since the influx of the pagans into the church in the fourth century.

10. INTERPRETING THE BIBLE

While the Roman Catholic people in the United States have access to the Bible, they are told that they cannot understand it and that it must be interpreted for them by the church speaking through the priest. People ordinarily do not waste their time reading a book that they are persuaded they cannot understand.

The priests in turn are pledged not to interpret the Bible for themselves, but only as the church interprets it, and according to "the unanimous consent of the fathers." But the church has never issued an official commentary giving that interpretation. And as we have pointed out earlier, the unanimous consent of the fathers is purely a myth, for there is scarcely a point of doctrine on which they do not differ. The doctrine of the immaculate conception, for instance, was denied by Anselm, Bonaventura, and Thomas Aquinas, three of the greatest Roman theologians. Yet Rome presumes to teach that Mary was born without sin, and that that is the unanimous teaching of the fathers.

In their insistence on following an official interpretation the Roman Catholics are pursuing a course similar to that of the Christian Scientists, who also have the Bible but insist that it must be interpreted by Mary Baker Eddy's book, *Science and Health, with Key to the Scriptures,* and that of the Mormons, who likewise have the Bible but interpret it by the *Book of Mormon.*

The practical result of the priests and people being told that they cannot interpret the Bible for themselves is that they read it but very little. Why should they? They cannot understand it. They may read a few pages here and there, but even among the priests there is scarcely one in twenty who reads it from beginning to end and really studies it. Instead the priests spend hours reading their breviaries, books of daily devotions and prayers, as required by their church, but which are of human origin. This practice of representing the Bible as a mysterious book is a part of Rome's over-all program of presenting Christianity as a mystery religion, in which the mass in particular as well as various other practices are set forth as mysteries which are not to be understood but which are to be accepted with implicit faith.

The priests and the people alike look upon the Bible as a mysterious book, and anyway the interpretation is given to them in pope's decrees and church council pronouncements which are declared to be clearer and more easily understood. Furthermore, these latter supersede Scripture. Experience proves that whenever an interpretation becomes more important than a document, the document becomes buried and the interpretation alone survives. For this reason the average Roman Catholic is faithful to his church but neglects his Bible. Instead of following the teachings of God the priests and people follow the traditions of men.

A fraudulent claim recently put forth by the Knights of Columbus in a series of newspaper and magazine ads designed to appeal to Protestants and others is that the Roman Catholic Church produced the Bible and that we received it from her. Some of her spokesmen attempt to say that the canon of the Bible was established in the fourth century, by the pope and council of Carthage, in 397 A. D. But that statement is erroneous on two counts. In the first place, there was no pope as such in 397 A. D. It was not until the Council of Chalcedon, in 451, that the bishop of Rome was designated pope, and the authority of the bishop of Rome never has been acknowledged by the Eastern churches. Previous to that time all priests and bishops were called popes (Latin, *papa*), and in the Eastern churches that title is applied to ordinary priests even to the present day. The Council of Chalcedon attempted to restrict the title exclusively to the bishop of Rome, who at that time was Leo I, and conferred it posthumously on all previous bishops of Rome in order to make it appear that an unbroken succession of popes had proceeded from Peter.

And in the second place, the New Testament was produced during the first century of the Christian era and had assumed its present form centuries before the Roman Catholic Church developed its distinctive characteristics. At that time the Eastern churches were dominant in Christian affairs, and the Church in Rome was relatively insignificant. Gregory I, called Gregory the Great, who was consecrated pope in 590 and died in 604, was in effect the founder of the papal system. He reorganized the church, revised the ritual, restored monastic discipline, attempted to enforce celibacy among the clergy, and extended the authority of the Roman Church into many countries adjacent to Italy. He more than anyone else gave the Roman Church its distinctive form and set the course that it was to follow in its later history.

Furthermore, long before the Council of Carthage the particular books now found in the New Testament, and only those, had come to be looked upon by the church at large as the inspired and infallible Word of God on the basis of their genuineness and authority. These particular writings, in distinction from all other books of that age, manifest within themselves this genuineness and authority as we read them; and the Council of Carthage did not so much choose the books that were to be accepted in the New Testament but rather placed its stamp of approval on the selection that by that time, under the providential control of the Holy Spirit, had come to be looked upon by the church as the New Testament canon. The Old Testament canon was completed and had assumed its present form long before the coming of Christ. The Roman Church, of course, had nothing whatever to do with that.

V. PETER

1.   THE ROMAN CATHOLIC POSITION

The controversial passage in regard to Peter's place in the Church is Matthew 16:13-19, which reads as follows:

"Now Jesus, having come into the district of Caesarea Philippi, began to ask his disciples, saying, 'Who do men say the Son of Man is?' But they said, 'Some say, John the Baptist; and others, Elias; and others, Jeremias, or one of the prophets.' He said to them, 'But who do you say that I am?' Simon Peter answered and said, 'Thou art the Christ, the Son of the living God.' Then Jesus answered and said, 'Blessed art thou, Simon Bar-Jona, for flesh and blood hath not revealed this to thee, but my Father in heaven. And I say to thee, thou art Peter, and upon this rock I will build my Church, and the gates of hell shall not prevail against it. And I will give thee the keys of the kingdom of heaven; and whatever thou shalt bind on earth shall be bound in heaven, and whatever thou shalt loose on earth shall be loosed in heaven" (Confraternity Version).

To this passage the Confraternity Version adds the following interpretation:

"The rock was Peter. . . . *The gates of hell:* hostile, evil powers. Their aggressive force will struggle in vain against the Church. She shall never be overcome; she is indefectible. And since she has the office of teacher (cf. 28, 16-20), and since she would be overcome if error prevailed, she is infallible.

"*Keys:* a symbol of authority. Peter has the power to admit into the Church and to exclude therefrom. Nor is he merely the porter; he has complete power within the Church. 'To bind and to loose' seems to have been used by the Jews in the sense of to forbid or to permit; but the present context requires a more comprehensive meaning. In heaven God ratifies the decisions which Peter makes on earth, in the name of Christ" (pp. 36, 37).

And the late Cardinal Gibbons, a former archbishop of Baltimore and one of the most representative American Roman Catholics, in his widely read book, *Faith of our Fathers,* set forth the position of his church in these words:

"The Catholic Church teaches that our Lord conferred on St. Peter the first place of honor and jurisdiction in the government of His whole church, and that the same spiritual supremacy has always resided in the popes, or bishops of Rome, as being the successors of St. Peter. Consequently, to be true followers of Christ all Christians, both among the clergy and laity, must be in communion with the See of Rome, where Peter rules in the person of his successor" (p. 95).

The whole structure of the Roman Church is built on the assumption that in Matthew 16:13-19 Christ appointed Peter the first pope and so established the papacy. Disprove the primacy of Peter, and the foundation of the papacy is destroyed. Destroy the papacy, and the whole Roman hierarchy topples with it. Their system of priesthood depends absolutely upon their claim that Peter was the first pope at Rome, and that they are his successors. We propose to show that, (1) Matthew 16:13-19 does not teach that Christ appointed Peter a pope; (2) that there is no proof that Peter ever was in Rome; and (3) that the New Testament records, particularly Peter's own writings, show that he never claimed authority over the other apostles or over the church, and that that authority was never accorded to him.

2. THE "ROCK"

"And I say to thee, thou art Peter, and upon this rock I will build my Church, and the gates of hell shall not prevail against it" (Matt. 16:18, Confraternity Version).

Romanists quote this verse with relish, and add their own interpretation to establish their claim for papal authority. But in the Greek the word Peter is *Petros,* a person, masculine, while the word "rock," *petra,* is feminine and refers not to a person but to the declaration of Christ's deity that Peter had just uttered—"Thou art the Christ, the Son of the living God."

Using Peter's name and making, as it were, a play upon words, Jesus said to Peter, "You are Petros, and upon this petra I will build my church." The truth that Peter had just confessed was the foundation upon which Christ would build His church. He meant that Peter had seen the basic, essential truth concerning His person, the essential truth upon which the church would be founded, and that nothing would be able to overthrow that truth, not even all the forces of evil that might be arrayed against it. Peter was the first among the disciples to see our Lord as the Christ of God. Christ commended him for that spiritual insight, and said that His church would be founded upon that fact. And that, of course, was a far different thing from founding the church on Peter.

Had Christ intended to say that the Church would be founded on Peter, it would have been ridiculous for Him to have shifted to the feminine form of the word in the middle of the statement, saying, if we may translate literally and somewhat whimsically, "And I say unto thee, that thou art Mr. Rock, and upon this, the Miss Rock, I will build my church." Clearly it was upon the truth that Peter had expressed, the deity of Christ, and not upon weak, vacillating Peter, that the church would be founded. The Greek "petros" is commonly used of a small, movable stone, a mere pebble, as it were. But "petra" means an immovable foundation, in this instance, the basic truth that Peter had just confessed, the deity of Christ. And in fact that is the point of conflict in the churches today between evangelicals on the one hand, and modernists or liberals on the other, whether the church is founded on a truly divine Christ as revealed in a fully trustworthy Bible, or whether it is essentially a social service and moral welfare organization which recognizes Christ as an example, an outstandingly great and good man, but denies or ignores His deity.

The Bible tells us plainly, not that the church is built upon Peter, but that it is "built upon the foundation of the apostles and prophets, Christ Jesus himself being the chief corner stone" (Eph. 2:20). And again, "For other foundation can no man lay than that which is laid, which is Jesus Christ" (I Cor. 3:11). Without that foundation the true Christian church could not exist.

If Matthew 16:18 had been intended to teach that the church is founded on Peter, it would have read something like this: "Thou art Peter, and upon you I will build my church"; or, "Thou art Peter, and upon you the rock I will build my church." But that is not what Christ said. He made two complete, distinct statements. He said, "Thou art Peter," and, "Upon this rock (change of gender, indicating change of subject) I will build my church."

The gates of hell were not to prevail against the church. But the gates of hell did prevail against Peter shortly afterward, as recorded in this same chapter, when he attempted to deny that Christ would be crucified, and almost immediately afterward, in the presence of the other disciples, received the stinging rebuke, "Get thee behind me, Satan; thou art a stumbling block unto me, for thou mindest not the things of God but the things of men" (vs. 23)—surely strong words to use against one who had just been appointed pope!

Later we read that Peter slept in Gethsemane, during Christ's agony. His rash act in cutting off the servant's ear drew Christ's rebuke. He boasted that he was ready to die for his Master, but shortly afterward shamefully denied with oaths and curses that he even knew Him. And even after Pentecost Peter still was subject to such serious error that his hypocrisy had to be rebuked by Paul, who says: "But when Cephas came to Antioch (at which time he was in full possession of his papal powers, according to Romanist doctrine), I resisted him to the face, because he stood condemned" (Gal. 2:11). And yet Romanists allege that their pope, as Peter's successor, is infallible in matters of faith and morals!

The Gospel written by Mark, who is described in early Christian literature as Peter's close companion and understudy, does not even record the remark about the "rock" in reporting Peter's confession at Caesarea Philippi (Mark 8:27-30). No, Christ did not build His church upon a weak, sinful man. Rather the essential deity of Christ, which was so forcefully set forth in Peter's confession, was the foundation stone, the starting point, on which the church would be built.

That no superior standing was conferred upon Peter is clear from the later disputes among the disciples concerning who should be greatest among them. Had such rank already been given, Christ would simply have referred to His grant of power to Peter. Instead we read:

"And they came to Capernaum: and when he was in the house he asked them, What were ye reasoning on the way? But they held their peace: for they had disputed one with another on the way, who was the greatest. And he sat down, and called the twelve; and he saith unto them, If any man would be first, he shall be last of all, and servant of all" (Mark 9:33-35).

And again:

"And there came near unto him James and John, the sons of Zebedee, saying unto him, Teacher, we would that thou shouldest do for us whatsoever we shall ask of thee. And he said unto them, What would ye that I should do for you? And they said unto him, Grant unto us that we may sit, one on thy right hand, and one on thy left hand, in thy glory. . . . And when the ten heard it, they began to be moved with indignation concerning James and John. And Jesus called them unto him, and saith unto them, Ye know that they who are accounted to rule over the Gentiles lord it over them; and their great ones exercise authority over them. But it is not so among you: but whosoever would become great among you, shall be your minister; and whosoever would be first among you, shall be servant of all" (Mark 10:34-44).

It is interesting to notice that some of the church fathers, Augustine and Jerome among them, gave the Protestant explanation of this verse, understanding the "rock" to mean not Peter but Christ. Others, of course, gave the papal interpretation. But this shows that there was no "unanimous consent of the fathers," as the Roman Church claims, on this subject.

Dr. Harris says concerning the reference to the "rock":

"Mark's Gospel is connected with Peter by all early Christian tradition and it does not even include this word of Jesus to Peter. Likewise in the Epistles of Peter there is no such claim. In I Peter 2:6-8 Christ is called a rock and a chief cornerstone. But Peter here claims nothing for himself. Indeed he is explicit in calling all believers living stones built up a spiritual house with Christ as the head of the corner.

"Christ is repeatedly called a Rock. The background for this is that around thirty-four times in the Old Testament God is called a Rock or the Rock of Israel. It was a designation of God. In the Messianic passages, Is. 8:14; 28:16; and Ps. 118:22, Christ is called a Rock or Stone upon which we should believe. These passages are quoted in the New Testament and for that reason Christ is called a Rock several times. It designates Him as divine. For that reason, every Jew, knowing the Old Testament, would refuse the designation to Peter or to anyone except insofar as we are children of Christ. He is the Rock. We are living stones built upon Him. Ephesians 2:20 says this plainly. We are built upon the foundation of the apostles and prophets, Jesus Christ himself being the chief cornerstone. Paul says of the Rock from which the Israelites drank that it typified Christ (I Cor. 10:4). In the New Testament there are twelve foundations and on them are the names of the twelve apostles— none of them are made pre-eminent" (*The Bible Presbyterian Reporter*, Jan. 1959.)

And Dr. Henry M. Woods says:

"If Christ had meant that Peter was to be the foundation, the natural form of statement would have been, 'Thou art Peter, and *on thee* I will build my church'; but He does not say this, because Peter was not to be the rock on which the church was built. Note also that in the expression 'on this rock,' our Lord purposely uses a different Greek word, *Petra*,

from that used for Peter, *Petros.* He did this to show that, not Peter, but
the great truth which had just been revealed to him, viz., that our Lord
was 'the Christ, the Son of the living God,' was to be the church's
foundation. Built on the Christ, the everlasting Saviour, the gates of hell
would never prevail against the Church. But built on the well-meaning
but sinful Peter, the gates of hell would surely prevail; for a little later
our Lord had to severely rebuke Peter, calling him 'Satan' " (*Our Priceless
Heritage*, p. 40).

3. THE "KEYS"

"And I will give thee the keys of the kingdom of heaven; and whatever
thou shalt bind on earth shall be bound in heaven, and whatever thou
shalt loose on earth shall be loosed in heaven" (Matt. 16:19, Confraternity
Version).

Admittedly this is a difficult verse to interpret, and numerous ex-
planations have been given. It is important to notice, however, that the
authority to bind and to loose was not given exclusively to Peter. In the
eighteenth chapter of Matthew the same power *is given to all of the
disciples.* There we read:

"At that hour the disciples came to Jesus. . . . Amen I say to you, whatever you bind on earth shall be bound also in heaven; and whatever you
loose on earth shall be loosed also in heaven" (Vss. 1, 18, Confraternity
Version).

Consequently Matthew 16:19 does not prove any superiority on Peter's
part. Even the scribes and Pharisees had this same power, for Jesus said
to them: "But woe upon you, scribes and Pharisees, hypocrites! because
ye shut the kingdom of heaven against men: for ye enter not in yourselves, neither suffer them that are entering in to enter" (Matt. 23:13).
And on another occasion He said: "The scribes and Pharisees sit on
Moses' seat: all things therefore whatsoever they bid you, these do and
observe: but do not ye after their works; for they say, and do not. Yea,
they bind heavy burdens and grievous to be born, and lay them on men's
shoulders; but they themselves will not move them with their finger"
(Matt. 23:2-4).

Here the expression clearly means that the scribes and Pharisees, in
that the Word of God was in their hands, thereby had the power, in
declaring that Word to the people, to open the kingdom of heaven to
them; and in withholding that Word they shut the kingdom of heaven
against people. That was Moses' function in giving the law. It was, there-

fore, a *declaratory* power, the authority to *announce the terms* on which God would grant salvation, not an absolute power to admit or to exclude from the kingdom of heaven. Only God can do that; and He never delegates that authority to men.

And in Luke 11:52 Jesus says: "Woe unto you lawyers! for ye took away the key of knowledge: ye entered not in yourselves, and them that were entering in ye hindered." Here, the key of the knowledge of the way of salvation, by which entrance into the kingdom of heaven is obtained, was in the hands of the Pharisees in that they had the law of Moses in their possession, and were therefore the custodians of the Word of God. In that sense they possessed the key to the kingdom. They took away that key in that they failed to proclaim the Word of God to the people. They were not entering into the kingdom of heaven themselves, and they were hindering those who wanted to enter.

Furthermore, we notice that in the words spoken to Peter, it was "things," not "persons," that were to be bound or loosed—"whatsoever," not "whomsoever"—things such as the ceremonial laws and customs of the Old Testament dispensation were to be done away with, and new rituals and practices of the Gospel age were to be established.

Thus the "keys" symbolize the authority to open, in this instance, to open the kingdom of heaven to men through the proclamation of the Gospel. What the disciples were commissioned to do, given the privilege of doing, was the opposite of that which the scribes and Pharisees were doing, that is, they were to facilitate the entrance of the people into the kingdom of heaven.

There was, of course, no physical seat which had been used by Moses and which now was being used by the scribes and Pharisees. But the scribes and Pharisees, who were in possession of the law of Moses, were giving precepts which in themselves were authoritative and good and which therefore were to be obeyed; but since they did not live up to those precepts the people were not to follow their example.

It is clear that the keys were symbolical of authority, which here is specified as the power of binding and loosing; and it is also clear that the consequences of what the disciples did in this regard would go far beyond earth and would have their permanent results in heaven. They were in a real sense building for eternity. In referring to the keys of the kingdom Jesus was continuing the figure in which He had been comparing the kingdom of heaven to a house which He was about to build. It would be built upon a solid rock (Matt. 7:24). Entrance into that house was through the door of faith. This door was to be opened, first to the Jews, and then to the Gentiles. And Peter, who had been the first of the disciples to comprehend the person of Christ in His true deity and to confess that deity before the other disciples, was commissioned to be the first to open that door. In this sense the keys were first given to him. To him was given the distinction and high honor among the apostles of being the first to open the door of faith to the Jewish world, which he did on the day of Pentecost when through his sermon some three thousand Jews were converted (Acts 2:14-42), and a short time later the distinction and high honor of opening the door of faith to the Gentile world, which he did in the house of Cornelius (Acts 10:1-48). And while the keys were in this respect first given to Peter, they were soon afterward also given to the other disciples as they too proclaimed the Gospel both to Jews and Gentiles. But while Peter was given the distinction and honor of being the first to open the kingdom to the Jews, and then to the Gentiles, he did not claim nor assume any other authority, and was in all other respects on precisely the same footing as were the other apostles.

Possession of the keys, therefore, did not mean that Peter had sovereignly within his own person the authority to determine who should be admitted to heaven and who should be excluded, as the Roman Church now attempts to confer that authority on the pope and priests. Ultimate authority is in the hands of Christ alone—it is He "that openeth and none shall shut, and that shutteth and none openeth" (Rev. 3:7). But it did mean that Peter, and later the other apostles, being in possession of the Gospel message, truly did open the door and present the opportunity to enter in as they proclaimed the message before the people. This same privilege of opening the door or of closing the door of salvation to others is given to every Christian, for the command that Christ gave His church was to go and make disciples of all the nations. Thus "the power of the keys" is a *declarative* power only.

It can almost be said that the Roman Catholics build their church upon these two verses which speak of the "rock" and the "keys." They say that the power given to Peter was absolute and that it was transferred by him to his successors, although they have to admit that there is not one verse in Scripture which teaches such a transfer. Under this "power of the keys" the Roman Church claims that "In heaven God ratifies the decisions which Peter makes on earth" (Footnote, Confraternity Version, p. 37).

But it is interesting to see how Peter himself understood this grant of power. In his exercise of the power of the keys he says: "And it shall be, that whosoever shall call on the name of the Lord shall be saved" (Acts 2:21). And at the house of the Roman centurion Cornelius he again gave a universal Gospel invitation: "To him (Christ) bear all the prophets witness, that through his name every one that believeth on him shall receive remission of sins" (Acts 10:43). So, in the preaching of Peter, as elsewhere in the New Testament, salvation is set forth as based on faith in Christ, and nowhere is obedience to Peter, or to the pope, or to any other man even hinted at.

Rome terribly abuses this "power of the keys" to insure obedience to her commands on the part of her church members and to instill in them a sense of fear and of constant dependence on the church for their salvation. This sense of fear and dependence, with constant references to "Mother Church," goes far to explain the power that the Roman Church has over her members, even cowing them to the extent that they are afraid to read or to listen to anything contrary to what their church teaches. And since that teaching is drilled into them from childhood the truly formidable power that the Roman Church exercises over the laity can be easily understood.

4. PAPAL AUTHORITY NOT CLAIMED BY PETER

The Roman Church claims that Peter was the first bishop or pope in Rome and that the later popes are his successors. But the best proof of a man's position and authority is his own testimony. Does Peter claim to be a pope, or to have primacy over the other apostles? Fortunately, he wrote two epistles or letters which are found in the New Testament. There he gives his position and certain instructions as to how others in the same position are to perform their duties. We read:

> "Peter, an apostle of Jesus Christ. . . . The elders therefore among you I exhort, who am a fellow-elder, and a witness of the sufferings of Christ, who am also a partaker of the glory that shall be revealed: Tend the flock of God which is among you, exercising the oversight, not of constraint, but willingly, according to the will of God; nor yet for filthy lucre, but of a ready mind; neither as lording it over the charge allotted to you, but making yourselves ensamples to the flock" (I Peter 1:1; 5:1-3).

Here Peter refers to himself as an apostle of Jesus Christ, an elder (the word in the Greek is *presbuteros*), which of course has nothing to do with a sacrificing priesthood. He does not claim the highest place in the church as some would expect him to do or as some would claim for him. He assumes no ecclesiastical superiority, but with profound humility puts himself on a level with those whom he exhorts. He makes it clear that the church must be democratic, not authoritarian. He forbids the leaders to lord it over the people, to work for money or to take money unjustly. He says that they are to serve the people willingly, even eagerly, and that by their general lives they are to make themselves examples for the people.

But the fact is that the Church of Rome acts directly contrary to these instructions. Can anyone imagine the proud popes of later times adopting such a role of humility? It was several centuries later, when the church had lost much of its original simplicity and spiritual power and had been submerged in a flood of worldliness, that the autocratic authority of the popes began to appear. After the fourth century, when the Roman empire had fallen, the bishops of Rome stepped into Caesar's shoes, took his pagan title of Pontifex Maximus, the supreme high priest of the pagan Roman religion, sat down on Caesar's throne, and wrapped themselves in Caesar's gaudy trappings. And that role they have continued ever since.

In regard to the title Pontifex, The Standard International Encyclopedia says this was: "The title given by the ancient Romans to members of one of the two celebrated religious colleges. The chief of the order was called Pontifex Maximus. The pontiffs had general control of the official religion, and their head was the highest religious authority in the state. . . . Following Julius Caesar the emperor was the Pontifex Maximus. In the time of Theodosius [emperor, died 395 A.D.] the title became equivalent to Pope, now one of the titles of the head of the Roman Catholic Church."

Peter refused to accept homage from men—as when Cornelius the Roman centurion fell down at his feet and would have worshipped him, Peter protested quickly and said, "Stand up; I myself also am a man" (Acts 10:25, 26). Yet the popes not only accept, but demand, such homage, even to the extent that men, including even the highest cardinals, prostrate themselves on the floor before a newly elected pope or when making ordination vows before him and kiss his foot. The popes accept the blasphemous title of "Holy Father" as theirs as a matter of right. And how the cardinals, bishops, and priests do like to set themselves apart from the congregations and to lord it over the people!

Surely if Peter had been a pope, "the supreme head of the church," he would have declared that fact in his general epistles, for that was the place of all others to have asserted his authority. The popes have never been slow to make such claims for themselves, or to extend their authority as far as possible. But instead Peter refers to himself only as an apostle (of which there were eleven others), and as an elder or presbyter, that is, simply as a minister of Christ.

5. PAUL'S ATTITUDE TOWARD PETER

It is very interesting to notice Paul's attitude toward Peter. Paul was called to be an apostle at a later time, after the church had been launched. Yet Peter had nothing to do with that choice, as he surely

would have had if he had been pope. Instead God called and ordained
Paul without consulting Peter, as He has called and ordained many
thousands of ministers and evangelists since then without reference to
the popes of Rome. Paul was easily the greatest of the apostles, with a
deeper insight into the way of salvation and a larger revealed knowledge
concerning the mysteries of life and death. He wrote much more of the
New Testament than did Peter. His thirteen epistles contain 2,023 verses,
while Peter's two epistles contain only 166 verses. And if we ascribe
the Epistle to the Hebrews to Paul, as does the Roman Catholic Church
(Confraternity Version, p. 397), he wrote an even larger proportion.
Peter's epistles do not stand first among the epistles, but after those of
Paul; and in fact his second epistle was one of the last to be accepted by
the church. Paul worked more recorded miracles than did Peter, and he
seems to have established more churches than did Peter. Apart from
the church at Rome, which we believe was established by laymen, Paul
established more prominent and more permanent churches than did
Peter. And, so far as the New Testament record goes, Paul's influence in
the church at Rome was much greater than was that of Peter. Paul mentions Peter more than once, but nowhere does he defer to Peter's authority, or acknowledge him as pope.

Indeed, quite the contrary is the case. Paul had founded the church at
Corinth, but when some there rebelled against his authority, even to the
extent of favoring Peter, he does not give even an inch on his own
authority. Instead he vigorously defends his authority, declaring, "Am I
not an apostle? have I not seen Jesus our Lord?" (I Cor. 9:1), and again,
"For in nothing was I behind the very chiefest apostles" (II Cor. 12:11)—
or, as translated in the Confraternity Version, "In no way have I fallen
short of the most eminent apostles." He declares that he has been
"intrusted with the gospel of the uncircumcision, even as Peter with the
gospel of the circumcision" (Gal. 2:7). He therefore put himself on a
par with all the other apostles. Certainly those ideas were incompatible
with any idea of a pope in Paul's day.

But beyond all that, on one occasion Paul publicly rebuked Peter.
When Peter at Antioch sided with the "false brethren" (vs. 4) in their
Jewish legalism and "drew back and separated himself" from the Gentiles
and was even the cause of Barnabas being misled, Paul administered a
severe rebuke. We read:

> "But when Cephas came to Antioch, I resisted him to the face, because
> he stood condemned. For before that certain came from James, he ate
> with the Gentiles; but when they came, he drew back and separated him-
> self, fearing them that were of the circumcision. And the rest of the

Jews dissembled likewise with him; insomuch that even Barnabas was carried away with their dissimulation. But when I saw that they walked not uprightly according to the truth of the gospel, I said unto Cephas before them all, If thou, being a Jew, livest as do the Gentiles, and not as do the Jews, how compellest thou the Gentiles to live as do the Jews? (Gal. 2:11-14).

He then impressed upon Peter some good, sound, evangelical theology, declaring that,

". . . a man is not justified by the works of the law but through faith in Jesus Christ . . . because by the works of the law shall no flesh be justified" (vs. 16).

In other words, Paul gave the "Holy Father" a "dressing down" before them all, accusing him of not walking uprightly in the truth of the Gospel. Surely that was no way to talk to a pope! Imagine anyone today, even a cardinal, taking it upon himself to rebuke and instruct a real pope with such language! Just who was Paul that he should rebuke the Vicar of Christ for unchristian conduct? If Peter was the chief it was Paul's duty and the duty of the other apostles to recognize him as such and to teach only what he approved. Obviously Paul did not regard Peter as infallible in faith and morals, or recognize any supremacy on his part.

6. ATTITUDE OF THE OTHER APOSTLES TOWARD PETER

The other apostles as well as Paul seem totally unaware of any appointment that made Peter the head of the church. Nowhere do they acknowledge his authority. And nowhere does he attempt to exercise authority over them. The only instance in which another man was chosen to succeed an apostle is recorded in Acts 1:15-26, and there the choice was made not by Peter but by popular choice on the part of the brethren who numbered about one hundred and twenty, and by the casting of lots.

On another occasion Peter, together with John, was sent by the other apostles to preach the Gospel in Samaria (Acts 8:14). Imagine the pope today being sent by the cardinals or bishops on any such mission. It is well known that today the popes seldom if ever preach. They do issue statements, and they address select audiences which come to them. But they do not go out and preach the Gospel as did Peter and the other apostles.

The important church council in Jerusalem (Acts 15) reveals quite clearly how the unity of the church was expressed in apostolic days. Differences had arisen when certain men from Judaea came down to Antioch, in Syria, where Paul and Barnabas were working and insisted that certain parts of the Jewish ritual must be observed. Had the present Roman Catholic theory of the papacy been followed, there would have been no need at all for a council. The church in Antioch would have written a letter to Peter, the bishop of Rome, and he would have sent them an encyclical or bull settling the matter. And of all the churches the one at Antioch was the last that should have appealed to Jerusalem. For according to Roman Catholic legend Peter was bishop in Antioch for seven years before transferring his see to Rome! But the appeal was made, not to Peter, but to a church council in Jerusalem. At that council not Peter but James presided and announced the decision with the words, "Wherefore my judgment is. . . ." (vs. 19). And his judgment was accepted by the apostles and presbyters. Peter was present, but only after there had been "much questioning" (vs. 7) did he even so much as express an opinion. He did not attempt to make any infallible pronouncements although the subject under discussion was a vital matter of faith. In any event it is clear that the unity of the early church was maintained not by the voice of Peter but by the decision of the ecumenical council which was presided over by James, the leader of the Jerusalem church. Furthermore, after that council *Peter is never again mentioned in the book of Acts.*

It is an old human failing for people to want to exercise authority over their fellow men. We are told that the disciples disputed among themselves which was to be accounted the greatest. Jesus rebuked them with the words: "If any man would be first, he shall be last of all, and servant of all" (Mark 9:35). On another occasion the mother of James and John came to Jesus with the request that her two sons should have the chief places in the kingdom. But He called the disciples to Him and said, "Ye know that the rulers of the Gentiles lord it over them, and their great ones exercise authority over them. Not so shall it be among you: but whosoever would become great among you shall be your minister; and whosoever would be first among you shall be your servant: even as the Son of man came not to be ministered unto, but to minister, and to give his life a ransom for many" (Matt. 20:25-28). And even on the night in which Christ was delivered up to die they contended among themselves "which of them was accounted to be greatest" (Luke 22:24). In each instance Jesus taught them that they were not to seek to exercise lordship, but rather to excel in service. But in no instance did He settle the dispute by reminding them that Peter was the Prince of the Apostles. In fact they could not have argued that question at all if

Peter had already been given the place of pre-eminence, as the Roman Church holds.

Christ alone is the head of the church. "Other foundation can no man lay than that which is laid, which is Jesus Christ" (I Cor. 3:11). The church is "built upon the foundation of the apostles and prophets, Christ Jesus himself being the chief corner stone" (Eph. 2:20). Paul says that God "gave him (Christ) to be head over all things to the church, which is his body" (Eph. 1:22,23). Besides Him there can be no earthly foundation or head of the church. Only a monstrosity can have two heads for one body.

7. WAS PETER EVER IN ROME?

According to Roman Catholic tradition Peter was the first bishop of Rome, his pontificate lasted twenty-five years, from 42 to 67 A. D., and he was martyred in Rome in 67 A. D. The Douay and Confraternity versions say that he was in Rome before the Jerusalem council of Acts 15, and that he returned to Jerusalem for that council, after which he went to Antioch, and then returned to Rome. In the Confraternity Version we read:

"After the resurrection the primacy was conferred upon him and immediately after the ascension he began to exercise it. After preaching in Jerusalem and Palestine he went to Rome, probably after his liberation from prison. Some years later he was in Jerusalem for the first church council, and shortly afterward at Antioch. In the year 67 he was martyred in Rome" (Introduction to the First Epistle of St. Peter).

The remarkable thing, however, about Peter's alleged bishopric in Rome, is that the New Testament has not one word to say about it. The word Rome occurs only nine times in the Bible, and never is Peter mentioned in connection with it. There is no allusion to Rome in either of his epistles. Paul's journey to that city is recorded in great detail (Acts 27 and 28). There is in fact no New Testament evidence, nor any historical proof of any kind, that Peter ever was in Rome. All rests on legend. The first twelve chapters of the book of Acts tell of Peter's ministry and travels in Palestine and Syria. Surely if he had gone to Rome, the capital of the empire, that would have been mentioned. We may well ask, If Peter was superior to Paul, why does he receive so little attention after Paul comes on the scene? Not much is known about his later life, except that he traveled extensively, and that on at least some of his missionary journeys he was accompanied by his wife—for

Paul says, "Have we no right to lead about a wife that is a believer, even as the rest of the apostles, and the brethren of the Lord, and Cephas" (I Cor. 9:5). (The Confraternity Version here reads "sister" instead of "wife"; but the Greek word is *gune*, wife, not *adelphe*, sister).

We know nothing at all about the origins of Christianity in Rome. This is acknowledged even by some Roman Catholic historians. It was already a flourishing church when Paul wrote his letter to the Romans in 58 A. D. Quite possibly it had been founded by some of those who were present in Jerusalem on the day of Pentecost and heard Peter's great sermon when some 3000 were converted, for Luke says that in that audience were "sojourners from Rome, both Jews and proselytes" (Acts 2:10). In any event there is nothing but unfounded tradition to support the claim that Peter founded the church in Rome and that he was its bishop for 25 years. The fact is that the apostles did not settle in one place as did the diocesan bishops of much later date, so that it is quite incorrect to speak of Rome as the "See of Peter," or to speak of the popes occupying "the chair" of St. Peter.

Legend was early busy with the life of Peter. The one which tells of his twenty-five years' episcopate in Rome has its roots in the apocryphal stories originating with a heretical group, the Ebionites, who rejected much of the supernatural content of the New Testament, and the account is discredited both by its origin and by its internal inconsistencies. The first reference that might be given any credence at all is found in the writings of Eusebius, and that reference is doubted even by some Roman Catholic writers. Eusebius wrote in Greek about the year 310, and his work was translated by Jerome. A seventeenth century historian, William Cave (1637-1713), chaplain to King Charles II, of England, in his most important work, *The Lives of the Apostles, says:*

> "It cannot be denied that in St. Jerome's translation it is expressly said that he (Peter) continued twenty-five years as bishop in that city: but then it is as evident that this was his own addition, who probably set things down as the report went in his time, *no such thing being found in the Greek copy of Eusebius.*"

Exhaustive research by archaeologists has been made down through the centuries to find some inscription in the Catacombs and other ruins of ancient places in Rome that would indicate that Peter at least visited Rome. But the only things found which gave any promise at all were some bones of uncertain origin. L. H. Lehmann, who was educated for the priesthood at the University for the Propagation of the Faith, in Rome, tells us of a lecture by a noted Roman archaeologist, Professor

Marucchi, given before his class, in which he said that no shred of evidence of Peter's having been in the Eternal City had ever been unearthed, and of another archaeologist, Di Rossi, who declared that for forty years his greatest ambition had been to unearth in Rome some inscription which would verify the papal claim that the apostle Peter was actually in Rome, but that he was forced to admit that he had given up hope of success in his search. He had the promise of handsome rewards by the church if he succeeded. What he had dug up verified what the New Testament says about the formation of the Christian church in Rome, but remained absolutely silent regarding the claims of the bishops of Rome to be the successors of the apostle Peter (cf., *The Soul of a Priest*, p. 10).

And, after all, suppose Peter's bones should be found and identified beyond question, what would that prove? The important thing is, Does the Church of Rome teach the same Gospel that Peter taught? Succession to Peter should be claimed, not by those who say they have discovered his bones, but by those who teach the Gospel that he taught—the evangelical message of salvation by grace through faith.

Furthermore, if mere residence conferred superiority, then Antioch would outrank Rome; for the same tradition which asserts that Peter resided in Rome asserts that he *first* resided in Antioch, a city in Asia Minor. It is well known that during the time of the apostles and for generations later the Eastern cities and the Eastern church had the greatest influence, and that the Roman church was comparatively insignificant. The first councils were held in Eastern cities and were composed almost altogether of Eastern bishops. Four of the patriarchates were Eastern—Jerusalem, Antioch, Constantinople, and Alexandria. Rome did not gain the ascendancy until centuries later, after the breakup of the Roman empire. If any church had a special right to be called the Mistress of all the churches, it surely was the church in Jerusalem, where our Lord lived and taught, where He was crucified, where Christianity was first preached by Peter and the other apostles, where Peter's great Pentecostal sermon was delivered, and from which went forth to Antioch and Rome and to all the world the glad tidings of salvation. Long before the Reformation Rome's claim to be the only true church was rejected by the eastern churches, which were the most ancient and in the early days much the most influential churches in the world.

Another interesting and very important if not decisive line of evidence in this regard is the fact that Paul was pre-eminently the apostle to the Gentiles, while Peter was pre-eminently the apostle to the Jews, this division of labor having been by divine appointment. In Galatians 2:7,8 Paul says that he "had been intrusted with the gospel of the uncircumcision, even as Peter with the gospel of the circumcision (for he that wrought for Peter unto the apostleship of the circumcision wrought for me also unto the Gentiles)." Thus Paul's work was primarily among the Gentiles, while Peter's was primarily among the Jews. Peter ministered to the Jews who were in exile in Asia Minor, "to the elect who are sojourners of the Dispersion in Pontus, Galatia, Cappadocia, Asia, and Bithynia" (I Peter 1:1), and in his journeys he went as far east as Babylon, from which city his first epistle (and probably his second) was addressed to the Jewish Christians in Asia Minor—"She that is in Babylon, elect together with you, saluteth you" (I Peter 5:13). As most of Paul's letters were addressed to churches he had evangelized, so Peter wrote to the Jewish brethren that he had evangelized, who were scattered through those provinces. While there is no Scriptural evidence at all that Peter went west to Rome, here is a plain statement of Scripture that he did go east to Babylon. Why cannot the Roman Church take Peter's word to that effect?

But his testimony, of course, must be gotten around by those who are so anxious to place him in Rome, and they take a curious way to do it. The Confraternity edition has an introductory note to I Peter which reads: "The place of composition is given as 'Babylon' . . . a cryptic designation of the city of Rome."

But there is no good reason for saying that "Babylon" means "Rome." The reason alleged by the Church of Rome for understanding Babylon to mean Rome is that in the book of Revelation Rome is called by that name (Rev. 17:5; 18:2). But there is a great difference between an apocalyptic book such as the book of Revelation, which for the most part is written in figurative and symbolic language, and an epistle such as this which is written in a straightforward, matter of fact style.

In regard to Peter's assignment to work among the Jews, it is known that there were many Jews in Babylon in New Testament times. Many had not returned to Palestine after the Exile. Many others, such as those in Asia Minor and Egypt, had been driven out or had left Palestine for various reasons. Josephus says that some "gave Hycannus, the high priest, a habitation at Babylon, where there were *Jews in great numbers*" (*Antiquities,* Book IV, Ch. II, 2). Peter's assigned ministry to the Jews took him to those places where the Jews were in the greatest numbers, even to Babylon.

8. PAUL'S EPISTLE TO THE ROMANS

The strongest reason of all for believing that Peter never was in Rome is found in Paul's epistle to the Romans. According to Roman Church tradition, Peter reigned as pope in Rome for 25 years, from 42 to 67 A. D. It is generally agreed that Paul's letter to the Christians in Rome was written in the year 58 A. D., at the very height of Peter's alleged episcopacy there. He did not address his letter to Peter, as he should have done if Peter was in Rome and the head of all the churches, but to the saints in the church in Rome. How strange for a missionary to write to a church and not mention the pastor! That would be an inexcusable affront. What would we think of a minister today who would dare to write to a congregation in a distant city and without mentioning their pastor tell them that he was anxious to go there that he might have some fruit among them even as he has had in his own community (1:13), that he was anxious to instruct and strengthen them, and that he was anxious to preach the Gospel there where it had not been preached before? How would their pastor feel if he knew that such greetings had been sent to 27 of his most prominent members who were mentioned by name in the epistle (Ch. 16)? Would he stand for such ministerial ethics? And if he were the most prominent minister in the land, as allegedly was the bishop of Rome, such an affront would be all the more inexcusable. This point alone ought to open the eyes of the most obdurate person blinded by the traditions of the Roman Church.

If Peter had been working in the church in Rome for some 16 years, why did Paul write to the people of the church in these words: "For I long to see you, that I may impart unto you some spiritual gift, to the end ye may be established"? (1:11). Was not that a gratuitous insult to Peter? Was it not a most presumptuous thing for Paul to go over the head of the pope? And if Peter was there and had been there for 16 years, why was it necessary for Paul to go at all, especially since in his letter he says that he does not build on another's foundation: "making it my aim so to preach the gospel, not where Christ was already named, that I might not build upon another man's foundation"? (15:20). This indicates clearly that Peter was not then in Rome, and that he had not been there, that in fact Paul was writing this letter because no apostle had yet been in Rome to clarify the Gospel to them and to establish them in the faith. At the conclusion of this letter Paul sends greetings to the 27 people mentioned above, including some women; also to several groups. But he does not mention Peter in any capacity.

And again, had Peter been in Rome prior to or at the time when Paul arrived there as a prisoner in 61 A. D., Paul could not have failed to have mentioned him, for in the epistles written from there during his imprisonment—Ephesians, Philippians, Colossians, and Philemon—he gives quite a complete list of his fellow-workers in Rome, and Peter's name is not among them. He spent two whole years there as a prisoner, and received all who came to visit him (Acts 28:30). Nor does he mention Peter in his second epistle to Timothy, which was written from Rome during his second imprisonment, in 67 A. D., the year that Peter is alleged to have suffered martyrdom in Rome, and shortly before his own death (II Tim. 4:6-8). He says that all his friends have forsaken him, and that only Luke is with him (4:10,11). Where was Peter? If Peter was in Rome when Paul was there as a prisoner, he surely lacked Christian courtesty since he never called to offer aid. Surely he must have been the first absentee bishop on a big scale!

All of this makes it quite certain that Peter never was in Rome at all. Not one of the early church fathers gives any support to the belief that Peter was a bishop in Rome until Jerome in the fifth century. Du Pin, a Roman Catholic historian, acknowledges that "the primacy of Peter is not recorded by the early Christian writers, Justin Martyr (139), Irenaeus (178), Clement of Alexandria (190), or others of the most ancient fathers." The Roman Church thus builds her papal system, not on New Testament teaching, nor upon the facts of history, but only on unfounded traditions.

The chronological table for Peter's work, so far as we can work it out, seems to be roughly as follows:

Most Bible students agree that Paul's conversion occurred in the year 37 A.D. After that he went to Arabia (Gal. 1:17), and after three years went up to Jerusalem where he remained with Peter for 15 days (Gal. 1:18). That brings us to the year 40 A.D. Fourteen years later he again went to Jerusalem (Gal. 2:1), where he attended the Jerusalem council described in Acts 15, in which Peter also participated (vs. 6). This conference dealt primarily with the problems which arose in connection with the presentation of the Gospel in Jewish and Gentile communities. Paul and Barnabas presented their case, and were authorized by the council to continue their ministry to the Gentiles (Acts 15:22-29); and this quite clearly was the occasion on which Paul was assigned to work primarily among the Gentiles while Peter was assigned to work primarily among the Jews (Gal. 2:7-8), since this same Jerusalem council is spoken of in the immediate context (Gal. 2:1-10). So this brings us to the year 54 A.D., and Peter still is in Syria, 12 years after the time that the Roman tradition says that he began his reign in Rome.

Sometime after the Jerusalem council Peter also came to Antioch, on which occasion it was necessary for Paul to reprimand him because of his conformity to Judaistic rituals (Gal. 2:11-21). And the same Roman tradition which says that Peter reigned in Rome also says that he governed the church in Antioch for 7 years before going to Rome. Hence we reach the year 61 A.D., with Peter still in Syria!

Indeed, how could Peter have gone to Rome, which was the very center of the Gentile world? Would he defy the decision reached by all the apostles and brethren from the various churches who met in the famous first Christian council in Jerusalem? Clearly the Scriptural evidence is that Peter accepted that decision, and that his work was primarily among the Jews of the dispersion, first in Asia Minor, and later as far east as Babylon—that in fact his work took him in the opposite direction from that which Roman tradition assigns to him!

And even if Peter had been the first bishop of Rome, that would not mean that the bishops who followed him would have had any of the special powers that he had. The apostles had the power to work miracles and to write inspired Scripture. Even if Peter had been granted special powers above those of the other apostles, there is nothing in Scripture to indicate that those powers could have been transmitted to succeeding popes. In his second epistle he makes a reference to his approaching death (1:14), and surely that would have been the appropriate place to have said who his successor should be and what the method of choosing future popes should be. But he gives no indication that he even thought of such things. Peter as an apostle had qualifications and gifts which the popes do not have and dare not claim. The fact of the matter is that with the passing of the apostles their place as guides to the church was taken not by an infallible pope but by *an inspired and infallible Scripture* which had been developed by that time, which we call the New Testament, through which God would speak to the church from that time until the end of the age.

We may be certain that if the humble, spirit-minded Peter were to come back to earth he would not acknowledge as his successor the proud pontiff who wears the elaborate, triple-decked, gold bejeweled crown, who wears such fabulously expensive clothing, who is carried on the shoulders of the people, who stands before the high altar of worship, who is surrounded by a Swiss military guard, and who receives such servile obedience from the people that he is in effect, if not in reality, worshipped by them. The dedicated Christian minister who serves his people faithfully and humbly, and not the pope, is the true successor of Peter.

9. CONCLUSION

Let it be understood that we do not seek to minimize or downgrade Peter, but only to expose the preposterous claims that the Roman Church makes for its popes and hierarchy. Peter was a prince of God, but he was not the Prince of the Apostles. He, together with the other apostles, Mary, and the early Christians, turned from the religion in which they were born, Judaism, and became simply Christians, followers of Christ. Not one of them was a Roman Catholic. Roman Catholicism did not develop until centuries later.

The doctrine of the primacy of Peter is just one more of the many errors that the Church of Rome has added to the Christian religion. With the exposure of that fallacy the foundation of the Roman Church is swept away. The whole papal system stands or falls depending on whether or not Peter was a pope in Rome, and neither the New Testament nor reliable historical records give any reason to believe that he ever held that position or that he ever was in Rome.

VI. THE PAPACY

1. The Rise of the Papacy. 2. The Claims of the Papacy. 3. Worldly Character of the Papacy.

1. THE RISE OF THE PAPACY

Much of what needs to be said in regard to the papacy has already been covered in the discussion dealing with the church, the priesthood, and Peter. But there remain some further points that should be clarified.

The word "pope," by which the head of the Roman Church is known, and the word "papacy," by which is meant the system of ecclesiastical government in which the pope is recognized as the supreme head, are not found in the Bible. The word "pope" comes from the Latin *papa,* meaning "father." But Jesus forbade his followers to call any man "father" in a spiritual sense: "And call no man your father on the earth: for one is your Father, even he who is in heaven" (Matt. 23:9). For centuries this term was applied to all priests, and even to the present day it is so used in the Eastern Church.

In Italy the term "pope" came to be applied to all bishops as a title of honor, and then to the bishop of Rome exclusively as the universal bishop. It was first given to Gregory I by the wicked emperor Phocas, in the year 604. This he did to spite the bishop of Constantinople, who had justly excommunicated him for having caused the assassination of his (Phocas') predecessor, emperor Mauritius. Gregory, however, refused the title, but his second successor, Boniface III (607) assumed the title, and it has been the designation of the bishops of Rome ever since.

Likewise, the title "pontiff" (as also the term "pontificate," meaning to speak in a pompous manner), which literally means "bridge builder" (*pons,* bridge, and *facio,* make), comes not from the Bible but from pagan Rome, where the emperor, as the high priest of the heathen religion, and in that sense professing to be the bridge or connecting link between this life and the next, was called "Pontifex Maximus." The title was therefore lifted from paganism and applied to the head of the Roman Catholic Church. As the high priest of the Old Testament was the mediator between God and men, so the pope also claims to be the mediator between God and men, with power over the souls in purgatory

125

so that he can release them from further suffering and admit them to heaven, or prolong their suffering indefinitely.

But Christ alone is the mediator between God and men: "For there is one God, one mediator also between God and men, himself man, Christ Jesus" (I Tim. 2:5). And He alone is the true Head of the church. It was He who founded the church and redeemed it with His own blood. He promised to be with His church always, even unto the end of the world. He alone has the perfect attributes needed to fill that high office, for "in him dwelleth all the fulness of the Godhead bodily" (Col. 2:9). "He put all things in subjection under his feet, and gave him to be head over all things to the church, which is his body" (Eph. 1:22-23). "And he is the head of the body, the church" (Col. 1:18). For the pope or any other man to claim to be the head of the church and the mediator between God and men is arrogant and sinful.

The papal system has been in process of development over a long period of time. Romanists claim an unbroken line of succession from the alleged first pope, Peter, to the present pope, who is said to be the 262nd member in that line. But the list is in many instances quite doubtful. The list has been revised several times, with a considerable number who formerly were listed as popes now listed as anti-popes. It simply is not true that they can name with certainty all the bishops of Rome from Peter to the present one. A glance at the notices of each of the early popes in the *Catholic Encyclopedia* will show that they really know little or nothing about the first ten popes. And of the next ten only one is a clearly defined figure in history. The fact of the matter is that the historical record is so incomplete that the existence of an unbroken succession from the apostles to the present can neither be proved nor disproved.

For a period of six centuries after the time of Christ none of the regional churches attempted to exercise authority over any of the other regional churches. The early ecumenical councils were composed of delegates from the various churches who met as equals. There is not a scholar anywhere who pretends to show any decree, canon, or resolution by any of the ecumenical councils which attempts to give pre-eminence to any one church. *The first six hundred years of the Christian era know nothing of any spiritual supremacy on the part of the bishops of Rome.* The papacy really began in the year 590, with Gregory I, as Gregory the Great, who consolidated the power of the bishopric in Rome and started that church on a new course. We quote two contemporary church historians, one a Protestant and the other a Roman Catholic, concerning the place of Gregory in this development. Says Professor A. M. Renwick, of the Free Church College, Edinburgh, Scotland:

"His brilliant rule set a standard for those who came after him and he is really the first 'pope' who can, with perfect accuracy, be given the title. Along with Leo I (440-461), Gregory VII (1073-1085), and Innocent III (1198-1216), he stands out as one of the chief architects of the papal system" (*The Story of the Church*, p. 64).

And the Roman Catholic, Philip Hughes, says that Gregory I,

". . . is generally regarded as the greatest of all his line. . . . It was to him that Rome turned at every crisis where the Lombards [the invaders from the north] were concerned. He begged his people off and he bought them off. He ransomed the captives and organized the great relief services for widows and orphans. Finally, in 598, he secured a thirty years' truce. It was St. Gregory who, in these years, was the real ruler of Rome and in a very real sense he is the founder of the papal monarchy" (*A Popular History of the Catholic Church*, p. 75, 1947. Used by permission of The Macmillan Company).

2. THE CLAIMS OF THE PAPACY

When the triple crown is placed on the head of a new pope at his "coronation" ceremony the ritual prescribes the following declaration by the officiating cardinal:

"Receive the tiara adorned with three crowns, and know that thou art the Father of Princes and Kings, Ruler of the World, the Vicar of our Saviour Jesus Christ. . . ." (*National Catholic Almanac*).

The New York Catechism says:

"The pope takes the place of Jesus Christ on earth. . . . By divine right the pope has supreme and full power in faith and morals over each and every pastor and his flock. He is the true Vicar of Christ, the head of the entire church, the father and teacher of all Christians. He is the infallible ruler, the founder of dogmas, the author of and the judge of councils; the universal ruler of truth, the arbiter of the world, the supreme judge of heaven and earth, the judge of all, being judged by no one, God himself on earth."

And pope Leo XIII, in his encyclical, *The Reunion of Christendom* (1885), declared that the pope holds "upon this earth the place of God Almighty."

Thus the Roman Church holds that the pope, as the vicar of Christ on earth, is *the ruler of the world*, supreme not only over the Roman Church itself but over all kings, presidents, and civil rulers, indeed over all peoples and nations. The fact is that on numerous occasions the popes have exercised that authority in countries where the Roman Church was strong. They have excommunicated and deposed kings and governors, and, as in the cases of Queen Elizabeth I of England, and Emperor Henry IV of Germany, they have attempted to arouse rebellions by releasing subjects from any allegiance to their rulers. They have been prevented from exercising such authority in the United States because they do not have control here and because our Constitution serves as a shield against such outside interference.

The pope thus demands a submission from his people, and indeed from all people in so far as he is able to make it effective, which is due only to God. Sometimes that submission takes a particularly servile form, with even the cardinals, the next highest ranking officials in the Roman Church, prostrating themselves before him and kissing his feet! The popes have gone so far in assuming the place of God that they even insist on being called by His names, e. g., "the Holy Father," "His Holiness," etc. Such titles applied to a mere man are, of course, blasphemous and unchristian. We cannot but wonder what goes through the mind of a pope when people thus reverence him, carrying him on their shoulders, kissing his hands and feet, hailing him as the "Holy Father," and performing acts of worship before him. By such means this so-called "vicar of Christ" accepts the position of ruler of the world which the Devil offered to Christ, but which Christ spurned with the command, "Get thee hence, Satan!"

The triple crown the pope wears symbolizes his authority in heaven, on earth, and in the underworld—as king of heaven, king of earth, and king of hell—in that through his absolutions souls are admitted to heaven, on the earth he attempts to exercise political as well as spiritual power, and through his special jurisdiction over the souls in purgatory and his exercise of "the power of the keys" he can release whatever souls he pleases from further suffering and those whom he refuses to release are continued in their suffering, the decisions he makes on earth being ratified in heaven.

It is impossible to denounce strongly enough the folly and guilt of such glorification of man. The papacy, however, is the direct consequence and end result of the exaltation of the priests as necessary mediators between God and men.

But who can really believe that Christ has built His church upon a man? The Bible teaches clearly that Christ's Vicar on earth is *the Holy Spirit*—"the Comforter, even the Holy Spirit, whom the Father will send in my name, he shall teach you all things" (John 14:26). The Holy

Spirit, since He is the third person of the Trinity, has the attributes of wisdom and power which enable Him to perform effectively and perfectly the work of guiding and developing the church of Christ. Christ does not need such a deputy as Rome claims that she has in the pope, and history shows that all men who have attempted to function in that capacity have failed miserably. Over against the claims of Rome the Reformers set the Word of God. Against Rome's "Thus saith the church," they placed a "Thus saith the Lord." Luther and Calvin were willing to recognize only Christ as the Head of the Church and denounced the pope as the Antichrist. Indeed, the claims of the pope to universal and total authority over the souls of men and over the church and nations are such that either he is all that he claims to be—the vicar of Christ and the vice-regent of God—or he is the biggest imposter and fraud that the world has ever seen!

3. WORLDLY CHARACTER OF THE PAPACY

The fallacy of the claim that the pope is the vice-regent of Christ is apparent in the glaring contrast between him and Christ. The pope wears, as a fitting symbol of the authority claimed by him, a jewel-laden, extremely expensive crown, while Christ had no earthly crown at all—except a crown of thorns which He wore in our behalf. In solemn ceremonies the pope is carried in a portable chair on the shoulders of twelve men, while Christ walked wherever He needed to go. We cannot imagine Christ, who came not to be ministered unto but to minister, being carried in luxury on the shoulders of men. The pope is adored with genuflections (a bowing of the knee in reverence), he is preceded by the papal cross and by two large fans of peacock feathers, and his garments are very elaborate and costly, all of which is out of harmony with the person and manner of Christ. The pope lives in luxury with many servants in a huge palace in Vatican City, while Christ when on earth "had not where to lay His head." Many of the popes, particularly during the Middle Ages, were grossly immoral, while Christ was perfect in holiness. Christ said that His kingdom was not of this world, and He refused to exercise temporal authority. But the pope is a temporal ruler, just like a little king, with his own country, his own system of courts, vassals, coinage, postal service, and a Swiss military guard (100 men in sixteenth century uniforms) which serves as a papal bodyguard. The popes claim political power, and for many years ruled the Papal States, which stretched all the way across Italy and contained 16,000 square miles and a population of approximately 3,000,000. Those states were confiscated by Italy, under the leadership of the patriot Garibaldi, in

1870, and since that time the popes have been limited to Vatican City, located within the city of Rome, which has an area of about one-sixth of a square mile and a permanent population of about 1,000, with some 2,000 more employed there. In maintaining his claim to political power the pope sends ambassadors and ministers to foreign governments, and in turn receives ambassadors and ministers from those governments. As of October 12, 1960, 31 nations maintained ambassadors at the Vatican and received ambassadors from the Vatican, and 11 nations maintained ministers there. In each country to which a papal ambassador is sent Rome seeks to have her ambassador designated as the dean of the diplomatic corps.

The affairs of the Roman Church are controlled by a bureaucracy that is tightly controlled, completely authoritarian, and self-perpetuating, all of which is in striking contrast with the New Testament principles of church government in which the affairs of the church were in the hands of the people. The pope is elected by the cardinals, who then disband and have no further power to censure any of his actions. New cardinals are appointed by the pope, without necessary consultation with anyone; nor is there any limit on the number of new cardinals that he may appoint, the full number of the college of cardinals having remained at 70 for centuries until recently when pope John XXIII increased the number to 85. The bishops too are appointed by the pope, and may be promoted, moved, demoted, or dismissed as he pleases. The priests and nuns are chosen by the bishops, and are promoted, demoted, or transferred by them, without explanation if they so choose. And the people must be obedient to the priests, although in all of that elaborate system they have no official voice at all, nor is there any official channel through which they can express their ideas or preferences in church affairs. The papacy, therefore, is not a spiritual unity in Christ, but an external unity under the pope, a cloak which covers divisions and dissensions between the various church orders which on occasions have emerged with much rivalry and bitterness.

We close this discussion of the papacy with a quotation from Dr. Harris which we believe states correctly the New Testament teaching concerning church government and inter-church affairs:

"The fact is that the early church had no head on earth. Christ was their head and they all were brothers. They did have an organization, however, and Presbyterians point to Acts 15 as a splendid example of how it operated. There was a doctrinal question at Antioch. What should the church of Antioch do to settle it? Should they write a letter to Peter asking his decision? This would be the Romanist position. But they did not. Should they write a letter to the 'college of Apostles'? This is the episcopal position that the bishops by apostolic succession have the whole authority in the church. But Antioch did not do that. Should they call a congregational meeting of the church at Antioch and have the matter decided by the vote of the congregation? That would be the independent theory of church government. But they did not do this either. Rather they sent representatives to a synod meeting held at Jerusalem where the apostles and elders came together to consider the matter. They considered it carefully with prayer and Scripture study. Finally the apostles and elders decided on a policy and gave out decrees to which all the churches were expected to submit (Acts 16:4). There was no primacy of Peter or of anyone else. There was instead a democratic meeting of the ordained leaders of the churches judging matters according to God's Word. This is the Scriptural answer to Roman Catholic pretentions on Peter" (*The Bible Presbyterian Reporter*, Jan. 1959).

VII. MARY

1. MARY'S PLACE IN SCRIPTURE

The New Testament has surprisingly little to say about Mary. Her last recorded words were spoken at the marriage in Cana, at the very beginning of Jesus' ministry: "Whatsoever he saith unto you, do it"— then silence. But the Church of Rome breaks that silence, and from sources entirely outside of Scripture builds up a most elaborate system of Mary works and Mary devotions.

Following Mary's appearance at the marriage in Cana, we meet her only once more during Jesus' public ministry, when she and His brothers came where He was speaking to the multitudes, seeking Him, only to draw the rebuke: "Who is my mother? and who are my brethren? . . . Whosoever shall do the will of my Father who is in heaven, he is my brother, and sister, and mother" (Matt. 12:46-50). She was present at the cross, where she was committed to the care of the disciple John for the remainder of her natural life (John 19:25-27). Finally, in Acts 1:14, she is mentioned as having been with the disciples and the other women and the Lord's brethren engaged steadfastly in prayer immediately after the ascension, but she has no prominent place.

The apostles never prayed to Mary, nor, so far as the record goes, did they show her any special honor. Peter, Paul, John, and James do not mention her name even once in the epistles which they wrote to the churches. John took care of her until she died, but he does not mention her in any of his three epistles or in the book of Revelation. We recall that Prime Minister Churchill used to make it a special point of honor to mention the Queen in his eloquent public addresses. Imagine the Prime Minister of England never mentioning the Queen in any of his addresses to Parliament or in any of his state papers!

When the church was instituted at Pentecost there was only one name given among men whereby we must be saved, that of Jesus (Acts 4:12). Wherever the eyes of the church are directed to the abundance of grace, there is no mention of Mary. Surely this silence is a rebuke to those who would build a system of salvation around her. God has given us all the record we need concerning Mary, and that record does not indicate that worship or veneration in any form is to be given to her. How complete, then, is the falsehood of Romanism that gives primary worship and devotion to her!

2. "MOTHER OF GOD"

The doctrine of "Mary, the Mother of God," as we know it today is the result of centuries of growth, often stimulated by pronouncements of church prelates. And yet the full-fledged system of Mariolatry is a comparatively recent development in Roman Catholic dogma. In fact the last one hundred years have quite appropriately been called the "Century of Mariolatry."

As late as the fourth century there are no indications of any special veneration of Mary. Such veneration at that time could begin only if one were recognized as a saint, and only the martyrs were counted as saints. But since there was no evidence that Mary had suffered a martyr's death, she was excluded from sainthood. Later the ascetics came to be acknowledged as among the saints. That proved to be the opening wedge for the sainthood of Mary, for surely she of all people, it was alleged, must have lived an ascetic life! The church acknowledged that Christ was born of the *virgin* Mary. Apocryphal tradition built on those possibilities, and slowly the system emerged.

The phrase "Mother of God" originated in the Council of Ephesus, in the year 431. It occurs in the Creed of Chalcedon, which was adopted by the council which met in that city in 451, and in regard to the person of Christ it declared that He was,

"Born of the Virgin Mary, the Mother of God according to the manhood"

—which latter term means: according to the flesh of human nature. The purpose of the expression as used by the Council of Ephesus was not to glorify Mary, but to emphasize the deity of Christ over against those who denied His equality with the Father and the Holy Spirit. A heretical sect, the Nestorians, separated the two natures in Christ to such an extent that they held Him to be two persons, or rather a dual person formed by the union between the divine Logos and the human person Jesus of Nazareth. They were accused of teaching that the Logos only inhabited the man Jesus, from which it was inferred that they held that the person born of Mary was only a man. It was therefore only to emphasize the fact that the "person" born to Mary was truly divine that she was called "the Mother of God."

Hence the term today has come to have a far different meaning from that intended by the early church. It no longer has reference to the orthodox doctrine concerning the person of Christ, but instead is used to exalt Mary to a supernatural status as Queen of Heaven, Queen of the Angels, etc., so that, because of her assumed position of prominence in heaven, she is able to approach her Son effectively and to secure for her followers whatever favors they ask through her. When we say that a woman is the mother of a person we mean that she gave birth to that person. But Mary certainly did not give birth to God, nor to Jesus Christ as the eternal Son of God. She was not the mother of our Lord's divinity, but only of His humanity. Instead, Christ, the second person of the Trinity, has existed from all eternity, and was Mary's Creator. Hence the term as used in the present day Roman Church must be rejected.

In the life and worship of the Roman Church there has been a long course of development, setting forth Mary's perpetual virginity, her exemption from original sin and from any sin of commission, and now her bodily assumption to heaven. In the Roman Church Mary is to her worshippers what Christ is to us. She is the object of all religious affections, and the source whence all the blessings of salvation are sought and expected.

The Bible calls Mary the "Mother of Jesus," but gives her no other title. All that the Roman Church has to substantiate her worship of Mary is a sheaf of traditions entirely outside the Bible telling of her appearances to certain monks, nuns and others venerated as saints. At first glance the term "Mother of God" may seem comparatively harmless. But the actual consequence is that through its use Roman Catholics come to look upon Mary as stronger, more mature, and more powerful than Christ. To them she becomes the source of His being and overshadows Him. So they go to her, not to Him. "He came to us through Mary," says Rome, "and we must go to Him through her." Who would go to "the Child," even to "the holy Child," for salvation when His mother seems easier of access and more responsive? Romanism magnifies the person that the Holy Spirit wants minimized, and minimizes the person that the Holy Spirit wants magnified.

Says S. E. Anderson:

"Roman priests call Mary the 'mother of God,' a name impossible, illogical, and unscriptural. It is *impossible,* for God can have no mother; He is eternal and without beginning while Mary was born and died within a few short years. It is *illogical,* for God does not require a mother for His existence. Jesus said, 'Before Abraham was born, I am' (John 8:58). It is *unscriptural,* for the Bible gives Mary no such contradictory name. Mary was the honored mother of the human body of Jesus—no more—as every Catholic must admit if he wishes to be reasonable and Scriptural. The divine nature of Christ existed from eternity past, long before Mary was born. Jesus never called her 'mother'; He called her 'woman'" (Booklet, *Is Rome the True Church?* p. 20).

And Meyer Marcus says:

"God has no mother. God has always existed. God Himself is the Creator of all things. Since a mother must exist before her child, if you speak of a 'mother of God' you are thereby putting someone before God. And you are therefore making that person God. . . . Mary would weep to hear anyone so pervert the truth as to call her the mother of her Creator. True, Jesus was God; but He was also man. And it was only as man that He could have a mother. Can you imagine Mary introducing Jesus to others with the words: 'This is God, my Son?'" (Pamphlet, *No Mother*).

Furthermore, if the Roman terminology is correct and Mary is to be called God's mother, then Joseph was God's step-father, James, Joseph, Simon, and Judas were God's brothers, Elizabeth was God's aunt, John the Baptist was God's cousin, Heli was God's grandfather, and Adam was God's 59th great grandfather. Such references to God's relatives sound more like a page out of Mormonism than Christianity.

3. HISTORICAL DEVELOPMENT

It is not difficult to trace the origin of the worship of the Virgin Mary. The early church knew nothing about the cult of Mary as it is practiced today—and we here use the word "cult" in the dictionary sense of "the veneration or worship of a person or thing; extravagant homage."

The first mention of the legend about Mary is found in the so-called *Proto-Evangelium* of James, near the end of the second century, and presents a fantastic story about her birth. It also states that she remained a virgin throughout her entire life. Justin Martyr, who died in 165, compares Mary and Eve, the two prominent women in the Bible. Irenaeus, who died in 202, says that the disobedience of the "virgin Eve" was atoned for by the obedience of the "virgin Mary." Tertullian, who was one of the greatest authorities in the ancient church, and who died in 222, raised his voice against the legend concerning Mary's birth. He also held that after the birth of Jesus, Mary and Joseph lived in a normal marriage relationship. The first known picture of Mary is found in the Priscilla catacomb in Rome and dates from the second century.

Thus the Christian church functioned for at least 150 years without idolizing the name of Mary. The legends about her begin to appear after that, although for several centuries the church was far from making a cult of it. But after Constantine's decree making Christianity the preferred religion the Greek-Roman pagan religions with their male gods and female goddesses exerted an increasingly stronger influence upon the church. Thousands of the people who then entered the church brought with them the superstitions and devotions which they had long given to Isis, Ishtar, Diana, Athena, Artemis, Aphrodite, and other goddesses, which were then conveniently transferred to Mary. Statues were dedicated to her, as there had been statues dedicated to Isis, Diana, and others, and before them the people kneeled and prayed as they had been accustomed to do before the statues of the heathen goddesses.

Many of the people who came into the church had no clear distinction in their minds between the Christian practices and those that had been practiced in their heathen religions. Statues of pagan gods and heroes found a place in the church, and were gradually replaced by statues of saints. The people were allowed to bring into the church those things from their old religions that could be reconciled with the type of Christianity then developing, hence many who bowed down before the images of Mary were in reality worshipping their old gods under a new name. History shows that in several countries Roman Catholicism has absorbed local deities as saints, and has absorbed local goddesses into the image of the Madonna. One of the more recent examples is that of the Virgin of Guadalupe, a goddess worshipped by the Indians in Mexico, which resulted in a curious mixture of Romanism and paganism, with sometimes one, sometimes the other predominating—some pictures of the Virgin Mary now appearing show her without the Child in her arms.

As we have seen, the expression "Mother of God," as set forth in the decree of the Council of Ephesus gave an impetus to Mary worship, although the practice did not become general until two or three centuries later. From the fifth century on the Mary cult becomes more common. Mary appears more frequently in paintings, churches were named after her, and prayers were offered to her as an intercessor. The famous preacher Chrysostom, who died in 407, resisted the movement whole-heartedly, but his opposition had little effect in stemming the movement. The Roman Catholics took as their text the words of the angel to Mary, found in Luke 1:28: "And he came in unto her, and said, Hail, thou that art highly favored, the Lord is with thee." It is to be noted, how-ever, that shortly after the angel spoke to Mary, Elizabeth, speaking by inspiration of the Holy Spirit, did not say, "Blessed art thou *above* women," but, "Blessed art thou *among* women" (Luke 1:42). Starting with the false premise that Mary was above all other women, there developed the practice of worshipping her.

Invocation of the saints had a similar origin. In the year 610 pope Boniface IV first suggested the celebration of All Saints festival and ordered that the Pantheon, a pagan temple in Rome that had been dedi-cated to all the gods, should be converted into a Christian church and the relics of the saints placed therein. He then dedicated the church to the Blessed Virgin and all the martyrs. Thus the worship of Mary and the saints replaced that of the heathen gods and goddesses, and it was merely a case of one error being substituted for another.

The spiritual climate of the Middle Ages was favorable to the develop-ment of Mary worship. Numerous superstitions crept into the church and centered themselves in the worship of the Virgin and the saints. The purely pagan character of these practices, with dates and manner of observance, can be traced by any competent historian.

The art of the Middle Ages represented Mary with the child Jesus, Mary as "mater dolorosa" at the cross, etc. The rosary became popular; poems and hymns were written in honor of the "god-mother." Stories of miracles performed by her started in response to prayers addressed to her.

Also during that period arose the custom of looking to "patron saints," who in fact were merely Christianized forms of old pagan gods. In polytheism everything had its own god: the sea, war, hunting, merchants, agriculture, etc. After the same fashion there developed the Roman Catholic gallery of "patron saints" for seamen, soldiers, travelers, hunters, and in modern times, for fliers, divers, cyclists, artillerymen, etc. This kinship with the pagan cults explains why Mary worship developed so rapidly after Constantine made Christianity the preferred religion.

4. CONTRAST BETWEEN ROMAN AND PROTESTANT TEACHING

We are indebted to Dr. Joseph Zacchello, editor of *The Convert*, Clairton, Pennsylvania, for the following statement concerning Mary's rightful place in the Christian church, followed by extracts in one column from Ligouri's book, *The Glories of Mary*, and in a parallel column extracts setting forth what the Bible teaches:

"The most beautiful story ever told is the story of the birth of our Lord Jesus Christ. And a part of that beautiful story is the account of Mary, the mother of our Lord.

"Mary was a pure virtuous woman. Nothing is clearer in all the Word of God than this truth. Read the accounts of Matthew and Luke and you see her as she is—pure in mind, humble, under the hand of God, thankful for the blessing of God, having faith to believe the message of God, being wise to understand the purpose of God in her life.

"Mary was highly favored beyond all other women. It was her unique honor that she should be the mother of our Lord Jesus Christ. Blessed was Mary among women. Through her, God gave His most priceless gift to man.

"But, though Mary be worthy of all honor as a woman favored of God beyond all others, and though she be indeed a splendid, beautiful, godly character, and though she be the mother of our Lord, Mary can neither intercede for us with God, nor can she save us, and certainly we must not worship her. There is nothing clearer in the Word of God than this truth.

"Let us notice this truth as it is diligently compared with the teaching of the Roman Catholic Church and the Word of God. The following quotations are taken from the book, *The Glories of Mary*, which was written by Cardinal Alphonse de Ligouri, one of the greatest devotional writers of the Roman Catholic Church, and the Word of God taken from the Douay Version which is approved by James Cardinal Gibbons, Archbishop of Baltimore. The Editor's notice says, 'Everything that our saint has written is, as it were, a summary of Catholic tradition on the subject that it treats; it is not an individual author; it is, so to speak, *the church herself that speaks to us* by the voice of her prophets, her apostles, her pontiffs, her saints, her fathers, her doctors of all nations and ages. No other book appears to be more worthy of recommendation in this respect than *The Glories of Mary*.'" (1931 edition; Redemptorist Fathers, Brooklyn). Note the following deadly parallel:

Mary Is Given the Place Belonging to Christ

Roman Catholic Church:

"And she is truly a mediatress of peace between sinners and God. Sinners receive pardon by . . . Mary alone" (pp. 82, 83). "Mary is our life. . . . Mary in obtaining this grace for sinners by her intercession, thus restores them to life" (p. 80). "He fails and is LOST who has not recourse to Mary (p. 94).

The Word of God:

For there is one God, and ONE Mediator of God and men, the man Christ Jesus" (I Tim. 2:5). "Jesus saith to him: I am the way, and the truth, and the life. No man cometh to the Father, but by me" (John 14:6). "Christ . . . is our life" (Col. 3:4).

Mary Is Glorified More Than Christ

Roman Catholic Church:

"The Holy Church commands a WORSHIP peculiar to MARY" (p. 130). "Many things . . . are asked from God, and are not granted; they are asked from MARY, and are obtained," for "She . . . is even Queen of Hell, and Sovereign Mistress of the Devils" (pp. 127, 141, 143).

The Word of God:

In the Name of Jesus Christ . . . For there is no other name under Heaven given to men, whereby we must be saved' (Acts 3:6; 4:12). His Name is "above every name . . . not only in this world, but also in that which is to come (Eph. 1:21).

Mary Is the Gate to Heaven Instead of Christ

Roman Catholic Church:

"Mary is called . . . the gate of heaven because no one can enter that blessed kingdom without passing through HER" (p. 160).

"The Way of Salvation is open to none otherwise than through MARY," and since "Our salvation is in the hands of Mary . . . He who is protected by MARY will be saved, he who is not will be lost" (pp. 169, 170).

The Word of God:

"I am the door. By me, if any man enter in, he shall be saved," says Christ (John 10:1, 7, 9).

"Jesus saith to him, I am the way . . . no man cometh to the Father but by me" (John 14:6). "Neither is there Salvation in any other" (Acts 4:12).

Mary Is Given the Power of Christ

Roman Catholic Church:

"All power is given to thee in Heaven and on earth," so that "at the command of MARY all obey—even God . . . and thus . . . God has placed the whole Church . . . under the domination of MARY" (pp. 180, 181). Mary "is also the Advocate of the whole human race . . . for she can do what she wills with God" (p. 193).

The Word of God:

"All power is given to me in Heaven and in earth," so that "in the Name of JESUS every knee should bow," "that in all things He may hold the primacy" (Matt. 28:18; Phil. 2:9-11; Col. 1:18).

"But if any man sin, we have an Advocate with the Father, JESUS CHRIST the Just: and he is the propitiation for our sins" (I John 2:1, 2).

Mary Is the Peace-Maker Instead of Jesus Christ Our Peace

Roman Catholic Church:

"Mary is the Peace-maker between sinners and God" (p. 197).

"We often more quickly obtain what we ask by calling on the name

The Word of God:

"But now in CHRIST JESUS, you, who sometimes were far off, are made nigh by the blood of Christ. For He is our peace" (Eph. 2:13,14).

of MARY, than by invoking that of Jesus." "She . . . is our Salvation, our Life, our Hope, our Counsel, our Refuge, our Help" (pp. 254, 257).

"Hitherto you have not asked anything in my name. Ask, and you shall receive," for "Whatsoever we shall ask according to His will, He heareth us" (John 16:23,24).

Mary Is Given the Glory that Belongs to Christ Alone

Roman Catholic Church:

"The whole Trinity, O MARY, gave thee a name . . . above every other name, that at Thy name, every knee should bow, of things in heaven, on earth, and under the earth" (p. 260).

The Word of God:

"God also hath highly exalted HIM, and hath given HIM a Name which is above all names, that in the Name of JESUS every knee should bow, of those that are in Heaven, on earth, and under the earth" (Phil. 2:9,10).

Ligouri, more than any other one person, has been responsible for promoting Mariolatry in the Roman Church, dethroning Christ and enthroning Mary in the hearts of the people. Yet instead of excommunicating him for his heresies, the Roman Church has canonized him as a saint and has published his book in many editions, more recently under the imprimatur of Cardinal Patrick Joseph Hays, of New York.

In a widely used prayer book, the *Raccolta,* which has been especially indulgenced by several popes and which therefore is accepted by Romanists as authoritative, we read such as the following:

"Hail, Queen, Mother of Mercy, our Life. Sweetness, and Hope, all Hail! To thee we cry, banished sons of Eve; to thee we sigh, groaning and weeping in this vale of tears."

"We fly beneath thy shelter, O holy Mother of God, despise not our petitions in our necessity, and deliver us always from all perils, O glorious and Blessed Virgin."

"Heart of Mary, Mother of God . . . Worthy of all the veneration of angels and men. . . . In thee let the Holy Church find safe shelter; protect it, and be its asylum, its tower, its strength."

"Sweet heart of Mary, be my salvation."

"Leave me not, My Mother, in my own hands, or I am lost; let me but cling to thee. Save me, my Hope; save me from hell."

Also in the *Raccolta* prayers are addressed to Joseph:

"Benign Joseph, our guide, protect us and the Holy Church."

"Guardian of Virgins, and Holy Father Joseph, to whose faithful keeping Christ Jesus, innocence itself, and Mary, Virgin of Virgins, were committed, I pray and beseech thee by those two dear pledges, Jesus and Mary, that being preserved from all uncleanness, I may with spotless mind, pure heart, and chaste body, ever most chastely serve Jesus and Mary. Amen."

The rosary, which is by far the most popular Roman Catholic ritual prayer, contains fifty "Hail Marys." The *Hail Mary* (or *Ave Maria*) is as follows:

"Hail Mary, full of grace, the Lord is with thee; blessed art thou amongst women, and blessed is the fruit of thy womb, Jesus. Holy Mary, Mother of God, pray for us sinners, now, and at the hour of our death. Amen."

5. MARY AS AN OBJECT OF WORSHIP

The devotions to Mary are undoubtedly the most spontaneous of any in the Roman Catholic worship. Attendance at Sunday mass is obligatory, under penalty of mortal sin if one is absent without a good reason, and much of the regular service is formalistic and routine. But the people by the thousands voluntarily attend novenas for the "Sorrowful Mother." Almost every religious order dedicates itself to the Virgin Mary. National shrines, such as those at Lourdes in France, Fatima in Portugal, and Our Lady of Guadalupe in Mexico, are dedicated to her and attract millions. The shrine of Ste. Anne de Beaupre, in Quebec, the most popular shrine in Canada, is dedicated to Saint Anne, who according to apocryphal literature was the mother of Mary. Thousands of churches, schools, hospitals, convents, and shrines are dedicated to her glory.

It is difficult for Protestants to realize the deep love and reverence that devout Roman Catholics have for the Virgin Mary. One must be immersed in and saturated with the Roman Catholic mind in order to feel its heart-beat. Says Margaret Shepherd, an ex nun:

"No words can define to my readers the feeling of reverential love I had for the Virgin Mary. As the humble suppliant kneels before her statue he thinks of her as the tender, compassionate mother of Jesus, the friend and mediatrix of sinners. The thought of praying to Christ for any special grace without seeking the intercession of Mary never occurred to me" (*My Life in the Convent,* p. 31).

The titles given Mary are in themselves a revelation of Roman Catholic sentiment toward her. She is called: Mother of God, Queen of the Apostles, Queen of Heaven, Queen of the Angels, The Door of Paradise,

The Gate of Heaven, Our Life, Mother of Grace, Mother of Mercy, and many others which ascribe to her supernatural powers.

All of those titles are false. Let us consider just two of them. When she is called "Queen of the Apostles," is that an apostolic doctrine? Where is it found? Certainly it is not in Scripture. When did the apostles elect Mary their queen? Or when was she appointed by God to be their queen? And the title, "Queen of Heaven," is equally false, or even worse. Heaven has no "queen." The only references in Scripture to prayers to the "queen of heaven" are found in Jeremiah 7:18; 44:17-19, 25, where it is severely condemned as a heathen custom practiced by some apostate Jews. This so-called "queen of heaven" was a Canaanitish goddess of fertility, Astarte (plural, Ashtaroth) (Judges 2:13). How shameful to impose a heathen title on Mary, and then to venerate her as another deity!

How can any one of the perhaps one hundred million practicing Roman Catholics throughout the world who desire Mary's attention imagine that she can give him that attention during his prayers to her, his wearing her scapulars for special protection, his marching in parades in her honor, etc., while at the same time she is giving attention to all others who are praying to her, attending to her duties in heaven, conducting souls to heaven, rescuing souls from purgatory, etc.? The average Roman Catholic acts on the assumption that Mary has the powers of deity.

There is nothing in the Bible to indicate that any departed human being, however good, has any further contact with affairs on this earth, or that he can hear so much as one prayer from earth. How, then, can a human being such as Mary hear the prayers of millions of Roman Catholics, in many different countries, praying in many different languages, all at the same time? Let any priest or layman try to converse with only three people at the same time and see how impossible that is for a human being. They impose on Mary works which no human being can do. How impossible, how absurd, to impose on her the works which only God can do! Since Mary is not omnipresent nor omniscient, such prayers and worship are nothing less than idolatry—that is, the giving of divine honors to a creature.

Nowhere in the Bible is there the slightest suggestion that prayer should be offered to Mary. If God had intended that we should pray to her, surely He would have said so. Worship is accorded to the infant Jesus; but never to His mother. When Jesus was born in Bethlehem, Wise-men came from the east, and when they came into the house, they saw the young child with Mary His mother. What did they do? Did they fall down and worship Mary? Or Joseph? No! ! We read: "They fell down and worshipped *him*" (Matt. 2:11). And to whom did they give their gifts of gold, frankincense and myrrh? To Mary? Or to Joseph? No! ! They presented their gifts to Jesus. They recognized Him, not Mary or Joseph, as worthy of adoration.

Furthermore, in Old Testament times the Jews prayed to God, but never to Abraham, or Jacob, or David, or to any of the prophets. There is never the slightest suggestion that prayers should be offered to anyone other than God. Nor did the apostles ever ask the early Christians to worship, or venerate, or pray to Mary or to any other human being.

The objections against prayers to Mary apply equally against prayers to the saints. For they too are only creatures, infinitely less than God, able to be at only one place at a time and to do only one thing at a time. How, then, can they listen to and answer the thousands upon thousands of petitions made simultaneously in many different lands and in many different languages? Many such petitions are expressed, not orally, but only mentally, silently. How can Mary and the saints, without being like God, be present everywhere and know the secrets of all hearts?

That living saints should pray to dead saints seems on the face of it to be the very height of the ridiculous. But the fact is that most Roman Catholics pray to Mary and the saints more than they pray to God. Yet they cannot explain how dead saints can hear and answer prayers. The endless prayers to the Virgin and to the countless saints cannot bring one closer to God. And particularly when we see all the gaudy trappings that are resorted to in Rome's distorted version of a glamour queen the whole procedure becomes, to Protestants, truly abhorrent.

The Roman Church commits grievous sin in promoting the worship of Mary. It dishonors God, first, by its use of images; and secondly, by giving to a creature the worship that belongs only to the Creator. We have here merely another example of Rome's persistent tendency to add to the divinely prescribed way of salvation. Romanism sets forth faith *and* works, Scripture *and* tradition, Christ *and* Mary, as the means of salvation.

Father Chiniquy, a former priest from Montreal, Canada, who became a Presbyterian minister, tells of the following conversation between himself and his bishop when doubts began to assail him regarding the place given to Mary:

"My lord, who has saved you and me upon the cross?"
He answered, "Jesus Christ."
"And who paid your debt and mine by shedding His blood; was it Mary or Jesus?"
He said, "Jesus Christ."
"Now, my lord, when Jesus and Mary were on earth, who loved the sinner more; was it Mary or Jesus?"

Again he answered that it was Jesus.

"Did any sinner come to Mary on earth to be saved?"

"No."

"Do you remember that any sinner has gone to Jesus to be saved?"

"Yes, many."

"Have they been rebuked?"

"Never."

Do you remember that Jesus ever said to sinners, 'Come to Mary and she will save you'?"

"No," he said.

"Do you remember that Jesus has said to poor sinners, 'Come to me'?"

"Yes, He has said it."

"Has He ever retracted those words?"

"No."

"And who was, then, the more powerful to save sinners?" I asked.

"O, it was Jesus!"

"Now, my lord, since Jesus and Mary are in heaven, can you show me in the Scriptures that Jesus has lost anything of His desire and power to save sinners, or that He has delegated this power to Mary?"

And the bishop answered, "No."

"Then, my lord," I asked, "why do we not go to Him, and to Him alone? Why do we invite poor sinners to come to Mary, when, by your own confession she is nothing compared with Jesus, in power, in mercy, in love, and in compassion for the sinner?"

To that the bishop could give no answer (*Fifty Years in the Church of Rome*, p. 262).

Even to this day the province of Quebec is almost solidly Roman Catholic. Throughout the province one can scarcely hear the Gospel in any church, or on any local radio broadcast, or obtain anything but Roman Catholic literature. Quebec is full of idols. The late pope Pius XII declared that the province of Quebec was the world's most Catholic country. But everywhere Mary, and not Christ, is represented as the only hope of the four million French-Canadians. And, let it be noticed further, the province of Quebec has the most illiteracy, the poorest schools, and the lowest standard of living of any province in Canada.

It is very difficult to convince Roman Catholic people that Christ has won for them the right to go directly to God in prayer. They read the Bible but very little. Instead they fall back on what their priests have taught them, that to obtain mercy and forgiveness they must cajole some saint, some close and favored friend of God, to intercede for them. And the most powerful intercessor of all, of course, is Mary, since she is the mother of Christ. But the absurd thing about saint worship is that neither Mary nor any of the others ever promised, when they were living, that they would pray for their devotees after reaching heaven.

According to New Testament usage, all true Christians are saints. Paul's letters to the Ephesians was addressed, "to the saints that are at Ephesus" (1:1); his letter to the Philippians, "to all the saints that are at Philippi" (1:1). See also: Rom. 1:7; 16:15; I Cor. 1:2; II Cor. 1:1. It has well been said, If you want a "saint" to pray for you, find a true Christian and make the request of him. His prayer will be more effective than any request that can be made through dead saints. We have no need for the intercession of Mary, or dead saints, or angels, for we ourselves have direct access to God through Christ. Furthermore, not only do we have no single instance in the Bible of a living saint worshipping a dead saint, but all attempts on the part of the living even to make contact with the dead are severely condemned (Deut. 18:9-12; Ex. 22:18; Lev. 20:6; Is. 8:19,20).

The Scriptures directly repudiate all saint worship. We have specific examples of Peter, and Paul, and even of an angel rejecting such worship. When Peter went to the house of Cornelius in response to the vision that he had while at prayer on the housetop, we read that "Cornelius met him, and fell down at his feet, and worshipped him. But Peter raised him up, saying, Stand up; I myself also am a man" (Acts 10:25, 26). Although Peter was one of the twelve, and had been personally associated with Jesus, he knew that he had no right to such worship for he was only a man. At Lystra, after Paul had healed a lame man, the multitude attempted to worship him and Barnabas. We read: "But when the apostles, Barnabas and Paul, heard of it, they rent their garments, and sprang forth among the multitude, crying out and saying, Sirs, why do ye these things? We also are men of like passions with you and bring you good tidings, that ye should turn from these vain things unto a living God, who made the heaven and the earth and the sea, and all that in them is" (Acts 14:14,15). And the apostle John writes concerning his experience on the island of Patmos: "And when I heard and saw, I fell down to worship before the feet of the angel that showed me these things. And he saith unto me, *See thou do it not:* I am a fellow-servant with thee and with thy brethren the prophets, and with them that keep the words of this book: worship God" (Rev. 22:8,9). But how different is the attitude of popes, bishops, and priests who expect people to kneel before them and to kiss their hands or rings! The pope allows or expects that under some conditions they shall even kiss his feet! But what nonsense that is, both on the part of the pope and on the part of those who submit themselves to such a servile practice!

6. IN ROMANISM MARY USURPS THE PLACE OF CHRIST

A striking phenomenon in Roman Catholicism is the effective way in which they have caused Mary to usurp the place of Christ as the primary mediator between God and men. Christ is usually represented as a helpless babe in a manger or in His mother's arms, or as a dead Christ upon a cross. The babe in a manger or in His mother's arms gives little promise of being able to help anyone. And the dead Christ upon a cross, with a horribly ugly and tortured face, is the very incarnation of misery and helplessness, wholly irrelevant to the needs and problems of the people. Such a Christ might inspire feelings of pity and compassion, but not of confidence and hope. He is a defeated, not a victorious, Christ. The Roman Church cannot get its people to love a dead Christ, no matter how many masses are said before Him or how many images are dedicated to Him. There can be no real love for Christ unless the worshipper sees Him as his living Saviour, who died for him, but who arose, and who *now lives gloriously and triumphantly*—as indeed He is presented in Protestantism. In the Roman Church the people prefer a living Mary to a dead Christ. And the result is that the center of worship has shifted from Christ to Mary.

Despite all protestations to the contrary, the fact is that the worship, intercessions, and devotions that are given to Mary obscure the glory of Christ and cause the church to set forth a system of salvation in which human merit plays a decisive part. While asserting the deity of Christ, Rome nevertheless makes Him subservient to the Virgin, and dispenses salvation at a price through the agency of the priest. This most blessed of women, the mother of Jesus, is thus made His chief rival and competitor for the loyalty and devotion of the human heart. In Romanism Mary becomes the executive director of deity, the one through whom the prayers of the people are made effective.

Mary has nothing whatever to do with our salvation. All who think she does are simply deceived. And yet in Romanism probably ten times as much prayer is directed to her as to Christ. The most popular prayer ritual of Roman Catholics, the *rosary*, has ten prayers to Mary for each one directed to God. The prayer book contains more prayers which are to be offered to Mary and the saints than to Christ. Mary is unquestionably the chief object of prayer.

7. MARY REPRESENTED AS MORE SYMPATHETIC THAN JESUS

The spiritual climate of the Middle Ages was favorable for the development of the Mary-cult. Particularly in that age Christ was represented as a Man of stern wrath, a strict Judge, avenging evil with an inexorable justice, while Mary was clothed with the virtues of lovingkindness and mercy. Where Christ would demand justice, Mary would extend mercy. The simple believer, who had been told that God was an angry Judge always ready to send the sinner to hell, wanted to flee to the protection of the tender-hearted and loving Mary. Even monks who lived ascetic lives and shunned or even hated women as instruments of their temptation and downfall wanted the protection of Mary.

In *The Glories of Mary* Ligouri pictures Christ as a stern, cruel Judge, while Mary is pictured as a kind and lovable intercessor. Among other things Ligouri says: "If God is angry with a sinner, and Mary takes him under her protection, she withholds the avenging arm of her Son, and saves him" (p. 124); "O Immaculate Virgin, prevent thy beloved Son, who is irritated by our sins, from abandoning us to the power of the devil" (p. 248); and again: "We often obtain more promptly what we ask by calling on the name of Mary, than by invoking that of Jesus" (p. 248).

In another instance Ligouri teaches that Mary is the saviour of sinners, and that outside her there is no salvation. He describes an imaginary scene in which a man burdened with sin sees two ladders hanging from heaven, with Christ at the head of one and Mary at the other. He attempts to climb the ladder at which Christ is the head, but when he sees the angry face he falls back defeated. As he turns away despondent, a voice says to him, "Try the other ladder." He does so, and to his amazement he ascends easily and is met at the top by the blessed virgin Mary, who then brings him into heaven and presents him to Christ! The teaching is, "What son would refuse the request of his mother?"

The same reasoning is found among Roman Catholics today. Christ still is looked upon as a stern Judge. But Mary, being a mother, is looked upon as having a mother's heart and therefore as more capable of understanding the problems of her children. She can go to her Son with her requests and petitions, and He can never refuse to grant any favor that she asks. She is represented as everywhere present. Romanists are taught to appeal to her with confidence to allay the fierce judgment of Christ, and to turn His serious frown into a friendly smile—all of this in spite of the fact that no prayer by Mary for a sinner can be found anywhere in the New Testament.

But what a travesty it is on Scripture truth to teach that Christ demands justice, but that Mary will extend mercy! How dishonoring it is to Christ to teach that He is lacking in pity and compassion for His people, and that He must be persuaded to that end by His mother! When He was on earth it was never necessary for anyone to persuade Him to be compassionate. Rather, when He saw the blind and the lame, the afflicted and hungry, He was "moved with compassion" for them and lifted them out of their distress. He had immediate mercy on the wicked but penitent thief on the cross, and there was no need for intercession by Mary although she was there present. His love for us is as great as when He was on earth; His heart is as tender; and we need no other intermediary, neither His mother after the flesh, nor any saint or angel, to entreat Him on our behalf.

8. ONE MEDIATOR

The Bible teaches that there is but one mediator between God and men. It says:

"For there is one God, one mediator also between God and men, himself man, Christ Jesus" (I Tim. 2:5). When this verse is understood the whole system of the Roman Church falls to the ground, for it invalidates the papacy, the priesthood, and all Mary worship.

Other verses which teach the same truth are:

"I am the way, and the truth, and the life: no one cometh unto the Father, but by me" (John 14:6).
"And in none other is there salvation: for neither is there any other name under heaven, that is given among men, wherein we must be saved" (Acts 4:12).
"He is the mediator of a new covenant" (Heb. 9:15).
"If any man sin, we have an advocate with the Father, Jesus Christ the righteous" (I John 2:1).
"Christ Jesus . . . who is at the right hand of God, who also maketh intercession for us"—Christ, not Mary, the Scripture says, is at the right hand of God making intercession for us (Rom. 8:34).
"Wherefore also he is able to save to the uttermost them that draw near unto God through him, seeing he ever liveth to make intercession for them" (Heb. 7:25).

Thus Christ, because He is both God and man, is the only Saviour, the only Mediator, the only way to God. Not one word is said about Mary, or a pope, or the priests, or the saints, as mediators. Yet Romanism teaches that there are many mediators, and the great majority of Roman Catholics, if asked, would say that our primary approach to God is through the Virgin Mary, and that only as she begs for us can we enter the presence of God.

The priests detract from the glory of Christ when they teach that

Mary is a mediator. Humanly speaking, that must grieve her who would want all honor to go to Christ. The priests have no right to place her in such an unscriptural position. Mary is presented in Scripture as a hand-maiden of the Lord who fulfilled her office in the church according to promise, just as did John the Baptist and others, but whose work has long since ceased. The great antithesis is not between Eve and Mary, as Rome sets it forth, but between Adam and Christ (Rom. 5:12-21; I Cor. 15:21,22,45-47). Roman tradition has so altered the picture of Mary that the Mary found in the New Testament and the Mary found in the Roman Catholic Church are two different and conflicting persons. Any fair-minded Roman Catholic knows that his church gives first place to Mary and that Christ is kept in the background.

The reason that Mary, the saints or angels cannot act as our priest or mediator is because they have no sacrifice, nothing to offer in behalf of our sins. Only a priest with a true sacrifice can serve as mediator between God and men. Christ alone has a true sacrifice, and He alone can act as our priest. In this connection Calvin says:

> "I deem it indisputable that the papal priesthood is spurious; for it has been formed in the workshop of men. God nowhere commands a sacrifice to be offered now to Him for the expiation of sins; nowhere does He command that priests be appointed for such a purpose. While then the pope ordains his priests for the purpose of sacrificing, the Apostle (Paul) denies that they are to be accounted lawful priests."

9. ADORATION OR IDOLATRY?

The Roman Church officially denies worshipping Mary. Officially she says that Mary is only a creature, highly exalted, but still a creature, in no way equal to God. Yet she tells us that Mary hears the prayers of millions and that she constantly gives attention to her followers through-out the world. It may well be that, as Rome says, she does not *intend* idolatry. But the intention and the practical working out of the system are two different things. We must insist that it *is* worship, and that therefore it is *idolatry* as practiced by millions of people who kneel be-fore Mary's statues and pray and sing to her. Most of these people know nothing at all of the technical distinctions made by their theologians between adoration and worship. It certainly is idolatrous to give her the attributes of omnipresence and omniscience and to give her titles and functions which belong to God, as when by the late pope Pius XII, she was officially designated the "Queen of Heaven," and "Queen of the World," and when prayers are made to her for salvation.

That the prayers addressed to Mary and the saints are idolatrous is clear from the fact that: (1) They are precisely the same kind, and are expressed in the same terms, as those addressed to God; (2) They are presented in the ordinary course of worshipping God; (3) They are offered kneeling; And (4) they form the bulk of the prayers offered.

We have mentioned the most famous prayer addressed to Mary, the *Ave Maria*, or *Hail Mary*. As commonly used this prayer follows the Lord's prayer, and is offered in precisely the same way. Assuming that there are one hundred million "practicing" Roman Catholics throughout the world, and that half of them say the rosary at least once each day—the rosary contains 50 "Hail Marys" and takes quite some time to repeat—Mary would have to have the attributes of deity to hear and answer such a mass of prayer. Surely Roman Catholics themselves can see the impossibility of all those prayers being heard and answered by one who by the admission of their own church is not God, but only human. The whole thing is a deceit and an illusion. Even if it were true that the spirits of the departed have access to this world, that could not be known except by divine revelation. And no such revelation exists.

The growth of Mariolatry is indeed a sad chapter in the history of the church. Like the brazen serpent of Moses, which at the time of Hezekiah had become an object of idolatrous worship and had to be destroyed, so in the Roman Church Mary has come to be looked upon as the instrumental cause of salvation, and as such is given divine honors. The Roman Church ascribes to her large numbers of miracles, fully supernatural and similar in all respects to those performed by Christ. Numerous appearances are claimed for her. On some occasions statues of Mary are said to have blinked or wept. Relics in abundance have been exhibited in European cathedrals. Samples of her clothing, hair, teeth, and milk have been exhibited in numerous places.

The worship of Mary is, of course, a great injustice to Mary herself, for it makes her the occasion for breaking the commandments of God. Nothing is more clearly revealed in Scripture than that divine worship is to be paid to God alone—"Thou shalt worship the Lord thy God, and him only shalt thou serve" (Matt. 4:10). Nothing is more severely rebuked than idolatry of every kind and form. If Mary could see all the Roman Catholics bowing down before her images in the thousands of churches and millions of homes, how great would be her grief! To pray to Mary is at the least a waste of time. And worse than that, it is idolatry, a direct product of the use of unscriptural doctrines and practices.

10. LATRIA—DULIA—HYPERDULIA

The Church of Rome, without any warrant whatever from Scripture, technically divides worship into three kinds: (1) *Latria,* the supreme worship, given to God alone; (2) *Dulia,* a secondary kind of veneration given to saints and angels; and (3) *Hyperdulia,* a higher kind of veneration given to the Virgin Mary.

The theory, however, is useless in practice, for the average worshipper is not able to make the distinctions, nor does he even know that such distinctions exist. The subtleties of definition only confuse the issue, for who can balance his feelings so nicely as to give God, the Virgin, and the saints their due proportion? This is particularly true in Roman Catholic countries such as Italy, Spain, and Latin America where so many of the people are illiterate and given to all kinds of superstitions. We must insist that any religious worship, whether inward or outward, consisting of prayer, or praise, and expressed by outward homage such as bowing, kneeling, or prostration, is properly termed worship and belongs to God alone.

The slogan, "Through Mary to Christ," does not change the fact that for many worshippers the devotion naturally stops with Mary. They pray to Mary, not to Christ. Their prayers are directed to her personally. Roman Catholics are taught that all grace necessarily flows through Mary. She is regarded as a kind of fourth person of the Blessed Trinity. To speak of Mary as "holy," as "the Mother of God," and as "co-redeemer with Christ," cannot but give the impression that she is more than human. Pope Benedict XV (1914-1922) gave expression to the thought that Mary suffered with her suffering and dying Son, and that with Him she has redeemed the human race. This pronouncement was also sanctioned by pope Pius XI in 1923.

The distinction that Rome makes between latria, dulia, and hyperdulia does enable her to maintain officially that she does not teach the "worship" of Mary. However, the lengths to which her apologists have gone in trying to distinguish between such devotions and actual worship is evidence that she feels uncomfortable about the lofty names given to Mary and about the actual results, and that she does not dare take responsibility for what goes on in her churches. And, subtleties aside, some Roman theologians acknowledge that they do worship Mary.

11. JESUS' ATTITUDE TOWARD MARY

It is particularly instructive to notice the attitude that the Lord Jesus Himself took toward Mary. The first recorded instance occurred when, at the age of 12, the boy Jesus after attending the Passover in Jerusalem with His parents remained in the temple. We read, in the Confraternity Version, that when His parents found Him, "His mother said to him, 'Son, why hast thou done so to us? Behold, in sorrow thy father and I have been seeking thee.' And he said to them, 'How is it that you sought me? Did you not know that I must be about my Father's business?' And they did not understand the word that he spake to them" (Luke 2:48,49).

Says *The New Bible Commentary* (Protestant) in explanation of this event: "The answer of Jesus is an expression of surprise. There was something about him which He was surprised His parents did not know. . . . He had always been occupied with His Father's affairs and had no interests of His own to engage Him. This was what His parents might have known" (p. 844).

On two later occasions, after Jesus had reached His maturity, Mary attempted to show her parental authority, but each time was held in check. The first occurred at the wedding in Cana of Galilee, when the wine ran out. We read, again in the Confraternity Version:

> "And on the third day a marriage took place at Cana of Galilee, and the mother of Jesus was there [Notice, it does not say, "Mother of God"]. Now Jesus too was invited to the marriage, and also his disciples. And the wine having run short, the mother of Jesus said to him, 'They have no wine.' And Jesus said to her, 'What wouldst thou have me do, woman? My hour has not yet come.' His mother said to the attendants, 'Do whatever he tells you' " (John 2:1-5).

In this instance, the first of its kind after the beginning of His public ministry, Jesus gave Mary to understand that no one, not even His mother, must dictate to Him concerning the time and manner of opening His public ministry, that thenceforth she was not to exercise any authority over Him, and that His working of miracles and the redemption of souls was, strictly speaking, none of her business. He was pointing out to His mother that from then on He had no dependence on her, but that she must depend upon Him. Mary's words to the servants, "Do whatever he tells you," indicate that she understood and accepted this new role. In any event, Mary is not to be worshipped, nor does she have authority with her Son in behalf of others. Had Jesus submitted to His mother's suggestion and leading, there might have been some grounds for "Mary worship," and for the claim of the Roman Church that "Mary is the hope of all." But here at the very beginning of His public ministry, the ground is cut from under any such claim.

On another occasion, apparently after weeks of absence, Mary came seeking Jesus at the place where He was preaching to the multitude, but could not get to Him because of the crowd. Apparently she sent word to Him by messenger, making known her desire that He would come to her, or perhaps making the direct request that He come to her without regard to how that might interrupt His work. But He ignored or refused her request. We read (Confraternity Version):

"While he was still speaking to the crowds, his mother and his brethren were standing outside, seeking to speak to him. And someone said to him, 'Behold, thy mother and thy brethren are standing outside, seeking thee.' But he answered and said to him that told him, 'Who is my mother and who are my brethren?' And stretching forth his hand toward his disciples, he said, 'Behold my mother and my brethren! For whoever does the will of my Father in heaven, he is my brother and sister and mother'" (Matt. 12:46-50).

Instead of granting Mary's request, He replied in such a way that it was in effect a public rebuke. Undoubtedly she felt it keenly. Perhaps Mary was even ashamed of the fact that her Son was attracting so much attention and wanted to withdraw Him from the crowd, for in Mark's account of this event we read, "And the multitude cometh together again, so that they could not so much as eat bread. And when his friends heard it, they went out to lay hold on him: for they said, He is beside himself" (3:20,21). As we read the New Testament we get the impression that neither Mary nor the brothers of Jesus understood His activities while He was on earth ("For even his brethren did not believe on him," John 7:5), and that while Mary believed on Him earlier, His brothers may not have joined the company of believers until after His resurrection, perhaps not until after His ascension.

As a boy growing up in the home of Joseph and Mary, Jesus was obedient to them. But after His public ministry began, after He had presented Himself as the Son of God and as the Saviour of the world, Mary had to sink into the background. It is to Jesus alone that the world must turn for salvation. Undoubtedly He gave this rebuke purposely, that the world might know that Mary was His mother as man, but not as God.

If Mary had had the influence and authority over Him that is claimed by the Church of Rome, He would not have answered her as He did but would have honored her request promptly. Here again we have Scriptural evidence that Mary has nothing to do with the ministry of the Son of God as regards the matter of salvation. By this statement He respectfully classes her and His brethren along with other converts. To Him they were all the same—"Who is my mother and who are my brethren? . . . Whoever does the will of my Father in heaven, he is my brother and sister and mother!" As the Son of God and the redeemer of men, His relation to Mary was identically the same as with any others who would hear His Word, and do it.

And on still another occasion a woman in the crowd raised her voice in praise of Mary (Confraternity Version):

> "Now it came to pass as he was saying these things, that a certain woman from the crowd lifted up her voice and said to him, 'Blessed is the womb that bore thee, and the breasts that nursed thee.' But he said, 'Rather, blessed are they who hear the word of God and keep it' " (Luke 11:27,28).

This was the most subtle attack of all, appealing, as it does to the sentiments and the emotions. It is a device that even today traps unstable souls into worshipping a woman, that is, Mariolatry. But here again Jesus gave a plain and decisive answer which should settle forever the question regarding the superiority of Mary or the promotion of any Mary cult. He utterly rejected the idea that Mary occupies a position of holiness above that of other women, or that she was to be crowned the "Queen of Heaven" and become the object of worship. After the ascension of Christ she is seen with the apostles and several other women in Jerusalem (Acts 1:14), but no special honor or position is recorded as having been given to her. She was not, in herself, more than any other virtuous woman, except that she was especially chosen to be the mother of Jesus, and to be the kind and loving parent which she was to the most wonderful Child that ever grew up in a home.

We notice further that throughout our Lord's public life He was ever careful to call Mary "woman," never "mother." Even when He was dying on the cross He addressed her thus. The Greek, Hebrew, and Latin each had a word for "mother," as well as for "woman." But the Scripture says "woman," not "mother." And of course He *never* used the term "Lady," which is so much used in the Roman Catholic Church. Let us follow the Scripture.

While Jesus always spoke respectfully to His mother, He nevertheless made it clear that neither she nor anyone else had any part in the work of salvation. No mere human *could* assist in that work, and the Scriptures are careful to point out that no assistance or dictation in any form was permitted. When Jesus stepped out of His home life at Nazareth and began His public ministry a new relationship was established. From that time on His supernatural parentage was emphasized. For He was the only begotten Son of the Father in heaven. He rebuked the mistaken tendency which seeks to exalt the human relationship at the expense of the divine, the physical at the expense of the spiritual.

12. THE PROTESTANT ATTITUDE TOWARD MARY

As evangelical Protestants we honor Mary, the mother of our Lord, with the honor the Scriptures give her as "blessed among women." No other member of the human race has received such a high honor as was conferred upon Mary in that she was chosen to be the mother of the Saviour of the world. She was truly a woman of virtue, and of extraordinary faith. She fulfilled admirably the office assigned to her. She was the chosen vessel to bring the Bread of Life to a sin-cursed world. But she was only the vessel, not the Bread of Life. We cannot eat the vessel; rather it is the Bread of Life that we need. It is not Mary the Jewish maiden, but Jesus the Son of God whom we need as Saviour.

We honor Mary, and all generations shall call her "blessed," because she believed the word of God and accepted the message of the angel Gabriel. But we do not deify her, nor worship her, nor pray to her, and we are bound to protest strongly when Christ is dethroned and Mary is elevated to that place which belongs to Him alone. We worship *with* her the Son of God, but we do not worship *her*, nor worship *through* her, as if she were a mediator. It is important that all understand the difference between the matter of honoring Mary, and the grossly unscriptural practice of *worshipping* her. We are constantly reminded of the words of Jesus: "Whosoever shall do the will of my Father who is in heaven, he is my brother, and sister, and mother" (Matt. 12:50).

Roman priests *say* that they honor Mary and accuse Protestants of failing to do so. There is the danger, of course, that in revolting against the recognized evil of Mariolatry, we may neglect to give Mary the distinguished and honored place which the Scripture itself accords her. And we should be on guard against that. But the priests do her a grave injustice in that they impose too much responsibility upon her. Peter, the alleged first pope, did not do that. He did not even mention her in any of his sermons or in his two letters. As is characteristic of Protestants, he said much about Christ as the only Saviour from sin, but he did not present Mary as a mediator. To present her in that capacity is to rob God of part of His glory and to pawn off a counterfeit salvation upon the people. There is no record in Scripture of anyone ever calling on Mary for salvation.

The false estimate of Mary's position on the part of the Roman Church is based in large measure on a mistaken interpretation of the words of Jesus spoken on the cross, when He said to John, "Behold, thy mother." Romanists say that these words were addressed to all men, present and future, and that He was committing all men to Mary as her sons. The truth, however, is that the New Testament is unmistakably clear on this point, and that the Lord committed His mother to John's care for the remainder of her natural life, and that He laid upon John as an individual the responsibility to serve as a son to her. It reads:

> "When Jesus therefore saw his mother, and the disciple standing by whom he loved, he saith to his mother, Woman, behold, thy son! Then saith he to the disciple, Behold, thy mother! and from that hour the disciple took her unto his own home" (John 19:26,27).

The natural meaning of those words is that they were addressed to Mary and to John as individuals, that from that time forward Mary should look upon John, the beloved disciple, as her son, as the one who in her life would take the place of Jesus, and that John should assume the duties of a son and care for Mary with filial affection, that he should comfort her in her loneliness, as a true son would. And that Mary and John so understood those words is clear from the immediately following verse, which reads: "And from that hour the disciple took her unto his own home" (vs. 27).

This, then is the Mary we honor—not a weeping statue of stone, not a half-goddess, nor a "Queen of Heaven," but the humble servant of God, who found favor with Him and became the mother of Jesus.

13. WERE THERE OTHER CHILDREN IN THE FAMILY OF JOSEPH AND MARY?

The Scriptures tell us that Jesus was virgin born. But what of the family of Joseph and Mary after the birth of Jesus? Did Joseph and Mary have other children? Or was Jesus the only Child? The answers to these questions pointedly divide Roman Catholics and Protestants.

In Matthew 13:54-56 we read:

> "And coming into his own country he taught them in their synagogue, insomuch that they were astonished, and said, "Whence hath this man this wisdom, and these mighty works? Is not this the carpenter's son? is not his mother called Mary? and his brethren, James, and Joseph, and Simon, and Judas? And his sisters, are they not all with us?"

Mark also names the brothers of Jesus and mentions his sisters (6:3).

The natural meaning of these verses is that there were other children in the family of Joseph and Mary. There were four sons; and there were at least two daughters, for the term is in the plural. Presumably there were three or more daughters, for the term used is "all." When there are only two we say "both," not "all." And the reference in John 7:5, "For even his brethren did not believe on him," also finds its most natural meaning in other sons of Joseph and Mary. It was self-evident that the people at large did not believe on Him, but here John says that even His own brothers, the members of His own family, did not believe on Him.

A prophecy about Christ in Psalm 69, "I am become a stranger unto my brethren, And an alien unto my mother's children" (vs. 8), also finds its natural fulfillment in the attitude of Christ's brothers toward Him. That this is a messianic psalm, prophetic of the coming and work of Christ, is clear from a number of New Testament references in which it is applied to Him. Compare verses 4, 8, 21, and 25 with John 15:25; 2:17; Rom. 15:3; Matt. 27:34; and Acts 1:20, in which other elements of the psalm are fulfilled. Luke's statement concerning Mary, "And she brought forth her firstborn son" (2:7), implies that there were other sons born after Jesus. Acts 1:14 refers to "Mary the mother of Jesus," and "his brethren," who are mentioned in addition to the disciples.

These would in fact have been half-brothers and half-sisters of Jesus since they were sons and daughters of Joseph and Mary, while He was the Son of Mary only. James, the half-brother of the Lord, became the head of the church in Jerusalem and presided at the Jerusalem Council (Acts 15:13,19). And two of the books of the New Testament, James and Jude, were written by the sons of Joseph and Mary.

The Roman Catholic Church attempts to explain these away as cousins, and therefore not children of Joseph and Mary at all. But the Greek has another word which means cousin, *anepsios,* as in Colossians 4:10: "Mark, the cousin of Barnabas."

Another reference indicating the same is Matthew 1:24,25: "And Joseph arose from his sleep, and did as the angel of the Lord commanded him, and took unto him his wife; and knew her not till she brought forth a son: and he called his name Jesus." All that the Scripture says is that Joseph knew her not *until after* the birth of Jesus. The inference is that after the birth of Jesus Mary became wholly and completely the wife of Joseph, that they then lived as normal husband and wife, and, taken in connection with the other references that we have cited, that other children were then born into their family.

The Scriptures affirm that Mary was a virgin until after Jesus was born. Nothing beyond that is needed to safeguard the Deity of Christ and the purity of Mary. What more is needed to prove that Jesus was virgin-born? What more do you need to prove that Joseph was not the father of Jesus? In going beyond that and teaching the "perpetual virginity" of Mary, the Roman Catholics go beyond Scripture and set up man made doctrine which has no authority.

The priests make repeated references to "the Virgin Mary." They acknowledge that Joseph and Mary were husband and wife and attempt to portray them as the ideal human family, but deny that they lived in a normal marriage relationship. But such an unnatural relationship is absurd on the face of it, and nowhere in Scripture is approval ever given for such an abnormal relationship. Such an arrangement would have been contrary to nature and simply a frustration for both parties. The priests must either give up the idea of Mary's perpetual virginity, or give up the idea that Joseph and Mary represent the ideal human family.

Back of Rome's insistence on the perpetual virginity of Mary, of course, is the desire to justify the celibate state of the priests and nuns. Rome teaches that the single state is holier than the married state, that there is something inherently unclean and defiling about marriage. Says one Roman Catholic writer concerning the Virgin Mary: "It cannot with decency be imagined that the most holy vessel which was once consecrated to be a receptacle of the Deity should be afterwards desecrated and profaned by human usage." According to this teaching a woman's body is "desecrated and profaned" when she becomes a mother in the normal course of family life! A nun is holier than the mother of lovely children! And since Rome thinks of marriage as unholy and unclean, and since she has set herself to maintain the holiness, even the sinless perfection, of Mary, she finds herself obliged to teach that Mary always remained a virgin.

14.   THE IMMACULATE CONCEPTION

The doctrine of the "Immaculate Conception" teaches that Mary herself was born without sin, that from the very first moment of her existence she was free from the taint of original sin. It holds that while all the rest of mankind are born into an inheritance of original sin, Mary alone, by a special miracle of God, was excepted. The original decree setting forth this doctrine was issued by pope Pius IX, on December 8, 1854, and reads as follows:

"We declare, pronounce and define that the Most Blessed Virgin Mary, at the first instant of her conception was preserved immaculate from all stain of original sin, by the singular grace and privilege of the Omnipotent God, in virtue of the merits of Jesus Christ, the Saviour of mankind, and that this doctrine was revealed by God, and therefore must be believed firmly and constantly by all the faithful" (From the papal bull, *Ineffabilus Deus*, quoted in *The Tablet*, December 12, 1953).

Many Protestants misunderstand this doctrine and assume that it relates to the virgin birth of Christ. It relates, however, to Mary's own birth, and has nothing to do with the virgin birth of Christ.

Side by side with the doctrine that Mary was born without sin, there developed the doctrine that she did not commit sin at any time during her life. Then, as one link reached out for another, they gave her the attribute of impeccability, which means that she *could not sin,* that her nature was such that it was impossible for her to sin! All of this was a natural outgrowth of their worship of Mary, a further step in her deification. Their Mariolatry demanded it! They sensed that if they were to give her the worship that is due our Lord, she must be sinless.

But this doctrine, like the other distinctive doctrines of the Roman system, completely lacks any Scriptural support, and in fact is directly opposed to the Scripture doctrine of original sin. The Bible teaches that all men, with the single exception of Christ who was deity incarnate and pre-existent, are sinners. Mary herself acknowledged her need of a Saviour, for she said:

"My soul doth magnify the Lord,
And my spirit hath rejoiced in God my Saviour" (Luke 1:46, 47).

Note particularly Mary's words, "my Saviour." No one other than a sinner needs a Saviour, for no punishment or evil in any form can be inflicted upon a sinless person. Roman Catholics will have to take Mary's word or accuse "Our Lady" of lying. For in those words she confessed that she was a sinner in need of a Saviour. That should settle once and for all whether or not a Christian should pray to her. Mary was an admirable character, to be sure. But she was not sinless, and she was only human. It was, therefore, necessary for her to be born again by faith and to participate in the redemption provided by her Son.

The Scriptures say clearly: "*All* have sinned, and fall short of the glory of God" (that includes Mary—Rom. 3:23); "Therefore, as through one man sin entered into the world, and death through sin; and so death passed unto *all* men, for that *all* sinned" (Rom. 5:12); "For as in Adam *all* die. . . ." (I Cor. 15:22); "If we say that we have no sin, we deceive ourselves, and the truth is not in us. . . . If we say that we have not sinned, we make him a liar, and his word is not in us" (I John 1:8,10); "There is none righteous, no, not one" (Rom. 3:10).

Scripture tells us that after the birth of Jesus Mary brought the two offerings prescribed in the law, one, a burnt-offering (symbolizing complete surrender of the will to God), and the other a sin-offering (a sacrifice acknowledging sin) (Luke 2:22-24; Lev. 12:6-8). The last time

Mary is mentioned in the New Testament she is praying *on the same plane* as other needy Christians, not being prayed to by them (Acts 1:13,14).

The doctrine of the immaculate conception has had a long and varied history. It was unknown to the apostolic church, and it was not even a matter of discussion until several centuries after the death of Mary. It did not become an official doctrine until the year 1854, more than 18 centuries after Christ was born of the virgin Mary, and so is one of the later doctrines of the Roman Church. The Council of Ephesus, 431, used the expression, "Mother of God," but its purpose was to emphasize the deity of Christ, not to set forth a doctrine concerning Mary. But popular opinion reasoned that since the birth of Christ occurred without any taint of sin, Mary herself must have been without sin, even without original sin, which is the lot of all other human beings.

Augustine, who died in 430, A. D., and who was admittedly the greatest theologian of the ancient church, contradicts the idea of immaculate conception, for he expressly declares that Mary's flesh was "flesh of sin" (De Peccatorum Meritis, ii, c. 24); and again that "Mary, springing from Adam, died because of sin; and the flesh of our Lord, derived from Mary, died to take away sin." He expressly attributed original sin to Mary in his *Sermon on Psalm 2*. The doctrine was opposed by Chrysostom, Eusebius, Ambros, Anselm, most of the great medieval schoolmen, including Thomas Aquinas, Bonaventure, Cardinal Cajetan (Luther's opponent at Augsburg), and also by two of the most outstanding popes, Gregory the Great, and Innocent III.

Thomas Aquinas says that while Christ did not contact original sin in any way whatsoever, nevertheless "the blessed Virgin did contact original sin, but was cleansed therefrom before her birth" (*Summa Theol.* III, ad 2; Quest. 27, Art. 1-5); and again that, "It is to be held, therefore, that she was conceived in original sin, but was cleansed from it in a special manner" (*Compendium Theol.*, p. 224). Geddes MacGregor, in his book, *The Vatican Revolution,* says:

> "So strong was St. Thomas (Aquinas') opposition to the doctrine that it became almost a point of honor throughout the Dominican Order to oppose the notion as theologically untenable. The Franciscans, however, following Duns Scotus, were more inclined to foster the notion, and the Jesuits, later on, made it one of their special concerns to do so. If pope Pius IX was right, let alone infallible, it seems regrettable that the learned theologians of Christendom should have been left for eighteen hundred years with such a marked lack of guidance on the subject that they not only erred on it but erred almost in proportion to their stature as the leaders of the Church's intellectual life, the luminaries in the firmament

of her mind" (p. 9; Beacon Press, Boston; Macmillan & Co., Ltd., London and Toronto).

The dispute between the Dominicans and the Franciscans became so bitter that pope Sixtus IV eventually took a hand and prohibited further discussion, without deciding the question in favor of either side. The Council of Trent, though called primarily to deal with the problems arising because of the Protestant Reformation, was asked by pope Pius IV to make a pronouncement, but left the matter untouched.

Nevertheless, the idea that Mary was sinless continued to gain ground. Members of the Jesuit order soon began to propagate the doctrine anew, and it was largely through their work that it was decreed by pope Pius IX, "the infallible successor of Peter," in 1854, and was officially ratified by the docile Vatican Council of 1870 (which council also ratified the decree concerning the infallibility of the pope in matters of faith and morals).

Most of the theologians of the Middle Ages opposed the doctrine because they were unable to harmonize it with the universality of original sin. Most of them held that if Mary were not a partaker of the sin and apostasy of the race, she could not be the point of contact between Deity and humanity as was required for the human nature of Christ. Hence in this case, even tradition, the usual refuge of the Roman Church in matters of doctrine, contradicts this papal dogma.

So, Mary is now placed on a plane of absolute equality with her adorable Son, Jesus Christ, so far as sinlessness is concerned. Like the other doctrines of Romanism, this one is said to be based on "the unanimous consent of the fathers." Though the dispute in reality continued for centuries and was at times bitter, it is accepted by all Roman Catholics today, for the official pronouncement by the pope leaves them no other choice. For along with the decree there was issued this condemnation of any who dare to disbelieve it:

"Therefore, if some shall presume to think in their hearts otherwise than we have defined (which God forbid), they shall know and thoroughly understand that they are by their own judgment condemned, *have made shipwreck concerning the faith,* and fallen away from the unity of the Church; and, moreover, that they, by this very act, subject themselves to the penalties ordained by law, if, by word, or writing, or by other external means, they dare to signify what they think in their heart."

What a flagrant example of false doctrine and ecclesiastical tyranny! That is the very thing that Peter condemned when he forbade "lording it over your charges" (Confraternity Version, I Peter 5:3). The Council of

Trent pronounced its anathemas primarily against Protestants who dared
to differ with its decrees. But the anathemas pronounced by the later
councils have been directed primarily against their own people, in order
to force them into line.

But why should any Roman Catholic embrace that doctrine when the
greatest teachers in his own church rejected it? Indeed, why should anyone believe it if the Bible does not teach it?

15. THE ASSUMPTION OF MARY

The latest addition to the long list of Roman Catholic beliefs ("inventions" might be a more accurate term) came on November 1, 1950, with
the *ex cathedra* pronouncement by pope Pius XII from St. Peter's chair
that Mary's body was raised from the grave shortly after she died, that
her body and soul were reunited, and that she was taken up and enthroned as Queen of Heaven. And to this pronouncement there was
added the usual warning that "anyone who may henceforth doubt or deny
this doctrine is utterly fallen away from the divine and Catholic faith."
That means that it is a mortal sin for any Roman Catholic to refuse
to believe this doctrine.

According to tradition Mary's assumption was on this wise:

> "On the third day after Mary's death, when the apostles gathered
> around her tomb, they found it empty. The sacred body had been car-
> ried up to the celestial paradise. Jesus Himself came to conduct her
> hither; the whole court of heaven came to welcome with songs of triumph
> the Mother of the divine Lord. What a chorus of exultation! Hark how
> they cry, 'Lift up your gates, O ye princes, and be ye lifted up, O
> eternal gates, and the Queen of Glory shall enter in.' "

This is the type of account that might be expected from a medieval
monk who was not satisfied with the information given in the Bible
concerning Mary, and who undertook to describe the events as he
imagined they might have happened. Here we are told that Mary was
not only received into heaven, but that she was raised to a pre-eminence
far above that which it is possible for any of the saints to attain. Because
of her alleged cooperation in the passion of her Son, she is assigned a
dignity beyond even the highest of the archangels. She was crowned
Queen of Heaven by the eternal Father, and received a throne at her
Son's right hand.

Thus Mary's body was miraculously preserved from corruption, and
her resurrection and ascension are made to parallel Christ's resurrection
and ascension. And she, like Him, is said to be enthroned in heaven

where she makes intercession for the millions of people throughout the world who seek her assistance. This was a natural consequence of the 1854 pronouncement of the immaculate conception of Mary—a supernatural entrance into life calls for a supernatural exit from life. A mysterious halo of holiness falls over her entire being. Whereas the glorification of the saints will take place at the end of the world, her glorification has already taken place.

The late pope Pius XII was called the "Marian pope" for his work in promulgating this doctrine of the assumption of Mary and in declaring her Queen of Heaven. By his decree a twelve month period was set aside for this purpose, involving Marian congresses, special services, and pilgrimages to Rome (which, of course, brought huge revenues to the Vatican, primarily from American pilgrims or tourists), with the avowed purpose of turning the eyes of the world more intensively toward Mary—which inevitably meant a proportionate turning away from Christ.

To a Protestant the most amazing thing about the doctrine of the assumption of Mary is that it has no Scripture proof whatever. Not one shred of evidence can Roman Catholics find in the Bible about Mary's death, burial, location of her grave, or when or how she ascended to heaven. And yet this troubles the Roman Church not in the least. Pope Pius XII made the pronouncement with the utmost confidence, relying on an alleged original "deposit of faith" given to the apostles by Jesus Christ —but which, we note, did not come clearly to light until some nineteen centuries later. The early church fathers, who were closest to those events, knew nothing at all about such an ascension. One marvels that such unscriptural, unhistorical, and senseless teachings could be embraced by any people and treated as if they were unchallengeable Scripture truth.

All that the Roman Church pretends to have from an early date supporting this doctrine is an apocalyptic legend, contained in a book, *De Gloria Martyrum,* written by Gregory of Tours, southern France, in the sixth century. On the face of it it is a mere fairy tale. This book narrates how as Mary lay dying with the apostles gathered around her bed, Jesus appeared with His angels, committed her soul to the care of Gabriel, and her body was taken away in a cloud. As Edward J. Tanis appropriately remarks, "There is no more evidence for the truth of this legend than for the ghost stories told by our grandfathers" (*What Rome Teaches,* p. 26). But this curious medieval folklore has now been made an official doctrine of the Roman Church, and any member who refuses to accept it is declared by papal decree to be "utterly fallen away from the divine and Catholic faith."

Here we have a typical example of how Roman Catholic doctrines develop. Millions of people are simply told to believe in the bodily assumption of Mary without the church furnishing any Scriptural or historical proof, and they do so even without a protest. Not even in the schools of learning is there any voice raised to demand proof for such a doctrine. Whether Scriptural or unscriptural, historical or unhistorical, scientific or unscientific, reasonable or unreasonable, every member of the church is under obligation to accept it and believe it. This shows the baneful effect of the kindred doctrines that the pope is infallible in his *ex cathedra* statements, and that the average church member is not to try to reason out his faith but to accept implicitly whatever the church teaches.

The doctrine of the assumption of Mary is merely one of the so-called "logical conclusions" that the Roman theologians have drawn to support their system. Since Mary was sinless it is illogical, we are told, to assume that her body remained in the grave. But the answer is: *If Mary was sinless, why did she have to die at all?* Death is the penalty for sin. And where there is no sin there can be no penalty. God would be unjust if He punished the innocent. Either Mary was sinless and did not die, or she did have sin, she died, and her body remains in the grave.

Rome has so built up the Mary role that it has become an indispensable part of the present day church, so much so that if Mary were placed back in the position given her in Scripture it would change the whole character of that church. Some have even suggested that the Roman Catholic Church should be called the "Marian Church," because in its life and practice it gives first place to her.

Following the *ex cathedra* pronouncements concerning the immaculate conception and the bodily assumption of Mary, there remains one major link to complete the process to which the Roman Church is committed in regard to Mary, that of her co-redeemership with Christ. This doctrine has been under discussion for several years. Some prominent churchmen have indicated that the next official pronouncement will declare that Mary, though technically not divine, is nevertheless associated with the Father, Son, and Holy Spirit in matters of salvation, and that she is the "Mediatrix of all Graces," or "Co-redemptrix with Christ." At the present rate we eventually shall have in heaven no longer a Trinity but a Quartet! Thus in every age Rome moves forward deliberately in the formulation of her doctrines.

16. ROME'S PURPOSE IN EXALTING MARY

In the development of this section extensive use has been made of an article, *The Secret Purpose of Mariolatry*, by Dee Smith, published in *Christian Heritage*, December, 1958.

In the Roman Church so much of myth and legend has been added to Mary's person that the real Mary has been largely forgotten. Although there are but few references to her in the Bible, she is there presented as a sublimely courageous character. In no other event is her true character brought out so clearly as in her vigil at Calvary. When most mothers would have been in a state of collapse, Mary persisted through a long and agonizing ordeal which only the most valiant spirit could have endured.

What a contrast there is between this noble, heroic woman and the gaudily dressed doll that we see in the Roman Catholic Church! Instead of the candid and forthright gaze of one conscious of the dignity and self respect of her womanhood, the "Blessed Virgin" shrinks in servility with lowered head and lowered eyes, as if ashamed of it. One searches the empty face for a single trace of such character as must have graced the one chosen to nurture the Christ. The astute observer soon realizes that this insipid caricature decked out in superfluous finery has no relationship at all to the Mary of Scripture, and is nothing more than a sheer fabrication, a fiction promoted with ulterior purposes.

What, then, is the purpose of the hierarchy in promoting this particular type of mannequin? In what way does she serve their interests?

It is obvious that the Blessed Virgin represents a model for Roman Catholic women, or to put it more accurately, a strait jacket in which the clergy would like to fasten them. She represents the type of woman most conducive to sustained clerical control over the minds of the Roman masses. Her outstanding qualities are humility, obedience, pliability—abject submission to authority. It is this ideal that the Roman Church wishes to instill—indeed must instill—in Roman Catholic womanhood if it is to retain its hold on the people and maintain the services rendered in its many institutional enterprises such as schools and hospitals which for the most part are run with unpaid labor.

The most important service rendered by this caricature of the Blessed Mary is that of maintaining the control of the Roman clergy over Roman Catholic women. For the promotion of the church program it is absolutely essential that they remain spineless, mindless, "meek and mild," as Mary is pictured, willing to accept dumbly a half-life in which their role is merely to bear and to drudge. In Roman Catholic countries this control remains as complete today as ever it was at any age in the past, and in countries such as our own any deviation from this norm is due to the good fortune of those women in being born in a Protestant country in which truly Christian influences make for the general uplift of womankind. The hierarchy exacts a service from the women of the church that it cannot obtain from the men, yet ironically its contempt for womankind is coupled with a full awareness that its whole power-system rests upon the Catholic woman, and that if she ever raises her bowed head, the world-wide political machine will lose its efficiency and collapse irreparably.

In Roman Catholic countries where women can be kept in total ignorance the priests, who are educated and intelligent men, have never hesitated to play upon their emotions, to instill fear into their souls, and to encourage superstition as that suited their purpose. In enlightened countries common knowledge prevents much of that deception, and Roman Catholic women to a large extent share with their Protestant sisters the blessings of a common culture.

It is well known that the Roman Catholic clergy in all countries urge their people to produce large families. This serves a double purpose. First, it keeps both mothers and fathers so fully occupied, the women in caring for the children, and the fathers in making a living, that they have little chance to look around and make undesirable comparisons between the ethics of their creed and that of the Protestant countries. And, secondly, this large family program serves to plug the hole in the dyke left by the defection of a large number who leave their church.

As an alternative to her child-bearing services for the glory of Rome, the Catholic woman is offered the privilege of becoming a holy drudge within the church, namely, a nun in a convent. Here again the Blessed Virgin plays a key role, that of recruiting officer. Add to this the masterly publicity job that has been done on the Roman Catholic girl from infancy to make the nun an object of holy glamour, almost a replica of the Blessed Virgin, and it is somewhat surprising to learn that in recent years the Roman Church is finding it increasingly difficult to persuade American girls to enter convents. It has become so difficult in fact that the Roman Church has been obliged to import sisters from Europe to meet the need for teachers and nurses.

In concluding the article previously mentioned Dee Smith says:

"Presiding over the two functions of Roman Catholic womanhood, the child-bearing program and the unpaid labor pool, stands the puppet figure of the Blessed Virgin, at once the instigator and the patroness.

"Compared with her services in insuring the cushioned privilege and power of the hierarchy by subjugating the Roman Catholic women, the enormous wealth brought to Rome's exchequer by the financial exploitations of Mariolatry is merely incidental. Yet it is worth a glance.

"From the sale of 'holy' pictures, leaflets, scapulars, candles burned before her altars, fees for masses, and so on, the staggering intake at commercialized shrines such as St. Anne de Beaupre, Our Lady of Guadalupe, and others, a steady stream of gold flows into hierarchical coffers. One might almost paraphrase the Roman title, 'Mother of God,' to 'Minter of Gold.'

"But all this is as nothing beside the Blessed Virgin's vital and indispensable function in maintaining the status quo. Without the inspiration of the Blessed Virgin, the Roman Catholic woman could not be kept at her business of child-bearing and drudging. Without the subjection of the Catholic woman, without her submissive acceptance of the yoke of Mary caricatured by the Roman Church, the all-powerful, self-indulgent ambitious men who constitute the Roman hierarchy would not be able to use their power as a weapon against human liberties and human rights.

"Without doubt, the devotion to the Blessed Virgin constantly impressed upon the Roman population by its clergy is inspired not by piety, but by expediency. For the clergy, devotion to Mary is not merely a matter of dollars and cents, but of survival. Their sinecure depends on it. That is the secret purpose of Mariolatry."

What, then, is the remedy for this situation, this entire problem of Mariology and Mariolatry? It is, indeed, very simple. Let the Roman Catholic people *read the Bible*, particularly the New Testament. There they will find the living, compassionate, redeeming Christ, with very little said about Mary. It is not without reason that the Roman priesthood has striven so hard to keep the Bible from the people, and that even now the people are strictly forbidden to read any Bible except one that contains the approved set of explanatory notes.

VIII. THE MASS

1. Definitions. 2. The Nature of the Mass. 3. The Mass the Same Sacrifice as on Calvary? 4. Transubstantiation. 5. The Cup Withheld from the Laity. 6. The Finality of Christ's Sacrifice. 7. The Mass and Money. 8. Historical Development. 9. Seven Sacraments. 10. Conclusion.

1. DEFINITIONS

"The Holy Eucharist And while they were at supper, Jesus took bread, and blessed and brake, and gave it to his disciples, and said, 'Take and eat; this is my body.' And taking a cup, he gave thanks and gave it to them, saying, 'All of you drink this; for this is my blood of the new covenant, which is being shed for many unto the forgiveness of sins'" (Confraternity Version, Matt. 26:26-28).

"Institution of the Eucharist For I myself have received from the Lord (what I also delivered to you), that the Lord Jesus, on the night in which he was betrayed, took bread, and giving thanks, broke, and said, 'This is my body which shall be given up for you; do this in remembrance of me.' In like manner also the cup, after he had supped, saying, 'This cup is the new covenant in my blood: do this as often as you drink it, in remembrance of me. For as often as you shall eat this bread and drink the cup, you proclaim the death of the Lord, until he comes'" (Confraternity Version, I Cor. 11:23-26).

In the New York Catechism we read: "Jesus Christ gave us the sacrifice of the Mass to leave to His Church a visible sacrifice which continues His sacrifice on the cross until the end of time. *The Mass is the same sacrifice as the sacrifice of the cross* [italics ours]. Holy Communion is the receiving of the body and blood of Jesus Christ under the appearance of bread and wine."

The Creed of pope Pius IV, which is one of the official creeds of the Roman Church, says: "I profess that in the Mass is offered to God a true, proper, and propitiatory sacrifice [that is, a sacrifice which satisfies the justice of God and so offsets the penalty for sin] for the living and the dead; and that in the most holy sacrament of the Eucharist there

168

is truly, really, and substantially, the body and blood, together with the soul and divinity, of our Lord Jesus Christ; and that there is a conversion of the whole substance of the bread into the body, and of the whole substance of the wine into the blood, which the Catholic Church calls Transubstantiation."

The Council of Trent declared: "The sacrifice [in the Mass] is identical with the sacrifice of the Cross, inasmuch as Jesus Christ is a priest and victim both. The only difference lies in the manner of offering, which is bloody upon the cross and bloodless on our altars."

A Roman Catholic, John A. O'Brien, whose books are widely read, says: "The Mass with its colorful vestments and vivid ceremonies is a dramatic re-enactment in an unbloody manner of the sacrifice of Christ on Calvary" (*The Faith of Millions*, p. 382).

2. THE NATURE OF THE MASS

The words of Matthew 26:26-28 and I Corinthians 11:23-26, particularly the words, "This is my body," and "This is my blood," may seem to be quite simple and easy to understand. But the fact is that they probably are the most controverted words in the history of theological doctrine, and probably have caused more division within the church than any others.

It is surprising how many Protestants do not understand the significance of the Roman Catholic mass. Some think of it as merely a church ritual and dismiss it as just another form of the Lord's supper or holy communion. But that is far from being the case. For Protestants and Roman Catholics alike the Lord's supper or holy communion is a sacrament. For Protestants it is a means of spiritual blessing and a memorial service, recalling to mind the glorious person of Christ and the great service that He rendered for us on Calvary. But for Roman Catholics it is something quite different. For them it is also a *sacrifice*, performed by a priest. And its sacrificial element is by far the most important. In fact the sacrifice of the mass is the central point in their worship, while even the preaching of the Gospel is assigned a subordinate role and is not even held to be an essential of the priestly office.

In the Roman Church this further distinction should be noted between the two parts of the mass, the mass proper, and holy communion. In the mass the so-called sacrifice is offered only by the priest and only he partakes of both the bread and the wine. In holy communion the people partake of the bread but not of the wine and have no other active part in the service.

According to Roman teaching, in the sacrifice of the mass the bread and wine are changed by the power of the priest at the time of consecration into the actual body and blood of Christ. The bread, in the form of thin, round wafers, hundreds of which may be consecrated simultaneously, is contained in a golden dish. The wine is in a golden cup. The supposed body and blood of Christ are then raised before the altar by the hands of the priest and offered up to God for the sins both of the living and the dead. During this part of the ceremony the people are little more than spectators to a religious drama. Practically everything is done by the priest, or by the priest and his helpers. The audience does not sing, nor are there any spontaneous prayers either on the part of the priest or the people. The liturgy is so rigid that it can be carried out mechanically, almost without thought.

In the observance of holy communion the priest partakes of a large wafer, then he drinks the wine in behalf of the congregation. The lay members go to the front of the church and kneel before a railing, with closed eyes, and open mouths into which the priest places a small wafer. Roman Catholic theology holds that the complete body and blood of Christ are in both the bread and the wine. At this point one is tempted to ask, If the priest can partake of the wine for the congregation, why may he not also partake of the bread for the congregation?

Formerly it was required that anyone partaking of the mass must have abstained from any form of food or drink, even water, since midnight—hence the need for early mass. That, however, caused many to become indifferent. Now one has to abstain from solid food for only three hours before receiving communion, and he does not have to abstain from water at all. Yet the New Testament tells us that Christ instituted the Lord's supper immediately *after* He and the disciples had eaten the passover feast. If Christ had no objection to the bread being mixed with other food, why should the Roman Church object?

The elaborate ritual of the mass is really an extended pageant, designed to re-enact the experiences of Christ from the supper in the upper room, through the agony in the garden, the betrayal, trial, crucifixion, death, burial, resurrection, and ascension. It is a drama crowding the detailed events of many days into the space of one hour or less. For its proper performance the priest in seminary goes through long periods of training and needs a marvelous memory. Witness the following: he makes the sign of the cross sixteen times; turns toward the congregation six times; lifts his eyes to heaven eleven times; kisses the altar eight times; folds his hands four times; strikes his breast ten times, bows his head twenty-one times; genuflects eight times; bows his shoulders seven times; blesses the altar with the sign of the cross thirty times; lays his hands flat on the altar twenty-nine times; prays secretly eleven times; prays aloud thirteen times; takes the bread and wine and turns it into the body and blood of Christ; covers and uncovers the chalice ten times; goes to and fro twenty times; and in addition performs numerous other acts. His bowings and genuflections are imitations of Christ in His agony and suffering. The various articles of clothing worn by the priest at different stages of the drama represent those worn by Christ; the seamless robe, the purple coat, the veil with which His face was covered in the house of Caiaphas, a girdle representing the cords with which He was bound in the garden, the cords which bound Him to the cross, etc. If the priest forgets even one element of the drama he commits a great sin and technically may invalidate the mass. Add to the above the highly colored robes of the clergy, the candles, bells, incense, music, special church architecture of the chancel often in gleaming white, and the fact that the mass is said or sung in an unknown tongue, Latin, which is not understood by the people, and you see something of the complexity of the program. Surely there was much truth in Voltaire's remark concerning the mass as practiced in the cathedrals of France in his day, that it was "the grand opera of the poor."

But what a miserable form of play-acting is all of that! What a poor substitute for the Gospel do the people depend on for eternal life! In contrast how simple was the scene in the upper room as Christ instituted the Lord's supper! In I Corinthians 11:23-26, in just four verses, Paul outlines the whole simple service: The Lord Jesus in the night in which He was betrayed took bread; He gave thanks; He broke the bread; and He gave it to them as a memorial of His body which was to be broken for them. Just four simple actions concerning the bread. Then two actions are recorded concerning the wine: He took the cup; and He gave it to them as symbolical of His blood which was to be shed for them. All that we are asked to remember is that He died to save sinners and that we are so to commemorate His death until He returns. But this simple event the Church of Rome has magnified into the glaring, elaborate, showy pageantry and drama of the mass!

The celebration of the mass is the chief duty of the Roman priesthood. Yet the New Testament gives no instruction as to how to offer mass, and in fact there is not so much as one line on the subject in Scripture. Christ sent the apostles to teach and to baptize, not to say mass. His final instructions to the church were: "Go ye therefore, and make disciples of all the nations, baptizing them . . . teaching them. . . ." (Matt. 28:19). Search the Gospels, the book of Acts, and the Epistles, and you find many admonitions to prayer, praise, preaching the Gospel, etc., but not one word about the mass. Paul gave many instructions and exhortations concerning the government and duties of the churches, but he says nothing about the sacrifice of the mass. For centuries the sacrificing priesthood of the Old Testament era had been typical of the one true Priest who was to come. But after He had come and had accomplished His work there was no further need to continue the empty forms. So the priesthood, having served its purpose, was abolished, and Christ made no provision for His apostles and ministers to continue any kind of sacrifice. The writer of the Epistle to the Hebrews has much to say about the endless repetition and futility of the ancient sacrifices. He shows that their only value was to symbolize and point forward to the one true sacrifice that was to be made by Christ. "We have been sanctified," he said, "through the offering of the body of Jesus Christ *once for all.* And every priest indeed standeth day by day ministering and offering oftentimes the same sacrifice which can never take away sins; but he, when he had offered *one sacrifice for sin for ever,* sat down on the right hand of God; henceforth expecting till his enemies be made the footstool of his feet. For by *one* offering he hath *perfected for ever* them that are sanctified" (10:10-14). The New Testament, therefore, announces the termination of all sacrifices, declaring that Christ alone is our true sacrifice, and that He offered Himself "once for all," thus forever ending all other sacrifices.

It staggers the imagination to realize that a merely human pantomime so absurd and so contradictory to Holy Scripture could be accepted and slavishly attended day after day and week after week by thinking men and women. Since the New Testament gives no instructions at all about the continuation of the Old Testament sacrifices, it was necessary for the Roman priesthood to invent a new kind of sacrifice. This they did by making a frivolous distinction between the "bloody" sacrifice of Christ on the cross, and the "unbloody" sacrifice which they pretend to offer in the mass. A priest, of course, must have a sacrifice, for that is the distinguishing mark of his profession. A priest without a sacrifice is simply no priest at all.

In the true observance of the Lord's supper the symbolism is found in the bread and wine. But in the Roman ceremony no place is left for that symbolism, for the bread and wine become the actual flesh and blood of Christ so that He is literally present. The newly developed symbolism in the Roman ceremony centers in the priest at the altar—his consecration of the host, his vestments, and his various movements which constitute "the drama of the mass." Rome destroys the symbolism of the elements, which recalls the sacrifice on Calvary, and substitutes the symbolism of the one who administers the sacrament.

Concerning the altar at which the priest ministers, Dr. Harris says:

"It was probably the invention of the priesthood which brought in the altar. The early churches had no altar. The Jewish altar, done away in

Christ, was a massive structure of brass on which a constantly burning fire consumed the Jewish offerings. It was a type, of course, of the cross on which Christ 'once for all' (Heb. 9:26) offered Himself. An altar without fire is a contradiction in terms, just as an 'unbloody sacrifice of the mass' is a contradiction of the clear teaching of Scripture that 'without the shedding of blood there is no forgiveness' (Heb. 9:22), and, 'we are justified by his blood' (Rom. 5:9; Confraternity ed.). The altar, as now used, is a Roman Catholic invention" (*Fundamental Protestant Doctrines*, II, p. 5).

The Protestant views concerning the elements in the Lord's supper can be stated very simply. They differ somewhat in regard to the symbolic significance of the bread and wine, but in regard to the event memorialized they agree that in the one sacrifice on Calvary Christ offered Himself once for all for the sins of His people. The following summary of Protestant views is given in the Christian Heritage Series, Book No. 1, pages 52 and 53:

"The Lutheran Church rejects the doctrine of transubstantiation and teaches that the elements are figurative. They insist, however, upon the *real presence* of Christ at the Supper; that is, He is present as the soul is in the body or magnetism is in the magnet. Theologians call this *consubstantiation*." [Luther expressed this by saying that Christ is "in, with, and under" the elements].

"Reformed [and Presbyterian] congregations understand the words of Christ *metaphorically*. 'This is (that is, signifies) my body.' Along with this metaphorical understanding of the elements, however, is the idea that Christ is present virtually, or as Dr. Hodge puts it: 'the virtues and effects of the sacrifice of the body of the Redeemer on the cross are made present and are actually conveyed in the sacrament to the worthy receiver by the power of the Holy Ghost, who uses the sacrament as His instrument according to His sovereign will.'

"All other Protestant churches hold that the bread and wine are mere symbols of the body and blood of Christ, nothing more. The observance is a memorial only of His death for our sins, to be commemorated until He comes again."

3. THE MASS THE SAME SACRIFICE AS ON CALVARY?

In a Roman Catholic Catechism of Christian Doctrine the question is asked: "Is the Holy Mass one and the same sacrifice with that of the Cross?" (Question 278). And the answer is given:

"The Holy Mass is one and the same sacrifice with that of the Cross, inasmuch as Christ, who offered Himself, a bleeding victim, on the Cross to His Heavenly Father, continues to offer Himself in an unbloody manner on the altar, through the ministry of His priests."

The Church of Rome holds that the mass is a continuation of the sacrifice that Christ made on Calvary, that it is in reality a re-crucifixion of our Lord over and over again, in an unbloody manner. It also holds that this sacrifice is just as efficacious to take away sin as was the sacrifice on Calvary. Christ supposedly is offered in sacrifice every time the mass is celebrated, that is, daily, in thousands of Roman Catholic churches throughout the world. The mass, therefore, is not a memorial, but a ritual in which the bread and wine are transformed into the literal flesh and blood of Christ, which is then offered as a true sacrifice. The only difference is the manner in which the two are made. Rome thus claims to continue an act which the Scriptures say was completed nearly two thousand years ago.

In the sacrifice of the mass the Roman priest becomes an "Alter Christus," that is, "Another Christ," in that he sacrifices the real Christ upon the altar and presents Him for the salvation of the faithful and for the deliverance of souls in purgatory. The Roman Church teaches that Christ, in the form of the "host" (the consecrated wafer), is in reality upon the altar, and that the priests have Him in their power, that they hold Him in their hands, and carry Him from place to place. There is even a ritual sometimes used at the close of a night service known as "Putting Jesus to bed."

We must, of course, take strong exception to such pretended sacrifice. We cannot regard it as anything other than a deception, a mockery, and an abomination before God. The so-called sacrifice in the mass certainly is not identical with that on Calvary, regardless of what the priests may say. There is in the mass no real Christ, no suffering, and no bleeding. And a bloodless sacrifice is ineffectual. The writer of the book of Hebrews says that "apart from shedding of blood there is no remission" of sin (9:22); and John says, "The blood of Jesus his Son cleanseth us from all sin" (I John 1:7). Since admittedly there is no blood in the mass, it simply cannot be a sacrifice for sin.

In the New Testament the ordinance of the Lord's supper is always presented as a sacrament, never as a sacrifice. Furthermore according to the Levitical law a sin offering was *never to be eaten,* and all eating of blood, even animal blood, and much more human blood, was strictly forbidden. The fact that in the Lord's supper the elements are eaten is proof in itself that it was never intended to be a sacrifice.

4. TRANSUBSTANTIATION

The word "transubstantiation" means *a change of substance*. The Church of Rome teaches that the whole substance of the bread and wine is changed into the literal physical body and blood of Christ. A Catechism of Christian Doctrine asks the question: "What is the Holy Mass?" and the answer is given:

"The Holy Mass is the sacrifice of the body and blood of Jesus Christ, really present on the altar under the appearance of bread and wine, and offered to God for the living and the dead."

The doctrine of transubstantiation and the power of the priests is clearly stated by Ligouri in the following words:

"With regard to the power of the priests over the real body of Christ, it is of faith that when they pronounce the words of consecration, the incarnate God has obliged Himself to obey and come into their hands under the sacramental appearance of bread and wine. We are struck with wonder when we find that in obedience to the words of His priests —*Hoc est corpus meum* (This is my body)—God Himself descends on the altar, that He comes whenever they call Him, and as often as they call Him, and places Himself in their hands, even though they should be His enemies. And after having come He remains, entirely at their disposal and they move Him as they please from one place to another. They may, if they wish, shut Him up in the tabernacle, or expose Him on the altar, or carry Him outside the church; they may, if they choose, eat his flesh, and give Him for the food of others. Besides, the power of the priest surpasses that of the Blessed Virgin because she cannot absolve a Catholic from even the smallest sin" (*The Dignity and Duties of the Priest*).

The priest supposedly is endowed with power by the bishop at the time of his ordination to change the bread and wine into the literal living body and blood of Christ, which is then known as the "host," and so to bring Him down upon the altar. And that body is said to be complete in all its parts, down to the last eyelash and toenail! How it can exist in thousands of places and in its full proportions, even in a small piece of bread, is not explained, but is taken on faith as a miracle.

It must not be supposed for a minute that modern Roman Catholics do not literally believe this jumble of medieval superstition. They have been taught it from infancy, and they do believe it. It is the very sternest doctrine of their church. It is one of the chief doctrines, if indeed it is not the chief doctrine, upon which their church rests. The priests preach it literally and emphatically several times a year, and Roman Catholic laymen do not dare express any doubt about it.

After the adoration of the consecrated "host," the uplifted hands of the priest pretend to offer to God the very body and blood of Christ as a sacrifice for the living and the dead. Then, in the observance of the eucharist he pretends to eat Him alive, in the presence of the people, also to give Him to the people under the appearance of bread, to be eaten by them.

This doctrine of the mass, of course, is based on the assumption that the words of Christ, "This is my body," and "This is my blood" (Matt. 26:26-28), must be taken literally. The accounts of the institution of the Lord's Supper, both in the Gospels and in Paul's letter to the Corinthians, make it perfectly clear that He spoke in figurative terms. Jesus said, "This cup is the new covenant in my blood" (Luke 22:20). And Paul quotes Jesus as saying: "This is the new covenant in my blood. . . . For as oft as ye eat this bread, and drink the cup, ye proclaim the Lord's death till he come" (I Cor. 11:25-26). In these words He used a double figure of speech. The cup is put for the wine, and the wine is called the new covenant. The cup was not literally the new covenant, although it is declared to be so as definitely as the bread is declared to be His body. They did not literally drink the cup, nor did they literally drink the new covenant. How ridiculous to say that they did! Nor was the bread literally His body, or the wine His blood. After giving the wine to the disciples Jesus said, "I shall not drink from henceforth of the fruit of the vine, until the kingdom of God shall come" (Luke 22:18). So the wine, even as He gave it to them, and after He had given it to them, remained "the fruit of the vine"! Paul too says that the bread remains bread: "Wherefore whosoever shall eat the bread and drink the cup of the Lord in an unworthy manner. . . . But let each man prove himself, and so let him eat of the bread, and drink of the cup" (I Cor. 11:27-28). No change had taken place in the elements. This was after the prayer of consecration, when the Church of Rome supposes the change took place, and Jesus and Paul both declare that the elements still are bread and wine.

Another and more important proof that the bread and wine are not changed into the literal and actual flesh and blood of Christ is this: the literal interpretation makes the sacrament a form of *cannibalism*. For that is precisely what cannibalism is—the eating of human flesh. Rome attempts to deny this, but not with much logic. Clearly there is a contradiction in the Romanist explanation somewhere.

Indeed, how can Christ's words, "This is my body," and, "This is my blood," be taken in a literal sense? At the time those words were spoken the bread and wine were on the table before Him, and in His body He was sitting at the table a living man. The crucifixion had not taken place. They ate the Lord's supper before the crucifixion took place. Furthermore, we do not, and cannot memorialize someone who is present, as the Romanists say Christ is present in the mass. But in the future, in His absence, these things would *symbolize* His broken body and shed blood. They would then call to mind His sacrifice, and would then be taken "in remembrance" of Him (I Cor. 11:25).

Jesus' words, "This do in remembrance of me," show that the Lord's supper was not some kind of magic operation, but primarily a memorial, instituted to call Christians throughout the ages to remember the wondrous cross of the crucified Lord and all its marvelous benefits and lessons for us. A memorial does not present the reality, in this case His true body and blood, but something quite different, which serves only as a reminder of the real thing.

We often show a friend a photograph and say, "This is my wife"; "This is my son"; "This is my daughter." Such language is readily understood in ordinary conversation. Nobody takes such words literally. The Bible is written in the language of the common people. Hence it is perfectly obvious to any observant reader that the Lord's Supper was intended primarily as a simple memorial feast, in no sense a literal reincarnation of Christ.

We believe that the real meaning of Christ's words can be seen when they are compared with similar figurative language which He used in John 4:13,14. There, speaking to the woman at Jacob's well, He said: "Every one that drinketh this water shall thirst again; but whosoever drinketh of the water that I shall give him shall never thirst; but the water that I shall give him shall become in him a well of water springing up unto eternal life."

On other occasions He used similar language. He said, "I am the door (John 10:7)—but of course He did not mean that He was a literal wooden door with lock and hinges. He said, "I am the vine" (John 15:5)—but no one understood Him to mean that He was a grapevine. When He said, "I am the good shepherd" (John 10:14), He did not mean that He was actually a shepherd. When He said, "Ye must be born again" (John 3:7), He referred not to a physical birth but to a spiritual birth. When He said, "Destroy this temple, and in three days I will raise it up" (John 2:19), he meant His body, not the structure of wood and stone. When He said, "He that eateth my flesh and drinketh my blood hath eternal life" (John 6:54), He was speaking of a spiritual relationship between Himself and His people in terms of the Old Testament type, that is, eating the passover lamb and drinking the passover wine; but His Jewish hearers, being literalists, as are the Roman Catholics, misunderstood His words. He said, "Ye are the salt of the earth" (Matt. 5:13), and "Ye are the light of the world" (Matt. 5:14). He spoke of "the leaven of the Pharisees and Sadducees" (Matt. 16:6). James said, "The tongue is a fire" (3:6); and again, "Ye are a vapor that appeareth for a little time, and then vanisheth away" (4:14). Moses spoke of "the bread of affliction" (Deut. 16:3); and Isaiah spoke of "the bread of adversity and the water of affliction" (30:20). None of these statements is true if taken literally. The disciples had no trouble understanding Jesus' figures of speech. Similarly, the expressions, "This is my body," and "This is my blood," are clear enough for all except those who will not see, or those who merely follow medieval theologians. It is unreasonable in the extreme to take these two expressions literally while taking the others figuratively.

The actual eating of human flesh and blood is repulsive, abhorrent to all right minded people, and it was especially so to the Jews. Such practice is contrary to Scripture and to common sense. "And whatsoever man there be . . . that eateth any manner of blood, I will set my face against that soul that eateth blood, and will cut him off from among his people," was the word of God through Moses (Lev. 17:10); "Ye shall not eat the blood" (Deut. 12:16); etc. In Jewish law a stern penalty was assessed against eating blood. In Peter's vision (Acts 10) when he was told to arise, kill and eat, he promptly protested that he had never eaten meat with the blood. A little later the Jerusalem Council, legislating for the Christian dispensation, ratified a provision against the eating of blood: ". . . that ye abstain from things sacrificed to idols, and from blood" (Acts 15:29). It is impossible to believe that when the apostles thus set forth the law of God they were themselves partakers, not merely of animal blood, but of human blood—as they would have been if in the Lord's Supper they regularly ate the literal flesh and blood of Christ.

The Roman Church acknowledges that in the mass there is no visible change in the bread and wine, that they continue to have the same properties: the same taste, color, smell, weight, and dimensions. It should be sufficient to refute this doctrine to point out that it involves an impossibility. It is impossible that the attributes or sensible properties of bread and wine should remain if the substance has been changed. It is self-evident that if the attributes of flesh and blood are not there, the actual flesh and blood are not there. When Jesus changed the water into wine at Cana of Galilee, there was no question but that it was wine. It had the properties of wine. But since the bread and wine in the eucharist do not have the attributes of flesh and blood, it is absurd to say that any such change has taken place. That which contradicts our reason must be pronounced irrational. Yet the adherents of Rome, under threat of eternal condemnation, are forced to believe what their church tells them, even though it contradicts their senses. The effect cannot be other than detrimental when men are forced to accept as true that which they know to be false. Says Henry M. Woods:

> "If men think at all, they know that what the papal church requires them to believe in the eucharist, under penalty of an eternal curse, is a monstrous untruth. They know they are eating bread, not human flesh: and they know that no human priest can offer a real atoning sacrifice for sin" (*Our Priceless Heritage*, p. 107).

When the Roman priest consecrates the wafer it is then called the "host," and they worship it as God. But if the doctrine of transubstantiation is false, then the "host" is no more the body of Christ than is any other piece of bread. And if the soul and divinity of Christ are not present, then the worship of it is sheer idolatry, of the same kind as that of pagan tribes who worship fetishes.

A curious and interesting item in connection with the doctrine of the Church of Rome is that the efficiency of a priest's action in performing any sacrament depends upon his "intention," and that if he does not have the right intention in doing what he professes to do the sacrament is invalid. The Council of Trent declared: "If anyone shall say that intention, at least of doing what the church does, is not required in ministers while performing and administering the sacraments, let him be anathema" (Sess. VII, Can. 11). The Creed of pope Pius IV says:

> "If there is a defect in any of these: namely, the due matter, the form with intention, or the sacerdotal order of the celibrant, it nullifies the sacrament." And cardinal Bellarmine, who is considered one of the foremost authorities, says: "No one can be certain, with the certainty of faith, that he has received a true sacrament, since no sacrament is performed without the intention of the ministers, and no one can see the intention of another" (Works, Vol. 1, p. 488).

Hence in the administration of the mass, baptism, or any of the other sacraments, if the right intention is lacking on the part of the priest, either through lack of attention to what he is doing, ill feeling toward the person before him, spite at his superiors, physical or mental distresses which distract him, etc., the sacrament is null and void. If at the time the priest is administering the mass, the bread and wine undergo no change, then when he elevates the "host" and the people bow down and worship it they are worshipping a mere creature, acknowledged by the Church of Rome to be such. And that, of course, is pure idolatry. How often that occurs we have no way of knowing. If one cannot be certain that he is partaking of a true sacrament, he cannot be sure but that he may be worshipping mere bread and wine. In view of the fact that so many priests eventually leave the priesthood—some say as many as one-fourth or one-third—it surely is reasonable to assume that many of those, for considerable periods of time before they leave and while they are in a state of doubt and uncertainty, are often lacking in sincere intention in performing the sacraments. It would indeed be interesting to know what proportion of the members of the Roman Church, according to Rome's own doctrine, have received invalid baptisms, ordinations, marriages, absolutions, etc. Undoubtedly it is considerable. It would also be interesting, if it were possible, to know who those individuals are. No doubt there would be many surprises as some of her most distinguished and ardent supporters were revealed as not legitimately ordained priests, nor even members of the Roman Church.

Dr. Joseph Zacchello, a former priest and editor of *The Convert,* points out that this doctrine of the intention of the priest undermines the doctrinal basis of the Roman Church. He says:

> "This teaching implies that no Roman Catholic, be he priest or laymen, can ever be sure that he has been properly baptized, confirmed, absolved in confession, married, received holy communion or extreme unction. . . . Suppose a child is baptized by a priest who lacks the proper intention. The baptism is then of no avail, and the child grows up a pagan. If he should enter a seminary and be ordained a priest, his ordination will be invalid. All the thousands of masses he says, all the sacraments he performs, will likewise be invalid. If he becomes a bishop, the priests he ordains and the other bishops he consecrates will have no such power. If by chance he should become pope, the Roman Catholic Church would then have as 'Vicar of Christ' and 'infallible' head a man who was not even a Christian to start with!" (*Secrets of Romanism,* p. 110).

5. THE CUP WITHHELD FROM THE LAITY

Another serious error of the Church of Rome is that in the eucharist or holy communion she withholds the wine from the laity. She thus deprives believers of half of the benefits of the sacrament. That decision was made without any command from the New Testament, there being no suggestion of any such distinction between clergy and laity.

Even in the Confraternity Version Christ's command that all believers partake of the cup is clear and unequivocal: "All of you drink this" (Matt. 26:27). And Mark says: "And they all drank of it" (14:23). Christ said,

"This is the new covenant in my blood' (I Cor. 11:25). Since all believers are in that covenant, and since all Christians should remember Christ's atoning death which was made for them, all should partake of the cup which is one of the seals of that covenant and one of the reminders of that death.

In Paul's directions for the observance of the Lord's Supper it is clear that the laity partook of both the bread and the wine. Writing to the church at Corinth he even found it necessary to admonish the people against gluttony and drunkenness. We read: "When ye come together in the church. . . . When therefore ye assemble yourselves together. . . ."; then follows the admonition: ". . . one is hungry, and another is drunken. What, have ye not houses to eat and to drink in?. . . . Wherefore whosoever shall eat the bread or drink the cup of the Lord in an unworthy manner, shall be guilty of the body and blood of the Lord" (I Cor. 11:18-27). How could anyone be guilty of drinking the cup of the Lord in an unworthy manner if the cup were not given to him? This is clearly one more instance in which the Church of Rome has taken it upon herself to alter the commands of the Gospel.

In the early church the people partook of both the bread and the wine, and that practice was continued through the first eleven centuries. Then the practice of permitting the priest to drink the wine for both himself and the congregation began to creep in. In 1415 the Council of Constance officially denied the cup to the people. That decision was confirmed by the Council of Trent (1545-1563), and that practice has been continued to the present day.

The reason given by the priests for withholding the cup from the laity are: (1) that someone might spill a drop (since the wine allegedly has been transformed into the literal blood of Christ that indeed would be a great tragedy)—the disciples too might have spilled some, but Jesus did not withhold it from them for any such flimsy reason; and (2) that the body of Christ, the flesh and the blood, is contained complete in either the bread or the wine—but there is no suggestion of that in Scripture.

O'Brien, acknowledges that "It was the common custom for the first twelve centuries to give communion under both kinds," and that "The present law of giving communion to the laity only under the form of bread dates from the Council of Constance in 1415" (*The Faith of Millions*, p. 223).

6. THE FINALITY OF CHRIST'S SACRIFICE

That Christ's sacrifice on Calvary was complete in that one offering, and that it was never to be repeated, is set forth in Hebrews, chapters 7, 9 and 10. There we read:

"Who needeth not daily, like those high priests, to offer up sacrifices, first for his own sins, and then for the sins of the people: for this he did *once for all,* when he offered up himself" (7:27).

". . . through his own blood, entered in *once for all* into the holy place, having obtained eternal redemption" (9:12).

"Apart from shedding of blood there is no remission. . . . Nor yet that he should offer himself often, as the high priest entereth into the holy place year by year with blood not his own; else must he often have suffered since the foundation of the world: but now *once* at the end of the ages hath he been manifested to put away sin by the sacrifice of himself. . . . Christ also, having been *once* offered to bear the sins of many, shall appear a second time, apart from sin, to them that wait for him unto salvation" (9:22-29).

"By which will we have been sanctified through the offering of the body of Jesus Christ *once for all.* And every priest indeed standeth day by day ministering and offering oftentimes the same sacrifices, the which can never take away sins: but he, when he had offered *one sacrifice* for sins *for ever,* sat down on the right hand of God; henceforth expecting till his enemies be made the footstool of his feet. For by *one offering* he hath *perfected for ever* them that are sanctified" (10:10-14).

Notice that throughout these verses occurs the statement "once for all," which has in it the idea of completeness, or finality, and which precludes repetition. Christ's work on the cross was perfect and decisive. It constituted one historic event which need never be repeated and which in fact cannot be repeated. The language is perfectly clear: "He offered one sacrifice for sins for ever" (10:12). Paul says that "Christ being raised from the dead dieth no more" (Rom. 6:9); and the writer of the Epistle to the Hebrews says that "By one offering he hath perfected for ever them that are sanctified" (10:14).

Christ's priesthood is contrasted with that of the Old Testament priests, and we are told that the ancient priesthood has ceased and that the priesthood of Christ has taken its place. We are told that Christ has sat down as token that His work is finished. Depend upon it, He never descends from that exalted place to be a further sacrifice upon Rome's altars or on any other; for of such sacrifice there is no need. The verses just quoted completely contradict all that Rome has to say about the mass. Thank God that we can look back to what our Lord did on Calvary and know that He completed the sacrifice for sins once for all, and that our salvation is not dependent on the whim or arbitrary decree of any priest or church. Any pretense at a continuous offering for sin is worse than vain, for it is a denial of the efficacy of the atoning sacrifice of Christ on Calvary.

Where there is a continual offering for sin, as when the sacrament of the mass is offered daily, it means that sins are really never taken away, and that those who are called priests pretend to continue the unfinished work of Christ. When on Memorial Day we lay a wreath on the tomb of a soldier we may speak of the sacrifice that he made to save his country. But his sacrifice cannot be renewed. He died once and his sacrifice was complete. So it is with the sacrifice of Christ. He died once, as the Scriptures so emphatically and repeatedly state; and since He was deity incarnate, He was a person of infinite value and dignity and His work therefore was fully efficacious and complete for the accomplishing of what He intended, namely, the redemption of those for whom He died. When Paul said, "For as often as ye eat this bread, and drink this cup, ye proclaim the Lord's death till he come" (I Cor 11:26), he did not say that we repeat the Lord's death, or supplement it, or make it finally effective, but that we proclaim it, that is, memorialize it.

Roman Catholics who take their church membership seriously and who in most cases have had it drilled into them from infancy that in the mass a daily sacrifice is offered for them, find it hard to leave the Roman Church precisely because in the Protestant church they find no mass, and they fear that without the mass they will lose their salvation. A devout Roman Catholic regards this matter of salvation through the mass far more seriously than most Protestants realize. And the hierarchy has been quick to realize that its main hold on the minds and hearts of the people through the centuries has been the mass, which is a visible re-enactment, by the use of symbols, of the suffering and death of Christ. Only when one begins to read the Bible thoughtfully and prayerfully does he discover that the only sacrifice necessary for his salvation was made for him by Christ on Calvary, and that the mass cannot possibly be a continuing sacrifice. Once he sees this point it becomes easy for him to accept the other doctrines of the Protestant faith.

The obligation that rests on a Roman Catholic to attend mass is a far different thing from the freedom that Protestants enjoy in the matter of church attendance. The Baltimore Catechism says:

"It is a mortal sin not to hear Mass on a Sunday or a holyday of obligation, unless we are excused for a serious reason. They also commit mortal sin who, having others under their charge, hinder them from hearing Mass without a sufficient reason" (Answer, 390).

The Roman Catholic, according to this authoritative standard, is obliged to attend mass every Sunday, and in the United States there are six special holydays. The mass is the most important ceremony of the Roman Church, the central and supreme act of worship. Everything else hinges on this. It becomes, therefore, the rule of discipline for all Roman Catholics, a mighty instrument in the hands of the clergy for the supervision of the laity.

Judged by outward appearances, Roman Catholics are quite faithful in attending Sunday mass, although on the acknowledgment of some there is nothing in the performance of a pleasing nature. But the Romanist, believing in the efficacy of good works, looks upon church attendance as a means of gaining merit for himself in the other world and as an offset to the evil charged against him. Attendance at mass gives him a sense of having fulfilled his duty. He has met the requirement. Regardless of how wicked a person he may be, if he continues to acknowledge the authority of the church by regular attendance at mass and by going to confession as required at least once a year, he remains a member "in good standing"—witness, for instance, the large number of gangsters and crooked politicians in the big cities who have maintained their standing in this church while continuing uninterruptedly their evil practices.

With the sagacity characteristic of her long career, the Roman Church takes advantage of that weakness in human nature which seeks some visible and outward object of worship. In the consecrated "host" she presents to her people a god whom they can see and feel. And it is generally accepted that Romanists, having been to mass, especially on Sunday, can do about as they please the remainder of the day. Rome is more concerned about the observance of a ceremony and the mark of allegiance which it implies than she is about holy living or about keeping a day holy to the Lord.

Another feature of the mass is that it is conducted in Latin, a language not spoken by the people in the Medieval church nor understood by people today unless they use a translation. Latin has been a dead language for centuries. Paul said: "Howbeit in the church, I had rather speak five words with my understanding, that I might instruct others also, than ten thousand words in a tongue" (I Cor. 14:19). In response to the criticism that at mass the worshipper is not a participant, not able to understand what is said, but merely an observer, the Roman Church in some places conducts the services in the vernacular, or makes translations available so that the people can participate intelligently, at least to the extent of knowing what is said. But such is not the general practice. In fact the Council of Trent directed one of its anathemas against those who say "that the mass ought to be celebrated in the vulgar tongue only." But the prayers of the Jews in Old Testament times were always offered in the Hebrew vernacular; and we read that the members of the early church, when they met for worship, "lifted up their voices to God with one accord" (Acts 4:24). Yet, as C. Stanley Lowell has appropriately observed: "It is not essential (in the mass) that they understand. Ideas are not integral to the mass, may even defeat its purpose. The objective here is to produce through the medium of the miracle allegedly performed by the priest an emotional ecstasy in which thoughts or ideas become superfluous" (Article, *Protestant and Papal Infallibility*).

7. THE MASS AND MONEY

One very prominent feature of the mass as conducted in the Roman Church is the financial support which it brings in. It is by all odds the largest income producing ceremony in the church. An elaborate system has been worked out. In the United States low mass, for the benefit of a soul in purgatory, read by the priest in a low tone of voice and without music, costs a minimum of one dollar. The high mass, on Sundays and holydays, sung by the priest in a loud voice, with music and choir, costs a minimum of ten dollars. The usual price for high mass is twenty-five to thirty-five dollars. The high requiem mass (at funerals), and the high nuptual mass (at weddings), may cost much more, even hundreds of dollars, depending on the number and rank of the priests taking part, the display of flowers, the music, candles, etc. Prices vary in the different dioceses and according to the ability of the parishioners to pay. No masses are said without money. The Irish have a saying: *High* money, *high* mass; *low* money, *low* mass; *no* money, *no* mass.

In regard to the various kinds of masses, there are: (1) Votive masses, made for various purposes, such as relief of one suffering in purgatory, recovery from sickness, success in a business venture, a safe journey, protection against storms, floods, drouths, etc; (2) Requiem or funeral masses, in behalf of the dead; (3) Nuptual masses, at marriages; and (4) Pontifical masses, conducted by a bishop or other dignitary. Each of these is available in high or low mass, and at various prices.

On Purgatory Day, November 2 of each year, three masses are said, two for the souls in purgatory and one for the "intentions" of the pope—which "intentions," we may assume, are directed for the good of the offerer. Every member of the church is urged to attend on that day. The priest of a church of 500 members may reasonably expect to take in from $500 to $5000 on that day.

The most popular mass is that to alleviate or terminate the suffering of souls in purgatory. The more masses said for an agonizing soul the better. Sometimes ads are placed in church papers in which multiple or repeated masses are offered for a price. Purgatorial societies and mass leagues offer blanket masses recited for beneficiaries *en masse,* in which anyone who sends, say, $10, can secure for a departed soul a certain number of high masses celebrated daily for a month, or longer. The present writer, who lives in Missouri, has for the past two Christmases received solicitations by mail from a priest and church in Maryland for a thousand masses, euphemistically called "spiritual bouquets," for the apparently reasonable price of $10.00. The need for such large numbers of masses, continued over long periods of time, surely casts doubt on the claim that the mass is of such high value in matters of salvation.

One consequence of this system is that the poor are left to burn in purgatory longer, while the rich can have more and higher grade masses said and so escape more quickly. People with property are sometimes urged to leave thousands of dollars to provide for prayers and masses to be said perpetually for their souls. According to the teaching of the Church of Rome the great majority of those dying within the pale of the church go to purgatory where they remain in a state of suffering with no known termination date before the day of judgment. Those outside the Roman Church are, for the most part, said to be hopelessly lost and therefore beyond help.

One of the worst features about the mass system is that the priest can never give assurance that the soul for which he has said mass is out of purgatory. He admittedly has no criterion by which that can be known. Hence the offerings may be continued for years—as long as the deluded Romanist is willing to continue paying. Says Stephen L. Testa:

> "It would not pay the priest to say that the soul for which he prayed is already out of purgatory and gone to heaven and needs no further masses. It would cut off a rich source of income. Like many unscrupulous physicians who would rather prolong the illness of a wealthy patient, so he could continue to need his treatments—a priest would never tell a bereaved mother that her daughter is 'with Jesus' in heaven and needs no more requiem masses. A Protestant minister would give that comforting assurance from the Word of God, but never a Catholic priest!" (*The Truth About Catholics, Protestants and Jews,* p. 13).

Dr. Zacchello says:

> "The only 'sacrifice' in the Roman Catholic mass is that of the money of the poor given to the priest to pay for the mysterious ceremonies he

performs, in the belief that he will relieve the suffering of their beloved ones in the fires of purgatory" (*Secrets of Romanism*, p. 82).

And L. J. King points out that,

"Death doesn't end all with the Roman Church. A member cannot avoid his church dues by dying. His estate or friends have to pay on and on. Even the tax collector lets up on a dead man, but the Roman Church never. It retains its grip on its dupes long after their bodies are reduced to ashes. The priestly threat that the soul is suffering in the 'devouring flames' of purgatory and will remain there for a long, long time, will bring the last dollar from the sorrowing mother, whose only son or daughter is detained in that fiery prison."

Those who contribute money for masses fail to appreciate the fact that the gifts of God *cannot be bought with any amount of money.* That was precisely the sin of Simon the sorcerer, who attempted to buy the power of God with money. But he received Peter's stern rebuke: "Thy money perish with thee, because thou hast sought to obtain the gift of God with money" (Acts 8:20). The term "simony" has entered the dictionary, meaning "to make a profit out of sacred things," "the sin of buying or selling ecclesiastical benefices," etc.

8. HISTORICAL DEVELOPMENT OF THE DOCTRINE

In view of the prominent place given the mass in the present day Roman Church, it is of particular interest to find that it was unknown in the early church, that it was first proposed by a Benedictine monk, Radbertus, in the ninth century, and that it did not become an official part of Romanist doctrine until so pronounced by the Lateran Council of 1215 under the direction of pope Innocent III. It was reaffirmed by the Council of Trent, in 1545. Transubstantiation is not mentioned in the Apostles' Creed, or in the Nicene or Athanasian creeds. Its first creedal mention is in that of pope Pius IV, in the year 1564.

Only since the year 1415, by decree of the Council of Constance, has the Roman Church refused to give the cup to the laity. On various occasions in the earlier history of the church popes have condemned as a sacrilege the serving of bread only in the holy communion. The decree that the bread only should be given to the laity was enacted on June 15, 1415, at a time when the Roman Church was without a head. For this same council had deposed pope John XXIII, on May 29, 1415, for crimes against the church and the state; and his successor, Martin V, was not elected until November 11, 1417.

The decree denying the cup to the laity contradicted Roman Canon Law of the preceding centuries. Pope Leo I, called the Great (440-

461), said in his condemnation of the Manichaeans: "They receive Christ's body with unworthy mouth, and entirely refuse to take the blood of our redemption; therefore we give notice to you, holy brethren, that men of this kind, whose sacrilegious deceit has been detected, are to be expelled with priestly authority from the fellowship of the saints."

Pope Gelasius I (492-496), in a letter addressed to some bishops, said: "We have ascertained that certain persons having received a portion of the sacred body alone abstain from partaking of the chalice of the sacred blood. Let such persons . . . either receive the sacrament in its entirety, or be repelled from the entire sacrament, because a division of one and the same mystery cannot take place without great sacrilege." The decree of the Council of Clermont, presided over by pope Urban II, in 1095, and pope Pascal II in 1118, also condemned the practice of giving the bread only in the sacrament. How can the Church of Rome claim to be catholic, apostolic, and unchanging when a council without a pope has deliberately overthrown the teaching of four popes concerning the matter of holy communion?

We can only conclude that the mass is a medieval superstition, designed to throw a veil of mystery over the sacrament of the Lord's Supper and to impress ignorant people. From a simple memorial feast it became a miraculous re-enactment of the sacrifice on Calvary, through which Christ was constantly dying for His people. A similar effect was designed in the use of the Latin language in the liturgy—for which it certainly cannot be said that it was intended to make the Lord's Supper more intelligible to the people, for practically none of them could understand Latin. The purpose of each of those innovations was to exalt the hierarchy, to clothe it with an air of mystery, and, particularly as regards the mass, to make the priest appear to have supernatural powers.

9. SEVEN SACRAMENTS

What is a sacrament? To this question the Shorter Catechism of the Westminster Standards answers:

"A sacrament is a holy ordinance instituted by Christ; wherein by sensible signs, Christ and the benefits of the new covenant are represented, sealed, and applied to believers" (Answer, 92).

According to the New Testament, and according to the teaching of the Protestant churches, two sacraments, and only two, were instituted by Christ. These are baptism and the Lord's Supper. In the upper room during the last night with His disciples Jesus instituted the Lord's Supper when He said: "This do in remembrance of me" (Luke 22:19). Baptism was practiced from the time of John the Baptist, and after His resurrection Christ specifically instituted it as a sacrament when He said: "Go ye therefore, and make disciples of all the nations, baptizing them into the name of the Father and of the Son and of the Holy Spirit. . . ." (Matt. 28:19).

To these two sacraments Rome has added five more, so that she now lists them as: (1) baptism, (2) confirmation, (3) eucharist (mass), (4) penance, (5) extreme unction, (6) marriage, and (7) orders (ordination of priests and consecration of nuns).

Rome holds that in the ordinary course of life five of these, baptism, confirmation, mass, penance, and extreme unction are indispensable to salvation, while marriage and orders are optional. But no church leaders nor any church council has the right to appoint sacraments. The church is Christ's church, and only He, as its Head, has that right. Furthermore, Rome has altered the form of the eucharist, making it a sacrifice as well as a sacrament.

Rome can give no proof for the additonal five sacraments, except that tradition holds them to be such. The number seven was arrived at only after centuries of drifting about. The early church fathers sometimes used the word in a broad sense, and spoke of the sacrament of prayer, the sacrament of the Scriptures, the sacrament of the Christian religion, the sacrament of weeping, etc., applying the term to various things that were regarded as in some way sacred or as designed to bring one closer to God, although it is evident from their writings that, strictly speaking, they recognized only two real sacraments. Peter Lombard (1100-1164), who published the famous book of "Sentences" from the writings of Augustine and other church leaders, which was regarded as a standard book on Theology until the time of the Reformation, was the first to define the number as seven. It is important to notice that no author for more than a thousand years after Christ taught that there were seven sacraments. It was not until the Council of Florence, in the year 1439, that the seven sacraments were formally decreed. Later the Council of Trent declared: "If any one saith that the sacraments of the New Law were not instituted by Jesus Christ, our Lord; or that they are more, or less, than seven, to wit, baptism, confirmation, the eucharist, penance, extreme unction, orders, and matrimony; or even that any one of these seven is not truly and properly a sacrament, let him be anathema."

What was the purpose of the Church of Rome in appointing seven

1. voluntary punishment for wrongdoing (to show repentance)
2. admit a person to full membership
3. anointing

sacraments? Probably in order that it might have complete control over the lives of its people from the cradle to the grave. This sacramental system is designed to give the priest control at the most important events of human life. From baptism as soon as possible after birth to the shadow of approaching death the laity is kept dependent on and under the control of the priests.

That the five sacraments added by the Church of Rome are spurious should be clear beyond doubt. Confirmation, penance, and extreme unction are not even mentioned in Scripture, and are therefore completely without authority. We shall discuss the seven in order.

1. *Baptism.* Rome has perverted the meaning of baptism so that instead of accepting it as a symbolical ordinance and an outward sign through which Christ and the benefits of the new covenant are represented and conveyed to the believer and received by faith, it is represented as working in a magical way to produce baptismal regeneration and securing automatically the forgiveness of all past sins, and as absolutely necessary to salvation. Rome teaches that it is not possible even for unconscious infants to be saved so as to enjoy the delights of heaven unless they are baptized. To that end they have even invented a means of prenatal baptism. In the words of the Trent Cathechism: "Infants, unless regenerated unto God through the grace of baptism, whether their parents be Christian or infidel, are born to eternal misery and perdition." But what a horrible doctrine that was! And what a contrast with the generally accepted Protestant doctrine that all those dying in infancy, whether baptized or unbaptized, are saved!

The Romish doctrine was so horrible and so unacceptable to the laity that it was found necessary to invent a third realm, the *Limbus Infantum,* to which unbaptized infants are sent, in which they are excluded from heaven but in which they suffer no positive pain. The ecumenical councils of Lyons and Florence and the canons of the Council of Trent declare positively that unbaptized infants are confined to this realm. The primary purpose of the Church of Rome in excluding unbaptized infants from heaven is to force parents to commit their children to her as soon as possible. The long range design is to bring all people into subjection to her, to put her stamp of ownership on every person possible. And the pressure put on Roman Catholic parents to see to it that their children are baptized early is almost unbelievable—a commitment which once she receives she never relinquishes.

2. *Confirmation.* In the so-called sacrament of confirmation the bishop lays his hands on the head of a person who previously has been baptized, for the purpose of conveying to him the Holy Spirit. But no

apostle or minister in the apostolic church performed that rite, and no man on earth has the Holy Spirit at his command. Roman theologians are uncertain as to the time when this so-called sacrament was instituted. The ritual leads confirmants to think they have received the Holy Spirit, whereas all they have received is the word and ritual of fallible priests. Confirmation is also practiced in the Protestant Episcopal Church, but they regard it only as a church ordinance, not as an institution established by Christ.

3. *Eucharist* (the mass), discussed throughout this chapter.

4. *Penance.* What is penance? An authorized catechism says:

"Penance is a sacrament in which the sins committed after baptism are forgiven by means of the absolution of the priest. . . . The priest gives a penance after confession that we may satisfy God for the temporal punishment due to our sins. We must accept the penance which the priest gives to us."

The Word of God teaches that the sinner must truly repent from the heart for his sin. Otherwise there can be no forgiveness. But the Church of Rome to a considerable degree substitutes penance for Gospel repentance. Penance consists of outward acts, such as repeating certain prayers many times, e.g., the Hail Mary or the rosary, self-inflicted punishments, fastings, pilgrimages, etc. Penance represents a false hope, for it relates only to outward acts. True repentance involves genuine sorrow for sin, it is directed toward God, and the person voluntarily shows by his outward acts and conduct that he has forsaken his sin. Rome cannot point to any event in the Bible in which penance was instituted.

5. *Extreme Unction.* Extreme unction is described as "the anointing by the priest of those in danger of death by sickness, with holy oil, accompanied with a special prayer. . . . It is called Extreme because administered to sick persons when thought to be near the close of life." In this ritual the priest anoints the eyes, ears, nose, hands, and feet of the dying person with "holy oil," as he pronounces an accompanying Latin prayer formula which offsets the sin committed by those members of the body. But no matter how good the priest or his prayer, he still cannot assure the dying person of heaven. The best he can do is to get him into purgatory, there to suffer the pains of fire. From that point his loved ones are supposed to purchase numberless masses to secure his early release. But how different that is from the Protestant assurance that all true believers at death pass into the immediate presence of Christ and into the joys of heaven! Christ said: "Verily, verily I say

unto you, He that heareth my word, and believeth him that sent me, *hath eternal life,* and *cometh not into judgment,* but hath passed out of death into life" (John 5:24). Christ gives liberty; the priest imposes bondage.

This sacrament in its present form was not introduced into the church until the twelfth century. And again the Roman theologians are uncertain as to the time of its institution. No instances of its practice are recorded in Scripture. Those persons anointed with oil by the apostles were not in danger of death. Extreme unction is intended only for those who are expected to die, not for those who are expected to recover, and it is intended as a preparation for the next life. The case recorded in James 5:14-15 cannot be claimed, for the purpose there was to restore the sick one to health.

6. *Orders.* The ordination of church officials was appointed by Christ, but not the specific orders adopted by the Church of Rome—priests, bishops, archbishops, cardinals, and popes. Furthermore, no sacramental sign was appointed to accompany the appointment of church officials.

7. *Matrimony.* Matrimony, too, is a divine ordinance, but it was given no outwardly prescribed sign. It was in fact instituted thousands of years earlier, even before the fall, and therefore is not an institution of the new covenant. The Church of Rome admits her uncertainty about the time of its appointment as a sacrament.

Rome's error in making marriage a sacrament came about because of a mistranslation in the Vulgate, Jerome's Latin translation of the Bible, which the Council of Trent made the official inspired version for the Roman Church. The passage in question is Ephesians 5:31-32, which correctly translated reads: "For this cause shall a man leave his father and mother, and shall cleave to his wife: and the two shall become one flesh. This mystery is great. . . ." But the Vulgate translated: "This is a great sacrament. . . ." Happily that error has been corrected in the new Confraternity Version, so that it reads: "This is a great mystery. . . ." But even so, Rome continues to teach that marriage is a sacrament. But cardinal Cajetan, Luther's opponent at Augsburg, made the frank admission: "You have not from this place, O prudent reader— from Paul—that marriage was a sacrament; for he does not say that it was a great sacrament, but a great mystery."

Furthermore, for six or seven centuries after the establishment of the Christian church the laity made no acknowledgment of any claim that the clergy alone could perform marriages, and they exercised the right of divorce on Scriptural grounds. It was through the influence of strong popes, such as Hildebrand, who, wishing to bring the laity under the more complete control of the clergy, at last secured for the church complete control over marriage. Such was the situation during the Middle Ages. As a "sacrament" the new type marriage could be performed only by a priest and was indissoluble. The low state of morals in countries where the Roman Church has been able to enforce its rule shows the result of that false doctrine. A fee, of course, has always been charged for the marriage ceremony. And where the fee has been excessive, as in some Latin American countries, the result has been an abnormally large proportion of common law marriages, in some areas as high as 70 percent. Had the Roman clergy been truly Christian it would have modified its claims and practices when the practical results of those claims and practices became evident, and would have sought first of all to safeguard the honor of the church and the family. But instead it has held doggedly to its privileged position, refusing to give up anything.

In regard to the multiplying of sacraments, the words which God spoke to Moses regarding the laws of the Old Testament are particularly appropriate: "Ye shall not add unto the word which I command you, neither shall ye diminish from it, that ye may keep the commandments of Jehovah your God which I command you" (Deut. 4:2).

The Church of Rome embodies further serious error in its doctrine of the sacraments in that it teaches that they confer divine grace automatically and mechanically, by their outward action, as fire burns by its heat, or as medicine cures by its chemical properties. But the Word of God teaches just the opposite. The blessing is not inherent in the sacrament as such, nor in him who administers it, but is bestowed directly by the Holy Spirit, and it is received by the one who exercises true faith—"Without faith it is impossible to be well-pleasing unto him; for he that cometh to God must believe that he is, and that he is a rewarder of them that seek after him" (Heb. 11:6). A sacrament is an outward visible sign of an inward invisible grace, through which the blessings of grace are conferred when appropriated by faith. As the Holy Spirit does not dwell in the pages of the Bible, yet warms the heart and enlightens the mind as we read, so grace does not reside intrinsically in the sacrament, but comes to the believer who receives it by faith.

10. CONCLUSION

In this chapter it has been our purpose to show that there is no transubstantiation in the mass and therefore no physical presence of Christ in the bread and wine; that there is no true sacrifice in the mass; and that the eucharist is instead primarily a means of spiritual blessing and a commemorative feast through which we are reminded of our Lord and what He has done for our salvation. We assert unqualifiedly that the mass as practiced in the Roman Catholic Church is a fraud and a deception—for the simple reason that it is the selling of non-existent values. The sale of masses to gullible people for various purposes has transformed the ministers of the Roman Church into sacrificing priests, and has been an effective means by which under false pretenses huge sums of money have been extracted from the people.

In all the pagan religions of the world it would be hard to find an invention more false and ridiculous than that of the mass. To assert that an egg is an elephant, or that black is white, would be no more absurd or childish than to assert that the bread and wine, which retain the properties of bread and wine, are actually and totally the body and blood, the deity and humanity, of Christ.

The Roman doctrine of the sacraments constitutes the most elaborate system of magic and ritual that any civilized religion ever invented, and from first to last it is designed to enhance the power and prestige of the clergy. In its fundamental ideas it is as alien to the whole spirit of Christianity and as out of harmony with modern times as the Medieval science of astrology is out of harmony with astronomy, or alchemy with chemistry. Yet these are the beliefs to which the Roman Catholic people give allegiance, and to which they hope some day to convert the United States and the world. For these beliefs they are willing to overlook all the horrors of the Middle Ages and all the corruption of the popes and the papacy of that period—in so far as they know anything at all about the history of that period.

The fact that the elaborate ritual of the mass is totally unknown to Scripture, and that it is highly dishonoring to Christ in that it makes His work on the cross largely ineffective until it is supplemented by the work of the priest, does not impress the average Roman Catholic layman seriously, for the simple reason that he has practically no knowledge at all of what the Bible teaches concerning these things.

We ask in all seriousness: What is there in the Roman service of the mass that compares with the beauty and simplicity of the Lord's supper as observed in Protestant churches? In the latter you have no pompous hierarchy separated from the laity and communing with themselves, partaking of the bread and wine while seated at the altar on a higher level and with their backs to the congregation, while the laity, like children, kneel before the clergy with closed eyes and open mouths and receive only the wafer which is dropped into their mouths. In the Protestant churches the minister comes from the pulpit and sits at the communion table on the same level with the people. Minister and people are a company of Christian brethren partaking together of the Lord's Supper as a simple memorial feast, each one eating of the bread and each one drinking of the cup as the rite was originally instituted. In the light of New Testament revelation surely the latter is much to be preferred.

IX. THE CONFESSIONAL

*1. The Nature of the Confessional. 2. Mortal
and Venial Sins. 3. The Priests Cannot Forgive
Sins. 4. Scripture Teaching Regarding Confession. 5. Alleged Roman Catholic Scripture
Proof. 6. Abuses of the Confessional.*

1. THE NATURE OF THE CONFESSIONAL

The Baltimore Catechism defines confession as follows:

"Confession is the telling of our sins to an authorized priest for the purpose of obtaining forgiveness."

It adds:

"An authorized priest is one who has not only the power to forgive sins by reason of his ordination to the priesthood, but also the power of jurisdiction over the persons who come to him. He has this jurisdiction ordinarily from his bishop, or by reason of his office" (p. 315).

The important words here are "authorized priest." And to be genuine a confession must be heard, judged, and followed by obedience to the authorized priest as he assigns a penance, such as good works, prayers, fastings, abstenance from certain pleasures, etc. A penance may be defined as a punishment undergone in token of repentance for sin, as assigned by the priest—usually a very light penalty.

The New York Catechism says:

"I must tell my sins to the priest so that he will give me absolution. I shall go to confession often . . . to fulfill a condition for gaining certain indulgences. . . . A person who knowingly keeps back a mortal sin in confession commits a dreadful sacrilege, and he must repeat his confession. . . . The sacrament of penance remits the mortal sins and their eternal punishment; it revives the merits annulled by the mortal sins, and gives a special grace to avoid sin in the future."

The French Catechism goes so far as to say:

196

"One must receive absolution in feelings of total humility, considering the confessor as Jesus Christ Himself whose place he takes."

The priests can scarcely make a greater demand than that! Canon Law 888 says: "The priest has to remember that in hearing confession he is a judge." Canon Law 870 says: "In the confessional the minister has the power to forgive all crimes committed after baptism." And a book, *Instructions for Non-Catholics,* primarily for use by those who are joining the Roman Catholic Church, says:

"The priest does not have to ask God to forgive your sins. The priest himself has the power to do so in Christ's name. Your sins are forgiven by the priest the same as if you knelt before Jesus Christ and told them to Christ Himself" (p. 93).

Thus Roman Catholics are required to confess all their mortal sins to a priest who sits as a judge and who claims to have the power to forgive sins in the name of God. The priest forgives the guilt of mortal sins, which saves the penitent from going to hell; but he cannot remit the penalty due for those sins and so the penitent must atone for them by the performance of good works which he prescribes. Priests, too, including the bishops, cardinals, and even the pope, receive forgiveness in this same manner, confessing their sins to other priests.

In the language of Romanism a "penitent" is one who confesses to a priest, not necessarily one who is repenting of sin, although that is implied; and the "confessor" is the priest, not the one who confesses.

The confessional "box" found in all Roman Catholic churches, is divided into two compartments. The priest enters one, and the penitent the other. In the wooden partition between them is a metal gauze about two feet square. The penitent kneels, and through the gauze whispers or speaks in a low voice his or her sins. The confession is secret, and is called "auricular," because spoken into the ear of the priest. It supposedly is a detailed confession of all the mortal sins committed since the last confession.

The penitent may be, and usually is, interrogated by the priest, so that he or she may make a full and proper confession. That, of course, gives the priest the opportunity to find out practically anything and everything that he may want to know about the person or about community affairs. Stress is placed on the fact that any sin not confessed is not forgiven, and that the omission of even one sin may invalidate the whole confession.

The form of confession is quite interesting. After kneeling before the priest and asking and receiving his blessing, the penitent must repeat the first part of the Confiteor:

"I confess to the Almighty God, to the blessed Virgin Mary, to blessed Michael the Archangel, to blessed John the Baptist, to the holy apostles Peter and Paul, to all the saints, and to you, father, that I have sinned exceedingly, in thought, word, and deed, through my fault, through my fault, through my most grievous fault" (latter, repeated three times).

The penitent must then confess all his mortal sins, concealing nothing. Venial sins, in most instances, may be omitted, since they are comparatively mild and may be expiated by other means.

We notice concerning this form of confession that: (1) It places Mary, Michael, John the Baptist, Peter, Paul, the Roman saints, and the officiating priest on a level with God Almighty. (2) It addresses the confession of sin to all of them, as if the sin was committed equally against all of them, and as if they were holy beings with power to forgive. And (3) it makes no mention whatever of Christ, through whom alone pardon is to be had, or of the Holy Spirit, by whom alone the soul can be cleansed. And there sits the priest, usurping the place of God and forgiving sins! Notice how the penitent is constantly put in a subordinate role and at the mercy of the priest.

Every loyal Roman Catholic is required under pain of mortal sin to go to confession at least once a year. The Fourth Lateran Council, 1215, decreed that every adult, man or woman, should confess all his or her sins to a priest at least once a year. This decree was ratified by the Council of Trent, 1546, and remains in force today. More frequent confession is advised, particularly if public or heinous sins have been committed. This decree has been elaborated and extended by various church laws so that considerable pressure rests on the average church member to go to confession more often, the preferable time period frequently being set at once a month.

Confession is facilitated through "societies," or "confraternities," which under the guidance of the priest urge their members to confess at least once a month. Young women may belong to an organization known as "Children of Mary." Boys and young men have similar organizations, most of which have a provision for confession at least once a month. Membership in such organizations supposedly is voluntary, but the social pressures may be such that one who fails to join is made to feel practically ostracized. Hence "voluntary" confessions are fairly frequent and fairly easy to secure. Ordinarily a child is required to begin going to confession at the age of seven, as though he comes to accountability at that age.

Historical development. We search in vain in the Bible for any word supporting the doctrine of auricular confession. It is equally impossible to find any authorization or general practice of it during the first one thousand years of the Christian era. Not a word is found in the writings of the early church fathers about confessing sins to a priest or to anyone except God alone. Auricular confession is not mentioned in the writings of Augustine, Origen, Nestorius, Tertullian, Jerome, Chrysostom, or Athanasius—all of these and many others apparently lived and died without ever thinking of going to confession. Those writers give many rules concerning the practice and duties of Christian living; but they never say a word about going to confession. Never were penitents forced to sit alone with a priest and reveal to him the secret history of all their evil thoughts, desires, and human frailties. No one other than God was thought to be worthy to hear confessions and to grant forgiveness. There were, to be sure, public confessions before local church groups, in order that offenders might be restored to fellowship. Such practice is found even in some Protestant groups of our own day. But such confessions were open, general, and voluntary, and were as different from auricular confession as light is from darkness.

But gradually as the church gained power the practice of seeking spiritual counsel and advice from the priest was turned into the confessional. Confession was first introduced into the church on a voluntary basis in the fifth century, by the authority of Leo the Great. But it was not until the Fourth Lateran Council, in 1215, under pope Innocent III, that private auricular confession was made compulsory and all Roman Catholic people were required to confess and to seek absolution from a priest at least once a year. At that council the twin doctrines of auricular confession and transubstantiation were decreed. It will be recalled that that was the period of the greatest extension of priestly and papal power over the people. It was, therefore, during the darkest days of the state and of the church that this masterpiece of deception was brought forth.

2. MORTAL AND VENIAL SINS

The Roman Church divides all sin into two classes, making an important and elaborate distinction between so-called "mortal" and "venial" sins. Mortal sin is described as "any great offense against the law of God," and is so called because it is deadly, killing the soul and subjecting it to eternal punishment. Even after a penitent has received pardon a large but unknown amount of punishment remains to be expiated in purgatory.

Venial sins, on the other hand, are "small and pardonable offenses against God, or our neighbor." Technically, venial sins need not be confessed since they are comparatively light and can be expiated by good works, prayers, extreme unction, purgatory, etc. But the priests are not to be outdone by this technicality. The terms are quite elastic, and permit considerable leeway on the part of those who want to probe more deeply into the affairs of the penitent. It is generally advised that it is safer to confess supposed venial sins also, since the priest alone is able to judge accurately which are mortal and which are venial. The Baltimore Catechism (written, of course, by priests) says: "When we have committed no mortal sins since our last confession, we should confess our venial sins or some sin told in a previous confession for which we are again sorry, in order that the priest may give us absolution" (p. 329). What chance has a poor sinner against such a system as that?

There is no agreement among the priests as to which sins are mortal and which are venial. But they all proceed on the assumption that such a distinction does exist. What is venial according to one may be mortal according to another. If the pope were infallible in matters of faith and practice, as claimed by the Roman Church, he should be able to settle this important matter by accurately cataloging those sins which are mortal as distinguished from those which are venial. But such a list no pope has ever been able to produce. Instead what they have is an elaborate system of compromise which is designed to promote the authority of the church and to give a considerable amount of leeway to the priest as to what seems expedient in individual cases.

Among mortal sins, however, are those committed in breaking the ten commandments, together with the so-called "seven deadly sins": pride, covetousness, lechery (lust, lewdness), anger, gluttony, envy, and sloth. Included are practically all sexual offenses, whether in word, thought, or deed, and a long list of transgressions down to attending a Protestant church, reading a Protestant Bible, eating meat on Friday, or "missing mass on Sunday morning" without a good excuse (which means that considerably more than half of the claimed Roman Catholic membership throughout the world is constantly in mortal sin). Sometimes violations of the rules of the church are treated as mortal sins, while transgressions of the commandments of God are treated as venial sins. All mortal sins must be confessed to the priest in detail or they cannot be forgiven. The theory is that the priest must have all the facts in order to know how to deal with the case and what penance to assign. The real reason, of course, is to place the penitent more fully in the hands of the priest.

But the Bible makes no such distinction between mortal and venial sins. There is in fact no such thing as venial sin. All sin is mortal. It is true that some sins are worse than others. But it is also true that all sins, if not forgiven, bring death to the soul, with greater or lesser punishment as they may deserve. The Bible simply says: "The wages of sin is death" (Rom. 6:23)—and there Paul was not speaking of any particular kind of sin, but of all sin. Ezekiel says: "The soul that sinneth, it shall die" (18.4). When James said, "For whosoever shall keep the whole law, and yet stumble in one point, he is become guilty of all" (2:10), he meant, not that the person who commits one sin is guilty of all other kinds of sin, but that even one sin unrepented of shuts a person out of heaven and subjects him to punishment, just as surely as one puncture of the eyeball subjects a person to blindness, or as one misstep by the mountain climber plunges him to destruction in the canyon below. In the light of these statements, the distinction between mortal and venial sins is shown to be arbitrary and absurd.

The Westminster Shorter Catechism (Presbyterian), in answer to the question, "What is sin?" says: "Sin is any lack of conformity unto, or transgression of, the law of God" (Question 14). And we are reminded that in the Garden of Eden eating the forbidden fruit appeared to be but a very trifling offense; yet the consequences were fatal, not only for Adam and Eve but for the entire human race.

Romanism presents a purely arbitrary classification of sins. The effect of that classification is in itself immoral. We know how quick corrupt human nature is to grasp at any excuse for sin, and how readily this distinction gives license for its commission. Furthermore, we may point out that a Roman Catholic who commits mortal sin shortly before his death, but who cannot find a priest to whom he can confess, by definition of his church, runs the risk of dying in mortal sin. It is so easy to commit mortal sin. As just stated, even failure to attend Sunday mass without a good excuse is a mortal sin.

Through the use of the confessional the priest has been able to pry into the conscience of each individual, so that no heretic might escape, and in the case of the faithful to gain entrance into the privacy of the domestic family circle. There is literally and in truth *no area* of life that is exempt from the scrutiny and supervision of the priest. "Knowledge is power," and that power can be wielded in many ways, to direct people along lines that will promote the church program, or for the personal benefit of the priest himself. It is perfectly evident that the priest to whom a person has confessed his thoughts, desires, and every sinful action just as it occurred, has placed that person largely under his control. For some that means little less than slavery. This is particularly true of women and girls who have even destroyed their self-respect in so surrendering themselves to the priest. The result is a sense of shame, worry, and of being at the mercy of the priest. Through the confessional Rome has been able to exercise an effective control not only over the family, but over political officials of every grade, teachers, doctors, lawyers, employers and employees, and indeed over all who submit to that discipline.

3. THE PRIESTS CANNOT FORGIVE SINS

The Scriptures teach that only God can forgive sins: "Who can forgive sins but one, even God?" (Mark 2:7); ". . . The Son of man hath authority on earth to forgive sins" (Matt. 9:6). It is because God is our Creator and Owner and Judge, and because it is His law that we have broken, that He can forgive sins. The Lord Jesus Christ has this power because He is God.

But the Church of Rome teaches that her priests also can forgive sins, and that "They pardon sins, not only as ambassadors of Jesus Christ, but as judges, and by way of jurisdiction" (Council of Trent, sess. 14,9; Bellarmine, *De Poenit,* 3,2). The Council of Trent declares further: "Whosoever shall affirm that the priest's sacramental absolution is not a judicial act, but only a ministry to pronounce and declare that the sins of the party confessing are forgiven, let him be anathema." And the priest, after hearing the confession, says to the penitent: "I absolve you from your sins, in the name of the Father, and of the Son, and of the Holy Ghost. Amen."

Thus the priest in the confessional claims not merely a declarative power through which the penitent's sins are pronounced forgiven, but a judicial power through which he assigns penances. Unlike the priests of the Old Testament who merely declared the leper cleansed from his leprosy, the Roman priest actually claims power as a minister of God to forgive sin. Though a mere human being, he exalts himself to a position as a necessary mediator between God and man, and insists that in his office as confessor he be considered as Christ Himself. Auricular confession therefore becomes a public act of idolatry in that the penitent bows down before a man, who is dependent on him for his living, and asks from him that which God alone can give. And on the part of the Roman Church it is the height of sinful pride and folly thus to put in the place of God a priest who himself is only a man and guilty of sin.

Even a priest who is in mortal sin still can forgive sin in the confessional. Bishop Fulton J. Sheen, after saying that "The Church asks that a priest who absolves a penitent be in the state of grace, a participant, himself, of the Divine Life," adds "This does not mean, however, that a priest in the state of mortal sin would not possess the power to forgive sins or that when exercised it would not be effective for the penitent" (*Peace of Soul*, p. 136; 1949; McGraw Hill Book Co., New York).

Dr. Zacchello tells of his experience in the confessional before conversion to Protestantism in these words:

"Where my doubts were really troubling me was inside the confessional box. People were coming to me, kneeling down in front of me, confessing their sins to me. And I, with a sign of the cross, was promising that I had the power to forgive their sins. I, a sinner, a man, was taking God's place, God's right, and that terrible voice was penetrating me saying, 'You are depriving God of His glory. If sinners want to obtain forgiveness of their sins they must go to God and not to you. It is God's law that they have broken, not yours. To God, therefore, they must make confession; and to God alone they must pray for forgiveness. No man can forgive sins, but Jesus can and does forgive sins.' "

In the United States the Roman hierarchy is much more reserved in its claims than it is in Roman Catholic countries, and the priests often say to uninformed people that they do not presume to forgive sins. But that is a deliberate falsehood, as is shown by the official decree of the Council of Trent, and by the formula of absolution which is, "I absolve thee. Go in peace." The Roman position is that through the power given to Peter, and received from him by apostolic succession, they have the power to forgive or to refuse to forgive sins. That was a power claimed by the priests of pagan Rome, and it was taken over by the priests of papal Rome. Many American Roman Catholics have been enlightened by their contacts with Protestantism to the extent that they refuse to believe such claims. But where Rome is unopposed the claims are asserted boldly.

In the Roman system the priest constantly comes between the sinner and God. In Father McGuire's edition of the New Catechism No. 1, with imprimatur by Cardinal Spellman, of New York, we read: "You must tell your sins to the priest to have them forgiven." And again, "Confession is telling your sins to the priest to obtain forgiveness." As the penitent confesses to the priest and does the penance assigned there is no direct contact with God, but only with the priest. A Roman Catholic does not pray to God spontaneously as to one who is a Friend, Comforter, Forgiver. To him God is exalted beyond the reach of ordinary mortals, and his contact is on a lower level, with the priest, who presents himself as God's representative. The result is that Roman Catholics never really settle the sin problem. The only solution they have is in their contact with the church: original sin is removed by baptism; and mortal and venial sins are confessed to the priest who absolves them in his own right. They may be punctual in prayer to God, but only to venerate and adore Him. The priest represents God in personal problems. Consequently, they have religion, but not the religion of the Bible. Martin Luther says that after becoming a priest, which he did primarily as a means of gaining assurance concerning his own salvation, he realized, as most priests eventually do, that forgiveness of sins in the Catholic confessional had no effect on him and that he was just the same after confession as before.

In this connection Dr. Paul Woolley, Professor of Church History in Westminster Theological Seminary, says:

"People today love authority. In a disordered and uncertain world that may blow up in their faces, they have a deep desire to listen to the man who knows or the church which knows. The Roman Catholic Church says that it knows. But the substitution of the authority of the Roman Church for the authority of God is exceedingly dangerous. It results in such phenomena as the denial of the freedom of Protestant preaching in Spain and in Colombia, in the physical persecution of Protestants in various areas where Rome is dominant. This is not the exercise of the authority of God; it is the tyrannous perversion of God's authority by sinful men. It is a denial of the New Testament teaching that the Gospel is to be preached by spiritual means, that violence cannot bring in the kingdom of God, that 'faith cometh by hearing and hearing by the word of God,' not by imposition from above.

"Catholicism is a refuge for the lazy thinker. The man who wants to be told the answers to everything, to be treated like a child, can find what he wants in the Roman Church. But God gave His Word to man to read, to study, to ponder, to apply. Only under the freedoms of modern Protestantism can this be done with a good conscience. These freedoms must be protected as of the vital core of our liberties. Rome claims the right not only to suppress free preaching but to deny civil liberties in general. Let us not barter away these freedoms" (*The Presbyterian Guardian,* Dec. 15, 1958).

The somber attitude of the confessional cannot be denied. The priest sits as judge of the eternal destiny of all who come before him. He may, at his own discretion, forgive or withhold forgiveness for every kind and number of sins. There are no witnesses to what is said. No record of the proceedings is kept. The penitent is merely given a promise that secrecy will be observed. For the devout, sincere Roman Catholic salvation depends upon his ability to call to mind while in the confessional all of his sins and to confess them. It is impressed upon him that only that which is confessed can be forgiven. The priest cannot forgive that which he does not know about. What spiritual agony that means for many a soul who fears he may have omitted some things that should have been told, and that he will have to make amends for them in purgatory! And even though he does his best he may, from one confession to another, fall into mortal sin and be lost.

On the other hand, no matter how serious the crime, whether murder, robbery, adultery, fraud, etc., no public jail sentence or fine is imposed, but instead only a few minutes of prayer, the saying of the rosary or of "Hail Marys," and a verbal promise of reform is imposed. This secret process of forgiveness and of hiding of crimes may be accomplished again and again as long as the sinner conforms to the church regulations. A consequence of easy absolution is that many take the moral law more lightly and sin more freely just because they know absolution is easy to obtain.

The Roman Church denies that anyone can have assurance of eternal life—such assurance, of course, would undermine the confessional itself, for the penitent must be made to feel his constant dependence upon the priest and the church. But how contrary is such teaching to the word of Christ: "Verily, verily I say unto you, He that heareth my word, and believeth him that sent me, *hath eternal life,* and cometh not into judgment, but hath passed out of death into life" (John 5:24). Here Christ clearly teaches that, (1) The believer now has eternal life, (2) He does not come into judgment, and (3) He has passed from death into life. All three of these blessings are given solely on the basis that one has heard and believed the promise of Christ. Not a single word is said about confession to a priest or about doing penance. And nowhere in the New Testament is there any record of forgiveness having been obtained from a priest.

We may well ask: If Roman priests have the apostolic power of binding and loosing, of granting or refusing absolution from sin, why do they not also possess the power to perform miracles which Christ conferred upon the apostles? Christ said that it was just as easy to say, "Arise, and walk," as to say, "Thy sins are forgiven" (Matt. 9:5). Why cannot Roman priests do the same? The fact is that all men are sinners, all have serious defects and faults, and none can exercise the powers of God. Those who play God are only acting foolishly.

4. SCRIPTURE TEACHING REGARDING CONFESSION

The Bible teaches that it is the privilege of every penitent sinner to confess his sins directly to God: "If we confess our sins, he is faithful and righteous to forgive us our sins, and to cleanse us from all unrighteousness" (I John 1:9). What did the Lord Jesus say when He spoke of the Pharisee and the publican? The publican had no priest; and he did not go to a confessional. All he did was to cry with bowed head, "God, be thou merciful to me a sinner." He went directly to God. And Jesus said that he went down to his house justified (Luke 18:9-14). Indeed, why should anyone confess his sins to a priest when the Scriptures declare so plainly: "There is one God, *one mediator* also between God and men, himself man, Christ Jesus" (I Tim. 2:5). And yet the priest presumes to say, "I absolve you," "I forgive your sins."

Confession of sins is commanded all through the Bible, but always it is confession to God, never to man. It is a striking fact that although Paul, Peter, and John dealt frequently with men and women in sin, both in their teaching and in their practice, they never permitted a sinner or a saint to confess to them. Paul wrote thirteen of the New Testament epistles, and in them he often speaks of the duties and practices of Christians. But never once does he mention auricular confession. Peter, John, and Jude wrote six epistles in which they have much to say about the matter of salvation. But not one of them ever mentions auricular confession. And certainly Christ never told anyone to go to a priest for forgiveness. Nowhere do the Scriptures tell us that God appointed a special class of men to hear confessions and to forgive sins.

If such an important tribunal as the confessional had been established, undoubtedly the apostles would have commented on it repeatedly. Had the power of forgiving sins been committed to the apostles, it would have been one of the most important parts of their office and one of the leading doctrines of Christianity. We cannot imagine that they would have been so remiss as never to have exercised that most important function, and nowhere even to have alluded to it. John, for instance, says: "If any man sin we have an Advocate with the Father, Jesus Christ the righteous" (I John 2:1). He does not say that we have a priestly tribunal to which we can go and having confessed our sins receive forgiveness. Everywhere throughout the Bible the remission of sins and the gaining of salvation is connected with faith in Christ. "He that believeth on the Son hath eternal life: but he that obeyeth not the Son shall not see life; but the wrath of God abideth on him" (John 3:36). "Being therefore justified by faith, we have peace with God through our Lord Jesus Christ," says Paul (Rom. 5:1). Everywhere the exhortation is, "Believe and be saved." Nowhere are we told to seek the absolution of a priest.

The statement of James, "Confess therefore your sins one to another, and pray one for another, that ye may be healed" (5:16), and that in Acts 19:18, "Many also of them that had believed came, confessing, and declaring their deeds," alleged by Roman Catholics to support their position, do not teach private confession to a priest, but are rather proof against it since they imply the duty of the priest to confess to the layman as well as for the layman to confess to the priest. These statements properly mean, "Confess your faults, your shortcomings, to your fellow Christians who have been injured by you." They mean that when one has wronged his neighbor he should acknowledge his fault and make restitution.

Public confession was practiced in the early church on occasions, as it now is in some Protestant churches when members wish to give a testimony of their lives. But secret auricular confession to a priest, with the priest privileged to draw out the individual and probe for details, to pronounce a judgment upon him and assign a penance, is an entirely different thing. The Bible does not require us to parade our sins before a priest or before the congregation, but only to confess to God. In any event, for one sinner to confess his sins to another sinner to obtain forgiveness is degrading and demoralizing, and beyond that it is dishonoring to God.

5. ALLEGED ROMAN CATHOLIC SCRIPTURE PROOF

In defense of the confessional the priests depend primarily on the two following Scripture references:

> "I will give thee the keys of the kingdom of heaven; and whatever thou shalt bind on earth shall be bound in heaven, and whatever thou shalt loose on earth shall be loosed in heaven" (Matt. 16:19).

> "He therefore said to them, 'Peace be to you! As the Father has sent me, I also send you.' When he had said this, he breathed upon them, and said to them, 'Receive the Holy Spirit; whose sins you shall forgive, they are forgiven them; and whose sins you shall retain, they are retained" (John 20:21-23; Confraternity Version).

In the chapter on Peter, and the section dealing with the "Keys," we have discussed the meaning of Matthew 16:19, and have pointed out that the power given to the apostles was symbolical and declarative, and that it related to the authority given to them to preach the Gospel which contains God's conditions for repentance and forgiveness. "Repentance and remission of sins" was to be "preached in his name unto all the nations" (Luke 24:47). "To him (Christ) bear all the prophets witness, that through his name every one that believeth on him shall receive remission of sins" (Acts 10:43). And again, "Be it known unto you therefore, brethren, that through this man is proclaimed unto you remission of sins: and by him every one that believeth is justified from all things" (Acts 13:38-39).

Christ often used figurative language, as when He said, "The scribes and Pharisees sit on Moses' seat: all things therefore whatsoever they bid you, these do and observe: but do not ye after their works; for they say, and do not" (Matt. 23:2-3); and, "Woe unto you, scribes and Pharisees, hypocrites! because ye shut the kingdom of heaven against men: for ye enter not in yourselves, neither suffer ye them that are entering in to enter" (Matt. 23:13).

The scribes and Pharisees were in possession of the law. In that sense they sat on Moses' seat. As the law was faithfully given to the people, or withheld from them, the way to heaven was opened before them, or closed to them. In the failure of the scribes and Pharisees to give the law to the people they were shutting the kingdom of heaven against men, not literally, but figuratively.

"The keys of the kingdom" was a symbolic expression for the Old Testament Scriptures which set forth the way of salvation. The Old Testament, of course, was the only Scripture they had at that time. It was the responsibility of the scribes and Pharisees, who were the custodians of the Scriptures to acquaint the people with that knowledge by making the Scripture truth available to them. But instead, they not only neglected that duty but actually veiled the Scriptures and perverted their meaning so that the people who wanted that knowledge were deprived of it. Similarly, in the Christian dispensation, the apostles were given "the keys of the kingdom," not a set of metallic keys, of course, and not that they could by a mere word admit certain individuals into the kingdom while excluding others, but that, in the words of Paul, they were "intrusted with the Gospel" (I Thess. 2:4), and so opened or closed the kingdom as they proclaimed the Word of Life or withheld it. In that sense every minister today, and indeed every Christian, who teaches the Word also possesses the "keys" and admits to, or excludes from, the kingdom. The key to the kingdom is *the Gospel of Christ*. Peter was given that key, and he used it to unlock the kingdom to those to whom he preached. We have that same key, and we must use it in the same way, by making known the message of salvation and so opening up to others the way into the kingdom of heaven.

The powers of binding or loosing, and of forgiving or retaining sins, were given to the apostles as proclaimers of the Word of God, not as priests. As we have shown elsewhere, there are no Christian "priests" in the New Testament dispensation. The apostles never claimed the power of forgiving sins by absolution as Roman priests do. Rather they preached the Gospel of salvation through Christ—which was a declarative power, by which they announced the gracious terms on which salvation was granted to sinful men.

As Dr. Woods has said:

> "These expressions indicate a *declarative* power only: the right to proclaim in Christ's name and with His authority, that all who truly repent of sin and trust in Him for pardon and salvation, shall surely be forgiven and saved. But it is Christ alone, and not the minister, who forgives. According to Scripture, the minister is only a herald to announce what the King will do, on condition of repentance and faith on the part of the sinner.
>
> "This was the teaching of the apostles, and of the early church before the papal party corrupted it; for Tertullian in the third century declared that all Christians have, like Peter, the power of the keys, to proclaim forgiveness and salvation through Christ. And this has always been the doctrine of the Reformed Church of all branches" (*Our Priceless Heritage*, p. 118).

That this is the true meaning of Matthew 16:19 and John 20:21-23 is clear from the practice and preaching of the apostles. They always directed sinners to Christ. Never once did any apostle say, "I absolve you," or, "Your sins are forgiven." Instead, we read that when Peter entered the home of the Roman centurion, Cornelius, and this man "fell down at his feet, and worshipped him," Peter "raised him up, saying, Stand up; I myself also am a man" (Acts 10:25-26). And when the people of Lystra attempted to confer divine honors upon Paul and Barnabas, these two Christian missionaries promptly stopped such procedure, saying, "We also are men of like passions with you" (Acts 14:15).

Language similar to that spoken to the Apostles was addressed to the prophet Jeremiah. We read: "And Jehovah said unto me, Behold, I have put my words in thy mouth: see, I have this day set thee over the nations and over the kingdoms, to pluck up and to break down and to destroy and to overthrow, to build and to plant" (1:9-10). But Jeremiah never literally plucked up, or broke down, or destroyed, or planted nations and kingdoms. His mission was to *declare to the nations* the *terms* on which God would build up or destroy, or reward or punish nations. His was *declarative*, not *executive*, power. Similarly, Peter and the other apostles were given authority to declare the terms on which God would save His people and forgive their sins.

It is perfectly obvious that the teaching of these verses regarding the forgiving or retaining of sins, and the binding or loosing, are not intended to contradict the clear teaching of the rest of the Bible on this subject, which states explicitly that only God has the power to forgive sin. If we read carefully Matthew's account, for instance, we find that the context deals with *disciplinary problems in a local church.* The immediately preceding verses, 15-17, read "And if thy brother sin against thee, go, show him his fault between thee and him alone: if he hear thee, thou hast gained thy brother. But if he hear thee not, take with thee one or two more, that at the word of two witnesses or three every word may be established. And if he refuse to hear them, tell it unto the church: and if he refuse to hear the church also, let him be unto thee as the Gentile and the publican." Then follows the statement: "Verily I say unto you, What things soever ye shall bind on earth shall be bound in heaven; and what things soever ye shall loose on earth shall be loosed in heaven."

Here we have a case in which a difference develops between two believers. This passage tells us how such a difference is to be settled. If our Christian brother has sinned, it is our duty first to go to him and tell him about it. If he hears us and mends his ways, well and good. But if he does not hear us, then we are to go back to him taking one or two Christian brothers with us. If that is unsuccessful, then we are to bring the matter before the local congregation. If he refuses to heed the admonitions of the church, i.e., the whole assembly of believers, then we are to treat him as a Gentile and a publican, as no longer a member of the congregation. In this manner disciplinary action is to be exercised, not secretly by a priest, but openly by the collective decision of the local church, the elders of course leading as they do in all other functions of the local church. If their efforts prove futile, then the "sin" of this member is to be "bound," that is, the offender is to be officially charged with it, pronounced guilty, and expelled from the membership. But if he is found innocent, he is to be "loosed" from the sin, that is, acquitted of the charge of which he was accused. In this sense, and in this sense only, not a priest, nor an elder, but the local congregation is to exercise discipline. And Christ has promised to honor such action in His church, so long as it is done in a Christian manner under the guidance of the Holy Spirit—what they bind on earth shall be bound in heaven, and what they loose on earth shall be loosed in heaven.

6. ABUSES OF THE CONFESSIONAL

If the confessional has no sanction in Scripture, how did it come to be established in the church? Let Dr. Woods answer:

"Because its establishment was greatly to the interest of the hierarchy. The confessional enormously increased the power of the pope and the clergy. The priests came to know the secrets of men from the emperor down to the humblest peasant, and all classes of society were thus placed in the power of their religious leaders, whom they did not dare to disobey or offend. Not only were the sins and scandals of each individual's life and that of families laid bare, but all the intrigues of State, the political schemes of the rulers of Europe, were in the possession of the confessor, who could use his knowledge for the advancement of the church, or to help a political party in which he was interested. What greater intellectual and moral bondage for human beings could be imagined, or what more dangerous power could be possessed, than that of the Roman confessional? History furnishes many impressive warnings; see Charles IX and the massacre of St. Bartholomew; or of Louis XIV and the cruel revocation of the Edict of Nantes, 1685" (*Our Priceless Heritage,* p. 129).

Listen again to the testimony of Lucien Vinet, who for years operated the confessional and who knows the Roman system well:

"A Roman Catholic, says his church, must, in order to obtain peace with God, declare all his sinful actions, omissions and his most secret thoughts and desires, specifying minutely the kinds of sins committed, the number of times and all the circumstances that might alter the gravity of a sin. A murderer is obliged to declare his crimes, a young girl her most intimate thoughts and desires. We have seen men tremble, women faint and children cry when the time to confess their sins to us had come. A priest cannot hear confessions for many months before he realizes that this ordeal cannot be requested by the kind and merciful Lord. On the other hand we have seen priests laugh and joke in referring to their embarrassed penitents. Confession is a usurpation of authority by priests who investigate the minds and souls of human beings. When an organization such as the Roman system can control not only the education, the family and policies of the civil government of its members, but even their very thoughts and desires, we do not wonder that it can prosper and succeed. Roman Catholics, whether they feel that they ought to admit it or not, are forced into submission to Romanism through the process of torturing auricular confession."

Vinet then gives the following specific examples of the abuse of the confessional:

(a) *"Confession of a Child.* The child may be only seven years of age. He has been told that he must tell all his sins to the priest. If he does not, he will commit a sacrilege and should he die, he cannot go to heaven. He is naturally very confused as to what really constitutes sin. He is naturally shy and reluctant to tell what he has done or thought. The result is that he omits to declare certain things that are really not sinful but he thinks they are. His conscience will reproach him for having hidden a sin in confession and he cannot make peace with his God. Confession has ruined the soul of many a child. How different is all this from the words of Christ who said, 'Suffer the little children to come unto me'!

(b) *"Confession of a Young Girl.* We now have a shy Roman Catholic young girl, passing through the state of childhood to puberty, who is about to enter the confessional. She is naturally embarrassed and her state of mind is just what a sordid confessor wishes to explore. The priest will now hear from a young woman the most secret thoughts and desires of her soul. Her mind and soul are sacrificed on the altar of Romanism. Many embarrassing questions are asked according to the sins accused. . . . These shameful details of a confession are mentioned here to illustrate what is meant by the torture of confession. Roman Catholics know very well that what we disclose is the crude truth.

(c) *"Confession of a Married Woman.* A married woman enters the confessional. She will tell a strange man secrets which she probably would not dare to reveal to her husband. She is even bound to reveal certain secrets of her husband. In the Roman Church birth control of all varieties is a sin and must be confessed with all its circumstances. The husband might be of Protestant faith and his Roman Catholic wife will have to disclose to the priest the most intimate relations of their marital life. The priest will know more about the wife than the husband. There are no family secrets because Rome has required that hearts and souls shall be fully explored by priests. In this manner Romanism controls the whole intimate lives of married couples.

"A married woman, who has any amount of natural discretion and honesty, will enter the confessional with apprehension and often despair. She fears that terrible infallible questionnaire. It is impossible to describe the mental inconvenience she now experiences by the spectre of compulsory confession. . . .

"Poor Roman Catholic women! We know well that your kind souls are tortured to death by this terrible Roman obligation of telling, not only your sins, but also the most intimate secrets of your married life. As an ex-priest we can tell you that these mental tortures imposed upon your souls are not a prescription of the Saviour of mankind to obtain forgiveness of your sins, but are pure inventions of men to keep your minds and hearts under the control of a system, the torturous Roman religious organization. We must admit that as a priest we had no power to forgive your sins. No priest has such powers" (*I Was a Priest*, pp. 62-67).

Father Charles Chiniquy, after spending twenty-five years as a Roman Catholic priest in Canada and the United States, renounced the Roman Church and the priesthood and in the following paragraphs

expressed his sense of humiliation and shame at having ever engaged
in the processes of the confessional.

"With a blush on my face, and regret in my heart, I confess before
God and man, that I have been through the confessional plunged for
twenty-five years in that bottomless sea of iniquity, in which the blind
priests of Rome have to swim day and night.

"I had to learn by heart the infamous questions which the Church of
Rome forces every priest to learn. I had to put these impure, immoral
questions to women and girls who were confessing their sins to me.
Those questions, and the answers they elicit, are so debasing that only
a man who has lost every sense of shame can put them to any woman.

"Yes, I was bound in conscience, to put into the ears, the mind, the
imagination, the memory, the heart and soul of women and girls, questions of such a nature, the direct and immediate tendency of which is to
fill the minds and hearts of both priests and penitents with thoughts
and temptations of such a degrading nature, that I do not know any
words adequate to express them. Pagan antiquity has never seen any
institution more polluting than the confessional. I have lived twenty-five
years in the atmosphere of the confessional. I was degraded and polluted
by the confessional just as all the priests of Rome are. It has required
the whole blood of the great Victim, who died on Calvary for sinners,
to purify me" (*The Priest, the Woman, and the Confessional*, pp. 67, 68).

This book by Father Chiniquy is, we believe, the best available dealing with all phases of the confessional, and should be read by everyone
who would have a clear understanding of the evils involved in that
institution. It describes conditions which existed in Montreal and in
other parts of Canada in the middle nineteenth century, and shows the
depths to which the confessional tends if unrestrained by evangelical
forces.

Such testimonies as we have cited make it clear that the confessional
is contaminating alike to the penitent and to the priest. The great orna-
ment of the woman is modesty and purity. But when a woman is taught
that modesty and restraint in the confessional are in themselves sins,
womanly virtue is bound to suffer. Most of the priests are educated,
trained, clever men, who know how and to what extent they can safely
ply their penitents. Appropriate here are the words:

> Vice is a monster of such hideous mien,
> As, to be hated, needs but to be seen;
> But seen too oft, familiar with her face,
> We soon approve, admire, and then embrace.

Husbands and fathers are not ordinarily asked such questions as are put to girls and women in the confessional, and it is not an unusual thing when they become enlightened as to what conversations are carried on between the priests and their wives and daughters that they absolutely forbid them to go to confession. The unfortunate thing, however, is that even after they become enlightened concerning this phase of Romanism they usually remain in that church and continue to try to fulfill all of the other requirements, despite the fact that failure to comply with the regulations concerning the confessional is in itself a mortal sin.

Another who grew up in the Roman Catholic Church describes the confessional and its effect on the people in these words:

> "The confessional is a system of espionage—a system of slavery. The priest is the spy in every home. Many Catholics are shocked by the character of the questions put to them. A Catholic woman said to a Protestant friend, 'I would rather take a whipping any day than go to confession.' One can readily understand why most Catholics are timid and afraid of the priest and are obedient to the letter of his wishes because they know that through the confessional the priest has secured a knowledge of their habits and life that no one else knows anything about. The average priest can stride along with that lofty air. When he meets his parishioners he often tosses his head as though he were a demigod. Why is it? Because he holds the secrets of the personal lives of all his flock—of all who trust him" (John Carrara, *Romanism Under the Searchlight,* p. 70).

Under the rules of the Roman Church the priest is forbidden to reveal anything told him in the confessional. This is known as the "seal of the confessional." Otherwise the practice of confession could not be maintained. But under certain circumstances he can pass on information gained: (1) With the consent of the penitent, which for the priest often times is not hard to obtain. (2) Anything revealed apart from the confession itself, that is, in further conversation, can be passed on. (3) Among themselves priests often discuss information gained in the confessional without mentioning names, and so stay within the limits of Canon Law. And (4) if a dispute arises as to whether or not permission was granted, the word of the priest is to be accepted in preference to that of the penitent. And, as the clergy is not permitted to tell what transpires in the confessional, so neither are those who confess permitted to repeat anything, since they too are a part of the church system. This, then, gives the priests an ideal situation for the secret direction of the personal affairs of their parishioners, including their family life, community affairs, voting, or the management of any political machines directed by them or political offices held by them.

The assertion of the priests that the confessional brings peace to the soul is cruel sarcasm. In most cases the result is exactly the opposite, and the penitents remain a certain period of time, sometimes longer, sometimes shorter, in a distressed state of mind. For the honest, conscientious person, young or old, the fear of not making "a good confession," of omitting or inaccurately reporting the various experiences, and so making the entire confession null and void, is in itself a tormenting worry. Believing that their salvation depends, as the priest tells them that it does, on a full and truthful recounting of all their sinful actions, those honest souls fear that they have not been sufficiently contrite, or that they have withheld some necessary details. Women in particular dislike the confessional, and usually restrict themselves to what they *must* say.

The Roman Catholic people pay dearly for this invention as they submit themselves to its discipline. Much depends, of course, upon the individual priest. Some are truly considerate of the sensitivities of their people and refrain from unreasonable probing, while others abuse the privilege. In any event, every priest knows that he proffers what is flagrantly false every time he dismisses his penitent with the benediction: "Go in peace, thy sins are forgiven thee." For Protestants the confessional is undoubtedly the most revolting feature of the Roman system.

Fortunately, in the United States, where Protestantism is the predominant religion, the abuses of the confessional do not reach such depths as in the Roman Catholic countries. Why is it, for instance, that the Roman Catholics of Southern Ireland are so inferior to their Protestant neighbors in Northern Ireland? Why so much poverty, ignorance, superstition, and immorality? Nearly a century ago Father Chiniquy wrote concerning the Roman Catholic nations of his day:

"The principal cause of the degradation of Ireland is the enslavement of the Irish women by means of the confessional. After the Irish woman has been enslaved and degraded, she, in turn, has enslaved and degraded her husband and sons. Ireland will be an object of pity; she will be poor, miserable, degraded, as long as she rejects Christ and is ruled by the father confessor." He added: "The downfall of woman in France, and her degradation through the confessional, is now an accomplished fact, which nobody can deny; the highest intellectuals have seen and confessed it. Why is it that Spain is so miserable, so weak, so poor, so foolishly and cruelly reddening her fair valleys with the blood of her children? The principal, if not the only cause of the downfall of that great nation is the confessional. There, also the confessor has defiled, degraded, enslaved women, and women in turn have defiled and degraded their husbands and sons" (*The Priest, the Woman, and the Confessional,* p. 64-66).

As regards the comparative status of Roman Catholic and Protestant nations, it is a fact that every Roman Catholic nation in the world today is bankrupt, and that every Roman Catholic nation in the world today is looking to Protestant United States for financial and economic aid in one form or another. The Protestant nations of Europe—England, Scotland, Holland, Norway, Sweden, Denmark, and northern Germany, have been far more enlightened and progressive than have their Roman Catholic neighbors. This is not mere chance, but a consistent pattern that has been in evidence since the days of the Reformation. Surely the facts speak for themselves. Someone has said: "Every Protestant nation is superior to every Roman Catholic nation." We believe that is true.

According to a decree of the Council of Trent it is not necessary, in order to obtain pardon in the confessional, that the sinner be sorry because his sin was an offense against God, but only that he be sorry for fear that unless he confesses before a priest and receives forgiveness he will go to hell forever. The decree reads:

"It is sufficient if he is sorry for fear of otherwise burning in hell for all eternity" (Sess. 14, C. H.).

Commenting on this phase of the confessional Dr. Zacchello says:

"Anyone can understand that this practice of the Catholic confession is no deterrent to crime, and can easily, in fact, be made an excuse for continuing in it. Big-time criminals and racketeers generally can find ways to circumvent the civil law and its penalties. If they are Roman Catholics and believe in confession, they have assurance of an easy way of also escaping punishment in the next life.

"Examples are plentiful of such big-time Catholic criminals and racketeers continuing in crime without any qualms of conscience. 'Big Tom' Pendergast of Kansas City who died after release from federal penitentiary was one of them. Under his rule Kansas City was a menace to the morals of young and old. Brothels flourished openly and criminal gangs enforced his edicts. Gambling houses were commonplace, and he himself was the biggest gambler of his age. Political corruption abounded and Pendergast, as the boss of it all, grew fabulously rich from the wealth that flowed into his pockets from this underworld traffic in crime. Yet, when he died on January 26, 1945, Monsignor Thomas B. McDonald who preached his funeral sermon after solemn high mass, publicly proclaimed him 'a man with a noble heart and a true friend,' because *'he went to mass every morning at 7:30 for 30 years.'*

"Tom Pendergast did not fear the penalties of the civil law, because he could escape them by bribing and corrupting judges and officers of the law whom he himself had appointed. He was assured by his church's teaching that he could also escape God's punishment as long as he went to confession regularly, told his crimes to the priest and said he was sorry merely because he was afraid of going to hell. He was assured that he could continue his life of crime with impunity as long as he made sure of having a priest to absolve him before he died and to say masses afterward for his soul in purgatory. . . . We former priests now know what true forgiveness of sins means in Christian teaching; that God alone forgives sin and with forgiveness comes a complete change of life. The Catholic practice of confession is merely a recital to a man of sins committed, with no guarantee of pardon from God, and nothing to prevent the repetition of the same sins over and over again" (*Secrets of Romanism,* pp. 123-125).

What a fraudulent, dishonest, futile, and unscriptural practice the operation of the confessional really is!

X. PURGATORY

1. ROME'S TEACHING CONCERNING PURGATORY

The Roman Catholic Church has developed a doctrine in which it is held that all who die at peace with the church, but who are not perfect, must undergo penal and purifying suffering in an intermediate realm known as purgatory. Only those believers who have attained a state of Christian perfection go immediately to heaven. All unbaptized adults and those who after baptism have committed mortal sin go immediately to hell. The great mass of partially sanctified Christians dying in fellowship with the church, but who nevertheless are encumbered with some degree of sin, go to purgatory where, for a longer or shorter time, they suffer until all sin is purged away, after which they are translated to heaven.

The Roman Church holds that baptism removes all previous guilt, both original and actual, so that if a person were to die immediately after baptism he would go directly to heaven. All other believers, except the Christian martyrs but including even the highest clergy, must go to purgatory to pay the penalty for sins committed after baptism. The sacrifices made by the martyrs, particularly those that reflect honor upon the church, are considered adequate substitutes for the purgatorial sufferings.

The doctrine of purgatory is not based on the Bible, but on a distinction which Rome makes by dividing sin into two kinds. This distinction is clearly set forth by Dr. Zacchello, who says:

"According to Roman teaching a person can commit two kinds of sin against God: *mortal* and *venial*. By mortal sin is meant a grave offense against the law of God or of the church. It is called 'mortal' because it kills the soul by depriving it entirely of sanctifying grace. Venial sin is a small and pardonable offense against God and the laws of the church. Then, this confusing and unscriptural doctrine continues: Two kinds of

218

punishment are due to mortal sin, eternal (in hell forever), and temporal (in purgatory). Eternal punishment is cancelled by the sacraments of baptism and extreme unction, or by an act of perfect contrition with promise of confession. Temporal punishment is not cancelled by these sacraments, but by works of penance, by almsgiving, by paying the priest to say mass, by indulgences, etc., which reduce the temporal punishment for mortal sins that would have to be suffered in purgatory. Thus even if all mortal sins of a Roman Catholic are forgiven in confession by a priest, and he does not perform enough of these 'good works,' he will go to purgatory and remain there in torture until his soul is completely purified" (*Secrets of Romanism*, p. 101).

The doctrine of purgatory rests on the assumption that while God forgives sin, His justice nevertheless demands that the sinner must suffer the full punishment due to him for his sin before he will be allowed to enter heaven. But such a distinction is illogical even according to human reasoning. For it manifestly would be unjust to forgive a criminal the guilt of his crime and still send him to prison to suffer for it.

The Roman Catholic people are taught that the souls of their relatives and friends in purgatory suffer great torment in the flames, that they are unable to help themselves, that not even God can help them until His justice has been satisfied, and that only their friends on earth can shorten or alleviate that suffering. Purgatory is supposed to be under the special jurisdiction of the pope, and it is his prerogative as the representative of Christ on earth to grant indulgences (i.e., relief from suffering) as he sees fit. This power, it is claimed, can be exercised directly by the pope to alleviate, shorten, or terminate the sufferings, and within limits it is also exercised by the priests as representatives of the pope. It is, of course, impossible but that power of this kind should be abused even in the hands of the best of men. Vested in the hands of ordinary men, as generally must be the case, or in the hands of mercenary and wicked men as too often has happened, the abuses were bound to be appalling. The evils that have flowed from this doctrine, and which are its inevitable consequences, make it abundantly clear that it cannot be of divine origin.

2. THE TERRIFYING ASPECT OF PURGATORY

Since none but actual saints escape the pains of purgatory, this doctrine gives to the death and funeral of the Roman Catholic a dreadful and repellent aspect. Under the shadow of such a doctrine death is not, as in evangelical Protestantism, the coming of Christ for His loved one, but the ushering of the shrinking soul into a place of unspeakable torture.

It is no wonder that millions of people born in the Roman Catholic Church, knowing practically nothing about the Bible but believing implicitly in the doctrines of their church, should live and die in fear of death, in fear of spending an unknown number of years in the pain and anguish of that place called purgatory. How tragic that these people live in fear and servitude to the priests, who they are taught to believe hold in their hands the power of life and death, when all the time Christ has paid for their redemption *in full*. Even their own Roman Catholic Bible says: "Wherefore because children have blood and flesh in common, so he in like manner has shared in these; that through death he might destroy him who had the empire of death, that is, the devil; and might deliver them, who throughout their life were kept in servitude by the fear of death" (Heb. 2:14, 15, Confraternity Version). These words, "Kept in servitude by the fear of death," describe the spiritual state of even devout Roman Catholics. All their lives they are kept in bondage through fear of this imaginary purgatory.

The sufferings in purgatory are said to vary greatly in intensity and duration, being proportioned to the guilt and impurity or impenitence of the sufferer. They are described as being in some cases comparatively light and mild, lasting perhaps only a few hours, while in others little if anything short of the torments of hell itself and lasting for thousands of years. They differ from the pains of hell at least to this extent, that there is eventually an end to the sufferings in purgatory, but not to those in hell. They are in any event to end with the last judgment. Hence purgatory eventually is to be emptied of all its victims.

As regards the intensity of the suffering, Bellarmine, a noted Roman Catholic theologian, says:

> "The pains of purgatory are very severe, surpassing anything endured in this life." The Manual of the Purgatorial Society, with the imprimatur of Cardinal Hayes, says:
>
> "According to the Holy Fathers of the Church, the fire of purgatory does not differ from the fire of hell, except in point of duration. 'It is the same fire,' says St. Thomas Aquinas, 'that torments the reprobate in hell, and the just in purgatory. The least pain in purgatory,' he says, 'surpasses the greatest suffering in this life.' Nothing but the eternal duration makes the fire of hell more terrible than that of purgatory."

And in another book with the imprimatur of archbishop Spellman (now cardinal), Bellarmine is quoted as saying:

> "There is absolutely no doubt that the pains of purgatory in some cases endure for entire centuries" (John M. Haffert, *Saturday in Purgatory*).

It seems that the Church of Rome has rather wisely refrained from making any official pronouncement concerning the nature and intensity of purgatorial suffering. Books and discourses intended for Protestant readers or hearers speak of it only in the mildest terms. But the Roman Church does not thereby escape responsibility, for it has always allowed free circulation, with its expressed or implied sanction, of books containing the most frightening descriptions, ranging all the way from comparatively mild disciplinary measures to a burning lake of billowing flames in which the souls of the impenitent are submerged. Among their own people and in the hands of the priests the doctrine of purgatory has been an instrument of terrifying power. We are reminded of the remark of Charles Hodge in this connection: "The feet of the tiger with its claws withdrawn are as soft as velvet; but when those claws are extended, they are fearful instruments of laceration and death."

Furthermore, as Dr. Augustus H. Strong has appropriately said:

"Suffering has in itself no reforming power. Unless accompanied by special renewing influences of the Holy Spirit, it only hardens and embitters the soul. We have no Scriptural evidence that such influences of the Spirit are exerted after death, upon the still impenitent; but abundant evidence, on the contrary, that the moral condition in which death finds men is their condition forever. . . . To the impenitent and rebellious sinner the motive must come, not from within, but from without. Such motives God presents by His Spirit in this life; and when this life ends and God's Spirit is withdrawn, no motive to repentance will be presented. The soul's dislike for God (we may even say, the sinner's hatred for God) will issue only in complaint and resistance" (*Systematic Theology,* p. 1041).

We ask: How can spirits suffer the pains of material fire in purgatory before they have resurrection bodies? In answer to this question the Roman theologians have invented a theory that in purgatory the soul takes on a different kind of body—the nature of which they do not define—in which the suffering can be felt. But that is like the doctrine of purgatory itself, a purely fictitious assumption without any Scripture proof whatever, and in fact contrary to Scripture.

Roman Catholicism is often described as a religion of fear. The doctrine of purgatory is where much of that fear centers—fear of the priest, fear of the confessional, of the consequences of missing mass, of the discipline of penance, of death, of purgatory, and of the righteous judgment of an angry God. L. H. Lehmann tells us concerning his boyhood in Ireland:

"A sense of constant fear overshadowed everything. Ingrained fear is, in fact, the predominant note running through the life of all children born and reared in Catholic Ireland. Few ever get rid of it completely in after life, even in America. That fear concerns everything in this life on earth, and still more terrible is the fear of the terrors in the life beyond the grave" (*The Soul of a Priest*, p. 34).

3. THE MONEY MOTIVE IN THE DOCTRINE OF PURGATORY

It is safe to say that no other doctrine of the Church of Rome, unless it be that of auricular confession, has done so much to pervert the Gospel or to enslave the people to the priesthood as has the doctrine of purgatory. A mere reference to the days of Tetzel, Luther, and the Protestant Reformation, not to mention present day conditions in the Roman Catholic countries in Southern Europe and Latin America where that church has had undisputed ecclesiastical control for centuries, is sufficient to illustrate this point. Every year millions of dollars are paid to obtain relief from this imagined suffering. No exact figures are available. In contrast with the custom in Protestant churches, in which itemized financial statements of income and expenses are issued each year, Roman Catholic finances are kept secret, no kind of budget or balance sheet ever being published which would show where their money comes from, how much it amounts to, how much is sent to Rome, how or where the remainder is spent. In this as in other things, the people must trust their church implicitly.

The doctrine of purgatory has sometimes been referred to as "the gold mine of the priesthood" since it is the source of such lucrative income. The Roman Church might well say, "By this craft we have our wealth."

In general it is held that the period of suffering in purgatory can be shortened by gifts of money, prayers by the priest, and masses, which gifts, prayers, and masses can be provided by the person before death or by relatives and friends after death. The more satisfaction one makes while living, the less remains to be atoned for in purgatory.

At the time of death the priest is summoned to the bed of the dying person. He administers extreme unction, and solemnly pronounces absolution. Yet after death occurs money is extracted from the mourning relatives and friends to pay for masses to be said in order to shorten the period of torment in purgatory. The result, particularly among ignorant and uneducated people, has been that the Roman Church sells salvation for money, not outwardly and directly, but nevertheless in reality. All understand that the service of the church in securing the salvation of a soul in purgatory is to be rewarded with appropriate gifts or services.

It has well been said that the Roman Church is a huge money-gathering institution, and that everything in Rome has a price tag on it.

It is due in no small measure to this doctrine of purgatory that the Roman Catholic Church has been able to draw in large sums of money and to build magnificent cathedrals, monasteries, and convents, even in regions where the people are poor. This has been particularly true in the Latin American countries. It is a common experience in Mexico, for instance, to find in almost every town an impressive Roman Catholic church surrounded by the miserable huts of the natives. The practical outworking of the system has been seen in several countries, e.g., France, England, Italy, Austria, Mexico, and others when a disproportionately large part of the property fell into the hands of the Roman Catholic Church, sometimes as much as a fourth or a third of all the property of the nation, and had to be confiscated and redistributed by the government in order to redress the economic situation. There is literally no limit to the amount of property that the Roman Church seeks for itself if it is not restrained. Those who contribute money for masses, particularly those who at the urging of the priests leave substantial portions of their estates to the Roman Church so that future masses can be said for them, are helping to keep in operation a lucrative and detestable system which became a regular practice in the church centuries after the time of Christ and which is a disgrace to Christianity.

At this point another question arises. If the pope, or the priest acting for him, really has the power to shorten or modify or terminate the suffering of souls in purgatory, why does he not, if he is a good man, render that service freely and willingly as a Christian service to humanity? In the hospitals the doctors and nurses try in every possible way to relieve the pain and misery of those who come to them. Why does the pope, or the priest, keep those poor souls suffering horrible pain in the fire if at any time he can pay all their debt out of his rich treasury of the merits of the saints? Why? Does Romanism have an answer?

If any one of us actually had the power to release souls from purgatory and refused to exercise that power except in return for a payment of money, he would be considered cruel and unchristian—which indeed he would be. By all Christian standards that is a service that the church should render freely and willingly to its people. No decent man would permit even a dog to suffer in the fire until its owner paid him five dollars to take it out. The insistence on a money transaction before a soul can be released, and sometimes money transactions over long periods of time, shows clearly the sinister purpose for which the doctrine of purgatory was invented. The simple fact is that if purgatory were emptied and all those suffering souls admitted to heaven, there would be little incentive left for the people to pay money to the priests.

The doctrine of purgatory is a horribly cruel doctrine in that the priests, all of whom in the United States at least, are educated, intelligent men, know how flimsy or how utterly lacking is all actual evidence for such a place. Under the pretense of delivering souls from that suffering large sums of money are wrung from the bereaved at a time when hearts are sore and when they are least able to think logically about such matters.

Says Stephen L. Testa:

"Purgatory has been called 'a gigantic fraud,' and 'a colossal racket,' for it deprives the poor of their last pennies and extorts large funds from the rich in exchange for *nothing*. During the Middle Ages the rich rivaled each other in leaving their estates to the Church, and the poor gave out of their poverty till the Church became the richest landowner in every country. In several countries the Church owned one-half of the land and one-third of all the invested funds. It built great cathedrals and bishops' palaces and left the poor to live in huts and shanties. You can see even today in Europe and in Mexico great massive cathedrals surrounded by the hovels of the poor who grovel in misery, ignorance, and wretchedness.

"But many of those Catholic nations during the last century had their wars of independence, beginning with the French Revolution, and the Church was deprived of its temporal power and the landed properties were seized by the State and partitioned among the poor farmers. In Italy this happened in 1870. But Mussolini restored the temporal power of the pope (in name only) in 1929. However, the church is not the rich land owner that it once was. The spirit of liberty and democracy is fatal to the autocracy and totalitarianism of the Roman Church" (booklet, *The Truth About Catholics, Protestants, and Jews,* p. 14).

And Dr. Robert Ketcham asks:

"How do you know, Mr. Priest, when to stop praying and taking money from your parishioners for a given case? How do you know when John Murphy is out of purgatory? His getting out is dependent upon the saying of masses paid for by his bereaved ones. If you stop one or two masses too soon, what then? If you keep on saying masses for the fellow after he is out, that is bad. It is bad either way you come at it. I ask seriously, Sir, Mr. Roman Catholic Priest, How do you know when to stop saying masses for a given individual? Do you have some kind of a connection with the unseen world?" (booklet, *Let Rome Speak for Herself,* p. 20).

The fact is that Roman Catholic priests admit that they have no way of knowing when a soul is released from purgatory. One former layman from that church writing on this subject says that it was the priests' abuse of this doctrine that finally turned him against Roman Catholicism. He tells of an incident that occurred 45 years after the death of a man in his congregation, when the then officiating priest again asked the widow for money that he might say mass for her husband. A succession of priests in turn had taken money from that widow, always on the pretense of getting her husband out of purgatory. But they had never gotten him out. And there, 45 years later, they were still extracting money on that fraudulent claim.

We charge in the strongest terms that the practice of saying mass for souls in purgatory is a gigantic hoax and fraud, a taking of money under false pretenses, because it purports to get people out of purgatory when actually no such place exists. We would not trust a judge who manipulated the law to make himself rich, nor would we trust a policeman who asked for a bribe. Why, then, should we trust a priest who presents an interpretation concerning the afterlife which is not only not in the Bible but which is contrary to the clear teaching of the Bible? Such practice is fraudulent and is designed primarily for only one purpose, that of keeping the people under the power of the priests and controlling their lives and property as far as possible.

4. SCRIPTURE TEACHING

That the doctrine of purgatory is unscriptural can be shown easily. The Bible says nothing about any such place, and in fact the most devastating arguments against purgatory come from those inspired pages. Christ made not even so much as a passing allusion to purgatory. Instead He said: "He that heareth my word, and believeth him that sent me, *hath* eternal life, and cometh not into judgment, but hath passed out of death into life" (John 5:24). Hence eternal life is already possessed by the soul that believes on Christ and there can be no possible condemnation of that soul. When Jesus said to the penitent thief on the cross, "Today shalt thou be with me in Paradise" (Luke 23:43), the clear inference was that at his death he would go immediately to heaven. Christ's words, "It is finished" (John 19:30), spoken at the end of His suffering on the cross, mean that the work of redemption which He came to perform has been accomplished, finished, not partially, but completely. Furthermore, there is no transfer from one realm to another after death. Those who go to the place of outer darkness cannot cross from that sphere to the other: "Between us and you there is a great gulf fixed, that they that would pass from hence to you may not be able, and that none may cross over from thence to us" (Luke 16:26).

The apostle John teaches the same: "The blood of Jesus his Son cleanseth us from *all* sin. . . . If we confess our sins, he is faithful and righteous to forgive us our sins, and to cleanse us from *all* unrighteousness" (I John 1:7, 9). Hence our sins, all of them, are forgiven through the sacrifice of Christ, and none are left to be purged away by human merit. And again: "And I heard a voice from heaven saying, Write, Blessed are the dead who die in the Lord from henceforth: yea, saith the Spirit, that they may rest from their labors; for their works follow with them" (Rev. 14:13).

Paul's teaching on this subject is quite full. He anticipated no purgatory, but said that to depart was to "be with Christ," and that it would be "very far better" (Phil. 1:23). While we are "at home in the body," we are "absent from the Lord"; but to be "absent from the body" is to be "at home with the Lord" (II Cor. 5:8). To the Philippians he wrote: "For me to live is Christ, and to die is gain" (1:21). In answer to the question, "What must I do to be saved?" he gives the straightforward and unqualified answer: "Believe on the Lord Jesus, and thou shalt be saved" (Acts 16:31)—no reference there to confession to a priest, penance, purgatory, or any other thing such as a works religion attaches. Those who put their trust in Christ's atoning death do not come into judgment: "There is therefore now no condemnation to them that are in Christ Jesus" (Rom. 8:1).

Peter, the alleged founder of Romanism, declared: "Christ also suffered for sins *once*, the righteous for the unrighteous, that he might bring us to God" (I Peter 3:18). Hence we cannot be made to suffer for that sin a second time. And the writer of the Epistle to the Hebrews says that God not only forgives, but *forgets*, our sin: "And their sins and their iniquities will I remember no more" (10:17).

What a contrast there is between these words of Scripture concerning the state of the righteous immediately after death, and that teaching which would have us believe that the sufferings of purgatory must be endured indefinitely, perhaps even for years! The Roman Church knows, of course, that this doctrine of purgatory, which is of such great importance to it, is not in the Bible. And that undoubtedly is one of the reasons that through the ages it has kept the Bible from the people.

Purgatory is, therefore, a travesty on the justice of God. God's justice has been fully satisfied *once and for all* by the sacrifice of Christ, and God cannot exact double punishment, once from Christ, and again from those for whom He died. Hence the redeemed soul goes not to any midway station between earth and heaven, but directly to heaven; and the sacrifice on Calvary was sufficient to "purge" all our sins without the need of any "purg"-atory.

A Roman Catholic cannot approach his deathbed and the certain prospect of the interminable fires of purgatory with anything other than fear and dread. For as he is true to the doctrines of his church he can see only great fires beyond. It is difficult to conceive of a belief so groundless and yet so frightening as that of the doctrine of purgatory. But what a marvelous, glorious thing it is at death to go *straight to heaven!* And what good news it is for Roman Catholics when they learn that there is no such place as purgatory, no suffering for the redeemed soul beyond the grave!

Where, then, does Rome find her authority for the doctrine of purgatory? Four Scripture verses are cited, but not one of them has any real bearing on the subject. They are (Confraternity Version): "He will baptize you with the Holy Spirit and with fire" (the words of John the Baptist concerning Christ) (Matt. 3:11); "If his work burns, he will lose his reward, but himself will be saved, yet so as through fire" (I Cor. 3:15); "And some, who are judged, reprove; and others, save, snatching them from the fire" (Jude 22-23); and "Christ . . . (who) was brought to life in the spirit, in which also he went and preached to those spirits that were in prison. These in times past had been disobedient when the patience of God waited in the days of Noe while the ark was building. In that ark a few, that is, eight souls were saved through water" (I Peter 3:18-20).

None of these verses mentions purgatory, nor gives any real ground for believing that such a place exists. I Peter 3:18-20 at first seems more plausible. But on closer examination these verses simply tell us that the Spirit through which Christ "was brought to life" (in the resurrection), which we believe refers to the Holy Spirit, was the same Spirit in which He preached to the people in Noah's day. The preaching referred to by Peter was long since past. It occurred while the ark was in process of construction; and the tragic thing about it is that only eight souls responded to that preaching. Those eight, and only those, were saved through water. Those who refused the testimony of the Spirit of Christ as He spoke through Noah were "those spirits that were in prison" (the American Standard Version translates more accurately: "the spirits in prison"), that is, in the prison house of sin, or in hell, at the time Peter wrote. And they still are imprisoned. These verses are, in brief, a warning against disobedience to God and rejection of the Gospel, but they have no bearing on the doctrine of purgatory. Thus the four passages cited by Roman Catholics surely are a very light cord on which to hang so heavy a weight.

But Rome bases her doctrine of purgatory primarily on a passage in II Maccabees, which is a Jewish book written after the close of the Old Testament. It is, of course, an apocryphal writing, and is not acknowledged by Protestants as having any authority. In order to show how flimsy this evidence is we quote this passage in full:

"And the day following Judas (Maccabeus) came with his company, to take away the bodies of them that had been slain, and to bury them with their kinsmen, in the sepulchres of their fathers. And they found under the coats of the slain some of the donaries of the idols of Jamnia, which the law forbiddeth to the Jews: so that all plainly saw, that for this cause they were slain. Then they all blessed the just judgment of the Lord, who had discovered the things that were hidden. And so betaking themselves to prayers, they besought him, that the sin which had been committed might be forgiven. But the most valiant Judas exhorted the people to keep themselves from sin, forasmuch as they saw before their eyes what had happened, because of the sins of those that were slain. And making a great gathering, he sent twelve thousand drachmas of silver to Jerusalem for a sacrifice to be offered for the sins of the dead, thinking well and religiously concerning the resurrection. For if he had not hoped that they that were slain should rise again, it would have seemed superfluous and vain to pray for the dead. And because he considered that they who had fallen asleep with godliness, had great grace laid up for them. It is therefore a holy and wholesome thought to pray for the dead that they may be loosed from sins" (12:39-45, Douay Version).

But these verses really do not teach the doctrine at all. Nowhere in this passage is there any mention of fire in which souls are tormented. All that is mentioned is prayers for the dead, from which the Roman Catholic theologians infer, first, that such prayers are proper, and secondly, that such prayers can be effective for the salvation of the dead. Furthermore, from the Roman Catholic viewpoint, these verses prove too much, for they teach the possible salvation of soldiers who had died in mortal sin, that of idolatry. And that contradicts Roman Catholic doctrine, which is that those dying in mortal sin go straight to hell and are permanently lost. They do not go to purgatory where they can be aided by the prayers of people still on earth. Surely one who had never heard of purgatory would not learn about it from this passage. The word purgatory is not found here. This, again, is a precarious passage on which to build such an important doctrine.

5. HISTORY OF THE DOCTRINE

The germ of what afterward grew into the doctrine of purgatory is to be found in the idea of a purification by fire after death among the ancients long before the time of Christ, particularly among the people of India and Persia. It was a familiar idea to the Egyptian and later to the Greek and Roman mind. Plato accepted the idea and gave expression to it in his philosophy. He taught that perfect happiness after death was not possible until one had made satisfaction for his sins, and that if his sins were too great his suffering would have no end. Following the conquests of Alexander the Great, Greek influences spread through all the countries of western Asia, including Palestine. We have seen that it found expression in II Maccabees. The Rabbis began to teach that by means of sin offerings children could alleviate the sufferings of deceased parents. Later Jewish speculation divided the underworld into two abodes— Paradise, a place of happiness, and Gehenna, a place of torment.

We need only read church history to discover how this doctrine developed by slow processes into its present form. In the early Christian era, following the Apostolic age, the writings of Marcion and the Shepherd of Hermes (second century) set forth the first statement of a doctrine of purgatory, alleging that Christ after His death on the cross went to the underworld and preached to the spirits in prison (I Peter 3:19) and led them in triumph to heaven. Prayers for the dead appear in the early Christian liturgies and imply the doctrine since they suggest that the state of the dead is not yet fixed. Origen, the most learned of the early church fathers (died 254 A.D.), taught, first, that a purification by fire was to take place after the resurrection, and second, a universal restoration, a purifying by fire at the end of the world through which all men and angels were to be restored to favor with God.

In the writings of Augustine (died, 430 A.D.) the doctrine of purgatory was first given definite form, although he himself expressed doubt about some phases of it. It was, however, not until the sixth century that it received formal shape at the hands of Gregory the Great, who held the papal office from 590 to 604 A. D. Thereafter eschatology entered upon what we may term its mythological phase, during the period of history known as the Dark Ages. The invisible world was divided into heaven, hell, and purgatory, with the imagination attempting to portray as vividly as possible the topography and experiences of each region. The doctrine was proclaimed an article of faith in 1438, by the Council of Florence, and was later confirmed by the Council of Trent, in 1548. But does any intelligent person believe that if such a place as purgatory is described in the Bible it would have taken the church fathers 600 years to discover it, and another 1,000 years to confirm it? At any rate the Protestant Reformation swept away those creations of terror and fancy, and reverted to the Scriptural antithesis of heaven and hell. The Eastern Orthodox Church, incidentally, does not teach the doctrine of purgatory.

The following paragraph by Dr. Charles Hodge shows the influence that this doctrine had in the lives and thinking of all classes of people during the Middle Ages:

"It was Gregory the Great who consolidated the vague and conflicting views circulating through the church, and brought the doctrine into shape and into such connection with the discipline of the church, as to render it the effective engine of government and income, which it has ever since remained. From this time onward through all the Middle Ages, purgatory became one of the prominent and consistently reiterated topics of public discussion. It took firm hold of the popular mind. The clergy from the highest to the lowest, and the different orders of monks vied with each other in their zeal for its inculcation, and in the marvels which they related of spiritual apparitions, in support of the doctrine. They contended fiercely for the honor of superior power of redeeming souls from purgatorial pains. The Franciscans claimed that the head of their order descended annually into purgatory, and delivered all the brotherhood who were detained there. The Carmelites asserted that the Virgin Mary had promised that no one who died with the Carmelite scapulary upon their shoulders, should ever be lost. The chisel and pencil of the artist were employed in depicting the horrors of purgatory, as means of impressing the public mind. No class escaped the contagious belief; the learned as well as the ignorant; the high and the low; the soldier and the recluse; the skeptic and the believer were alike enslaved. From this slavery the Bible, not the progress of science, has delivered Protestants. . . . All experience proves that infidelity is no protection against superstition. If men will not believe the rational and true, they will believe the absurd and false" (*Systematic Theology*, III, p. 770).

Dr. Harris says:

"It is well to remember that the doctrine of purgatory which rests like a heavy burden upon the heart of every Roman Catholic was not taught by any of the early church fathers and had a very slow growth until the fifth century. Its beginnings in prayers for the dead and a difference in status between the martyred dead and the ordinary Christian departed may be found as early as 200 A.D. in Tertullian. Mention of the penal fires comes much later, and the masses for the poor souls in purgatory still later. The doctrine of purgatory is another one of those foreign growths that has fastened itself like a malignant tumor upon the theology of the Roman Catholic Church" (*Fundamental Protestant Doctrines*, V, p. 7).

And Alexander Hislop, in his exhaustive study of the origin of Roman Catholic doctrines, finds that the doctrine of purgatory was adopted from paganism—from Babylonian, Greek, and Roman mythology:

"In every system except that of the Bible the doctrine of a purgatory after death, and prayers for the dead, has always been found to occupy a place. Go wherever we may, in ancient or modern times, we shall find that Paganism leaves hope after death for sinners, who, at the time of their departure, were consciously unfit for the abodes of the blest. For this purpose a middle state has been feigned, in which, by means of purgatorial pains, guilt unremoved in time may in a future world be purged away, and the soul be made meet for final beatitude. In Greece the doctrine of purgatory was inculcated in the very chief of the philosophers (Plato). . . . In pagan Rome, purgatory was equally held up before the minds of men.

"In Egypt, substantially the same doctrine of purgatory was inculcated. But when once this doctrine of purgatory was admitted into the popular mind, then the door was opened for all manner of priestly extortions. Prayers for the dead ever go hand in hand with purgatory; but no prayers can be completely efficacious without the interposition of the priests; and no priestly functions can be rendered unless there be *special pay* for them. Therefore, in every land we find the pagan priesthood 'devouring widows' houses,' and making merchandise of the tender feelings of sorrowing relatives, sensitively alive to the immortal happiness of the beloved dead" (*The Two Babylons*, p. 168).

6. CONCLUSION

As we have indicated, there is surprisingly little revealed in Scripture concerning the intermediate state. This has led some to resort to conjecture and imagination in order to fill out the picture that revelation has given only in the barest outline.

The Roman Catholic theologian Newman cites the doctrine of purgatory as one of the clearest instances of "development" from a slight Scriptural germ. But in reality it is an instance of the development from a germ of that which was never in it to begin with—as if from a mustard seed one could derive an oak tree.

In defense of this doctrine Roman Catholics lay considerable stress upon the fact that the custom of praying for the dead prevailed early and long in the church. Such prayers, it is said, take for granted that the dead need our prayers, and that they are not immediately in heaven. But the fact is that prayer for the dead is merely another superstitious practice which is entirely without Scriptural support. That was one of the early corruptions introduced into the church from heathenism. It will not do to argue from one corruption to support another.

One thing that has given the doctrine of purgatory a certain amount of plausibility is the fact that we all are sinners and none attain perfect holiness in this life, while heaven is a place of perfect holiness where nothing evil can enter. The question naturally arises, How is the soul cleansed from the last remnants of sin before it enters heaven? Since this deals with something that is outside the realm of our experience it might seem reasonable to believe that there would be a place of further purification. In this case the Bible is our only trustworthy source of information. But a careful examination of all the passages relating to this subject show that there are only two abodes for the dead: a heaven for the saved, and a hell for the lost. And in response to the question as to how the Christian is made ready for heaven, the Bible teaches that perfect righteousness is not to be had by any process at all, but only through faith in Christ (Gal. 2:16). We are not justified by the works of the law. As expressed in the Westminster standards: "The souls of believers are at their death made perfect in holiness." And if it be doubted that holiness can be attained in a single moment, let it be remembered that recovery from disease is ordinarily a process but that when Christ said, "I will; be thou made clean," even the leper was cleansed in an instant (Matt. 8:3).

Belief that one can maintain contact with the dead, and that he can influence them for good or bad, has been a common element in the pagan religions. When the Israelites came into the land of Canaan, Moses strictly charged them that they were not to follow the customs of the land in making gifts to or sacrificing for the dead, nor were they to allow any marks to be made in their flesh to appease or facilitate contact with the spirits of the dead. In Deuteronomy 26:13-14 we read: "And thou shalt say before Jehovah thy God, I have put away the hallowed things (objects of heathen veneration and worship) out of my house. . . . I have not eaten thereof in my mourning, neither have I put away thereof, being unclean, nor given thereof for the dead." The Roman practice of gifts for the dead and prayers to and for the dead (to Mary and the saints and for deceased relatives and friends) is not far removed, if indeed it is removed at all, from such customs.

Mr. Norman Porter, of Belfast, Northern Ireland, tells of a conversation that occurred during a visit to a Roman Catholic monastery in connection with a course of instruction offered on Roman Catholic beliefs. "I asked the priest, 'Sir, when you die, where do you hope to go?' He replied, 'I hope that when I die I shall go at least to the lowest place in purgatory.' That was his hope. I said, 'Tell me, when the pope dies, where will he go?' He said, 'He will be just as I am. He hopes that he will go to purgatory.' I said, 'The so-called Vicar of Christ, the man who has claimed for himself the right to represent Christ on earth, is going to purgatory?' He said, 'Yes.' I then said, 'Sir, when do you get out of purgatory? When will you be in heaven?' He answered, 'I don't know.' So not even the Roman priests know when a soul escapes from this mysterious place. What a message for a perishing world!"

Furthermore, the doctrine of purgatory represents God as a respecter of persons, which the Bible says He is not. Because of money a rich man can leave more for prayers and masses and so pass through purgatory and into heaven more speedily than many a poor man who is more deserving and who has more to commend him in the sight of God. The Bible teaches that God's judgment is based on character alone, not on outward circumstances of wealth, position, or special standing.

This doctrine turns to commercial gain the sorrow of relatives and friends for their departed loved ones, and prolongs indefinitely the hold of the priest over the guilty fears and hopes of people which otherwise would end at death. It is not difficult to imagine the anguish in the heart of a devout Roman Catholic who accepts the teachings of his church and believes that his father or mother, son or daughter, is suffering in the flames of purgatory. Millions of people are steeped in that superstitious system, and those who sincerely believe it will do almost anything to provide relief. It is not strange that the Roman Church accumulates wealth.

What a striking contrast there is between a Protestant and a Roman Catholic funeral! For the Protestant death is his promotion to glory-land, his coronation. He has gone to heaven to be with Christ. He has preceded us to the Father's house. We gather not primarily to mourn a loss, but to celebrate a victory. The Scriptures are read, and the words of Christ comfort our hearts: "Let not your hearts be troubled: believe in God, believe also in me. In my Father's house are many mansions; if it were not so, I would have told you; for I go to prepare a place for you. And if I go and prepare a place for you, I come again, and will receive you unto myself; that where I am, there ye may be also." And the words of Paul, such as these: "For me to live is Christ, and to die is gain . . . having the desire to depart, and be with Christ; for it is very far better"; ". . . willing rather to be absent from the body, and to be at home with the Lord"; etc. Christian hymns about heaven are sung, such as: "Safe in the arms of Jesus"; "O think of the home over there"; "When we all get to heaven"; "And I shall see Him face to face, and tell the story, 'Saved by grace'"; "Beyond the sunset"; hymns which speak of heaven as our home. Then words of comfort and consolation are spoken to the bereaved family, words of inspiration and warning to the congregation, urging them to accept Christ as Saviour and to walk in His way as He is the way that leads to heaven.

But how different is the Roman Catholic funeral! We quote the words of Stephen L. Testa as he describes a funeral that he attended recently:

"It was a high requiem mass, with three priests officiating, all in black robes, chanting a dirge of penitential psalms in Latin, in lugubrious tones which heighten the wailing and crying of the bereaved family especially if they come from Latin countries. The friends of the family read the prayer on the prayer card given to them at the door by the undertaker, praying to Jesus to have mercy on the soul of the deceased and release it soon from the 'devouring flames' (of purgatory) where it is supposed to be imprisoned. At one point during the mass the priest will sprinkle the casket with holy water and pronounce the 'absolution of the dead,' and then he will fumigate it with sweet smelling burning incense, walking around the casket or catafalque, mumbling Latin prayers.

"No hymns about heaven are sung. It is a fact that *Catholic prayer books have no songs about heaven.* And no sermon or words of consolation are spoken by the priest to the bereaved family, for the whole service is intended to appease God, that He may have mercy on the soul of the deceased and deliver him soon from the flames of purgatory. If any words are spoken in English it is to induce the friends of the bereaved family to pay for more requiem masses to be said in the future at $5.00 per, for the refreshment and repose of that soul in purgatory."

The strong public sentiment that is found everywhere against obtaining money under false pretenses should apply to the Roman Catholic priests who extort money from deceived relatives for prayers and masses which they pretend will better the condition of the dead. And the church that maintains this species of dishonesty should be held in disrepute and contempt by all honest people regardless of denominational differences.

Our conclusion, therefore, after an extensive survey of the doctrine of purgatory is that it is not in the Bible, that it is a human invention and contrary to what the Bible teaches. Redeemed souls are cleansed, not by the fires of purgatory, but by the blood of Christ and in this present life; for the Bible says, "The blood of Jesus his Son cleanses us from *all* sin" (I John 1:7)—thereby eliminating once and for all any need for such a horrible place as purgatory. We do not say that any person who believes in purgatory cannot be a Christian. Experience shows that Christians as well as unbelievers sometimes are very inconsistent, that they may accept without thinking it through a doctrine or theory that is contrary to what the Bible teaches and to what their hearts know to be true. But how thankful we should be that we are not under the false teaching of a misguided church or priesthood that threatens us with the torments of purgatory, that instead we have the assurance that at death we go immediately to heaven and enter into its joys.

XI. THE INFALLIBILITY
OF THE POPE

1. Definition. 2. The Nature of the Pope's Infallibility. 3. Infallibility not Taught in the Bible. 4. History of the Doctrine Before 1870. 5. The Vatican Council of 1870. 6. Errors of the Popes.

1. DEFINITION

The Vatican Council which met in Rome, in 1870, defined the doctrine of the infallibility of the pope as follows:

". . . We teach and define that it is a dogma divinely revealed that the Roman Pontiff, when he speaks *ex cathedra*, that is, when in discharge of the office of pastor and doctor of all Christians, by virtue of his supreme Apostolic authority, he defines a doctrine regarding faith and morals to be held by the universal Church, by the divine assistance promised him in blessed Peter, is possessed of that infallibility with which the divine Redeemer willed that His Church should be endowed for defending doctrines regarding faith and morals, and that therefore such definitions of the Roman Pontiff of themselves—and not by virtue of the consent of the Church—are irreformable."

To this pronouncement there was attached the inevitable anathema of the church on all who dare to disagree:

"But if any one—which may God avert—presume to contradict this our definition: let him be anathema."

It will be noticed that in this pronouncement there are three important restrictions: (1) Infallibility is not claimed for every statement made by the pope, but only for those made when he is speaking *ex cathedra*, that is, seated in his papal chair, the chair of St. Peter, and speaking in his official capacity as the head of the church. (2) The pronouncement must be intended as binding on the whole church. Infallibility is not claimed for statements addressed to particular segments or groups within the church which may relate more or less to local conditions. And (3) the

235

pronouncements must have to do with matters pertaining to "faith and morals." In actual practice, however, the term "faith and morals" is broad enough and elastic enough to cover almost any and every phase of religious and civil life. Practically every public issue can be looked upon as having some bearing on faith or morals or both. The Vatican takes full advantage of this, and the result is that within the Roman Church almost any statement issued by the pope is assumed to be authoritative.

2. THE NATURE OF THE POPE'S INFALLIBILITY

The doctrine of papal infallibility does not mean that the pope is infallible as a man. It does not relate to his personal habits. It does not mean that he is sinless. Nor does it mean that he is inspired as were the apostles so that he can write Scripture. It means rather that in his official capacity as teacher of the church he has the guidance of the Holy Spirit so that he can interpret and state clearly and positively doctrines which allegedly have been a part of the heritage of the church from the beginning. Theoretically he cannot produce new doctrines, but some of the decrees issued have had that effect.

That the alleged infallibility cannot relate to personal morals is perfectly clear in the light of history. We merely state a fact when we say that some of the popes have been grossly immoral. That was one of the contributing factors in the rapid progress of the Protestant Reformation. Roman Catholic historians readily admit these facts. Some of the popes have been so illiterate that it would be absurd to attribute to them scholarly ability sufficient to propound doctrine. Even Cardinal Bellarmine, a Jesuit and a papal champion, now a canonized saint, frequently warned pope Clement VIII (1592-1605) that, not being a theologian, he could not expect to understand the Molinist controversy (concerning semi-Pelagianism). Words such as those of Pius V (1566-1572), to the effect that all the Huguenots should be exterminated, are explained away on the ground that in such cases the pope was not speaking *ex cathedra.*

It is interesting to notice that the popes, in issuing their decrees or pronouncements, do not label them *ex cathedra* or *not ex cathedra.* We may be sure that if this power were a reality they would not hesitate so to label them, that in fact they would find it very advantageous to do so. Surely it would be of inestimable value to know which deliverances are *ex cathedra* and which are not, which are infallible and authoritative and which are only private observations and therefore as fallible as those of anyone else. It seems impossible to secure such a list. We may safely assume that the proclamation of pope Pius XII regarding the assumption of the Virgin Mary (1950) was *ex cathedra*. According to some Roman Catholic writers such utterances are relatively infrequent. It is also interesting to notice that neither the Church of Rome in her corporate capacity, nor any of her infallible popes, have ever given the world the benefit of their sanctity and infallibility in a commentary on the Bible, which assuredly would be a blessing of inestimable value. In fact they have never published an infallible exposition of even one chapter.

How then is anyone to know whether any given pronouncement is *ex cathedra* and therefore infallible? The pope presumably would be the most likely person to know his own intentions. How does he distinguish between pronouncements? Can he call up this peculiar kind of inspiration at any time? Does he have a particular sensation or feeling of any kind when exercising it?

A rather amusing aspect of this whole affair is the extreme reluctance of all the popes since 1870, when this decree went into effect, to use this amazing gift. The church and the world have passed through many controversies and have been faced with many perplexing problems in the solution of which some infallible pronouncements with divine authority behind them would have been of inestimable blessing. But instead the hierarchy as well as others have often been perplexed and have made many mistakes—we need recall only such events as the support given by the Vatican to Mussolini in his rise to power and in his military campaigns in Ethiopia and Spain, the concordat signed with Hitler, and the unfailing support given the Spanish dictator Franco since he first came to power. During these perplexing times the popes have been as confused as anyone else. They have merely issued "encyclicals" (formal letters, in Latin, addressed to all the bishops), for which no infallibility is claimed, and which can be modified or set aside by a successor. But of what conceivable value is papal infallibility unless it be to insure clarity and certainty of statement when circumstances make it desirable that the church should speak with authority? Furthermore, the procedure now followed when a pope wants to make an important statement is that he asks certain theologians or bishops to make a study of the subject and to give him their report. The report is then submitted to many others, whose opinions over a long period of time are considered. Last of all he decides on the matter. But if he possesses the attribute of infallibility why should he consult with theologians and bishops who individually are subject to error? Why is he not able to make the pronouncement merely upon his own authority? We take this reluctance as *prima facie* evidence that all concerned know that in reality no such infallibility exists, and that they do not want to risk being caught up by such statements.

The average Roman Catholic layman usually assumes that anything

the pope puts in writing relating to faith and morals is as infallible as
if it had been uttered by Christ Himself. But representative churchmen
are more cautious and warn that it is not easy to distinguish between
ex-cathedra and non-*ex cathedra* statements.

The notion that any human being is in any way infallible does not
commend itself to the mind of a Christian. To most people such a claim
does not seem worthy of serious consideration. There can hardly be any
more brazen exhibition of arrogance, bigotry, and intolerance than this
claim that the pope, who in reality is a mere man, is the very mouthpiece
of God on earth, God's sole deputy, and that he can impose dogmatic
decrees under pain of excommunication and death in this life and the
loss of eternal salvation in the next. How true the words of England's
Lord Acton, himself a Roman Catholic, who after visiting Rome and
seeing at firsthand the workings of the papacy wrote: "All power corrupts, and absolute power corrupts absolutely."

How utterly different is this attitude of the popes from that of Peter,
in whose succession they claim to follow, who humbly called himself a
"fellow-elder" and who warned so clearly against "lording it over the
charge allotted to you"! (I Peter 5:1-3). And, more importantly, how
utterly different from the attitude set forth by Christ, who said: "Ye know
that the rulers of the Gentiles lord it over them, and their great ones
exercise authority over them. Not so shall it be among you: but whosoever would become great among you shall be your minister; and whosoever would be first among you shall be your servant: even as the Son
of man came not to be ministered unto, but to minister, and to give his
life a ransom for many" (Matt. 20:25-28).

The doctrine of infallibility appeals to many people who are poorly
informed and who are drifting spiritually. These people know practically nothing about the Bible. Consequently, they have no sound
theology on which to base their actions. Oftentimes they are bewildered
by the conflicting claims of the various churches and by the disappointing
conduct of some church members. Particularly in the spiritual realm a
state of uncertainty is a state of misery; so the Roman Church finds this
situation ideally suited for her purpose. She skillfully presents her claims
to speak with divine authority, and it is not surprising that there are
those who respond. These people are fascinated by the call of a church
which promises stability and calm. If the priest or the church says a thing
is all right, then for them it is all right. Their consciences are relieved
in that they no longer have to worry about the right or wrong of certain
actions. They tend to surrender without first examining the promised
certainty, only to find after it is too late that they have been cruelly
deceived and that they cannot surrender their consciences to the rule of
any man or church.

3. INFALLIBILITY NOT TAUGHT IN THE BIBLE

The silence of Scripture concerning an infallible church or concerning Peter as an infallible pope is sufficient to disprove the idea. Yet the most prominent characteristic of the papacy, the thing that sets it apart from all other churches, is its claim to supremacy, authority, infallibility. Had there been an infallible source of authority in the church, it is inconceivable that Peter, the alleged bishop of Rome, writing two general epistles and mentioning his departure which he indicated was close at hand (II Peter 1:15), would not have acquainted the members of the church as to what guide or authority they were to follow after he was taken from them, or how that guide or authority was to be chosen. But he does not even mention the subject. On the other hand Christ and the apostles warned against false Christs, false prophets, false teachers who would arise and make such claims.

The Bible says: "For as many as are led by the Spirit of God, these are sons of God" (Rom. 8:14). But the Church of Rome demands that all follow blindly and with implicit faith the interpretation of the Bible given by the pope and his hierarchy. In doing so it usurps the place of the Holy Spirit as teacher and leader. That Peter, the alleged first pope, was not infallible as a teacher of faith and morals is evident from his conduct at Antioch when he refused to eat with Gentile Christians lest he offend certain Jews from Jerusalem (Gal. 2:11-16). Instead, he would have fastened the ritual requirements of Judaism on the new Christian church. This should have been no problem at all for him if he had the special guidance of the Holy Spirit claimed by the Church of Rome for the pope. Furthermore, if any one of the apostles was to be chosen as the infallible head of the church, it would seem that that one should have been Paul, and not Peter. For both as a man and as a teacher Paul was a far greater personality. But the fact is that the New Testament nowhere gives the slightest indication that any man was to be chosen for that position.

In the New Testament, in addition to the two letters written by Peter, we have thirteen written by Paul. But in none of those does he refer to Peter as the bishop of Rome, or of any other church. In Paul's most important letter, that to the church of Rome, he does not so much as mention Peter. In his letter to Timothy he mentions the office of bishop or elder, but he does not mention that of archbishop, supreme bishop, or pope. Surely if such an important office as supreme bishop or pope existed he would have mentioned it. Nor in the literature of the early church during the second or third century is there any mention of a supreme bishop or pope. There are references to Christ as the Chief Shepherd, but none to any man as having that or any similar title.

The fact is that we have our infallible rule of faith and morals in the New Testament Scriptures. And having that it is not necessary to bestow infallibility on any man. For one who wants to know the truth, we point him to the Scriptures and say: "Here it is. Read and practice what is taught here and you will live. The one who turns aside from this rule will not have life."

4. HISTORY OF THE DOCTRINE BEFORE 1870

We may well ask: If the doctrine of infallibility was taught by Christ or by any of the apostles, why did the Roman Catholic Church wait for more than eighteen centuries before giving it acknowledgment? Dr. Geddes MacGregor, in his book, *The Vatican Revolution,* says:

"In spite of the early recognition of the importance of the See of Rome and the consequent prestige of its bishop, there is not even a hint of an *ex cathedra* notion before the eleventh century. Even in the fourteenth, in the lively debates on the nature of papal pronouncements, no such common notion was being either combatted or upheld" (p. 137).

And Edward J. Tanis, in his booklet, *What Rome Teaches,* says:

"*Ireneus,* who was a disciple of Polycarp (a disciple of John the apostle), died about the year 200. He knew what the early church believed and taught, and he wrote many books against heresies of various kinds, but Ireneus never taught that Christ intended any bishop to be the infallible head of the church.

"*Tertullian* was the greatest theologian of the early church before Augustine, the learned scholar who developed the doctrine of the Trinity, emphasizing the equality of the Father, Son and Holy Spirit. He died in the year 220. If any man knew what Christ and the apostles taught, Tertullian knew it. But Tertullian never heard of an infallible head of the church.

"One of the ablest scholars in the early church was *Jerome,* who died in 420. He provided the church with a new and better translation of the Scriptures, and until this day his Latin translation of the Bible has been in use in the Roman Catholic Church, evidence that this scholar is held in high esteem among Roman Catholics. But even so great a scholar did not teach that the church had an infallible head.

"*Gregory the Great* was one of the most powerful and influential popes, bishop of the congregation in Rome from 590 to 604. He made a large contribution to the improvement of the preaching and music of the church and was an ardent defender of the Catholic traditions, but Gregory never taught that he was the infallible head of the whole church. Foakes-

Jackson, the scholarly historian, quotes Gregory the Great as saying that the title of pope as 'Ecumenical Bishop' (bishop of the whole church) was 'proud and foolish' and 'an imitation of the devil' " (p. 17).

The clear teaching of history is that the office of pope was a gradual development. The early bishops in Rome knew nothing of it. They neither claimed the title nor exercised the power. But as time went on, particularly after the fall of the Roman empire, more and more power, political as well as ecclesiastical, fell into the hands of the bishop of Rome, and so the papacy developed.

For centuries before the doctrine of papal infallibility was adopted there was much difference of opinion as to where that infallibility lay. Some held that it rested in the councils speaking for the church. Two councils, that of Constance (1415), which deposed the first pope John XXIII after he had held the office for five years and had appointed several cardinals and bishops who continued to hold their offices, and that of Basle (1432), declared that "even the pope is bound to obey the councils." At another time it was held that infallibility lay in acts of the councils approved by the pope. But in 1870 it was declared to reside in the pope alone, and all good Roman Catholics now are compelled to accept that view. The Jesuits, because of their influence at the Vatican and their ability to influence the popes, supported that view. But the principal question remains: Which council pronouncement was "infallible," that of Constance and Basle? Or that of the Vatican Council? Clearly they are contradictory and cannot both be right.

That the popes have not always been considered infallible is made clear by a review of events in the late 14th and early 15th centuries. Such a survey is given by Dr. Harris as follows:

"In the 1300's, the popes moved to Avignon, France, and for seventy years were manifestly subservient to the French kings. This has been called the 'Babylonian Captivity' of the papacy. Following this time, Gregory XI went back to Rome. His successor, Urban VI (1378-1389) made an election promise to return to France, but election promises are not always kept and he later refused. The French then called his election illegal and elected a new rival pope, Clement VII (1378-1394). This schism continued until a council was called at Pisa in 1409 which deposed both rival popes and elected a new one, Alexander V (1409-1410). The rival popes refused to accept the council and so three popes were on the scene. After the death of Alexander V, he was succeeded by John XXIII whom Roman Catholics do not acknowledge and whose name the present pope has taken to show the illegality of the first John XXIII. Roman Catholics do not accept the Council of Pisa as an ecumenical council (that is, one representative of the whole church). But most of them accept Alexander V whom it elected! ('Hefele, *History of the Church Councils,* Vol. 1, p. 58). The Council of Pisa declared that a council is superior to a pope.

"The schism continued and the Council of Constance (1414-1418) was called. This council deposed all three popes and elected a new one, Martin V (1417-1431). . . . The Council of Constance also declared that a council is superior to a pope, and thus it acted to depose three popes at once. Hefele, one of the best known Roman authorities, takes the odd position that the first forty sessions of the council were not ecumenical but that sessions 41-45, presided over by Martin V whom they elected, were ecumenical. Martin proceeded to confirm all the decrees of the first forty sessions except those which minimized the papacy. Here, of course, was the pope's dilemma. If the earlier sessions were valid, the Council was supreme over the pope. If not, the other popes were not deposed and Martin V was not rightly elected! The Vatican Council of 1870 declared: 'They err from the right course who assert that it is lawful to appeal from the judgment of the Roman Pontiff to an ecumenical council, as to an authority higher than that of the Roman Pontiff.' This is wonderful. The pope is higher than a council. The Vatican Council made him so! But a previous council, just as regular, had denied him to be so" (Article, *The Bible Presbyterian Reporter,* Dec., 1958).

The Council of Constance declared that "every lawfully convoked ecumenical council representing the church derives its authority immediately from Christ, and every one, the pope included, is subject to it in matters of faith, in the healing of schism, and the reformation of the Church." But the Vatican Council of 1870 has decreed that infallibility is vested in the pope as head of the church, when speaking *ex cathedra.*

There were times during the Middle Ages when the popes increased their power until they were the unquestioned rulers in both the church and the state. Some deposed kings and lesser civil officials and could imprison or commit individuals to servitude for life. The decree of excommunication, directed against individuals, in which those excommunicated were cut off from the church and were placed outside the protection of the civil law, and the interdict, by which whole nations were branded as outlaws and placed under the ban, were terrible things. Some popes took it upon themselves to declare any political action not pleasing to them null and void, as Innocent III did with Magna Carta after it had been won by the people of England from a despotic king, or as Pius V did in 1570 when he attempted to "uncrown" Queen Elizabeth I, of England, and to release the people of England from allegiance to her. The Roman Catholic ideal is that the pope should be able to crown and uncrown kings, and that kings and other civil rulers should acknowledge that their power comes from God through the pope as God's representative on earth. Where the Roman Church has been able to realize its ideal it has made civil rulers vassals of the pope.

Before 1870 the ultimate authority commonly acknowledged in the Roman Church was the church speaking through its councils. While the doctrine of papal infallibility had been discussed for some centuries, it had never met with general favor. Instead, it had been repugnant to many of the most eminent scholars and theologians and to a large majority of the hierarchy. For nearly two hundred years before the Vatican Council the Roman Catholic bishops, clergy and laity of England and Ireland had denied that infallibility was a doctrine of the church. In 1825, for instance, when the restoration of political privileges to English Roman Catholics was under discussion in Parliament, a British government commission asked a panel of Irish Roman Catholics if the Roman Church held that the pope was infallible. The bishops correctly replied that it did not. On the basis of that assurance the privileges were restored.

Two catechisms in general use before 1870 verify this position. Keenan's *A Doctrinal Catechism,* asks: "Must not Catholics believe the pope in himself to be infallible?" And the answer is: "This is a Protestant invention; it is no article of the Catholic faith; no decision of his can oblige, under pain of heresy, unless it is received and enforced by the teaching body, that is, the bishops of the church" (p. 305). When papal infallibility was decreed by pope Pius IX in 1870, this question and answer were quietly omitted from the catechism without note, comment or explanation. The *Catechism of the Catholic Religion* gave substantially the same reply (p. 87).

It is well known that Cardinal Newman was strongly opposed to the promulgation of the doctrine of infallibility. But having left the Church of England in order to join the Roman Church and having given it such fulsome praise, he was powerless to prevent the change and did not have the courage to come back out of it. Shortly before the decree was issued he wrote to a friend, comparing the impending decree with that setting forth the Immaculate Conception which was issued in 1854: "As to the Immaculate Conception, by contrast there was nothing sudden, or secret, in the proposal. . . . This has taken us all by surprise." And on January 28, 1870, while the council was in session, he wrote to Bishop Ullathorne, deploring what seemed imminent, and asked: "What have we done to be treated as the Faithful never were treated before? Why should an aggressive and insolent faction (by which he meant the Jesuits) be allowed to make the hearts of the just to mourn whom the Lord hath not made sorrowful?" It was a bitter pill for Newman to swallow, but he submitted and acknowledged papal infallibility.

5. THE VATICAN COUNCIL OF 1870

The council which ratified the infallibility decree was clearly stacked in favor of the Jesuit controlled papal party. MacGregor, who has made a special study of this council and its effect on the Roman Church, says:

"Out of the 541 prelates from Europe, the Italian peninsula, with a population of 27 million, was represented by 276, or 11 more than the whole of the rest of the continent including Britain and Ireland. . . . Even more horrifying is the fact that those of the Papal States that had not at that time been seized, and which had a population of less than three-quarters of a million, were represented by sixty-two bishops, while five million Roman Catholics elsewhere were represented by only three bishops—those of Paris, Cambrai and Cologne—all three critical of the standpoint of the papalist party. . . . It was calculated in an anonymous pamphlet circulated in Rome after the Council had been in operation for five months and attributed to Mgr. Darboy, Archbishop of Paris, that one hundred ninety-one members of the Council had no constitutional right to be there at all" (*The Vatican Revolution*, p. 28, 29).

The church historian, Philip Schaff, says there was strong opposition to the call for the council, and that delegates representing 80 million Roman Catholics were opposed to it. A preliminary vote in secret session gave the delegates a limited opportunity to express themselves. Eighty-eight delegates voted against it, 65 voted for it with reservations, and over 80 abstained. But the papal party was in firm control and easily carried the final voting. To take sides against the strong-willed pope and against the Jesuits a minority had to be particularly courageous to express itself at all. It was a foregone conclusion that the decree would be passed. Opposition clearly was futile, and could mean reprisals affecting the delegates' present positions or injury to any chances for future promotion. Before the final vote was taken 410 bishops petitioned in favor of the dogma, and 162 against it.

Among those who opposed the decree was the scholarly archbishop Strossmayer, who made a famous speech in which he declared boldly:

"I have set myself to study with the most serious attention the Old and New Testaments, and I have asked these venerable monuments of truth to make known to me if the holy pontiff, who presides here, is the true successor of St. Peter, vicar of Christ, and the infallible doctor of the church. I find in the apostolic days no question of a pope, successor to St. Peter, the vicar of Jesus Christ, any more than a Mohammed who did not then exist. Now having read the whole New Testament, I declare before God, with my hand raised to that great crucifix, that I have found no trace of the papacy as it exists at this moment."

And in concluding his speech he said:

"I have established: (1) that Jesus gave to His apostles the same power that He gave to St. Peter. (2) That apostles never recognized in St. Peter the vicar of Jesus Christ. (3) That Peter never thought of being pope, and never acted as if he were a pope. (4) That the councils of the first four centuries, while they recognized the high position which the bishop of Rome occupied on account of Rome, only accorded to him the pre-eminence of honor, never of power or jurisdiction. (5) That the holy fathers in the famous passage, 'Thou art Peter and upon this rock I will build my church,' never understood that the church was built on Peter (*super Petrum*) but on the rock (*super petram*), that is, on the confession of the faith of the apostle. I conclude victoriously, with history, with reason, with logic, with good sense, and with a Christian conscience, that Jesus Christ did not confer any supremacy on St. Peter, and that the bishops of Rome did not become sovereigns of the church, but only by confiscating one by one all the rights of the episcopate."

The bishops from the United States and Canada had very special reasons for disliking the infallibility decree. Lord Acton, of England, a Roman Catholic historian and editor whose scholarship cannot be questioned, recognized the peculiar circumstances under which this decree placed the American bishops and wrote in their defense:

"The Americans ask how they are to live under the free constitutions of the Republic, and maintain their position of equality with their fellow-citizens, after committing themselves to the principles attested by papal infallibility, such as: (1) Religious persecution and the coercive power of the church. (2) The claim of Catholicism to exclusive mastery in the state. (3) The pope's right to dispense from oaths. And (4) The subjection of the civil power to his supreme dominion."

The discussion was abruptly closed before all the opponents had been heard. When the vote was to be taken practically all of those who were opposed to the decree absented themselves, since they did not want to be officially on record against it. Five hundred thirty three delegates answered in the affirmative, 2 answered in the negative, and 106 were absent. And well might any delegate hesitate before voting against the decree, for to it would be attached the anathema: "If any one—which may God avert—presume to contradict this our definition, let him be anathema."

The decree having been passed, all the bishops were required to give their consent. MacGregor writes:

"Some of the recalcitrant bishops were exceedingly dilatory in sending in their submission. But they did, and the papalists have ever since made a great deal of this fact. The alternative to submission was excommunication. This extreme penalty is terrible for a devout layman, since it deprives him of the sacraments, the greatest solace in a Catholic life. It is even worse for a priest for it cuts him off absolutely from every friend he is likely to have, not to mention his livelihood, making him at worst an object of contempt, at best an object of pity. But for a bishop excommunication is a sentence almost past endurance. Even the most heroic could hardly be expected to face it" (*The Vatican Revolution*, p. 63).

Thus the Roman Church, having no sure Scriptural anchorage concerning the problem of authority, drifted about for centuries before solving this problem. As we have indicated, some of the strongest opposition to the infallibility decree came from within the Roman Church. The leading German theologian, Dollinger, who had been a teacher of theology for 47 years, strenuously opposed the decree, and insisted that the three leading criteria in all such controversies—universality, antiquity, and consent—were clearly lacking. He could not be induced to change his mind, and was excommunicated on April 17, 1871. A further result of the decree was that a small group of anti-infallibilists met in Munich, Germany, in September, 1871, withdrew from the Roman Catholic Church, and formed the "Old Catholic" Church, which, although not as well known as it should be, continues to this day and serves as a salutary and inconvenient reminder of the outrage perpetrated against the leading German theologian of the Roman Catholic Church.

By its vote the Council in effect abdicated its power and acknowledged that there was nothing that any future council could do that could not be done as well or better by the pope himself. Since the pope is acknowledged to have the guidance of the Holy Spirit and therefore to possess every power that a council could have, he has no particular need to call a council. This was clearly foreseen by Dollinger who, in a monumental work, *Papal Infallibility* (1871) wrote:

"Councils will for the future be superfluous: the bishops will no doubt be assembled in Rome now and then to swell the pomp of a papal canonization or some other grand ceremony, *but* they will have nothing to do with the dogma. If they wish to confirm a papal decision . . . this would be bringing lanterns to aid the light of the noon-day sun.

"If the bishops know the view and will of the pope on any question, it would be presumptuous and idle to vote against it. An ecumenical assembly of the church *can have no existence,* properly speaking, in the presence of an 'ordinarius ordinariorum' and infallible teacher of faith, though, of course, the pomp, ceremonial, speeches, and voting of a council may be displayed to the gaze of the world. . . .

"Bishops who have been obliged to swear 'to maintain, defend, increase, and advance the rights, honors, privileges, and authority of their Lord the Pope—and every bishop takes this oath—cannot regard themselves, or be regarded by the Christian world, as free members of a free council."

The practical effect of the infallibility decree has been to stifle the development of theological doctrine within the Roman Church. For only the pope can speak with authority, and when he speaks there can be no opposition. No longer can a church council or a theologian appeal to the Scriptures as against the pope. Paul says: "The word of God is not bound" (II Tim. 2:9). But by this decree the Word of God is frozen and chained down by a well-nigh unbreakable chain.

It is interesting to notice that in the early Christian and later Roman Catholic Church history there have been but twenty-one ecumenical councils, the latest having been the Second Vatican Council, which was called by pope John XXIII, and which began its sessions in Rome, in October, 1962. It would seem, however, that such a council can be little more than a puppet gathering, since any action that it may take can become effective only after that action has been approved by the pope. It is safe to say that nothing will be done contrary to the pope's wishes.

MacGregor calls the infallibility decree "the most momentous decision in the history of the Roman Church" (p. 3). He says that it "sounded the death knoll to the democratic element in the Roman Catholic tradition"; and adds that, "So absolute is the papal authority that not even the entire church may dare to review or modify the pope's judgment in any way. If the whole of the rest of the church should disagree with the pope, the whole of the rest of the church would be in error" (p. 6).

That the Vatican Council does mark a turning point in the history of the Roman Church is clear. For centuries the popes avoided church councils like the plague, because they regarded them as rivals to their own authority. But the Vatican Council changed all of that by absolutizing the pope's power and thus making all councils practically superfluous. The papacy today tolerates no criticism from its own people. There was a time in the early history of the church when priests, monks, and even the laity could express their criticisms of the church and be heard. But that has all disappeared and today the Roman Church is a total dictatorship with an infallible pope at its head. Says Dr. Walter M. Montano, former editor of *Christian Heritage,* "All voices are silenced; protests are crushed; dissenters are excommunicated. A total dictatorship—in spirit and letter—rules every aspect of the Roman Catholic Church" (booklet, *Can a True Catholic Be a Loyal American?*, p. 14).

6. ERRORS OF THE POPES

It is difficult to say whether a claim such as that of infallibility is more wicked or ridiculous. It certainly is wicked, because it gives to a man one of the attributes of God and usurps the headship of Christ in the church. And it is ridiculous, because the history of the popes reveals many grievous errors, moral and doctrinal, with one often denying what another has confirmed. The claim to infallibility is so fantastic that it is hard to take seriously since the "infallible" church and the "infallible" popes have made so many mistakes. Many of their solemnly worded decrees are contradictory to the Word of God. And much of the prestige and temporal power of the Roman Church was gained through the use of forgeries such as the alleged "gift of Constantine," or the Isadorian decretals.

Many of the popes have taught heretical doctrines. Some have been grossly immoral, although the theologians say that this does not affect their official powers. Several have been condemned by later popes and church councils, and some have been declared "antipopes," that is, fraudulently chosen or elected, and later dropped from the official record. Among popes committing serious errors are the following:

Callistus (bishop of Rome, 221-227) is said by Hippolytus, a third century writer, to have been a kind of unitarian, identifying the Father and the Son as one indivisible Spirit.

Liberius, in 358, subscribed to a heretical Arian creed in order to gain the bishopric of Rome under the heretical emperor Constantius. He broke with and anathematized Athanasius, the great trinitarian defender of the Nicene Creed, who records him as an opponent.

Zozimus (417-418) pronounced Pelagius an orthodox teacher, but later reversed his position at the insistence of Augustine.

Vigilinus (538-555) refused to condemn certain heretical teachers at the time of the monophysite controversy, and boycotted the fifth Ecumenical Council which met at Constantinople in 553. When the Council proceeded without him and threatened to excommunicate and anathematize him, he submitted to its opinions, confessing that he had been a tool of Satan (Cf. Hefele, one of the best known Roman Catholic writers, *History of the Christian Councils*, Vol. 4, p. 345).

Honorius (625-638). The heresy of Honorius was clearly official. Dr. Harris has treated this case quite fully in the following paragraph:

"The greatest scandal of this nature is pope Honorius. He specifically taught the monothelite heresy in two letters to the patriarch of Constantinople [that is, that Christ had only one will, which by implication meant that he denied either His deity or His humanity]. The opinion was condemned by the sixth ecumenical council (680) which condemned and excommunicated Honorius by name (*Honorio haeterico anathema,* Session XVI). The Roman breviary contained this anathema until the sixteenth century (until the time of Luther, when apparently the Reformers made so much of it that it was quietly dropped). . . . Honorius was a heretic according to Roman Catholic standards and was condemned by church councils and popes for 800 years. Such facts are not known to most Protestants as they arise from the technical study of history. They naturally are not publicized by Roman Catholics. But facts they are. And they entirely disprove the papal claims" (*Fundamental Protestant Doctrines,* II, p. 13).

This condemnation of Honorius as a heretic shows clearly that the bishops of that time had no idea whatever of papal infallibility. For how can a pope be infallible and at the same time be condemned as a heretic? Also let it be noticed that Honorius held the papal chair for thirteen years.

Gregory I (590-604) called anyone who would take the title of Universal Bishop an antichrist; but Boniface III (607) compelled the emperor Phocas to confer that title upon him, and it has been used by all later popes.

Hadrian II (867-872) declared civil marriages to be valid; but Pius VII (1800-1823) condemned them as invalid.

A curious case arises in regard to Hadrian IV (1154-1159), who authorized the invasion and subjugation of Ireland by the British king, Henry II. That conquest marks the beginning of British rule in Ireland, a thing which has been bitterly resented by the Irish. It is of more than passing interest to note that Hadrian was an English pope, the only Englishman ever to hold that position. But that should make no difference. A pope is a pope regardless of nationality or race. In view of the attitude of later Roman Catholics toward British rule in Ireland, they evidently will have to say that in sanctioning the invasion the pope's decree did not relate to morals. Or perhaps the problem is to be solved by saying that when the pope authorized that much to be regretted invasion he was not seated on the papal chair, but was perhaps at the dinner table, or perhaps reclining on a sofa! Indeed, if at the moment the pope did not happen to be seated on the papal chair we may have to forget the whole matter. For by such means the Roman Church seeks to escape from its embarrassing position as regards this invasion of

Ireland, and to hold that there was no infallible mistake after all. But it will hardly do to say that the pope was not speaking *ex cathedra*. For if he has that great power but fails to use it in such momentous decisions, or uses it carelessly, he surely is culpable.

How can one infallible pope, Eugene IV (1431-1447), condemn Joan of Arc (1412-1431) to be burned alive as a witch, while another pope, Benedict XV, in 1919, declares her to be a saint?

There has been some dispute in the Roman Church concerning which version of the Vulgate should be used. Pope Sixtus V (1585-1590) preferred the old version, personally supervised every sheet of an edition then being published, and prefixed an editorial bull to the first volume excommunicating anyone who in republishing the work should make any alterations in the text. But it turned out that the work contained so many errors that it had to be recalled, and another infallible pope published another version, altered in many particulars.

The condemnation of Galileo for his theory that the earth moves around the sun is a special case in point. Dr. Zacchello has stated this well:

"Were popes Paul V (1605-1621) and Urban VIII (1623-1644) infallible when they condemned Galileo for holding a true scientific theory? Did they not declare the Copernican theory was false, heretical, and contrary to the word of God? Did they not torture and imprison Galileo in the dungeons of the Inquisition for not sharing their erroneous views? In their decree prohibiting the book of Copernicus, *De Revolutionibus,* the congregation of the index, March 5, 1619, denounced the new system of the mobility of the earth and the immobility of the sun as 'utterly contrary to the Holy Scriptures'" (*Ins and Outs of Romanism*, p. 28).

How is the decree of Clement XIV (July 21, 1773) suppressing the Jesuits to be harmonized with the contradictory decree of Pius VII (August 7, 1814) restoring them?

Sixtus V (1585-1590) recommended the reading of the Bible, but Pius VII (1800-1823) and various other popes condemned that practice.

As regards infallibility in the moral sphere, consider these cases. Pope John XI (931-936) was the illegitimate son of pope Sergius III by a wicked woman named Marozia. The nephew of John XI, who took the name John XII (956-964), was raised to the papacy at the age of 16 through the political intrigue of the Tuscan party which was then dominant in Rome, and proved to be a thoroughly immoral man. His tyrannies and debaucheries were such that, upon complaint of the people of Rome, the emperor Otho tried and deposed him. Some of the sins enumerated in the charge were murder, perjury, sacrilege, adultery, and incest. Yet he is reckoned as a legitimate pope through whom the unbroken chain of apostolic authority descends from Peter to the pope of the present day.

Alexander VI (1492-1503) was one of the Borgia popes, from Spain, and had been made a cardinal at the age of 25. He had six illegitimate children, two of whom were born after he became pope. The charge of adultery was brought against him repeatedly. His third son, Caesar Borgia, was made a cardinal and was appointed to command the papal armies. The intrigues and immoralities of his daughter, Lucretia Borgia, brought a full measure of disgrace upon the papal office. The Roman Catholic historian, Ludwig Pastor, in his *History of the Popes*, grants that he lived the immoral life of the secular princes of his day, both as cardinal and as pope (V, 363; VI, 140); that he obtained the papacy by the rankest simony (V, 385); and that he brought that office into disrepute by his unconcealed nepotism and lack of moral sense (VI, 139). The eloquent reformer, Savonarola, urged his deposition, whereupon Alexander had him condemned as a heretic, hanged, and publicly burned in 1498.

John XXIII (1410-1415) was deposed by the Council of Constance because of simony and immorality, and the Roman Church now attempts to deny that he ever was a legitimate pope. Apparently the present John XXIII will have to be known as pope John XXIII, the Second. During the period of history known as the Middle Ages many of the popes were guilty of nearly every crime in the catalogue of sin. Twenty-nine of those who held the office at one time or another but who are now said to have obtained it by fraud or otherwise to have been unfit for it are now listed as "anti-popes." Repeatedly the papal office was bought and sold by cardinals and popes as unworthy men sought to gain control. These abuses, together with many others, are described with surprising frankness and detail in a recent book, *The Papal Princes*, by a Roman Catholic, Glenn D. Kittler, with the Nihil Obstat of Daniel D. Flynn, S.T.D., Censor librorum, and the Imprimatur of cardinal Spellman (1960; 358 pages; Funk & Wagnalls, New York).

Just recently still another pope has been deposed. The Pontifical Year Book for 1961 eliminates pope Stephen VIII (929-931) from the authentic line of popes. The present pope was registered in 1958, after his election, as the 263rd pope. By the "ousting" of pope Stephen VIII he becomes the 262nd in the official list.

We have called attention to the numerous false doctrines set forth by pope Pius IX in his Syllabus of Errors (1864). We single out just one for special mention as completely contrary to our American ideals of civil and ecclesiastical relations, namely, that which declares that the church and the state should be united, with the church in the dominant position. In fact he went so far as to declare that the separation of church and state is one of the principal errors of our age. Recently, however, the Knights of Columbus have circulated a pamphlet in which they declare that the pope in condemning the separation of church and state did not have in mind the kind of separation that exists in the United States. But the Syllabus made no exception for the United States. It was an unqualified assertion of the basic principles that should govern the church and the state everywhere in the world. The United States has the same form of government today that it had in 1864. Hence the Knights of Columbus are quite clearly resorting to subterfuge, and are simply attempting to shield the Roman Church from responsibility concerning one of its official doctrines which is diametrically opposed to our American form of government. The almost universal feeling today, even among enlightened Roman Catholics, is that the issuance of the Syllabus of Errors was in itself a serious error.

And yet despite these cases of error and many others that could be cited, the infallibility decree, which was retroactive and therefore applies to all earlier as well as later popes, officially pronounces all of the popes infallible as teachers of faith and morals.

We should point out that there have been several popes who expressly disclaimed the attribute of infallibility (we may even say, the divine attribute of infallibility, for only God is infallible as regards faith and morals), most conspicuous of whom have been Vigilinus, Innocent III, Clement IV, Gregory XI, Hadrian VI, and Paul IV.

Thus Rome's claim to infallibility is contradicted by Scripture, logic, and history. Dr. Harris writes appropriately:

> "The fact is, the popes are not infallible. They preach and teach another gospel. They not only contradict themselves, but contradict the Bible as well. All the fanfare of wealth, the tinsel of ceremony, and the prestige of power which we witness at Rome cannot avail before God. The present pope John XXIII is neither infallible nor orthodox nor the successor of Peter, nor of any other of the holy apostles of Jesus Christ. He is an imposter as was the first John XXIII of the fifteenth century."

As we have indicated, this alleged attribute of infallibility has been used only very sparingly by the popes, evidently because they do not want to risk being caught up by false statements. Apparently it has been formally invoked on only three occasions—twice by pope Pius IX, once when he proclaimed his own infallibility, and once when without benefit of a church council he set forth the doctrine of the immaculate conception of the Virgin Mary; and once by pope Pius XII, when he promulgated the doctrine of the assumption of the Virgin Mary. And, we would say, in each instance the pope employing it set forth colossal error. Indeed the pope must be quite a practical joker if, possessing such power, he so seldom gives any indication that he is using it, but keeps the people guessing whether or not he is speaking authoritatively.

Probably no other element of the papal system causes the Romanists more embarrassment than this doctrine of papal infallibility. In the first place it asserts a doctrine that can be easily disproved; and in the second place it serves to focus attention on the utter unreasonableness of the powers claimed by and for the pope. To Protestants the whole *ex cathedra* business appears, on the one hand, as particularly monstrous and vicious, and on the other, as just a big joke—a joke perpetrated on the Roman Catholic people who are so docile and unthinking and so poorly informed as to believe in and submit to such sophistry.

XII. PENANCE; INDULGENCES— SALVATION BY GRACE OR BY WORKS?

1. Definition. 2. Penance as a System of Works. 3. Salvation by Grace. 4. Further Scripture Proof. 5. Indulgences. 6. Historical Development of the Doctrine of Indulgences. 7. Assurance of Salvation.

1. DEFINITION

In the Roman system penance is one of the seven sacraments, the fourth in the series. The word, however, is used in two different senses. As a sacrament and in the broad sense it refers to the act of confession on the part of the penitent, together with the priest's pronouncement of absolution and his assigning of certain works to be done by the penitent. In the narrow sense penance has reference only to the works assigned by the priest and their performance by the penitent.

The Baltimore Catechism defines penance as follows:

"Penance is the sacrament by which sins committed after baptism are forgiven through the absolution of the priest" (p. 300).

Another catechism, published in New York, says:

"The priest gives penance in Confession, to help me to make up for the temporal punishment I must suffer for my sins. The penance given to me by the priest does not always make full satisfaction for my sins. I should, therefore, do other acts of penance . . . and try to gain indulgences" (Indulgences are remissions of so many days or months or years of punishment in purgatory).

And in a Roman Catholic training book, *Instructions for Non-Catholics,* we read:

"In the sacrament of penance, God gives the priest the power to bring sinners back into the state of grace and to prevent them from falling into

254

the abyss of hell. Moreover, after confession some temporal punishment due to sin generally remains, and some of this punishment is taken away in the penance (prayers) the priest gives you to say. You should perform other acts of penance also so that you can make up for the temporal punishment due to sin and to avoid a long stay in purgatory. The Church suggests to us these forms of penance: prayer, fasting, giving alms in the name of Christ, the spiritual and corporal works of mercy, the patient sufferings of the ills of life, and the gaining of indulgences" (p. 95).

2. PENANCE AS A SYSTEM OF WORKS

Penance, as the catechisms say, involves confession of one's sins to a priest and the doing of good works as the only way by which sins committed after baptism can be forgiven. According to the Roman system God has established a tribunal on earth in which the priest sits as judge, through which the penitent receives absolution and an assignment of works to be performed, in doing which he shows his sorrow for sin. According to this view God does not cancel out all the punishment due to the sinner when he forgives his sins. No limit is set to the works and services that can be demanded. The poor sinner is always left at the mercy of the priest.

The Church of Rome thus demands acts of penance before she grants forgiveness, inferring that the sacrifice of Christ was not sufficient to atone fully for sin and that it must be supplemented to some extent by these good works. But what God demands is not acts of penance, but *repentance,* which means turning from sin, vices, injustice and all wickedness in whatever form: "Let the wicked forsake his way, and the unrighteous man his thoughts; and let him return to Jehovah, and he will have mercy upon him; and to our God, for he will abundantly pardon" (Is. 55:7). From the Greek New Testament edited by Erasmus, Luther discovered that Jesus did not say, "Do penance," as interpreted by the Roman Church, but "Repent."

Protestantism is primarily a reassertion of New Testament Christianity, the teaching that salvation is by faith rather than works. Romanism on the other hand teaches that salvation depends ultimately upon ourselves, upon what we do, that one can "earn" salvation by obedience to the laws of the church, indeed that the saints can even store up excess merits in heaven beyond the requirements of duty, through such things as regular attendance at church, masses, rosary prayers, fastings, the wearing of medals, crucifixes, scapulars, etc. These excess merits Rome calls "works of supererogation." Mary and the saints are said to have stored up vast treasures of merit, from which the pope can draw and dispense to the faithful as they perform the works assigned by the priests.

Bishop Fulton J. Sheen expresses this doctrine in the following words:

"Through them, the Church gives her penitents a fresh start. And the Church has a tremendous spiritual capital, gained through centuries of penance, persecution, and martyrdom; many of her children prayed, suffered, and merited more than they needed for their own individual salvation. The Church took these superabundant merits and put them into the spiritual treasury, out of which repentant sinners can draw in times of spiritual depression" (*Peace of Soul*, p. 208).

Here indeed is *salvation by works*. This is the bondage in which the Church of Rome keeps its millions of adherents. But against all this futility of human works stand the simple words of Scripture. In response to the question, "What must I do to be saved?" the Scripture answers simply and clearly: "Believe on the Lord Jesus, and thou shalt be saved" (Acts 16:30-31).

Dr. Woods has well said:

"Penance is a wholly different thing from Gospel repentance. Penance is an outward act; repentance is of the heart. Penance is imposed by a Roman priest; repentance is the work of the Holy Spirit. Penance is supposed to make satisfaction for sin. But nothing that the sinner can do or suffer can satisfy the divine Justice. Only the Lord Jesus Christ can do that, and He did it once for all when He made atonement on the cross and completely satisfied the divine law. Rome's error is like that of the heathen religions, seeking to win forgiveness or deliverance from sin by self-inflicted or priest-imposed punishment. Such are the tortures of Buddhist and Hindu devotees.

"What God desires in the sinner is not a punishment of oneself for sins, but a change of heart, a real forsaking of sin, shown by a new life of obedience to God's commands.

"In short, penance is a counterfeit repentance. It is the work of man on his body; true repentance is the work of God in the soul. The divine Word commands: 'Rend your heart, and not your garments' (Joel 2:13). Penance is 'rending the garments'; an outward form without inward reality, which Christ commands His people not to do" (*Our Priceless Heritage*, p. 132).

In all Roman Catholic catechisms and theological books which deal with this subject it is taught that God grants forgiveness only to those who, on their part, try to atone for their sins through worthy fruits of penance. In the words of the French catechism, "Our satisfaction must be in proportion with the number and measure of our sins." This false teaching, that forgiveness is only partial and that it is given only for a price, is the real basis of the Roman Catholic doctrine of salvation, and must always be kept in mind in any effective controversy with Roman Catholics.

In other words, while Romanism teaches that Christ died for our sins, it also teaches that His sacrifice was not sufficient, that our sufferings must be added to make it effective. In accordance with this, many have tried to earn salvation by fastings, rituals, flagellations, and good works of various kinds. But those who attempt such a course always find that it is impossible to do enough to earn salvation.

Self-inflicted suffering cannot make atonement for sin. To suffer as a Christian in defense of a righteous cause serves to identify one with his Lord and Master. But we cannot choose our own course of discipline, for "We are *His* workmanship." We can only submit to His will. Each receives a discipline divinely suited to him and, as a living stone, each is polished for his unique setting when the Lord of Glory makes up His jewels. It has been the sad history of the Roman Church that while making much of outward evidences of humility and suffering on the part of its people as administered through its doctrine of penance, its priests, bishops, cardinals, and popes have flouted those principles and usually have lived in luxury and splendor.

The easy way in which the Church of Rome deals with sin is seen in this doctrine of penance. She does not require genuine repentance and sorrow for sin, nor any genuine purpose to turn from it, but accepts as a substitute an act of allegiance to the church and the penitent's "fear of punishment." Accordingly, the penitent receives pardon on comparatively easy terms, particularly so if he is on good terms with the priest. He is assigned some task to perform, usually not too hard or irksome, sometimes merely the recital of a given number of "Hail Marys." The result is that he has no scruples about resuming his evil course. But the Bible teaches that the first duty of a sinner who is moved to true repentance is to confess his sin to God, and to Him alone, and to turn effectively from his sin. "If we confess our sins," says John, "he is faithful and righteous to forgive us our sins, and to cleanse us from all unrighteousness" (I John 1:9).

"The basic and fatal error of Romanism," says Dr. C. D. Cole, "is the denial of the sufficiency of Christ as Saviour. It denies the efficacy of His sacrifice on the cross. Romanism has a Christ, but He is not sufficient as a Saviour. What He did on Calvary must be repeated (in the mass) and supplemented (through works of penance), and this makes priestcraft and sacramentarianism necessary. Romanism is a complicated system of salvation by works. It has salvation to sell, but not on Isaiah's terms— without money and without price (Is. 55:1). It offers salvation on the installment plan, and then sees to it that the poor sinner is always behind in his payments, so that when he dies there is a large balance unpaid, and he must continue payments by sufferings in purgatory, or until the debt is paid by prayers, alms and sufferings from his living relatives and friends. The whole system and plan calls for merit and money, from the cradle to the grave, and even beyond. Surely the wisdom that drew such a plan of salvation is not from above, but is earthly and sensual" (Sermon delivered in the Jarvis Street Baptist Church, Toronto).

Good works, of course, are pleasing to God, and they have an important and necessary place in the life of the Christian. They naturally follow if one has true faith, and they are performed out of love and gratitude to God for the great salvation that has been bestowed. If any professing Christian does not want to obey the Bible and live a good Christian life, that is proof that his faith is not sincere. Good works, in other words, are not the cause and basis of salvation, not what the person does to earn salvation, but rather the fruits and proof of salvation—"Not by works done in righteousness, which we did ourselves, but according to his mercy he saved us, through the washing of regeneration and the renewing of the Holy Spirit" (Titus 3:5).

The born again Christian produces good works as naturally as the grape vine produces grapes. They are a part of his very nature. He performs them not to get saved but because he is saved. And it is to be observed further that the distinguishing mark of a saint is not, as in the Roman Church, what one has done for God, but what God has done for him.

Penance is, therefore, merely another clever tool or scheme to control those who are ignorant of the Biblical way of salvation. We should confess all our sins to God, and to Him alone; and we need confess our personal shortcomings only to those who may have been injured by us.

3. SALVATION BY GRACE

The Bible declares that the salvation of sinners is a matter of grace. From Ephesians 1:7-10 we learn that the primary purpose of God in the work of redemption was to display the glory of this divine attribute so that through succeeding ages the intelligent universe might admire it as it is made known through His unmerited love and boundless goodness to guilty, vile, helpless creatures. Accordingly all men are represented as sunk in a state of sin and misery, from which they are utterly unable to deliver themselves. When they deserved only God's wrath and curse, He determined that He would graciously provide redemption for a vast number. To that end Christ, the second person of the Trinity, assumed our nature and guilt, and obeyed and suffered in our stead; and the Holy Spirit was sent to apply that redemption to individual souls. On the same representative principle by which Adam's sin is imputed to us, that is, set to our account in such a way that we are held responsible for it and suffer the consequences of it although not personally responsible for it, our sin in turn is imputed to Christ, and His righteousness is imputed to us. This is briefly yet clearly expressed in the Westminster Shorter Catechism (Presbyterian), which says: "Justification is an act of God's free grace, wherein He pardoneth all our sins, and accepteth us as righteous in His sight, only for the righteousness of Christ imputed to us, and received by faith alone" (Ans. to Q. 33).

The word "grace" in its proper sense means the free and undeserved favor of God exercised toward the undeserving, toward sinners. It is something that is given irrespective of any worthiness in man; and to introduce works or merit into any part of the system vitiates its nature and frustrates its design. Just because it is grace, it is not given on the basis of preceding merits. It cannot be earned. As the very name imports, it is necessarily gratuitous; and since man in his fallen nature is enslaved to sin until it is given, all the merits that he can have prior to it are bad merits and deserve only punishment, not gifts, or favor.

Because of His absolute moral perfection God requires spotless purity and perfect obedience in His intelligent creatures. This perfection is provided for His people in that Christ's spotless righteousness is imputed to them, so that when God looks upon the redeemed He sees them clothed not with anything properly their own, but with this spotless robe. We are told that Christ suffered as a substitute, "the just for the unjust." And when man is encouraged to think that he owes to some power or art of his own that salvation which in reality is all of grace, God is robbed of part of His glory. By no stretch of the imagination can a man's good works in this life be considered a just equivalent for the blessings of eternal life. We are, in fact, *nothing but receivers;* we never bring any adequate reward to God, we are always receiving from Him, and shall be unto all eternity.

All men naturally feel that they should earn their salvation, and a system which makes some provision in that regard readily appeals to them. But Paul lays the ax to such reasoning when he says: "If there had been a law given which could make alive, verily righteousness would have been of the law" (Gal. 3:21); and Jesus said to His disciples, "When ye shall have done all the things that are commanded you, say, We are unprofitable servants; we have done that which it was our duty to do" (Luke 17:10). We have no righteousness of our own; for as Isaiah says: "All our righteousnesses are as a polluted garment"—or as the King

James Version expresses it, "as filthy rags" (64:6). Salvation is based solely on the merits of Christ who suffered and died for His people. It is for this reason that God can demand perfection of all who enter heaven and yet admit into heaven those who have been sinners.

When Isaiah wrote, "Ho, every one that thirsteth, come ye to the waters, and he that hath no money; come ye, buy and eat; yea, come, buy wine and milk without money and without price" (55:1), he invited the penniless, the hungry, the thirsty, to come and to take possession of, and to enjoy the provision, free of all cost, as if by right of payment. And to buy without money must mean that it has already been produced and provided at the cost of another. The farther we advance in the Christian life, the less we are inclined to attribute any merit to ourselves, and the more to thank God for all.

Paul says concerning some who would base salvation on their own merit, that, "being ignorant of God's righteousness, and seeking to establish their own, they did not subject themselves to the righteousness of God" (Rom. 10:3), and that they were, therefore, not in the church of Christ. He makes it plain that "the righteousness of God" is given to us through faith, and that we enter heaven pleading only the merits of Christ. Time and again the Scriptures repeat the assertion that salvation is of grace, as if anticipating the difficulty that men would have in coming to the conclusion that they could not earn it by their own works.

The reason for this system of grace is that those who glory should glory only in the Lord, and that no redeemed person should ever have occasion to boast over another. Romanism destroys this purely gracious character of salvation and substitutes a system of grace plus works. No matter how small a part those works may be said to play (and in the Roman system they play a conspicuously large part), they are decisive and ultimately they are the basis of the distinction between the saved and the lost; for he that is saved can then justly point the finger of scorn and say, "You had as good chance for salvation as I had. I accepted, and you rejected the offer; therefore you deserve to suffer." But if saved by grace, the redeemed remembers the mire from which he was lifted, and his attitude toward the lost is one of sympathy and pity. He knows that but for the grace of God he too would be in the same state as those who perish, and his song is, "Not unto us, O Jehovah, not unto us, But unto thy name give glory, For thy lovingkindness, and for thy truth's sake" (Ps. 115:1).

And yet the Council of Trent, in its opposition to the Reformers' doctrine of justification by faith alone, and in defense of its doctrine of penance, declared:

"If anyone saith that justifying faith is nothing else but confidence in the divine mercy which remits sin for Christ's sake alone; or, that this confidence alone is that whereby we are justified, let him be anathema" (Sess. VI, Can. 12).

In taking this stand Rome rejects the teaching of Augustine, one of the church fathers whom she is most anxious to follow; for Augustine taught that salvation is purely by the grace of God, not by human merit.

Against Rome's anathema Paul declares: "But though we, or an angel from heaven, should preach unto you any gospel other than that which we preached unto you, let him be anathema" (Gal. 1:8). And again he says: "For as many as are under the works of the law are under a curse: for it is written, Cursed is every one who continueth not in all the things that are written in the book of the law, to do them" (Gal. 3:10)— by which he teaches that anyone who would earn salvation by keeping the law must render perfect obedience—"all the things that are written in the book of the law, to do them," which manifestly is impossible for any human being. Hence Paul's anathema shatters that of Rome, for it is the curse of God upon those who teach salvation by works in any form.

It was this great truth of justification by faith alone that flashed through the mind of Martin Luther when, while still a monk, on a pilgrimage to Rome he was climbing the *scala sancta,* the "sacred stairway," one step at a time and on his knees, trying to find peace with God. Suddenly the truth burst upon him and he saw the real meaning of the verse, "The just shall live by faith" (Rom. 1:17; Gal. 3:11, KJV). Immediately he got up on his feet and walked down the steps. How wrong it was for anyone to think that he could earn salvation through works of penance! Although Luther did not make a formal break with the Roman Church until some years later, his action in Rome that day was in reality the prelude to the Protestant Reformation.

4. FURTHER SCRIPTURE PROOF

New Testament Christianity repudiates the doctrine that the believer must, or can, earn his salvation through good works assigned by a priest, or that saving grace can be conferred by a priest regardless of his moral character, or that such grace is given because of allegiance to any church organization. Instead it teaches that we have only to receive it in simple faith. Witness the following:

"By grace have ye been saved through faith; and that not of yourselves, it is the gift of God; not of works, that no man should glory" (Eph. 2:8-9).
"The righteous shall live by faith" (Rom. 1:17).

"Knowing that a man is not justified by the works of the law but through faith in Jesus Christ . . . because by the works of the law shall no flesh be justified" (Gal. 2:16).

"But if it is by grace, it is no more works: otherwise grace is no more grace" (Rom. 11:6).

"If righteousness is through the law, then Christ died for naught" (Gal. 2:21).

"And Abraham believed God, and it was reckoned unto him for righteousness. Now to him that worketh, the reward is not reckoned as of grace, but as of debt. But to him that worketh not, but believeth on him that justifieth the ungodly, his faith is reckoned for righteousness" (Rom. 4:3-5).

"Being therefore justified by faith, we have peace with God through our Lord Jesus Christ" (Rom. 5:1).

"He that believeth on the Son hath eternal life; but he that obeyeth not the Son shall not see life, but the wrath of God abideth on him" (John 3:36).

"Believe on the Lord Jesus, and thou shalt be saved, thou and thy house" (Acts 16:31).

"But now apart from the law a righteousness of God hath been manifested, being witnessed by the law and the prophets; even the righteousness of God through faith in Jesus Christ unto all them that believe. . . . We reckon therefore that a man is justified by faith apart from the works of the law" (Rom. 3:21, 22, 28).

What a significant coincidence it is that this doctrine of justification by faith is given such prominence in the Epistle to the Romans, since Rome later became the seat of the papacy! It seems to be written there as if intended as a strong and permanent protest against the errors of the Roman Church. For if we believe that we are justified by faith in Christ, who died "once for all," we certainly cannot believe in "the sacrifice of the mass" as so many repetitions of that sacrifice on Calvary.

5.   INDULGENCES

Another subject closely related to penance is that of *indulgences*. The Baltimore Catechism defines an indulgence as follows:

"An indulgence is the remission in whole or in part of the temporal punishment due to sin. . . . There are two kinds of indulgences—plenary and partial. . . . A plenary indulgence is the full remission of the temporal punishment due to sin. . . . A partial indulgence is the remission of a part of the temporal punishment due to sin. . . . To gain an indulgence we must be in the state of grace (the result of a satisfactory confession to a priest) and perform the works enjoined."

Another catechism defines an indulgence more briefly as "a remission of that temporal punishment which even after the sin is forgiven, has yet to be suffered either here or in purgatory."

An indulgence, therefore, is an official relaxation of law which shortens or cancels one's sufferings which are due to sin, and it usually has reference to the sufferings in purgatory.

Indulgences are granted by the pope, who the Roman Church teaches has personal jurisdiction over purgatory; and they usually are granted through the priests in return for gifts or services rendered to the church or as a reward for other good deeds.

This release from punishment is said to be possible because the church has a vast treasury of unused merits which have been accumulated primarily through the sufferings of Christ but also because of the good works of Mary and the saints who have done works more perfect than God's law requires for their own salvation. Thus not only the suffering and death of Christ, but also the good works of Mary and the saints, are the grounds of forgiveness of sins. The church claims to be able to withdraw merits from that store and to apply them to any member of the church just as if he had suffered what was necessary for the forgiveness of sins.

An indulgence is not, as many think, and as the term might suggest, a license to commit sin, although that has been done on numerous occasions particularly among the more backward and ignorant people. That was one of the abuses that developed during the Middle Ages. An indulgence is rather a limited period of release from punishment (1 day, 10 days, 30 days, etc.) which the person would have to suffer in purgatory. Indulgences are like prison paroles. A man sentenced to imprisonment for one year may be released at the end of eight months if he manifests true repentance and good behavior. In the same manner an indulgence affords release from a part or the whole of the punishment due because of sin.

Indulgences are not available to those guilty of mortal sin until they confess to a priest and receive absolution. The priest forgives only mortal sins in the confessional, which saves the soul from hell. He does not forgive venial sins. Those have to be atoned for in the present life, or they have to be suffered for in the flames of purgatory after death.

According to Roman doctrine, all those dying in mortal sin go straight to hell, where prayers, masses, etc., cannot affect any alleviation of their pains. For those who go to confession, the absolution of the priest removes mortal sin and thereby releases from eternal punishment; but temporal punishment remains and must be atoned for by good works, prayers, etc., in this life, or by sufferings in purgatory in the next. In practice this means that every Roman Catholic, if he escapes hell, must reckon on going through purgatory. As we have indicated earlier, there seems to be no very definite catalogue of what sins are mortal and what are venial. The classification varies from place to place and from priest to priest, depending on the priest's definition and the nature of the purpose to be served.

Only the pope can grant a plenary indulgence, cancelling out all suffering. Bishops can grant up to forty days, and parish priests shorter periods. During the Middle Ages plenary indulgences were granted to persons who visited the holy sepulcher in Jerusalem, or joined the crusades to regain the Holy Land, or helped in the work of persecuting Protestants and extirpating heresy. Partial indulgences were granted for lesser services, such as reciting the rosary, ritual prayers to the Virgin Mary or to some saint, self-denials, gifts of money or property, etc. The list is almost endless.

Technically, indulgences must not be sold by the church. But that rule has been violated on many occasions, and the spirit of it on many more. The sale is still carried out in countries where Rome is supreme, and where it is not calculated to revolt public opinion. The first pope John XXIII sold indulgences openly, but was condemned for it by a church council. The present pope John XXIII, in 1958, granted a plenary indulgence to all who attended his coronation ceremony or listened by radio or viewed the ceremony by television or news reel. And again, on Easter Sunday, 1961, he granted a plenary indulgence to all who attended the Easter observance in St. Peter's Square in Rome. Most indulgences, however, are partial. The Roman Church is careful to point out that "only God knows exactly how much of the temporal punishment is taken away by an indulgence." Hence no one can ever be sure that he has done enough and that he needs no further indulgences.

Likewise many "dispensations" or permissions to do certain things not approved by the Roman Church are granted each year, such as marriage between a Roman Catholic and a Protestant, annulments, and even, as in Spain until recently, permission on payment of a small fixed sum, to eat meat on Friday, which otherwise would be a mortal sin. There is no fixed price for "dispensations," but it is understood by both parties that there are to be gifts and that for the more important ones the gifts are to be generous.

6. HISTORICAL DEVELOPMENT OF THE DOCTRINE OF INDULGENCES

The practice of granting indulgences was unknown in the early church. It arose in the Middle Ages in connection with penances imposed by the

Roman Church. At first they were applicable only to the living. Gelasius, bishop of Rome in 495, said: "They demand that we should also bestow forgiveness of sins upon the dead. Plainly this is impossible for us, for it is said, 'What things soever ye shall bind upon earth.' Those who are no longer upon the earth He has reserved for His own judgment." Now if this pope was infallible in his exegesis of Scripture, the current Roman practice is false. In the year 1096, at the Synod of Clermont, Urban II promised a plenary indulgence for all who would take part in the crusades. From that time on indulgences became a fixed and remunerative part of the religion of Rome. Pope Clement VI (1342-1352) proclaimed the doctrine that the church has control of a treasury of merit, and that it can give to one believer the excess merits of another. And in 1477 pope Sixtus IV declared that indulgences were available for souls in purgatory. Since that time indulgences have been considered helpful to the dead as well as to the living.

The abuses connected with the granting or sale of indulgences became so flagrant that clear-thinking men in the clergy and laity alike came to despise the practice. Many of the promoters played heartlessly on the credulity of the bereaved. The great majority of mankind was pictured as suffering in the flames of purgatory until their survivors provided the money for their release. The demoralization which resulted from this evil practice spread like poison through the church. In 1250 Grosseteste, bishop of London, England, protested to the pope that the low morality of the priesthood was due to the purchasable pardon. A commission of cardinals reported to pope Paul III (1534-1549) that pardons and dispensations produced indescribable scandals, and begged him to put an end to them.

For years indulgences were sold openly. When pope Leo X (1513-1521) needed money to complete the great cathedral of St. Peter's in Rome he offered plenary indulgences for sale and sent his preaching monk emissaries to every nation, promising forgiveness of sins to the living and release from the flames of purgatory for the dead. Those found a ready market in many parts of Europe. It was for this purpose that the monk Tetzel came through the region around Wittenburg, Germany, making the claim: "A soul is released from purgatory and carried to heaven as soon as the money tinkles in the box."

It was this corrupt practice of taking money from the people that revolted Martin Luther against the whole system of indulgences and led to his posting the 95 theses on the cathedral door in Wittenburg, October 31, on the eve of All Saints Day, 1517. That act marked the beginning of the Protestant Reformation. The 86th thesis read: "The pope's riches at this day far exceed the wealth of the richest millionaires; cannot he therefore build one single basilica of St. Peter out of his own money, rather than out of the money of the faithful poor?"

Luther's action was in effect a daring challenge to the papal authorities for public debate on each of the propositions listed. Needless to say, his challenge was not accepted. But it did arouse intense excitement and it met with a ready response in the hearts of the people over a wide area. And well might he challenge the indulgence system; for in so doing he was simply taking his stand for first century Christianity. We wonder how many who visit St. Peter's cathedral in Rome today realize that the construction of that church was the event that set in motion the Protestant Reformation.

The question may well be asked: If indulgences are so clearly opposed to the Gospel plan of salvation, why did the popes persist in selling them? Or why do they still uphold the practice? The answer is: Because indulgences have been a source of enormous revenue to the Vatican. Although the popes knew there was no warrant whatever in Scripture for such practice, they could not resist the temptation to acquire easy money. By appealing to the superstitions and fears of the people, high and low, they collected large sums. Not only St. Peter's cathedral, but many other projects have been financed in considerable measure by money raised in this manner. Papal indulgences are not sold today; but they still are granted, and it is understood that "the faithful" who come seeking them must not come empty handed.

Having examined the tenets and practices of the Roman Church as regards the matter of individual salvation, we have no hesitation at all in branding as false the entire system of penance and indulgences. And that for the simple reason that those who trust Christ for salvation are justified by faith, not by works. They have no need for penances or indulgences from any priest or pope. The superabundant merits of the saints, alleged to have been accumulated by those who have done more than was required, are purely imaginary. No man can earn his own salvation by good works, much less can he have merits left over which can be transferred to others. The penances and indulgences which the people receive are not only worthless but are clever frauds and are without any foundation whatever in the Bible.

Such a system represents God as forgiving sins, yet holding the sinner guilty and subjecting him to punishment both here and after death. What an arrogant assumption that is on the part of the priests when they presume to take charge of and to dispose as their own the merits of the saints, and even those of Christ Himself! It is readily apparent what effective weapons the assigning of penances and the granting of indulgences really are for keeping a spiritually unenlightened people under the power of the priesthood.

7. ASSURANCE OF SALVATION

The first consequence of the doctrine of penance and indulgences is that the Roman Catholic, though baptized and confirmed, can never have that assurance of his salvation and that sense of spiritual security which is such a great blessing to the Protestant. In proportion as he is spiritually sensitive the person who holds to a works religion knows that he has not suffered as much as his sins deserve, and that he can never do as much as he should in order to be worthy of salvation. The dying Roman Catholic, after he has done all that he can do and after the last rites have been given to him, is told that he still must go to purgatory. There he will suffer unknown torture, with no assurance as to how long it will continue, but with the assurance that if his relatives pay with sufficient generosity his suffering will be shortened.

But what a contrast with all of that is the death of the true believer, who has the assurance that he goes straight to heaven into the immediate presence of Christ! What a marvelous blessing is the evangelical faith, both in life and at the time of death!

The Council of Trent even pronounced a curse upon anyone who presumed to say that he had assurance of salvation, or that the whole punishment for sin is forgiven along with that sin. Such assurance is pronounced a delusion and a result of sinful pride. Rome keeps her subjects in constant fear and insecurity. Even at death, after extreme unction has been administered and after thousands of rosary prayers have been said "for the repose of his soul," the priest still cannot give assurance of salvation. The person is never "good enough," but must serve in purgatory prison to be purified of venial sins before he can be admitted to the celestial city. No one can be truly happy without the assurance of salvation; and particularly in spiritual matters a state of doubt and uncertainty is a state of misery.

The simple truth, however, is that one can be saved and can be sure that he is saved. All he has to do is to trust in the finished work of Christ and to receive from Him the gift of eternal life. For His Word declares: "He that heareth my word, and believeth him that sent me, *hath eternal life,* and cometh not into judgment, but hath passed out of death into life" (John 5:24). "He that believeth on the Son *hath eternal life;* but he that obeyeth not the Son shall not see life, but the wrath of God abideth on him" (John 3:36). The Bible tells us that "the blood of Jesus his Son cleanseth us from *all* sin" (I John 1:7), and that to be

"absent from the body" is to be "at home with the Lord" (II Cor. 5:8).
Paul expected that at his death he would go into the immediate presence
of Christ, for he wrote to the church in Philippi: "But I am in a strait
betwixt the two, having the desire to depart and be with Christ; for it
is very far better (no purgatory there!): yet to abide in the flesh is
more needful for your sake" (Phil. 1:23). And in the parable that Jesus
gave of the rich man and Lazarus, Lazarus was carried by the angels
directly from earth to Abraham's bosom (Luke 16:19-31).

Furthermore, Christ is able to *keep His people saved,* not because of
their goodness or faithfulness, both of which are very erratic, but because of His power and grace: "And I give unto them eternal life; and
they shall never perish, and no one shall snatch them out of my hand.
My Father who hath given them unto me, is greater than all; and no one
is able to snatch them out of the Father's hand" (John 10:28-29). This
eternal life of which Christ speaks is a gift (John 3:16); it is made
effective by a supernatural work of the Holy Spirit in the soul which is
called "regeneration" (Titus 3:5), or a new birth, a being "born anew" or
"from above" (John 3:3), and as such it is irrevocable—"for the gifts and
the calling of God are not repented of" (Rom. 11:29). Nothing less than a
supernatural act on the part of God (regeneration) can bring a soul from
a state of spiritual death to a state of spiritual life; and nothing less than
another supernatural act of God could reverse that condition. This is the
true "perseverance of the saints"—not that we persevere in holding on
to God, but that He perseveres in holding on to us.

Thus God wants us to be saved, and He wants us to know that we are
saved. He has told us so in His Word. We have a salvation that is complete, a salvation that meets all the needs of the sinner. In Protestantism
salvation is *present,* when one accepts Christ as Saviour. In Romanism it
is *future,* after he has been through purgatory, and only then if he has
"good works" added to confession, penance, and communion. In Protestantism salvation is a matter of grace. In Romanism one must work hard
for it and must pay dearly for it, and after he has done all that the priest
has prescribed he still cannot know whether he has it or not. And through
it all there stands the anathema of the Council of Trent against all who
affirm the certainty of their salvation. Hence there is not to be found anywhere a consistent Roman Catholic who enjoys the assurance of eternal
life. Nor can Modernism or Liberalism give that assurance, nor Judaism,
nor Mohammedanism, nor any of the pagan religions. Evangelical
Protestantism alone can give that assurance. That was the message of
the Reformation in the sixteenth century when it proclaimed justification
by faith alone.

A very curious thing happened in connection with the death of pope

Pius XII, in 1958. His personal physician, Dr. Galeazzi-Lisi, shortly afterward wrote an article for publication in a Rome newspaper in which he described "the agonizing death of Pope Pius XII," and told of the pope's fear and insecurity regarding the future. But the article met strong disapproval on the part of the church authorities. Copies of the newspaper were confiscated before they could be distributed, and Dr. Galeazzi-Lisi was promptly dismissed from his position. Dr. Walter M. Montano, at that time editor of *Christian Heritage,* recalled that when pope Benedict XV died in 1922 a similar report was given of his death, and added:

"One can feel only a sense of pity for the last end of such a man. How is it possible that the ecclesiastical demigod who had the keys of heaven and earth is unable to use those keys to gain entrance into his own eternal salvation? What a pathetic ending for a man who has devoted his life to religion; who has directed, as they say, 'the barque of St. Peter'; who was infallible; who has elevated the Virgin Mary to a state that no other pope had dared to imagine.

"At the end of his life he dies in fear and agony, not knowing what the future holds in store for him. All the pomp and ceremony, all the masterfully devised rituals in his honor may impress the people, especially Roman Catholics, but they cannot gain him one inch of heaven. And what about his soul and his eternal destiny? What Roman Catholic knows where this pope is right now? The doctrine of the Roman Church established that anyone who can say 'I am saved' at any time in his life commits a mortal sin.

"If pope Pius XII had had the courage to express faith in the only One who died for our sins; if he had realized that there is only one Mediator between man and God; if he had accepted the fact that Christ's death invalidated any other sacrifice and that once for all He died for the sins of the world—then pope Pius XII would not have faced a death of fear and desperation, an 'agonizing death.' Instead, he would have been able to say: 'I know whom I have believed!' " (Issue of December, 1958).

XIII. RITUALISM

1. RITUALISM

If we search for the factors that account for the power and influence of the Roman Catholic Church, not only over its own members but over many others who have no personal connection with that church, we find that one of the most important is its ritualistic worship. The gorgeous vestments, colorful processions, pageantry and mystifying symbolism, the stately music, the solemn intonations of the priests in a singsong voice, the flickering candles, the tinkling bells, the sweet smelling incense, the dim light of the cathedral where Mary holds sway—all are designed to impress the senses and the emotions. Witnessed in a great cathedral, Roman Catholic worship appeals to the senses as much as any spectacular on the stage of the Roxy Theatre in New York. Hollywood could never outdo, nor even equal, the colorful coronation of pope John XXIII, in November, 1958, as that ritual was presented directly to some fifty thousand persons in Rome and to millions more by television and movie film. One news source described the coronation spectacle in part as follows:

"... Swiss guards in polished breastplates and scarlet-and-gold uniforms, and a scarlet-robed ecclesiastic carrying the pontifical tiara. Chaplains in violet soutanes, bishops in white mitres and robes decorated with silver; ecclesiastics in scarlet capes, and the College of Cardinals in cream colored vestments heavy with gold embroidery, followed each other in measured procession. Finally, amid renewed shouts of enthusiasm, the pope was carried in by 12 bearers, seated in the gestatorial chair beneath a richly embroidered canopy. The pontiff wore a gem-studded mitre and the ritual falda. To right and left were members of the noble guard and Palatine Guard in gala uniforms."

All of that in a purely man-made religious display, a ritualistic ceremony that is not even hinted at anywhere in the Bible!

An American observer describes a public appearance of the pope in St. Peter's basilica in Rome in these words:

"First, soldier guards with rifles enter—perhaps 50 of them, then the papal officials. Then borne by 12 men on their shoulders, a huge chair on which the pope sits. He has a white skull cap and is dressed in white robes. We see the light flash on the diamond of his crucifix. Twenty thousand people shout, 'Viva il Papa!' 'Long live the Pope!' He begins to salute the people genially on all sides, scattering his blessings with great liberality. He is carried through the full length of the great church to the great altar and steps from his chair to a red throne on a platform raised above the heads of the people.

"The people are wild with enthusiasm. They cheer and raise their children to see his face. As one looks about at the beaming faces, one wonders if the participants understand the difference between *latria* and *dulia*—one permits devotion to a holy thing, and the other, devotion due only to God. We fear the devotion given him is the type one would give only to his God! . . .

"As he mounts his chair to be borne out again on the shoulders of 12 men dressed in red, the children cry and women plead not to be crushed. The pope is carried out, scattering his greetings all about him. As he is about to pass the curtain, he rises and again gives the apostolic blessing. The vast crowd pours out into the Piazza San Pietro, having seen a man who, to most of them, stands in the place of God. It has been the highest point in their experience—the most exquisite emotion of their lives.

"One wonders what passed through the mind of the old man as the delirious crowds did him such great honor. Once before crowds exclaimed, 'It is the voice of a god and not of a man' (Acts 12:22), but God strikingly demonstrated His displeasure.

"How striking was the dissimilarity between the Lord of heaven and His pretended viceregent in Rome! Jesus was a humble itinerant preacher, but this gentleman rides into the church on the shoulders of 12 men. All the pomp, the ostentation, the lights, the ceremony, all the wealth imaginable, are employed to enhance the grandeur of an institution which in every sense is the opposite of the simple church of the Gospels and the book of Acts" (Article, Henry F. Brown).

Eucharistic and Marianistic congresses, with priests, bishops, and cardinals wearing gorgeous robes and bejeweled mitres, present similar spectacles. In February, 1946, when thirty-two new cardinals were created by pope Pius XII, Americans were surprised to learn that the scarlet robes alone of each new American cardinal's outfit cost $10,000. The pope's robes, of course, are much more expensive. The jewels in the pope's triple-decked crown alone are said to be worth $1,300,000. What a contrast with the manner in which Protestant ministers dress! And what a contrast with the words of the alleged founder of the Roman Church, the apostle Peter, who said to the lame beggar: "Silver and gold have I none" (Acts

3:6). Peter warned against the "wearing of jewels of gold, or of putting on apparel" (I Peter 3:3). Paul, too, could say, "I coveted no man's silver, or gold, or apparel" (Acts 20:33).

Some people, however, want to be dazzled with a theatrical display of religion, and the Roman Church readily obliges. But the total effect of such ritualistic displays, so lacking in spiritual instruction, is usually repulsive to thoughtful minds, and is entirely outside the bounds of true Christianity. What spiritually sensitive souls most condemn seems often to have been the chief attraction for the great mass of people who, without interest in religion as such, are moved by the spectacular display of what seems to be a union of the human and the divine. To the ignorant and uneducated, and also to a considerable extent to the educated, the splendor of the Roman Church appears as something awesome, fascinating, and inspiring. But many a spiritually weary traveler has found after all that such ritual and ceremony is only a mirage seen from a distance, a gorgeous display promising rest for the traveler on his way through a desert land, but failing utterly to supply the water of life that could bring peace and joy to his thirsty heart. Gradually the mirage fades on the horizon, and the desert that was to have bloomed as the rose yields only briars and thorns. How different from all that is the evangelical Protestant service, where with a minimum of ritual the emphasis is on the sermon which is designed to impart Biblical knowledge and to nurture and edify the spiritual and moral nature of man!

Concerning the rituals and ceremonials of Romanism, Stephen L. Testa says:

"Pagan Rome and Jewish Jerusalem had these ceremonials. But when Christ came to save the world He did not copy or adopt any of them; rather He disdained them. He founded His church, not as a hierarchy, but as a simple brotherhood of saved souls, commissioned to preach the Gospel to all the world. The early church, the church of the catacombs, for 300 years had no such ceremonials. It was in the fourth century, after the so-called conversion of Emperor Constantine, that he made Christianity the State Church and those pagan ceremonials were introduced. It was then that the Catholic Church became the Roman Catholic Church. Italy and the other Catholic countries have derived no benefit whatever, spiritual or material, from them, as anyone can see for himself. The Reformation of course rejected them."

We are often amazed at the magnificence of Roman Catholic churches and cathedrals, even in areas where the people are comparatively poor or even in poverty. The following account of how the Roman Church developed in one area is given by August Vanderark, in the booklet, *Christ the Hope of Mexico:*

"The American visitor to Mexico is often amazed to discover an abundance of large beautiful churches in almost every part of the nation. Frequently the question arises, 'How could they afford to construct such a vast number of imposing edifices?' The answer, of course, is slave labor.

"Following the conquest by Cortez, the Indians were forced into slavery by the Roman Church and put to work building its places of worship and other religious structures. In Henry Bamford Parkes' most excellent work, *A History of Mexico*, we read: 'Twelve thousand churches were built in Mexico during the colonial period; and though they testify to the triumph of Christ over Huitzilopochtli (chief god of the Aztecs), they also testify to the skill of the missionaries (Jesuits) in obtaining unpaid labor from the Indians.' Many of the Indians died as a result of being forced into the strenuous labor to which they were not accustomed."

Romanism is largely a religion of ceremonials and rituals, and as such it is a far departure from the purity and simplicity of the Gospel. The supposed blessing is mysterious and magical. No really intelligent participation is required on the part of the people. They are largely spectators watching the pageantry, and are supposed to be blessed simply because they are there. The mystifying mannerisms of the priests, and the mumble-jumble of the unknown tongue used at the altar, tend more toward credulity and superstition. Fifteen centuries of history make it clear that the Roman ritual is powerless to uplift the world. Indeed, is it any wonder that Roman Catholic countries are proverbially impoverished, illiterate, and degraded? We charge Rome with obscuring rather than revealing the simple truth of the way of salvation as set forth in the Bible, and with the addition of many doctrines and practices not found in the Bible. When we tear aside the gaudy trappings of Romanism we find only an ugly skeleton, which because it cannot find support in Scripture, is not able to stand on its own feet. Applicable here are the words of Joel: "Rend your heart, and not your garments" (2:13); and especially the words of Isaiah:

"What unto me is the multitude of your sacrifices? saith Jehovah: I have had enough of the burnt-offerings of rams, and the fat of fed beasts; and I delight not in the blood of bullocks, or of lambs, or of he-goats. When ye come to appear before me, who hath required this at your hand, to trample my courts? Bring no more vain oblations; incense is an abomination unto me; new moon and sabbath, the calling of assemblies, —I cannot away with iniquity and the solemn meeting. Your new moons and your appointed feasts my soul hateth; they are a trouble unto me; I am weary of bearing them" (1:11-14).

Elaborate ritual and ceremony, which theoretically are designed to aid the worshipper, usually have the opposite effect in that they tend to take the mind away from things which are spiritual and eternal and to center it on that which is material and temporal. Artistic ritual and exquisite music often become ends in themselves, and can easily become instruments which prevent the people from joining in the worship of God. The reason the Roman service tends to become more and more elaborate, liturgical, and ritualistic, is that the heart of the exercise, true adoration of God, is missing, and a persistent effort is made to fill up the emptiness and unsatisfactoriness of it all by piling one ceremony and ritual upon another. But ironically, the more that is done the more difficult it becomes to worship God, and so the vicious circle goes round and round.

We object to the elaborate ceremonials and gorgeous furnishings of Romanism, not because of any lack of aesthetic taste, but on theological grounds. Such things may be all right in a theater, but they are out of place in a Christian church. Within proper limits dignity and beauty are characteristics which are proper in the worship of God, as indeed is clear from the prescriptions for worship which were given to the children of Israel. But the various elements of the Old Testament ritual were types and shadows portraying God's plan of salvation. Their purpose was to present the Gospel in picture to a primitive people. But those things were done away in Christ, and no others were put in their place (Heb. 8:5; 9:23; 10:1). The only references to incense, for example, in connection with the New Testament church are found in the book of Revelation where it is used figuratively, referring to the prayers of God's people (Rev. 5:8; 8:3-4). Romanism is in this respect a recrudescence of Judaism, and in its ceremonialism stands much closer to Judaism than to New Testament Christianity. It has a delight in the picture language of ceremonies that were designed for the childhood of the church, and it still is fascinated with the beauty of the temple and its gorgeous ritual.

We maintain that the New Testament assigns *no liturgy at all* for the church. We maintain further that there is a beauty in chaste simplicity, that this characterized the early church, that the departure from this simplicity in the fourth and later centuries was the result of spiritual deterioration, and that most of the ritualism and ceremonialism was taken over from the pagan religion of ancient Rome. But while no required form is demanded, it is necessary that some systematic form be developed, so that "all things" may be done "decently and in order" (I Cor. 14:40). Most churches develop an order of service sufficient to give order and dignity to the service without going to the extreme of Romanism.

Let Protestants not be deceived by the outward splendor of Romanism. The most elaborate rituals will not save one if the heart is not right. Neither the two thousand proscriptions of the Canon Law, nor all the absolutions of the priests, can open the kingdom of heaven for one who is not first of all a true believer.

2. CEREMONIALS

Some of the ceremonials of Romanism are of special interest. First of all and most important is the *Ave Maria,* or "Hail Mary," which was used in part as early as 1508, completed 50 years later, and finally approved for general use by pope Sixtus V at the end of the sixteenth century. It reads as follows:

"Hail, Mary, full of grace; the Lord is with thee; blessed art thou among women, and blessed is the fruit of thy womb, Jesus. Holy Mary, Mother of God, pray for us sinners, now and at the hour of our death. Amen."

The "Hail Mary" is thus a prayer. It is repeated many times in the churches, in the schools, and by individuals in private as a work of penance and as one of the most effective means of storing up merit.

Another ceremonial, always used by Roman Catholics in entering a church as well as in various personal acts, is the sign of the cross. This is considered both a prayer and a public profession of faith. In entering a church they dip the forefinger of the right hand in holy water, and touch the forehead, the breast, and the left and right shoulder, thus tracing upon their person the figure of the cross while reciting aloud or in silence the words, "In the name of the Father, and of the Son, and of the Holy Ghost. Amen."

Fasting has a prominent place in Romanism. When carried out according to the rules of the church it is supposed to gain certain merits for the person fasting. A fast day is not one on which no food at all is eaten, as the name might imply, but one on which persons over twenty-one and under sixty years of age are allowed but one full meal, and are forbidden meats, unless granted a special dispensation. A day of abstinence is one on which meat is forbidden, but the usual number of meals is allowed. Fasting is required during Lent (the forty week days preceding Easter), and on certain other appointed days. Fish, but not other meat, is allowable on Fridays. This, like the days of fasting and the days of abstinence, is of course an empty formalism, a purely arbitrary rule, without any New Testament authority, and can be set aside at any time by a dispensation from the priest because of hard work, sickness, or for various other reasons. Yet the people are taught that under normal conditions it is a mortal sin to eat meat on Friday and on other days of

abstinence. In 1958 pope John XXIII granted Roman Catholics throughout the world a special dispensation to eat meat on Friday, December 26,
the day after Christmas, because of continued Christmas festivities and
celebrations.

The fasts commanded by the Church of Rome are wholly different from
those in the Old Testament. Rome's fasts are purely arbitrary and mechanical, not spiritual, appointed by the popes. They are not necessarily connected with any religious observances. The wild revelry, drinking, and
feasting which precedes Lent and other occasions in Roman communities,
particularly that best known one, the Mardi Gras carnival in New Orleans
and some other cities, proves this beyond dispute. True fasting is a
spiritual exercise usually connected with prayer, repentance, and meditation.

Mere arbitrary fasting is denounced in Scripture as an abomination. To
Jeremiah God said concerning the people of Israel, who were outwardly
religious and observed forms but who in heart rejected Him and broke
His commandments: "Pray not for this people for their good. When they
fast, I will not hear their cry" (14:12). Christ rebuked the Pharisees because they were particular about keeping the fasts but neglected obedience
to God (Matt. 6:16), and Paul warned against man-made commandments
"to abstain from meats" as a mark of apostasy (I Tim. 4:3). How completely arbitrary and unchristian are commandments which impose fasts,
making certain meats edible on some days but not on others, edible at certain times of the day but not at other times, and for some people but not
for others! Paul's words concerning food dedicated to an idol are equally
applicable here: "But food will not commend us to God: neither if we eat
not, are we the worse; nor if we eat, are we the better" (I Cor. 8:8).
That, in fact, is the New Testament principle as regards eating or
fasting.

Still another Roman ceremonial is flagellation, or self-torture. This
is not to be thought of as merely a barbaric and stupid custom practiced
back in the Middle Ages. In some places it still is a reality in our twentieth
century. Emmett McLoughlin, in his *People's Padre* (p. 17), tells how
three times a week, at a certain hour in the evening, the students in the
seminary where he obtained his training were required to go to their
rooms, disrobe, and practice flagellation. And in a recent popular movie,
The Nun's Story, produced under Roman Catholic supervision, the
mother superior is pictured handing the novitiate girl a whip which she is
to use on herself, with the admonition that she should use it "neither too
little, nor too much"; "for," said the mother superior, "the one is as bad
as the other." In the Philippine Islands the fanatical "Flagellantes," at the
Lenten season each year can be seen in processions, carrying heavy

crosses, chanting Latin hymns, and beating their bodies with a scourge until the flesh is raw and bleeding, in a blind hope that through that kind of suffering merit will be stored up and their souls will be released sooner from purgatory. How can an intelligent and professedly *Christian* priesthood allow such things to continue? Flagellation, however, has never been practiced by the rank and file of Roman Catholics.

Another important peculiarity of the Roman Church is its use of the Latin language. It has been a long standing rule that the mass cannot be celebrated in any language other than Latin, that it is better not to celebrate mass at all than to do so in the language of the people. In some places, however, in recent times this rule has been modified so that the mass can be celebrated in the common tongue, or a translation is provided so that the people can follow intelligently what is being said. Early in the Middle Ages, about the year 600, preaching in the Latin tongue was instituted—which surely was one of the most ridiculous things in the world. Latin had been the basis of the Italian language, but was no longer understood by the people. However, preaching never was a very important part of the Roman service, and it is no longer conducted in Latin. But the mass, which is the very heart of the service, still is in Latin, although the great majority of present day congregations know nothing about Latin. A little reflection should convince anyone that neither the Lord's supper as instituted by Christ, nor His passion, which is re-enacted in the mass, was done in Latin. Christ spoke the Aramaic of His day, which was the language of the people. Yet Roman priests hold that it is a sacrilege to commemorate that experience in anything but Latin!

The apostle Paul, who himself was a scholar and who probably could speak more languages than anyone in his audiences, nevertheless insisted that a few words spoken with the understanding were better than many spoken in a tongue that could not be understood: "Howbeit in the church I had rather speak five words with my understanding, that I might instruct others also, than ten thousand words in a tongue" (I Cor. 14:19); and again: "If any man speaketh in a tongue, let it be by two, or at the most three, and that in turn; and let one interpret: but if there be no interpreter, let him keep silence in the church" (I Cor. 14:28); and further: "So also ye, unless ye utter by the tongue speech easy to be understood, how shall it be known what is spoken? for ye will be speaking into the air" (I Cor. 14:9). Protestants always conduct their services in the language of the people, and that surely is more uplifting.

There are certain benefits, however, which in a way seem to accrue to the Roman Church as it conducts its ceremonials under the veil of a dead language. Most importantly, it adds to the air of mystery that surrounds the service, and helps to set the priest apart from the people as a man with special wisdom and special powers. Every priest at times has to bless the "holy water" with which Roman Catholics sprinkle themselves, and which is sprinkled on various objects to purify or consecrate them. The prayer by which that is done intimates that its object really is to drive the devils out of this common water, and indirectly to keep them from the people who are sprinkled. Probably not one priest in a hundred really believes that, and it doubtless would seem rather crude and awkward to go through the ritual in English. But they do not seem to mind doing it in Latin. In Medieval times it was customary for the priest to do a preliminary devil chase before the service began by going back through the audience and sprinkling holy water on the people while calling on all demons and devils to depart. The baptism of infants is an elaborate ritual in which the Devil is exorcised and commanded to depart from the child, and undoubtedly would be somewhat embarrassing if done in English. Yet the Latin ritual is accepted without question. Also, the mother who has given birth to a child is considered polluted and unfit to enter the church with respectable people until she has been "churched" through the use of an ancient ritual which if spoken in English probably would cause so much resentment that it would have to be abandoned. And in theological books detailed instructions to the priests concerning questions relating to sex to be asked of women and girl penitents in the confessional are given in Latin, and so in the main are kept concealed from the public.

Still another problem to be considered in this connection is the appearance of priests and nuns in public in their church garb, which of course is offensive to Protestants. Recently C. Stanley Lowell wrote:

"In long-suffering Mexico which finally rose up in wrath against the church, to this day the clergy are not permitted to appear on the streets in clerical garb. Resentment mounted to such a pitch that the people did not even want to look at the clergy."

And again:

"Roman Catholic politicians dote on public demonstrations of their denominational symbols and observances. Roman Catholicism is a majority faith in many areas of this country. As a majority faith Catholics frequently show insensibility to the religious sensitivities of those who do not share their faith. They may flaunt their religious practices and virtually force them on the entire community. They have an astonishing faculty for never suspecting that the symbol or observance which inspires them may be shocking and abhorrent to persons of another faith."

The fact is that Romanist religious regalia is almost always offensive to those who do not belong to that church. Oftentimes the tendency toward forcing their religion on other people of the community is also carried out by dedicating public statues, parks, schools, etc., to Roman Catholic saints or church leaders. We submit that in fairness to all the people of a community statues, parks, schools, etc., should not be given names that are offensive to the people of the community who are of other faiths.

3. IMAGES

In the first commandment we are commanded to worship God, and none other. In the second commandment we are commanded to worship directly and not through any intervening object: "Thou shalt not make unto thee a graven image . . . thou shalt not bow down thyself to them, nor serve them. . . ." (Ex. 20:4,5).

Literally hundreds of other passages also condemn the making or worshipping of images. A few examples are:

"Ye shall make you no idols, neither shall ye rear you up a graven image, or a pillar, neither shall ye place any figured stone in your land, to bow down unto it: for I am Jehovah your God" (Lev. 26:1). "Cursed be the man that maketh a graven or molten image, an abomination unto Jehovah, the work of the hands of the craftsman, and setteth it up in secret" (Deut. 27:15). "My little children, guard yourselves from idols" (I John 5:21). ". . . the works of their hands . . . the idols of gold, and of silver, and of brass, and of stone, and of wood; which can neither see, nor hear, nor walk" (Rev. 9:20). "What agreement hath a temple of God with idols?" (II Cor. 6:16).

The Jerusalem Conference warned the Gentiles

". . . that they abstain from the pollution of idols" (Acts 15:20).

How very clearly, then, the commandment against the making or use of images or idols (for they are the same thing if used in worship) is written into the law of God!

But in direct opposition to this the Council of Trent decreed:

"The images of Christ and the Virgin Mother of God, and of the other saints, are to be had and to be kept, especially in Churches, and due honor and veneration are to be given them" (Sess. 25).

Where can a more deliberate and willful contradiction of the command of God be found than that?

The practice of the Church of Rome is that she solemnly consecrates images through the blessing of her priests, places them in her churches and in the homes of her people, offers incense before them, and teaches the people to bow down and worship before them. It cannot be denied that the Roman Church has made the second commandment of no effect among her people, and that she teaches for Christian doctrine her own precepts, which are the commands of men. She has not dared to remove the commandment from her Bible, but she has withdrawn it as much as possible from view. Since her practices are contrary to the Bible, she covers up her guilt *by simply omitting that commandment* from her version of the Decalogue and from her catechisms and text books! She then re-numbers the commandments, making the third number two, the fourth number three, and so on. And in order to cover up this deficiency, she splits the tenth commandment in two, thus making two separate sins of coveting—that of coveting one's neighbor's wife, and that of coveting one's neighbor's goods. As a result of this sophistry multitudes of people are misled and are caused to commit the sin of idolatry.

With this official encouragement it is not surprising that images of Christ, Mary, the saints and angels are very common in Roman Catholic circles. They are found in the churches, schools, hospitals, homes, and other places. Occasionally one even sees a little image of Jesus or Mary or some saint on the dashboard of an automobile (often the image of St. Christopher, the patron saint of travelers). Thus as one drives he supposedly has the protection of Jesus, or Mary, or the saint.

Roman Catholics tell us that they do not pray to the image, or idol, but to the spirit that is represented by it. But that is the answer given by idol worshippers the world over when they are asked why they pray to their idols. That was the answer given by the Israelites when they worshipped the golden calf in the wilderness; for after making the idol they said: "These are thy gods, O Israel, which brought thee up out of the land of Egypt" (Ex. 32:4). They did not intend their worship to terminate on the image. They were worshipping their gods *through the use of an image,* or idol, a likeness which they thought appropriately represented their gods. But on other occasions the Israelites worshipped idols as such. Hosea's condemnation of idolatry in Israel: "The workman made it; therefore it is not God" (8:6), implies that the calf of Samaria was worshipped in the Northern Kingdom as a God. See also Ps. 115:4-8. Undoubtedly the better educated do make the distinction between the idol and the god or spirit which it is designed to represent. But in actual practice in Roman

Catholic countries and among the ignorant the tendency is for this distinction to disappear and for such worship to become simply idolatry. The Old Testament prophets and the Bible as a whole makes no distinction between false gods and their images; and the cult practices of the heathen tend to identify them completely. The Israelites were severely condemned for using idols in their worship of God. It cannot be otherwise with the Roman Catholics.

On numerous later occasions the Israelites attempted to worship God through the use of images, but such practices were always severely condemned. Even if it were true that Roman Catholics pray only to the person or spirit represented by the image, it still would be sin, for two reasons: (1) God has forbidden the use of images in worship; (2) there is only one mediator between God and men, and that one is Christ, not Mary, or the saints.

Historically, when men have made images or idols which they could see, as an aid to worship, they later came to think of the images themselves as indwelt by their gods. The images became the centers of attention rather than that which they were supposed to represent. Instead of helping the worshippers they confused them. This has been particularly true in regard to the larger images which are preserved from one generation to another. In the same manner as the heathens, the Romanists make gods of wood and stone, dress them up, paint them with gaudy colors, bow down before them and worship them. The priests encourage the people to have little shrines in their homes at which they can worship. Millions of illiterate people in Europe and in the Americas attribute supernatural qualities to those images. In doing so they feel that they have the full approval of their church—which of course they do have. But the Bible calls such practice idolatry and condemns it. The Bible teaches that God is a Spirit, and that they that worship Him must worship in spirit and truth (John 4:24). We should never forget that one of the most heinous sins of ancient Israel, in fact the besetting sin of ancient Israel, was the worship of idols, and that Israel paid a fearful price for that practice.

Were the apostles to return to earth and enter a Roman Catholic church, they would scarcely be able to distinguish between the pagan worship of idols that they knew and the present day practice of kneeling before images, burning incense to them, kissing them, praying to them, and carrying them in public processions. The Roman Church today is about as thoroughly given over to idolatry as was the city of Athens when Paul visited there. Many priests do not believe in images, but they keep them in their churches because it is established custom and because, they say, it helps the worshippers, particularly if they are uneducated, to have a visual representation of the person they are worshipping.

But how very foolish is the practice of idolatry—
For life man prays to that which is dead.
For health he prays to that which has no health or strength.
For a good journey he prays to that which cannot move a foot.
For skill and good success he prays to that which cannot do anything.
For wisdom and guidance and blessing he commits himself to a sense-less piece of wood or stone.

Romanism, with its image or idol worship, has no appeal at all for the Mohammedan world, which is so strongly opposed to all forms of idolatry. In fact it has made practically no attempt to win Mohammedans. The great mission field of North Africa lies only a short distance across the Mediterranean from Italy, practically on Rome's doorstep. But through the centuries that field has remained almost untouched and unchallenged by Roman Catholicism. Yet Rome sends thousands of missionaries across the oceans to India, Japan, South America, and even to the United States, which even by Roman standards is in much less need of them than is North Africa.

Nor does Roman Catholicism have any attraction for the Jews, who also are strongly opposed to all forms of idolatry. Instead, the Roman Church persecuted the Jews for some fifteen centuries. The evangelization of both Jews and Mohammedans has been left almost exclusively to Protestants.

As we have indicated earlier, Roman Catholics attempt to justify the use of images by making a distinction between what they term *latria,* which is devotion given only to God, *hyper-dulia,* which is given to Mary, and *dulia,* a lower form of devotion which is given to the saints, images, and relics. But in practice that distinction breaks down. The people, particularly those who are illiterate, of whom the Roman Catholic countries have so many, know nothing of the technical distinctions made by the theologians. They worship the images of Mary and the saints in the same way and often with more fervency than they worship those of Christ, or the "Blessed Sacrament" which they believe is the actual body, soul, and divinity of Christ. The only name for their practice is idolatry.

The Old Testament strictly forbade image worship, and in time such practice came to be an abomination to the Jews. With that background it seems incredible that idols should ever have been admitted into the more spiritual worship of the Christian church. But in the fourth century, with the granting of preferred status to the Christian church and the great influx of pagans, the heathen element in the church became so strong that it overcame the natural opposition to the use of images. Most of the people could not read. Hence it was argued that visible representations of Scripture persons and events were helpful in the church.

At the beginning of the seventh century pope Gregory the Great (590-604), one of the strongest of the popes, officially approved the use of images in the churches, but insisted that they must not be worshipped. But during the eighth century prayers were addressed to them and they were surrounded by an atmosphere of ignorant superstition, so that even the Mohammedans taunted the Christians with being idol-worshippers. In 726 the Eastern emperor, Leo III, first attempted to remedy the abuse in his dominion by ordering that the images and pictures be placed so high that the worshippers could not kiss them. But when that failed to achieve the desired ends he issued an order forbidding the use of images in the churches as heathenish and heretical. To support his action a council was called in Constantinople, in 754, which gave ecclesiastical sanction to his actions. This great controversy became known as the "iconoclastic" dispute, a word which means the breaking of images. The Eastern church banned all use of images or icons, and to this day that remains one of the great contrasts between the Eastern Orthodox and the Roman Catholic Church.

But in 787 a council met at Nice, France, repudiated the work of the earlier council, and fully sanctioned the worship of images and pictures in the churches. This action was defended on the principle on which image worship, whether among the heathens or Christians, has generally been defended, namely, that the worship does not terminate on the image but on the object that it represents.

Thomas Aquinas, who is generally acknowledged as the outstanding medieval theologian of the Roman Church, fully defended the use of images, holding that they were to be used for the instruction of the masses who could not read, and that pious feelings were excited more easily by what people see than by what they hear. The popes of the Roman Church have strongly supported the use of images.

The argument in favor of the use of images, that in the Old Testament God commanded the making of the cherubim and the brazen serpent, ignores the fact that the cherubim were not to be used in worship, whereas the images are. The cherubim were placed in the holy of holies where they were not seen by the people but only by the high priest, and then only as he entered once each year, whereas the images are displayed in public. A further and most important difference is that God commanded the making of the cherubim, but He strictly forbade the making of images. Likewise the brazen serpent was not made to be worshipped. When it later became a sacred relic and was worshipped by the people who offered incense to it, good king Hezekiah destroyed it.

The moral and religious effects of image worship are invariably bad. It degrades the worship of God. It turns the minds of the people from

God, who is the true object of worship, and leads them to put their trust in gods who seem near at hand but who cannot save.

Closely akin to the use of images is that of pictures of Christ. And these, we are sorry to say, are often found in Protestant as well as Roman Catholic churches. But nowhere in the Bible, in either the Old or New Testament, is there a description of Christ's physical features. No picture of Him was painted during His earthly ministry. The church had no pictures of Him during the first four centuries. The so-called pictures of Christ, like those of Mary and the saints, are merely the product of the artist's imagination. That is why there are so many different ones. It is simply an untruth to say that any one of them is a picture of Christ. All that we know about His physical features is that He was of Jewish nationality. Yet He more often is represented as having light features, even as an Aryan with golden hair. How would you like it if someone who had never seen you and who knew nothing at all about your physical features, resorted to his imagination and, drawing on the features of his own nationality, painted a picture and told everyone that it was a picture of you? Such a picture would be fraudulent. Certainly you would resent it. And certainly Christ must resent all these counterfeit pictures of Him. He was *the* truth; and we can be sure that He would not approve of any form of false teaching. No picture can do justice to His personality, for He was not only human but divine. And no picture can portray His deity. All such pictures are therefore fatally defective. Like the grave of Moses, the physical features of Christ were intended to be kept beyond the reach of idolatry. For most people the so-called pictures of Christ are not an aid to worship, but rather a hindrance, and for many they present a temptation to that very idolatry against which the Scriptures warn so clearly.

4. ROSARY—CRUCIFIX—SCAPULAR

The rosary may be defined as (1) a series of prayers, in its long form consisting of 15 Paternosters (the Lord's prayer, addressed to God the Father), 15 Glorias, and 150 Hail Marys addressed to the Virgin Mary; or (2) the mechanical device used in counting the prayers, the shorter and more common form being a string or chain of beads divided into five sections, each consisting of one large bead and ten small ones. The large rosary consists of fifteen sections. But usually one who wishes to say the complete rosary goes over the short form three times. In some religious orders the large rosary is used, and is worn as a part of the religious habit. Holding the large bead of each section in turn, one says the Our Father, and holding the small ones the Hail Mary for each separate bead. Between each section the Gloria is said: "Glory be to the Father, and to the Son, and to the Holy Ghost. As it was in the beginning, is now, and ever shall be, world without end. Amen." The Apostles' Creed may also be recited with the rosary.

As for the origin of the term "rosary," a book, *Things Catholics Are Asked About,* by Martin J. Scott, S. J., says: "Rosary means a garland of roses. A legend has it that Our Lady was seen to take rosebuds from the lips of a young monk when he was reciting Hail Marys, and to weave them into a garland which he placed on her head" (p. 237). Another explanation is that the beads originally were made of rosewood. But they may also be of glass, stone, or other hard material.

The rosary has ten times as many prayers addressed to Mary as to God the Father, with none addressed to Christ or the Holy Spirit. It is designed primarily as a devotional to Mary, thus exalting a human being more than God. It is more commonly used by girls and women, and is by far the most popular and universal devotion in the Roman Church.

Peter the Hermit invented the rosary, in the year 1090, more than a thousand years after the time of Christ. It is acknowledged by Roman Catholics not to have come into general use until after the beginning of the thirteenth century, and was not given official sanction until after the Protestant Reformation in the sixteenth century.

The rosary represents a form of prayer that was expressly condemned by Christ, for He said: "And in praying use not vain repetitions, as the Gentiles do: for they think that they shall be heard for their much speaking. Be not therefore like unto them: for your Father knoweth what things ye have need of before ye ask him" (Matt. 6:7-8). Yet the priests encourage their people to use the rosary frequently, and in giving penances after confession they often assign a certain number of Hail Marys to be said. The more such prayers are said the more merit is stored up in heaven.

The Bible teaches that the true believer should pray to God reverently, humbly, and with a believing and thankful heart, thinking of what he is doing and of the great King to whom he is praying. It is a distinguishing mark of Romanism, and also a matter of primary importance between Romanism and Protestantism, that a Roman Catholic "says" or "recites" his prayers, while for the most part the Protestant speaks extemporaneously, with his own words, thinking out his praise, petitions, requests, and thanks as he prays. For a spiritually minded person the mechanical use of beads destroys the true spirit of prayer.

A mechanical device similar to the rosary and used for counting prayers had been in use among the Buddhists and Mohammedans for centuries before the rosary was introduced, so its origin is not hard to trace. It is simply another device borrowed from paganism. And, strange as it may seem, Roman Catholics who condemn as pagan and foolish the use of prayer wheels by the Buddhists in Tibet (wheels with attached prayers, placed in a stream of water or in the wind so that each time the wheel turns over the prayer is repeated), nevertheless display great devotion in counting their repetitious rosary prayers as one bead after another is pushed across the string. But surely the principle is exactly the same. A similar practice is the use of eight-day candles in little red cups, usually placed at the front and to one side in the churches, which are sold to those who are so busy they do not have time to pray. Indeed, why should Roman priests condemn the chanted incantations of African and West Indies priests while continuing the practice of sprinkling holy water with solemn exorcisms of the devils?

Crosses and crucifixes. The most widely used religious symbol both for Roman Catholics and Protestants is the cross, much more so in Roman Catholic than in Protestant churches. The crucifix is a cross with the figure of Christ crucified upon it. In the Roman Church the sign of the cross has to be in every altar, on the roofs of all Roman Catholic churches, in the school and hospital rooms, and in the homes of its people. For interior use the crucifix is often displayed rather than the cross. Small crosses four or five inches long and suspended on a chain are often worn as part of the religious garb of priests and nuns, and a small gold cross on a chain suspended around the neck is often worn by the women.

But as regards the cross as a symbol of Christianity, we must point out that the Scriptures do not give one single instance in which a mechanical cross was so used, or in which it was venerated in any way. There are, of course, numerous instances in Scripture in which the cross is spoken of figuratively. Nor is there any evidence that the cross was used as a Christian symbol during the first three centuries of the Christian era. A Roman Catholic authority asserts:

"It may be safely assumed that only after the edict of Milan, A.D., 312, was the cross used as a permanent sign of our redemption. De Rossi (a Roman Catholic archaeologist) states positively that no monogram of Christ, discovered in the Catacombs or other places, can be traced to a period anterior to the year 312" (*The American Ecclesiastical Review,* p. 275; Sept., 1920).

The cross as a symbol of Christianity, then, it is generally agreed, goes back only to the days of emperor Constantine, who is supposed to have turned from paganism to Christianity. In the year 312 he was engaged in a military campaign in western Europe. According to tradition he called upon the pagan gods, but there was no response. Shortly afterward he saw in the sky a pillar of light in the form of a cross, on which were written the words, "*In hoc signo vinces,*" "In this sign conquer." Shortly afterward he crossed into Italy and won a decisive victory near Rome. Taking this as a token of divine favor, he issued various edicts in favor of the Christians. Whether he ever became a Christian or not is disputed, some holding that he remained a pagan all his life and promoted paganism and Christianity alternately as best served his purposes, although he professed Christianity and was baptized shortly before his death in 337. At any rate, the alleged sign in the sky, like so many other signs of that and later times, undoubtedly will have to be explained on other grounds. The idea that Christ would command a pagan emperor to make a military banner embodying the cross and to go forth conquering in that sign, is wholly inconsistent with the general teaching of the Bible and with the spirit of Christianity.

In any event the cross, in pre-Christian as well as in Christian times, has always been looked upon as an instrument of torture and shame. Christians do not act wisely when they make such an instrument an object of reverence and devotion. Paul spoke of what he termed "the offense of the cross" (Gal. 5:11; KJV). And in Hebrews 12:2 we read that Jesus "endured the cross, despising the shame." In view of these things we should not regard the device on which Christ was crucified as holy or as an object of devotion. Rather we should recognize it for what it is, a detestable thing, a pagan symbol of sin and shame.

When Jesus said: "If any man would come after me, let him deny himself, and take up his cross, and follow me" (Matt. 16:24), He did not mean that one should have a gold representation of it hanging from a chain about his neck or dangling from long cords at his side. He meant rather that one who is a faithful follower should be willing to do His will, to serve and to endure suffering as He did, since all those who sincerely follow Him will meet with some degree of hardship and suffering and perhaps even with persecution. Ever since the time that the emperor Constantine allegedly saw the sign of the cross in the sky, and took that as his banner, that banner has been raised over a half Christian and half pagan church. Protestant churches, too, have often offended in this matter, and, like Lot, who pitched his tent too close to Sodom, these bodies have camped too close to the gates of Rome. The true Christian conquers, not through the sign of a fiery cross or the charm of a jeweled crucifix, but through the Gospel of Christ, which is "the power of God unto salvation to every one that believeth" (Rom. 1:16).

Scapulars. Another object of special devotion in the Roman Catholic Church is the scapular. This can best be described as a "charm" which is designed to give the wearer protection against all kinds of perils, such as accidents, disease, lightning, fire and storms, and to ward off witchcraft and enchantments, and put devils to flight.

The scapular was invented by Simon Stock, an English monk, in the year 1287. According to tradition this holy man withdrew into a wood where he lived in great austerity for twenty years, at the end of which time the Virgin Mary appeared to him in celestial splendor, with thousands of angels, and, holding the scapular in her hand, commissioned him to take this as the sign of the Carmelite Order to which he belonged.

The scapular consists of two pieces of brown cloth about four inches square, on which are pictures of the Virgin Mary, to be worn next to the skin, suspended over the shoulders by cords fore and back. Normally it must be of wool or other cloth, but not of silk, since it is worn in honor of the Virgin Mary and it is said that she never wore silk. It is to be worn day and night, never to be taken off until death, and it is good even to be buried with it. During the Second World War a metal scapular was supplied to Roman Catholic service men and was called the "Scapular Militia." On one square were printed the words, "S. Simon Stock, pray for us," and on the other, "Our Lady of Mt. Carmel, pray for us."

Paul Blanshard cites the following use (or misuse) of the scapular:

> "I have before me as I write a four-page circular called *The Scapular Militia,* issued by the Carmelite National Shrine of Our Lady of Scapular, of 338 East 29th St., New York. It bears the official Imprimatur of Archbishop (now Cardinal) Spellman, and it was issued at the height of the war in 1943. The slogan emblazoned on its cover is 'A Scapular for Every Catholic Service Man,' and it carries, underneath a picture of Mary, Joseph, and St. Simon Stock, the specific guaranty in heavy capitals: WHOSOEVER DIES CLOTHED IN THIS SCAPULAR SHALL NOT SUFFER ETERNAL FIRE" (*American Freedom and Catholic Power,* p. 248).

That, we assert, is pure fetishism, the same kind of thing practiced by primitive tribes in many pagan countries. By such means do priests (and cardinals) substitute charms and superstitions in place of the New Testament which contains no such deceptions.

5.　RELICS—PILGRIMAGES

A relic is a piece of bone or other part of a saint's body or some article which a saint touched during his life. Each of these supposedly has some degree of the supernatural attached to it and is regarded with more or less reverence, depending to a considerable extent on the education or lack of education of the worshipper. Such relics have an important place in the worship of the Roman Church. Paul Blanshard writes:

"Many non-Catholics imagine that relics are used by Catholicism merely as symbols of faith and devotion. Nothing could be farther from the truth. The Church, even the American Church of the present day, still operates a full-blown system of fetishism and sorcery in which physical objects are supposed to accomplish physical miracles. Sometimes it is claimed that these physical objects also accomplish spiritual miracles and change the physical or spiritual destiny of any fortunate Catholic who relies on them" (*Ibid.*, p. 248).

Relics range from pieces of the true cross, the nails, thorns from the crown of thorns, the seamless robe of Christ, the linen of Mary, her wedding ring, locks of her hair, vials of her milk, and her house miraculously transplanted from Palestine to Italy, to the more common and more abundant bones, arms, legs, hair, garments, and other possessions of the saints and martyrs. Many of the alleged relics have been proved false and have been dropped, but others continue to the present day. Some of the bones have been exposed as those of animals. In one instance the alleged bones of a famous Neapolitan saint, which it was claimed had worked countless miracles, were found to be those of a goat.

As for the actual cross on which Christ was crucified, the *Catholic Encyclopedia* says: "The so-called true cross of Christ was found in the mount Calvary by the mother of Constantine (in the fourth century), and taken to Jerusalem by Constantine himself" (Vol. 8, p. 238). But since that time hundreds of pieces of the true cross have been scattered over the earth for the veneration of superstitious Roman Catholics and for the enrichment of the clergy. Calvin wrote concerning the fragments of the cross alleged to exist in Roman churches in his day: "If all the pieces . . . were collected into a single heap, they would form a good ship-load, although the Gospel testifies that a single individual was able to carry it. What effrontery, then, to fill the whole earth with fragments which it would take more than 300 men to carry." St. Paulinus, one of the Roman Catholic apologists for the veneration and defense of relics, says that "a portion of the true cross kept at Jerusalem gave off fragments of itself without diminishing." That would seem to be the only way in which the facts in question can be accounted for.

There is an abundance of nails from the true cross, and almost every city in Italy and France has one or two thorns from the true crown of thorns. Nearly every town in Sciliy has one or more teeth of Saint Agatha, the patron saint of the island. The duplicates of nearly every article of primary interest should, of course, be sufficient to convince even the most credulous that these are nothing but pious frauds.

A report in *The Kansas City Star*, September 21, 1959, said that the Holy Robe of Christ, in a glass-inclosed case, was displayed for the first time in 26 years in the cathedral at Trier, Germany, the oldest cathedral in Germany, that during the two months of its public viewing it drew 1,800,000 pilgrims, and that the final display was attended by more than 35,600 people including cardinal Ottaviani, pro-secretary of the Holy Office at the Vatican. About ten years ago there was returned to this country an arm of Saint Francis Xavier, famous Spanish Jesuit missionary to the Orient in the sixteenth century, which attracted large crowds at public showings in Los Angeles and other cities. In Spain there have been exhibited in different cathedrals two heads of John the Baptist, and in one of the cathedrals there is a magnificent ostrich feather preserved in a gorgeous case, which it is said fell from a wing of the angel Gabriel when he came to make the announcement to Mary. Perhaps the best known present day event in connection with any relic is that of the liquefaction of the blood of St. Januarius, patron saint of Naples, Italy, which we are told liquefies three times annually, proving that their saint still watches over the city. In Rome the *Scala Sancta*, the sacred stairway, exhibited as the one Jesus mounted going up to Pilate's judgment hall, is crowded continually with devout pilgrims who climb the steps on their knees, saying a prayer on each step to gain indulgences. It will be recalled that this was the stairway that Martin Luther was climbing when there dawned upon him the truth of the words, "The just shall live by faith." Luther arose from his knees, walked down the steps, and from that time did no more works of penance.

Most intriguing of all relics is "the House of Mary," or "the Holy House of Loretto," in Italy. This house is said to have been the house of the Virgin Mary at Nazareth, in Palestine. It is a stone structure about twenty-eight feet long and twelve feet wide. A booklet purporting to give the authentic history of the house as sanctioned by the Roman Church is sold to visitors. The booklet says that in this simple apartment the Virgin Mary lived with Jesus until He grew to manhood and departed on His mission. After the crucifixion Mary continued to live in it until her death, visited frequently by the apostles and other disciples of Jesus. When Nazareth was plundered by the Roman soldiers the house was miraculously preserved in that the soldiers could not enter it or touch it. In 1291, when Palestine was overrun by the Saracens, so the booklet relates, the house was detached from its foundation by the angels, and was carried by them across the sea to Dalmatia, in Macedonia, where it was deposited on a hill. The Dalmatians gave it a friendly welcome, devoutly worshipped it, and for three years and seven months it was visited by many pilgrims. Then suddenly it removed and flew over the sea to eastern Italy, first coming to rest near the town of Loretto, about two miles from the coast. A few months later it removed again a short distance to its present home, on a hill in the town of Loretto, where it has been enshrined in a beautiful church. The Dalmatians lamented its departure, and for a long time in their prayers were wont to say: "Return to us, O beautiful lady; return to us, O beautiful lady; come back to us, O Mary, with your house." But it would not come. In its present location it is visited by many pilgrims, some of whom climb the hill leading to it on their knees, kissing the stones of the walk as they move themselves forward. This same account regarding the house of Mary is recorded by Ligouri in his book, *The Glories of Mary*, 1902 edition, pp. 72, 73.

The Standard International Encyclopedia says concerning the town of Loretto:

> "It is noted as the seat of the Holy House, which according to tradition, was occupied as a dwelling by the Virgin Mary at Nazareth and, in 1295, was removed to Loretto. The building was originally of simple construction, but it has been adorned by marble sculptures. The town is visited annually by many tourists, who go there to view the structure and to witness an image of the Virgin which is reputed to be a carving by St. Luke."

That the legend concerning the house now existing in Loretto is a mere fabrication should be clear on two points: (1) Some brick in the structure were made in an oven, while in the time of Christ brick were sun baked. (2) The house has a chimney, while the houses of Palestine did not have chimneys, the smoke escaping through holes in the sides or roofs of the buildings.

What a varied collection of relics the Roman Church maintains to assist the faithful of its members! The whole Roman Catholic world is full of frauds of this kind, exhibited as openly and as often as seems advisable. Every Roman Catholic church is supposed to have at least one relic. The only justification that the more intelligent Romanists can give for this situation is that it is justifiable to deceive the people for their own good. But as Dr. Woods has said:

> "The Church of Rome asserts that relics are intended 'to excite good thoughts and increase devotion.' But instead of doing this, for the most part they excite irreverent curiosity in careless sightseers, and disrupt true religion by exhibiting as genuine what men know to be counterfeit. The right way to 'excite good thoughts and increase devotion' is by the

reverent study of God's Word and prayer. The right way to honor a good man who has passed away, is not to venerate one of his bones, but to emulate his virtues in the service of God and our fellow men" (*Our Priceless Heritage,* p. 169).

Fraud is practiced in the Roman Church not only in exhibiting relics of the saints, but also in attributing supernatural powers to them. Each time a new saint is canonized the church comes into possession of a new collection of relics which are alleged to have performed miracles. All of this is on a par with the customs in the pagan religions. Interestingly enough, an AP dispatch from Kandy, Ceylon, published in *The Kansas City Star,* August 20, 1959, reported that a temple elephant had run amuck through Buddhist crowds during a ceremony at the Temple of the Holy Tooth, killing 20 people and injuring 250 others. The temple houses a tooth relic of the Buddha who founded that religion 25 centuries ago, and is considered one of the most sacred spots in Buddhism. The Roman devotion to sacred relics cannot be looked upon as one whit better than the same misguided devotion paid to relics in pagan temples.

Many priests have little or no faith at all in relics, even though it is part of their work to recommend them and to supervise their use by the pious faithful. Priests who have been to Rome for any length of time lose any reverence they may have had for such things when they see the shameless traffic that is carried on in that city in bits of bones and pious objects of all kinds.

The amazing thing about this whole business is that presumably intelligent and educated Roman Catholics, clerical and lay alike, even in an enlightened country such as the United States, either tacitly accept such relics as genuine or fail to denounce them for the gross superstition that they know them to be. Veneration of such articles is of the same order as that of the heathen who, in their blindness, "bow down to wood and stone." The great lesson taught by the history of image worship and the reverencing of relics is the importance of adhering strictly to the Bible as the only rule of faith and practice.

Closely akin to the subject of relics is that of "Holy Water," so-called, which is nothing more than ordinary water with a pinch of salt added and blessed by a priest. A holy water font is found just inside the entrance in every Roman Catholic church. That is another empty superstition from the Dark Ages, borrowed from paganism, and introduced into the church in the ninth century. Pagan temples in Rome had holy water stoups or basins long before they were introduced into the Christian churches, and all of those entering were expected to sprinkle themselves.

If the reader has ever visited a Roman Catholic goods store he doubtless has seen the hundreds of statues of Mary and the saints on sale there, row on row, some highly ornamented and expensive, others quite plain, in various sizes and colors and prices. All of those are, or become, small Roman gods; for when blessed by the priest they are thought to have deep religious significance and are worshipped and given places of honor in the churches and homes. Then there are literally thousands of rosaries, crucifixes, crosses, sacred pictures, candle sticks, holy oils, incense, medals, and little charms and gadgets which the Roman Church blesses and encourages the people to use. For a Protestant it is a disturbing experience, for he cannot help but feel that he is indeed in the house of the idols.

Pilgrimages. Another characteristic of Romanism is the idea that special merit attaches to pilgrimages made to holy places. This too is an idea that was entirely foreign to first century Christianity. Most important of the pilgrimages in our day is that to Rome. And of course no one must go empty handed. Pope Boniface VIII (died 1303) proclaimed a jubilee with plenary indulgences granted to all who visited Rome, and the project brought such crowds and such a great amount of money that it has been repeated periodically ever since, the most recent having been the Marian year proclaimed by pope Pius XII, in 1954, this after having promulgated the doctrine of the assumption of Mary in 1950. During the Middle Ages much virtue was thought to attach to a pilgrimage to Jerusalem. Plenary indulgences were offered to those who joined the Crusades in an attempt to wrest the Holy Lands from the Mohammedans. Pilgrimages have been much in vogue in pagan religions, such as Buddhism, Hinduism, and Mohammedanism (that to Mecca being the most famous), as a means of pleasing the god or gods who are worshipped and of accumulating merit.

Famous, too, as pilgrimage cities, are Lourdes, in extreme southwestern France, and Fatima, in Portugal. At Lourdes the Virgin Mary allegedly appeared to a 14 year old peasant girl, Bernadette Soubirous, in 1858. When Bernadette dug in a certain place as commanded by Mary, a spring of water with curative powers was uncovered. The Basilica of the Rosary was later erected on the site, and every year tens of thousands of pilgrims visit the place in search of cures. Thousands of cures have been claimed, but the Roman Church officially claims but very few. Hardly more than one person in a thousand is actually helped, and those evidently are psychological cures, on the order of those sometimes achieved by the Christian Scientists and other faith healers. Yet the Roman church promotes pilgrimages to Lourdes. The place is now highly commercialized, and directly and indirectly is a source of revenue for the church. We notice, however, that when a pope gets sick he does not go to Lourdes, but instead secures the best medical help available—as was the case with the late Pius XII.

In recent years the shrine of Fatima, Portugal, has become even more popular than that at Lourdes, with as many as 700,000 people said to have visited it in a single month. There, in 1917, shortly before the Bolshevik revolution in Russia, the Virgin Mary appeared to three children, ages seven, nine, and ten, who had never gone to school and, curiously enough, in messages subsequently released by the church, gave warnings against the evils of Communism, messages having more to do with present day relations between the Vatican and Russia than with anything that might be thought to concern children of those tender ages. Rome's promotion of the Fatima shrine has been coupled with her crusade against Communism.

In our western world the two most important shrines are Our Lady of Guadalupe, on the outskirts of Mexico City, and Ste. Anne de Beaupre, in Quebec. After Cortez' conquest of Mexico the Romanists practically forced their religion upon the Mexican people. Cortez and his soldiers took Mexico City. With them were a number of priests. Some of the Indians eventually were converted, despite the greed and cruelty of the Spanish soldiers. But not many could be persuaded to worship the Virgin Mary because she was not an Indian—hence the invention of "The Virgin of Guadalupe," in reality a Mexican goddess who was absorbed into the Roman system.

According to tradition "The Virgin" appeared to Juan Diego, an uneducated Indian, who was one of the converts, and told him that the Indian people should build a temple in her honor and that she would be their protector. At first no one would believe his story. But an allegedly miraculous picture of the Virgin imprinted on his cloak proved convincing. A giant church eventually was erected in honor of the Virgin at the place where he had seen the vision. The cloak with its picture is still preserved in the church. All indications are, however, that priestly influence was behind the entire project, and that Juan Diego was merely their tool. At any rate, today thousands of Mexicans, some of whom "walk" on their knees for miles before reaching the church, visit the shrine to bow to the image of the Virgin and to those of the saints.

The shrine of Ste. Anne de Beaupre is located on the north bank of the St. Lawrence River, about 20 miles northeast of the city of Quebec. It was dedicated to Saint Anne, who according to early legend was the mother of Mary. It is visited annually by thousands from the United States and Canada. Large numbers of crutches and canes are exhibited, allegedly left by cripples who received miraculous cures.

Religious parades or processions are common to all Roman Catholic countries. In Spain they have the procession in which the image of the "Senor Jesus del Gran Poder" is paraded; and in Portugal that of the "Senor de los Pasos." In Peru they have the procession of "The Lord of Miracles," in which a large image of Jesus is carried through the streets, to which the people give special veneration and of which they ask all kinds of favors—healings, success in business, happiness in love, luck in the lottery, etc. Thousands of people participate in these parades, carrying burning tapers, counting their rosaries, forming a guard of honor for the painted and clothed images. But such images and parades are totally ineffective in teaching anything about Christ and the way of salvation, for the people know practically nothing about who He is or what He taught.

6. PRAYERS FOR THE DEAD

A common practice in the Roman Church is that of praying for the dead. This is closely connected with and is a logical consequence of their doctrine of purgatory. The high Anglican Church, which holds a position about half way between Roman Catholicism and representative Protestantism, also follows that custom. But practically all Protestant churches reject it.

Prayers for the dead imply that their state has not yet been fixed, and that it can be improved at our request. We hold, however, that there is no change of character or of destiny after death, and that what the person is at death he remains throughout all eternity. We find an abundance of Scripture teaching to the effect that this world only is the place of opportunity for salvation, and that when this probation or testing period is past only the assignment of rewards and punishments remains. Consequently we hold that all prayers, baptisms, masses, or other rituals of whatever kind for the dead are superfluous, vain, and unscriptural.

As for the righteous dead, they are in the immediate presence of Christ, in a perfect environment of holiness and beauty and glory where their every need is satisfied. They have no need of any petitions from us. They lack nothing that our prayers can satisfy. Their state is as perfect as it can be until the day when they and we receive our resurrection bodies. To petition God to change the status or condition of His loved ones in glory, or to suggest that He is not doing enough for them, is, to say the least, highly presumptuous, even though it may be well intended.

As for the wicked dead, their state too is fixed and irrevocable. They have had their opportunity. They have sinned away their day of grace, and the uplifting and restraining influence of the Holy Spirit as directed toward them has been withdrawn. It is understandable that remaining relatives and friends should be concerned about them. But the determination of their status after death is the prerogative of God alone. The holiness and justice of God are all-sufficient guarantees that while some by His grace will be rewarded far above their deserts, none will be punished beyond their deserts. Consequently, the dead in Christ have no need of our prayers; and for the dead out of Christ, prayers can avail nothing.

It is very significant that in Scripture we have not one single instance of prayer for the dead, nor any admonition to that end. In view of the many admonitions for prayer for those in this world, even admonitions to pray for our enemies, the silence of Scripture regarding prayer for the dead would seem to be inexplainable if it availed anything.

7. CONCLUSION

Such is the background of ritualism and superstition against which the Roman Catholic people have to struggle. Forms and ceremonies and rich clerical vestments impress the eye, but they deaden the soul to spiritual truth. They are like opiates in that they take the attention of the worshipper and cause him to forget the truths they were originally intended to convey. By absorbing his attention they tend to hide God rather than to reveal Him. And the people, like wide-eyed children at a circus, see the showy ritualism but nothing of the shoddy meanness that lies behind it.

Most Roman Catholics have a fear of entering a Protestant church. They have been forbidden by their priests to do so, under penalty of mortal sin. It is a revealing experience, therefore, when for the first time they are persuaded to do so. They find no images, no musing angels, no confessional, no incense, no mention of purgatory or of salvation by good works, no penance, indulgences, etc. Instead they hear the simple Gospel message and a plain invitation to accept Christ as Saviour. The sermon is delivered in English, not in Latin which they cannot understand, as in the mass. And with a minimum of ritualism, they find that the sermon is the principal part of the service. How rich they find the hymnology of the Protestant church, and how free and spontaneous the singing! The Roman Church has nothing to sing about. The best it can promise is the flames of purgatory, of greater or lesser intensity and of longer or shorter duration, depending on how good or bad their works have been.

Multitudes of Roman Catholics, ensnared in a religion that teaches salvation by works and merit, are searching for the truth that makes men free. Protestantism has that truth, due largely to its emphasis on the reading and study of the Bible. That truth is set forth as a life to be lived, not as a formula or a ritual. Its emphasis is upon a change of heart and a life of fruitful service. It behooves us as Protestants, therefore, to see to it that when Roman Catholics do come to our churches where they miss the ritual and pageantry and the outward things that so appeal to the senses, they find compensating values, first of all an evangelical sermon, and then a group fellowship that is spiritually uplifting and rewarding beyond anything that they have experienced in the more formal church.

XIV. CELIBACY

1. Definition and Presuppositions. 2. The Monastic System. 3. Imposed Celibacy a Hindrance to Personal Sanctity. 4. History of the Doctrine of Celibacy. 5. Scripture Teaching. 6. Immorality Often a Result of Celibate Restrictions. 7. Nuns and Convents. 8. Entering the Convent. 9. Convent Life. 10. Conclusion.

1. DEFINITION AND PRESUPPOSITIONS

By celibacy, in the present discussion, is meant the sectarian requirement of the Roman Catholic Church that its priests, monks, and nuns abstain from marriage. It is not to be confused with the vow of chastity, which is also taken by the members of these groups, and which means abstention from sexual relations.

According to Canon Law the vow of celibacy is broken if the priest marries, but not if he engages in sexual relations. Pardon for sexual relations can be had easily at any time by confession to any fellow-priest. But absolution for any priest who marries can be obtained only from the pope, with accompanying severe penalties. And to obtain such pardon it is required that he forsake his wife.

The requirement for celibacy, as we shall see shortly, is entirely without Scriptural warrant, and was not generally enforced in the Roman Church until more than 1,000 years after the time of Christ.

Protestant clergy may marry, and most of them do. Eastern Orthodox priests also may marry, provided they do so before they are ordained, and most of them are married men. They are not allowed to marry after ordination. Nor if they are married can they become bishops. Bishops are chosen from among the celibate priests. Jewish rabbis, too, may be and usually are married men.

By a strange inconsistency the Church of Rome holds that marriage is a sacrament, that is, something regarded as in a special sense sacred or holy, yet she denies marriage to her priests, monks, and nuns, who supposedly are the most holy people. She holds that celibacy is a state superior to marriage, and the Council of Trent even pronounced an anathema against all who teach that the married state is preferable to that of virginity or celibacy. Thus on the one hand she exalts marriage, while on the other she degrades it.

In the eyes of Rome there is something unclean about marriage. The boy who enters a monastery to study for the priesthood, and the girl who enters a convent, are taught, not that sex is the normal reproductive instinct found in every healthy person and animal, but that these romantic desires are sinful, something to be ashamed of. Under the misleading name of "virginity" the Church of Rome has promoted the notion that the instinct of procreation is in itself a foe to spiritual advancement and that it should be suppressed. L. H. Lehmann says concerning the seminary training of those who are being prepared for the priesthood:

"Young men thus kept apart from the ordinary mode of life of the people, of necessity fall short of full sympathy with the people and of intimate understanding of the needs of common folk. During the years of their blossoming youth they are immured in closely-guarded seminaries. Every indication of the adolescent urgings, which in other young men find healthful expression in the practical affairs of life and in romantic response to sweet and wholesome affection, are crushed out at their inception. The promptings of such urges to affectionate companionship are even taught to be regarded as sinful. A cold, stoical, and indifferent attitude toward the life that other men and women lead, is cultivated in them as of the highest virtue and as essential for the exalted position which they are to occupy as priests.

"As a safeguard for the celibate life imposed upon them they are counselled to harden themselves against the tenderness of domestic happiness enjoyed by ordinary men with loving wife and growing children. Although they are commissioned as guides and counsellors, especially in the confessional, in everything that concerns the relations between the sexes, priests personally must abhor the tender glances of women as an instrument of the Devil's guile to lead them into sin" (*The Soul of a Priest*, p. 152).

To the same effect Emmett McLoughlin writes concerning an event that occurred after he left the priesthood:

"The announcement of my marriage brought out another facet of the Roman Catholic mind, both clerical and lay—its preoccupation with sex. Of the thousands of letters that I received, the majority even from married Catholics, spoke of matrimony as if physical glorification were its only purpose. And they wrote of natural love as a deplorable, filthy, unnatural thing" (*People's Padre*, p. 194).

Mr. McLoughlin says concerning his own seminary training that a compendium of Roman Catholic moral theology that they used, which was merely a summary of the several volumes studied, contained thirty-two pages devoted to the infinitesimal details of the multiplicity of sexual sins, while only twelve pages were required to set forth the hierarchy's teachings on assault, suicide, murder, duelling, capital punishment, the relations among nations, and the morality of war from the stone age to the atomic era. He also quotes Dr. Alfred C. Kinsey, after his exhaustive studies in the field of sex, as having said that the largest collection of books in the world on the subject of sex is in the Vatican Library in Rome.

In opposition to that attitude we hold that the sex urge is a gift imparted to man by the Creator Himself, and that consequently there is nothing unclean or sordid about it. Men and women have been so created that they are instinctively drawn to someone of the opposite sex. This natural attraction of one sex toward the other is God's way of assuring the propagation of the race. It is as wholesome as the forces which operate in seedtime and harvest. The natural instinct of every normal man and woman is to give expression to the romantic side of his or her nature, to marry, and to have a family. God planned it that way. All through Scripture the blessing and dignity of parenthood is extolled and exalted, and the refusal to assume the responsibilities and blessings of parenthood are vigorously condemned. The disposition of some people to surround sex with impure associations is a travesty on life as God meant it to be. Historically, celibacy had its roots in the Gnostic and Manichaean heresies of the second and third century which taught that matter was inherently evil and that salvation consisted in resisting and overcoming it.

2. THE MONASTIC SYSTEM

In order to understand the Roman Catholic position regarding the grouping of men and women in monasteries and convents we must understand the basic viewpoint which underlies that system. During the Middle Ages the idea developed in Roman theology that man's work was to be divided into the natural (i.e., the secular) and the spiritual. Only the spiritual was thought to be pleasing to God. Consequently, while the natural man might be satisfied with the common virtues of daily life, the ideal was that of the mystic who in deep contemplation reached out for the spiritual. In achieving this higher life the natural was thought of not as a help but as a hindrance. The life of the monk and the nun who withdrew from society and from the workaday life of the world and retired into the quiet of the cloisters, thus losing themselves in mystic contemplation, was thought to be the higher life. There, in seclusion from the world, the image of God, which had been lost in the fall, was to be restored in its beauty. The monastic system is thus based on two false principles, namely, that celibacy is a holier state than matrimony, and that total withdrawal from the social intercourse and business life of the world is conducive to true religion.

That type of thinking remains a part of the Roman system even to the present day and is particularly prominent in two different aspects:

(1) The vow of celibacy which is required of the priests, and the vows of poverty, chastity and obedience, which are required of the monks and nuns in the different monastic and convent orders.

(2) The ceremony that is performed before anything can be used for sacred purposes. All such things must undergo a ceremony of purification and consecration, the prominent part of which is sprinkling with holy water. All priests and clergy, as well as churches, crosses, images, garments, bells, cemeteries, etc., must be sprinkled with holy water and consecrated.

The ascetic viewed the natural world as in itself sinful, a sphere to be avoided as much as possible. Consequently he developed a contempt for the things of the world and sought to withdraw from it in order that he might practice the heavenly virtues. The most effective way to do that was to seek the seclusion of the cloister. Hence the rise of monasteries and convents, and the unmarried state of the priests and nuns.

But the Reformation swept away all such erroneous views for Protestants. In contrast with Romanism, Protestantism looks upon all phases of life, the secular as well as the ecclesiastical, as sacred, all as a part of God's plan, and so to be lived under His blessing and to His glory. Whether in the church, or in science, politics, art, or the various professions, whether married and in the life of the family or in the single state, the Protestant was to serve God not by withdrawing from the world but by going out into the world, ministering to the spiritual and physical needs of the people, and by using his time and talents efficiently in his chosen occupation. Whatever his work he was to perform it to the glory of God, and so to have a part in the advancement of the kingdom of God.

The Protestant holds that the world, though fallen, has been in principle redeemed through the work of Christ, that this is our Father's world, that it does not belong to the Devil although he has usurped much authority, and that our duty is to live so as to recapture it for our Lord who is the rightful King over the redeemed creation. This view casts a sacredness over all of life, and stimulates the natural virtues such as thrift, industry, fidelity, loyalty and order, and so remakes people and nations. Only as we see this contrast between Romanism and Protestantism shall we be able to understand why the Roman Church establishes monasteries and convents, and why Protestantism has no use for them.

The New Testament makes it clear that Christ was no monk. He did not withdraw Himself from the world, nor did He teach His disciples to do so. He prayed for His disciples, not that they should be taken out of the world, but that they should be kept from the evil one (John 17:15). True Christian service is manifested most efficiently by going out into the world and ministering to its needy men and women, not by withdrawing into a monastery or convent and donning funereal garments which tend only to keep one in bondage. The risen Lazarus is not to wear grave clothes, and the born again Christian is not to be a recluse.

The inmates of monasteries are unmarried men, whose interests by training and profession are alien not only to the family and society, but to the civil and ecclesiastical institutions of the country. Convents too promote an abnormal type of life. The many monasteries that sprang up in Europe during the Middle Ages often accumulated such wealth and encouraged such idlesome and luxurious living among the monks that the church at large was brought into disrepute.

No doubt some monasteries did much good in keeping alive the lamp of learning during the dark centuries. We hold, however, that the Roman Church was in large measure responsible for the darkness of that era in that it withheld the Bible from the people. It may at least be questioned whether the well-intentioned monks and nuns might not have done much more to promote the church and to uplift society had they gone out to evangelize a rude world instead of withdrawing from it. In any event the monastic system represented a far different spirit and practice from that found in first century Christianity.

As a matter of historical interest, the most prominent orders, the Dominican, Franciscan, and Jesuit, arose during the later Middle Ages. St. Dominic and St. Francis of Assisi lived around 1200 A. D. The Jesuit order was founded by Ignatius Loyola, a Spanish soldier priest, in 1534. The Jesuit order was suppressed throughout Roman Catholic Europe by pope Clement XIV, in 1773, but survived in Russia where the pope's authority did not reach, and finally was re-established in 1814 by pope Pius VII. The monastic orders within Roman Catholicism probably have been as numerous as the major denominations within Protestantism, and oftentimes they have differed as sharply as ever did the Protestant denominations. Witness for instance the prolonged and often bitter rivalries between the Dominican and Franciscan orders, and particularly the rivalries between both of these and the Jesuit order. Protestant churches often unite; but who can imagine a union between the Dominicans and

Franciscans, or between either of these orders and the Jesuits? There are various orders of nuns, although rivalry between them to a considerable extent is kept down since they are under the control of the bishops. At the present time the Jesuits, although not so numerous, are the most powerful order, and for more than a century they have dominated the papacy, much to the chagrin of the other orders. One of their goals has been the strengthening of the papacy while weakening the powers of the bishops. And in that they have been eminently successful.

3. IMPOSED CELIBACY A HINDRANCE TO PERSONAL SANCTITY

Voluntary celibacy on the part of those who are dedicated to a great cause and who have what we may term "the gift of celibacy," can be a real blessing. The Bible commends such practice. But celibacy enforced indiscriminately against whole groups of men and women is shown by its fruits to be not only difficult and irksome but productive of untold evils. The quite uniform testimony of those who have experienced it and who are free to talk is that it does not suppress desire, but on the contrary increases and heightens it. Priests and nuns are not superhuman, as has so often been represented, nor are they even normally human, but because of the unnatural laws under which they live they are particularly susceptible to temptation. Both groups are denied normal family life. Both groups therefore live in contravention of the deepest cravings of their nature, and are subject to needless temptations. God has said, "It is not good that the man should be alone" (Gen. 2:18). And that also means that it is not good for a woman to be alone. The practical effects of the monastic system down through the ages shows clearly that the forced and unnecessary restrictions are a hindrance, not a help, to personal sanctity.

Celibacy in the Roman Catholic Church is, of course, merely a church regulation, not a command of Scripture. But this fact is cleverly concealed from the submissive Roman Catholic people. They refuse to believe that their clergy are following anything other than a divinely instituted role. Nor will they believe without the most explicit proof that the apostle Peter was a married man, although that fact is recorded three times in the New Testament (Matt. 8:14; Luke 4:38; I Cor. 9:5).

Dr. Charles Hodge has well said:

"It is only in the married state that some of the purest, most disinterested, and most elevated principles of our nature are called into exercise. All that concerns filial piety, and parental and especially maternal affection, depends on marriage for its very existence. It is in the bosom of the family that there is a constant call for acts of kindness, of self-denial, of forbearance, and of love. The family, therefore, is the sphere the best adapted for the development of all the special virtues; and it may be safely said that there is far more of moral excellence and of true religion to be found in Christian households, than in the desolate homes of priests, or in the gloomy cells of monks and nuns" (*Systematic Theology*, III, p. 371).

L. H. Lehmann repeatedly referred to the bitter disappointment and broken lives of the priests under the monastic system. Said he:

"The saddest experiences of my years as a priest are the evidences I found everywhere of the broken hopes and crushed ideals of priests, young and old, the same in every country that I visited. Imposed celibacy is the primary cause of the failure of which priests themselves are most fully conscious. Not that the physical implications of celibacy are a matter of great moment; it should never have been made a matter of importance. Had it not been imposed to serve the ends of the papal power, but left to free, voluntary choice, priestly celibacy might have been a real service. Instead it has been made the cause of scandal and shame to the Christian church. Forced as it is by human and not divine law, it has perverted any good that otherwise might come from it. It has had the effect of belittling the sanctity of the marriage relation; for the only object which it can attain is the denial to priests of legal marriage rights, not abstention from sexual indulgence. The pope alone can absolve a priest who avails himself of civil sanction to contract a legal marriage relation; private sexual aberrations can be either concealed, or absolved by recourse to an ordinary confessor.

"But the real evil consequent upon forced clerical celibacy is its enervating effect upon the bodily and mental faculties. It saps all the vigor of manhood from those who must employ the continual force of mind and will against the natural bodily urge. Its victims have to confess that, far from freeing them from the sexual urge, it actually breeds a very ferment of impurity in the mind. It is the boast of the Roman Catholic Church that priestly celibacy makes its clergy something more than men— that it makes them supernatural, almost angelic. The simple people readily believe this. In truth it makes them something less than men.

"It is almost impossible for the laity to understand to what extent Roman Catholic priests fail to live up to the celibate state imposed upon them. . . . The general public today knows enough about sex, and the part it plays in the lives of all normal men and women, to judge for themselves. If priests were as celibate as they appear, then the conviction of the simple Irish about them must be more than an induced pious belief, namely, that priests are especially endowed with a kind of angelic continence at their ordination ceremony.

"Totally at variance with that induced pious belief of the Irish about their priests, which I had shared from my youth, were my findings among them during my ministry upon three continents. Not one in a hundred was free from a tense bodily and mental struggle with the sex urge.

"Among the priests in the United States who became my co-workers were many companions of my seminary days in Ireland and in Rome. Of the religious enthusiasm, the intense Christian idealism, even the personal sanctity, which had possessed them, little remained. The soul-destroying process which I had seen working in my brother-priests in other lands, had also been at work in these others from whom I had been separated by thousands of miles of ocean. All without exception groaned out their confession of disillusionment. Invariably they expressed their desire to escape from the bondage, to go far away to some place where they could forget that they ever had been priests.

"Not that these young men had become bad. They were just sick, tired, and disappointed; once imbued with a saintly, self-sacrificing Christian idealism, worthy indeed to serve a better cause than that of Roman Church propaganda in modern countries, they had succumbed to a state of indifferent lethargy. They could see no recognized, respectable retreat out of it. They had, therefore, submitted to the loyal soldier's rule: 'Theirs not to ask the reason why; theirs but to do and die' " (*The Soul of a Priest,* pp. 120-124).

To the same general effect is the testimony of Emmett McLoughlin, who writes of present day conditions in the United States:

"The life of a priest is an extremely lonely one. If he lives in a large rectory, he is still lonely. Other priests are not interested in him or in his doubts and scruples. If he is the only priest in a solitary parish or desert mission, he is still more alone.

"As his years slip by and the memories of seminary and its rigidity fade away, the realization may dawn that his life is not supernatural but a complete mental and physical frustration. He sees in his parish and his community the normal life from which he has been cut off. He sees the spontaneous childhood which he was denied. He sees the innocent normal companionship of adolescence which for him never existed. He performs the rites of matrimony, as starry-eyed young men and women pledge to each other the most natural rights and pleasures. He stands alone and lonely at the altar, as they turn from him and confidently, recklessly, happily step into their future home, family, work, and troubles and the successes of a normal life.

"More than anything else, he seeks companionship, the companionship of normal people, not frustrated, disillusioned victims like himself. He wants the company of men and women, young and old, through whom he may at least vicariously take part in a relationship with others that

has been denied him and for which, at least subconsciously, the depths
of his nature craves.

"No priest who has heard priests' confessions and has any respect for
the truth will deny that sexual affairs are extremely common among the
clergy. The principal concern of the hierarchy seems to be that priests
should keep such cases quiet and refrain from marriage. . . .

"The number who rebel against the frustration and unnaturalness of
this form of life is far greater than anyone realizes. No one knows how
many priests have quit the Roman Catholic Church in America. I know of
approximately one hundred. Most ex-priests do not reveal their identity
for fear of persecution by the hierarchy. There are no official records, as
far as I know. The bishops and the orders are so jealous of one another
that they do not reveal the 'defections' in their areas" (*People's Padre*,
pp. 93-94).

The subject of birth control has aroused much debate in recent years.
The priests profess to be strongly opposed to all mechanical and medical
methods, while at the same time they violate the principle which they
profess to hold by approving the rhythm method which supposedly ac-
complishes the same result through "natural" methods. The absurdity of
a celibate, bachelor priesthood, the members of which have not even
the ordinary man's understanding of the complexity of woman, pre-
suming to dictate the practices of married couples in regard to their
sex life and family arrangements is well set forth in the following paragraphs by Mr. McLoughlin, who himself married after leaving the priesthood. He says:

"The Roman Catholic priest is supposed to teach his parishioners how
to live in marriage, when marital relations should or should not be had,
how to solve the big and little problems of conjugal life. His word is
final, above that of the trained counselor, the family physician, or the
psychologist.

"But the Roman Catholic priest can no better teach or counsel people
about marriage than the paint salesman can advise the artist, or a stone-
cutter guide the sculptor. The blind cannot teach art. Those born deaf
cannot conduct symphonies.

"The Roman Catholic priest actually knows nothing about marriage
except that sex is involved and lots of little Catholics are its desired
results. The priest, in his thinking, contrasts celibacy with marriage.
Celibacy means simply the inhibition of sex. Marriage, to him, means the
satisfaction of its urge—little more.

"Many things happen in marriage besides the act that leads to procreation, but the Roman Catholic priest's ignorance makes him unequipped
to advise others about them. He has no concept of the softer, enduring,

satisfying, non-sexual aspects of marriage, such as the intellectual comple-
ment between two people, the emotional balancing between a man and a
woman" (*People's Padre*, p. 91).

4. HISTORY OF THE DOCTRINE OF CELIBACY

The practice of celibacy had a gradual development. An unnatural
asceticism was manifesting itself even in the days of St. Paul, and was
condemned by him: ". . . forbidding to marry, and commanding to abstain from meats" (I Tim. 4:3); and again: "Why, as though living in
the world, do ye subject yourselves to ordinances? . . . Which things
have indeed a show of wisdom in will-worship, and humility, and
severity to the body; but are not of any value against the indulgence of
the flesh" (Col. 2:20,23). Such practices were present in the East, and
were strongly developed especially in Buddhism which had its monks
and nuns long before the Christian era.

Asceticism was practiced by individuals, of both sexes, who dedicated
themselves to God through vows of perfect obedience. This was promoted by the heresy of justification by human efforts, human suffering,
and so-called merits. The practice of withdrawing from society, or from
"the world," seems to have originated in southern Egypt, where various
ones established themselves in warm desert abodes. Around such hermits,
especially around those who were considered saints, there often gathered
a group of disciples. This was considered the highest form of Christian
piety. One of the earliest of the hermits was St. Paul of Thebes. Around
him there developed a community of monks who imitated him. His
famous disciple, St. Anthony, about the year 270 placed his sister in a
"convent." Originally the movement was confined to Egypt, then spread
to Palestine, Syria, and Asia Minor. St. Basil of Cappadocia (329-379),
who refused to recognize the primacy of the church in Rome, and who is
regarded as the founder of eastern monasticism, drew up a reform code
for monasteries, including a novitiate trial period, and limited monasteries
to groups of from 30 to 40.

From the fourth century asceticism was more widely practiced, and in
time, in spite of vigorous protest, it came to be the rule for the clergy.
The Spanish council of Elvira, in 305, enacted decrees against the
marriage of the clergy. These decrees, however, were of limited extent,
and no serious effort was made to enforce them. St. Patrick of Ireland,
for instance (died, 461), declared that his grandfather was a priest. But
the Roman Church was persistent in requiring a celibate priesthood. In
the year 1079, under the strong hand of Hildebrand, known as pope
Gregory VII, the celibacy of the priesthood was again decreed and was

made reasonably effective, although Gregory could not curb all of the abuses. Popes Urban II (1088-1099) and Calixtus II (1119-1124) made a determined fight against clerical concubinage. The decree of the First Lateran Council (1123) declared the marriage of all in sacred orders invalid, and the Council of Trent (1545) made strict pronouncements concerning the celibacy of the clergy. According to those decrees a priest who married incurred excommunication, and was debarred from all spiritual functions. A married man who wanted to become a priest was required to leave his wife, and his wife was also required to take the vow of chastity or he could not be ordained. The Council decreed:

> "Whoever shall affirm that the conjugal state is to be preferred to a life of virginity or celibacy, and that it is not better and more conducive to happiness to remain in virginity or celibacy, than to be married, let him be accursed" (Canon 10).

Thus during the first centuries of the Christian era the clergy were permitted to marry and have families, and for more than a thousand years after the time of Christ the Roman priesthood, without too much opposition, exercised the privilege.

The immorality of the priests was the special target of the reformers who appeared from time to time, such as William of Occam, John Wycliffe, John Hus, Savonarola, and especially Luther, Calvin, Zwingli, and Knox, at the time of the Reformation. The churches of the Reformation restored the liberty of marriage to the clergy, citing in particular Paul's injunction to Timothy: "The bishop therefore must be without reproach, the husband of one wife" (I Tim. 3:2).

It is easy to see why the pope and the hierarchy are so insistent on enforcing the law of celibacy against the priests, monks, and nuns. The reasons are both ecclesiastical and economic. In the first place it gives the pope and his prelates a higher degree of control over the priests and nuns, so that, not having wives or husbands or families which must be consulted in making their plans, they are more responsive to the orders of the hierarchy and can be transferred more readily from one parish to another or to different points around the world. And secondly, property owned by the priests, which in some cases is quite considerable, and which if they were married would go to their families, either automatically falls to the church or likely will be left to it by choice in much larger proportion. Thus the pope has secured for himself an army readily available to carry out his commands. That in accomplishing this purpose the priests and nuns are doomed to a life of celibacy, oftentimes to a life of misery in contending against nature, appears to be of little concern to the hierarchy.

A curious situation has arisen in the Roman Church in that several Uniate churches, Eastern Rites, which permit a married clergy, are united with the Roman Church under the pope. There are about nine million Catholics in those, divided into seventeen sects, with somewhat different doctrines and practices. They are located primarily in the Near East, but are not connected with the Eastern Orthodox Church. For the most part they are dissident groups which have broken with the Eastern Church. Most prominent among them is the old church in Lebanon, making that country about 55 percent Christian, and about 45 percent Mohammedan. The most striking difference between them and the Western Church is that their priests may be married men. Also, their services are conducted in their native tongues rather than in Latin, they have no images, in the eucharist the communicants receive both the bread and the wine, and baptism is by immersion. Priests from those churches and Roman Catholic priests may exchange places in conducting church services, or may transfer from one church to another. Even in the United States there are a few Roman Catholic priests who have come in through those churches and who still are permitted to retain their married status and to have families—showing that in reality the celibacy of the priesthood is nothing but an arbitrary church regulation which the pope can modify or abolish any time he pleases. The one thing required of the Uniate churches is that they acknowledge the authority of the pope.

5. SCRIPTURE TEACHING

Christ imposed no rule against the marriage of Christian ministers, nor did any of the apostles. On the contrary, Peter was a married man, and his wife accompanied him on his missionary journeys. The same is true of the other apostles, and of the brothers of Jesus. This information we have from the writings of Paul, who in I Corinthians 9:5 says: "Have we no right to lead about a wife that is a believer, even as the rest of the apostles, and the brethren of the Lord, and Cephas?" The Confraternity Version reads: "Have we not a right to take about with us a woman, a sister, as do the other apostles, and the brethren of the Lord, and Cephas?" But in the Greek the word is *gune*, wife, not *adelphe*, sister.

Moreover, Peter continued in the married state for at least 25 years. Early in His public ministry Jesus had healed Peter's wife's mother, who was sick with a fever (Matt. 8:14-15). Hence Peter was a married man at that time, and therefore at the time Jesus addressed to him the words which Rome says constituted his appointment as pope (Matt. 16:18).

And Paul's first epistle to the Corinthians, just quoted, was written about the year 58 A. D. Hence Peter was a married man during a considerable part of the time that the Roman Church says that he was a pope in Rome (42-67 A. D.); and his wife was there with him. But as we have indicated earlier, we think Peter never was in Rome at all, that instead his ministry, which was primarily to the Jews, took him to the provinces of Asia Minor and to the east, as far as Babylon (I Peter 1:1; 5:13).

Rome claims that she never changes. But the popes are all single men, therefore Peter was no pope, certainly not in the sense that the present day head of the Roman Church is a pope. It would indeed be a first rate scandal if the pope were to get married. We can scarcely imagine anything more revolutionary. Yet if he were to do so he would merely be following the example of Peter. If celibacy properly has the place that is given to it in the Roman Church, it is incredible that Christ would have chosen as the foundation stone and first pope a man who was married.

The fact is that when Christ established His church He took no account at all of celibacy, but instead chose for the apostolic college men who were married. In the verse that we have just quoted Paul defended his own right to have a wife and to take her with him on his missionary journeys if he chose to do so. In this same verse he tells us that "the rest of the apostles," and "the brethren of the Lord," also were married men, and that their wives accompanied them on their missionary journeys. That ought to settle forever the question as to whether or not is is permissible, yes, and advisable, for the clergy to marry.

In his first letter to Timothy Paul says that a bishop should be "the husband of one wife, temperate, sober-minded . . . one that ruleth well his own house, having his children in subjection with all gravity" (3:2,4). Likewise the elders (I Titus 1:5-6) and the deacons (I Tim. 3:12) should each be the husband of one wife, "ruling their children and their own houses well." In the light of those statements, what right has the Roman Church to infer that the apostles were single men and that the single state is holier than the married state? Certainly no Roman Catholic wrote those verses!

The patriarchs, prophets, and priests of the Old Testament era were for the most part married men. During that period marriage for the priests was practically obligatory, since the priesthood was hereditary, that is, perpetuated by the descendants of the priests. It is assumed by many that Paul too had been married, and that his wife had died. At any rate, in telling of his persecution of the Christians before the time of his conversion he said: "And when they were put to death I gave my vote against them" (Acts 26:10)—which vote presumably was cast as a member of the Jewish Sanhedrin, one of the requirements for membership in that body being that the person should be a married man.

If celibate priests are more holy, or more industrious, or if they set a better example in the community, why did not Jesus choose unmarried men for that apostolic group upon which such great responsibility was to rest? All the excellencies and advantages that Roman Catholic writers ascribe when they try to show the need for the celibate state would have been equally applicable for the patriarchs, prophets, and priests of the old dispensation. But we know that such was not the case, that the very opposite was true. We may even say that Christ apparently chose married men to be the first ministers and missionaries of the church *by way of example* of what the later clergy should be, and as a safeguard against the very scandals and abuses that have been so common in the Roman priesthood.

It is true, of course, that in certain ministries under the old covenant the priests were to dedicate themselves exclusively to spiritual activities, separated from all fleshly intercourse and from all worldly affairs. But those were only temporary parentheses in their matrimonial life, accepted as such and blessed of God. Likewise under the new covenant there are special situations in which an unmarried person may render more efficient service, or in which it may be temporarily inexpedient to marry. Both Christ and Paul made exceptions for such cases. But they did not make them the rule, and there is no reason to believe that they expected any large number of Christians to refrain from marriage for those purposes. To conclude from the exceptions that lifelong continence is a necessity is to make a baseless assumption.

Continence, said Jesus, is for those to whom the capacity has been given to receive it. "For there are eunuchs, that were so born from their mother's womb: and there are eunuchs, that were made eunuchs by men: and there are eunuchs, that made themselves eunuchs for the kingdom of heaven's sake. *He that is able to receive it, let him receive it*" (Matt. 19:12). And Paul said, "If they have not continency, let them marry" (I Cor. 7:9). Continency is a gift, even as are certain talents and skills (I Cor. 7:7). But it is not given to all men, nor to all women. Hence no church should make it compulsory on those to whom it has not been given. And it is evident that it has not been given to all the priests, for not all of them understand it, nor are all of them able to practice it consistently.

There is nothing sinful about marriage in itself. Instead, God instituted marriage as a holy ordinance: "And Jehovah God said, It is not good that the man should be alone; I will make him a help meet for him. . . . Therefore shall a man leave his father and his mother, and shall cleave unto his wife: and they shall be one flesh" (Gen. 2:18,24); "The bishop (and, we may also say, the priest) therefore must be without reproach, the husband of one wife" (I Tim. 3:2); "Let marriage be had in honor among all, and let the bed be undefiled: for fornicators and adulterers God will judge" (Heb. 13:4).

The Holy Spirit uses marriage as a type of that most sacred of all relationships, the union of the church and the believer with his Lord (Eph. 5:23-33). Yet many Roman authorities extol the celibate state as peculiarly holy, and the Roman Church presumes to teach that the marriage of churchmen is "a pollution and a sacrilege." But if marriage is a sacrament, as the Roman Church teaches, it is difficult to see why it should be considered the worst kind of sin and a most abominable thing for a priest to have a legitimate wife.

Dr. Charles Hodge has given an excellent summary of this whole teaching in the following paragraphs:

> "The very fact that God created man, male and female, declaring that it was not good for either to be alone, and constituted marriage in paradise, should be decisive on this subject. The doctrine which degrades marriage by making it a less holy state, has its foundations in Manichaeism or Gnosticism. It assumes that evil is essentially connected with matter; that sin has its seat and source in the body; that holiness is attainable only through asceticism and 'neglecting of the body'; that because the 'vita angelica' is a higher form of life than that of men here on earth, therefore marriage is a degradation. The doctrine of the Romish Church on this subject, therefore, is strongly anti-Christian. It rests on principles derived from the philosophy of the heathen. It presupposes that God is not the author of matter; and that He did not make man pure, when He invested him with a body.
>
> "Throughout the Old Testament Scriptures marriage is presented as the normal state of man. The command to our first parents before the fall was, 'Be fruitful, and multiply, and replenish the earth.' Without marriage the purpose of God in regard to our world could not be carried out; it is therefore, contrary to the Scriptures to assume that marriage is less holy, or less acceptable to God than celibacy. To be unmarried was regarded under the old dispensation as a calamity and a disgrace (Judges 11:37; Ps. 78:63; Is. 4:1; 13:12). The highest earthly destiny of a woman, according to the Old Testament Scripture, which is the word of God, was not to be a nun, but to be the mistress of a family, and a mother of children (Gen. 30:1; Ps. 113:9; 127:3,4; Prov. 18:22; 31:10,28).
>
> "The same high estimate of marriage characterizes the teaching of the New Testament. Marriage is declared to be 'honorable in all' (Heb. 13:4). Paul says, 'Let every man have his own wife, and let every woman have her own husband' (I Cor. 7:2). In I Tim. 5:14, he says, 'I

will that the younger women marry.' In I Tim. 4:3, 'forbidding to marry' is included among the doctrines of devils. As the truth comes from the Holy Spirit, so false doctrines, according to the Apostle's mode of thinking, come from Satan, and his agents, the demons; they are the 'seducing spirits' spoken of in the same verse. Our Lord more than once (Matt. 19:5; Mark 10:7) quotes and endorses the original law given in Genesis 2:24, that a man shall 'leave his father and his mother, and shall cleave unto his wife, and they shall be one flesh.' The same passage is quoted by the Apostle as containing a great and symbolical truth (Eph. 5:31). It is thus taught that the marriage relation is the most intimate and sacred that can exist on earth, to which all other human relations must be sacrificed. We accordingly find that from the beginning, with rare exceptions, patriarchs, prophets, apostles, confessors, and martyrs, have been married men. If marriage was not a degradation for them, surely it cannot be for monks and priests" (*Systematic Theology*, III, p. 369).

6. IMMORALITY OFTEN A RESULT OF CELIBATE RESTRICTIONS

A charge that the Roman Church has had to contend with down through the ages is that of immorality in the monasteries and convents, and between some of the priests and certain of their parishioners. Undoubtedly in the United States, where the Roman Church is in competition with Protestantism, and where restrictions are more severe, there is comparatively little of such practice. But even here the church authorities constantly warn priests and nuns against scandal. There is, of course, no way of knowing how many priests and nuns violate the vows of chastity. But it is revealing to read what struggles the great saints of the Roman Church, themselves unmarried, have endured in order to keep themselves pure. There is no difference, of course, between the human nature of priests and nuns and that of laymen and laywomen, and certainly the temptations in the modern world are many and deceptive.

Forced celibacy and auricular confession are by their very nature conducive to sex perversion. To all outward appearances, and, we believe, in reality, the behavior of the Roman Catholic clergy in the United States is far superior to that of their counterpart in Italy, Spain, France, and Latin America. But there is abundant evidence that in the predominantly Roman Catholic countries, particularly during the Middle Ages, the monasteries and convents sometimes became cesspools of iniquity.

L. H. Lehmann, after saying that the primary purpose for which the custom of celibacy has been retained is, (1) to maintain the principle of centralized power, and (2) to retain property for the church that otherwise would go to the priest's family, says:

"It is not for spiritual reasons that the Roman Catholic Church has for so many centuries denied legitimate marriage to its priests. Those in power have always known that it is only the legality of the marriage relation that can be denied them, and that the custom of clerical concubinage, with resultant generations of illegitimate offspring, has always taken its place. Loss of centralized power and property titles, disruption of its authoritarian system of government, would have been the result if these generations of priests' children in the past had been legalized. Clerical concubinage has thus been tolerated in preference to this loss of undisputed power centered in Rome.

"The children of a priest in the past had the right to call him 'Father' only in the spiritual sense of the word. The illegitimate sons of popes, cardinals and bishops, however, were often enabled to rise to high positions in the church and state. Several popes were themselves sons and grandsons of other popes and high church dignitaries. My researches among the collection of papal bulls reveals that concubinage among the clergy of Europe was so prevalent that it was necessary to regulate the practice by law—lest clerical concubinage itself should ever become a legal right" (*Out of the Labyrinth,* pp. 99, 100).

In the ninth century, an age in which ignorance and superstition were prevalent even among the clergy, the emperor Charlemagne, in an attempt to suppress vice among ecclesiastics, issued this edict:

"We have been informed to our great horror that many monks are addicted to debauchery and all sorts of vile abominations, even to unnatural sins. We forbid all such practices and command the monks to cease wandering over the country" (T. Demetrius, *Catholicism and Protestantism,* p. 26).

The Irish historian, William Lecky says:

"An Italian bishop of the tenth century described the morals of his time, saying that if he were to enforce the canons against unchaste persons administering ecclesiastical rites, no one would be left in the Church except the boys. A tax was systematically levied on princes and clergymen for license to keep concubines" (*History of European Morals*).

Bernard of Clairvaux protested against enforcing celibacy on the clergy as contrary to human nature and divine law, saying:

"Deprive the Church of honorable marriage, and you fill her with concubinage, incest, and all manner of nameless vices and uncleanness."

John Calvin, in his *Institutes,* inveighed with all the power of his vast learning and all the passion of his scorn against the papal requirement of celibacy. Said he:

"In one instance, they are too rigorous and inflexible, that is, in not permitting priests to marry. With what impunity fornication rages among them, it is unnecessary to remark. Imboldened by their polluted celibacy, they have become hardened to every crime. This prohibition has not only deprived the Church of upright and able pastors, but has formed a horrible gulf of enormities, and precipitated many souls into the abyss of despair. . . . Christ has been pleased to put such honor upon marriage as to make it an image of his sacred union with the Church. What could be said more, in commendation of the dignity of marriage?" (IV, p. 24).

Henry VIII of England, in 1536, appointed commissioners to inspect all monasteries and nunneries in the land, and so terrible were the cruelties and corruptions uncovered that a cry went up from the nation that all such houses without exception should be destroyed. The fall of the monasteries was attributed to "the monstrous lives of the monks, the friars, and the nuns." This suppression of the monasteries undoubtedly did much to widen the gap between the Roman Church and this British monarch who already had declared his independence of the pope.

Henry Bamford Parkes, in his *A History of Mexico,* says:

"Clerical concubinage was the rule rather than the exception, and friars openly roamed the streets of cities with women on their arms. Many of the priests were ignorant and tyrannical, whose chief interest in their parishioners was the exaction of marriage, baptism, and funeral fees, and who were apt to abuse the confessional."

Many more such testimonials might be given. The widespread looseness of domestic manners in European and Latin American countries where that system has prevailed has been a disgrace to religion and a scandal to Christendom. It is extremely difficult to bring a priest into a civil court for punishment because the Roman Church forbids all Roman Catholics to testify against a priest. And most such crimes have been committed against their own people—another evidence that the Roman Catholic people are themselves the first and primary victims of their own church.

Numerous Roman Catholic historians have acknowledged that the law of celibacy for priests and the vows of chastity for monks are historical failures. What we are most concerned to criticize is not the sins of individual men, but the system as imposed by the Roman Church which leads to and tolerates such abuses. When will the Roman Catholic people throughout the world open their eyes and see that the boasted holiness of their church and of their priests is a pure fiction?

7. NUNS AND CONVENTS

There are some 168,000 Roman Catholic nuns in the United States alone, according to *The Official Catholic Directory*. All of these are under strict vows of poverty, chastity, and obedience, in their various orders, and constitute a vast pool of unpaid labor with which the Roman Church operates the thousands of parochial schools, hospitals, orphanages, and in some instances commercial establishments, which are under her control. This army of obedient, self-sacrificing nuns gives the Roman Church an immense advantage over establishments which pay their employees regular salaries or wages. To keep this labor force is of vital importance to the Roman Church, and to that end the priests usually are promoted by their bishops on two counts: first, the amount of money they turn in to the diocese; and second, the number of "vocations" (commitments to church service) they muster.

We have little criticism of the nuns as a class, except for their blind, unreasoning submission to orders from the priestly caste. As a rule they are kind, gentle, courteous, sincerely trying to practice their professions. They are far more human, less religious, and much less happy than the people of their own church, or others for that matter, are led to believe. While we regard the system as evil, we regard the nuns as primarily its victims, not its instigators.

The nuns have to fight a hard battle to crush out the natural and maternal instincts, to give up all prospects of marriage and family, which means so much to a woman, in order to enter the stoical convent system. The burden assumed by them is far heavier than is generally realized. In most cases the nuns are so helpless, so fearful of the persecution, ostracism, and other consequences which they have been led to believe will be visited upon them if they leave the convent, and so poorly prepared to make their way in the outside world, that they have no choice but to stay where they are. The course of convent training is purposely planned to fit them only for the work that the church has for them, deliberately excluding those courses that might be of value to a girl if she decided to leave the convent and turn to some other occupation.

In the normal course of life, marriage is a woman's natural, God-given privilege. Playing on this matrimonial instinct, the church deceives the nun with the fiction that she is the "bride of Christ," or "wife of Christ." She is even given a "wedding" ring, which she wears as a symbol of her union with Christ. Furthermore, the priests have imposed on the nuns a medieval church garb consisting of a long, black dress, the very symbol of grief and death, and a grotesque headgear which is awkward to wear and which is totally unfit for either hot or cold weather. We say the priests are to blame for this form of dress, for they are the real masters and owners in the Roman Church, and the nuns obey them. Convent orders are subject to the bishop of the diocese. The distinctive garb keeps, and is designed to keep, both priests and nuns constantly aware of the fact that they are committed totally to the service of the church, and places an impassable gulf between them and the world. The pope in Rome has the supreme and final authority over all nuns, and could relieve their hardships if he chose to do so.

The testimony of Emmett McLoughlin concerning the place of the nun in the Roman Church is very enlightening. He writes:

"The nun is one of the most remarkable products of the Roman Catholic Church. She is an absolute slave; one whose willingness to offer her life should fill Communist leaders with jealousy; one from whom the hierarchy conceals her slavery by the wedding ring on her finger; one who believes that in shining the bishop's shoes, waiting on his table, or scrubbing the floor, she is gathering herself 'treasure in heaven.' She is the one who makes possible the Church's hundreds of hospitals; the one who teaches in its thousands of parochial schools and orphanages; the one who (with her 156,695 sisters in 1952) does the drudgery behind the scenes in the hierarchy's drive to 'make America Catholic.' She is also a woman, with all the desires, instincts, loyalties, and hatreds of which a woman is capable; subservient to her 'man' through her indoctrination of her 'wedding' to Christ; often catty and gossipy toward her sister nuns and hospital nurses; maternal in her hoverings over priests and children; matriarchal in her petty policies for the control of her hospital or convent; and magnificent in her spirit of abasement, poverty, and self-annihilation in behalf of God and the Roman Catholic Church.

"In many seminaries in the United States, nuns—living in walled-off sections to prevent contact with the priests or seminarians—spend their lives performing the domestic services of cooking, laundry, and cleaning. During the persecutions of the Roman Catholic Church in Mexico in recent decades, many nuns sought refuge in the United States. The Bishop of Tuscon, the Most Rev. Daniel J. Gercke, offered some of them refuge in his episcopal mansion. He dispensed with his servants. The Mexican nuns took over all the household duties. If he merely rang a bell, a nun slipped in with bowed head to receive his orders, and on bended knee kissed his episcopal ring in appreciation of the privilege. As a dinner guest in his home, I personally witnessed this scene" (*People's Padre,* pp. 107, 108).

The position of the cloistered nuns, those committed to certain convents for life, is quite different from that of the regular nuns. They usually have gone into this seclusion because of some great sorrow or disappointment. Dr. Montano says concerning them:

"There are 100,000 nuns in the world living in strict seclusion in convents. Subsisting in these retreats are nuns who have retired behind closed doors for life. Young women who accept the vows of the cloistered nuns renounce their homes, their loved ones, their families, never to see them again. They will stay behind bars for the rest of their lives, shut away from the world.

"These unfortunate souls have cloistered themselves thinking that the fact they are not in touch with the world will save them from temptations. But again and again, throughout my lifetime, some of the most prominent nuns and monks have confessed to me that it is precisely behind the walls of these convents and monasteries that temptation has tortured them more than it ever did when they lived in the world. Here temptation has beset them until they have finally succumbed, because of the unnatural life they lead. Many poor souls have become tools of Satan, victims of the most monstrous sins.

"Severe discipline is inflicted upon these nuns by the Mother Superior, and flagellation and mortification of the body is practiced. Self-inflicted suffering is for the purpose of gaining indulgences by works, a striving to achieve salvation by merits. These poor souls are taught that they are putting treasures in the bank of indulgences. . . .

"The psychological disturbances that have resulted from this type of existence are such that not a few of these poor creatures have had to live out their days within the walls of mental institutions. To confirm this, Father More, of the Catholic University of America, Washington, D. C., states: 'Insanity among priests and nuns (compared with a general population ratio of 595 per 100,000) . . . among sisters who were cloistered rather than active showed a rate of 1,034, nearly twice the general population ratio.'

"Father Bief, president of the American Catholic Psychiatric Association, writes: 'Schizophrenia is by far the most frequent disorder among institutionalized priests and religious.' "

Dr. Montano adds:

"Of all the devices that Satan has employed to mislead souls who desire to serve God, this is the most perverted and institutionalized program in existence. That it should have been permitted to continue in a land of freedom, where governmental agencies have more and more reached a protective arm into all institutions to defend the physical and spiritual well-being of its sons and daughters, is most astonishing" (*Christian Heritage,* September, 1959).

8. ENTERING THE CONVENT

Why do girls enter convents? The large majority of girls have no desire to become nuns, and few would do so if left to their own choice. They instinctively shrink from the prospect of a long life spent within the walls of a convent. The fact is that in recent years the Church of Rome in the United States has found it increasingly difficult to secure enough American Catholic girls to staff her schools, hospitals, churches, etc., and has been obliged to import sisters from Europe. So serious has become this shortage that in some areas plans have been considered for dropping part of the lower grades in parochial schools in order to concentrate on the upper grades.

Why do girls enter convents? Let Helen Conroy, an ex-nun, give the answer:

"The truth is that girls go into convents because they are recruited. They are recruited for the convents and nunneries because the Church of Rome must have an unlimited number of pauper laborers to insure a fair return on the billions of dollars she has invested in 'charitable' institutions, such as schools, hospitals, orphanages, and laundries" (*Forgotten Women in Convents*, p. 32).

In the setup of the Roman Catholic Church it is the confessional box that feeds the nunneries. The ground work is done on the Catholic girl in the parochial school, where the nun is made an object of holy glamour, almost a replica of the Blessed Virgin Mary. The institution of the confessional makes it easy for the priests to find the ones they want, and of course they try to select the very choicest ones. That, in brief, is the reason the young nuns, as a rule, are above average in beauty, personality, and ability.

Ordinarily confessions begin at the age of seven. Through this means the priests come to know the very hearts and souls of those who confess before them, which would be desirable in the service of the church and which would not, which can be persuaded and which cannot. "Vocations" is the term euphemistically applied to the pressure that is put upon adolescent girls, with the object of persuading them to become nuns.

At this most susceptible age, when a girl's kaleidoscopic enthusiasm for becoming now a nurse, now a nun, now a stewardess, is at its height, it is easy for a trained priest to seize upon a passing fancy and blow it up into a full scale vocation. Once the victim has been chosen, pressure is applied directly and indirectly until the battle is won. Appeals are made to the girl's Christian sense of duty. Visits may be arranged on the part of those who already are nuns, or who are in training. Week-end retreats may be arranged at convents where she is royally entertained. Special favors and even flattery may also be used. The girl's natural reluctance to enter such a life is pictured as the evil influence of the world, or more directly of the Devil, attempting to hold her back from her divine calling, and she is warned that those who refuse their vocations quite possibly will be lost. She is told that within the convent she will be secluded from the evil influences of the world, and assured of everlasting happiness in heaven.

There is a sharp contrast between the exhortation Rome gives to her masses, to raise large families, and that given to the girl who is a prospect for the convent. To the latter, virginity is held up as the perfect state, and as more pleasing to God. Marriage and motherhood are spoken of disparagingly, as a lower form of morality, designed for the less perfect. The girl who may be matrimonially inclined is warned of the problems of home, childbearing, care of children, problems of in-laws, annoyances of all kinds. She is told that if she turns down this offer of "marriage" to Christ she will be committing a terrible sin and will have to take the consequences.

Usually the most opportune time for persuading a girl to enter the convent comes just after she has been disappointed in love. Blighted romance often affords the priest his most valuable opportunity. Says Helen Conroy:

> "A jilted girl, in the first rush of shame and agony at the shattering of her romance, is an easy victim of any priest. Knowing that such intense grief cannot last long, the girl is urged to go into a convent at once. The poor girl sees in it a chance to get away from an embarrassing situation, and this, coupled with the fact that she is assured she can leave any time she wishes, has led thousands to rush headlong into the convent" (*ibid.*, p. 3).

Often the priest can count on the support of the girl's family, which stands to gain social prestige and other favors in the Catholic community by giving a nun to the church. The deference which the Church of Rome teaches the people to pay to the priests and nuns extends itself to the families from which the priests and nuns come. Families of such are often showered with social and financial favors through which Rome cleverly makes them her allies. Should any boy or girl renounce his or her profession, that becomes a reflection on the family, and many a family that has owed its prosperity to the influence of the church has marked its decline from the day a son or daughter abandoned the religious life, particularly so if the parents sympathized with them and helped them to that end.

For parents who resist the idea that a son or daughter should enter the religious life the Church of Rome also has a word. In a book, *The Parents' Role in Vocations,* by Poage and Treacy, parents are encouraged to do what they can toward furthering such vocations. "Parents who without just cause prevent a child from entering a religious state," they are told, "cannot be excused from mortal sin" (ch. 10). Thus the threat of mortal sin, which to a Roman Catholic means the loss of salvation, is held over the heads of any parents who seek to keep a boy or girl from becoming an inmate of a monastery or convent!

The practice of the Roman Church is to persuade boys to enter monasteries and girls to enter convents at an early age. Rome well knows the value of this early training. In the book just referred to, the question is asked: "Which is preferable, entering a convent after high school or after college?" and the authors reply: "The Church recommends that the entrance be made as soon as possible." The Council of Toledo laid down the rule that, "As soon as a child has arrived at adolescence, that is to say, at the age of twelve for girls and fourteen for boys, they may freely dispose of themselves by entering religion." Thus the uninformed, inexperienced, immature mind is molded toward the religious vocation before it has a chance to develop independent ways of thinking and acting.

The normal practice in convent training is that during the first two years a girl may leave any time she pleases. Some do leave. Others are sent home because they are not found satisfactory. Following that period, the girl takes a vow for one year. If she first entered a convent near her home, she probably now will be sent to one some distance away. Even then she still can leave if she is unhappy or wants to leave. At the end of the third year the permanent vow is taken. This commits one for life. Some, however, refuse to commit themselves permanently, and will renew the vow for only one year at a time. The Roman Church does not like this practice, but when pressed for teachers or nurses often has no choice but to tolerate it. The nuns who commit themselves only for one year at a time usually do about as they please.

The Church of Rome well knows the influence that strong family ties can have on the nun, pulling her back to an independent life. Consequently a determined effort is made to break all her ties with home and relatives. The first step in that program is to change her identity. This is done at one stroke by dropping her real name and giving her a fictitious one, usually the name of some obscure saint. Thenceforth she is known as Sister So-and-so, symbolical of the fact that she now is a new person and that she is breaking all ties with the old life. Experience proves, however, that the man or woman who finds it necessary to use an assumed name loses self-respect, and with it courage and initiative. The mere use of a false name tends to make one feel that he can escape obligations. And by what authority does the Church of Rome arrogate to herself the right to change the names of her members without recourse to civil law? Photographs, even of the girl's mother and father are taken away from her. For photographs are strong reminders of the old life and tend to make "dying to the world" harder and slower by prolonging the agony. Even the memory of her parents pulls her back to the old life, and so must be obliterated as far as possible. Her incoming and outgoing mail is censored by the Mother Superior, and may be mutilated or withheld if it contains unfavorable comments about the convent or convent life. Again, by what authority does the Church of Rome tamper with the mail? Why, by the authority of the pope, of course. He is a law unto himself and above all civil law. He is the representative of God on earth, and is not to be hampered by the civil laws of the various nations!

Concerning the matter of breaking relations with home and family Ligouri, the most noted moral theologian in the Church of Rome, utterly perverting the true sense of Scripture, says:

> "If attachment to relatives were not productive of great mischief, Jesus Christ would not have so strenuously exhorted us to estrangement from them. 'If,' He says, 'any man comes to me, and hates not his father and mother, and brethren and sisters, he cannot be my disciple' (Luke 14:26). And again, 'I came to set a man at variance against his father, and the daughter against her mother' (Matt. 10:35)."

We point out, however, that the true explanation of Luke 14:26 and Matthew 10:35 is found in Matthew 10:37, where we read: "He that loveth father or mother more than me is not worthy of me; and he that loveth son or daughter more than me is not worthy of me." Luke 14:26 and Matthew 10:35, in which our obligation to Christ as compared with that to our closest relatives and friends is stated negatively, and Matthew 10:37, in which it is stated positively, simply mean that we are not to put any other person *before* Him. They do not mean that we are not to continue to have a proper love and regard for our relatives and friends as such.

Ligouri continues:

> "But why does the Redeemer insist so strongly on alienation from relatives? Why does He take so much pains to separate us from them? He, Himself, assigns the reason: it is because 'A man's enemies shall be those of his own household' (Matt. 10:36). Relatives are the worst enemies of the sanctification of Christians, and particularly of religious; because they are, according to St. Thomas (Aquinas), the greatest obstacle to achievement of virtue. 'Frequently,' says the Holy Doctor, 'carnal friends oppose the progress of the spirit; for in the affairs of salvation, the nearest of kin are not friends, but enemies' (p. 189).
> "The truth of this assertion is fully established by experience. . . .

He who desires to walk in the way of perfection must fly from relatives, must abstain from taking part in their affairs, and when they are at a distance, must not even inquire about them. The religious who tells her parents, and her brothers, and her sisters, that she knows them not, is the True Spouse of Christ."

To the same effect St. Jerome says:

"It is a great advantage to forget your parents; for then 'the King shall greatly desire your beauty.'" And again, "How many monks have by compassion towards their father and mother, lost their own souls! A religious who is attached to her relatives has not yet left the world."

And St. Teresa, who is held up as a model for nuns, says:

"For my part, I cannot conceive what consolation a nun can find in her relatives."

But to such reasoning Helen Conroy gives this devastating reply:

"This infamous system, not satisfied with getting the girl away from her parents, poisons the mind and heart of the girl against the mother who bore her, as well as against the father, sisters and brothers. Of all the crimes committed in the name of religion, this forcing of hatred of parents is the blackest. Siva (a Hindu deity) may have been the Great Destroyer, but Rome is the Great Dehumanizer. This doctrine of hatred of parents by nuns and sisters fully explains why a girl is not allowed to dispose of her property until sixty days before she is to take the veil and the vows. The church fully expects that by that time the girl will have learned the hymn of hate, and refuse to leave them anything" (*Forgotten Women in Convents*, p. 82).

We have mentioned the fact that a girl entering a convent takes solemn vows of poverty, chastity, and obedience. The vow of poverty reduces those who take it to the status of paupers. Giving up all property rights, the girl thenceforth has in common with the other members of the Order only what is given them by the mother superior. Canon Laws 568 and 569 relate to any property that the novitiate may have, and provides that it must all be given up. Ligouri says:

"All the money, furniture, clothes, and whatever species of property you possess, all that you receive from your parents or relatives, or the fruit of your industry, belong, not to you, but to the convent. You have only the use of what the superior gives you. Hence, if you dispose of anything without her leave you are guilty of theft, by violating the vow of poverty" (*The True Spouse of Christ* p. 159).

The prospective nun is forbidden to dispose of her property before she enters, or at the time she enters, the convent. Instead, she must wait until within sixty days of the time she is to make her solemn, permanent profession. The reason behind this rule is that it is assumed that by that time she will be sufficiently alienated from her family, and sufficiently committed to the convent, that she will give her property, in large amount at least, to the convent. These two rulings are of great importance to the Roman Church, for through them a great amount of property falls into her hands.

There is a widespread belief among Protestants, and even among Roman Catholics, that the convents are financed by the Roman Church, so that those who wish may retire from the world and spend their lives in seclusion. Nothing could be farther from the truth. Canon Law requires that the girl bring with her a specified amount of money or property, depending on her status in life, which money is known as "the dowry," or marriage portion of the spouse of Christ. This money is invested, and if for any reason she leaves the convent, it must be returned to her, but not the interest that may have been derived from it. There are exceptions, however, in which no dowry is required, in which other considerations prevail, such as education, special talents, the church's need for teachers, nurses, etc. But one of the usual considerations in selecting a girl who is to be urged to become a nun is that she come from a family in which she will have some inheritance.

Those who on entering the convent bring money, or education, or special talents, are known as "choir sisters"; those who bring neither money, nor education, nor special talents are known as "lay sisters," and may be assigned to menial work such as cooking, sweeping, scrubbing, waiting on the choir sisters, etc. No girl lacking good health will be accepted. If the novitiate breaks down, she is promptly returned to her family. The Church of Rome has no intention of spending money on a nun who is not a good investment. Thus in the Roman Church even the privilege of working for one's salvation has a price tag on it—and oftentimes it is a very high price tag. Going to heaven via the Roman route calls for money first, last, and all the time. Money is the golden key that most effectively unlocks the pearly gates.

9. CONVENT LIFE

The Roman Church seeks to convey the idea that a nun is the happiest of women, and that a convent is the most holy, delightful, and peaceful place of abode. "No girl can be a nun or stay a nun unless she herself desires it," says Charles F. X. Dolan, in a Roman Catholic Questionnaire.

"Nobody," he continues, "can make her stay in the convent. Convent walls are not to keep the nuns in, but to keep the world out." On the strength of such promises many a poor, deluded girl has sought shelter in a convent.

But quite a different picture is presented by some of those who have left the convents through the regular procedures, or who have escaped from them. For instance, Helen Conroy says:

"The fact is that the average convent is a hornet's nest of intrigue. In them are cliques and factions, and many an ambitious sister gets to be superior, the most coveted position in a convent, not by an honest election, but by crushing all opposition ruthlessly, and by catering to the priest. . . . The convent system is honeycombed with spies, who are known by the name of 'discretes.' They are the G-men, the undercover agents. They are seldom known. This is what makes real friendship among sisters and nuns an impossibility" (*ibid.*, p. 56).

Conditions in convents in the United States, where the Roman Church is subject to restraining influences from Protestantism, and where abuses are more likely to be publicized, are far better than in the Roman Catholic countries where restraints are at a minimum and where the ecclesiastical, governmental, and police power are all under Roman domination. A majority of the nuns here undoubtedly are sincere, hard-working, well-meaning women. Those who are engaged in teaching and nursing still have some contact with the outside world, but they too are carefully restricted in their social contacts, their reading, travel, living quarters, etc. There is no reason to believe that immorality in any appreciable degree exists in these convents. But the basic principles of convent life are the same everywhere and the convents here have many of the undesirable characteristics that are commonly found in such institutions.

The best analysis of convent life that we have seen is given by Dee Smith, formerly a layman in the Roman Church. He divides the nuns into four distinct groups. Concerning these he says:

(1) "It must not be supposed that all nuns are unhappy and wish to leave the convent. Temperaments differ inside the convent as well as outside of it. Some nuns enjoy communal life and find all the fulfillment their natures require in doing the work they love. I believe these to be a fairly large minority."

He then divides the remaining majority into three groups as follows:

(2) "The largest group consists of those who are disillusioned with convent life, depressed by the spite, petty politics, and lack of charity within the convent walls. But they have lost none of their faith in the

Roman Catholic Church, believing it their duty to stay on and endure. They are totally unaware that their lives are being worse than wasted— used in fact as a commodity to keep unscrupulous men in power. These sad, empty-hearted, betrayed souls sincerely believe they are serving God.

(3) "Next comes the group who are not only disillusioned with the convent but wish to leave it. They do not, however contemplate leaving the church nor do they attach any blame to convent life, believing themselves simply to have misjudged their 'vocation.' What are their chances of getting out? If they come from influential families sufficiently broad-minded to support their plea for release and to welcome them back with understanding, their chances are good. While leaving the convent is not a common event, no few individuals have done so, and have lived a normal life within the Roman Catholic fold afterward.

"If, however, the nun comes from the superstitious and fanatical type of Catholic family which supplies most of the church's vocations, she may find her family itself opposing her release, and her superiors, mindful of the impending loss of a trained drudge, will not be slow to take advantage of this. She will find her Mother Superior and her Confessor both pleading the dangers of a vocation relinquishment.

"Under the circumstances the nun gives up hope of getting out. What else can she do? She has no money, no clothes except her convent garb, no means of communicating with the outside world since her mail is censored, nowhere to go if she did get out. When Catholics say that any nun can leave the convent at any time she wishes, they are simply talking nonsense. Many a nun who would love to get out is spending her life within convent walls because she has no alternative and is making the best of it.

(4) "The nun in the last group is the one who has the least chance of all to find freedom. She is almost hopelessly incarcerated. These are the alert, intelligent women who have seen through the whole scheme and have been injudicious enough to say so. They want not only to get out of the convent but out of the Roman Church. Their families seldom support their stand, but if they seem likely to, communication between the family and the recalcitrant is shut off. At first the usual pleas and admonitions are used on them, but if these fail to impress, a Roman Catholic doctor or psychologist obligingly examines them and they disappear forever into a Catholic mental institution.

"The only way this type of individual ever frees herself from the convent is by shrewdness and diplomacy, by withholding all criticism of church and convent and concentrating on concern over her vocation. If sufficiently convincing she may sometimes be able to secure her release. Once outside, these are among the most valiant fighters against Roman tyranny."

Dee Smith then concludes: "The convent has its full quota of hard, malicious characters who take out their frustrations on the gentler and more sweet-tempered of their associates. If these women have ability they quite often become Superiors, as they are usually endowed with a capacity for driving others" (*Christian Heritage*, December, 1958).

With particular reference to cloistered nuns Dr. Montano says:

"Having been won to the cloister by the promise of being wedded to Christ, she takes part in the binding. After the organ music is silenced, after the congratulations of loved ones have died away, alone in her cell the poor victim awakens to the sad reality that the mirage which drew her behind these walls has faded. She finds herself on the lonely road between life and death. What of her future? To remain there, shut away from human experience, human fellowship, human love, human service. She finds herself surrounded by utter disillusionment as her eyes are opened to the petty jealousies, enmities, cruelties, and the spiritual un- balance. In her vows she has pronounced the words, 'until death.' She is chained behind the walls of the convent until she dies.

"Any visitor to those cloistered must be appointed by Roman Catholic dignitaries. Only the priests of the monasteries have access to these cloistered nuns. They go to inspect the convent, to attend a sick nun, or to hear their confessions. Secular justice has no entree behind the barred doors and windows of the cloisters. No one from the outside can reach inside these walls to help free these souls, nor can those within escape unless, as a few have done, they manage to flee by risking their lives" (*Christian Heritage*, September, 1959).

Throughout the world there are some 100,000 cloistered nuns. Speaking of one of the more extreme orders, and quoting the regulations under which they live, Dr. Montano says:

"The discalced (barefoot) Carmelite sisters, for example, neither teach, nor nurse, nor care for the old, the orphans, the infirm. They take a vow of silence—complete silence.

"At 5:30 A.M. the nuns arise from their pallets, which are wooden boards across saw-horses, covered with a straw-filled tick—for they have also talken a vow of poverty.

"At 8:30 A.M. they eat a slice of bread and drink one cup of black coffee. The table is set with plain wooden utensils and a covered water pitcher. The mask of death, a skull, is on the table, to symbolize thoughts of death, that we are mortal beings, soon to pass into the unknown.

"Their main meal may be of fish and vegetables, and their evening meal is soup and bread. Their day ends at 11 P.M., when they silently return to their cells furnished with only pallet, table and chair" (*Christian Heritage*, September, 1959).

How, then, are these pitiful souls to be reached? That is indeed a very difficult, and in most cases an impossible, task. Civil governments are extremely reluctant to interfere in church affairs. And even the communities in which convents are located usually know practically nothing about what goes on behind convent walls.

Fortunately the working nuns are not bound so tightly by their convent regulations. But their case is difficult enough. Many a young, impressionable girl has gotten worked up into an enthusiastic hysteria, has been swept off her feet, and has taken the veil. By the time she sobers down and regrets her decision she finds herself so deeply involved that it is next to impossible to retrace her steps. Perhaps she entered the convent against the protest of her parents, who wanted her to think it over a while longer. Now she regrets her unwise haste. What is she to do?

Probably her property commitments are so binding that she cannot renounce them, for she has signed legal documents that in most cases turn her property over to the convent. She finds that the course of training that she has received has been designed to fit her only for the work of the church. She has been left completely unequipped to meet the problems of every day living in the world. She is told that if she turns back she will be branding herself a traitor to God and to her church, and that public opinion will be strongly against her—which in most cases is not true. The stigma that the Roman Church in Catholic communities attaches to those who abandon convent life is another powerful reason why she feels that, happy or unhappy, she must remain where she is. Furthermore, her vows of service were made to the pope, and official release from them must be obtained from him—a procedure which may involve endless red tape. Under such circumstances many a girl has felt completely helpless and has concluded that she had no choice but to continue in the convent.

In regard to the problems that one who leaves the convent has in re-establishing herself in life, listen to the testimony of Helen Conroy:

"I shrink at the memory of the awful struggle back to normalcy which I, in common with every other ex-nun, went through. With no business training, no knowledge of homemaking, no sense of values without which any life is a failure; with no decision, a prey to a thousand terrors, afraid of myself and everyone else; timid, cringing, physically emancipated, but mentally chained, the unfortunate ex-nun in too many cases returns to her cell voluntarily, because, 'there are no decisions to be made.' Rome clips the wings of her victims so that they cannot fly, then tells the believing world that they stay because they like it" (*Forgotten Women in Convents,* p. 109).

And Daniel March says:

"The vows of a nun are fetters of brass. Around the nun is an invisible wall so high she cannot scale it, so strong she cannot pierce it. If she abandons the convent she abandons the only friends she knows. The years she has spent in the convent, far from fitting her to cope with reality, have made her a creature without a will of her own."

In this connection it is interesting to read that the Roman Catholic Teresa Foundation recently made application to establish a convent for Carmelite (cloistered) nuns in Glumslov, Sweden. No Roman Catholic convents have been permitted in Sweden since the Reformation. The Swedish Advisory Council is opposed to the move, and has declared that "if permission is granted" it will be only "in consideration of personal freedom" for the women who have taken the vows, and that they must have permission to "leave the convent if they wish without fear of punishment."

What a pity it is that in the United States, in this fabled "land of the free," we do not have a requirement that convents can exist on our soil *only* if the nuns are assured "personal freedom," and *only* if they may "leave the convent if they wish without fear of punishment."

10. CONCLUSION

Freeborn Protestant women can have little idea of the spiritual, mental, and physical slavery in which their unfortunate Roman Catholic sisters in some instances have been held and still are held by that church. Even in the United States thousands of broken-hearted convent girls and women are shut away from parents, friends, and homes, forbidden to appear alone in public, forbidden even to carry on an ordinary conversation with other people. That this slavery is in many cases voluntary or semi-voluntary does not make it any less real. Those who have lost the sense of freedom, or the desire for freedom, or who never had it in the first place, do not know what it is. Rome claims some 168,000 nuns in the United States, and many more thousands throughout the world. Keep the girls and women from the confessional box and take them out of the convents, and Romanism will wither. It is well known that in the confessional the priests do not make one-tenth the progress with men that they do with women, nor do they waste much time attempting it.

Christ established no convents, no nunneries. In the true Christian church there are no high stone walls, no locked doors and barred windows such as so often have been a part of the Roman convent system. Instead, the convent system is of pagan origin. Practically every Buddhist temple in India has its "virgins" consecrated to the service of the god worshipped there, complete with holy water, holy ashes, charms, bones, bells, and pictures, all blessed by the priests. The historical fact is that the Buddhist convent system antedated the Roman Catholic system of pious slavery of women by more than 500 years.

What, then, must be our conclusion regarding the convent system? That it is abominably cruel, unnatural, un-American, and unscriptural, and that it should be abolished by law. In our own country the so-called "sanctity" of those institutions is honored, so that secular justice and the protective agencies of government have no entrance. If there is a convent in your community, ask the sheriff what he knows about the things that go on inside those walls. He will have to acknowledge that he knows practically nothing about how many people are there, who they are, what they do, how they are treated, or whether or not they are there of their own volition. The government of the United States should give the women in American convents a new status, based not on Roman Catholic Canon Law, but on the Constitution of the United States.

In her book, *Forgotten Women in Convents*, Helen Conroy suggests an eleven point program for convent reform. It is as follows:

(1) "It should be made illegal to accept into any convent or monastic institution of any kind any boy or girl under eighteen years of age, with or without the consent of their parents.

(2) "No person should be allowed to make vows until twenty-one years of age. This would end the exploitation of mere children in the name of religion.

(3) "Every state where monastic institutions exist should have on file a sworn statement of the exact number of inmates in the house. This list should be kept up-to-date.

(4) "All arrivals and departures of members of these colonies should be reported (even hotels and motels are required to keep a record of their guests).

(5) "The state should have a certified list of the real names of the inmates, together with the names and addresses of their parents, or of their nearest kin.

(6) "Since the act of entering a monastic institution is, to all intents and purposes, a renunciation of the rights of citizenship, for no man can serve two masters (the pope and the state), members of monastic communities are no longer free citizens and should be debarred from voting in any election, state, county, or national, and from teaching in public schools.

(7) "Members of religious orders entering the country should be required to take out citizenship papers within the time specified by law. Do they all stay in the convents? No one knows.

(8) "All persons entering a monastic institution should be required to

make a will and file the same. The renunciation which the Church of Rome forces all religious to make sixty days before profession should be null and void.

(9) "The use of special regalia should be confined to the premises.

(10) "The board of public health should have full control of monastic institutions, and should make regular visits to them.

(11) "Death certificates of all persons dying in monastic institutions should be signed by a non-Catholic doctor as well as by a Catholic doctor" (pp. 119, 120).

To these suggestions we would add the further provision, that inmates of such institutions should be free to leave at any time without fear of punishment. Surely the adoption of these recommendations would go far toward eliminating the most objectionable features of the convent system.

XV. MARRIAGE

1. The Christian View of Marriage. 2. The Roman Doctrine that Marriage is a Sacrament. 3. Roman Denial of the Validity of Protestant and Civil Marriage. 4. The Pre-Marital Contract. 5. The Injustice of the Pre-Marital Contract. 6. A Fraudulent Contract. 7. Mixed Marriage Difficulties. 8. The Roman Catholic Attitude Toward Divorce.

1. THE CHRISTIAN VIEW OF MARRIAGE

The teaching of Scripture concerning marriage can be set forth in the four following propositions:

1. Marriage is a holy and sacred relationship between one man and one woman, designed to continue as long as they both live.
2. Marriage is the normal state for the average adult both from the social and the hygienic standpoint.
3. Children are a gift from God.
4. The family (not the individual) is the fundamental unit of society.

In the Christian view of marriage sex is set forth as one of the powers divinely implanted in human nature. It is, therefore, not to be looked upon as something evil, something to be suppressed and put down like a plague. The Bible tells us: "God created man in his own image, in the image of God created he him; male and female created he them" (Gen. 1:27). In that same passage we also read: "And God saw everything that he had made, and, behold, it was very good" (vs. 31).

God, then, is the author of sex. He created mankind with that particular power, and when He had done so He pronounced it good. He also made clear that the purpose of sex was: (1) that the human race might be perpetuated and that it might increase upon the earth; and (2) that it might provide a special kind of companionship among human beings. Viewed in this light, marriage is a gift that not even the angels know, and sex is a high and wholesome gift from God to the highest of His earthly creatures. Sex, therefore, can become evil only when it is perverted.

Says one writer: "The attraction which men and women and boys and girls feel for each other is a normal, natural thing. It is part of the nature that God has put within us, but it must be governed by the ideals and

332

rules that He has given us. The fullness of human relationship is to be shared by only one man with one woman and vice versa. It is intended that this human partnership shall be on a lifetime basis. It is a union which is physical and spiritual, and it is the ultimate in human relationships" (B. Hoyt Evans, *The Presbyterian Journal*, Aug. 5, 1959).

For the Christian man and woman marriage properly begins in the church. Most Christians realize the importance of religion for marriage, and they want to have the ceremony solemnized and blessed by the church. The vows taken are religious. The spiritual aspect of marriage and the blessing of God upon the new union are the very heart of the matter. For Christians it just does not seem right or sufficient to be married before a civil official even though such marriage is legal. A mere civil ceremony seems cold and lacking in that spiritual aspect which can do so much to enrich and ennoble the new union and make it permanent. For non-Christians, however, the civil ceremony is both legal and proper.

2. THE ROMAN DOCTRINE THAT MARRIAGE IS A SACRAMENT

Because the supposedly infallible Vulgate mistranslated Ephesians 5:32 to read, "This is a great sacrament," the Roman Church for ages has taught that marriage is a sacrament. But the correct translation is: "This is a great mystery."

In his broader teaching in Ephesians, chapter 5, Paul is speaking of the union that exists between Christ and the church, and he points to marriage as a symbol of that union. He teaches that as Christ loved the church, and gave himself up for it (vs. 25), so should husbands love their wives as their own bodies (vs. 28). He says: "For this cause shall a man leave his father and mother, and shall be joined unto his wife, and they two shall be one flesh"; and then he adds: "This is a great mystery: but I speak concerning Christ and the church" (vss. 31,32)—King James Version. The American Standard Version reads: "This mystery is great," which is substantially the same. Today even Roman Catholic writers acknowledge that the old translation was in error. The new Confraternity Version translates it correctly: "This is a great mystery"—which is the same as the King James Version. But the Church of Rome continues to hold zealously the doctrine that was formulated on the erroneous Vulgate translation, namely, that marriage is a sacrament. Marriage is now firmly established as one of the seven sacraments of the Church of Rome, and evidently cannot be relinquished.

A vital consequence of the erroneous translation has been that the Roman Church has attempted to control everything pertaining to marriage. Since marriage was held to be a sacrament, that placed it entirely under the control of the church; for only the church can administer a sacrament. Civil marriage was declared to be unlawful. And since at the time of the Council of Trent the Roman Church did not acknowledge the validity of Protestant marriage, the Council simply declared that any marriage not performed by a priest was null and void. The 73rd article of the *Syllabus of Errors* issued by pope Pius IX, which even today forms a part of the ordination vow of every Roman Catholic priest, says: "Marriage among Christians cannot be constituted by any mere civil contract; the marriage contract among Christians must always be a sacrament; and the contract is null, if the sacrament does not exist." In another statement Pius IX declared that marriage without the Roman sacrament was "low and abominable concubinage."

The Catholic Almanac for 1954 says: ". . . a Catholic who goes through a marriage ceremony before a minister or justice of the peace contracts no marriage." And America's most distinguished Roman theologian, Monsignor Francis J. Connell, for many years Dean of the School of Sacred Theology at Catholic University, in Washington, D. C., sets forth the rule that Roman Catholics who are married before a Protestant minister must be punished even to the graveyard. In answer to the question, "Is it correct to tell Catholics that they will be denied Christian burial in the event that they attempt marriage before a non-Catholic minister?" he replied: "Such a statement can be made correctly, as long as the clause is added, 'unless before death they give signs of repentance' (Canon 1240, Section 1). The reason is that by such a sinful act a Catholic becomes a public and manifest sinner, and to such a one Christian burial is denied (Canon 1240, Section 1, Note 6)" (*American Ecclesiastical Review,* October, 1959, p. 266). And *The Sign,* a Roman Catholic magazine, issue of May, 1958, expresses typical Roman Catholic bigotry on this subject when it refers to marriage not performed by a priest as merely "attempted" marriage, and rates a marriage ceremony performed by a Protestant minister as inferior even to that of a civil official. It says: "The attempted marriage of two Catholics, or of even one Catholic, before a civil official is invalid. On that score, however, excommunication is not incurred, as would be the case were the marriage attempted before a non-Catholic religious minister." A practical *Commentary on the Code of Canon Law* (1925), by S. Woywod, page 563, carrying the imprimatur of Cardinal Hayes, sets forth this same view, as does another book, *Catholic Principles of Politics,* by Ryan and Boland, a widely used text in Roman Catholic colleges and universities. Hence it is clear that the Roman Church claims exclusive jurisdiction over the marriage contract and the marital state of Christians, and that all civil laws that contradict Canon Law are held to be null and void.

But the fact is that Rome's own teaching is null and void, for Paul does not say that marriage is a sacrament, nor is that statement found anywhere in the Bible. Marriage was not instituted by Christ, which is a requirement for a true sacrament, but instead was instituted in the Garden of Eden thousands of years before the time of Christ. Hence Rome's attempt to bring all marriage under her exclusive jurisdiction stands revealed as merely another of the methods which she uses in her attempt to nullify an important area of civil control and to bring all human relationships under her own control. Her clearly revealed purpose is to rule the entire life of the family.

The fact that Roman Catholicism holds that marriage is a sacrament does not mean that it holds marriage in greater reverence than does Protestantism. Protestantism holds that marriage was divinely instituted in the Garden of Eden, and so was established by God's blessing. For a Christian, therefore, it is a sacred ordinance that should be performed by a minister and blessed by the church.

3. ROMAN DENIAL OF THE VALIDITY OF PROTESTANT AND CIVIL MARRIAGE

During the Middle Ages when the Roman Church had a monopoly over all religious affairs, her control over marriage was effective and ruthless. Civil law was conformed to Canon Law, and no form of marriage other than that performed by a priest was recognized as valid or legal. Even after the Reformation the Roman Church for centuries continued to deny the validity of all marriage performed by Protestant ministers or by officials of the state. She asserted that all couples not married by a priest were living in adultery and that their children were illegitimate.

Few Protestants seem to know that even today the Roman Church still claims authority over the marriage of all Christians everywhere, over Protestants as well as Roman Catholics, and that it is only since the *Ne Temere* decree, issued by pope Piux X, April 19, 1908, that the marriage of Protestants, performed by Protestant ministers, has been regarded as valid by the Roman Church. And even today in several countries where there is a concordat between the Vatican and the civil government, as in Spain and Colombia, Protestant marriages still are illegal. Civil marriages are legal for Protestants, but they have to be approved by judges who usually are Roman Catholics and they often are hindered by all kinds of impediments. If one party has been baptized into the Roman Church even in infancy (as most people in those countries have been), even though he has long since left that church Rome still opposes the marriage and seeks to bring it within her own jurisdiction. That, of course, is Roman practice everywhere, never to give up to another church one who has been baptized in the Roman Church. In the concordat countries the marriage of two Roman Catholics, or of a Roman Catholic and a Protestant, or of a Roman Catholic and an unbeliever, before a Protestant minister or official of the state is strictly forbidden by the Roman Church and is illegal in the state. That is a consistent pattern in countries where Rome has the power to enforce her will, and that is what we can expect in the United States if this ever becomes a Roman Catholic nation.

The *Ne Temere* decree of 1908, while granting that the marriage of Protestants by Protestant ministers after that date would be considered valid, was not retroactive and did not validate such marriages performed before that date. On the other hand it defined more specifically the rule of the Roman Church regarding its own members, in that anywhere the marriage of two Roman Catholics, or of one Roman Catholic and a Protestant, before a Protestant minister or an official of the state was pronounced null and void, even though the marriage had occurred years earlier and had brought forth several children. Furthermore, the decree of 1908 was made only as a concession, largely because of pressure brought to bear on the hierarchy in the United States and other Protestant countries. Hence the pope may revoke that decree any time he deems expedient and declare that no marriage of Christians anywhere is valid without the special blessing of his priests.

Because of the pope's asserted authority over all Christian marriage, he claims the authority to annul any Protestant marriage anywhere and at any time. That authority is no idle boast, and is exercised today in some cases in which Protestants wish to be free from present mates in order to marry Roman Catholics. Though professing to be unalterably opposed to divorce, the Roman Church gets around that obstacle quite easily by declaring those marriages null and void, that is, never to have existed in the first place. She simply grants an "annulment." Surely it would be hard to find bigotry and intolerance in a more exaggerated form than is thus displayed officially and continually by the Roman Church.

There is a strange inconsistency in the application of the *Ne Temere* decree. Under that decree if two Protestants are married by a Protestant minister the marriage is held to be valid. But if two Roman Catholics, or a Roman Catholic and a Protestant, are married by the same minister, using the same service and taking the same vows, she calls it "attempted" marriage, and pronounces it null and void. By all the rules of logic if the ceremony is valid in one case it is also valid in the other. Such a distinction in Canon Law is merely another evidence of the compromising nature of the Roman Church, conceding as much as seems expedient under certain circumstances, but enforcing her rule wherever she is able.

That the Roman Church in Protestant countries today does not interfere directly with marriage when only Protestants are concerned is due only to the fact that she does not have the power, not because she willingly and freely makes that concession. Let it never be doubted that if Rome gains the power she will again enforce her claim over all marriage as she did before the Reformation. She would like nothing better than to return to that period, which even yet she refers to nostalgically as "the age of faith."

An example of what Roman Catholic domination in the field of marriage can mean, and of the ideal that Rome would like to put into effect everywhere, is set forth in the report of the Evangelical Confederation of Colombia, dated August 24, 1959. It reads as follows:

> "*Protestant marriage not legal.* As the Roman Catholic and the civil ceremonies are the only forms of marriage which produce legal effects in Colombia, Protestants are first married by a magistrate and then solemnize their union with a religious service in their church.
>
> "The Roman Catholic clergy is jealous of its privileged position in the performance of the marriage ceremony. It brands as 'public concubinage' the union produced by civil marriage. It puts pressure on the civil authorities to delay and obstruct the civil ceremony, if not to prevent it altogether. Against those couples who have the courage and tenacity to carry through with the civil ceremony the church hurls its penalty of excommunication in an attempt to force the pair, through social ostracism and economic pressure, to renounce their sin and return to the Catholic Church in repentance."

For members of the Roman Catholic Church in Colombia only a church ceremony is valid. However, a national law states that if both parties to the marriage declare that they have never been members of the Roman Catholic Church, or that they have formally separated from it, a civil ceremony is valid. But the process is a difficult one. The magistrates must notify the priest in whose parish the couple are resident, and then a delay of one month is required, during which time the priest has opportunity to try to dissuade the parties from their contemplated step. At the request of the priest the civil ceremony may be postponed indefinitely. Conditions in Spain are similar to those in Colombia.

Marriage of a Roman Catholic and a Protestant before a Protestant minister opens the way for easy divorce on the part of the Roman Catholic. Suppose a Roman Catholic man marries a Protestant girl. If the marriage proves to be satisfactory, well and good; he is content to let it stand. But if it does not turn out well, he can easily accept the teaching of his church that it was not a valid marriage in the first place. He does not see it as the solemnly binding union that the Protestant holds it to be. If he finds himself forbidden absolution from sin by the priest because of a Protestant marriage, he may feel obliged in conscience to separate from the Protestant partner. But if the couple wishes to remain together he may proceed to obtain from the pope a dispensation or a "revalidation" of the marriage. An effort usually will be made to persuade the Protestant to submit to a Roman Catholic wedding. But if that fails, a curious thing happens. The Roman Catholic party then goes *alone* to the priest. Lucien Vinet describes this process as follows:

> "He or she will be married 'validly' without the consent or knowledge of the Protestant party. This wonderful Roman invention is called, in Latin, 'Revalidatio in radice' (Cure from the very root). The pope in Rome will give his consent to this marriage in union with that of the Roman Catholic party, using also the original marriage consent of the Protestant party, and this will render valid the marriage of this unfortunate couple. The cure has been effected. The 'Sanatio' of the pope has validly married the two persons without the knowledge of the Protestant party. Now the couple can live together and the Roman Catholic party has no more conscientious troubles" (*I Was a Priest,* p. 56).

Recently a case arose in Italy in which a man who was not a member of the Roman Catholic Church and a woman who was a member were married in a civil ceremony. At the direction of the bishop of Brato the local priest read a letter to the congregation in which the legality of the marriage was denied and the relationship was denounced as "low and abominable concubinage." The case was taken to court by the husband, on the charge of slander, and in March, 1958, a verdict was obtained against the bishop and the priest. The court was composed of three judges who were Roman Catholics. The bishop was fined 40,000 lire ($64) and costs of the six day trial, and was ordered to pay the injured couple $672 damages. The $64 fine, however, was suspended. The bishop appealed the case and strong pressure was brought to bear on the court by the hierarchy from the pope down. The pope declared a period of mourning, because a fine had been laid on a bishop of the Roman Church by a civil court. That apparently was more pressure than the court could stand. The result was that the verdict was reversed, the claim for damages was denied, and the couple was ordered to pay the court costs. There the case ended, but not without a great deal of very unfavorable publicity for the Roman Church.

There is, of course, nothing in Scripture that gives to church authorities the exclusive right to perform the marriage ceremony. According to American law the legal right and privilege of performing marriage ceremonies is given to the ministers of all churches who qualify and to certain officials of the state. No person or church should attempt to usurp that power, or to say that marriages performed by rituals other than their own are illegal and that the people who employ them are not married but are living in sin. Such procedure is a vicious repudiation of American law, and should be punishable as slander in the courts. In New Zealand it is a felony punishable in the courts for any church or individual to declare or teach that a marriage contracted in accordance with the civil law is not a true marriage. Certainly church laws made in a foreign country and utterly lacking in Scriptural authority, should not be allowed to supersede American laws, resulting in the vilification of the ministers of other churches, our court officials, and many of our people whose good name is injured by such laws. But Roman Church law, based on Canon 1094, does precisely that. In Roman Catholic countries it is a common occurrence for the civil laws to be conformed to or based on the Roman Church Canon Law. The Roman Church thus claims that she is above all civil authority, that to her belongs the authority to legislate on matters pertaining to marriage, and that any conflict between the church and the state is to be resolved in favor of the church.

4. THE PRE-MARITAL CONTRACT

Since the Roman Church denies the validity of the marriage of a Roman Catholic before a Protestant minister, there is strong pressure on Roman Catholics, if they wish to remain in good standing with their church, to be married only by a priest. When a Protestant consents to marry a Roman Catholic before a priest he finds that he must agree, first, to take a series of religious instructions. This course, given by the priest, consists of at least six one-hour lessons in which the doctrines of that church are favorably presented in the hope that the Protestant will be persuaded to become a Roman Catholic. Ten to fifteen such lessons are preferred if the Protestant will consent to take them. He is also given some books to study which glorify the Roman Church and condemn Protestant churches. He soon learns that he must sign away all of his religious rights and privileges in the home, and that he must make all of the concessions while the Roman Catholic party makes none at all. He also learns that the Roman Catholic party must secure a dispensation from the bishop (the priest cannot grant it) before a mixed marriage can be performed, for which dispensation a payment must be made (every service in the Roman Church seems to have a fee attached to it, and this fee is in addition to the regular marriage fee). This payment normally is made by the man. But if the man happens to be a Protestant, and particularly if he might be expected to resent a request for such a payment, it is made by the future wife.

The following contract must be signed by the Protestant:

"I, the undersigned, not a member of the Catholic Church, wishing to contract marriage with _____ _____, a member of the Catholic Church, propose to do so with the understanding that the marriage thus contracted is indissoluble, except by death. I promise on my word of honor that I will not in any way hinder or obstruct the said _____ _____ in the exercise of _____ religion, and that all children of either sex born of our marriage shall be baptized and educated in the Catholic Church, even though the said _____ _____ should be taken away by death. I further promise that I will marry _____ _____ only according to the marriage rite of the Catholic Church; that I will not either before or after the Catholic ceremony present myself with _____ _____ for marriage with a civil magistrate or minister of the gospel."

Signature _____

Signed in the presence of Rev. _____

Date _____

Witnesses (_____

(_____

(_____

The following promise is to be signed by the Roman Catholic party:

"I, _____ _____, a Catholic, wishing to marry _____ _____, a non-Catholic, hereby promise that, if the Most Reverend Bishop grants me a dispensation, I will have all my children baptized and reared in the Catholic Church, sending them, if possible to a Catholic school, and will practice my religion faithfully, and do all in my power, especially by prayer, good example, and frequentation of the Sacraments, to bring about the conversion of my consort."

Place _____ Date _____

Signature:

Witnesses (_____

_____

(_____

(_____

This promise by the Roman Catholic party, containing among other things a pledge to work for the conversion of the Protestant party, is not necessarily brought to the attention of the Protestant party, but may be signed in secret. Resentment has often arisen when it has been discovered, sometimes years afterward, that such a pledge was made a part of the wedding contract without the knowledge or consent of the Protestant party.

After these pledges have been signed the wedding ceremony can be performed only by a Roman Catholic priest. It cannot, however, take place in the church, but only in the rectory or church vestry. No organ will be played, and no singing will take place. The girl, if she is the Roman Catholic party, is purposely deprived of the glamour of the ritual and of the blessing of her church, which means so much to a Roman Catholic girl. Thus in her eyes her marriage is made to fall short of a true wedding. She is made painfully aware that it is a defective wedding. And for a Roman Catholic man who values his church the wedding is equally marred. By these restrictions the official sorrow of the Roman Church is expressed, because a Protestant is becoming a proximate cause of the loss of a Roman Catholic to the Roman Church—by means of his or her life long association with a member of another church. Such impediments, promises, and dispensations illustrate and emphasize in a very practical way the hierarchy's determination to isolate Roman Catholics from other people so far as possible. The Roman Church thus recognizes the evils of a mixed marriage, and is as set against it as is any Protestant church. She seems to feel that in a mixed marriage she probably will be the loser, that the Roman Catholic party if exposed to Protestant influences is more likely to leave his or her church than is the Protestant to be won to it. And indeed statistics show that such is the case.

In some dioceses, because of the fact that the pre-marital contract so often is not carried out, a new method has been adopted—the Milwaukee diocese form—which gives the archbishop the authority to enforce all the promises made by either or both parties. This form reads:

"The parties hereto expressly state that they do hereby give to the Most Reverend Archbishop of _____, as the representative of the Roman Catholic Church or his delegates, or representatives, the right to enforce each and every promise herein contained in the event of the violation by either party or both, and empower him to give full force and effect to the agreement herein contained."

Such a marriage becomes in fact a three-cornered affair. The two young people not only marry each other, but admit into their married

life a third party, the archbishop, who is given specific legal authority
to enforce the provisions between them as individuals, or between them
and the Roman Church. In the event that they do not fulfill the terms of
the agreement he can, by his own authority, revoke the dispensation, if
he does nothing more, and so, as far as the Roman Church is concerned, dissolve the marriage.

But even before the present method was thought of, the Roman Church
was attempting to deal with the situation. Because so many Roman
Catholics who signed the pre-marital contract were disregarding it, the
Holy Office of the Inquisition, in Rome, in 1922, issued a more drastic
decree which declared that if the conditions were not adhered to, the
dispensation must be counted "null and void." Thus if parties to a mixed
marriage fail to have their children baptized and educated in the Roman
religion, their marriage is automatically dissolved so far as the Roman
Catholic Church is concerned. And that has proved to be a powerful
weapon for keeping Roman Catholics in line, for, since they trust to
their church for salvation, there is nothing they fear more than condemnation by their church. But when marriages of many years standing,
which have produced families and which the husband and wife want
to preserve, are dissolved for such frivolous and selfish reasons, how
clearly that reveals the hierarchy's lack of appreciation of the true sacredness of marriage! And how clearly it reveals the basically unchristian
character of that church! We can only conclude that such action is another product of a celibate priesthood which knows nothing of the
pleasures and responsibilities of home and family.

It is well known that many Roman Catholics resent these stringent requirements. Some authorities tell us that in the Protestant parts of
the United States, Canada, Australia, and South Africa, approximately
one-fourth of the Roman Catholics contract Protestant or civil marriages,
and that in so-called Roman Catholic France, and in Italy, Spain, and
Portugal before those countries became fascist the proportion was even
higher.

5. THE INJUSTICE OF THE PRE-MARITAL CONTRACT

No Protestant who has any respect for his church will sign such a contract. When he is asked to sign he is in effect asked to acknowledge
that his own church, which he holds to be a true church of Christ, is
no church at all, but instead a dangerous organization. And he is also
asked to do a further unreasonable and even sinful thing, namely, to
surrender his right to any voice in the religious affiliation or the
spiritual training of his own children. To sign such a pledge is to betray

his Christian heritage. Such action invariably brings not happiness but heartache and tragedy.

It is the duty of a Protestant minister, when any member of his congregation is being led into or is contemplating marriage with a Roman Catholic, to enlighten him or her concerning the situation that will result, and to do all within his power to prevent such a marriage. He should challenge the right of any Roman Catholic priest to instruct any member of his congregation, particularly if he himself is not also present at such meetings. If such instruction is given any member of his congregation he should invite personally the Roman Catholic party for a series of lessons on the Bible or demand an equal opportunity to give him instruction in the Protestant faith. In view of the Roman practice, no Roman Catholic should be allowed to marry a Protestant without knowing what Protestant life and doctrine is, and this provision should be made effective through church discipline against the Protestant member if necessary. And beyond that the Protestant minister should see to it that the young people of his church are properly instructed, through their group meetings or special study classes, concerning the nature and practices of Roman Catholicism.

How shameful for a Protestant boy or girl to sign a pre-marital contract forever surrendering the religious freedom of his or her children in order to marry someone, no matter how attractive, in the Roman Church! To such we say: "The Roman Catholic Church wants your children. It wants them more than you want them, for it extracts a pledge for them while you are willing to give them up. In signing that contract while yourself refusing to join that church you are saying in effect that the Roman Church is not good enough for you but that it is good enough for your children." Let any Protestant who contemplates signing that contract realize that it bars Protestant parents from their precious children completely and forever in that most sacred of all relationships, spiritual guidance. Let him also realize that financially it means that in time his family inheritance will pass into Roman Catholic hands. This latter, of course, is one of the primary aims that the Roman Church has in forcing through such a contract.

Too often when young people fall in love everything else, including the church, becomes secondary. Wrapped up in each other, and in a mood to be magnanimous and charitable, they are at that time peculiarly susceptible to pressure and are in a mood to sign anything. So, at the opportune moment the priest presents his exorbitant demands, mixing love with religious proselyting. Pledges are made that under normal conditions would not be made. The marriage ceremony is performed. Then gradually disillusionment sets in. The Roman Catholic member is pledged to do everything possible to convert the Protestant, but the Protestant is forbidden to do anything to convert the Roman Catholic or to have any voice in the religious life of the home. This makes for disharmony from the beginning. Children come, and the Protestant parent awakens to the fact that his child is already contracted to the Roman Church. The pre-marital pledge casts its evil shadow, and in many instances leads to broken hearts and bitter family relations. Under normal conditions children serve to bring parents closer together. But in mixed marriages they tend to tear them apart. The threat of ecclesiastical discipline makes family unity more difficult. And the Christian religion, which should be a means of binding the family more closely together, serves instead to tear it apart and to make family unity impossible except on the basis of total surrender. The chance for separation, annulment, or divorce is greatly increased. And most unfortunate of all, the children become the victims of sectarian exploitation.

Furthermore, the Protestant who enters into such a marriage with a loyal Roman Catholic finds that the priest, in the confessional as frequented by the other party, deems it his privilege and duty to inquire into the most intimate habits and practices of the home and to give advice and commands regarding them. It is the priest who will forever stand between those two people, and, if that influence is not resisted, it is he who will win the battle of minds in that marriage.

Let the Protestant who is engaged to marry a Roman Catholic make a serious attempt to lead him or her to become a true Christian, with sincere faith in Christ and in Christ alone as Lord and Saviour, to be proved by a consistent manner of life over a period of time. If possible, let him persuade the Roman Catholic to join a Protestant church. The Protestant cannot get fair play in the Roman Church; therefore the Roman Catholic should be persuaded if possible to join a Protestant church. Otherwise the engagement should be broken off. Such procedure will go far toward avoiding the tragedy of a mixed marriage.

Any unprejudiced person will readily understand how intolerant and cruel is a system which takes advantage of the noblest and most intimate affections of two young people in order to force one of them into submitting to the authority of a religious system which he cannot accept. Protestant churches have never attempted to control and exploit marriage so as to increase the membership and wealth of their denominations as the Roman Church has. They instinctively expect and practice fair play in such matters, while the Roman Church, under threat of eternal damnation, demands all of the children and so attempts to rob Protestants of the heritage of their faith, their children, and their family fortunes.

6. A FRAUDULENT CONTRACT

If a Protestant has had the misfortune to have signed the Roman Catholic pre-marital contract, is he legally and morally bound to keep it?

The answer is that in Roman Catholic countries, where civil law is based on or conformed to Canon Law and the courts are under the domination of the Roman Catholic Church, it can be enforced. Children often are taken from one or both parents, allegedly for their own good, when the terms of the contract are not complied with, and are given to the Roman Catholic parent or placed in Roman Catholic institutions. Homes have been broken up by this cruel practice. But in democratic and Protestant countries it usually cannot be enforced. In the United States, for instance, the Roman Church, sensing that trouble might arise if attempts were made to enforce such agreements, has made but little effort toward that end. But the Canon Law which is the basis for that practice remains a part of the system, ready to be applied if and when Roman influence increases so that it can be made effective.

In the few cases in which court tests have been made the courts have quite consistently held that no agreement as to the religious education of children entered into by the father and mother, before or after marriage, is binding. The welfare of the child takes precedence in such cases. In most such cases the Roman Church has simply been running a bluff when it has insisted on enforcement of the contract through the courts. Whenever the Protestant parent has had the courage to assert his rights rather than surrender his children, the presiding judge almost invariably has ruled in favor of religious freedom and has refused to allow his court to be used to promote the membership of an ecclesiastical organization.

Furthermore, in the United States where the Constitution guarantees freedom of religion to every person, it is the privilege of either parent *to change his or her mind in matters of religion,* and to teach his or her children those moral and religious truths which at the time seem best. If outside pressure is brought to bear upon a person so that he signs away his constitutional rights, the transaction is fraudulent and should be repudiated. For any church or individual to attempt to freeze a person's religious thinking is a violation of those constitutional rights.

But above and beyond the legal aspects of the case, the Roman Catholic pre-marital contract is morally fraudulent, and as such it should be repudiated. In the first place it is fraudulent because it compels the Protestant husband to abdicate his divinely appointed right to be the head of the family in the realm of faith and morals, and it is unchristian for the Roman Church to attempt to usurp that right. The Bible says: "The husband is the head of the wife, as Christ also is the head of the church" (Eph. 5:23); and again, "But I would have you know, that the head of every man is Christ; and the head of the woman is the man" (I Cor. 11:3). But in signing that pledge the Protestant husband abdicates his God-given right to be the head in that most important realm, the spiritual, and instead makes his wife the head. And the Protestant girl simply should not marry a man who will claim the right to make Roman Catholicism the religion of the home.

Secondly, it is fraudulent because no church has a right to compel parents to sign over their children to it for religious training. The Scriptures expressly place upon the parents, not the church, the primary responsibility for the right training of their children.

Thirdly, it is fraudulent because the Roman Church represents itself as a true Christian church, indeed as the only true church, which it most certainly is not, as is proved by many events in its past history and by the fact that it teaches numerous doctrines which are contrary to the Bible.

And fourthly, it is fraudulent because under threat of excommunication it is forced upon young people who want to get married. Yet the Roman Church itself, in its system of granting annulments, separations, or divorces, acknowledges that coercion invalidates the marriage. And since it so readily and pointedly recognizes the illegality of a contract that has been entered into through coercion, the pre-marital contract that is forced upon all Protestants who marry Roman Catholics by a priest is equally invalid.

Is it, then, morally wrong to break such a contract? The answer is: NO! It was a fraudulent contract, obtained under duress, and therefore invalid even by Rome's own standards.

Sooner or later most people who have been foolish enough to sign such a contract wake up to the fact that they have done something that is morally wrong. What they should do then is to repent of their sin, ask God to forgive them, repudiate the contract, and from there on do as the Bible and their consciences direct. The primary guilt for such a situation rests on the church that has taken advantage of a delicate situation and has sown the seeds of matrimonial disharmony by coercing a couple to sign away their Christian privileges.

C. Stanley Lowell, in a splendid article dealing with this subject says:

> "Any moral code makes allowance for actions taken under duress. A trusted bank teller would not ordinarily hand over a bag of the bank's money

to a stranger. But when the stranger demands the money at gun point, he may do that very thing. The bank does not discharge the teller for dereliction of duty. It recognizes that the act was done under dire coercion.

"The Roman Catholic ante-nuptial pact is an agreement at gun point. When a man and woman are in love they are notoriously unable to think straight. More than that, they are under the influence of the most tender and powerful emotions. Sign the agreement? Of course they will sign! They will sign anything; they're in love! Such an agreement can hardly be expected to stand, however, once reason has reasserted itself.

"When the day of awakening comes, as it always comes for the Protestant or Jew who has been coerced, there is only one thing to do. Let the two persons involved sit down together and look clear-eyed into a problem that is uniquely their own. Let arrogant clerical counsel be disregarded for the interference it patently is. Let these two—and no others —think the problem through and arrive at their solution. This is a hard thing; perhaps it is impossible. But there is one thing more impossible— the attempt to stand slavishly upon an agreement that was coercive from the first" (Pamphlet, *Is the Catholic Ante-Nuptial Agreement Binding?*).

7. MIXED MARRIAGE DIFFICULTIES

A happy home must be built on a firm foundation. Harmony in religious belief is a great asset toward that end. Every couple will find that marriage presents plenty of problems without adding to them an unnecessary and unsolvable religious problem. A mixed marriage is in itself a cause for alarm, and all groups, whether Protestant, Roman Catholic, or Jewish, strongly advise against it. Almost invariably those couples who have been so involved will advise against it. That an occasional mixed marriage works out well does not disprove the general rule, and in those cases it probably will be found that one or perhaps both parties did not take their religion seriously, or that each was willing to go more than halfway in giving in to the other.

In most cases mixed marriage means civil war, whether hot or cold. The most difficult problems usually come with the arrival of children. The Protestant father is reminded that he signed an agreement to allow all of his children to be brought up in the Roman Catholic faith. So they are baptized in that church. When Sunday comes the mother and children go to one church, while he disheartedly makes his way to another. There he sees other families, parents and children, worshipping together. But he sits alone, and feels more lonely. Church attendance may cease to have any pleasure for him, and he may even stop going to church. The children go to parochial school where their training is in the hands of the nuns. They are taught to kneel before images and crucifixes, to pray to the Virgin Mary, and to confess to a priest. They are also taught that all non-Catholics, including their own father, have no chance for salvation, and in general are given a philosophy of life and a code of ethics that outrages his conscience. Disagreement is certain to arise between husband and wife regarding the support of the churches. The husband may want to support Protestant missions in Latin America, or Japan, or particularly in Italy, while the wife probably will want to support Roman Catholic churches and convents and schools.

The home is the most important influence in the life of a child. But children are quick to sense it when there is trouble between parents. Quite often they are the chief casualties in a religiously mixed home. Caught up in the crosscurrents of conflict between father and mother, they are more or less forced to take sides. There is scarcely anything in the world more painful than that, and they rebel against having to make such a choice. Their tendency is to reject both, and to turn to irreligion. It then becomes easier to take the next step, rebellion against civil authority and against society itself. Social workers tell us that much juvenile delinquency arises because of religious conflict and religious indifference in the home. It is significant that the divorce rate in mixed marriage families is as high as among non-religious people, while it is considerably lower where husband and wife are of the same faith.

Some very interesting and significant facts were brought out recently in the Harvard Survey of 60,000 homes, by two prominent sociologists, Dr. Carle C. Zimmerman, of Harvard University, and Dr. Lucius F. Cerventes, S.J., of St. Louis University. The findings were as follows:

1. "Couples with different religous affiliation have fewer children than those who marry within their own faith.

2. "Children of interfaith marriages are much less likely to finish high school than those whose parents are of the same religious faith.

3. "Six out of every ten children of a Catholic-Protestant marriage end by rejecting all religions—Catholic, Protestant, and others.

4. "About half of the Catholic men who marry non-Catholics abandon their faith [No doubt this is one of the primary reasons the Roman Catholic Church is so opposed to interfaith marriages, and why it seeks to restrict them with such stringent rules].

5. "Men and women of all faiths showed a higher divorce rate when they married someone of a different religion. In an interfaith marriage by a Protestant, the divorce rate was two to three times as great as in an all-Protestant marriage. Among Catholics, the increase was three to four times. Among Jews, five to six times. Among other religions, two to three times.

6. "In this survey, Jewish men had the highest percentage of interfaith marriages. Twenty-four per cent of those studied had married non-Jews.

7. "Teen age arrests are much higher in mixed-marriage families. When Protestant men married outside their faith in St. Louis, Omaha, and Denver, their youngsters suffered twice as many arrests as youngsters in single-faith homes. In marriages between Catholics and non-Catholics, the arrests of teenage children in every city doubled or tripled. The children of Jewish husbands and Gentile wives in Boston, St. Louis, Denver, and Omaha, had four to ten times as many arrests for juvenile offenses as the children of all-Jewish marriages in those cities" (*This Week,* September 20, 1959).

A report from the United Lutheran Church of America, issued by Dr. E. Epping Reinartz, of New York, secretary and statistician for the denomination, showed that mixed marriages between members of the United Lutheran Church and Roman Catholics totaled 3,343 in 1958, and that two-thirds of the couples so married went to Lutheran pastors for the ceremony. It also showed that four times as many Roman Catholics joined the United Lutheran Church as United Lutherans joined the Roman Catholic Church, and that the United Lutheran Church gained 3,566 in baptized members from Roman Catholic congregations while losing 868 members to the Roman Catholic Church.

The General Assembly of the Presbyterian Church in the U. S., in 1959, counseled its church members as follows concerning mixed marriages:

"The Roman Catholic attitude with reference to mixed marriages makes it impossible for a wholesome family religious life to exist and continually requires the Protestant to surrender or compromise his personal convictions. What is even more serious it involves the signing away of the spiritual birthright of unborn children by denying them the possibility of any religious training in the home other than that prescribed by the Roman Catholic Church. It is far better that the parties concerned not marry than that these tragic results should follow."

A man needs a wife who can stand at his side and back him up in all of the important things in life, one who attends the same church, hears the same sermons, and prays the same prayers. And a woman needs a husband who can give her spiritual as well as material support in all of the trials and problems of life. But even the standard of authority is different for Protestants and Roman Catholics. For Protestants the Bible is the only rule of faith and practice, while Roman Catholics believe that the church sets forth that rule, that whatever the church teaches must be received implicitly, and that what the priest commands should be done. Long ago the prophet asked: "Can two walk together, except they be agreed?" (Amos 3:3).

From every side comes the warning that religiously mixed marriages are sources of trouble. Many of these marriages might turn out more happily if they were left to themselves. But constantly there rises up between husband and wife, and between parents and children, the black robed priest of the church. He comes armed with the anathemas which are so dreaded by devout Roman Catholics, and presumes to give instructions concerning church obligations, financial affairs, and the rearing of children, depending in each instance on how far he considers it expedient to go. Such interference makes normal family relationships impossible.

The most important decision one makes in life is whether or not he will accept Christ as Saviour. For most people the second most important decision is the choice of a life partner. Christian marriage involves not only a civil union of two people, but also a spiritual union of two souls. Yet how can there be a union of religious ideals when one is governed by Protestant principles and the other by Roman Catholic principles? Obviously the difference is too great and the antagonisms too strong for any such union. A Protestant, therefore, should not allow himself to fall in love with a Roman Catholic, but should regard that as forbidden territory unless he can win the Roman Catholic to his faith. The time to settle the matter of religion is *before,* not *after,* marriage. Those who carefully and prayerfully study God's Word and then come to marriage in a unity of spiritual understanding are far more likely to find that the blessing of God will rest upon their home than are those who attempt to disregard this problem.

The Bible strongly warns against mixed marriages, against marriage with one of another religion, or one with no religion. In the Old Testament the Jews were strictly forbidden to intermarry with the people around them. And in the New Testament Paul says: "Be not unequally yoked with unbelievers: for what fellowship have righteousness and iniquity? or what communion hath light with darkness?" (II Cor. 6:14).

Let anyone who is contemplating a mixed marriage stop and count the cost before he mortgages his own future and sells the birthright of his children. What heartache, what bitter remorse, is suffered by those who are caught in this dilemma! Many would give almost anything if they could undo what they have done—if they could go back and listen to the warnings they once spurned. There is no solution for this problem after marriage. The only way to solve it is avoid it in the first place.

8. THE ROMAN CATHOLIC ATTITUDE TOWARD DIVORCE

The Roman Catholic Church boasts of her strictness regarding divorce, and seeks to create the impression that divorces are much less common among Roman Catholics than among Protestants. In order to understand her claims it is necessary to distinguish between the different classifications which she makes of marriage as *legitimate, ratum,* and *consummatum.*

A marriage between Protestants, or between those who profess no religion, performed by a Protestant minister or official of the state, is called *legitimate.* A marriage between Roman Catholics performed by a priest is called *ratum.* And a marriage between those married by a priest is called *consummatum* after they have exercised their marital rights.

We have seen that for many centuries the Roman Catholic Church held that any marriage performed by a Protestant minister or by an official of the state was invalid, and that pope Pius IX setting forth these principles condemned all marriage not performed by a priest as "low and abominable concubinage." We have also seen that in 1908 the Roman Church reluctantly issued the *Ne Temere* decree through which it would recognize future Protestant marriages as valid, but that that decree was not retroactive.

Let it be remembered that while the pope has conceded the validity of Protestant marriage since the new Canon Law in 1908, he has never given up the claim of superior authority over all Christian marriage everywhere. By virtue of that power he claims the right to annul any Protestant or civil marriage. Since the concession in Canon Law was made only as a concession and under pressure, it may be withdrawn at any time that the Roman Church feels itself strong enough to enforce its claims, and all Christian marriage again be placed in the hands of the priests.

In the Roman Church every diocese has its divorce court. It refuses to recognize civil divorce of its members in certain instances, and holds that marriage of one of its members performed by a Protestant minister or civil official is not valid. On the basis of the so-called "Pauline privilege" as set forth in I Corinthians 7:15, in which a believer is declared to be under no further obligation to a deserting unbeliever, the Roman Church teaches that a marriage between Protestants, or between unbelievers, can be dissolved when one member is converted to Roman Catholicism. A marriage between a Roman Catholic and a Protestant, or between a Roman Catholic and an unbeliever, performed by a Protestant minister or official of the state, comes under this classification. This provides an easy "out" when a Roman Catholic wants to be free from a non-Roman Catholic in order to marry another Roman Catholic. This device is not called a divorce, but an "annulment." It says that in such cases a true marriage never existed in the first place. As such it opens the way for the dissolution of a large number of marriages by the simple expedient of giving another definition to what we term divorce, and exposes the hypocrisy of the claim that the Roman Catholic Church is unalterably opposed to divorce.

Even a marriage that is *ratum* (between two Roman Catholics before a priest), but which one or both participants claim is not *consummatum*, can be dissolved, (1) by profession of religious vows in a religious order approved by the Roman Church, e.g., entering a convent as a nun, or becoming a monk or a priest; or (2) by a dispensation from the pope. There is, of course, no Scripture warrant for such exceptions, nothing but man made decrees by the hierarchy.

Paul Blanshard, in his *American Freedom and Catholic Power*, discusses quite fully the teaching of the Roman Catholic Church concerning separation and divorce. He says:

"Legal and permanent separation without remarriage is permitted in the Catholic system for many reasons. . . . The Canon Law permits separation not only for adultery and habitual crime but also for simple difference in religious conviction 'if one party joins a non-Catholic sect; or educates the offspring as non-Catholics.' This rule is so sweeping that it is a ground for separation if a parent who has been married by a priest sends a child to an American public school without the priest's permission. In some cases it is also ground for the complete nullification of a mixed marriage. . . .

"There is almost no type of marriage that cannot be annulled under the complex rules of the Catholic marriage courts if a determined spouse is willing and able to go to the expense of prolonged litigation, and uses sufficient patience and ingenuity in constructing a plausible case.

"The annulment process is used eagerly and frequently by American Catholics as a kind of Catholic substitute for divorce. Hundreds of annulments of valid civil marriages are granted each year by the Catholic hierarchy in the United States without reaching public attention. The Church's annulment statistics tell only a fragment of the real story. The rest of the story is contained in tables and reports that never reach the public. . . .

"Any Catholic who has married a non-Catholic without getting his spouse to promise that all their children will be reared as Catholics can easily secure an annulment from a local bishop without any judicial formalities by proving that his original marriage was not 'correct in form.' The Canon Law says that such marriages are null and void from the beginning, so the priest does not need to submit the case to a tribunal. He delivers a one-sheet Decree of Nullity after making sure that the former marriage was actually performed in the way described. A modest fee— usually $15—is asked for this service. . . .

"When short cuts to annulment are unavailable, the Church provides a number of special elastic interpretations of marriage vows that can be used to dissolve marriages. One of these elastic devices is the theory that there must be an 'interior consent' to a marriage or it is void from the beginning. . . . The priests have stretched this to include many cases of apparent valid marriage in which a married person changes his attitude toward his spouse long after marriage, and then announces that he never consented to the marriage in the first place. . . . Any Catholic can obtain an ecclesiastical annulment if he can prove that in entering marriage he made it a condition that he would not have children, or that the parties agreed that they *could* get a divorce if the marriage proved to be unsuccessful. In such cases the hierarchy holds that the parties to a marriage never actually consented to full marriage. They made a mental reservation about two essentials of marriage, children and indissolubility" (pp. 198-208).

Thus the Roman Church, while pretending to be zealous in maintaining the marriage bond, makes exceptions on the basis of excuses so flimsy that they would not be given serious consideration in a civil court. Fortunately in the United States these church decrees do not give legal annulments or divorces, since American civil law is superior to Roman Catholic Canon Law. But they are effective in countries where church law has the force of civil law, either because civil law has been written to conform to church law or because it readily approves and supplements church law. We have already pointed out that since the Roman Church acknowledges coercion as invalidating a marriage, therefore, on the same principle, the pre-marital contract which is forced upon a Protestant in a mixed marriage, is equally invalid.

L. H. Lehmann makes the following comparison between marriage relations in Protestant and Roman Catholic countries:

"Despite the obvious evils of divorce in modern democratic countries . . . the number of divorces is no greater than the number of unfaithful husbands in Catholic authoritarian countries where the church's prohibition against divorce is upheld by the civil law. In such countries there is no check on the waywardness of men and no recourse to the law by wives to obtain either freedom or support from adulterous husbands.

"In Latin Catholic countries especially, the priests have always indulgently ignored the traditional custom of married men having one, if not many, mistresses, but have always fought relentlessly against divorce, by which wives could free themselves from such men. The result is a very high rate of illegitimacy in such countries as compared to Protestant countries.

"Safeguarding property rights, social status and legitimacy, has always been considered of greater importance to the Roman theologians than individual morality. This accounts for the extraordinarily high rate of illegitimacy in Catholic countries such as Italy, Spain, Portugal, France and all Latin American countries. . . . In Latin American countries the rate of illegitimacy ranges from 25% to 50%, and the illiteracy is correspondingly high. North of the Rio Grande, in Protestant democratic countries, even though it includes Catholic Canada, the rate of illegitimacy is only 2.4%, and the illiteracy rate only 6%" (*Out of the Labyrinth*, p. 190).

Any departure from Scripture invariably works evil in one form or another. The first and most detrimental result of the Roman Catholic doctrine that not even adultery is a proper ground for dissolution of the marriage bond (although annulments are granted for much less serious offenses), is to render that crime easier of accomplishment and more frequent. An unscrupulous husband or wife knows that his or her partner cannot obtain a divorce on the ground of adultery and so feels less restraint. As just pointed out in the quotation from Mr. Lehmann, it is notorious that in the Latin American countries the men are more lax in their extra-marital relations, it being not an uncommon practice and one accepted without serious protest for men of wealth and prominence to have a "mistress" in addition to a lawful wife. Another result, again particularly prominent in Latin America where the priests attempt so much interference in family affairs, is the abnormally large number of "common law" unions. And still another result is that numerous causes are allowed for permanent separation, *a thoro et mensa*, from bed and board. Certainly it is not the mark of a true church for divorce to be disguised under other terms and treated so lightly. In actual fact the sacred institution of marriage is handled in a quite arbitrary manner in the Roman Church. The whole matter of marriage and divorce is in the hands of the hierarchy, which exercises the right of setting up or removing impediments at its pleasure, supported only by papal decrees. And the inevitable result, far from rendering marriage a more sacred institution among Roman Catholics than among Protestants, is exactly the opposite.

XVI. THE PAROCHIAL SCHOOL

1. The Roman Church Claims the Right to Supervise All Education. 2. Parochial Schools Compulsory for Roman Catholics. 3. Parochial School Indoctrination. 4. Narrow View of the Parochial School. 5. Public Schools Sometimes Taken Over by the Roman Church. 6. Roman Catholic Opposition to Public Schools. 7. The Two Systems Compared. 8. State and Federal Aid for Parochial Schools. 9. Education in Romanist Dominated Countries. 10. The Christian School.

1. THE ROMAN CHURCH CLAIMS THE RIGHT TO SUPERVISE ALL EDUCATION

Webster's New International Dictionary defines "parochial" as "(1) of or pertaining to a parish . . . ; (2) confined or limited to a parish; as of parochial interest; hence limited in range or scope; narrow; local; as a parochial mind or point of view. . . ."

When we apply this term to a school we mean one created and governed by a church organization. Such a school may be created because the parent body does not consider the existing school system adequate (in most cases because it omits or gives unsatisfactory religious instruction), or because no other school is available. In the United States the motive for parochial schools is clearly the former.

One of the totalitarian claims made by the Roman Catholic Church, as professedly the only true church and the only organization on earth that has a right to speak for God, is the right to control *all* education, outside as well as inside its membership. Its ideal is that education should be the exclusive monopoly of the priesthood. Repeatedly it has denounced public education, that is, education organized and controlled by a public authority such as a local, state, or national government. Pope Pius IX, in his *Syllabus of Errors*, in 1864, condemned the public school system in these words:

"The direction of public schools in which the youth of Christian states are brought up . . . neither can nor ought to be assumed by the civil authority alone, or in such a manner that no right shall be recognized on the part of any other authority to interfere in the dispositions of the schools, in the regulation of the studies, in the appointment of degrees, and in the selection and approval of masters. . . . It is false that the best conditions of civil society demand that popular schools be open to the children of all classes, or that the generality of public institutions should be free from all ecclesiastical authority. Catholics cannot approve a system of education for youth apart from the Catholic faith, and disjointed from the authority of the church" (Propositions 45, 47, 48).

In another statement pope Pius IX declared: "Education outside of the Catholic Church is heresy." But we may well ask, Just what has education *in* the Roman Church done for the masses of Italy, France, Spain, and Latin America? And again we ask: If the direction of the public schools, which are paid for with tax money, should not be in the hands of the community which pays for it, where should it be? Certainly it should not be in the hands of a foreign pontiff of a different faith, nor should it be turned over to a totalitarian church which is under foreign control.

Pope Pius XI, in his encyclical, *On the Education of Youth* (1929), declared:

"In the first place, education belongs pre-eminently to the Church for two supernatural reasons. . . . As for the scope of the Church's educative mission, it extends over all people without any limitations, according to Christ's command: 'Teach ye all nations.' Nor is there a power which can oppose or prevent it."

The present pope, John XXIII, on December 30, 1959, reiterated the papal claim in substantially the same words.

Rev. J. A. Burns, president of Holy Cross College, Washington, D. C., in his book, *The Growth and Development of the Catholic School System in the United States,* says:

"We deny, of course, as Catholics, the right of the civil government to educate, for education is a function of the spiritual society. . . . It (the state) may found and endow schools and pay the teachers, but it cannot dictate or interfere with the education or discipline of the schools" (p. 223).

In these statements we have the claim of the Roman Church that it is the only rightful educator in the world. It denies the right of the state even to establish secular schools for its own order. According to this teaching the sole right and duty of the state in this field is to collect taxes for the establishment and maintenance of Roman Catholic schools.

It does not hesitate to claim openly, even in the Protestant and democratic United States, that education is exclusively a function of the Roman Catholic Church—as indeed it also claims that preaching and the administration of the sacraments are functions of the Roman Church only. This claim implies that education should be denied to all those outside the Roman Church. And indeed that is the policy that the Roman Church puts into effect in areas where she is in control—another means by which Rome seeks to maintain her control over the people.

What the Roman Church really wants is a concordat between the Vatican and each nation, such as that under which Italy, Spain, Portugal, and various other nations have been or are governed, through which a large part or perhaps all of the educational process is turned over to the Roman Church while being paid for by the state. Her aim is to dominate public and private schools to the exclusion of all other churches and religions. The teaching of the Roman Catholic religion in the public schools becomes compulsory, even for Protestant children, as in present day Spain, if the Roman Church has her way. The first step in that process in a country such as ours is to undermine the public schools by making her parochial schools tax supported, while at the same time placing as many Roman Catholics as possible in the public schools as teachers. But such a condition destroys the very foundation of democratic and representative government. Concerning this problem MacGregor says:

"A country such as America cannot expect to come to any reasonable terms with the Roman Catholic hierarchy on the subject of education. The Church is avowedly opposed not only to public schools but also to independent schools and universities that are not under the control of the Roman Catholic Church, to which alone, it is affirmed, belongs the right to teach anything.

"In practice, however, in a country such as the United States, the Church is unable, for obvious reasons, to enforce this principle. So the hierarchy has to content itself with the more practical aim of securing Roman Catholic parochial schools at the public expense." After saying that the Roman Church thus seeks "to make its own educational system a charge on the American public," he adds: "Financially it would hardly be better news to the hierarchy if Congress were to pass a bill appropriating money from the Treasury for the payment of mass stipends to all Roman Catholic clergy throughout the country. . . .

"It is by means of censorship and boycott, and above all, educational indoctrination at public expense, that it is hoped to transform America into a country that is predominantly Roman Catholic in spirit; that is to say, one in which it would be very imprudent to speak openly against anything uttered by a Roman Catholic bishop, and exceedingly dangerous to speak even privately in favor of anything uttered by anyone who was explicitly under the ban of the Church" (*The Vatican Revolution,* pp. 148-150).

It is important to remember that historically the American system of free, universal public education was exclusively a product of Protestantism. Practically all of the people in colonial America were Protestant. The Puritans of New England contributed most toward developing the ideal that all classes should have equal educational opportunities. Having come to America to secure religious freedom for themselves, it was only natural that they should turn to education as one means of promoting their faith.

Our first college, Harvard, was established in 1636, just 16 years after the landing at Plymouth Rock, and it was intended primarily as a school to train those preparing for the ministry. The first elementary schools were in the homes and churches, usually with the local pastor as the instructor. So keenly was the need felt for grammar schools that in 1647 a legislative act provided that every town having as many as fifty householders should appoint a teacher and provide for his wages, and that every community having as many as one hundred householders should provide a grammar school.

The next colleges of earliest origin, William and Mary (Episcopal) in 1693, Yale (Puritan) in 1701, Princeton (Presbyterian) in 1746, as also Dartmouth, Brown, Rutgers, and the University of Pennsylvania, were established through church influences during the colonial period, before the Constitution was written and before those generally recognized as the champions of our American way of life were born. Those schools were not the product of government but of the church.

2. PAROCHIAL SCHOOLS COMPULSORY FOR ROMAN CATHOLICS

The First Plenary Council of Baltimore, in 1853, called upon all bishops to establish parish schools in every church in their dioceses. The Second Plenary Council of Baltimore, in 1866, repeated that call and took steps to make it effective.

Canon Law 1374 denies freedom of choice to Roman Catholic parents in regard to schools, and says that they *must* send their children to parochial schools under pain of mortal sin unless excused from doing so by the bishop. Canon Law 1381 decrees concerning the school set-up:

> 1. "In all schools the religious training of the young is subject to the authority and inspection of the Catholic Church" (i.e., the priest or bishop).

2. "It is the right and duty of the Bishops to take care that nothing is taught or done against the Faith or sound morals in any school in their territory."

3. "The Bishops have also the right to approve the teachers of religion and the textbooks and further to require that texts be dropped or teachers removed, when the good of religion or morality demands this action."

Thus the curriculum, staff, and operation of the parochial school are under the complete domination of the bishop. Parents have no choice, no rights at all as regards teachers, texts, or methods of instruction, as over against the bishop, if he chooses to exercise his authority. Nor has any school board or committee any choice in the management of the school except as that choice may be delegated to it by the bishop.

The fact is that the parochial school has been promoted primarily by the priests and bishops as a means of keeping the children of their church separate from Protestant children and from public school influences during their formative years, the better to indoctrinate and control them. If left to themselves most Roman Catholic parents would send their children to the public schools, and many do so in spite of the pressure from the priests. After more than one hundred years of effort by the hierarchy to impose the parochial school system on their people less than half of their children attend those schools.

In the United States there are some 10,000 parochial grade schools with an enrollment of approximately 4,200,000, and some 2400 high schools with approximately 600,000 students. The National Department of Health, Education and Welfare has indicated that the total grade and high school enrollment in all schools is approximately 35,000,000. That means that the parochial schools enroll approximately one out of seven, or about 15 percent. And that of course includes some who are not Roman Catholics. Also there are about 260,000 students enrolled in 216 Roman Catholic colleges and universities. The parochial school enrollment has risen from about 5 percent in 1900 to the present figure, with the primary increase having come since the close of the Second World War in 1945. All of these students, of course, are taught Roman Catholic polity (political, economic, and social) as well as Roman Catholic doctrine. Approximately 90 percent of all parochial and private elementary and high schools in this country are under the control of the Roman Catholic Church.

Let it be clearly understood that we do not object to church related schools as such, as they are conducted, for instance, in the Lutheran and some other churches, but only to that form of parochialism that is found in the Roman Catholic Church.

3. PAROCHIAL SCHOOL INDOCTRINATION

In view of the fact that some 5,000,000 Roman Catholic children at the grade and high school level are being trained in the parochial schools, what is the hierarchy teaching these future Americans? It is well known that such schools do not confine their indoctrination to religion. History books are rewritten to present a "Catholic version." Roman Catholic schools do not share a mutual pride and appreciation with the public schools in setting forth the problems and difficulties and progress of the early colonists, such as the Pilgrims, Puritans, Quakers, etc., practically all of whom were Protestants. Protestant national heroes, such as Washington, Jefferson, Franklin, Roger Williams, William Penn, and others are minimized, and comparatively unimportant Roman Catholics are glorified and their deeds presented as accomplishments of Roman Catholicism. The struggles that our forefathers went through and the sacrifices they made to establish freedom of religion, freedom of speech and of the press, the right to vote, etc., are minimized or omitted. What we consider a victory and a great step forward, they consider a defeat and a step backward. We point with pride to the constitutional provision for the separation of church and state; they brand that a mistake and say that this and other nations should have remained under the authority of the pope. A few years ago the government of Mexico by constitutional provision closed all papal sectarian schools in that country, to the end that every boy and girl should be given a true statement of the history of Mexico as taught in the public schools. Certainly every boy and girl who is to become a good American citizen should be taught a fair and truthful account of American history.

In the parochial schools Roman Catholic indoctrination is included in every subject. History, literature, geography, civics, and science are given a Roman Catholic slant. The whole education of the child is filled with propaganda. That, of course, is the very purpose of such schools, the very reason for going to all of the work and expense of maintaining a dual school system. Their purpose is not so much to educate, but to indoctrinate and train, not to teach Scripture truths and Americanism, but to make loyal Roman Catholics. The children are regimented, and are told what to wear, what to do, and what to think.

Most of the teaching in the parochial schools is done by the nuns. They teach the children to revere and worship the Virgin Mary and to trust in images and rosaries whether they know anything about faith in Christ or not. All nuns are under solemn vows to promote their religion in every course they teach. They work year in and year out without receiving anything more than their board and keep, and without the personal freedom that every American has the right to enjoy. They are kept in abject poverty, while money flows freely to the priests, bishops, and especially to the Vatican in Rome.

As regards the content of the curriculum at the high school and college level, in the text book, *Christian Principles and National Problems,* by Ostheimer and Delaney, under the imprimatur of cardinal Spellman, we read:

> "The doctrine of the Church . . . is that the State must profess and teach not any religion, but the one true form of worship founded by Christ and continuing today in the Catholic Church alone" (p. 98).
>
> "The non-Catholic and the non-baptized should be permitted to carry on their own form of worship as long as there would be no danger of scandal or perversion of the faithful. In a country where the majority are Catholics, the practice of Protestantism or paganism by an inconspicuous minority would be neither a source of scandal nor perversion to the adherents of the true faith" (p. 99).

Here we have the threat that freedom of worship will be denied to Protestants if the Roman Church gains the ascendancy. Only as long as the Protestant minority remains small and "inconspicuous" will it be allowed to exist peacefully, and even then it must not seek to carry on evangelistic work among Roman Catholics and others. But just how small and how inconspicuous it would have to be to receive this tolerance is not stated. Presumably that would rest with the individual Roman Catholic leaders. Judging by the active persecution that still is carried on against an inconspicuous minority of Protestants in Spain, it would have to be near the vanishing point. That the rising generation of Roman Catholics should be taught that when their church reaches an anticipated majority in the United States they are to start oppressing and persecuting other churches is monstrous and diabolical. And yet this is set forth under the imprimatur, and therefore with the approval of, the most prominent American Roman Catholic, cardinal Spellman.

A similar view is taught in another widely used text, *Living Our Faith,* by Flynn, Loretto, and Simeon, also with Spellman's imprimatur. It says:

> "The question of union or separation of Church and State has perplexed men since the Protestant revolt. The ideal situation exists when there is perfect union and accord between Church and State, with each supreme in its own field. . . . In a Catholic country, when a dispute arises and settlement is unattainable the rights of the Church should prevail, since it possesses the higher authority" (p. 247).

This book also tells the students that "non-Catholic methods of worshipping must be branded counterfeit"—and the inference is that the state should assist the church in making the brand effective.

A widely used college and seminary text, with the official Nihil Obstat (nothing objectionable) of Arthur J. Scanlan, S.T.D. (Censor Liborum), and the official Imprimatur of archbishop (now cardinal) Francis J. Spellman, says:

"Suppose that the Constitutional obstacles to persecution of non-Catholics have been legitimately removed and they themselves have become numerically insignificant: What then would be the proper course of action for a Catholic State? Apparently, the latter State could logically tolerate only such religious activities as were confined to the members of the dissenting group. It would not permit them to carry on general propaganda nor accord their organization certain privileges that had formerly been extended to all religious corporations, for example, exemption from taxation" (p. 320; from *Catholic Principles of Politics*, by John A. Ryan and Francis J. Boland. Copyright 1940 by the National Catholic Welfare Conference. Used by permission of The Macmillan Company).

The general thrust of that book is that the Roman Catholic Church must establish itself as the state church in the United States, that it must be made to prevail and eventually to eliminate all other churches.

Thus the rising generation of Roman Catholics is being indoctrinated with the belief that church-state separation is unwise and un-American in principle, that the Roman Church is the only true church, and that it is the right and privilege of that church to suppress others by force as it has opportunity. And we are even asked to subsidize such teaching with tax money! This same teaching is also being given more or less directly to three million other students in various public schools through this nation that are staffed in part with nuns and brothers.

When these millions of students are being trained in that kind of mental climate, how can we doubt that if and when the opportunity comes they will attempt to put those ideas into practice? The bigoted and shocking teaching that goes on in schools using such text books as the above mentioned is a betrayal of American freedom and democracy. It is treasonable, and it certainly should not be allowed by any group or in any schools in this nation. If such teaching were being given in a set of schools established by the Communists there would be an immediate outcry against it. But when given in Roman Catholic schools it attracts little attention, and indeed some are even willing to assist in promoting it with tax money.

Roman Catholics often pretend to Protestants that their schools for all practical purposes are the same as the public schools except that at certain periods religion is taught. But as we have shown by quotations from their own texts, the facts are quite the contrary. We particularly warn Protestant parents against sending their children to such schools. The training given can have no other effect than to undermine the faith of Protestant children. And for parents who send their children to such schools the time surely will come when they will regret their decision with bitter tears. Many Protestant parents who pay little attention to school affairs have suddenly been amazed to find their children praying to the Virgin, crossing themselves, and attending Roman Catechism classes. And when that stage is reached it may be too late to reclaim them.

The secret of the success achieved by the dictators such as Hitler, Mussolini, and Stalin, in leading a majority of their countrymen to accept ideologies that were detrimental even to their own interests, was to concentrate on the training, or the so-called education, of youth. Each sought to control the schools and youth organizations, and both Hitler and Mussolini, although Roman Catholics themselves, had sharp disagreements with the Roman Church concerning that problem. Each of the dictators realized that if he could control the youth of the land, the nation soon would be under his control. The Roman Church had operated on that principle for centuries, and the dictators simply took that method over as a part of their own system.

Some Roman Catholic leaders say that a school in a community is more important than a church. And indeed that is the principle on which the hierarchy is now working in Japan, Korea, Formosa, in Lutheran Sweden and Finland, and in various other places where their people are few in numbers. In various places it is now putting the building of schools ahead of the building of churches. And that policy apparently pays off since it trains a group of followers who in time form the nucleus of a church. In established communities Roman churches usually do not bother to separate church and school finances but treat them as one operation. The parochial schools, with their intense indoctrination of the young are, in a word, the "secret weapon" by which the Roman Church hopes to control the nation's future citizens and so to win the victory over Protestantism.

4. NARROW VIEWPOINT OF THE PAROCHIAL SCHOOLS

One feature of the Roman schools that calls for comment is the very narrow outlook presented. This applies particularly to schools at the high school and college level. While Protestantism encourages free investigation, Romanism restricts the investigative process and is concerned primarily with its own advancement. It suppresses truth as does any totalitarian power. In the ages before the Reformation free inquiry was prohibited and men were even put to death for possessing the Bible translated into their own tongue. The Index of Forbidden Books, still in effect as rigidly as ever, proscribes all the controversial books, magazines, and other publications of Protestants and others who oppose Romanism, and so makes it impossible for Roman Catholics to know both sides of a question.

Graduates from parochial high schools who enroll in state colleges or universities are surprised to find, for instance, that their history books do not agree with the ones they have been studying. They read instead about the decadence and moral corruption of the papacy during the Middle Ages, the cruel tyranny of the Inquisition, and, on the other hand, the accomplishments of Protestant leaders and nations, and many other embarrassing facts. The Roman Church wants obedience, and to that end it withholds from its people that broader knowledge and outlook on the world that makes for a well-informed and well-rounded personality. Many Roman Catholic laymen, as well as some priests, resent the narrow, un-American atmosphere of the parochial schools. But few have the courage to express their views openly or to do anything about it. Those who expect to stay in the Roman Church simply accept the situation and keep their mouths shut.

Throughout the entire Roman Catholic system of "education," from the parochial schools to the colleges and seminaries, the teachers, who for the most part are nuns and priests, have studied practically nothing except what has borne the official *Imprimatur* ("Let it be published") of the church. The Index of Forbidden Books limits and controls their libraries. The most important qualification for teachers and professors is not knowledge and teaching ability, but indoctrination and loyalty to the church. Roman Catholic students, therefore, in a real sense are forbidden to think. They let the priests think for them. But the fallacy of that system is that the priests too are forbidden to think. They too are limited by the Imprimatur and the Index. Freedom of thought and research have very little place in such schools. And the students in such schools are, for the most part, not educated but merely trained.

Various instances can be cited showing how this narrow attitude toward learning has worked out in the past. Copernicus, a Polish-born astronomer who died in 1543, wrote a book, *On the Revolutions of the Heavenly Bodies,* in which he set forth the view that the sun was the center of the solar system and that the planets including the earth revolved around it. But the Roman theologians were bitterly opposed to that view. The idea that the earth was not fixed at the very center of all things was more than they could stand, and they were not open to demonstration. To make the earth a mere satellite, indeed only one among several satellites, seemed to diminish the importance of the pope, who allegedly was the ruler of the earth. Copernicus was excommunicated, and his book was put on the *Index* where it remained for centuries. But his scientific discoveries later proved to be true.

Thomas Aquinas, most prominent of all Roman theologians, taught that the earth was fixed in its position, and his writings tied up that false doctrine with the doctrines of the Church of Rome. In 1600 Galileo, another brilliant astronomer who supported the views of Copernicus and who discovered the telescope, was brought to trial by the Jesuits before the Inquisition. His work was examined by a committee and was condemned as dangerous to the church. He was forced to recant. But it is said that as he rose after the recantation he reiterated his views concerning the earth, saying, "Nevertheless it does move." The Inquisition sentenced him to the dungeon for three years. Later this was changed to house arrest, under which he spent the remainder of his life. The church put an end to his scientific investigations, but the learned man was right. The Roman Church persecuted Harvey who discovered the circulation of the blood, and it anathematized Pascal, the famous French mathematician and scientist, because he dared to question some of its doctrines.

5. PUBLIC SCHOOLS SOMETIMES TAKEN OVER BY THE ROMAN CHURCH

In some communities in the United States where Roman Catholics are in a majority they have taken control of the public schools. This usually is accomplished by gaining a majority on the school board. In view of the fact that so few people vote in school elections, it frequently is easy for pressure groups to elect their candidates. The schools are then staffed with nuns, or in some cases with priests or brothers, the study of Roman Catholic doctrine is introduced and is practically made compulsory, and all the while the school remains on the public pay roll. Pupils who object are subjected to social and economic reprisals, and sometimes are told that if they cannot adjust to the school they should go elsewhere.

Such schools are known as "captive schools." A report in *The Christian Century*, July 15, 1959, said there were at least 281 such schools in 21 states. The report also said that at least 2,055 nuns were teaching in these schools. Conditions of this kind exist in Ohio, Maine, Connecticut, Illinois, Wisconsin, Massachusetts, Michigan, Texas, and Arkansas, with the worst conditions in Indiana, Kansas, and Kentucky. In some of these states nuns teach in their church garb, and the classrooms display religious pictures, crucifixes, and other symbols of the Roman Catholic Church which by no stretch of the imagination can be called legitimate teaching devices. Salary checks of the nuns, who have taken vows of poverty and who therefore cannot own property, and who have no family obligations, are commonly made payable to the religious orders to which they belong, even without being subject to withholding tax deductions. But the salaries of Protestants teaching in the same or similar schools and with family obligations are subject to all of the tax deductions. This same situation has also been found to exist in regard to chaplains in the armed forces. This practice means that in reality the nuns' salaries and those of the chaplains are paid to the Roman Catholic Church, which in turn merely furnishes them with living expenses. For all practical purposes such schools are parochial schools supported by public taxation. This illustrates again the relentless drive of the hierarchy to get tax money for its private institutions. This practice of turning the nuns' and chaplains' salaries over to the order to which they belong, even without tax deductions, is permitted through a special ruling by H. F. O'Connell, Chief of Technical Reference Branch, U. S. Treasury Department, which seems to have been made for the special benefit of the Roman Catholic Church. His ruling reads:

> "Members of a religious order who have taken vows of poverty, are not required to report as income, for federal tax purposes, their earnings which, in accordance with their vows, they turn over to their orders.
> "Members of a religious order who have taken vows of poverty are bound absolutely to obey the commands of their superiors and have no discretion as to where they will perform their duties and in what capacity; and they are further bound to turn over their entire compensation (or the amount less living expenses), to the order. By reason of the stringency of these requirements and the lack of discretion on the part of the members, such members are considered agents of the order they represent. . . . This is the general rule applicable where one person performs services and receives compensation as agent for another" (Ruling issued December 19, 1956).

We point out first of all, however, that the restrictions under which the nuns and priests work are merely Roman Catholic Church regulations for which the government has no responsibility whatever. The nuns and priests accept those restrictions willingly and are responsible for them. In the second place, how can nuns and priests who are so completely under the control of their church organizations that they have no discretion as to where or in what capacity they perform their duties be considered free agents fit to teach in our public schools? In the third place, while the government can legitimately contract with private companies for such things as construction projects, carrying the mail, etc., under our constitutional provision for the separation of church and state it has no right to hire the religious orders of a church to provide teachers for the public schools or chaplains for the armed forces. And in the fourth place, in view of the official doctrines of their church how can these nuns and priests be expected to teach the true principles of American freedom and democracy? How can they be expected *not* to teach their religion?

C. Stanley Lowell reported the following situation as existing in 1956:

"In Indiana more than two million dollars in tax funds went to 'public schools' that were in effect parochial schools of the Roman Church. There are 152 garbed nuns teaching in the public schools of Kansas with their salaries going to their church" (*Christianity Today,* January 7, 1959).

In some states long and expensive legislation has been instituted to clear up abuses of this kind. Much more is needed. Schools such as those just mentioned—public in name but parochial in purpose and operation—patently violate the religious rights of Protestant and other children who do not belong to the Roman Church. Such schools are an affront to our Constitutional principle of separation of church and state.

Glenn L. Archer, executive director of Protestants and Other Americans United for Separation of Church and State, cites the following as a typical example of church-state abuse:

"In Bremond, Texas, the 'public school' is conducted in a parish-owned building with six nuns and two priests as teachers. A suit filed there recently charged that public funds were being illegally used in support of this sectarian institution. The Bremond school is only one of 22 such 'public schools' in Texas that are being supported by tax funds" (*The Convert,* November, 1959).

In numerous instances school boards friendly to Roman Catholicism or under Roman Catholic domination have sold school buildings and grounds to the Roman Catholic Church for a mere fraction of their true values, sometimes for only $1.00, a mere token sale. At Rome, New York, an old school was "abandoned" by the city, sold for $25,000, and reopened as the Transfiguration parish school. Catholic sources admitted that the true value of the property as "estimated by experts" was not $25,000 but $300,000. In St. Louis, Missouri, publicly acquired property was resold to St. Louis University, a Jesuit institution of the Roman Catholic Church, at an alleged loss to the public in excess of $6,000,000.

Even when nuns in a public school are instructed by the school board not to teach their religion it is vain to expect that they will not do so either directly or indirectly. They are under vows to teach their religion to all who come before them. Indeed that is the very purpose of their profession, and they will refrain from it only to the extent to which they are restrained. Protestants justly protest teaching which seeks to make Roman Catholics out of their children in the public school classrooms.

As just indicated, in several states nuns are even allowed to wear their religious garb while teaching in the public schools. In 1960 a ruling was handed down in Ohio permitting this practice. And the Roman Church pushes this practice just as far as it can without arousing too much opposition. Such symbolism inevitably has its effect on the impressionable young minds, identifying the teachers with the Roman Catholic Church and turning the pupils in that direction. Even if religion is not mentioned, even if the name "Roman Catholic" is never spoken, the church garb in itself carries the message: "This is Roman Catholicism; this is what the Roman Catholic Church teaches." The pupils grow up looking up, perhaps unconsciously, to the nuns and priests as their mentors and guides. As a rule children tend to admire what they see in their teachers, and under normal conditions it is proper that they should do so. But it is most highly improper for the Roman Church to take advantage of this situation and to propagandize in schools that are paid for at public expense and which contain children from Protestant and other homes.

We oppose the employment of nuns in the public schools under any conditions, for the simple reason that they are not free agents. Their allegiance to their church is stronger than their allegiance to any school board. At the very least they should be required to exchange their church garb and insignia for dress that is without distinctive suggestion and which does not in itself propagandize in behalf of their religion. But even this is less than a halfway measure toward correcting the problem.

6. ROMAN CATHOLIC OPPOSITION TO PUBLIC SCHOOLS

The Roman Church not only promotes her own school system, but is strongly opposed to the American system of free public education. She would like nothing better than to see it destroyed. This is true first of all because the Roman Church claims for herself and as a matter of right the privilege of supervising *all* education, so that the youth of the land can be effectively directed toward that church. Typical of this attitude are the words of Paul L. Blakely, S.J., in an article, *May an American Oppose the Public School,* which bears the imprimatur of the late cardinal Hayes:

> "Our first duty to the public school is not to pay taxes for its maintenance. We pay that tax under protest, not because we admit an obligation in justice. . . . The first duty of every Catholic father to the public school is to keep his children out of it. . . . For the man who sends his children to the public school when he could obtain for them the blessing of a Catholic education is not a practicing Catholic, even though he goes to mass every morning. . . . 'Every Catholic child in a Catholic school,' is the command of the church."

In the late 19th century the Roman Church began a vigorous campaign to drive Bible reading and all discussion of religion out of the public schools. The real objection, of course, was not to the teaching of religion as such, but to the fact that the Roman Catholic religion was not taught. And now that the Bible and religion have been driven out of the public schools the Roman Church denounces them as "godless," "pagan," "socialistic," "immoral," "un-American."

C. Stanley Lowell writes:

> "Roman Catholics undertook to drive religion out of the schools not because they were atheistic or secularistic people, but because they were not powerful enough to determine the kind of religion to be taught. They preferred no religious teaching at all if they could not have Roman Catholic dogma. The provincial council of the Roman Catholic Church in Baltimore, 1840, imposed on priests the responsibility of seeing to it that Catholic children attending public schools did not participate in any religious exercises there. They were also to use their influence to prevent any such practice in the public school. The 'secular public school' was in substantial part an achievement of the Roman Catholic Church" (*Christianity Today*, January 7, 1957).

In some places, however, where Roman Catholics are able to dominate the public school moral and spiritual teaching with their own dogma, as in New York City, or where they have been able to secure public funds for their own schools, they have done an about-face and now call for a return of religion in education.

Another practice, we may even say a standard procedure, of the parochial schools is that of "dumping" delinquent, problem children on the public schools. Acknowledgment of such practice, even from a Roman Catholic source, is found in an article in the Paulist magazine, *Information*, November, 1959, by Louise Edna Goeden, a public school administrator in an un-named American city. She says:

> "As a teacher and administrator in a large public high school I am constantly dealing with pupils the parochial school expels or refuses to enroll or re-enroll. From experience, I know without looking that a large percentage of these entrants will be from parochial schools. From experience I also know that many will become our problem cases—because of poor scholarship or conduct or both.
>
> "I call in the parents, and the story is always the same. The students were 'asked' to leave the parochial school because they had poor grades or didn't follow directions or were behavior problems. Or they were 'advised' not to enroll in any Catholic school.
>
> "As a teacher and a Catholic, I take exception to the parochial schools 'dumping' the dullards, the sluggards, and the delinquents on the public school doorstep. When my non-Catholic colleagues say about problem students, 'These are the very ones the Catholic schools should keep; they *need* religious training,' I agree."

7. THE TWO SYSTEMS COMPARED

Far from being "godless," or "immoral," or "un-American," as the Roman Catholics charge, the public school, in which all students meet as equals regardless of race, color, or creed, is uniquely designed to be a bulwark against narrow sectarianism, bigotry, intolerance, and race prejudice. The record is clear that an undue proportion of the gangsters, racketeers, thieves, and juvenile delinquents who roam our big city streets come, not from the public schools, but from the parochial schools. The Roman hierarchy must be aware of the preponderance of malefactors among their own people, and evidently they are attempting to hide their guilt behind the "godless school" smoke screen. It is time that the American people wake up to the fact that the real godless schools are the parochial schools that are turning out more than their proportionate share of the moral misfits.

C. Stanley Lowell, writing on this subject, has well said:

"Our public school system has been the keystone of democracy. It is the one place where Protestant, Catholic and Jew meet on common ground and get to know and understand each other. Very early the Romanists began to establish their own sectarian schools, although millions of Roman Catholic youth continued to attend public schools. In an endeavor to correct this situation, Romanist leaders have launched a campaign to undermine and discredit the public school. Father Francis P. Le Buffe has declared: 'Thanks to our godless American public school . . . we have a generation today which does not know God.' The Rev. Robert I. Gannon, president of Fordham University, has charged the public school is responsible for juvenile delinquency and suggests that there would be none if Roman Catholic moral teaching were given to all. Unfortunately, it just happened that at the time Dr. Gannon was making this speech in New York City, three-fifths of all the juvenile delinquents being arrested in that area were Roman Catholics (Roman Catholics make up only one-fifth of the population of New York City). It just happens, too, that Roman Catholics supply more than twice their proportionate share of the prison population of this country" (pamphlet, *A Summons to Protestants*).

And to the same general effect Dr. Walter M. Montano says:

"Let me disabuse those Protestants who send their children to Catholic schools in the fond belief that they 'receive a better education.' Actually, the education in Catholic schools is poor to a degree that would shock our educational authorities if they were ever permitted to find out about it. The deficiencies of our public schools, over which we are concerned, do not compare for a moment with the abysmal ignorance which passes as Catholic education.

"Many American Catholic children are being taught by ignorant European peasants in this country solely through the connivance of Catholic politicians. Too often their teachers are nuns who know nothing of American democracy or American institutions, who cannot speak grammatically even in their own tongue. Add to this the suppression and distortion of facts which constitute history, literature, and such little of the arts and humanities as are 'taught' in the Catholic schools, and you have the quality of Roman Catholic education.

"For instance, the word 'Inquisition' is hardly known to Catholic students. If mentioned at all, the Inquisition is represented as a political project in which Holy Mother Church's office is merely to turn over troublesome political undesirables to the proper authorities. The same explanation is given of the burning of Joan of Arc, with the church's responsibility played down to nullity and that of the political participants played up.

"This policy is also followed in dealing with current Colombian persecutions. Never is it revealed that the political authorities in all those cases held or hold their posts only by sufferance of the Roman Church and only as long as their decisions reflect her will.

"While whitewashing Rome, Catholic education loses no opportunity to vilify Protestants and Protestantism in a way calculated to engender resentment and hatred, even in the trusting heart of a child.

"Turning from the social to the natural sciences, we find them faring as poorly. It is no accident that the United States fails to boast a single major Catholic scientist. The fact is that the Roman Church is afraid of science and would suppress it if she could as in the days of Galileo's recantation. Her justified dread is based on the fact that science has so often proved her wrong. The need of private tutoring before they are able to meet matriculation requirements at standard colleges and universities is a common experience for Catholic students" (*Christian Heritage,* May, 1959).

One of the set purposes of the parochial school is to erect a wall between Roman Catholics and the other people of the community, not only the students but the parents as well, and so to isolate them to some extent from the liberalizing tendencies in American life.

Children in a parochial school are taught that only the Roman church has the "truth," that all others are in "error," and that it is "a sin against faith and a rebuff to God" even to attend another church (see: *Living Our Faith,* p. 114). They are also taught that any marriage ceremony involving a Roman Catholic is "null and void" unless performed by a priest, and that the marriage of a Roman Catholic before a minister or an official of the state is only "an attempt at marriage" (p. 290). Such teaching is bigotry of the worst kind. Add to this the fact that 90 percent of the teaching in the parochial school is done by brain-washed nuns and priests who throughout their lives are kept in a rigid mental straight jacket in which they are forbidden to read books or magazines not approved by the hierarchy, or to attend or listen by radio to religious services other than those of their own church, or even to carry on an ordinary conversation with people from other churches concerning religious matters, and that these teachers are not under a school board but under the absolute authority of one man, the bishop of the diocese, and the narrowness of the parochial school becomes so evident that it cannot be denied.

Since the Roman Catholic Church is so opposed to the public schools, the question arises: Should Roman Catholics—laymen, nuns, or priests—be allowed to teach in the public schools? Our answer is that they should not as long as they maintain their allegiance to the hierarchy. Protestants are not allowed to teach in the schools in Spain. In the other Roman Catholic countries it is very difficult, if not impossible, for Protestants to secure teaching positions. But the fact is that many Romanists are allowed to teach in this country. And not only that but in some places they are given a perference. In 1933 a law was passed in New York State making it an offense, punishable by a fine or imprisonment, even to inquire concerning the religious affiliation of applicants for teachers' positions! Thus the citizens of that state were deprived of one of the safeguards of civil and religious liberty, that is, the right of free speech and inquiry, and the way opened for teachers who are opposed to the public school system to be forced upon a community contrary to the wishes of the majority of the people of that community. Concerning this general subject Dr. Zacchello says:

"The Roman Church—popes, bishops, priests, and laymen—do not hesitate in opposing and denouncing our public schools. Then why should the followers of Romanism be allowed to teach in public schools? Would you employ in your business a man who would tell your customers that your merchandise is rotten and that they should buy from his relatives' store? And would you want to finance that rival store?

"No business man in his right mind would do this. Yet our government is not only employing teachers who are deliberately and publicly against our educational system, but is considering the financing of private Roman Catholic schools.

"If the public schools of this country are not good enough for the children of Roman Catholic parents, then the true American parents should consider their children too good to be taught by Roman Catholic teachers. I am referring, of course, to Roman Catholics who take orders from the Vatican" (*Ins and Outs of Romanism,* p. 170).

In most states there is no requirement that private or parochial schools:

1. Meet the standards of the public schools;
2. Meet any minimum requirements;
3. Report their attendance;
4. Make annual reports to the department of public instruction;
5. Be inspected by state officials;
6. Be licensed or registered under state regulations; or,
7. That the teachers have the same qualifications as those in the public schools; or,
8. That the teachers or their teaching qualifications be registered with the department of public instruction.

8. STATE AND FEDERAL AID FOR PAROCHIAL SCHOOLS

As the Roman Church has grown in this country the parochial schools also have grown. Often they have been staffed with poorly equipped nuns who served without pay, and often they have been conducted in inferior buildings with inferior equipment. In recent years, however, the Roman Church has made a considerable effort to improve its schools, particularly in the larger cities. In fact the aggressive actions of the hierarchy indicate that their ultimate goal is to take over the public school system here as they have done in the predominantly Roman Catholic countries. But before they can do that they must undermine it. This they attempt to do, first by securing fringe benefits. Usually they begin by asking for bus transportation. In some places this is now provided, sometimes through state or local law, oftentimes without benefit of law if there is no public protest. But free bus transportation does not satisfy them. Instead it only serves as a springboard for further demands. So consistently has this plan been followed that it has been appropriately termed "the school bus wedge." The next step is to ask for free lunches, free text books, free equipment, etc. The plan then calls for state or federal aid in erecting school buildings and in paying teachers' salaries, but never with state supervision, so that eventually the state pays for the schools and the Roman Church operates them.

Regarding the school bus problem the magazine *Church and State* recently said:

"One in three children in school today must be transported to and from the institution. The bill for public school transportation is $417 million annually. On the basis of the claimed attendance at parochial schools, and the national transportation average cost of $37 per pupil for those who need transportation, the subsidy to the (Roman) Church for transportation to its schools would run in excess of $61 million."

In various communities efforts to vote bonds for the erection of badly needed public school buildings have been defeated by an organized Roman Catholic vote, with the purpose of forcing equal appropriations for parochial schools. The hierarchy has made it clear to the U.S. Congress that it will oppose any federal aid to education bill unless aid to parochial schools is included. It is interesting to notice that in Puerto Rico, in the summer of 1960, the failure of the Roman Church to get legislation giving it the right to conduct classes in religion in the public school as well as certain other benefits was the occasion for the launching of a new Roman Catholic political party as a direct means to achieve those goals. But the new party fared rather badly in the 1960 election.

The campaign to shift the cost of Roman Catholic schools to the American taxpayer has been vigorously pushed, but up until now it has met with only minor success. Most Protestant denominations are strongly opposed to the use of public funds to aid parochial schools, and it has been particularly galling to the Roman hierarchy that it has not been able to put its hands into the public treasury in the United States as it is so accustomed to do in many other countries. To provide federal aid for parochial schools would mean that a nation which is four-fifths non-Catholic would build private religious schools for about one-seventh of the children who attend those schools. But the never ending campaign for tax money goes on.

The Supreme Court of the United States has quite consistently upheld the principle of separation of church and state as set forth in the first amendment to the Constitution. Free bus transportation has been permitted, but only by a divided opinion, the judges voting five to four to permit it. In this connection we think that logic is on the side of Judge Ralph M. Holman, in a Circuit Court, in Oregon, who in a suit regarding the furnishing of text books to parochial schools, ruled against such aid and indicated that in his opinion the five Supreme Court justices who voted in favor of the constitutionality of parochial school bus appropriations were wrong, and that the four who constitued the minority were right. In that decision he said:

"Anything that assists a religious sect to conduct a separate school where all instruction is permeated with religious overtones is an aid to religion. The proof in this case is conclusive that the sole purpose in maintaining the private school is to promote religion.

"It makes no difference whether books, teachers, equipment, transportation, or buildings are furnished, nor does it make any difference to whom they are furnished. In truth, all are an integral part of the whole which makes up the school and the educational process. You cannot logically distinguish one from the other. They constitute the elements of an educational process permeated with religious purpose" (*Church and State,* April, 1960).

It should be clear to all that a Roman Catholic parochial school is an integral part of that church, as definitely so as is the service of worship. A parochial school is usually developed in connection with a church. In many cases the church and school monies are not even separated. Such a school is in no sense a public school, even though some children from other groups may be admitted to it. The buildings are not owned and controlled by a community of American people, not even by a community of American Roman Catholic *people.* The title of ownership in a public school is vested in the local community, in the elected officers of the school board or the city council. But the title of ownership in a parochial school is vested in the bishop as an individual, who is appointed by, who is under the direct control of, and who reports to the pope in Rome.

Another contrast is that in the public school the selection of a faculty and the administration of the school usually rests with a school board which is subject to election and recall by the voters, but in the parochial school the selection of a faculty and the administration of the school is in the hands of the bishop alone, and usually is administered through the local priest. If a faculty member in the public school believes that he has been treated unjustly in being disciplined or dismissed, he can seek redress through the civil court and he is guaranteed a hearing. But if a faculty member in a parochial school is disciplined or dismissed he has no recourse whatsoever. The word of the bishop or priest is final, even without explanation if he so chooses. The tax payers have a voice in the way their money is used in the public school, but the people who support a parochial school have no voice at all in such affairs.

The argument is often made that Roman Catholic parents are the victims of double taxation since they pay the regular levy for public schools and also the cost of the parochial schools. But it is hardly accurate to call this double taxation. They pay the regular levy as does everyone else, and they have the privilege of sending their children to the public school. There is no discrimination against them. But if instead they choose to use the parochial school where the principal course is Roman Catholic polity and doctrine, that is their privilege, and they should be willing to pay for it. That is entirely a matter between them and their church. If they have any protest it should be made to their priest or bishop who orders them to build and maintain such a school. The other side of the picture, of course, is that if those of us who pay taxes to support the public schools are also required to support the Roman Catholic schools, that would constitute a double burden on us.

Furthermore, many people who have no children at all, or whose children are not ready for school or are past school age, are also required to pay the regular levy. And usually they do so gladly as a service to the community. If the Roman Catholic objection were valid, then only those families who have children in the public school should be required to pay the school tax, and they should pay in proportion to the number of children they have in school.

To use a simple illustration: Suppose the state builds a road. It is paid for with state funds. It is open to the public, and anyone may use it. But if another group does not like the public road and wants to build their own private road paralleling the public road, they may do so. But they have no right to expect the rest of us to pay for it. It is their road. Let them pay for it or use the public road.

In the United States we have "freedom of religion." In many other nations the people do not enjoy this high privilege. But freedom of religion has always had a price tag attached to it: *Pay the bill.*

Let us have public funds for public causes and private funds for private causes, whether it be for roads, schools, libraries, swimming pools, or anything else. And let Roman Catholics remember that in their country of Spain they do not allow Protestants to have private schools even though the latter would gladly pay all the costs.

The Detroit News has commented concerning the school problem:

> "All the states decree . . . that all children shall be educated at public expense because an educated citizenry is essential to our form of government. . . . No one is being taxed for the education of his own children; all are being taxed for the education of everyone's children, to everyone's ultimate benefit. They decree as well that what the community pays for on such a vast scale it must control. . . . Like it or not, that is what our state constitutions provide. No child is a 'second class citizen,' for no child is barred from these schools."

Cardinal Spellman recently demanded that federal aid for education be extended to parochial as well as public schools, and argued that the government would be guilty of "coercion" and "discrimination" if it denied federal funds to Catholic schools. This was promptly and effectively answered by Glenn L. Archer, who said:

> "Actually the government would be guilty of coercion and discrimination if it compelled the 140 million non-Catholic people of the United States to pay for schools which are maintained primarily to promote the doctrines

of one church. . . . The Catholic people of the United States have been offered free access to the schools of all the people without religious discrimination. If they choose under the pressure of their bishops to decline this invitation, they should not ask the taxpayers to pay the bill for their own separation" (*The Evening Star,* Washington, D. C., Jan. 19, 1961).

If the Romanists achieve a breakthrough at the parochial school level, it can be confidently expected that that will be followed by demands for bigger and better Hill-Burton Hospital Construction Acts, G. I. Bills with generous tuition grants to sectarian schools, National Defense Education Acts, and, in the not too distant future, sectarian political parties and candidates at state and local levels.

Under our American system of separation of church and state, all Protestant churches have financed their own projects by voluntary gifts from their adherents. The Roman Catholic Church should be willing to do the same. It is manifestly unfair for it to claim federal and state subsidies for its private projects. If such appropriations were granted, then Protestants, in proportion to their numbers, should receive similar appropriations, to be used in their church programs as they see fit. But Protestants do not want such help, and in most cases do not take it even if it is available. They are opposed on principle to government support for any denomination.

On repeated occasions in recent years programs providing for federal aid to education have been blocked by Roman Catholic spokesmen because parochial schools were not included. Whether federal aid to education is in itself a wise or an unwise policy we do not here attempt to say, although we think that as a general rule educational problems can be handled more economically and more efficiently by local communities or at most with state aid. But in any event the fact of the matter is that throughout the nation more than half of all Roman Catholic children attend public schools. Roman Catholics are represented on school boards, often out of proportion to their numbers in the community. And the percentage of Roman Catholic teachers in public schools often is in excess of their proportion in the community. So they are benefiting quite materially from our public school system.

The argument that the parochial school saves the community money is also largely false. In the first place, the community does not ask the Roman Church to aid in this matter. Secondly, the Roman Church develops such schools, not as an aid to the community, not to teach American principles of citizenship, but strictly to serve its own purpose. And thirdly, many people would rather pay the tax to provide an adequate and unprejudiced education for all of the young people than to experience the divisions and rivalries that almost invariably result from such schools. Usually they feel that the Roman Church is doing the community a disservice in restricting the children to the kind of training that they receive in the parochial schools.

Something is to be learned by observing the school situation in Britain, which is quite different from that in the United States. The British government has agreed to provide up to 75 percent of the funds needed for the building and maintenance of Anglican and Roman Catholic schools, and up to 95 percent of certain other school expenses. But even so the hierarchy is not satisfied. It is demanding complete financial equality with the public schools. In France, under President De Gaulle, a Roman Catholic, the Roman hierarchy, early in 1960, precipitated a governmental crisis by demanding full school aid without governmental supervision, and with De Gaulle's assistance received most of what it asked for. The ideal toward which the Roman Church strives is found in Spain where, under a concordat with the Vatican, the schools are financed by the government while the Roman Church supervises the curriculum, selects the teachers, and directs the administration of the schools. Protestant schools are prohibited. Why should anyone believe that the Roman Catholic Church in the United States would be satisfied with anything less?

An interesting light is thrown on this problem of state and federal aid to parochial schools in a recent issue of *Church and State* magazine. Under the title, *Do They Need The Money?*, we read:

"The spectacle of the hierarchy of the mighty Roman Catholic Church pleading poverty is one to give us pause. This church is, by its own admission, the largest and wealthiest of all Christian bodies. It is literally richer than Croesus.

"The Roman Church has assets so vast that it has never dared to make a public report of them. This is the organization which now comes pleading that it must have Federal grants or credit if it is to carry on. . . .

"The credit rating of the Buffalo diocese provides financial information about the Roman Church that is rarely disclosed. The Church's assets in this one diocese alone are placed at $236,000,000. Its average gross income is $24½ million. Taking the Buffalo membership of 860,000 in ratio with the claimed total American membership of 40 million, a total wealth close to 11 billion is indicated.

"When one adds to this the income producing potential of the 40 million contributors of Roman Catholic faith, we are confronted with a financial power that can be discussed in the same breath with the United States government itself. This is the organization which claims to stand in desperate need of government aid. . . . Why does the hierarchy insist on Federal aid to its denominational schools? We think we know the reason. And that reason is not financial" (May, 1961).

In regard to Vatican finances a recent book by Corrado Pallenberg reveals some interesting but little known facts. For twelve years Mr. Pallenberg has been engaged in journalistic work in Rome for Italian, English, and American newspapers and magazines and has had an excellent opportunity to observe Vatican policies and personalities. He recalls, for instance, that under the terms of the treaty between the Vatican and Mussolini, in 1929, the Vatican, in return for giving up its claim to the Papal States which it had ruled for many years and which comprised some 16,000 square miles in central Italy, was paid 1,500,000,000 lira, a sum which at that time was worth about $90,000,000. That sum has been kept intact and invested, much of it in the United States, England, and Switzerland, and it has increased greatly in value. No balance sheets are ever made public and it is impossible to discover its present value, but Mr. Pallenberg says that, "In Roman Banking quarters the figure of £200,000,-000 has been mentioned tentatively." That would be approximately $550,-000,000. In any event, what a vast sum that is for a church to maintain as a reserve, particularly when the spiritual and material needs of so many people, even Roman Catholic people in southern European and Latin American countries, are so great! In view of Rome's past history and present aggressive tendencies, what a threat such power poses for free institutions everywhere! And what a contrast that policy presents with the policies of the Protestant churches, which usually maintain a fairly close balance between income and expenses! (*The Vatican From Within;* 1961; pp. 191-201; George G. Harrap & Co., Ltd., London, publisher).

9. EDUCATION IN ROMANIST DOMINATED COUNTRIES

It is not by accident that the people in countries that have been dominated by Roman Catholicism for centuries have an abnormally high percentage of illiteracy. Some 50 percent of the Portuguese cannot read or write. Spain, which is the most Roman Catholic nation in Europe, is also the most backward and has the lowest standard of living of any nation in Europe. In Italy illiteracy is high, and Roman Catholic domination of education has been so oppressive that it has been almost impossible to establish even a primary school apart from the Roman Church. In Mexico, Central and South America, where the Roman Church has been dominant and practically without religious competition for four hundred years, the illiteracy rate until very recently was from 30 to 60 percent and in some places as high as 70 percent. Brazil, for instance, with 58 million people has more than 30 million who are illiterate. Only 42 percent of the people of Colombia, according to a government survey, can read and write, and most of those have not had schooling beyond the fourth grade. In Canada the Roman Catholic province of Quebec has lagged far behind the other provinces in education. Even primary education was not compulsory in Quebec until 1943. A program is now under way to remedy the lamentable conditions that were exposed by *Life* magazine in the issue of October 19, 1942. Throughout these countries we see the practice, so typical of all Roman Catholic countries, of gathering large sums of money for the building of magnificent cathedrals to overawe the people and for the enrichment of the priesthood, while leaving the people in indescribable ignorance and poverty.

Through the centuries the Roman Catholic Church has found that illiterate and superstitious people are much more obedient to her rule, and until she was forced by Protestant competition to make a change her deliberate policy seems to have been designed to keep them in that condition. But thanks to the mission work that has been carried on in Latin America and to the generally enlightening influences that have come from the Protestant nations, the illiteracy rate in that area is now decreasing. Nevertheless the record of the Roman Church in Latin America remains one of miserable and undeniable failure so far as the general enlightenment of the people is concerned, and Rome must take full responsibility for that condition. Many of her leading men in the governing classes and many of her priests have been distinguished for learning and logical skill, for "knowledge is power." But she has not entrusted that knowledge to the masses of her followers. Instead, she has reserved it for her office holders that they might use it to her advantage. It is important to keep in mind that the Roman Catholic Church the world over is one solid, monolithic organization, all closely knit and under the absolute power of the pope in Rome, and that the same pope who appoints all of the cardinals and bishops in the United States also appoints all of the cardinals and bishops in Latin America, and that the church, working through the hierarchy in Rome, has perfect freedom to send men and money and to promote or to refrain from promoting schools in any area under its control.

In Protestant countries the Roman Church has been driven, partly by shame and partly by a spirit of rivalry, to follow quite a different policy from that in Latin America. In the United States, which already possessed the most efficient system of universal education to be found anywhere in the world and where we might suppose that a parochial system was least needed, the Roman Church has been prompted to engage in extensive educational work. Much the same policy has been followed in Britain. In these countries her people cannot be kept in darkness, and she is forced to minister to them or lose them. In these countries her people are demanding high schools and colleges, and she is giving them what she does not give her people in Spain or Italy or Latin America. In the United States she has established hundreds of hospitals, colleges and various special institutions such as Dismas House in St. Louis, Boys Town in Nebraska (built to a considerable extent with money solicited indiscriminately from Protestants). But we do not find comparable institutions in the typical Roman Catholic countries. Hence we must to a considerable extent label these "showcase religion," designed to meet Protestant competition.

To discover what a system *really* is, what its true fruits are, we must look at countries where it is fully established and where it has been in operation for long periods of time. And when we apply that test to the Roman system we find the invariable products: ignorance, superstition, poverty, and immorality.

10. THE CHRISTIAN SCHOOL

Many Christian people are disturbed because the Bible cannot be read and Christianity cannot be taught in the public schools, and because in many instances the texts used present an anti-Christian viewpoint. This condition in the schools represents a radical departure from that which prevailed in the early days of our country and which in fact was common until comparatively recent times. The state, however, is a secular institution, and in a free society such as ours in which church and state are separate the state cannot promote any particular religion in its tax supported and politically controlled schools. Hence it follows that whenever the government undertakes to provide education, whether at the local, state, or national level, it tends to secularize the schools. The result is that today most of the schools tend to ignore the subject of religion, with many of them assuming a completely secular attitude, as if God did not exist, while others are actually irreligious, teaching an evolutionary philosophy in a man-centered world.

One of the privileges enjoyed by the people of the United States is that of establishing and operating private or parochial schools if they so wish. This right has been affirmed by the United States Supreme Court. While we strongly disapprove of the parochial school as conducted by the Roman Catholic Church, there is another type of school designed to provide a Christian atmosphere and course of instruction of which we approve most heartily. This is generally known as the "Christ-

ian School." It is supported and controlled not by a church or by a
group of churches, but by an organization of Christian parents in the
local community. It is usually interdenominational in nature, designed
to serve the children of all of the evangelical churches in the community and such others as are given permission to attend. Since no
church has any official connection with the project no compulsion is put
upon any families in those churches to send their children to the Christian school if they prefer the public school.

The first schools in America were private, usually in the homes or in
the churches. Often they were organized and taught by the local minister as a service to the community. The Bible was the most important
book studied, sometimes almost the only book. As it came to be realized
how valuabe such training was, the local communities, and later the
states, took over the work, broadened the course of study, and in time
such education was made universal and compulsory.

We believe that Christian training is the most important thing in a
child's life. Responsibility for such training rests first of all upon the
parents in the home. Early in the Old Testament the command was
given that there should be oral teaching of the Scriptures in the home by
the parents: "And these words, which I command thee this day, shall
be upon thy heart; and thou shalt teach them diligently unto thy children,
and shalt talk of them when thou sittest in thy house, and when thou
walkest by the way, and when thou liest down, and when thou risest up"
(Deut. 6:6,7). The command is that the home shall be literally saturated
with the Word of God.

But because many parents are so poorly equipped to give that training, perhaps never having had it themselves, it is a very great blessing
if it can be given in the schools. The ideal situation would be a Christian
state in which true Bible teaching could be given as a part of the regular
school course. But that condition does not now prevail, and it cannot be
realized in the foreseeable future.

While we insist that there must be separation of church and state,
that does not mean that we acknowledge any area of life in which
Christianity should not play a dominant role. It only means that it is
better that neither the government nor the schools should be dominated
by any religion than that they should be dominated by a false religion,
better that they not aid any religion than that they aid a false religion.
Due to the fact that in the United States most communities are composed
of Protestants, Roman Catholics, Jews, and other minority groups, in
order not to offend any the public schools are forbidden by law to give
any type of religious training.

But it is not enough merely to educate children in the arts and sciences.

They must also be trained in things relating to the spirit if they are to fulfill their true mission in life. To leave religion out of the curriculum is to omit the most important subject, and tends to give students the impression that religion is of little value or importance.

In order to meet this need various plans have been suggested. One is that in the public schools a certain number of Scripture verses be read each day without comment, followed perhaps by the Lord's prayer or some other suitable prayer. But such teaching can only be most elementary. And a further difficulty arises as to which version of the Bible should be used, and to whom or in whose name the prayer should be offered. Another plan that has met with fairly wide support is that of "released time," in which perhaps once each week the children are excused for a part of the school period in order to attend Christian training classes usually held in their own churches. The Supreme Court, in a case brought before it in 1952, gave the legal "go ahead" to released time religious classes, provided they are not held on school property. In accordance with that ruling approximately 4,000,000 children of all faiths are released from the public schools each week to attend such classes.

This latter plan, however, still leaves much to be desired, particularly if other courses in the school are taught from a non-Christian or anti-Christian viewpoint. Much the best plan, we believe, is that of the Protestant Christian school. For that purpose an organization of Christian parents builds or leases its own buildings, hires its own teachers, teaches in general the same courses and seeks to meet the same academic standards as does the public school. Such schools may include only the grades, or the high school, or both. All courses are taught from the Christian viewpoint. And in addition they also have courses in Bible study in which the Bible is presented as the inspired and authoritative Word of God.

But the question naturally arises: Can the "private" school survive? The answer is: Yes, it can, if the people of a community are genuinely interested in its success. In numerous communities such schools are proving remarkably successful. The Christian Reformed Church, with headquarters in Grand Rapids, Michigan, has done much to promote this type of school. We need only point out that for long ages it was generally thought that the churches in the various countries could not survive if they were cut off from state funds. But in those nations in which they have been "dis-established" they have gained new vitality and perspective and have prospered much more than where they still are dependent on state aid. In like manner Christian schools can be productive of true scholarship and can develop with more freedom and originality if Christian people take their work seriously. R. J. Rushdoony, who has made a special study of this problem, points out that, "The school society, as a voluntary organization, operates on a radically more economical basis than the public school in building, operational, administrative, and maintenance costs. On this basis it can still produce superior results" (*Intellectual Schizophrenia*, p. 24; The Presbyterian and Reformed Publishing Co., Phila., 1961.)

The hundreds of Protestant colleges with their splendid buildings and large endowment funds show what Protestant people can do when they set their minds to it. Such schools have rendered a most valuable service over the years.

There are valid reasons for establishing Christian schools at the elementary and high school levels. First of all there is the teaching of Christian truth and the building of Christian character. That, of course, can be done much more effectively in schools in which the Bible is honored rather than in those in which it is ignored or even attacked and ridiculed. In the second place a dedicated Christian faculty leaves an indelible impression on the lives and characters of the students who attend such schools. And in the third place fellowship with other students whose background and purpose in life is Christian does much to inspire students to better ways of living.

Ministers and laymen usually find a place in such schools as principals, teachers, and members of the school boards. Many teachers prefer the atmosphere of the Christian school to that of the public school. And the evangelical churches of a community usually give moral and sometimes financial support, although as churches they have no control over the schools.

It should be emphasized that the Christian school is not designed to operate as a rival of the public school but rather to cooperate with it in a friendly way for the benefit of the entire community. It was never the wish of the Protestant churches that Bible reading and Christian training should be excluded from the public school. But the fact must be faced that that condition now exists, and that remedial measures are needed. We insist that the public school with its secular viewpoint must not claim the right to teach every child under all conditions, nor the exclusive right to teach any child—that education is primarily the responsibility of the parents, and that the parents may provide that education privately if they wish.

(For assistance in starting and operating Christian schools contact: Christian Schools Service, 10119 Lafayette Avenue, Chicago 28, Illinois.)

XVII. BY WHAT MORAL STANDARD?

1. Basic Principles. 2. Liquor. 3. Oaths. 4. Theft. 5. Gambling. 6. The Roman Church and the U. S. Prison Population. 7. Questionable Hospital Practices. 8. Conclusion.

1. BASIC PRINCIPLES

One of the strong contrasts between Protestantism and Roman Catholicism is found in the moral codes which distinguish the two systems. In Protestantism this code is taken directly from the Bible. Nothing can be laid on men as a moral requirement unless it can be shown to be contained in the Bible. Such requirements thereby become a matter of conscience for the Christian.

But in Roman Catholicism the moral code is based primarily on Canon Law and only secondarily on the Bible, and in the main is imposed on the person from without. The authority of the church as interpreted by the priest is what counts. The result is that the Roman Church has developed a standard of morality that is designed, not to stir the conscience, but to maintain papal power. Many of the dogmas and rites of Romanism are antagonistic to the teachings of Scripture and directly or indirectly conducive to immorality. Drinking, gambling, and other habits considered as vices by Protestants are not counted as evil by Romanists except when indulged in to excess.

In the study of morals the Roman Church takes the teachings of the Jesuit theologian Ligouri as authoritative. Ligouri was canonized among the saints in heaven by the pronouncement of pope Gregory XVI, in 1839, and was declared a doctor of the universal Roman Church by pope Pius IX. Thomas Carlyle, the famous British author, had good reason for saying that the Jesuits have "poisoned the well-springs of truth." And he added:

> "More terrible still is the 'moral theology' of Alphonsus Ligouri, who is counted a saint and 'doctor' of the Church—of equal rank with Augustine, Chrysostom and others—whose textbooks are standard on moral questions in all Roman Catholic seminaries. The 'moral' teachings of Ligouri, if they could be read in their original Latin, would fill every right-minded person with horror. For there he outlines the ways in which

falsehood can be used *without really telling a lie;* the ways in which the *property* of others *can be taken without stealing;* how the *Ten Command-ments can be broken without committing deadly sin."*

Samples of Ligouri's "moral" teaching are:

"A servant is allowed to help his master to climb a window to commit fornication" (St. Alphonsus, 1, 22, 66).

"It is not a mortal sin to get drunk, unless one loses completely the use of his mental faculties for over one hour" (1, 5, 75).

"It is lawful to violate penal laws" (hunting, fishing, etc.).

"It is asked whether prostitutes are to be permitted. . . . They are to be permitted because, as a distinguished priest says, 'Remove prostitutes from the world, and all things will be disordered with lust. Hence in large cities, prostitutes may be permitted" (3, 434).

In this connection it is interesting to note that legalized prostitution was not abolished in the city of Rome, the very city which is head-quarters of the Roman Church, until September, 1958, and that even today almost every city of any size in South America has its legalized houses of prostitution. Dr. Walter Montano, returning from a conference of Protestant leaders in Colombia, reported that according to information given him the city of Cali, which has a population of 520,000, has 2600 houses of prostitution and 13,000 registered prostitutes. He adds that the Roman Catholic Church in that country has done practically nothing to lift the morality of the people or to bring a solution to the country's problems (*Christian Heritage,* February, 1960).

Ignatius Loyola (1491-1566), another famous teacher in the Roman Church and founder of the Jesuit order which today so largely controls Roman Catholic policy, wrote some rules for his order which he com-mended as conducive to complete obedience and as a "help in attaining the right attitude toward the Church." One of them reads:

"Laying aside all private judgment the spirit must be always ready to obey the true doctrine and therefore, *if anything shall appear white to our eyes which the Church has defined as black, we likewise must declare it to be black.* . . . If you receive from your superior a command which appears to go against your own judgment, your own conviction, or your own wellbeing, then you must fall on your knees, putting off all human principles and considerations and renew, when you are alone, your vow of obedience."

In accordance with this it is not uncommon in the Roman church to refer to one as a "good priest" if he does his work efficiently, even though it may be known that his moral character is bad. He is a "good priest" in the same sense that one may be a "good doctor," or a "good mechanic," entirely apart from his moral character. Under such a standard obedience to the church becomes the supreme virtue and takes precedence even over conscience. But for the Protestant such action does not make sense. The Protestant can not force his will to believe that which he knows to be irrational, nor his conscience to approve that which he knows to be wrong.

2. LIQUOR

We do not need to belabor the point that the Roman Catholic Church fights almost every movement throughout the nation that is designed to restrict the use of alcoholic liquors. The big cities, in which the Roman Catholic population is concentrated, are notoriously "wet." The three things that appeal most to the weakness of human nature and that bring large profits to those who control them, are drinking, gambling, and prostitution. Protestants are often regarded as "killjoys," because they oppose even a limited license for any of these. The Roman Church, however, holds that drinking and gambling are not sinful in themselves, but that they become so only when carried to excess. And who is to say at what point they become excessive? Why, the priest, of course. It is he who, in the confessional, decides for Roman Catholics at what point a man or woman is to be considered as drinking to excess, and how much may be spent on gambling without committing a sin.

A case in point occurred in Steubenville, Ohio, in the fall of 1946. It was public knowledge that drunkenness, gambling, and prostitution were rampant in that city and that a "clean up" was needed. A group of Protestant ministers undertook the job. But the Roman Catholic bishop openly opposed the clean up and issued a pastoral letter to be read in all of his churches, condemning the campaign of the ministers. According to *The New York Times* of November 28, of that year, the bishop called the ministers "narrow little people," and declared that "Drinking and gambling are not in themselves sinful or evil." The bishop then proceeded to lecture the ministers on the proper interpretation of the Christian moral code as follows: "These so-called leaders simply do not know the moral structure of Christianity. As a result they make themselves pitiable objects in a community." A Steubenville judge, apparently under the bishop's influence, backed him up and condemned the ministers as "fanatics insistent upon senseless arrests" (L. H. Lehmann, booklet, *The Secret of Catholic Power*, p. 7).

We have called attention to the De La Salle Institute, at Napa,

California, which is only one of several church owned properties in the United States producing commercial wine or brandy or both.

3. OATHS

According to Ligouri, a Roman Catholic can lie. Says he:

> "Notwithstanding, indeed, although it is not lawful to lie, or to feign what is not, however, it is lawful to dissemble what is, or to cover the truth with words, or other ambiguous and doubtful signs, for a just cause, and when there is not a necessity for confessing. These things being settled, it is a certain and a common opinion among all divines, that for a just cause it is lawful to use equivocation in the modes propounded and to confirm it (equivocation) with an oath" (Less. 1, 2, c. 41).

The right to hold a "mental reservation" is claimed by Roman theologians. The *Summa Theologia* of Thomas Aquinas, on which Roman theology relies so heavily, says that when the interests of Holy Mother Church require it, one may make a statement while holding a mental reservation which qualifies it into nullity.

The Roman Catholic Dictionary, 15th edition, published in London, in 1951, with the imprimatur of the cardinal of Westminster, under the subject *Oath*, says that the Roman Church has the right to dispense anyone from the provision of an oath: "Though generally speaking, no earthly power can dispense from keeping an oath made in favor of another, still in other cases a dispensation may be valid."

Under Canon Law 1320 the pope can dispense from *any* oath (see the authoritative book, *Canon Law: Text and Commentary* (1946), by Bouscaren and Ellis, p. 679). A Roman Catholic judge who obtains a papal dispensation in order to violate his judicial oath in case of conflict between church law and civil law is considered blameless by the Roman Catholic theologians. The most notable examples of papal release from oaths were the attempt of pope Pius V, in 1570, to "uncrown" Protestant queen Elizabeth I, of England, by releasing her court officials and all subjects from civil allegiance to her—which attempt failed because the British people in the main remained loyal to their queen—and the attempt of pope Gregory VII to depose Henry IV, of Germany, which attempt succeeded to the extent that Henry was forced to do obeisance to the pope, although he later regained his power and drove the pope out of Rome.

The principle to which the Roman Church resorts in freeing men from their oaths is that it does so in obedience to a "higher law." On the grounds that no man can justly bind himself to do that which is sinful, the church may decide that an oath of allegiance to a ruler who is disobedient to the pope, or a pledge made to a "heretic," is sinful and need not be kept.

It is Roman Catholic doctrine that the conscience is subject to the teaching of the church and is to be determined by that teaching rather than by private judgment. A pledge made during a political campaign, or an oath of office, is secondary to Canon Law. A Roman candidate for office may declare himself in favor of separation of church and state, or against federal and state aid to parochial schools. But even though he does so in all good conscience, the Roman Church teaches that in the final analysis his conscience must be governed by and be subject to its authority.

Edwin F. Healy, in his book, *Moral Guidance,* published by the Loyola University Press, declares: "A promise under oath to do something sinful does not bind at all." The Roman Church sets itself up as the judge to determine what things are sinful; hence an oath to perform some action that is later judged to be against the best interests of that church may be abrogated by a Roman Catholic office holder. What the church holds to be right, e.g., things which promote its welfare, restrict heretics, etc., are judged to be right. When personal judgment of conscience conflicts with the dictates of the church, personal judgment must be set aside. We have seen this principle set forth by Loyola for the members of his Jesuit order. The same general principle holds throughout the Roman Church.

Under the subject of mental reservation Healy says:

"For sufficient reason we may thus permit others to deceive themselves by taking the wrong meaning of what is said; and this remains true though the listener, because of his ignorance, does not know that there is another meaning to the word that is employed."

In other words, a Roman Catholic is not necessarily bound to the strict form of the words spoken. If the person to whom a promise is made, or before whom an oath is taken, does not know that the one making it may attach a different meaning to the words, that is his fault, and the promise or oath is not necessarily binding.

4. THEFT

In regard to theft, Ligouri teaches that a Roman Catholic may steal, provided the value of the thing stolen is not excessive. He says:

"If any one on an occasion should steal only a moderate sum either from one or more, not intending to acquire any notable sum, neither to injure his neighbor to any great extent, by several thefts, he does not sin grievously, nor do those, taken together, constitute a mortal sin. However, after it may have amounted to a notable sum by detaining it, he can commit mortal sin, but even this mortal sin may be avoided, if either then he be unable to restore, or have the intention of making restitution immediately of those things which he then received" (Vol. 3, p. 258).

This doctrine has been interpreted for American Roman Catholics to mean that it is not a mortal sin if one steals less than $40.00 worth at any one time. Msgr. Francis J. Connell writes as follows in *The American Ecclesiastical Review*, official magazine of instruction for priests, published at Catholic University, Washington, D.C.

"Question: What would be regarded nowadays as the absolute sum for grave theft in the United States?

"Answer: By the absolute sum for grave theft is meant that amount of money, the stealing of which constitutes a mortal sin, irrespective of the financial status of the individual or corporation from which it is taken, however wealthy they may be. Naturally this sum varies with the fluctuation of the value, or the purchasing power, of money. In a country like ours it is quite possible that this sum might be different in different sections. To lay down a general norm, in view of actual conditions and the value of money, it would seem that the absolute sum for grave theft would be about $40.00" (January, 1945, p. 68).

The condoning of theft and robbery under certain circumstances is known among Roman Catholic theologians as "secret compensation," and is contained in catechisms and textbooks used in Roman Catholic schools. In *The Manual of Christian Doctrine*, which has gone through many editions, and which bears the *nihil obstat* of M. S. Fisher, S.T.L., *censor liborum*, and the imprimatur of cardinal Dougherty of Philadelphia, the Preface states: "This book is intended as a manual of religious instruction not only in the novitiate and scholasticate of teaching congregations, but also in the classes of high schools, academies and colleges." On page 295 this textbook discusses the problem of theft, its nature and various forms, including larceny, robbery, cheating, fraud, and extortion, and on page 297 we find theft condoned in the following words:

"Q. What are the causes that excuse from theft?

"A. 1. *Extreme necessity*, when a person takes only what is necessary, and does not thereby reduce to the same necessity the person whose property he takes. 2. *Secret compensation,* on condition that the debt so cancelled be certain, that the creditor cannot recover his property by any other means, and that he take as far as possible, things of the same kind as he had given."

L. H. Lehmann comments very appropriately on such conduct:

"Moral conduct can be no better than the moral principles upon which it is based. Most crimes are distinctly connected with thievery and robbery. If a Roman Catholic youth, for instance, can persuade himself that he has 'extreme necessity' for an automobile, he will consider himself justified in stealing it legitimately according to the above teaching, provided he knows that the owner will not be thereby impoverished. The doctrine of 'secret compensation' applies mostly to employees who consider they are being underpaid for their labor. A twenty-dollar-a-week cashier in a sidestreet cafeteria may consider herself underpaid and apply this principle to justify her pilfering of odd dimes and quarters from the cash register whenever she can safely do so. Many a cashier in a large bank or commercial business corporation has done just this until he found himself in jail for large-scale embezzlement. A desperate man could also easily argue himself into thinking that he is justly entitled to some of the surplus money of a rich victim and will go after it with a gun. Likewise grafting politicians seize upon the argument implicit in this teaching to justify their conviction that they are worth much more to the community than their elected offices pay them. [And it surely does not take much imagination to guess how this principle might be applied by judges and clerks whose duty it is to count votes at the polling places. Just how many votes might be stolen in order to aid one's candidate without committing mortal sin? We should like to know.]

"This doctrine of 'secret compensation' was, of course, unheard of in Christianity, even in the Catholic Church, prior to the Jesuit casuists of the seventeenth century. It was invented by them along with other unethical doctrines such as 'mental reservation,' 'the end justifies the means,' 'the end sanctifies the means,' etc., to make Catholicism popular among the masses. It also helped to rationalize their own exploits. Thus Catholic textbooks of moral theology today make no pretention of showing that these principles of conduct take their origin from the Ten Commandments or from Christian revelation. They merely propound them as accepted Catholic doctrine and trace them back to Gury, the Jesuit fountainhead. . . .

"The blunt fact, confirmed by countless cases, is that many Catholics get the one idea from this teaching, namely that stealing is not essentially evil at all times, but, on the contrary, fair and reasonable if one needs something badly enough and the owner does not. How this conviction can be stretched to cover untold cases is easy to imagine. It is limited

only by the envy and self-prejudice of the individual circumstances—
which varies immeasurably from person to person.

"All in all, it is most unfortunate that any religion is permitted to teach
such a principle as part of the curriculum of American school education,
much more if it should ever be taught in the public schools on the pretext
of helping to lessen crime among the youth of America" (Booklet, *Catholic Education and Crime*).

5. GAMBLING

Another very serious defect in the moral armor of Roman Catholicism
is its penchant for games of chance, particularly its strong defense of
bingo as played in the churches, which, in whatever light it may be
viewed, is a form of gambling. The primary feature about gambling,
bingo, raffles, etc., is that each is a game of chance in which the ownership of money or some other article of value is decided by a lucky
number, a turn of a wheel, a throw of the dice, or some such device. And
gambling is gambling, no matter what form it takes. Basically, it is an
attempt to get something for nothing, an attempt to live not by honest
toil but at the expense of others. As such it is a moral disease, a covetous
greed or lust to get possession of what another has. Just because other
equally covetous people agree to the arrangement does not make it
moral. Even when a gambler wins he realizes that others have lost. Anything that induces people to take money needed for food and clothing
and risk it on games of chance is wrong in principle. And the "easy come,
easy go" principle involved seldom leaves anyone permanently enriched.
It is notorious that gamblers almost invariably end up broke. And usually
bingo, under the guise of charity for a church or school, is an opening
wedge for the more professional types of gambling. But whether
gambling takes the form of bingo, raffles, lucky numbers, or the more
outright forms with dice, cards, or roulette, it surely is unworthy of a
Christian, who should always be ready to give a comparable value in
return for what he seeks.

The fact that the article may not be of great value, and that the
"chances" cost only a few cents each, does not change the principle involved, nor make it right to participate. The principle is the same and
the practice is sinful whether one gambles for thousands of dollars at
roulette or whether he participates in the raffle of a $1 box of candy for
"chances" sold at 5 cents each. Sin remains sin, whether committed
outside the church or inside. The righteous robes of religion do not cover
it up in the sight of God.

Historically, organized gambling has meant organized crime. Recently
a top federal prosecutor, Malcolm Anderson, assistant U. S. attorney

general in charge of the criminal division of the Justice Department, speaking before the National Association of Attorneys General, declared that gambling is the life blood of organized crime, and that if gambling could be wiped out syndicated crime would die for lack of sustenance. Organized gambling flourishes in a twilight zone of society where the muscle man is boss and where threats, coercion, and corruption are the methods of doing business. An evil atmosphere envelopes such a community and eats into the fabric of law and order. Bribery and corruption of officials with attendant social abuses is a common result. Yet the Roman Church, which receives substantial revenues from gambling games, has not only failed to oppose legalized gambling but frequently has itself run afoul of state anti-gambling laws. On the other hand Protestant groups, which believe that it is a sin to gamble, have taken the lead in a great many places and have succeeded in having bingo, and particularly professional gambling, outlawed. In the bingo-pinball devices commonly found in taverns, the millions of nickels flow into millions of dollars. Usually these devices return the tavern owners 50 percent of the take, and the operators greedily reach for the profits. So the foundation for the underworld is built.

Gambling is a violation of one of God's first commands to man: "In the sweat of thy face shalt thou eat bread" (Gen. 3:19). It is also a violation of other Scripture commands and of the general spirit of Scripture teaching: "Thou shalt not steal" (Ex. 20:15); "Thou shalt not covet" (Ex. 20:17); "Thou shalt love thy neighbor as thyself" (Matt. 19:19); "Wherefore do ye spend money for that which is not bread? and your labor for that which satisfieth not?" (Is. 55:2). "Whether therefore ye eat, or drink, or whatsoever ye do, do all to the glory of God" (I Cor. 10:31); etc.

The ideal constantly held before us in Scripture is that we should earn our property by honest labor and fair exchange. To try to give gambling an aura of respectability, and even a certain kind of spirituality through church sponsorship, is at once a sign of spiritual degeneration and of abysmal ignorance or deliberate disregard of what the Scriptures really teach.

In 1958 the state of New York legalized bingo by a constitutional amendment, primarily because of pressure brought to bear by the Roman Catholic Church and a few other groups. A news dispatch from Albany, New York, May 31, 1960, reported that New York residents had spent more than 40 million dollars playing bingo since the game was legalized. It added that the state lottery control commission reported that of that total, 29 million was returned to the players in the form of prizes and that the non-profit sponsoring organizations retained 9 million.

Bingo is illegal in Pennsylvania. Interestingly enough, the magazine,

Church and State, April, 1960, carried this report: "Philadelphia police have stepped up their campaign against bingo games in Roman Catholic churches. Latest to feel the hand of the law were St. Agatha's and Church of the Gesu. . . . St. Agatha's budget is $90,000 a year; $50,000 has come from bingo." Interesting, too, is the fact that Pennsylvania's long ban on legalized gambling was broken in December, 1959, when the Roman Catholic governor signed a bill which permitted betting on harness races, subject to county option. An outright ban on bingo-pinball in Ohio was upheld by the United States Supreme Court in 1958. And the United States Post Office Department has ruled that the game of bingo is a lottery and that as such it cannot be promoted through the mails. The mailing of periodicals or circulars containing advance notice of lotteries is banned under postal regulations. Postal officials have ruled that bingo has all the classic elements of a game of chance as set forth in the Supreme Court's lottery definition, and, though legal in some states, the state laws do not affect the federal laws under which the department operates.

If there ever was a travesty on the Christian religion it is that of a church raising money by encouraging its people to engage in a form of gambling. Such practice cannot give stability to a church, and the effect on its spiritual and educational program is bound to be detrimental. Morally it is no better than was the sale of indulgences during the Middle Ages, which was one of the religious corruptions that brought about the Protestant Reformation.

6. THE ROMAN CHURCH AND THE U. S. PRISON POPULATION

When we mention prison statistics it must be acknowledged, of course, that men and women in all denominations occasionally go wrong, that no denomination is above criticism, and that good and bad people are found in all denominations. There are, however, certain points of contrast between the Roman and the Protestant churches, points which, we believe, arise primarily because of their different moral codes.

Various studies indicate that of the white prison population Roman Catholics constitute a higher percentage than do those of any other church operating on the American scene, and that while the Roman Catholic percentage in the general population is about 22 percent, their percentage in the jails and penitentiaries and in juvenile delinquency is approximately twice that.

An examination of the crime records of any large city in the United States shows that the gangster type criminal turns out with surprising frequency to be Roman Catholic or to have a Roman Catholic background. The Annual Reports of the Commissioner of Correction of the State of New York, for the years 1940 through 1946, shows that a consistent 50 percent of the criminals committed to New York's two largest prisons, Sing Sing and Dannemora, year after year, were Roman Catholic, while the Roman Catholic population in the state was approximately 27 percent. An analysis of criminal records in Sing Sing, which was made by a Roman Catholic chaplain and published in the magazine *Commonweal*, December 14, 1932, revealed that of a total of 1581 prisoners no less than 855 were Roman Catholics.

Emmett McLoughlin says concerning his work in Phoenix, Arizona:

"As chaplain of the local jail, I was shocked at the percentage of Roman Catholics among the unwilling guests. Wondering if the same incidence prevailed in other jails and penitentiaries, I found a study written by a Franciscan, the Roman Catholic chaplain of Joliet Penitentiary in Illinois. He discovered that the Catholic percentage among prisoners in America is about twice their percentage in the total population.

"If the Roman Catholic Church is the mother of learning and of holiness, how could this be? Priests answer that these prisoners and gangsters do not represent *American* Catholicism but mostly Irish, Polish, Italian, Spanish, and Mexican—unfortunate immigrants from backward countries. This is the stock answer to the question of Roman Catholic crime and illiteracy in America. It will be found routinely in the 'question boxes' of the hierarchy's publications" (*People's Padre*, p. 86).

We would point out that the countries mentioned in the above paragraph are Roman Catholic countries par excellence, that for centuries they have been almost exclusively Roman Catholic, and that they are precisely the countries in which we expect to find the true fruits of Romanism.

Paul Blanshard, in another best seller, his well documented *American Freedom and Catholic Power*, says that the Roman Catholic Church as a denomination "has the highest proportion of white criminals in our American prisons of any denomination" (p. 105). And in a footnote he says:

"This has been established by many studies of crime and juvenile delinquency, but it would be wrong to say that Catholicism is primarily responsible. Poverty and bad housing affect the lives of Catholic workers as well as others in our large cities. . . . Catholic pre-eminence in the field of crime and juvenile delinquency is notable in our Northern cities, especially in New York. A study, *Crime and Religion*, by Father Leo Kalmer, Franciscan Herald Press, Chicago, 1936, showed that the rate of Catholic criminals committed to prisons in forty-eight states was about twice that of the Catholic proportion in the population. See Leo H. Lehmann, *The Catholic Church and Public Schools,* Agora Publishing Co. Bishop Gallagher of Detroit declared in 1936, according to *The New York Times* of December 8, 1936, 'It is a matter of serious reproach to the Church that more Catholic boys in proportion to the total number, get into trouble than those of any other denomination. One-fifth of the people of Michigan are Catholics, but 50 percent of the boys in the Industrial School for Boys at Lansing are Catholics.' "

The New York Times, March 13, 1947, published an amazing admission by bishop John F. Noll, of Fort Wayne, Indiana, as given before the National Catholic Conference on Family Life, in Chicago the previous day. In this "chastening" confession, as the *Times* called it, this crusading bishop of the Roman hierarchy acknowledged that, "Nearly all the evils of society prevail where we (Roman Catholics) live, and not where Protestants live," that Roman Catholics are concentrated largely in the big cities of America where they constitute from one-third to two-thirds of the population, while the rural communities "where family life is most wholesome," are "eighty percent Protestant." He said:

"There are only 7,000,000 members of Protestant churches in the fifty biggest cities of the country, but 20,000,000 Catholics. Eighty percent of Protestantism is rural. And it is in rural America where family life is most wholesome and where the divorce rate is still low. On the other hand, where the bulk of Catholics live, one-half of the marriages end in divorce. It is where they live that the big motion picture houses are located, the filthy magazine racks, the taverns and the gambling halls."

Arthur Tenorio, staff psychologist of the New Mexico Boy's School, reports that 85 percent of the boys committed to that institution are of Spanish-American background, and that 71 percent are Roman Catholics, while only 41 percent of the state's total population is Roman Catholic (*Christian Century,* Sept. 4, 1957).

In Britain *The Sunday Times* recently dealt with the subject of crime and its causes. An article declared frankly that, "In this country (England) Roman Catholics, who have the most intensive religious training, have also the highest delinquency rates." To support that statement it was pointed out that the proportion of Roman Catholics population-wise was no more than ten percent, but that the proportion in boys' Borstal institutions of correction was 23 percent, and in Holloway prison about 26 percent. It was further declared that during the war delinquency rates among Roman Catholics were approximately twice as high as among those of other faiths, and that in Scotland in 1957 the 15 percent of Roman Catholics in the population provided 35 percent of those committed to Borstal institutions, and 40 percent of those committed to prison.

Chief among the devices used by the Roman Catholic Church in its policy of isolating its youth from childhood contacts with non-Catholics is the parochial school. In order to justify in the eyes of Roman Catholics the necessity for supporting these "hothouses of Catholicism," as they have been appropriately called, the Roman hierarchy condemns as godless the public school system which makes no distinction of race or creed. Surely the above statistics are at one and the same time a cause for alarm and a grave indictment of Roman Catholic education. They should be seriously considered by the Protestant people of this nation who are constantly being called upon to provide more and more support, through taxation and government handouts, for these Roman schools. Here we have a church making pretentious and bigoted claims about being "the only true church," yet turning out a product that is responsible for approximately twice its proportionate share of juvenile delinquency and adult crime. Tolerant Americans would like to avoid this subject. No one likes to connect crime with a specific system of church training. Yet if it could be proved that crime is more prevalent, say, among the Presbyterians, or Baptists, or Methodists proportionately than among other religious groups, certainly the Roman Catholic authorities would not hesitate to point out that fact and to use it in justification of their church and their schools. But since the facts are so clear we should not hesitate to question the value of the parochial school, and to insist that the Roman Church must stand responsible for the influence that it exerts. And surely the above facts should make any open-minded Roman Catholic want to inquire more carefully into the real nature of his church and the effect that it is having on society at large.

We must point out that the *Mafia*, probably the most notorious of all crime organizations, had its origin hundreds of years ago in Italy where for centuries the Roman Catholic Church almost exclusively has provided the religious background. It originated in Sicily in the late thirteenth century, as a semi-vigilante, semi-patriotic organization, designed to free Italy from French rule. Its rallying cry was: "Death to the French is Italy's Cry!" In Italian the words were: Morte Alla Francia Italia Anela!, and the initials of these words spell MAFIA.

With the passage of time the Mafia became a secret criminal organization, preying on its own countrymen, specializing in murder, robbery, extortion, blackmail, and arson. It turned up in the United States as early as 1860, but not until the end of the century did it become a serious threat in this country. It found easy entrance because of the extremely lax immigration laws which made little effort to strain out criminal elements. It spread across the country from New York to California, being centered primarily in the big cities, working through organized gangs, and specializing in big money crime, such as narcotics, gambling, prostitution, bootlegging, murder, and robbery. In 1959 a book, *Brotherhood of Evil,* by Frederic Sondern, Jr., was published which goes into considerable detail concerning its origin, history, international workings, and recent activities.

The recent Senate crime investigation committee, headed by Senator McClellan, of Arkansas, and the earlier committee, headed by Senator Kefauver, of Tennessee, sought to show that the Mafia was the main support of organized crime in the United States. With a monotonous regularity the witnesses who were called for questioning turned out to be Italians of Roman Catholic background.

The underworld convention which met at Appalachin, New York, November 14, 1957, was alleged to have Mafia connections and resulted in an intense drive by law enforcement officials to suppress that organization. A lengthy editorial in *The Kansas City Times,* December 16, 1959, gave some interesting facts concerning that meeting. Among other things it said:

> "A singular fact about the 60 men surprised at what turned out to be the best publicized barbecue in history is that all were of Southern Italian birth and ancestry, most of them Sicilian . . . the royalty of the underworld. Chief among the Mafia leaders who gathered at Joe Barbara's $150,000 mountain top mansion that fateful November day was the recognized leader of vice and corruption in the United States, Vito Genovese, whose Mafia title is Don Vitone. As far back as 1939 he was dubbed 'King of the Rackets' by Thomas E. Dewey, former New York governor."

Emmett McLoughlin remarks concerning the attitude of the Roman Catholic Church toward the Mafia:

> "Its leaders, the cardinals and bishops, are conspicuously silent in the face of the Roman Catholic Sicilian Mafia's complete defiance of decency and morals in the promotion of prostitution, narcotics, gambling, and labor racketeering in America. The same bishops and archbishops who vociferously condemn a young Catholic girl for entering a beauty contest say nothing about the traffic in narcotics and whoredom so long as good Catholics run the business" (*American Culture and Catholic Schools,* p. 232; 1960; Lyle Stuart, publisher; New York).

Prominent with Mafia or similar gangland connections have been the very royalty of the underworld, such as Al Capone, Lucky Luciano, Joe

Adonia, Albert Anastasia, Frank Costello, Frank Scalise, and others. The fact stands out clearly that the worst criminal element that we have received from any nation during the past several decades has come from Italy, and that the religious background of those men has been Roman Catholic. We have never had a comparable group from England, or Scotland, or Holland, or any other Protestant nation. Another editorial in *The Kansas City Times* made this comment:

> "In the last 15 years nearly a thousand Italian-born 'unwanteds' have been shipped back to their native land since the attorney general undertook to rid the United States of dope peddlers and an endless variety of thugs associated with the Mafia" (Sept. 25, 1959).

Supporting this contention that in hundreds of years with practically no Protestant competition Roman Catholicism has failed to raise the moral and spiritual standards of the Italian nation is the testimony of Stephen L. Testa, himself a former Roman Catholic of Italian birth. He says:

> "We see that in a population 96% Roman Catholic, the percentage of crime and illiteracy is very high. In Naples, for instance, filthy language, blasphemy, cursing and lying is very prevalent among the populace, and so is drinking, gambling, thieving and low morals. Yet they attend mass, go to confession, wear scapulars and religious medals around their necks and pray to images in their homes. The Church has had them for hundreds of years and it has not benefited them in the least. On the other hand those who are converted to Protestantism immediately abandon those vices and sins and live cleaner lives. They are completely changed, they are 'born again,' and are new creatures in Christ. The idea of salvation is different in the two religions" (Booklet, *The Truth About Catholics, Protestants and Jews*, p. 31).

Another series of events to which we must call attention, which surely cannot be pure coincidence, is that of the assassination of three presidents of the United States, all three of whom were killed by Roman Catholics educated in parochial schools: Lincoln, by John Wilkes Booth; Garfield, by Charles J. Guiteau; and McKinley, by Leon Czolgosz. Theodore Roosevelt was shot and wounded by a Roman Catholic in Milwaukee, while a candidate for president in 1912. In Florida a Roman Catholic shot at Franklin Roosevelt, then president elect, missed him but killed the mayor of Chicago who was riding beside him in the same car. Two Roman Catholics, Griselio Torresola and Oscar Collazo, Puerto Rican Nationalist party members, tried to kill Harry Truman in a shooting fray at Blair House, in Washington, D. C., while Truman was president (1950), and did kill one of his guards. Torresola was killed and Collazo is now serving a life term in Leavenworth penitentiary. And in 1954 Roman Catholic members of the Puerto Rican Nationalist party, in a wild shooting fray in the House of Representatives, attempted to kill members of that body and wounded five congressmen.

The Roman Catholic Church, of course, had no connection with the Mafia or its activities, nor with the actions of the others mentioned here. But as the system that almost exclusively provided the religious background out of which those men came, it bears a heavy responsibility and must be judged accordingly.

7. QUESTIONABLE HOSPITAL PRACTICES

A Roman Catholic hospital practice which very definitely has a moral aspect to it is that of baptizing Protestants and others who are thought to be in danger of death. An article by Fr. John R. Connery, S. J., in *Hospital Progress* (April, 1959), which magazine carries on its front cover the words, "Official Journal of the Catholic Hospital Association," sets forth in considerable detail the procedure to be followed by the chaplain or nurse in such cases. According to this article it is proper, and in some cases even mandatory, to baptize into the Roman Church, and even without their knowledge or consent, unbaptized persons or patients concerning whom it is not known whether they have been baptized or not, if they are thought to be in danger of death. The patient need not be actually dying, but perhaps unconscious or so critically ill that death is a possibility. This practice applies particularly to new born babes and to unconscious or critically ill persons if their parents or relatives are not available for consultation. Information concerning the baptism need not be given to anyone other than the local priest who records it. In this article we read:

> "Q. Are you obliged to tell the parents of an infant baptized in danger of death, if the parents are not Catholics? What if the parents resent it and refuse to raise the child a Catholic?"
>
> "A. Ordinarily it is not permitted to baptize children of non-Catholic parents against their wishes. To do so would be to violate the rights of these parents. . . . When there is danger of death, however, the Church makes an exception, although even in this emergency primary responsibility for the child's spiritual welfare belongs to the parents. . . . It is only when the parents, through neglect or for reasons of their own, fail to provide for the baptism of the child, or when the emergency does not allow even sufficient time to warn the parents, that the Church permits a

Catholic minister to baptize the child. In this case the Church's concern over the future religious education of the child . . . yields to the child's immediate spiritual need. Similarly *the wishes of parents must give way in these circumstances* to the child's own right to the means of salvation. *It will be permissible to baptize the child even without the knowledge or permission of the parents.* . . . If a child in these circumstances lives through the emergency, the question arises about the advisability of informing the parents of the baptism. . . . We can say that it would not be necessary, or even advisable, to acquaint non-Catholic parents with the fact that their child had received an emergency baptism unless there is good reason to believe that they would not resent it" (italics ours).

In regard to unconscious adults who are baptized Fr. Connery writes:

"In most cases it will not be advisable to acquaint the person with the fact that he was baptized unless it becomes clear that he would have wanted baptism under the circumstances."

He goes on to say that those baptized become members of the Roman Catholic Church and that if children they should be trained as Catholics, but that it will not be wise to insist upon it if the parents do not agree, because resentment might be aroused against the church. He defends such baptism by saying that in any event it will not hurt anything, and that in some cases it might prove helpful, as for instance if the person married before a Protestant minister later was converted to Catholicism and wanted to get an annulment in order to marry a Roman Catholic. In such an event the first marriage would be held invalid.

This forced and secret baptism of the helpless—"baptism by stealth," as some have called it—is justified by the Romanists on the basis of their doctrine that there is no hope of salvation for one who has not been baptized.

There are nearly 1000 Roman Catholic hospitals in the United States. Most of the patients in these hospitals are not Catholics, yet their treatment is governed by the Roman Catholic code of ethics in which the doctors and nurses are minutely instructed. Those instructions are set forth in detail by the Jesuit scholar, Father Henry Davis, in his *Moral and Pastoral Theology,* and by Father Patrick A. Finney, in his *Moral Problems in Hospital Practice* (1947 ed., imprimatur by the archbishop of St. Louis). Concerning one particular phase of that code Paul Blanshard, in his *American Freedom and Catholic Power,* says:

"One of the most important doctrines in the Catholic medical code is the doctrine of the equality of mother and fetus. This doctrine is of special interest to every potential mother who has a Catholic physician.

"When the average American woman approaches the ordeal of child-bearing, she takes it for granted that her physician will do everything possible to save her life in the event of complications. I am sure that 99 percent of all American husbands would consider themselves murderers if, confronted with the choice between the life of a wife and the life of her unborn child, they chose the life of the fetus. This is particularly true in the early months of pregnancy when such risks most frequently develop. Most of our citizens assume without discussion that every possible effort should be made to save the life of both mother and child, but that if a choice is forced upon the physician the mother should be given first consideration.

"The Catholic hierarchy does not endorse this choice, nor can a good Catholic physician leave such a choice to the husband and father and be true to the dogmas of his church. 'The life of each is equally sacred,' said pope Pius XI in his encyclical, *Casti Connubii*, 'and no one has the power, not even the public authority, to destroy it' " (pp. 139, 140).

Father Finney, in the book just mentioned, states the doctrine in question and answer form:

"If it is morally certain that a pregnant mother and her unborn child will both die, if the pregnancy is allowed to take its course, but at the same time, the attending physician is morally certain that he can save the mother's life by removing the inviable fetus, is it lawful for him to do so?"

Answer. "No, it is not. Such removal of the fetus would be direct abortion."

Mr. Blanshard remarks:

"It should be noted that under this statement of the complete doctrine, *both* mother and child must be allowed to die rather than allow a life-saving operation that is contrary to the code of the priests. There is no choice here between one life and another; it is a choice between two deaths and one. The priests choose the two deaths, presumably in order to save the souls of both mother and child from a sin that would send the mother's soul to hell and the child's to the twilight hereafter known as limbo. The fetus in Father Finney's question would die anyway. It is described as 'inviable,' which means incapable of life. It may be a six-weeks embryo about the size of a small marble, without a face. Nevertheless, the life of the mother must be sacrificed for this embryo that, by definition, is dying or will die.

"This doctrine is not a matter of opinion that priests or doctors are free to reject. It has been repeated over and over by Catholic authorities and incorporated into positive church law. Pope Pius XII reiterated the doctrine before the International College of Surgeons in Rome in May, 1948, when he declared that in spite of 'the understandable anguish of husbandly love' it is 'illicit—even in order to save the mother—to cause directly the death of the small being that is called, if not for the life here below, then at least for the future life, to a high and sublime destiny.' " (pp. 141).

Such practices we consider reprehensible. And yet about eighty percent of all federal funds being given to non-profit hospitals are going to Roman Catholic hospitals. The code of ethics under which those hospitals operate is not that of the laws of the United States of America, nor of the states in which they are located, nor the code of the American Medical Association, but that of the Roman Catholic Church. Surely Protestants and others should not enter Roman Catholic hospitals if they can avoid it.

We have been struck repeatedly throughout the study of this religion, the basic policies of which have been formulated almost 100 percent by celibate priests, with the various phases of it which inflict such callous, inhuman, even brutal treatment upon women. That has come out in the abuses practiced in the confessional, the enslavement of women as nuns, the exclusion of women from any policy making function in the church, the almost complete lack of educational facilities for women in Roman Catholic countries, and again here in regard to hospital practice. This trait Roman Catholicism has in common with Mormonism, Buddhism, Hinduism, and Mohammedanism. Each of these, as the present writer once heard a guide in the Mormon tabernacle in Salt Lake City, Utah, explain concerning Mormonism, is a "man's religion." How utterly unchristian such practices are!

8.   CONCLUSION

L. H. Lehmann, in his booklet, *The Secret of Catholic Power,* shows why the Roman Church often is able to exert an influence far beyond that of its actual numbers. He says:

"As a system of power, the Roman Catholic Church has no equal and is likely to retain its influence as long as mankind remains spiritually unregenerate. For its entire structure is geared to an earthly, human realism that is admirably suited to the weakness of human nature. It possesses elements of power that are strictly empirical and tangible, of the kind that weigh far more with the multitudes than logical arguments or spiritual insight. On the one hand, it gains all the advantages accorded to religion, and on the other, all the benefits, profits, and power that accrue to political and business organizations.

"These elements of power appeal not only to the Catholic Church's own membership, but even more so to the great mass of people outside its membership who have little or no interest in any particular religion. This fact in itself constitutes an element of power that is more effective than all the others combined. It explains why a country such as the United States, whose population is fully 80 percent non-Catholic, is controlled to such a great extent by the Catholic Church which claims the direct obedience of less than 20 percent of its inhabitants.

"Neither in Protestant countries such as the United States, nor in so-called Catholic countries such as Italy, Spain, France, Portugal and South America, does the Catholic Church derive its power from the actual numbers of devout church-going Catholics in good standing. This is small compared to the number of its mere *adherents* who though baptized in the Catholic Church fail to live up to its requirements of actual membership or 'communion' as understood by Protestant bodies. It is much smaller still compared to the vast number of unchurched people who admire it at a distance and are influenced, willy-nilly, by its political power, by its control of the press, movies, and radio, by its pageantry and grandeur, and, above all, *by its moral code*. Italy, Spain, France, Portugal, and the Latin American countries are regarded as almost 100 percent Roman Catholic and their destinies are tied to the Catholic Church's social, cultural, and moral code. Yet, only about one-fifth of the Italian population are devout, church-going Catholics; in France only about 17 percent are practicing Catholics; and were it not for Franco's forced application of the Catholic Church laws and decrees, the percentage in Spain would be even less. Cardinal Spellman confessed in his *Letters to My Father*, written in 1944 during his visits to Italy, Spain and other countries, that at a dinner with high prelates at the Nunciature in Madrid, he remembered the 'striking and terrifying remark' of a friend who was an authority on Spain that: *'Twenty-four hours of disorder in Spain could mean the assassination of every bishop, priest and nun that could be found.'*"

But, granted that the situation outlined by Mr. Lehmann is true, and we believe that it is, what is the remedy? How are Protestants to meet the challenge of Roman Catholicism? The solution, of course, is for Protestants to take their religion seriously, to work for it, propagate it, and so to evangelize effectively their own communities and eventually the world, as they are capable of doing with the true Gospel in their possession. Christ's command to His church was: "Go ye therefore, and make disciples of all the nations. . . ." (Matt. 28:19-20). That Romanism has flourished so luxuriously, and that it is to a large extent unopposed in many places, is due primarily not to Romanist strength but to Protestant indifference, as Modernism and Liberalism have weakened the churches and some of them have lost their evangelical witness.

However, there are some encouraging signs. The Roman Church has lost its grip on many of the traditionally Roman Catholic countries of Europe, and in those where it still has control it is hanging on by means of the artificial respiration of United States dollars. Various degrees of anti-clericalism are manifesting themselves in France and Italy, and in Spain the Roman Church retains control only through the support of a fascist political dictatorship. In Latin America it has lost the support of the laboring classes and also of the educated classes, and probably can claim the support of not more than 15 percent of the people.

On the other hand, in the United States the Roman Church has increased its power significantly. It is an ironic turn of events that as other countries are throwing off the yoke of Rome, this "Land of the Free" is crawling under that yoke almost without a murmur. This has been a most fortunate break for the Vatican, and has enabled it to maintain far more strength in other countries than otherwise would have been possible. Its financial support from the United States has been enormous. To what extent it has gained control in the United States is difficult to estimate. But it clearly has made extensive gains not only in the political realm but also through its indirect pressure group control of our press, radio, television, and movies. Many of our biggest cities are so firmly controlled by Roman Catholic political machines that it is practically impossible for a Protestant to be elected mayor, e.g., New York, Chicago, Boston, San Francisco, and others. In some places the Roman Church is now the *de facto,* if not the *de jure,* ruler of this country.

When Protestantism fails there is one other source of relief, howbeit, a long-range and a very unpleasant one, namely, that *Roman Catholicism carries within itself the seeds of its own destruction.* It is a false system, and therefore it cannot ultimately succeed any more than can Nazism, or Fascism, or Communism, or any of the pagan religions. But like those systems it can deceive millions, and it can cause untold misery and destruction while it does hold sway.

Where Romanism becomes the dominant religion for generations, poverty and illiteracy become the rule, and private and public morals become a scandal. Eventually there comes a reaction. In Latin America today, for instance, we see such a reaction taking place. Weakened by the moral and spiritual condition of its clergy, and by the ignorance, superstition, poverty, and lethargy of its people, the Roman Church becomes an easy prey to its enemies, foremost of which is Communism. The Roman hierarchy has just recently waked up to the fact that it must clean up the church in Latin America or lose the whole area.

Such reactions as we are talking about have occurred ,in England,

France, Spain, Mexico, and other countries, in which the people eventually rose up and disestablished or even abolished this misnamed Holy Roman Catholic Church. What a tragedy that a professedly Christian church should so degenerate that public opinion would hold it in contempt! The great rebellion that occurred against the Roman Church at the time of the Protestant Reformation in the 16th century, when in disgust and hatred for the old system the people rose up and more or less *en masse* threw it out of whole countries, was such a reaction. It is to be noted that a popular uprising against Protestantism has never occurred in any of those countries; for Protestantism does not enslave, but liberates and enlightens the people.

XVIII. INTOLERANCE—
BIGOTRY—PERSECUTION

1. "The Only True Church." 2. Roman Catholic Intolerance. 3. Freedom of Conscience. 4. Bigotry. 5. Persecution. 6. Present Day Spain. 7. Italy; Yugoslavia. 8. Latin America. 9. Contrast Between the British-American and the Southern European-Latin American Culture.

1. "THE ONLY TRUE CHURCH"

We have had occasion through the earlier chapters of this book to cite numerous cases of Roman Catholic intolerance in practice, and we shall have occasion to cite others. In this section we cite examples as set forth in the official creeds and authoritative statements of church leaders.

The most authoritative of all Roman Catholic creedal statements is that of the Council of Trent. Concerning the pope it declares: "He hath all power on earth. . . . All temporal power is his; the dominion, jurisdiction, and government of the whole earth is his by divine right. All rulers of the earth are his subjects and must submit to him."

The 14th article of the Creed of pope Pius IV, which is an abbreviated form of the Creed of the Council of Trent, refers to what it terms, "This true Catholic faith, out of which none can be saved."

"Heretics may be not only excommunicated, but also justly put to death" (Catholic Encyclopedia, Vol. XIV, p. 768).

"Protestantism of every form has not, and never can have, any rights where Catholicity is triumphant" (Bronson's Review).

"Non-Catholic methods of worshipping God must be branded counterfeit" (*Living Our Faith*, by Flynn, Loretto, and Simon; a widely used high school textbook; p. 247).

"In themselves all forms of Protestantism are unjustified. They should not exist" (*America*, January 4, 1941).

The Baltimore Cathechism, after declaring that the four marks by which the church can be known are, that it is one, that it is holy, that it

407

is Catholic, and that it is apostolic, asks: "In which Church are these marks found?" (Question 133), and it answers: "These attributes and marks are found in the Holy Roman Catholic Church alone."

Pope Boniface VIII made the claim: "We declare it to be altogether necessary to salvation that every human creature should be subject to the Roman Pontiff."

The late pope Pius XII had the impudence to tell an American audience in a radio broadcast that the pope in Rome is "the only one authorized to act and teach for God." In 1953 he declared that, "What is not in accord with truth (i.e., Roman Catholicism) has objectively no right of existence, propagation, or action."

Pope John XXIII, the Second, was no sooner inaugurated in November, 1958, than in his coronation address he gave expression to the same sentiment. Speaking of the "fold" of Jesus Christ, by which is meant the company of the saved, he said: "Into this fold of Jesus Christ no one can enter if not under the guidance of the Sovereign Pontiff; and men can securely reach salvation only when they are united with him, since the Roman Pontiff is the Vicar of Christ and represents His person on this earth."

We have already cited arrogant and intolerant statements from the Syllabus of Errors of pope Pius IX.

The following excerpts in a similar vein are taken from the more than 500 items compiled by Raywood Frazier in his book, *Catholic Words and Actions*, all documented and based on writings approved by the Roman Catholic Church or on statements of Roman Catholics in positions of authority:

"The true (Roman Catholic) Church can tolerate no strange churches besides herself" (*Catholic Encyclopedia*, Vol. XIV, p. 766).

"The Roman Catholic Church . . . must demand the right of freedom for herself alone (*Civilta Cattolica*, April, 1948; official Jesuit organ; Rome).

"The pope has the right to pronounce sentence of deposition against any sovereign" (*Bronson's Review*, Vol. I, p. 48).

"We declare, say, define, and pronounce that every being should be subject to the Roman Pontiff" (Pope Boniface VIII; Catholic Encyclopedia, Vol. XV, p. 126).

"No Catholic may positively and unconditionally approve of the separation of church and state" (Msgr. O'Toole, Catholic University of America, 1939).

"The pope is the supreme judge, even of civil laws, and is incapable of being under any true obligation to them" (*Civilta Cattolica*).

"Individual liberty in reality is only a deadly anarchy" (Pope Pius XII; April 6, 1951).

"All Catholics, therefore, are bound to accept the Syllabus (of Errors, of pope Pius IX)" (Catholic Encyclopedia, Vol. 14).

These claims are precise and clear. The official doctrine of the Roman Catholic Church, therefore, is that it alone is the true church, that all other churches and religious groups are in error, either heretical or pagan, and that such churches and groups have not even the right of existence. Without hesitation it consigns them to perdition. Truly Romanism, like Diotrephes, "loveth to have the pre-eminence" (III John 9). In sharp contrast with that teaching and practice, no Protestant church holds that it is the only way of salvation. Protestants hold rather—and they find this teaching written clearly in the Bible—that all who accept Christ as their personal Saviour, all who obey and worship Him as Lord and Master, will be saved, regardless of what church they belong to. To hold that only those who belong to a particular group can be saved, and only because they belong to that group, marks that group as merely a sect. For a sect, in the strict sense of the term, is a group that cuts itself off from the main stream of Christianity, a group which attempts to shut itself in as the Lord's people, while shutting all others out. Such practice reveals, in the first place, a narrow-minded attitude, and in the second place, an inexcusable ignorance of what the Bible really teaches.

It is from that false premise, that the Roman Church is the only true church, that the well-known Roman Catholic intolerance logically springs. If Rome is the only true church, then it automatically becomes her duty to suppress and destroy all other churches which, not being true churches, are, of course, false churches. In order to accomplish that purpose she invariably seeks a union of church and state, in order that she may use the power of the state to that end. And any government to which the Roman Church becomes legally joined, through a concordat or otherwise, is inevitably led into that course of action. Throughout the centuries that has been the method employed by the Roman Church in her efforts to destroy Protestantism.

Freedom of religion logically involves separation of church and state. Such separation precludes the state from making concordats or treaties of any kind with the Vatican or any other spiritual power. But Rome does not like that limitation, nor does she like being treated as an equal among the various churches. During the Middle Ages she was mistress of most of Europe through her alliances with and control over civil governments; and she maintained that position for centuries, suppressing all opposition, usually with the help of the civil authorities. Yet she failed utterly to Christianize those lands. Instead that unchristian monopoly produced the "Dark Ages" when ignorance, superstition, illiteracy, and immorality reached their worst state.

2. ROMAN CATHOLIC INTOLERANCE

The practice followed by the Roman Catholic Church in the countries where it has been in power confirms that it means what it says in the statements just quoted. We need only look at the countries of southern Europe and Latin America where Rome has had control to see what will happen in the United States if she gains control here. In this country where Protestantism is dominant Roman Catholics enjoy all the advantages of freedom of religion. But in countries where they have control they limit or prohibit any religion other than their own. In various countries today it is practically impossible for the dissenter to hold public office, or to practice his profession, or even to secure employment unless he gives some allegiance to the Roman Church. He has to pay taxes to support a creed in which he does not believe. If he is a member of the Roman Church and leaves it, he is likely to find himself discriminated against at every turn. Under such conditions he becomes a second class citizen. True religious freedom includes *the right to change one's religion,* as well as the right to practice it—a right which Roman Catholics themselves insist upon as they seek to make converts in Protestant countries.

The apostle Paul said: "If any man hath not the Spirit of Christ, he is none of his" (Rom. 8:9). And the Lord Jesus was kind, loving, and peaceful, even to sinners. He never persecuted anyone, not even those who were in error. But the arrogant Roman Church, with the blood of the Inquisition on its hands, unrepentant and defiant, presumes to set itself up as the final authority in the realm of faith and morals, and has cruelly slaughtered tens of thousands and has persecuted millions of others merely because they did not submit to its domination.

It is interesting to notice the difference between the Roman Catholic and the Protestant definition of the term "heresy." For Protestants it means something contrary to what the Bible teaches, while for Roman Catholics it means lack of conformity to the practice of the Roman Church—which may be something quite different. Roman Catholics, for instance, are forbidden to attend "heretical" services, that is, services in any other church. Thus a Catholic cannot take part in a Protestant service without committing a mortal sin and so offending the hierarchy! And having committed such a sin he would be bound to go to a priest, confess his sin, promise not to repeat the offense, and receive a penance by way of punishment.

In free Protestant America the Roman Catholics have the right freely to preach their beliefs and to promote their church. They receive the full privileges of tax exemption for their churches, schools, and other properties on precisely the same basis as do Protestants. But they are frank to tell us that if ever the tables are turned and they become the dominant power things will be different. They will deny us the privilege of preaching the Gospel according to what we believe, and they will deny tax exemption to our churches. A frank statement of their attitude toward other churches—as frank as Marx's *Communist Manifesto* against capitalistic nations, or Hitler's *Mein Kampf* against the German Republic—is found in the official Jesuit organ, *Civilta Cattolica*, published in Rome. This journal enjoys high prestige among church scholars, and is known to be close to the pope. It is, therefore, one of the most authoritative of all Roman Catholic sources. Listen to these words:

"The Roman Catholic Church, convinced through its divine prerogatives, of being the only true church, must demand the right of freedom for herself alone, because such a right can only be possessed by truth, never by error. As for other religions, the Church will certainly never draw the sword, but she will require that by legitimate means they shall not be allowed to propagate false doctrine. Consequently, in a state where the majority of people are Catholic, the Church will require that legal existence be denied to error, and that if religious minorities actually exist, they shall have only a *de facto* existence without opportunity to spread their beliefs. . . . In some countries Catholics will be obliged to ask full religious freedom for all, resigned at being forced to cohabit where they alone should rightfully be allowed to live. But in doing this the Church does not renounce her thesis which remains the most imperative of her laws, but merely adapts herself to *de facto* conditions which must be taken into account in practical affairs. . . . The Church cannot blush for her own want of tolerance as she asserts it in principle and applies it in practice" (April, 1948).

This is the "classic" Roman Catholic position in regard to religious liberty. It is echoed by numerous other sources. Msgr. Francis J. Connell, whom we have referred to as the highest ranking Roman Catholic theologian in the United States, says:

"We believe that the rulers of a Catholic country have the right to restrict the activity of those who would lead their people away from their allegiance to the Catholic Church. . . . They possess the right to prevent propaganda against the Church. This is merely a logical conclusion from the basic Catholic tenet that the Son of God established one religion and commanded all men to accept it under pain of eternal damnation" (*American Ecclesiastical Review*, January, 1946).

At the college and seminary level a textbook with Imprimatur by archbishop (now cardinal) Francis J. Spellman, after saying that the state should acknowledge and support the Roman Catholic religion to the exclusion of all others, has this to say concerning religious toleration:

"Does State recognition of the Catholic religion necessarily imply that no other religion should be tolerated? Much depends upon circumstances and much depends upon what is meant by toleration. Neither unbaptized persons nor those born into a non-Catholic sect should ever be coerced into the Catholic Church. This would be fundamentally irrational, for belief depends upon the will and the will is not subject to physical compulsion. Should such persons be permitted to practice their own form of worship? If these are carried out within the family, or in such an inconspicuous manner as to be an occasion neither for scandal nor of perversion of the faithful, they may properly be tolerated by the State. . . . Their participation in false worship does not necessarily imply a willful affront to the true Church nor a menace to public order or social welfare. In a Catholic State which protects and favors the Catholic religion whose citizens are in great majority adherents of the true faith, the religious performances of an insignificant and ostracized sect will constitute neither a scandal nor an occasion of perversion to Catholics. Hence there exists no sufficient reason to justify the State in restricting the liberty of individuals.

"Quite distinct from the performance of false religious worship and preaching to the members of the erring sect is the propagation of the false doctrine among Catholics. This could become a source of injury, a positive menace, to the religious welfare of true believers. Against such an evil they have a right of protection of the Catholic State. On the one hand, this propaganda is harmful to the citizens and contrary to public welfare; on the other hand, it is not among the natural rights of the propagandists. Rights are merely means to rational ends. Since no rational end is promoted by the dissemination of false doctrine, there exists no right to indulge in this practice" (p. 317; from *Catholic Principles of Politics*, by John A. Ryan and Francis J. Boland. Copyright 1940, by The National Catholic Welfare Conference. Used by permission of The Macmillan Company).

Professors Ryan and Boland, after noting that at present the Constitution of the United States guarantees freedom of religion, make this statement (cited previously, *re.* schools):

"Suppose that the constitutional obstacle to proscription of non-Catholics has been legitimately removed and they themselves have become numerically insignificant: what then would be the proper course of action for a Catholic State? Apparently, the latter State could logically tolerate only such religious activities as were confined to the members of the dissenting group. It could not permit them to carry on general propaganda nor accord their organization certain privileges that had formerly been extended to all religious corporations, for example, exemption from taxation" (p. 320).

Here the method of dealing with the problem of religious liberty in the event that the Roman Catholic Church becomes the dominant power in the United States is that of changing the Constitution so that every word about religious liberty is wiped out! The writers then ask what protection Protestants would have against the Roman Catholic state, and go on to say that they would have none at all. They say that dissenting churches would lose their exemption from taxation, while the Roman Catholic Church would retain such exemption. They also say that the Roman Catholic state could logically tolerate only such religious activities as were confined to the members of the dissenting group— which means that no public meeting of any Protestant church would be allowed. The only meetings tolerated would be those of the members held in private. Under such an arrangement the church would die of strangulation. Ryan's and Boland's assurance that they are talking about an idealized Roman Catholic state which presumably is some considerable distance in the future, and that Protestants therefore need not worry for a long time to come, is completely worthless, and even frivolous. Actually what they are saying is that Protestants need not worry until it is too late to worry.

Ryan's and Boland's comment, of course, is not merely a personal one, but one that is in harmony with the general tenor of Roman Catholic thinking. We might point out in behalf of Protestantism that during the economic emergency that has existed in so many countries following the Second World War, this nation has distributed much food and other supplies freely among needy nations without discriminating against religious beliefs, and that in numerous instances Roman Catholic relief agencies in those countries have distributed those supplies as if they were gifts from the Roman Catholics of the United States. No such acts of friendship and generosity were ever extended by a Roman Catholic nation to a Protestant nation in the entire course of world history, and we can be sure that they never will be. But how utterly devoid of any sense of gratitude and fair play Romanism is toward Protestantism! What Ryan and Boland threaten is indeed the kind of treatment that we can expect from the Roman Church after having nurtured it in our free land—if and when it becomes dominant. Protestants at least have had fair warning, for these things have not been plotted in secret, but published openly and taught in the schools.

Rome still follows the policy set forth by the French Roman Catholic writer, Louis Veuillot, who said to a group of Protestants:

> "When you are in a majority we ask for religious liberty in the name of your principles. When we are in a majority we refuse it to you in the name of ours."

There is in this regard a close parallel between the Roman Catholic demand for full religious freedom in the United States so that they can build their church and lay the groundwork for the destruction of religious liberty, and that of the Communists as they claim the protection of our Constitution and demand full civil liberties while building a system which if successful will destroy ours. This land still is predominantly Protestant and free. But if we are indifferent we can lose all of our freedoms, either to a totalitarian church or a totalitarian state.

We know that today Rome is seeking by every means at her disposal to "Make America Catholic"—that is her motto—and thus to eliminate the world's stronghold of Protestantism. But for many centuries the Roman Church had a monopoly in Europe, and the results were deplorable. In the countries that she controls she continues to fail to raise either the religious or the social standards of the people. Almost invariably monopoly is bad, whether in religion, business, manufacturing, labor unions, or government. And an ecclesiastical monopoly is worst of all. There is too much greed in the human heart and too much pride in the human mind, for any such system to work, whether in the church or in the state.

In Protestant countries the Roman Church hides her true character. When confronted by an alert and watchful Protestantism she becomes reasonably tolerant. She establishes schools, hospitals, orphanages, and at times even holds out a fraternal hand to those of differing views. In many an American town or village the Roman Church seems much like any Protestant church. The priest is friendly, as also are the people, and there is little outward difference between them and their Protestant neighbors. The Roman Catholic people in such communities are for the most part perfectly sincere, sharing in general the American ideals of freedom and liberty. Occasionally a local priest, or even a leader of prominence, makes a high-minded pronouncement on the subject of religious liberty—as even cardinal Spellman has done on occasions. Many Protestants have been deceived by such semblances of charity. But as the Roman Church gains strength the priests invariably indoctrinate their people with a more aggressive attitude, and they begin to place restrictions on Protestantism and to outlaw it as far as possible. Those who want to know what Roman Catholicism *really* is should look at the clerical system that it has developed in those countries where it has control, not at the restrained, half-Protestant and comparatively mild form that is found in many American communities.

American Roman Catholics, like their fellow church members in all other parts of the world, belong to a completely totalitarian church. Policy in their church is not made at the local level or national level, but at the top, in Rome. The people are not consulted; they are told. We had that brought to our attention quite forcibly in the 1960 election when the Roman Catholic people of Puerto Rico were threatened with excommunication if they did not follow the political advice of the hierarchy. When in deference to popular opinion American priests and bishops sometimes express themselves as favoring religious freedom and toleration, they do not speak for anyone—not even for themselves. They are allowed to proceed on a certain course as long as that seems expedient; but when the appropriate time comes Rome issues an official policy statement and that settles the matter.

While the Roman Church manifests a degree of good will and tolerance in the United States, her real nature is revealed in the cruelties and intolerance that she practices on those of other faiths in countries where she is dominant—at the present time most clearly seen in Spain and Colombia. The pope could stop the persecutions and abuses in those lands at once if he wanted to do so. Let it be remembered by all Americans that no matter how friendly individual Roman Catholics are now, once their church gains control even the laymen will have to change their attitude. They will not be permitted to mingle freely with Protestants and be cooperative and friendly. This deceptive pose, not primarily on the part of the people but on the part of the hierarchy, is what makes that church so dangerous. Such diverse behavior is based not on the teaching of Scripture nor on principle, but on expediency and Canon Law. It should arouse only disgust and resentment on the part of all informed people.

The famous British historian, James Anthony Froude, analyzed the character of Romanism well when he wrote:

"Where it has been in power, the Church of Rome has shown its real colors. . . . In Protestant countries where it is in opposition, it wears the similitude of an angel. It is energetic and devoted; it avoids scandal; it appeals for toleration, and, therefore, pretends to be tolerant. Elsewhere it has killed the very spirit of religion, and those who break from it believe nothing."

Most American Roman Catholic writers seek to point to some sources of religious freedom within Roman Catholicism. Almost invariably they mention the Religious Toleration Act of Maryland as an event contributing to the establishment of religious freedom in America. They are fond of pointing out that Maryland was established with a Roman Catholic majority and that its legislature passed the act just mentioned. But the passage of that act becomes rather amusing when we remember that Roman Catholicism in Maryland was at that time only a small island in a sea of Protestantism, and that most of the colonists having come to America to escape religious persecution in the various European countries were strongly opposed to any church controlled state. It is, after all, standard Roman procedure to speak up for religious toleration when they are in the minority, and to deny it when they are in the majority. Furthermore, the Maryland colony, which was founded in 1634 under Roman Catholic sponsorship, soon lost that distinction; for after 1691 the Protestants were in the majority. At the time of the American Revolution the Roman Catholics numbered only about two percent of the population of the thirteen colonies.

A further consequence of Roman Catholic intolerance in the European countries was that it alienated the Jews and turned them strongly against Christianity. Nearly all evangelistic work among the Jews has been done by Protestants. Rome has avoided the really hard mission work of the world, that among the Mohammedans and among the Jews. For 1200 years the Roman Church persecuted the Jews, so that they came to look upon Christians as their natural enemies. On different occasions the Jews were forced to flee from Rome, and one of the most cruel persecutions came in Spain at the time of the Inquisition. In some countries they had to live in ghettos, and sometimes had to wear hated yellow identification badges. Many occupations were closed to them. Often they were denied education. Because the Roman Church was for so long dominant in Europe, the average Jew doesn't differentiate between the different branches of Christianity. To him even yet *Romanism is Christianity*, and he therefore is quite sure that Christianity is anti-Semitic. Because of that past record the cause of Jewish evangelism suffers an historic handicap. The persecutions are not easily forgotten.

3. FREEDOM OF CONSCIENCE

The First Amendment to the Constitution reads:

"Congress shall make no laws respecting the establishment of religion, or prohibiting the free exercise thereof; or abridging the freedom of speech, or of the press; or the right of the people peacefully to assemble."

What a sharp contrast there is between these sentiments and the categorical statement of pope Leo XIII (1903) in *Libertas* that,

"It is not lawful to demand, to defend, or to grant unconditional freedom of thought, or speech, or writing, or religion, as if these were so many rights given by nature to man."

Persecution of those who conscientiously differ with us is so out of harmony with Protestant ideals that we can scarcely realize the vigor with which that practice, together with that of excommunication and the interdict, was carried out by the Roman Church in former ages. Yet so bowed down were the people and nations during the Middle Ages that usually little more than the mere threat of such action was required for the church to secure whatever obedience or property it wanted.

Freedom of religion, as we have indicated earlier, must include the right to change one's religion. The United Nations Charter of Human Rights has quite properly insisted upon this, even in the face of strong opposition from Romanist countries. The right of private judgment is one of the most precious benefits that we have received from the Protestant Reformation. Even in Protestant states which have established churches, as in Sweden, for instance, where all the people are supposed to belong to the Lutheran Church, anyone who wants to withdraw can do so merely by stating his desire to that effect. That is the sensible course to follow, for certainly the person knows his own mind better than does anyone else. No priest or governmental official should attempt to make that decision for him. And yet it is almost impossible anywhere to secure a release from the Roman Catholic Church. Even after one announces that he has changed his views and asks for a dismissal the Roman Church still attempts to hold him, to persuade him, perhaps even over a period of years, and her policy is never to give up one who has been baptized into that church. We do not see the principles of democracy and freedom in that church, but rather those of totalitarianism and dictatorship.

One of the most flagrant denials of freedom in the Roman Church is the *Index of Forbidden Books*, a device which deprives the people of freedom of judgment as to what they may read. This restriction is imposed on the pretense of shielding them from error; its real purpose is to isolate them from liberal and Protestant ideas, to maintain control over them, and so to hold them in the Roman Church. Even the Bible was put on the Index by the Council of Valencia, in 1229, and was not removed until centuries later. And to the present day all versions of the Bible except those which contain the official Roman Catholic explanatory notes still are on the Index. It is for this reason that in Roman Catholic countries the priests seek to confiscate and destroy all copies of the Bible put out by the Protestant churches or by the Bible societies. All editions of the Bible, all portions of it, and all Biblical commentaries in any language that do not show the Imprimatur or Nihil Obstat of some Roman official are forbidden. A long list of books and other publications are blacklisted, not always because they are anti-Christian, but because they are or are suspected of being anti-Romanist. The laws of the Index are binding on the priests as well as on the people. Only the bishops, cardinals, and others whose rank is not below that of bishop are free from the Index.

The intolerance of the Roman Catholic Church even toward its own people is perhaps seen most clearly in this restriction which forbids them to read anything that others write about its history or doctrines. And well do they keep their people in the dark concerning its history; for most of the people, if they knew its real history, probably would leave it immediately. This one church alone in the civilized world follows such an obscurantist rule and tells its people that they commit mortal sin if they so much as read what others say about them. A Roman Catholic young man who reads a criticism of his church, or who attends a lecture criticizing his church will be rebuked more severely by the priest than if he commits a sexual irregularity or some other crime against society. The reasoning is that the latter may be repaired, but the former leads to irreparable loss of faith.

This attitude on the part of the hierarchy and priesthood shows a glaring lack of scholarship and of confidence in their own doctrinal position. Although they claim to have the truth, and even to be the only true church, they do not dare risk a comparison of that "truth" with the supposed error which they oppose. They choose rather to keep their people in as complete ignorance as possible concerning all other systems. But that is the position of the special pleader. True scholars who are sure of their own position do not hesitate to state the position of an opponent, and then to expose its errors if such there are. Even in dealing with Communism and atheism we want to know what they hold, then we proceed to show their falsity. Protestants do not hesitate to acquaint their people with the Roman Catholic system, and then to point out its errors. In fact it is Protestant practice to study and discuss all of the other religions. Failure on the part of the Romanists to do the same reveals a conscious weakness, a reluctance to join the battle in a fair and open way and face logical conclusions. We challenge the Roman hierarchy to let its priests and its people investigate Protestantism fairly and openly or to give up the claim that it alone has the truth. It has often been said that a person who does not know both sides of a question really does not know either side. Not until he knows what his own doctrinal system sets forth, and what can be said against it, does he know what he believes and why.

The reader may wonder how it is possible in countries such as the United States, England, Holland, etc., for the Roman Church to fence its people away from the learning of modern times. If the facts of papal history and of European and American history are as we have represented them, it may be thought incredible that any church could maintain in its schools and in its churches a version radically at variance with those facts. The explanation, however, is just this, that the Roman Catholic is restricted to the literature of his own church. Every book he reads must have been passed by the censor. He has been taught from childhood that the reading of forbidden books is a grave sin, a sin against faith and morals. The Index has indeed proved to be an effective weapon for keeping both the clergy and the laity in obedient submission. It keeps them from thinking, and therefore from rebelling.

The devout, sincere Roman Catholic, priest or layman, finds it very difficult to change his religion. The church, of course, has planned it that way. Even though he may have doubts concerning some things, he finds it hard to make an investigation. He must not even carry on a conversation with a Protestant about religious matters unless his priest is also present. Even among the priests many would not dare to read a heretical book, or carry on such a conversation without permission from a bishop. Some, however, whose duty it is to defend their religion against attacks do find it necessary to investigate evangelical Christianity. And not infrequently one of them is won by the sublimity and simplicity of its teaching. But in the main the Roman Church withholds from its priests and people that broader knowledge and outlook on the world which makes for a well-rounded personality. Incidentally the minister of the Methodist church in Rome, Rev. Reginald Kissack, reports that some Roman Catholic priests in Italy are unsettled and are making tentative inquiries about Protestantism, and that nearly always the question, "What started your unrest?" gets the answer, "I started to read the Gospels."

4. BIGOTRY

The dictionary defines a "bigot" as, "one obstinately or intolerantly devoted to his own church, party, belief or opinion." And the adjective "bigoted" is defined as, "so obstinately attached to some creed, opinion, or practice as to be illiberal or intolerant."

A strange thing happened in the United States during the 1960 political campaign, in which the candidates for president were a Roman Catholic, John F. Kennedy, and a Protestant, Richard M. Nixon. In this land that had been comparatively free from religious prejudice in past elections the Roman Catholics attempted and, because there was no organized or effective Protestant reply, succeeded to a surprising extent in muzzling free men by the cunning use of the word "bigot." A widespread campaign was launched to popularize the idea that anyone who for whatever reason voted against their candidate was a "bigot," and the term was freely used over the radio and television, in the newspapers, and in political discussion. Along with this they sought to label as a "hate monger" and as "hate literature" any person or any literature that even so much as mentioned the Roman Catholic Church in connection with the political campaign. This was their strategy in the Protestant United States, although in all Roman Catholic countries the religious issue immediately becomes a prominent feature in any campaign if a Protestant is involved—if indeed they do not forbid by constitutional requirement any Protestant from even being nominated for the position of head of state, as is the case in Spain, Colombia, Argentina, and Paraguay. In various other countries where Romanism is strong practical considerations make it next to impossible for a Protestant to become head of the state.

Early in that campaign Mr. Nixon announced that he would not discuss religion, nor would he allow his workers to bring the religious issue into the campaign. Mr. Kennedy, too, gave lip service to that principle; but on repeated occasions he "defended" his right to belong to the Roman Catholic Church, a point which of course was not lost on his fellow Roman Catholics. Also, his national party campaign committee made extensive and effective use of a television film and recording that was made during an appearance which he made before a group of Protestant ministers in Houston, Texas, which film had been edited to present him and his religion in a very favorable light. Whether it was wise to attempt to keep religion out of the campaign is open to question. Personally we think it was not, for two reasons: first, a man's religion *does* affect his actions, particularly his conduct of an office such as the presidency; and, secondly, from a practical standpoint it clearly was impossible to suppress such an important factor.

When the facts became known it was shown that the charge of bigotry that had been brought against Protestants was for the most part groundless. The Gallup Poll, which after repeated surveys forecast the closeness of the election with remarkable accuracy, showed that the proportion of Roman Catholic Republicans who switched their votes to Kennedy was approximately twice that of the Protestant Democrats who switched to Nixon. The veteran political commentator, David Lawrence, observed that, "It is obvious that something has happened to stir up the Catholic voters and cause a big number apparently to disregard all other considerations and support the Democratic nominee, who happens to be of their faith" (*The Kansas City Times*, Nov. 2, 1960). These same sources indicated that the Roman Catholic vote went about 80 percent, or approximately four to one, for Kennedy, while the Protestant vote went about 60 percent, or approximately three to two, for Nixon. An impartial post-election analysis by the Survey Research Center of the University of Michigan, as published in *U. S. News and World Report*, May 1, 1961, reached substantially the same conclusion. Hence the evidence is that Roman Catholics showed themselves twice as "bigoted" in voting their religion as did Protestants. And certainly it is just as much an act of bigotry to vote for a man because of his religion as it is to vote against him because of his religion.

But is it bigotry to oppose the election of a Roman Catholic for president of the United States, or for other positions of influence? The basic doctrines of the Roman Catholic Church as they affect political and social life are diametrically opposed to our American ideas of freedom and democracy. The Roman Church has repeatedly condemned the separation of church and state, which is one of the basic principles of our American way of life; and it attempts to regulate even in detail the lives of its members. Roman Catholic officials are inevitably subjected to pressures from their church which could not be brought against other men. Believing that theirs is the only true church, that their eternal welfare is dependent on obedience to their church, and that it is their duty to promote their church so far as practicable, loyal Roman Catholic office holders are subject to what are sometimes unbearable pressures in the confessional and from the hierarchy at large. We submit that because of these obligations which rest in a peculiar way upon all members of that church it is unwise to entrust high office to any member of that church unless he gives convincing evidence that he will not allow his church to influence his conduct—assurance which a "good" Roman Catholic cannot give, and which a "poor" Roman Catholic should not need to give, for the simple reason that if he does not accept those principles he should not be in that church.

But further as regards the charge of bigotry as directed by the Roman Church against all who oppose it: In its announced goal to "Make America Catholic," the Roman Catholic Church proposes to force its doctrines and practices upon our nation regardless of their truth or falsity and regardless of the desires of the majority of our people. This it plans to do by silencing everyone who disagrees with it. And how does it propose to do that? One important item in that plan is to label everyone who opposes it a "bigot." A former Roman Catholic who studied for the priesthood in a Jesuit seminary, and who knows that church well, wrote in 1957 (three years before the 1960 political campaign got under way):

"The Roman Catholic Church, whatever may be its other faults, is never lacking in shrewdness or in good strategists. . . . The Jesuits have urged the Catholic Church in America to label every criticism of the Roman Church as 'bigotry' " (*Christianity Today*, issue of October 28).

But when the facts of history are examined Protestants stand forth clearly not as "bigots," but as *the real champions of religious and political liberty*, while on the other hand Roman Catholicism has maintained a religious despotism wherever it has been in power, even to the extent of putting to death those who disagree with it. The facts are so clear that they cannot be denied. And yet the recent propaganda campaign was conducted so skillfully and persistently that the Roman Church actually came to be looked upon by many as the victim of bigotry and intolerance. When the facts are presented the Roman Church itself stands forth as the biggest bigot of all time. In proof of that statement we submit the following. It is *bigotry:*

To claim to be the only true church.

To teach that all outside the Roman Church are lost.

For the pope to claim infallibility, or that he is the very mouthpiece of God on earth.

For the pope to claim for himself the title "Holy Father"—a claim which is simply blasphemous.

For the Roman Church in its official pronouncements, such as those of the Council of Trent, to pronounce anathemas upon all who dare to differ with it.

For the Roman Church to persecute or kill those who dare to differ with it, as it has done on so many occasions in the past.

For the Roman Church to refer to Protestants as "heretics."

For the Roman Church to teach its people that it is a mortal sin to attend a Protestant church.

For the Roman Church to restrict and persecute Protestants in Spain, Portugal, Italy, and various Latin American countries while it is accorded full freedom of religion in Protestant countries.

For the Roman Church to teach its people that it is a mortal sin to read any Bible other than their own annotated one.

For the Roman Church to force its pre-marital agreement upon Protestants who wish to marry Roman Catholics.

For the Roman Church to teach that the marriage of a Roman Catholic and a Protestant before a Protestant minister or an official of the state is null and void, that such is only "attempted marriage," that the parties thereafter are living in sin, and that their children are illegitimate.

For the Roman Church to teach its people to "detest" other churches and groups, as in the pledge which converts to Romanism take as a part of the induction ceremony, which reads: "With a sincere heart, therefore, and with unfeigned faith, I detest and abjure every error, heresy and sect opposed to the said Holy Catholic and Apostolic Roman Church."

For the Roman Church to maintain the Index of Forbidden Books.

For the Roman Church in Latin America to tell its people that Protestantism and Communism are the same thing.

Many other such practices could be cited.

There is a striking parallel between the practice of the Russian Communists who, knowing themselves to be the promoters of a system which resorts to violence, untruth, treachery, and every immoral practice as it serves their purpose, attempt to cover up their shortcomings by representing themselves and their allies as the "peace loving nations" and as the champions of the world's downtrodden masses, while accusing us of being "imperialists," "war-mongers," and "militarists" who are attempting to "enslave" the less developed nations, and the practice of the Roman Catholics who, knowing that for the most part their distinctive doctrines and rituals are not found in the Bible or are even contrary to the Bible, persistently designate themselves as "the only true church," and hurl the epithet "heretic" at all who differ with them. The Communists claim to "liberate" people when they take possession of a country, but what they actually do is to enslave them. They talk of "the People's Democratic Republic" (i.e., of Red China and East Germany), and of the "People's Courts" (as in Russia and China), while in fact the people of those countries have no voice at all in their government or in their courts. In similar manner the Roman Catholics, where they are in control, consider it their privilege and duty to "Christianize" or "convert" all others and to conform them to their church practices, by persuasion if possible, by force if necessary. The Communists hold that men will be free only when they are governed by the Communist state, and Roman Catholics hold that men are really Christian and can be saved only when they submit to the Roman Catholic Church and acknowledge the authority of the pope. Such terminology involves an absolute reversal of the meaning of words. Both groups, as smokescreens to cover up their own misdeeds and errors, accuse their opponents of the very things of which they know themselves to be guilty.

When Protestantism is stronger than Romanism, and when democracy is stronger than communism, the latter groups talk of tolerance and freedom. They want us to co-exist peacefully until they become stronger than we are—then they will really put the screws on. Peaceful co-existence means peaceful co-existence as long as we are stronger; but when they become stronger it means peaceful submission.

A further parallel between these two groups is that the Communists often are able to do their most effective work through "pinkos" and fellow travelers, and Roman Catholics often are most effective when they can persuade gullible Protestants under the pretense of being broad-minded and liberal to parrot their charges for them. But the facts of history are clear, and the doctrinal tenets and practices of both of those groups are a matter of public record. Any informed person knows that the terms used by both of those groups in the present controversies are falsely used, that the accusations are baseless, and that the facts are exactly the reverse of what they allege. In the light of history as manifested in the nations of Europe, the Communist charge of "war-mongers" as brought against the democratic nations, and the Roman Catholic charge of "bigotry" as brought against Protestants, are so ridiculous that no one should be deceived by them.

Let Protestants protest orally and in writing whenever these fraudulent charges of "bigotry," "hate-mongering," and "hate literature" are made over the radio, television, in public discussion, or in print, and their falsity and injustice will soon be exposed.

5. PERSECUTION

It has been said that,

> Rome in the minority is a lamb.
> Rome as an equal is a fox.
> Rome in the majority is a tiger.

The Roman Church has never acknowledged that the use of force to compel obedience is wrong in principle, although she has been compelled to abandon the practice in Protestant countries and the fires of the Inquisition are no longer burning. Even in those countries that have remained under her control an enlightened public opinion indirectly influenced by Protestantism has been sufficient to bring about a considerable degree of restraint.

While in the United States the priests often are friendly to Protestants, in Romanist countries they continue to be the instigators and leaders of riots against them. Regardless of attempts by some Roman Catholics to deny that Protestants are to be hated or persecuted, the fact is that they are charged with heresy by the Roman Church; and heresy, by Roman Canon Law, is punishable by death if need be. The undeniable fact is that today Protestant ministers behind the Iron Curtain, in such countries as Poland, Czechoslovakia, and East Germany, have more freedom to hold church services and to distribute Christian literature than they have in Spain.

Even today every Roman Catholic bishop at the time of his consecration takes an oath of allegiance to the pope which contains these words:

"With all my power I will persecute and make war upon all heretics, schismatics and those who rebel against our lord (the pope) and all his successors . . . So help me God and these the holy gospels of God" (*Pontificale Romanum Summorum* Pontificum. Belgium. Mechlin, p. 133. Cited by Emmett McLoughlin, in *American Culture and Catholic Schools,* p. 125).

Thomas Aquinas, prominent in the Dominican Order and the most authoritative philosopher and theologian of the Roman Church even to the present day, held that the church had the right to hunt out and kill heretics as a means of maintaining its purity. He wrote:

"Though heretics must not be tolerated because they deserve it, we must bear with them, till, by a second admonition, they may be brought back to the faith of the church. But those who, after a second admonition, remain obstinate in their errors, must not only be excommunicated, but they must be delivered to the secular power to be exterminated" (*Summa Theologia,* Vol. IV, p. 90).

And again:

"So far as heretics are concerned, heresy is a sin, whereby they deserve not only to be separated from the church by excommunication, but also to be severed from the world by death" (Vol. II, p. 154).

And still further:

"If counterfeiters of money or other criminals are justly delivered over to death forthwith by the secular authorities, much more can heretics, after they are convicted of heresy, be not only forthwith excommunicated, but as surely put to death" (Vol. II, Q. 2, Art. 3).

Dr. Marianus de Luca, S. J., Professor of Canon Law at the Georgian University in Rome, said in his *Institution of Public Ecclesiastical Law*, with a personal commendation from pope Leo XIII, in 1901:

"The Catholic Church has *the right and duty to kill heretics* because it is by fire and sword that heresy can be extirpated. Mass excommunication is derided by heretics. If they are imprisoned or exiled they corrupt others. The only recourse is to *put them to death*. Repentance cannot be allowed to save them, just as repentance is not allowed to save civil criminals; for the highest good of the church is the duty of the faith, and this cannot be preserved unless heretics are put to death."

The official newspaper of the large Roman Catholic diocese of Brooklyn, New York, *The Tablet*, in its issue of November 5, 1938, declared:

"Heresy is an awful crime . . . and those who start a heresy are more guilty than they who are traitors to the civil government. If the State has the right to punish treason with death, the principle is the same which concedes to the spiritual authority the power of capital punishment over the arch-traitor to truth and Divine revelation. . . . A perfect society has the right to its existence . . . and the power of capital punishment is acknowledged for a perfect society. Now . . . the Roman Catholic Church is a perfect society, and as such has the right and power to take means to safeguard its existence."

In the following words by a present day American Roman Catholic theologian, Francis J. Connell, with Imprimatur by Cardinal Spellman, even the right of existence is denied to other churches:

"The Catholic Church is the only organization authorized by God to teach religious truth and to conduct public religious worship. Consequently, they (Roman Catholics) hold that any creed which differs from that of the Catholic Church is erroneous, and that any religious organization which is separated from the Catholic Church lacks the approval and the authorization of God. The very existence of any other church is opposed to the command of Christ, that all men should join His one church. From this it follows that, as far as God's law is concerned, no one has a real right to accept any religion save the Catholic Church" (Pamphlet, *Freedom of Worship, the Catholic Position*).

These are representative samples of the "tolerance" that can be expected when the Roman Church has things its own way. Add to these the more than one hundred anathemas—"Let him be anathema," which means, "Let him be accursed"—pronounced by the Council of Trent, the most authoritative of Roman Catholic councils, upon all who dare to differ with its pronouncements. Such violent, intemperate language in a creed which purports to set forth the basic principles of the Christian system reveals clearly the unchristian nature of the men who pretend so to speak. How alien is all of that to the noble sentiments expressed in the American Declaration of Independence, which says:

"We hold these truths to be self-evident, that all men are created equal, that they are endowed by their Creator with certain inalienable rights, that among these are life, liberty, and the pursuit of happiness—that to secure these rights, governments are instituted among men, deriving their just powers from the consent of the governed."

Pope Boniface VIII, in 1302, issued the *Unam Sanctam,* a document in which he claimed to be the representative of God on earth, and concurrently claimed authority over every nation and government on earth. This decree, which sets forth the doctrine of "the two swords," reads as follows:

"In her (the Church) and within her power there are two swords, we are taught in the Gospels, namely, the spiritual sword and the temporal sword . . . the latter to be used for the Church, the former by the Church; the former by the hand of the priest, the latter by the hand of the princes and kings, but at the nod and sufference of the priest. The one sword must of necessity be subject to the other, the temporal authority to the spiritual . . . . For truth being the witness, the spiritual power has the function of establishing the temporal power and sitting in judgment on it if it would prove not good . . . but if the supreme power (the papacy) deviate, it cannot be judged by man but only by God alone."

This power of control over the two swords is assumed to be inherent in the papal office and superior to all other such powers. Men are to be compelled to submit to the Roman pontiff by the sword of the state, as wielded by kings and soldiers, but at the direction of the priesthood. This is, in fact, the traditional position of the Roman Church, that the actual persecution or execution of those judged by the church to be heretical should be done, not by the church, but by the state at the direction of the church. By such subterfuge the church seeks to escape responsibility for her crimes.

The doctrine of "the two swords" was the basis for the persecution and massacre of thousands of the Waldensians in Italy and France, one of the worst massacres having taken place in France, in 1545, when twenty-one of their towns were burned and the inhabitants plundered, tortured, and murdered in circumstances of the utmost cruelty. Two years later the dying monarch, Francis I, remembering with bitter remorse his ultimatum to the Waldensians that they embrace Roman Catholicism or be destroyed, pleaded with his son that the men who persuaded him to that course and led the massacre be given their just deserts.

Perhaps the most notorious of all massacres was that which was carried out against the Protestants of France, beginning on St. Bartholomew's Day, August 24, 1572, and continuing throughout France for five or six weeks. Some 10,000 "Huguenots," as the French Protestants were called, were killed in Paris alone, and estimates of the number killed throughout the country run from 40,000 to 60,000. *The Standard International Encyclopedia* places the number at 50,000. Hundreds of thousands more fled from France to other countries. Many of their descendants eventually made their way to the United States. When the news of the massacre reached Rome church bells were rung and there was wild rejoicing in the streets. Not long before that time Germany had become Protestant, as had also parts of Switzerland; and the new movement had made such progress in France that nearly a fourth of the population was Protestant and there was a real possibility that if it remained unchecked the whole country might become Protestant. So pleased was the pope, Gregory XIII, to be rid of the Protestants in France that he ordered *Te Deums* (hymns of praise and thanksgiving) sung in the churches of Rome, and had a medal struck with his own profile on one side and the destroying angel on the other. He also sent cardinal Ursini to convey his felicitations to the queen mother of France, Catherine de Medici, who at the promptings of the Jesuits had organized the plot. Primarily through that massacre France was preserved a Roman Catholic country, and has remained such, nominally at least, to the present day.

The Inquisition was created by the Roman Catholic Church to search out, examine, and punish heretics. Its worst excesses took place in Spain, under the inquisitor Torquemada, whose appointment was made by Ferdinand and Isabella in 1483 and confirmed by pope Alexander VI. The Jews too were driven out of Spain by Torquemada. As Columbus set sail from Palos in 1492 for his explorations in the new world he saw other ships in the harbor taking the Jews into exile.

An earlier Spanish king, Ferdinand III of Castile (died, 1252), had so pleased the Roman Church by his vigorous actions against dissenters that he was made a saint in 1671 and the church inserted in the Breviary (book of daily readings and prayers for the priests) these words in praise of him:

"He permitted no heretics to dwell in his kingdom, and with his own hands brought wood to the stake for their burning" (*The Stability and Progress of Dogma,* by cardinal Lepicier, p. 202; 1910).

The Inquisition also carried on its work with great effectiveness in Italy, where thousands of Protestants were put to death simply because they would not give up their faith and become Roman Catholics. Today Spain, Italy, Portugal, and to some extent France, Quebec, and Latin America, remain the devout children of the Inquisition. That, at any rate, was the method by which whole nations were made, or kept, Roman Catholic. Indeed, when we see the medieval attitude of the hierarchy still manifesting itself in the present day persecutions in some of those countries we are forced to conclude that the Roman Catholic Church is either the most decadent of all anachronisms, or the most dangerous of all survivals from a past that we wish were dead and buried.

The Inquisition was Rome's masterpiece for the control of people and nations, and the tribunal of the Inquisition has never been abolished. Today in Rome it is known as the Congregation of the Holy Office. It is composed of cardinals and prelates, with the pope himself as its head, and its principal work is that of maintaining the doctrines of the Roman Church against errors and heresies. The excesses of the Inquisition are no longer practiced, but the principles which made those excesses possible still are in effect. The late bishop Segura, of Seville, Spain, who was prominent in the recent persecutions in that country, said shortly before he died: "I regret I was not born in the days of the Holy Inquisition."

For another authoritative voice in Romanism let us listen to that of Ignatius Loyola, founder of the Jesuit order and held in high honor by the Jesuits who today are the real masters in the Roman Church. Said he:

"It would be greatly advantageous, too, not to permit anyone infected with heresy to continue in the government, particularly the supreme government, of any province or town, or in any judicial or honorary position. Finally, if it could be set forth and made manifest to all, that the moment a man is convicted or held in grave suspicion of heresy he may not be favored with honors of wealth but put down from these benefits. And if a few examples could be made, punishing a few with the penalty of their lives, or with the loss of property and exile, so there could be no mistake about the seriousness of the business of religion, this remedy would be so much more effective. . . .

"It would be advisable that whatever heretical books might be found, on diligent search, in the possession of dealers or individuals, should be burned or removed from all the provinces of the kingdom. The same may be said of books written by heretics, even when not heretical themselves, such as those which treat of grammar or rhetoric or dialectic, which it seems, ought to be cast aside utterly out of hatred toward the heresy of their authors. . . .

"Of all rectors and public professors in universities and academies, and likewise rectors of private schools and schoolteachers as well, and even tutors, it should be required that long before being accepted in their posts they should all be found true Catholics, through examination or secret information, and should be recommended by the testimony of Catholics; and they should swear that they are and will always remain Catholics; and if any such men should be convicted of heresy, they should be severely punished if only on the grounds of perjury" (*Obras Completas de San Ignacio de Loyola,* edicion Biblioteca de Autores Cristianos. Translated by Dwight Cristoanos; Madrid; 1952; 880 p.).

We need not ask ourselves what the Roman Catholic Church would do in the United States if it came into power. All we need do is to look at what it has done where it has been in power. Even the children in the parochial schools are being taught that the Roman Church has the right to suppress other churches and that it has the right to punish with death anyone who is a traitor to it. And history teaches that when people have the power they usually do what they have a right to do. Before the Reformation the Roman Church was able to quench all opposition in blood and violence. But since that time it has lived under the eyes of an alert and fiercely critical body of writers who have been free to express their opinions without fear of reprisal. But the doctrines concerning the temporal domain of the pope, and the right of the Roman Church to use physical force to attain spiritual ends, have never been renounced by any pope or church council. Nor has that church ever repented of or apologized for the crimes that she has committed. And we may be sure that she never will.

6. SPAIN TODAY

The Protestant population of Spain today is estimated at only 20,000, about half of whom are foreigners, with a constituency of about 10,000 others who may be termed sympathizers, out of a total population of approximately 28,000,000. There are about 230 organized Protestant groups, with only 70 or 80 pastors in the entire nation. That means that Spanish Protestants number only about .035 of one percent of the population. The government is clerical-fascist. Only one political party exists, that of dictator Franco. In present day Spain Protestants are not permitted to:

1. Establish a Protestant church.
2. Be elected to any public office, national, provincial, or municipal.
3. Obtain employment as teachers in the public schools.
4. Obtain employment as nurses.
5. Establish a Protestant school for their children.
6. Establish a theological seminary to train their ministers.
7. Publish or distribute Protestant literature.

8. Be married in a Protestant wedding service—only civil marriage is legal for Protestants.
9. Have a Protestant funeral service in many towns.
10. Bury their dead in the established cemeteries.

All but a few of the Protestant churches that were in existence when Franco came to power in 1936 are now closed. New churches cannot be established without government permission, which under Franco's concordat with the Vatican is almost impossible to obtain. Meetings in private homes and in unmarked buildings are permitted within limits, but often are spied upon by the police and frequently stopped if they appear to be having too much success, that is, making converts to Protestantism.

In 1958 a Baptist minister, Jose Nunez, held services in a church that had been closed, and after a trial that attracted international attention was sentenced to a month in prison. Protestant churches are not allowed to have distinctive church architecture, nor a church bell, nor to locate on a prominent street, nor to broadcast their services by radio, nor to advertise their services in the newspapers.

Since the Franco regime came to power the government, at the instigation of the Roman Catholic Church, has forced the closing of all Protestant schools, including the Union Theological Seminary, in Madrid. Protestants are not allowed to have Christian schools even for their own children, but must send them to parochial or government controlled schools where religion is taught by priests and nuns, or obtain private schooling for them if they can afford it. The established cemeteries usually are owned or controlled by the Roman Catholic Church; Protestants are excluded from "holy ground," and are required to bury in public plots set aside for atheists, criminals, and paupers.

Civil law in Spain conforms closely to Roman Catholic Canon Law. Protestant marriage services are illegal, and a license for a civil ceremony is difficult, sometimes impossible, to obtain if either or both parties have been baptized in the Roman Catholic Church, even in infancy, as most people in Spain have. Even if they have left the Roman Church and have become Protestants, the record stands against them. They are claimed by the Roman Church unless they can "prove" that they have severed all connection with it—which places a meddlesome power of investigation not only in the hands of professional judges, if they choose to abuse it, but often in the hands of municipal justices of the peace in every town and village, many of whom are next to illiterate. Some young couples have been forced to wait for years for permits to be married outside the Roman Church. Some have gone to England or France to be married, only to find when they return that their marriages are not recognized in Spain.

Protestants who press their case with court action usually obtain the permit. But that involves from $150 to $200 expense, and few can afford it.

The public professions, such as medicine, law, teaching, banking, and nursing are for the most part closed to Protestants. Often it is difficult to obtain any kind of employment unless they pay some allegiance to the Roman Church. Trusted men and women who have been employed by a firm for years have been dismissed when it has been found that they have joined a Protestant church. The unemployed and destitute find it difficult, in some cases impossible, to get public relief. Protestants in the army are not allowed to attain officer rank. Sometimes even non-Christians receive better treatment; a Moslem has been promoted to lieutenant-general. Young men, obliged to do military service, are expected to kneel before the image of the Virgin Mary during special mass. To disobey is a military offense which may mean up to two years imprisonment. The controlled press tells the people that Protestants are not only heretics, but subversive Leftists, Communists, and Masons; and Protestants are not allowed to purchase space in the newspapers to reply to attacks made upon them. Jews too are restricted, but in general are treated better than are Protestants because they do not try to make converts. The Jews are few in number and for the most part can be ignored.

The spirit of the Inquisition still lives in Spain. It hardly seems possible that such conditions could exist in a country that professes to be Christian and civilized. But the arrogant intolerance of clericalism is ever the same. Back of these restrictions are the so-called "charter of the Spanish People," of 1945, and the concordat between Franco and the pope. The key clause of the Charter reads:

"The profession and practice of the Catholic religion, which is that of the State, shall enjoy official protection. No one shall be disturbed because of his religious beliefs or the private practice of his worship. No other outward ceremonies or demonstrations than those of the Catholic religion shall be permitted."

Articles 1 and 19 respectively of the Concordat read:

"The Catholic Apostolic Roman Religion will continue to be the sole religion of the Spanish nation and will enjoy the rights and prerogatives which are due it in conformity with the Divine Law and the Canon Law. . . .

"The State, by way of indemnification for past confiscations of Church property and as a contribution to the Church's work for the good of the nation, will provide the Church with an annual endowment."

The major part of the salaries of the priests and other church officials is paid by the state. Thus Protestants and others are taxed to support a religion in which they do not believe.

If anyone has any doubt about what the Roman Catholic Church wants, we have an excellent, made-to-order demonstration in Franco's Spain. There, through the working of an official concordat, Protestants are treated exactly as the pope thinks they should be treated. The Roman Church never tires of referring to what it terms "Christian Spain"; and its ideal, the establishment of the Roman Catholic religion and the elimination of all other religions, is more closely approximated in Spain than in any other present day nation. What a contrast all of that is with the liberty that Roman Catholics enjoy in Protestant United States!

Concerning the Spanish situation Paul Blanshard has written:

"The same pope who appoints every bishop and cardinal in the United States also appoints every bishop and cardinal in Spain. The same pope who permits American bishops to declare in the United States that they favor the separation of Church and State in this non-Catholic country encourages his Spanish bishops to pursue a directly opposite policy in Catholic Spain. It is the Vatican and the Franco government that jointly deny to all Protestant churches and Jewish synagogues those liberties which leaders of the church in the United States profess to believe in. Between them they have abolished both political and religious democracy by a union of church and state which is the pluperfect negation of American principles" (Pamphlet, *Ecclesiastical Justice in Spain*).

And Walter M. Montano, writing in *Christian Heritage,* says:

"Spain has had a long history of intolerance. The number of victims sacrificed by the Inquisition in Spain almost exceeds credulity. Yet it has been shown by Llorente, who carefully examined the records of the Tribunal, and whose statements are drawn from the most authoritative sources, that 105,285 victims fell under the inquisitor general Torquemada; 51,167 under Cisneros; and 34,952 fell under Diego Perez. It is further reckoned that 31,912 were burned alive! Half that number, 15,659 suffered the punishment of the statute, and 291,450 were sent to penitentiaries. Half a million families were destroyed by the Inquisition, and it cost Spain two million children!"

And concerning the present day restrictions and persecutions in Spain he says:

"Let it never be forgotten that this is the heritage of the Roman Catholic Church, the end result of the dread Inquisition in a country that never knew Reformation" (September, 1959).

Small wonder it is that the Protestant population of Spain is almost infinitesimally small! And yet in spite of all of these persecutions and abuses, the Protestant United States continues to pour into Spain great sums of relief money as well as supplies distributed by voluntary relief agencies. Under the Eisenhower administration non-military aid has been at the rate of more than $200,000,000 a year (*Church and State*, Sept., 1959). The United States maintains military bases in Spain, and the military aid has been vast and varied. Our governmental officials know of the abuses practiced there—such have been called to their attention many times. The clerical-fascist government of Spain has been bankrupt for years, and has been able to survive only because of American aid. The United States, therefore, has been responsible for its continuance. Back of this policy, of course, is the political influence of the Roman Catholic Church on our government in Washington. This American branch of the Roman Church is not only a friend of the Franco regime, but is an integral part of that world system which makes such regimes possible and supports them.

7. ITALY; YUGOSLAVIA

In Italy there are approximately 300,000 Protestants in a population of 50,000,000, a ration of about 1 to 165. The Inquisition there, too, did its work almost as ruthlessly as in Spain. Since the Second World War Protestant work in Italy has increased to some extent.

The new Italian Constitution, adopted under pressure from the western democracies after the Second World War, declared for freedom of religion. But practical considerations, primarily the power of the Roman Catholic Church, have made it ineffective much of the time. However, in 1958 there were two different court decisions which were favorable to Protestants. The Constitutional High Court, Italy's highest tribunal, invalidated a provision in Italian law which made it necessary to secure a government permit to operate a house of worship such as was required under the concordat that was signed between Mussolini and the Vatican and which had been continued in force ever since. And in another case a complaint had been brought by Roman Catholic owners of an estate against three Protestant tenant farmers who had refused to permit a local priest to bless their cattle. The court decision was in favor of the defendants, and declared: "If a citizen associates himself with another citizen of different religious creed he must not force on him the rites of his own faith with regard to things that concern both of them."

Protestants in Italy have found it almost impossible to establish schools for their children even in the primary grades, despite the desperate need for schools throughout the country. Before the 1958 decision Protestants were not allowed to put signs on their churches designating them as such. To post such signs was regarded as an illegal "public display" of religion, and the police promptly tore them down and arrested the people responsible.

On the other hand within the Roman Catholic Church early in 1960 a new "constitution" for the diocese of Rome was proclaimed by pope John XXIII tightening the ecclesiastical discipline for both priests and laymen. This is the pope's own diocese, and its provisions usually are followed in other dioceses throughout the world. Among other things it forbids laymen to join or vote for political parties or persons disapproved by the Roman Church, under threat of excommunication; forbids them to enact any laws detrimental to the Roman Church; and makes them liable to excommunication if they support doctrines or ideas in the press or publicly which differ from those of the Roman Catholic Church.

In Italy remarks concerning the pope which the Vatican considers "slanderous" are punishable by law. Article 297 of the Italian Penal Code provides sentences up to three years for "whoever on Italian territory offends the honor and prestige of the head of a foreign state"—the pope in Vatican City qualifies as the head of a foreign state. In December, 1960, an Italian newspaper editor was given a five-month suspended sentence by a court in Rome for asserting that the pope and the hierarchy had acted unconstitutionally by interfering in Italian civil affairs when its daily newspaper, *L'Osservatore Romano*, upheld the right of the Roman Church to "guide the faithful" through ecclesiastical directives concerning political affairs.

In Yugoslavia there occurred during the Second World War one of the cruelest episodes in history, in the massacre of Eastern Orthodox Serbs by Roman Catholic Croats, in an effort to make the province of Croatia solidly Roman Catholic. So hideous were the massacres that they surpass even those of the Duke of Alva in the Netherlands and those of St. Bartholomew's day in France. Most astonishing was the manner in which those crimes were ignored or hushed up at the time by the news services even in the United States, although similar massacres of Jews in Germany were given the widest publicity—another demonstration of how subtly and efficiently Roman clericalism exerts its influence over the press and radio. But now a French author, M. Henri Mauriere, himself a Roman Catholic, has told the story in a well-documented book, *Assassins in the Name of God*. Miss Monica Farrell tells the same story in her book, *Ravening Wolves*. Both Mr. Mauriere and Miss Farrell put the responsibility squarely on the priests of the Church of Rome.

By way of background, after the First World War the Roman Catholic states of Croatia and Slovenia were united with the Eastern Orthodox state of Serbia to form the nation of Yugoslavia. Croatia had approximately 5,000,000 Roman Catholics and 3,000,000 Eastern Orthodox. At once the Croats began to intrigue against the Serbs. Terrorist Ustashi bands were organized. They received support from Mussolini, who financed them. When king Alexander I of Yugoslavia visited France in 1929, he was assassinated at Marseilles. The leader of the gang was Ante Pavelich, who escaped to Italy where Mussolini gave him protection and refused to surrender him to the Yugoslav government although he was convicted of the crime in both French and Yugloslav courts.

When in 1941 the Nazis invaded Yugoslavia the Croats, with Pavelich as their leader, joined them. As a reward Hitler made Pavelich the puppet head of the new "Independent State of Croatia." His minister of religion was Andrija Artukovic, another Roman Catholic. Then began a war of suppression or extermination of all Serbs and Jews. Nearly 70,000 of the 80,000 Jews in the new state were killed or forced to flee, their property being confiscated. Official records and photographs show that Pavelich and archbishop Stepinac were closely associated in governmental, social, and ecclesiastical affairs. Stepinac was appointed supreme military apostolic vicar of the Ustashi army led by Pavelich. He was, therefore, in a position to know of the atrocities that were constantly taking place.

In May, 1941, after innumerable massacres had been committed, Pavelich went to Rome and was received by pope Pius XII, and on the same occasion signed a treaty with Mussolini. In June of that year more than 100,000 Orthodox Serbian men, women, and children were killed by the Ustashi. In all some 250 Orthodox churches were destroyed or turned over to Roman Catholic parishes and convents. Documents requesting and authorizing such transfers are now in the state prosecutor's office at Zagreb and Sarajevo, bearing the signature of archbishop Stepinac. In February, 1942, a *Te Deum* was sung in Stepinac's church in Zagreb, the then capital of Croatia, with special honors paid to Pavelich. In a pastoral letter Stepinac declared that in spite of complexities, what they were seeing in Croatia was "the Lord's work," and called on his priests to support Pavelich. Stepinac twice visited pope Pius XII, in Rome, in 1942. He reported that 244,000 Serbs had accepted (forced) conversion to Roman Catholicism. So the pope, too, was well informed as to what was going on in Serbia and Croatia. Some estimates place the total number of Serbian men, women, and children killed by the Ustashi at 200,000. Others place it even higher.

When it became necessary for the Nazis to retreat from Yugoslavia, Pavelich, Artukovic, and almost all of the Roman priests went with them. After the war ended Yugoslav courts sentenced Stepinac to sixteen years imprisonment for his Nazi-Fascist collaboration. After serving five years he was released, but was kept under house arrest. The pope, however, rewarded his services by naming him a cardinal. Until his death in 1960, he was played up in Roman Catholic circles, particularly in the United States, as a "martyr," even to the extent that cardinal Spellman, in New York, named a parochial high school after him.

Pavelich again fled to Italy, where for some time he lived in disguise as a monk in a monastery, and later escaped to Argentina. Artukovic too avoided capture, and eventually entered the United States under a false name and with a forged certificate of identity from Southern Ireland, and settled in California. Both Pavelich and Artukovic successfully resisted all efforts of the Yugoslav government to extradite them as war criminals. Pavelich eventually returned to Spain, where he died in 1960. Los Angeles newspapers reported that through two court trials the principal support for Artukovic to prevent his extradition came from the Roman Catholic Church, of which he had been a lifelong member. So reads another chapter of church-state intrigue as dark as any played out during the Middle Ages. Let it also be noted that both Hitler and Mussolini were Roman Catholics, but that despite their crimes against humanity neither was ever excommunicated, nor even severely censored, by the Roman Church.

8. LATIN AMERICA

The most glaring example of persecution in our western hemisphere in recent years, and continuing to some extent to the present day, is found in the nation of Colombia. There a reactionary government with the support of the Roman Catholic Church came into power in 1948. A concordat was signed with the Vatican, under which severe restrictions were placed on Protestants. 60 percent of the country was declared "mission territory" and closed to Protestant work of any kind. During this period 116 Protestants have been killed, 66 Protestant churches or chapels have been burned or bombed, and over 200 Protestant schools have been closed. (Report of the Evangelical Confederation of Colombia, Bulletin No. 50; June 26, 1959). Protestants, however, have refused to acknowledge the validity of the concordat, because certain features of it are in open violation of the Colombian constitution, and it has never been submitted to the congress for ratification as is required by law for all treaties with foreign powers. Evidently its supporters doubt that they could secure ratification. But the course that has been followed by the Roman Church in Colombia in recent years seems to have had the full approval of the Vatican, for the archbishop of Bogota was promoted to cardinal by pope John XXIII in December, 1960.

Originally all of Latin America was intolerant toward Protestantism. But

during the past fifty years the area as a whole, through more or less open
conflict with the Roman Church, has been moving toward religious freedom. Some of the countries now have almost as much freedom of religion
as is found in the United States. Practically all of the Latin American nations, following the example of the United States, have written into their
constitutions articles guaranteeing freedom of religion. But the continuing
power of the Roman Church often makes their enforcement impractical or
impossible. About half have separation of church and state. In general the
people are proud of this liberalism and resent the machinations of the reactionary minority which in some areas is trying to restore the old order.

Almost invariably the anti-Protestant demonstrations and riots that have
taken place have been incited or led by local priests. In some areas the
priests have undue influence with the civil officials, police, editors, and
radio executives, and too often it happens even yet that the most powerful
man in a Latin American town is not the mayor, nor the chief of police,
but the Roman Catholic priest who controls them both. But the Roman
Catholic people, if left to their own desires, prefer to live in peace with
their Protestant neighbors. One telephone call from the pope could put
an end to all of the harassment, slander, and opposition on the part of his
priests within an hour if such were his desire. But no such call ever comes.
The responsibility for continued persecution rests squarely with him.

For the most part the masses of the Latin American people, sensing the
superstition and sham connected with the only kind of religion that they
have ever known, have forsaken it and have become largely agnostic to all
religion. The laboring class has become largely anti-Catholic, as have also
the educated classes. The colleges and universities, though few in number,
are largely independent and impartial as regards religion. As even North
American Roman Catholics know only too well if they are willing to
admit it, the Latin American Roman Catholic Church has proved to be
one of the major spiritual derelictions in the history of Christianity.

In colonial days the Roman Church became a powerful political force.
Vast amounts of land and wealth came into its hands, and complaints
were often heard about the excess accumulation of wealth on the part of
the clergy. The Inquisition was transplanted to Latin America—the original "Gestapo," as John Gunther calls it—and every movement of the mind
toward new truth and greater freedom was immediately crushed out.
Clerical politicians helped maintain the hold of the church on the masses,
while the church in turn supported their ambitions. With few exceptions
the Latin American dictators have been aided by the church, and in turn
have given their support to it. These are simply the facts of history, part of
the heavy impedimenta under which Latin America began her struggle
toward freedom.

For years the Roman Catholic hierarchy in the United States, through the power that it was able to exert on our government and through the press and radio, carried on an aggressive campaign to discredit Protestant mission work in Latin America and to deprive American Protestant churches of their right to carry on missionary work there. They sought to create the impression that such missions were not needed and not wanted by the people. Strong pressure was brought to bear on the State Department to refuse passports to Protestant missionaries, while at the same time every facility was placed at the disposal of Roman priests and nuns who applied for such passports. Repeatedly Protestant mission board secretaries tried to find out why their missionaries were discriminated against. This was particularly the situation in the 1930s and 1940s, during the Roosevelt and Truman administrations. But fortunately Protestantism is now making progress in almost all parts of Latin America. A new day is dawning for the church in most of those lands. The old feudal system, with its few large land owners and the poor peasant masses, is crumbling. A new middle class is emerging.

Many Latin Americans find it difficult to understand why the United States took part in the destruction of the Spanish Republic in the late 1930s, why it refused to sell supplies to the legitimate nationalist government and by so doing enabled Franco, with help from Mussolini and Hitler, to overthrow that government. They also find it hard to understand why so often our influence has been on the side of the dictators in the Latin American republics instead of following the principles that inspired the democratic founders of our nation. It became almost a fixed policy for this nation to appoint Roman Catholic ambassadors and consuls to represent it in Latin America. Such men obviously were unfitted properly to represent a Protestant nation in its dealings with other nations. In this connection both Mr. Roosevelt and Mr. Truman showed themselves very responsive to Roman Catholic pressures. Mr. Roosevelt, for instance, in defiance of public opinion, appointed a personal representative to the Vatican, with a $12,000 a year allowance. And Mr. Truman proceeded to nominate an American ambassador to the Vatican, receiving, of course, an ambassador in return, and to have congress make that a permanent diplomatic arrangement. But the plan was defeated in the Senate. It is difficult to explain to our South American neighbors the machinations of the Roman Catholic Church in Washington and why the hierarchy should have such a big influence in our government. But certainly it is not unreasonable for them to expect that our foreign policy would reflect those principles of religious and civil liberty which have contributed so much to this nation's greatness.

Actually the competition that the Roman Catholic Church in Latin

America has received from Protestantism has been a stimulus to it. When it held a monopoly as the state religion in most of those countries and other churches were excluded, it stagnated and decayed. But as has been the case in the United States where it is faced with an alert Protestantism, in recent years it has been forced to give better service, to build more and better schools and hospitals, and to provide better trained priests and nuns. In many Latin American countries two-thirds or more of the priests regularly have come from Spain. Separation of church and state, though strongly opposed by the Roman Church, has been for it a blessing in disguise both in the United States and in Latin America.

Ask the average thoughtful Latin American, "What is Latin America's most serious problem?" and the answer usually is: "The spiritual problem." Far from opposing Protestant missions, most Latin Americans welcome them and see in Protestantism many elements that they desire for their own religious life but which they do not find in Roman Catholicism. Many of them have reacted bitterly against a religion based on ignorance and superstition, and realize that what their people desperately need is a religion that is more than formalism, a faith that issues in purity of life and in strengthened moral character.

George P. Howard, in his book, *Religious Liberty in Latin America,* written a generation ago, said:

> "Nowhere is Christianity so devoid of inner content or real spiritual life as in Latin America. There is a vast difference between the Latin American Catholic Church and the Roman Catholicism of Northern Europe or North America." And then he adds: "Never has Christianity had such a magnificent missionary opportunity as was given the Roman Catholic Church in the period of the conquest and colonization of the Indes, as Latin America was then called. The field was wide open, support from the civil authorities was complete, no other rival church was on the ground, there was no opposition. And yet, after four centuries of undisturbed possession, the Christianization of the continent still lags. It is, therefore, no exaggeration to say that Latin America is Christianity's most shocking failure" (p. 42; The Westminster Press, Philadelphia; 1944).

Concerning the relation of the schools in Latin America to Christianity, Mr. Howard says:

> "A very large proportion of the student and educated classes as well as the new middle class, which is just emerging in Latin America, has not been won to Christianity. These people are traditionally indifferent and even hostile to religion. To be religious or to go to church is still the sign of inferiority among the large numbers of the intellectuals. They threw

off the shackles of obscurantist religious faith weighted with superstition and they have not yet been shown that a man can be a Christian and preserve his intellectual respectability. Will Durant remarked that 'the failure of the Reformation to capture France left Frenchmen no halfway house between infallibility and infidelity.' The reaction in university centers of Latin America against religion and all that was reminiscent of churchly influence was so radical that all forms of academic garb were barred. It is necessary to go to Protestant countries to find the cap and gown in use" (p. 28).

In Colombia, where Roman Catholic persecution of Protestants has been worst during the past 12 years, a recent survey by the Ministry of Education shows that 42 percent of the entire Colombian population is illiterate, that only 44 percent of the children of primary age are enrolled in any school, and that a serious shortage of schools and teachers exists. And yet during these past 12 years the Roman Church, which poses as the guardian of education in that nation, has forced the closing of more than 200 Protestant mission schools. The attitude of the Colombian Roman Catholic Church is: *Better an illiterate Colombian than one educated by Protestant teachers.*

The Director of UNESCO (United Nations Educational, Scientific and Cultural Organization) has said:

"In 1956, the average level of education for Latin America as a whole did not exceed the first grade; those who did enter school did not stay, on an average, beyond the fourth grade. After the first three years UNESCO, with the grudging support of most of the Latin American governments, could count nearly 25 million children at school (some 19 million still get no schooling at all) and 90 thousand more teachers at work in new classrooms. The major project is scheduled to run until 1968; on the horizon, by the end of the decade, is the goal: Decent primary education for every child in Latin America" (Quoted in *Christian Heritage*, May, 1961; p. 6).

Commenting on this situation, Stuart P. Garver, editor of *Christian Heritage*, says:

"The deficiencies of Roman Catholic education are of such a nature that an aroused national spirit retaliates against the Church like a man reacts upon discovering he has been cheated by some slick salesman. . . . The failure of the hierarchy to educate for responsible exercise of freedom by the people themselves has produced a world-wide pattern of trouble for Catholic education" (May, 1961).

Undoubtedly the present trouble in Cuba is to be explained in part by this very cause. The Roman Church in that island, which under earlier regimes enjoyed a favored position and which always has had control of education, sensed that change in the political and social areas threatened its position. It opposed the revolutionary movement and encouraged student demonstrations against it. Castro in turn took over the schools and carried the movement over into Communism—a not unfamiliar pattern where the people have known no church other than the Roman. Castro himself is a member of that church, as are 90% of the Cuban people. By a strange anomaly Roman Catholicism fights Communism, but because of the ignorance and poverty that develop in Roman Catholic countries itself become a seedbed for Communism. On more than one occasion this has proved to be a serious embarrassment for the hierarchy.

And yet in both Europe and Latin America our government officials, in a more or less open bid for the Roman Catholic vote in this country, have been backing dictatorial and oppressive governments with generous American aid. Dee Smith stated this problem well when he wrote that we have,

". . . a State Department which deliberately backs with American tax dollars the Roman Catholic party in foreign countries against much more liberal and democratic non-Catholic elements, a State Department which sanctions with silence outright tyrannies, pouring millions into countries where persecution of Protestants is in full swing, while exacting no promise whatever that such persecution will cease. In fact, our State Department takes a position which cannot fail to be recognized by both persecutors and persecuted as tacit endorsement of religious persecution" (*Christian Heritage,* May, 1960).

9. CONTRAST BETWEEN THE BRITISH-AMERICAN AND THE SOUTHERN EUROPEAN-LATIN AMERICAN CULTURES

How are we to explain the glaring contrast that over the centuries has developed and which continues to manifest itself so prominently between Protestant and democratic Britain and the United States on the one hand and the Roman Catholic countries of southern Europe and Latin America on the other? The former are known for the stability of their governments, the latter for the ease and rapidity with which they overthrow their governments. Mr. Howard has given an explanation that is for the most part unknown even to Protestants, but which we believe gets at the very heart of the matter. He first calls attention to the difficulty that the people in southern Europe and Latin America have even today in governing themselves, and points out that the political institutions in those countries are largely servile copies of Anglo-Saxon models. A constitutional monarchy such as existed for a time in Spain and Italy, the republics of France and Portugal, or the federal governments in Latin America are only imitations, and poor ones at that, of the constitutional forms found in Great Britain and the United States. The Anglo-Saxons have been able to carry forward and strengthen a movement which the Latins have found almost unworkable.

"The Latins and the Anglo-Saxons," says Mr. Howard, "have followed two different traditions whose synthesis has never yet been accomplished. The one is the Greco-Roman classic tradition. The other is the Hebrew-Christian tradition. The democracies were the product of Christianity. The classic tradition made no contribution. Democracy did not exist in the Greek republics. They were true aristocracies, or oligarchies, composed of a minority that exercised authority over a great mass of slaves on whose labor that handful of citizens lived. Even less democracy can be found in the imperial tradition of Rome.

"Democracy has existed, and can exist, only among men who believe in but one God, in human equality and fraternity. A political democracy has never yet appeared outside of the bounds of Christianity nor will it prosper where 'personal religion' is unknown.

"The seed of Christianity fell among the Latin people of Europe and, with the development of this new spiritual leaven, a movement toward democracy was started. Then came the Renaissance with the powerful resurrection of interest in the Greco-Roman pagan culture and ideals. The pagan aspect of the Renaissance never reached the northern countries of Europe with much strength. But southern Europe fell under the spell of the new culture. No enthusiasm was felt in the northern countries for the pagan aspects of the Renaissance, hence it never took such deep root. The Renaissance had the tragic effect in the Latin countries of killing the incipient movement toward democracy which Christianity had started.

"In the northern countries Christianity was able to continue its quiet work. Thus the Reformation appeared, and we must not forget that, just as the Renaissance meant the coming to life of the old paganism, so part of the deep significance of the Protestant Reformation lies in the fact that it was a strong protest against the pagan elements that were so powerfully leavening life in the countries of southern Europe.

"As a reaction against this pagan tendency of their day, some great spiritual personalities appeared in Latin countries, but they constituted only a small majority. The trouble with Latin America is that neither the saving influence of these great Latin mystics nor the invigorating breezes of the Reformation ever reached its lands. Only the spirit of the Renaissance, the materialism and vanity of a superficial culture, reached South America. The vast majority of those who landed on the shores of the southern continent were dominated by the sensual pagan influences of the Renaissance. The settlement of the continents of North and South America thus assumed widely divergent patterns" (pp. 103-105).

To the same effect an editorial which appeared in the great daily, *La Prenza,* in Buenos Aires, in October, 1943, summarized these two different historical trends and interpreted them:

"Let it not be forgotten that the stream of immigration that flowed toward the northern continent was entirely spontaneous. In lands that fell to the Spanish crown immigration was of a totally different sort. To North America went groups of settlers who on their own initiative left their native lands seeking freedom, and above all freedom of conscience. . . .

"Here on our continent, on the other hand, a different system was established and very diverse also were the effects of three centuries spent under the authority of the mother country. Absolutism characterized the government. Everything that was fundamental was kept under the control of the sovereign with the advice of the Crown Councils. Immigration was limited only to those of Hispanic origin and those who professed the religious faith which not only dominated the Spanish peninsula but which excluded all other faiths. Education was so completely neglected by the government that at the commencement of the 19th century the number of literates among the population was very scarce.

"The influence of all these diverse factors weighed heavily on our slow and painful social and economic revolution, which never went very far beyond the most rudimentary conditions. Thus poorly equipped were we on the eve of our struggle for independence.

"There we have the great results of the two different policies; the one held liberty as its norm, the other exercised its greatest zeal in suffocating the most elementary manifestations of liberty."

Another Latin-American statement emphasizing the religious variance between North and South America was published in *America,* a liberal magazine in Havana, Cuba (May, 1943). It said:

"As the history of the Americas has developed in two different ways, so there are two different types of Christianity in the new world. Anglo-America is a child of the Reformation: Latin America is the product of Catholic sculpturing. . . . The thirteen American colonies were founded by pilgrims who fled from religious and political intolerance and who reached the shores of America with the purpose of establishing a new society based on respect and liberty for man. Their first governments were pure democracies and a very significant detail is the fact that the first assemblies of those simple austere colonials for the purpose of dealing with the affairs of government were held in the same buildings that served as a place of worship. Such was the intimate relation between their faith and their social and political ideas.

"Latin America is the reverse of the coin. Among us Roman Catholicism has always been incompatible with democracy. During the period of the conquest and in colonial times the official religion served the purpose of weakening the conscience so that the people would more easily tolerate despotism and be more ductile under oppression. Clerical and absolutist Spain employed the physical force of her soldiers and the moral influence of her priests in a perfect partnership which led to the enchaining of these embryonic settlements and their more easy exploitation. Democracy appeared in our lands in answer to the intuitive cry of popular agony and under the inspiration of Anglo-Saxon democracy and the emotional impulse of the French Revolution. In the north democracy was born under the shadow of religion; here, among us, it appeared in spite of religion."

In these penetrating analyses we have the problem of Latin America. It is the problem of a bad start—religiously, politically, economically, and socially. We may add further that the Spanish Inquisition had the effect of developing a hard, ruthless character, and that this was reflected in Spain's treatment of her colonies. The Inquisition sanctified cruelty in the service of the church. Having become accustomed to plundering and murdering their neighbors whose orthodoxy was questionable, they did not hesitate to deal ruthlessly and selfishly with their colonists, and particularly with the Indians whose land they had seized. The uncivilized natives could be enslaved and plundered at will. The conquistadors had not been nurtured in a religion that issued in ethical living and moral character. The cross and the sword were supposed to advance together. Usually the sword led the advance. Latin America had a bad start.

We want to emphasize again that the Roman Catholicism that we see in the United States is not representative Roman Catholicism, but a modified form that has been greatly influenced by our ideals of democracy and freedom and which has adjusted itself to life with a Protestant majority. And still more important, it has been influenced by evangelical moral standards. Romanism has the ability to compromise and adjust itself to conditions as it finds them. It has, for example, one form in Spain, another in England, another in France, another in Latin America, and still another in the United States. For the sake of expediency and for the time being it acquiesces in the American principle of freedom of religion, while at the same time working to change this system.

We call particular attention to two facts, mentioned earlier: (1) Every Roman Catholic nation in the world today is bankrupt. (2) Every Roman Catholic nation in the world today is looking to Protestant United States for help, in the economic, social, educational, and financial spheres. We submit, therefore, that in view of the incomparably greater progress that this nation has made through the relatively short 186 years of its national existence with a free church in a free state, surely the logical course would be for the Roman Catholic nations to follow our example and grant full freedom of religion to their people, not for us to follow theirs in granting a religious monopoly to one church and in denying freedom of religion to the people.

We submit further that as regards our western hemisphere what Latin America needs more than anything else is not more foreign aid from the United States, nor more priests from Spain and Portugal, but *a change of religion,* specifically a change to evangelical Christianity; and that not until such a change takes place can there be substantial and permanent progress in those nations.

XIX. A SYSTEM TESTED
BY ITS FRUITS

1. A Fixed Pattern. 2. The Present Problem.
3. Is the Roman Catholic Church a True Church?

1. A FIXED PATTERN

The Roman Church has long boasted that she never changes—*Semper Idem*—"Always the Same," is her motto. We accept that motto at face value, not that she has not changed or added to the Christian faith which she inherited from the apostolic church, for she certainly has done that; but that the Roman Church has now been frozen into a definite pattern from which she cannot change and which is basically the same today as it was in the days of the Inquisition. What sometimes looks like change is merely a policy of caution which she has been forced to adopt because of public opinion. She changes her methods, but not her spirit. Her Canon Law has not undergone any essential change, nor has her ancient policy of suppressing or persecuting those who differ with her. No pope has ever declared himself in favor of freedom of religion or issued a decree to that effect, nor has the Roman Church ever established a free society anywhere. In view of what the Roman Church teaches her children in the parochial schools concerning her mission as the only true church, her right to suppress all other religions by force if necessary, together with her political and economic policies in those lands where she presently is in control, why should anyone doubt that a new Inquisition merely awaits the supremacy of Roman power when it will again burn and pillage and slaughter the "heretics"—all in the name of religion as it did in the earlier ages? Her position is that that which opposes her, that which she terms "error," has no rights, and that its mere existence is a crime against the Catholic state. If and when the times comes to "Make America Catholic," there is no reason to believe that she would hesitate to use her traditional methods. There is far too much history behind the Roman Catholic Church for us to believe otherwise.

It is hard to believe that Christianity actually has in its record the dark chapters of persecution that we read of. But the facts cannot be denied. How much better and how much more in the real spirit of Christianity it

447

would be if the Roman Church, instead of fighting the evangelical faith with the base methods of intolerance, bigotry, and persecution, would bend her efforts cooperatively to instruct her people, and unbelievers as well, in the basic truths of the Christian faith! But no matter how sincerely and Scripturally Protestants preach the Gospel, Romanists force them to stop if they have the power to do so.

The Christian method of promoting the faith is persuasive, kindly, and peaceable. It seeks to win people by love and by the power of truth. As Dr. Woods has said:

> "Persecution on account of religious belief is both foolish and wicked. It is foolish because the use of force never makes an honest man change his beliefs. His convictions are really deepened by suffering for conscience sake. Only weak men yield to persecution, and are made hypocrites by it; they profess to change their faith merely to escape torture. It is wicked because it is unjust and cruel. Torture, imprisonment, confiscation of property, disgrace and death, not only cause suffering to the individual, but also to his innocent family and friends" (*Our Priceless Heritage,* p. 181).

Most Roman Catholic people, in the United States at least, have no animosity toward their Protestant neighbors and no desire to persecute them. Most of the people do not know what the traditional policy and practice of their church is. And they know practically nothing of the 2414 statutes embodied in their Canon Law. Unfortunately they have no part in determining policy. Policy is imposed on them and they are indoctrinated by the hierarchy as the occasion arises. Since they have been taught from childhood that their salvation is dependent on obedience to the church, it is extremely difficult for any organized resistance to develop within the Roman Church. Some may become indifferent or even leave their church when policies which violate their consciences are put into effect. But it is a rare thing for Roman Catholics to organize and resist their church openly.

Protestantism does not fear competition. It does not need to persecute. It believes that true religion is too strong to be shaken by the attacks of atheists, doubters, or advocates of rival religions. It asks no special aid from the state, either to suppress its rivals or to pay its bills, but only to be left free, that it may present its case openly and fairly. That there have been instances in which Protestants persecuted Roman Catholics is not to be denied. Romanists point to these and attempt to make much of them in their own defense. But such persecutions have been comparatively few and comparatively mild, and in most instances in retaliation for wrongs inflicted by the Roman Church. But most important of all, such persecutions have been in violation of basic Protestant principles. No Protestant persecutions have even remotely approached those of the Inquisition in Spain, the extermination of the Waldensians in Italy, the St. Bartholomew's Day massacre in France, or the recent slaughter in Yugoslavia, to mention only a few.

There is scarcely anything more destructive of national unity than is religious intolerance. National unity flourishes in an atmosphere of peace, fraternity, and tolerance. This is demonstrated, for instance in the United States when after a national election all differences are put aside and the outgoing and incoming administrations cooperate in a friendly way for the orderly transfer of the powers of government. In the 186 years since the founding of this nation we have never had a governmental change that was brought about by force. The British, Dutch, and Scandinavian governments, too, have been very stable, continuing over periods of centuries. But what a contrast these governments present with the unstable governments of southern Europe and the Latin American countries, where in almost every nation such changes occur repeatedly! At the basis of political stability and freedom and giving permanence to it is religious faith and religious freedom.

The unity and prosperity of a country depends upon the freedom and diversity with which its religious, economic, educational, and cultural life is allowed to develop. The United States, with the most Protestantism and the most religious freedom, has the highest standard of living of any nation in the world and has brought more of the good things of life to the rank and file of its people than has any other nation. At the opposite extreme as regards these features is Spain, with the most Roman Catholicism, the least religious freedom, and the lowest standard of living in Europe. Spain is held together only by a military dictatorship, and is really one of the most disunited nations in the world. Even Roman Catholicism prospers most and is at its best in Protestant lands. What further proof is needed to show the superiority of religious freedom over religious bigotry and intolerance?

2. THE PRESENT PROBLEM

We have now examined the distinctive features of Roman Catholicism and have found that each one of them is false and truly formidable in its consequences of leading people astray from the Gospel. These things have been shown to be not peripheral but to concern the very heart of the Christian message as set forth in the New Testament. To an unbelievable extent Rome has apostatized from the faith. While she has been so quick to hurl the epithet "heretic" at others, she herself is honeycombed with heresies.

All of this is a strong indictment of the Roman system. But it is no stronger than the facts justify. How incredible that a religious system so obviously false as judged by the standard of Scripture should attain such power, hold that power for centuries, and be so widespread as the Roman system is today!

We have attempted to show that the Achilles heel of Romanism is the false theological basis on which the system rests, and that the strength of evangelical Protestantism is its rigid adherence to what the Scriptures teach. Protestantism can never defeat Romanism, nor even defend itself against Romanism, merely by pointing out the latter's corrupt political alliances, its inordinate greed for money, and its suppression of political and religious liberties. All of these things are true and should be exposed. But they relate only to external methods and practices. Romanism is basically a religious system and must be challenged and forced to defend its doctrines on the basis of Scripture. This method, and this method alone, can bring victory to the evangelical faith.

We have shown that Romanism, in distinction from other churches, is a dual system, *a church and a political state.* Its appeal to the rank and file of its members is religious in nature. On that basis it asks for their loyalty and their financial support. But the hierarchy is primarily a political organization, constantly trying to exert its power through civil agencies at the national, state and local level. It wants the state to support its churches, schools, hospitals, and other institutions. It also wants the state to help enforce its religious principles by restricting and suppressing all opposition.

The time has come to put aside false tolerance and to let the world know the facts about Romanism. The public has been duped too long, and it must be given the facts that it may know what is true Christianity and what is falsely so called. Before the true Christian doctrines of the evangelical faith can be accepted, the false and unscriptural doctrines of Romanism must be bluntly exposed and its superstitions destroyed. Protestants must be made to see the great danger that threatens them. The hierarchy makes no secret of the fact that it is out to "Make America Catholic." The Knights of Columbus, at the direction of the hierarchy, spend millions of dollars for propaganda in newspaper and magazine advertising. The hierarchy seeks to gain control, and to a remarkable degree is gaining control, by placing its agents in key positions in the government, the press, radio, television, movies, education, and labor movements, all over the nation. And for the most part Protestants are fast asleep!

We must, therefore, be prepared to engage in controversy. We possess a priceless heritage in Protestant America—"the American dream," as some here have termed it; the "Golden Land," as some in other countries call it—something God has given us, not something formulated in the minds of men. The Scriptures exhort us to "contend earnestly for the faith which was once for all delivered unto the saints" (Jude 3). We must carry the battle to our adversaries. Not one Roman Catholic in a hundred, priest or layman, knows the true story of his own church. They are forbidden to read the truth. What they are given under the name of "Catholic Truth" is a gross perversion of theology, church history, science, and secular history. There are millions of Roman Catholics who were born and raised in that church but who find its doctrines of Mariolatry and papal dominance repugnant to the Scriptures, to common sense, and to all concepts of freedom and democracy. There are millions who haven't been to mass for years and who are quite ready to say that they do not believe the doctrines of their church. Many of these can be won to the Gospel. Yet they are almost completely ignored, or even shunned, by Protestants.

One who signs himself "A Former Jesuit Trainee," tells us:

"When Luther rang the tocsin bell, thousands of disillusioned Catholic believers of his day rallied to him. They came out of the church by the thousands—nuns, priests, monks, lay people. Early Protestantism didn't hesitate to say exactly where, when, and how they thought the pope had erred in interpreting the Bible. They did not hesitate to condemn the Vatican's amoral politics, and its greed for gold. Thousands of Catholics listened and followed the Protestant Reformers. More thousands would have had not the church used the power of the state to threaten with death all heretics within Italy, Spain and other areas. Only ruthless use of the sword saved Rome.

"The Roman Church in free America ought to be challenged by Protestants to defend her dogmas, particularly her bigoted assertion that she alone is the true church of Christ. The type of bigotry which is taught in Catholic parochial schools should be castigated as a positive subversion of America's heritage of freedom—which it is.

"If the Roman Catholic Church were compelled to engage in debate in the free forum of ideas, if her communicants were regularly presented with the Protestant side of issues as well as the Catholic, she would soon be on the defensive. It cannot hold the minds of its adherents if they are given freedom of choice. . . . Rome would lose adherents by the millions in free America if she had to defend her dogmas" (*Christianity Today*, Oct. 28, 1957).

Protestantism must meet this challenge if it is to survive. Many Protestants have been misled into a form of Modernism or Liberalism which stresses a social gospel and tends to ignore the supernatural. Christians in all the churches should return to and confess their faith in the basic doctrines of the Scriptures, as set forth, for instance, in the Apostles' Creed, and reassert their belief in the Bible as the uniquely inspired and authoritative Word of God. A skeptical Protestantism can be no match for a dogmatic Romanism. We need a return to Bible study, to catechism instruction, and to faithful ministers of the Gospel who preach individual regeneration by the grace of God through faith in the vicarious, substitutionary atonement of Christ, men who will meet an infallible church with an infallible Bible, the sacramentarianism of Rome with the free and sovereign grace of the Gospel, and the political machinations of Rome with an enlightened and aroused Christian church.

In regard to the large membership which the Roman Catholic Church claims in the United States, on the basis of which it seeks to exert and does exert an influence in various fields much beyond that which its actual numbers justify, Mr. McLoughlin gives some interesting and enlightening facts. He says:

"Probably the greatest lie of the Roman Catholic press is the elaborate annual reporting of Catholic statistics regarding the Church's growth, as represented by the *Official Catholic Directory* published by P. J. Kenedy & Sons of New York.

"The Arizona *Register*, May 24, 1957, figures showed 34,536,851 Roman Catholics in America. The figure used in 1960 is 40,000,000. This is enough to make every Catholic proud of his faith and enough to scare every politician in the nation. That is exactly the result the hierarchy wishes to achieve by publishing the figures.

"An analysis of how these statistics are compiled will show how unreliable they are. In the first place no one is ever dropped from Catholic figures. As one priest wrote about me: '. . . there are no ex-Catholics, there are merely bad Catholics.' Furthermore, contrary to the custom of most Protestant churches, all baptized babies are considered as part of the Catholic populace. [In most Protestant church statistics children under 12 years of age are not included.]

"These accounting procedures are, however, not the important aspect of the utter falseness of Catholic statistics and therefore of Catholic political strength.

"The truth is that Catholics in the United States are, in most dioceses, not counted at all. The pattern of the compilation of Roman Catholic statistics should interest Protestants who are so precise in their membership rolls.

"There are, as such, no membership rolls in Catholic churches. Some parishes have a census of sorts, some have lists of regular contributors. But practically no Catholic pastor of a large parish in America knows how many good, bad or indifferent Catholics live within the geographical boundaries of his parish.

"This is, in the first place, due to the fact that, when Roman Catholics move from one parish to another or from one city to another, there is no constituted machinery in Catholicism to keep track of them. There are no letters of transfer or 'demit' so common in Protestant organizations.

"All a Catholic has to do when he moves to a new area is to go to Mass on Sunday—anywhere. Nor is it customary in Catholic churches to ask newcomers or visitors to rise or to fill out a card that might be used for statistical control. Only when there is a baptism, a wedding or a funeral to be performed need a Catholic identify himself to any priest. Barring these functions, a Catholic might well attend a large Catholic church for half a century without the clergy knowing that he is there or who he is.

"The annual publication of the Roman Catholic 'strength' in America is for several purposes. One is so that the hierarchy of America can scare the politicians and businessmen of the nation. Another is so that the Roman pastors can impress their bishops and the bishops can impress the Pope. The success of all these clerics is based largely on the numerical growth of the faithful under their care, not on their fidelity or their devotion to the Church" (*American Culture and Catholic Schools*, pp. 157, 158).

After saying that in their Memorial Hospital in Phoenix, Arizona, each new patient is asked if he will permit his clergyman to visit him, and that only ten percent of those who give their affiliation as Roman Catholic will permit a priest to see them, Mr. McLoughlin adds:

"The Catholic press might tone down its boasting, if it realized how weak is its control over its own people. Our Protestants and politicians might take heart enough to be real Americans if they could only realize that the Catholic press of America is nothing but 'sounding brass or a tinkling cymbal' and that Roman Catholic loyalty in America is confined to an unthinking minority and its alleged strength is purely a myth. The great strength of the Catholic hierarchy rests only in the fear of Protestant ministers with their boards and the fear of merchants who shrink from losing a Catholic dollar" (p. 161).

In another connection Mr. McLoughlin makes this statement:

"In their wildest untruthful exaggerated claims, Catholics do not constitute twenty-five percent of the population. Ten percent would be closer to the truth" (p. 235).

The fantastic claim of the Roman Church that it has a world membership of some 400 to 500 million is arrived at by counting practically *en masse* the populations of the Southern European and Latin American countries while actually not more than 15 to 20 percent of the populations of those countries are practicing Roman Catholics. About a third of the total number claimed are illiterate, and hardly should be counted; and of the remainder considerably more than half by Rome's own definition are in mortal sin, not having gone to mass or to confession within the prescribed time limits, having eaten meat on Fridays, or attended Protestant church services, etc. Many others have simply left the Roman Church without formal announcement. In any event an honest count would reduce the number drastically.

We have a suggestion to offer which we believe will prove very helpful to the Protestant churches if it is followed, namely, that these churches should send missionaries and Christian workers of all kinds to Italy and to the other Roman Catholic nations of Europe. Italy, the home of the pope and the seat of the papacy, is today one of the most forgotten mission fields, yet one with very great possibilities. Says one Italian evangelical:

> "The people of Italy live in an unbelievable spiritual ignorance. Most of them have never read the Bible; many do not even know that such a book exists. Besides this, they live in indescribable superstition as it is taught and practiced by the Church of Rome. People worship images, carry them on their shoulders, and pay great sums of money for the privilege. There are those who make pilgrimages, walking hundreds of miles to special shrines. The Virgin Mary is the central object of the teaching of the priests and the worship of the people" (Michele Tancredi, booklet, *The Burden for Italy,* p. 3; 1957).

For many decades Protestants have been establishing mission centers and founding Bible schools among the primitive tribes of Africa, South America, and the Orient. How much more reason there is for such work in Italy, among people of our own white race who are in such need and with whom we have so much more in common! Most of the people in Italy can read and write, hence they can read the Word of God for themselves and find the truth if it is presented to them. They have a language that is comparatively easy to master; and a knowledge of that one language makes it possible to reach the entire 50 million of the population, while throughout most of the other mission fields each tribe speaks a different language or dialect. And throughout most of Italy a favorable disposition on the part of the people welcomes evangelical work. Opposition can be expected, of course, from the Roman clergy; but when we allow Italian priests and nuns to operate freely in the Protestant United States we should insist firmly that we have the same freedom in operating there. The Roman Church in Italy, despite the great need for Christian and educational work in that land, has sent tens of thousands of missionaries, priests and nuns to the United States. On the other hand the great mass of our missionaries have gone to India, China, Japan, and Africa, to people of other races and with languages which are very difficult to master and customs so different from ours. Only the merest trickle of our missionaries have gone to Italy and to the other Roman Catholic countries of Europe, and only a tiny fraction of our money has been invested in evangelical work in those countries. The result is that Roman Catholicism is conquering the United States while Protestantism is not conquering the Roman Catholic countries. Let us redress this situation and, beginning with Italy, send a substantial number of missionaries to that country which in reality is almost as needy as are the outright pagan nations of the orient.

As regards the church in her world wide mission, we cannot match Rome's political scheming, her propaganda machines, nor her appeals to prejudice and greed and intolerance; but we have something much more effective. We have the truth as set forth in the Word of God. And that truth, if fairly and sympathetically presented, will break down the walls of prejudice and greed and intolerance. We also have a definite superiority in wealth, education, ingenuity, and especially in the spiritual intangibles which give depth and stability to Christian endeavor. If we can but reach the free, inquiring mind and present the truth we can win the world for the Christian faith.

3. IS THE ROMAN CATHOLIC CHURCH A TRUE CHURCH?

The elaborate system of doctrine and ritual that has been developed by the Roman Catholic Church apart from or even contrary to the Bible, together with her policy of persecution and her failure to raise the spiritual and economic standards in countries where she has long been in control, has caused many people to ask: Is the Roman Catholic Church a true church?

That the Roman Church has within it much of truth is not to be denied. It teaches the inspiration of the Scriptures, the deity of Christ, the virgin birth, the miracles, the resurrection of the body, a future judgment, heaven and hell, and many other Scripture truths. In every instance, however, it nullifies these truths to a considerable extent by adding to or subtracting from what the Bible teaches.

In regard to the inspiration of the Scriptures, the Roman Church accepts the Bible as the Word of God but adds to it a great body of tradition as of equal authority although in many instances tradition contradicts the Bible and in any event largely supplants it. Tradition is in fact made superior to the Bible since it gives the official interpretation of the Bible. Whereas evangelical Christianity accepts the Bible as its one and only authoritative standard of faith and practice, a standard which consistently calls it back to a true norm when it is inclined to go astray, the Roman Church gives the Bible only a secondary place and in actual practice is governed by a pope who allegedly is infallible in his pronouncements concerning faith and morals and by a rigid system of Canon Law. Coupled with this is Rome's traditional policy of withholding the Bible from the people; or if under pressure from Protestantism she must give the Bible to the people, only those editions which contain her interpretative notes are allowed.

The Roman Church teaches the deity of Christ. But it places Mary and the priest as mediators between Him and the believer, so that there is no way of access to Him except through them. He is usually presented either as a helpless babe in His mother's arms or as a dead Christ upon a cross. In either case He is effectively removed as a strong, virile, living personality, or as a daily companion or Saviour who hears and answers prayer. He has little to do with the problems of everyday life. All are urged to pray to Mary and the saints, who in turn present the prayers to Christ or to the Father and intercede for them.

The Roman Church teaches the forgiveness of sin, but only as it is confessed to a priest and absolution is received from him. It places a human priesthood between the people and God, while the Bible teaches that the sacrifice of Christ ended forever the work of the priests, that Christ alone is now our High Priest, and that we are to go directly to God in prayer. The complete dependence of the Roman Church upon the priesthood as the heart of the system, while the New Testament teaches that the sacrificing priesthood was abolished and that the universal priesthood of believers was established in its place, means that the system is false at its very center. Though some liberal churchmen talk of an eventual union of the Protestant churches and the Roman Catholic Church, this point alone, apart from that of acknowledging the authority of the pope, which is the one point that Romanists insist upon above all others, should be sufficient to show how impossible any such union is.

Instead of the Scripture doctrine of salvation by grace through faith alone, the Roman Church substitutes a system of grace plus works, in which works have a larger place than faith, and in which one works long and hard for his salvation. In actual practice it has become a system of absolutism, claiming to admit souls to or exclude them from heaven as they meet or fail to meet its demands for confession and penance. Its saving truths are covered over with a mass of human inventions and throughout most of its ritual and practice they are not savingly presented. It gives such false and misleading answers to the crucial questions about the way of salvation that the large proportion of those who trust themselves to it fail to show by their lives that they have undergone a true spiritual change.

The Roman Church teaches that Christ established the church, but it places a man, the pope, at its head and invests him with absolute power. It develops the mass and an elaborate ritualism which had no counterpart in the apostolic church, and makes salvation dependent on obedience to the church. And since the Vatican is itself a union of church and state, it seeks to promote that kind of organization wherever possible.

And finally, the Roman Church teaches a final judgment with rewards and punishments. But its promise of rewards in heaven for the righteous is largely overshadowed with other teaching concerning a hideous place of torment called purgatory, which is of much more immediate concern as throughout his life the person tries to alleviate or shorten his sufferings there through the purchase of indulgences and by doing works of penance. The Bible contains not even the slightest evidence for the existence of purgatory, but instead teaches that the redeemed soul goes straight to heaven.

The condition of the present day Roman Church would seem to be in many ways similar to that of Judaism at the time of Christ. There was much truth in Judaism and there were many sincere believers among the people. But the priesthood was largely indifferent to the needs of the people, as were the ruling classes, the Pharisees and the Sadducees. Like the Roman priests, the Jewish priests withheld the Word of God from the people, and their chief concern was their own advancement. The primary opposition that Christ encountered came from the priests, and it was they whom He denounced most severely, as it was also they who were primarily responsible for having Him put to death. Similarly in the Roman Church the priesthood has departed so seriously from the simplicity of the Gospel, and the teachings of the Bible have been so thoroughly covered over with man-made rituals and canon laws that the features of the apostolic church are hardly recognizable. The record shows that in those countries where Romanism has been dominant and unopposed for long periods of time it has not advanced but instead has become corrupt, and that its tendency has been downward with a consequent weakening of those countries. That was most clearly shown in the first place during the Middle Ages, from about 500 A.D., until the Protestant Reformation, a period of roughly one thousand years when darkness covered the land and the people were largely helpless under the rule of a corrupt, tyrannical church that was more concerned about securing political power and vast wealth for itself than it was about promoting the spiritual and moral welfare of the people. Those conditions of poverty, ignorance, superstition, and illiteracy have continued to some extent even until the present time in Rome-dominated Italy, Spain, Portugal, Southern Ireland, and Latin America. Wherever Rome rules the people become enslaved to the priest. Where it is dominant it establishes but few schools, and in many places none at all unless spurred on to that work by competition from Protestantism. Rather it allows ignorance and superstition to continue among the people as a means of controlling them, and so promotes an anti-Christian way of life.

This is the stinging rebuke to Romanism, which it cannot deny or evade: That in four centuries of undisputed control in Latin America it has failed utterly to raise the spiritual, moral, social, and economic standards of the people, and that most of the progress that has been made during the past two generations has been the direct or indirect result of evangelical missions and of economic aid given to those countries by the Protestant United States. At the present time the United States government is engaged in a vast aid program to those countries which for the most part simply by-passes the Roman Catholic Church.

We have said that Romanism carries within itself the seeds of its own destruction. This has been shown in one European country after another where, after gaining complete control, it has proved morally defective and has degenerated. Unrestrained by the power of strong civil governments, it perpetrated the horrors of the Inquisition in Spain and Italy. The excesses of the French Revolution were the end result of a long period of degeneration, and the hatred of the people was directed as much against the Roman Catholic Church as against the oppressive state as hundreds of priests were killed and hundreds of churches were burned. At the close of the Second World War the Roman Catholic Church in Italy found itself very unpopular because it had supported Mussolini's fascist policies, and today one-third of the Italians vote Communist. Although present day Spain is quiet under dictator Franco, the situation there apparently is not much different. We have cited the report of cardinal Spellman concerning the remark of a well informed Spaniard some eight years ago to the effect that if police protection in Spain were withdrawn the life of every priest and nun would be in danger. What a tragedy that an organization professing to be the church of Christ should be guilty of such flagrant abuse that the people would want to kill its clergy and destroy its edifices! What a tragedy that the church should be the principal source of strength for a clerical-fascist police state! And what a tragedy that in one country after another its actions have incited anticlericalism!

In most of the Latin American countries today the Roman Church has lost its hold, with the rank and file of the people indifferent toward it and the intellectuals openly opposed to it. A few years ago the government of Mexico confiscated the vast properties of the Roman Church in that land and put serious restrictions on its clergy, particularly on the foreign priests who were living in luxury at the expense of the people. Even today the government retains ownership of the churches. So strong was the resentment of the people that they made it illegal for the priests to appear on the streets in clerical garb—many did not want to see a priest anywhere.

The Roman Church thus has such serious inherent defects that over the broad course of history it cannot possibly emerge successful. Clearly it has lost its power to evangelize the world, and instead has become so confirmed in its present course that it cannot be reformed either from within or from without. In the main it is as antagonistic and as much an obstacle to evangelical Christianity as are the pagan religions. Admittedly there have been many high-minded and saintly souls in the Roman Church, as on the other hand many in the evangelical churches have not been true to their profession. In every church some are better and some are worse than their creed. But a church must be judged, not by individuals, but as a *system*.

The admonition in Scripture is: "By their fruits ye shall know them." Surely the fruits of Romanism as they have been manifested throughout history and in the various parts of the world are sufficient to disprove its arrogant claim that it is "the only true church." Indeed, when seen at its best it is a badly deformed type of Christianity, and when seen as it more often manifests itself in lands where it has long been dominant it is primarily not a church at all but a gigantic business and political organization that merely uses religion as a cloak. In those lands it makes little effort to hide its greed for power and its avarice for wealth. It victimizes first of all its own people and then all others who come under its sway. In general it has sought to weaken or destroy free governments. Its traditional policy toward other churches and other Christians who do not acknowledge its authority has been one of bitter opposition, oppression, and, when expedient, persecution, with tens of thousands having been put to death for their faith and millions more subjected to unspeakable physical torture and mental anguish. Such actions are contrary to the teachings of the Bible and they certainly are not the marks of the true church. Its interpretation of the Scriptures is so erroneous and its practices are so persistently unchristian that over the long period of time its influence for good is outweighed by its influence for evil. *It must, therefore, as a system, be judged to be a false church.*

ACKNOWLEDGMENTS

Our Priceless Heritage, Henry M. Woods; The Evangelical Press, Harrisburg, Pa.; 1941.

People's Padre, Emmett McLoughlin; The Beacon Press, Boston; 1954.

American Culture and Catholic Schools, Emmett McLoughlin; Lyle Stuart, publisher; New York; 1960.

American Freedom and Catholic Power, Paul Blanshard; The Beacon Press, Boston; revised edition, 1958.

Out of the Labyrinth, L. H. Lehmann; Angora Publishing Co., New York; 1947.

The Soul of a Priest, L. H. Lehmann; Angora Publishing Co., New York; 1933.

Ins and Outs of Romanism, Joseph Zacchello; Loizeaux Publishers, New York; 1956.

The Vatican Revolution, Geddes MacGregor; The Beacon Press, Boston; 1957; Macmillian & Co., Ltd., London, and Toronto.

The Story of the Church, A. M. Renwick; Wm. B. Eerdmans Publishing Co., Grand Rapids; 1958.

Religious Liberty in Latin America, George P. Howard; The Westminster Press, Philadelphia; 1944.

The Vatican in World Politics, Avro Manhattan; Gaer Associates, New York; 1949.

A Popular History of the Catholic Church, Philip Hughes; Doubleday & Co., Garden City, N. Y.; 1949.

Catholic Principles of Politics, John A. Ryan and Francis J. Boland; The Macmillan Co; New York; 1960.

Peace of Soul, Fulton J. Sheen; McGraw Hill Book Co., New York.

Forgotten Women in Convents, Sister Mary Ethel; Christ's Mission, Sea Cliff, New York.

The Priest, the Woman, and the Confessional, Charles Chiniquy; The Gospel Witness, Toronto.

Faith of Our Fathers, Cardinal Gibbons; John Murphy & Co., Baltimore; 1876.

Things Catholics Are Asked About, Martin J. Scott; J. P. Kennedy & Sons, New York; 1927.

The Papal Princes, Glenn D. Kittler; Funk & Wagnalls, New York; 1960.

Revelation Twenty, an exposition, J. Marcellus Kik; Presbyterian and Reformed Publishing Co., Philadelphia; 1955.

Magazines (monthlies):

Christian Heritage, Sea Cliff, New York.
Church and State, Washington, D.C.
The Convert, Clairton, Pennsylvania.

INDEX OF AUTHORS

INDEX OF SUBJECTS

DATE DUE